ALSO BY DAVID S. BROWN

A Hell of a Storm:
The Battle for Kansas, the End of Compromise,
and the Coming of the Civil War

The First Populist:
The Defiant Life of Andrew Jackson

The Last American Aristocrat:
The Brilliant Life and Improbable Education
of Henry Adams

Paradise Lost:
A Life of F. Scott Fitzgerald

Moderates:
The Vital Center of American Politics
from the Founding to Today

Beyond the Frontier:
The Midwestern Voice
in American Historical Writing

Richard Hofstadter:
An Intellectual Biography

"I have had," Roosevelt once remarked, "far more than the normal share of human happiness."

IN THE ARENA

THEODORE ROOSEVELT *in*
WAR, PEACE, *and* REVOLUTION

DAVID S. BROWN

SCRIBNER
New York   Amsterdam/Antwerp   London
Toronto   Sydney/Melbourne   New Delhi

Scribner
An Imprint of Simon & Schuster, LLC
1230 Avenue of the Americas
New York, NY 10020

For more than 100 years, Simon & Schuster has championed authors and the stories they create. By respecting the copyright of an author's intellectual property, you enable Simon & Schuster and the author to continue publishing exceptional books for years to come. We thank you for supporting the author's copyright by purchasing an authorized edition of this book.

No amount of this book may be reproduced or stored in any format, nor may it be uploaded to any website, database, language-learning model, or other repository, retrieval, or artificial intelligence system without express permission. All rights reserved. Inquiries may be directed to Simon & Schuster, 1230 Avenue of the Americas, New York, NY 10020 or permissions@simonandschuster.com.

Copyright © 2025 by David S. Brown

All rights reserved, including the right to reproduce this book or portions thereof in any form whatsoever. For information, address Scribner Subsidiary Rights Department, 1230 Avenue of the Americas, New York, NY 10020.

First Scribner hardcover edition December 2025

SCRIBNER and design are trademarks of Simon & Schuster, LLC

Simon & Schuster strongly believes in freedom of expression and stands against censorship in all its forms. For more information, visit BooksBelong.com.

For information about special discounts for bulk purchases, please contact Simon & Schuster Special Sales at 1-866-506-1949 or business@simonandschuster.com.

The Simon & Schuster Speakers Bureau can bring authors to your live event. For more information, or to book an event, contact the Simon & Schuster Speakers Bureau at 1-866-248-3049 or visit our website at www.simonspeakers.com.

Manufactured in the United States of America

1   3   5   7   9   10   8   6   4   2

Library of Congress Cataloging-in-Publication Data has been applied for.

ISBN 978-1-6682-0419-1
ISBN 978-1-6682-0420-7 (ebook)

IMAGE CREDITS: All embedded images and insert images 4, 7, 9–27, and 29–37 courtesy of the Library of Congress, Prints and Photographs Division; insert images 1–3, 5–6, 8, and 28 courtesy of the Theodore Roosevelt Birthplace National Historic Site; insert image 38 courtesy of the National Archives.

He was a much bigger man than his people understood or ...
knew how to use.
                    Rudyard Kipling, 1935

Contents

Introduction: The Wide Horizon   1

PART I: YOUTH

1. North and South   11
2. Casualties of War   18
3. The Invalid   23
4. Traveling Cure   27
5. Father of the Man   33
6. The Jackals of Damascus   37
7. College Brahmin   43
8. These Terrible Three Days   49

PART II: SUNSET, SUNRISE

9. Alice Lee   57
10. The Scholar in Politics   63
11. Enter the Dude   71
12. The Vanishing West   75
13. A Curse on This House   81
14. Picking Up the Pieces   85
15. Cowboy Blues   91
16. Back on Track   96

PART III: SONG OF THE STRENUOUS LIFE

17. The Historian   105
18. Washington Entrée   112

19	Elliott's Story	119
20	The Top Cop	124
21	In the Navy	131
22	By Jingo	138
23	And the War Came	144
24	Rough Rider	151

PART IV: PREACHER TO PULPIT

25	Turns to Gold	161
26	Kicked Upstairs	169
27	Keys to the Kingdom	175
28	Shifting American Scene	179
29	The Dinner	184
30	Playing Monopoly	189
31	Bred of Empire	195
32	King Coal	200

PART V: CULT OF CHARISMA

33	A Gentleman's Place	209
34	Into the Heart	216
35	Taking Panama	222
36	Atop the GOP	230
37	When Goliaths Go to War	238
38	Peace in the East	244

PART VI: DRAMATIS REX

39	Roosevelt and the Regulatory State	253
40	Alice in White	259
41	Brownsville	265
42	Cuban Encore	273

43	Genuine Race Feeling	277
44	A Ship in Every Port	281
45	Panic Attack	289
46	Thunder from On High	294

PART VII: AFTER THE MAGIC

47	Successor Politics	301
48	Regime Change	306
49	African Exile	313
50	Storming Europe	319
51	Lay of the Land	326
52	Widening Divide	333
53	The Battle Begins	337
54	Armageddon Arrives	345
55	The Lord's Candidate	351
56	The Last Hurrah	356

PART VIII: QUICKER THAN THE ROSE

57	The Wages of Doubt	367
58	Wilson's Washington	375
59	Rumors of War	381
60	Forever Jingo	388
61	Mortal After All	396
	Coda: Patrimonies	403
	Acknowledgments	409
	Notes	411
	Index	449

IN THE ARENA

Said to be "the first truly national political hero," Roosevelt captured the public's imagination like no president before him.

Introduction: The Wide Horizon

> To me he had ceased to be an American, but had become a world citizen. His horizon seemed to be greater, his mental scope more encompassing. I don't think this was in our imaginations alone. . . . He is bigger, broader, capable of greater good or greater evil, I don't know which.
>
> Archie Butt, aide to Roosevelt, 1910

American presidents occasionally perform roles that extend well beyond the formal obligations of their office. Thomas Jefferson's tenure (1801–1809) embodied the broader progress of antebellum southern agrarian power, while Abraham Lincoln's term (1861–1865) anticipated the growth of postbellum northern industrial might. More than engaging in tussles over elections, budgets, and boss fights, these men, the former a quasi-aristocratic slaveholder, the latter a largely self-educated model of midwestern social mobility, typified the dominant if transitory directions of nineteenth-century American development. Jefferson's states' rights vision collapsed in the Civil War, while a dawning age of corporate monopolization mocked Lincoln's quaint "free soil, free labor" convictions.

In their wake, Theodore Roosevelt, a conservative drawn to progressive ends, captured the imaginations of Americans caught in the anxieties of the modern—urbanized, industrialized, imperialized—quandary. Many of his achievements as a reformer were partial and incomplete, though he retained a remarkable hold on public opinion. With 56.4 percent of the popular vote in the 1904 election, he claimed the highest percentage in a contested presidential race since 1816 when James Monroe, the last chief executive to wear knee breeches, won over a largely Atlantic-facing electorate. In contrast to the sectional complexions of Jefferson's and Lincoln's respective constituencies, "TR's great political strength," so his cousin Nicholas Roosevelt once observed, "lay in his millions of devoted followers, especially in rural and small-town America. In a sense he was the first truly national political hero."[1]

The power of Roosevelt's popularity stemmed, ironically, from a raft of contradictions. Though a silver-spooned Manhattan dandy born into a wealthy merchant and banking family, he lived for extended periods after college (Harvard, naturally) on a cattle ranch in the Dakota Territory, became an unlikely military hero in the Spanish-American War, and, despite endorsing martial glory as a "strenuous life" antidote to the "ignoble ease" offered by a highly commercialized civilization, was the first American to receive the Nobel Peace Prize.[2] Above all, he represented to numerous constituencies concerned with an economy dominated by factory owners and financiers the dreamy promise of a precapitalist hero—hunter, warrior, explorer—who might yet infuse the country with an updated iteration of the old frontier ideals.

Domestically, Roosevelt's progressive reforms—breaking up dozens of monopolies, modifying railroad rates, setting aside public lands for conservation—cut against the long run of industrial oligarchy enjoyed by assorted oil, timber, and coal kings in collusion with their congressional retainers. "We demand," TR barked, "that big business give the people a square deal"; this Square Deal liberalism served as a corrective to classical (unregulated, let-the-buyer-beware) liberalism, thus anticipating a cluster of future government public assistance programs, including Franklin Delano Roosevelt's New Deal, Harry Truman's Fair Deal, and Lyndon Johnson's Great Society. By turns loathed and distrusted by any number of plutocrats—"We bought the son of a bitch," complained the disgruntled steel tycoon Henry Clay Frick, "and then he didn't stay bought"—Theodore Roosevelt was the first president to attack the problem of industrial fiat.[3]

In foreign affairs, TR presided over America's emergence as a global power. Leading a volunteer cavalry unit up Kettle Hill in Cuba, he earned his spurs in a war against a fading Spain that brought the island, an "empire of sugar," into the expanding U.S. sphere; as president he oversaw the conquest of the Philippine Republic, a struggle that foreshadowed the United States' hit-or-miss entry into future conflicts in Asia against Japan, North Korea, and North Vietnam. Schooled in social Darwinism, Roosevelt wielded a big-stick diplomacy in the Western Hemisphere that betrayed a barely concealed disdain for Latin peoples not atypical for its time. His great achievement in this corner of the world—construction of the Panama Canal—is inescapably paired with the controversial Roosevelt Corollary to the Monroe Doctrine, by which TR announced America's right to monitor the internal affairs of the Caribbean countries in the manner, so he told Congress, "of an international police power."[4] The groundwork was thus laid for a series of interventions and occupations, often by the Marine Corps, and usually to do with securing U.S. dominance over tropical trade in Haiti, the Dominican Republic, Honduras, Mexico, Panama, and elsewhere. Reflecting on these so-called Banana Wars, the Nicaraguan-born poet Rubén Darío offered a defiant 1904 ode "To Roosevelt":

> You are the United States,
> You are the future invader . . .
> You think life is fire,
> That progress is eruption;
> Where you put your bullet
> You put the future.[5]

Roosevelt's strong domestic program and personalized foreign policy—he said, of severing Panama from Colombia to forward the canal project, "the vital work . . . was done by me without the aid or advice of anyone"—helped ignite a contentious competition between the branches of government. For many years Capitol Hill had claimed rank. But TR proved to be the nation's strongest peacetime president since the notoriously combative Andrew Jackson, who had vetoed more bills than all his predecessors combined.[6] In Old Hickory's long shadow a series of failed 1850s administrations, followed by Lincoln's assassination and the near impeachment of Andrew Johnson, reinforced the course of congressional preeminence until Roosevelt, a progressive powerhouse, a State Department of one, became the dominant figure in U.S. politics. After a generation of Grants and Garfields, the modern presidency had arrived in time with the new century. Some critics would come to call its sharp enlargement of executive authority the imperial presidency.

Theodore Roosevelt is among our most relentlessly caricatured public figures. Standing five feet, ten inches, with a thickening trunk, he possessed a brown brush of a walrus mustache, pince-nez eyeglasses to correct severe myopia, and, most flagrantly, flashing white Chiclets-like teeth that, so one New York Times reporter swore, "seem to be all over his face." The overall impression is eye-catching if perhaps less than flattering. Photographs and portraits capture a bull neck, bulbous nose, and close-cropped hair that always looked a little on the short side. Belying the heavy set of his frame, TR's bodily extremities were by contrast a shade off—evident in elfin ears and tiny feet. "Mr. Roosevelt's clothes were always made for him and always at the same place," his personal valet noted. "His shoes, too, were made to order. But this was because he was particular about the fit. He had an unusually small foot for a man of his size—indeed, the smallest I have ever seen."[7]

Aside from questions of cobbling and couture, such imperfections compromised Roosevelt's athletic prowess. Though an avid hiker, tennis player, and college pugilist who liked to spar in the White House for exercise, he struck observers as clumsy, an active sportsman unable to master a single sport (leaving big-game hunting, at which he was perfectly lethal, aside). "His eye and hand do not go together," a British ambassador to the United States once remarked confidentially to a colleague. "He is very energetic and full of keenness, but not skillful. He is conscious of the fact and deplores it." Neither did TR fancy what the writer H. G. Wells called "his unmusical voice," a thin pitch that Roosevelt blamed in a letter to his mother on "not speak[ing] enough from the chest, so my voice is not as powerful as it ought to be."[8]

As if in compensation, Roosevelt fairly oozed charisma—Greek for the "gift of grace," the word denotes a magnetic personality radiating "confidence, exuberance, optimism, a ready smile, [and] expressive body language," among a host of less easily encompassed qualities. The German sociologist Max Weber thought a rare breed of leaders the likely keepers of charisma, evident in such as Julius Caesar and the emperor Charlemagne, Martin Luther, Mohandas Gandhi, and the oil magnate John D. Rockefeller.[9]

Those in Roosevelt's orbit invariably commented on the twenty-sixth president's unusual energy if not ebullience. "One of his charms lay in a certain boyish zest with which he welcomed everything that happened to him," remembered the writer Margaret Terry Chanler. "I never knew anyone more pleased with things as they were—life was the unpacking of an endless Christmas stocking." Edith Wharton, invoking Emily Brontë's iconic Catherine and Heathcliff, opined, "Our Theodore is a good deal more saga-like than anything in *Wuthering Heights*," while the British diplomat Cecil Spring Rice said upon TR's Pennsylvania Avenue encampment, "It is extraordinary to think of Theodore Roosevelt as President. He will make things hum. I don't suppose there will be a war but there will be plenty of amusement."[10]

Audience responses could and did vary. From Cambridge's rare air, a white-whiskered Charles W. Eliot remembered TR as sui generis: "Of the five Presidents who have visited Harvard while I was President of the University, Roosevelt was the only one who possessed the faculty of attaching all sorts of men to him with a deep sense of personal devotion, although their contact with him might have been but slight. Most of the American Presidents have had nothing of this faculty. Roosevelt possessed it in a supreme degree." Less charitably, the historian Henry Adams, descended from America's most celebrated political dynasty, refused to be blinded by the shine of TR's swollen star, writing in a memoir that this preening, peacocking "boy" lacked conviction and substance; "he was," Adams sniffed, looking down his blue nose, "pure act."[11]

Beyond the political game, Roosevelt, who believed his transient contact with rural peoples while cowpoking after college in the Dakota Territory "enabled me to get into the mind and soul of the average American," led a very unaverage American life. In youth he had spied from his wealthy grandfather's Manhattan home the progress of Lincoln's black-draped funeral procession (then snaking its dramaturgical way through seven states over 1,700 miles) and luncheoned on the Nile River with the ancient Transcendentalist Ralph Waldo Emerson; he had twice toured Europe with his family before the age of fifteen, on one occasion taking a pope by the hand. While on his first honeymoon he scaled the pyramid-shaped Matterhorn in the Pennine Alps, only sixteen years after it had first been ascended; and late in a not overly long life he nearly died in a Brazilian jungle exploring the previously uncharted River of Doubt, whose dark waters flowed into the Amazon. Given his many overseas trips, it is perhaps fitting that he became the first sitting president to travel abroad—inspecting, in a white linen suit and period-piece boater hat, the progress of the Panama Canal.[12]

A moralist at heart and hungry to put his personal philosophy on record, Roosevelt wrote some three dozen books, among them *The Naval War of 1812*, *The Winning of the West*, and *The Wilderness Hunter*, whose titles accurately convey their author's interest in, as he called it, "the life of strife." An insatiable reader, he enjoyed a wide range of literary acquaintances, some of whom—Rudyard Kipling, Owen Wister, and Joel Chandler Harris—became personal friends, and others, including Mark Twain ("a man wholly without cultivation") and Upton Sinclair ("the socialist"), he never quite cottoned to.[13]

Most Americans—including scholars—have liked Roosevelt. In the parlor game of presidential rankings, he often comes in fourth, just below the de rigueur demigods of Abraham Lincoln, George Washington, and TR's fifth cousin Franklin Roosevelt. It is from contrary opinions, however, that we often come upon insight, balance, and unexpected perspective. Writing in 1948 in the blasted shadow of European dictatorships, the Holocaust, and the unsettling popularity of mass propaganda, the historian Richard Hofstadter cannily observed of Roosevelt in his influential study *The American Political Tradition*:

> Despite his sincere loyalty to the democratic game, this herald of modern American militarism and imperialism displayed in his political character many qualities of recent authoritarianism—romantic nationalism, disdain for materialistic ends, worship of strength and the cult of personal leadership, the appeal to the intermediate elements of society, the ideal of standing above classes and class interest, a grandiose sense of destiny, even a touch of racism.[14]

A generation earlier, the jurist Oliver Wendell Holmes Jr., appointed to the Supreme Court by TR, recognized his patron's astonishing presence, but qualified it with caution: "He was very likeable, a big figure, a rather ordinary intellect, with extraordinary gifts, a shrewd and I think pretty unscrupulous politician. He played all his cards—if not more."[15]

Invariably, this harbinger of American Century wars and interventions was disappointed by not having a crusade of his own to attend. How it bothered him to watch a mere professor, the former Princeton University president Woodrow Wilson—initially angling for neutrality in what Roosevelt called a "diluted-mush policy"—luck into the Great War. His own administration, rather, oversaw a period of comparative peace. And thus, unlike the supreme trio who rank ahead of him in the presidential sweepstakes, and who are identified most clearly with the Revolutionary, Civil, and Second World Wars, Theodore Roosevelt holds his place principally, ironically, because of his progressivism, domestic reforms, and successful effort to mediate an end to the Russo-Japanese War. All of life is a compromise, of course, and Roosevelt, "saga-like" leanings to the contrary, seemed to grasp this fact as well as anyone. "Whatever comes hereafter," he wrote a British friend, shortly before exiting the White House with what can only be described as mixed feelings, "I have had far more than the normal share of human happiness."[16]

Part I

YOUTH

He was so alive at all points . . . like a tiny morsel of radium.
Edith Wharton, 1934

A ginger-whiskered Roosevelt in sculling gear at Harvard—
the culmination of a gilded youth.

1

North and South

On, so the *Chicago Tribune* noted, an "intensely hot" June evening in 1858, the year of Theodore Roosevelt's birth, a lanky, gray-eyed, and improbably tall Abraham Lincoln accepted the Illinois Republican Party's senatorial nomination. Following the balloting, the newly anointed candidate delivered a few remarks on the dangers of disunion before a crowd inside Springfield's Greek Revival–style capitol building, thus launching his surprising ascent into the stormy antebellum political heavens. "A house divided against itself cannot stand," he quoted from the Gospel of Mark. "I believe this government cannot endure, permanently half *slave* and half *free*."[1] His rural Kentucky roots etched indelibly on a dry and finely weathered face, Lincoln soon became, even before a martyred presidency, a symbol of Yankee possibilities. Taking a southern bride, the Lexington-bred Mary Todd, a stocky five feet, two inches, with long lashes and luminous blue eyes, only accentuated his private Mason-Dixon Line drama—as did, on a far greater scale, the Civil War, in which several of Mary's unreconciled siblings sided with the Confederacy. This splintered ménage fractionally captured the conflict's tragic brother-against-brother quality, the logical conclusion of a no longer habitable house.

Many American families experienced similar tensions during these fateful years, some becoming open sores of identity. Among these hard-pressed clans and their offspring, young Theodore absorbed his parents' contrasting sectional sympathies with a deep and keenly felt interest, only to augment over time.

The Roosevelts—to trace the boy's paternal bloodline—arrived on the shores of New Amsterdam/Manhattan Island about 1649; Claes Martenszen van Rosenvelt, a young Zeeland farmer of Dutch Reformed persuasion, and his wife, Jannetje Samuels, constituted the charter generation. Though but modest pioneers in an otherwise unkempt outpost of the Dutch West India Company, the family proceeded to find distinction over several decades as merchants, bankers, and importers, with a modest real estate empire ripening on the side. This particular iteration of the American dream, the moment when European discoverers relinquished their exhausted feudal heritage, is canonized in the final haunting pages of F. Scott Fitzgerald's 1925 novel *The Great Gatsby*, whose narrator, Nick Carraway, reflects on the perishability of the past: "As the moon rose higher the inessential houses began to melt away until gradually I became aware of the old island here that flowered once for Dutch sailors' eyes—a fresh, green breast of the new world."[2]

In time, the Roosevelt family's economic advancement found its metropolitan complement in civic engagement. Its sons sat in the then-colony's assembly, and, in the case of Isaac Roosevelt, owner of a thriving Wall Street sugar mill, served on the Committee of One Hundred, a would-be rebel organization formed in 1775 to oversee the city's boycott of British goods as enacted by the First Continental Congress. Following the Revolutionary War, Isaac joined Alexander Hamilton and John Jay (coauthors, along with James Madison, of *The Federalist Papers*) at a convention in Poughkeepsie, where New York's delegates ratified the proposed U.S. Constitution. By the fifth generation—that of merchant Cornelius Van Schaack Roosevelt (C.V.S.), the last of the full-blooded Dutch line and grandfather to the future president—the family had accrued considerable wealth and influence. In the 1850s, Theodore Roosevelt Sr., called "Thee" and one of C.V.S.'s six sons, joined the family's extended business concerns as a partner in a thriving importing firm; the company's diversified earnings amplified handsomely when put toward the purchases of various New York properties and lands.[3]

Wealthy and good-looking, highly sociable yet steeped in a pious sensibility that played well among midcentury Manhattan's tightly connected elite, Thee was a man in full. Leonine with a generous beard and strong gaze, he sported impeccably cut clothing, close-cropped hair, and a thick if firm build. "He was a large, broad, bright, cheerful man," a nephew reported, while his youngest child, the adoring Corinne, described Thee as "sunny, gay, dominant, unselfish, forceful and versatile, he ... was the most intimate friend of each of his children, and in some unique way seemed to have the power of responding to the need of each, and we all craved him as our most desired companion." A reverent Theodore concurred, calling his father "the best man I ever knew. He combined strength and courage with gentleness, tenderness, and great unselfishness."[4]

The southern, maternal line of Theodore Roosevelt's twining family tree evoked something more distant, colorful, and inaccessible than the small galaxy of hirsute Manhattan Dutch merchants. These were the Bullochs, whose American antecedent, James, an educated Scot from Glasgow said to know his Latin from his Greek, came to Charleston about 1729. A clergyman and owner of enslaved people who worked his Pon Pon plantation, James joined the South Carolina Assembly in 1754, before moving a few years later to coastal Georgia along the Savannah River and establishing a farmstead at Mulberry Grove, consisting of, so the *Georgia Gazette* noted in 1770, "800 acres, of which about 250 are tide land, and the rest good corn and timber land."[5]

James's son Archibald, a lawyer by trade, embraced the American Revolution, leaving for his heirs a storied history. He served in Georgia's provincial assembly as well as the Continental Congress, corresponded with John Adams on the progress of American arms, and organized a company of patriots to man the marshy coastal Sea Islands' defense. As Georgia's first governor, he implored his fellow citizens in a June 1776 address to strike for independence—"this is no time to talk of moderation"—and to aid "our northern brethren" in opposition to the "enemies of American liberty."[6]

Years later, in 1838, Archibald's industrious grandson James Stephens Bulloch, a well-connected Savannah cotton shipper, moved his family and slaves inland to present-day Roswell, twenty miles north of Atlanta along the serpentine Chattahoochee River. There he built Bulloch Hall. Erected on a slight rise, the still-standing rosemary-pine mansion, done up in Greek Revival with simple Doric columns before a whitewashed front, contains several fireplaces, high ceilings, and a downstairs hall accented by a graceful elliptical arch. A silver knob dominated the front door.[7]

Bulloch Hall is the well-appointed home in which James and his second wife, Martha ("Patsy"), widow of a Georgia senator, raised their four children, including Martha ("Mittie"), mother of the future president. The house and grounds further held over the years more than forty enslaved persons who were, in a 1921 account given by Corinne, mythologized in classic moonlight-and-magnolia-ese: "The ... slaves were treated as friends of the family and they became to us ... figures of great interest.... There was [a] young slave who went by the name of 'Black Bess,' and she was the devoted companion of her two young mistresses, Martha, my mother, and her sister, Anna Bulloch. She slept on a mat at the foot of their beds and rendered the devoted services that only the slave of the old ... days ever gave to his or her mistress." Referring to herself and her three siblings (Anna, Theodore, and Elliott Roosevelt), Corinne recalled their being told "stories of the ... plantation" in the family's Manhattan home.[8]

Presumably these nursery tales never explored the unexplained murder of a Roswell slave by Mittie's half brother Daniel, who, said to be in a fit of temper, shot his "little shadow." To soothe his conscience or his shame, he was sent abroad for a year. Neither, apparently, were Mittie's offspring aware that to pay for their parents' costly wedding, the Bullochs sold four of the Hall's enslaved. The children, rather, knew of Roswell only in stories, and these embroidered by the vanities of time. Shortly after assuming the presidency, Theodore wrote to one of his favorite authors, Joel Chandler Harris, the longtime associate editor of the *Atlanta Constitution*, though far better known as a folklorist for his popular Uncle Remus stories based on African American oral tradition. "When I was young," Roosevelt blithely observed, "my Aunt Annie Bulloch of Georgia, used to tell me some of your brer rabbit stories.... Your art ... [has] always been an addition to the forces that tell for decency, and above all for the blotting out of sectional antagonism." The much-hunted rabbit—small, vulnerable, and utterly dependent upon his wits to survive in a world of lashings and lynchings—can be seen as an expression of the antebellum enslaved negotiating a pack of predatory wolves, and one might wonder to what extent Roosevelt (or Harris) grasped this prickly fact.[9]

Thee Roosevelt and Mittie Bulloch met in 1850 through his older brother Weir, whose brother-in-law Dr. Hilborne West of Philadelphia was then courting Mittie's half sister Susan Elliott. Corinne, perhaps touching upon the trace of Huguenot ancestry in the Bulloch family— Archibald's wife was Mary De Veaux, daughter of a Savannah planter— later wrote in some detail of her mother's fair appearance: "She was very beautiful, with black, fine hair ... with a glow that sometimes seemed to have a slightly russet shade ... and her skin was the purest and most delicate white, more moonlight-white than cream-white, and in the cheeks there was a coral, rather than a rose, tint." Thee, all of nineteen and determined to meet this much-talked-of girl of fifteen, asked to visit Bulloch Hall. His stopover included picnic parties and gossip about Savannah's elite, though apparently no suggestion of marriage; perhaps the evident differences in their personalities—she, vague if lively, and he, argumentative and perhaps a little self-serious—defeated them at this early date. Three years later, however, in May 1853, the would-be couple reconnected in Philadelphia, he just returning from a European sojourn and she visiting her now-wed half sister. Presumably heavy courting ensued—Thee referred to the "almost sacred ... sofas" upon which they sat, while Mittie considered herself "entirely yours."[10] Returning to Roswell in June, she was engaged.

Thereupon ensued several months of separation as Thee returned north, triggering a difficult period for the intendeds. "Thee, Dearest Thee," Mittie wrote in late July, "I promised to tell you if I cried when you left me. I had determined not to do so if possible, but when the dreadful feeling came over me that you were, indeed, gone, I could not help my tears from springing and had to rush away and be alone with myself. Everything now seems associated with you." Thee replied days later with an open heart: "How can I express to you the pleasure which I received in reading your letter! I felt as you recalled so vividly to my mind the last morning of our parting, the blood rush to my temples; and I had, as I was in the office, to lay the letter down, for a few minutes to regain command of myself.... O, Mittie, how deeply, how devotedly I love You!"[11]

Faithful correspondents, the affianced practiced a largely lettered friendship, their time in each other's corporeal company—sacred sofas aside—acutely abridged and typically attenuated by chaperones. This underlying lack of intimacy is perhaps evident in a sober if lightly put Mittie-to-Thee missive written a few weeks before their wedding on the ticklish subject of the husband-to-be's deportment in front of the Bullochs: "Dear Thee, how are you going to behave when we meet? If I see you first before them all, mind seriously please, don't kiss me or anything of the kind. I would not let Brother see you do so for worlds. I am in earnest. I would regard my affections as misplaced if you should take any liberties."[12] More generally, and considering their rather sharp contrasts—he the product of an urban, commercial environment, and she a plantation appendage—certain tensions attending this union of burgher and belle were likely. In the face of such divisions, it seems clear that a strong and mutual attraction sustained their quick courtship.

Matters did, however, momentarily bristle as the late-December wedding date neared. Plans for a small ceremony, the couple's original preference, were put aside in October when Mittie, almost certainly yielding to parental pressure, wrote in some mixed attitude of explanation and frustration: "I said I would have no Bridesmaids at all—well, then I did not think it would be necessary—but since we have been thinking over things in general and have come to the conclusion that some of my five dozen *intimate friends* must be asked to officiate . . . I must submit to having four attendants." In reply, Thee gave in by degrees, bowing to the enlargement of the wedding party—"As to the four groomsmen I don't object to them in the slightest"—though pondering a little peevishly over the sudden need to invite half of Fulton County: "I must acknowledge that the utter change in your views with regard to other spectators is utterly incomprehensible."[13] Receiving this note, which was, Mittie anxiously surmised, "written in the heat of your displeasure," the bride-to-be offered her northern beau a swift tutorial on southern etiquette:

> Thee, I grant they may be different entirely, your Northern customs, but will I ever be able to impress upon you the *fact* that it is a southern young lady and in a Southern village that the wedding is to occur; consequently I must observe the rules and customs prevalent in that village. I cannot imagine you for one moment supposing I would take the step decided upon unless I had thought well of what I was doing. . . . As far as I am concerned I would infinitely prefer being married in the morning and leaving on the same day, but to this Mother was very much opposed. Consequently I was obliged to have all the Roswellites.[14]

Her sister Anna having perused the note with some skepticism, Mittie added a postscript: "Anna says [it] is not at all as she would write to her *Lover* and she thinks it sounds cross. Well, Thee, I do not mean any such thing, only you wrote 'your change is incomprehensible, do explain it,' and this letter is the only way I can explain.... You might have known I would have acted properly."[15]

The evening wedding took place on December 22, 1853, in the warmed dining room at Bulloch Hall; sliding doors opened upon an adjoining parlor filled with guests. Mittie wore white satin; her much-discussed bridesmaids sported muslin with narrow basque waists. A supper heavy on baked and roast meats followed, with ice cream and several kinds of cakes capping the nuptial feast; a few days later the Roosevelts, having obliged the Roswellites, made their nearly nine-hundred-mile journey to Manhattan, settling into a house near Union Square Park.[16]

There, thirteen months later, Mittie, bereft of her mother and only nineteen, had her first child, Anna (called "Bamie," a quaint corruption of "bambina," courtesy of an uncle who had traveled to Europe). In October 1858 a second infant—Theodore, called "Teedie"—arrived. His grandmother Bulloch, now in residence, thought the toddler "as sweet and pretty a young baby as I have ever seen," though a doubtful Mittie supposed her son a little "hideous" with a slight overbite (to be hidden in adulthood by a mustache) and more akin to a "terrapin."[17] Two years later Mittie gave birth to her second son, Elliott; her final child, Corinne, came the following year. By that late date the Roosevelts constituted a cohesive unit of six—its rare mix of northern hustle and southern Huguenot suddenly, implicitly censured in a nation rapidly coming undone.

2

Casualties of War

In late January 1861 Mittie's native Georgia became the fifth southern state to leave the Union, the first tremoring domino, South Carolina, having fallen in December. By June, eleven states had seceded, four of these following the stunning April assault on Fort Sumter, a pentagon-shaped brick sea citadel in Charleston Harbor piled upon an artificial island reclaimed by several thousand tons of New England granite. Its surrender to Confederate forces prefaced Lincoln's call for seventy-five thousand volunteers to stem the unfolding rebellion. Only in his late twenties, Thee might have served in the U.S. Army, though the delicacy of his domestic situation—Mittie, Anna, and their widowed mother, Martha, who had sold Bulloch Hall in 1856 a few years after her husband's death from heart disease, were all now living in Manhattan among the Roosevelts—argued otherwise. Rather, he hired a substitute in 1863, once the federal government implemented a draft. Giving some unintended veracity to the stinging expression "a rich man's war but a poor man's fight," Thee paid $1,000 (about $24,000 in today's dollars) to maintain a safe distance from the gathering storm.[1]

It is conceivable, of course, that even without a southern spouse, he might have sought an alternative form of service. Numerous wealthy and well-placed young men followed such a path, including Thee's brothers, none of whom fought in the conflict. The Bullochs, by contrast, were more active combatants. Mittie's brother Irvine, an officer in the Confederate navy, served on the CSS *Alabama*, a notorious screw sloop-of-war sunk outside the port of Cherbourg, France, in June 1864 after capturing or burning dozens of Union merchant ships; her half brother James, possessed of a bushy Hulihee beard (mustache and muttonchops), operated as a foreign agent for the Confederacy in Britain, overseeing the movement of commerce raiders and helping to smuggle southern cotton into the country. Both he and Irvine, their Stars and Bars sins considered irredeemable, were denied amnesty after the war and operated a successful cotton emporium in Liverpool. Flush with sibling affinity, Mittie is said, on at least one occasion, to have displayed the rebel flag to her Yankee neighbors following a Confederate triumph.

According to Bamie, Thee regretted his decision to avoid the front lines. Her father "always," so she wrote many years later, "felt that he had done a very wrong thing in not having put every other feeling aside and joined the absolute fighting forces." It is difficult to determine the accuracy of this after-the-event sentiment on Thee's (or Bamie's) part, though certainly the difficulties he faced within his marriage were daunting. "I wish we sympathized together on this question of so vital moment to our country," he wrote Mittie near the end of a dispiriting secession winter in early 1861. "I know you cannot understand my feelings and of course do not expect it." Invariably, their children adopted the sensitivities of their surroundings, which tilted, uprooted Georgia kin to the contrary, toward a deep Union blue. Though caught up in the romance of "dear old" Uncle Jimmy, as Teedie remembered his England-based uncle, the Roosevelt litter, when given a stocky sorrel Shetland in 1865, hesitated not to name it "Pony Grant."[2]

Despite heading a house divided, Thee performed a service of considerable consequence for the Union. Along with two New York allies, Theodore Bronson, an official on the state board of charities, and William Dodge Jr., a partner in a lucrative mining corporation, he devoted three months in 1861 to securing the passage of a bill in Congress creating a class of allotment commissioners who encouraged soldiers to send a portion of their pay to their families. Lincoln appointed Thee one of the roving commission agents. Accordingly, he spent nearly a year sojourning in the saddle, enduring often-inclement weather, giving speech after speech, and collecting signatures by the thousands. "This resulted," so Dodge later remembered, "in sending many millions of dollars to homes where it was greatly needed, kept the memory of wives and children fresh in the minds of the soldiers, and greatly improved their morale." The effort seems to have emboldened Thee's outlook as well. "It is a great luxury," he wrote Mittie, "to feel I am at last doing something tangible for the country."[3]

His father's connection to Lincoln offered young Teedie a vicarious brush with history that meant more to the boy than any comparatively narrow Bulloch heroism. Possessed of prized Lincoln letters and some small social acquaintance with the president, Thee came to be linked in the child's fecund mind with the turn of great events. Attending a White House supper in February 1862, Thee wrote his family that while some capital city grandees snootily "complained of the supper," for its necessary nod to wartime frugality, he insisted on having "rarely seen a better [one]" and described a candlelit feast of "terrapin, birds, ducks, and everything else in great profusion when I was in the dining room." To Teedie, "Father Abraham," selflessly engaged in preserving the Union, became his lifelong beau ideal of a statesman. "Lincoln is my hero," he wrote unabashedly to an uncle while in his forties, and he ached to frame his presidency in the key of Civil War campaigning. "Just as Lincoln got contradictory advice from the extremists of both sides at every phase of the struggle for unity and freedom," he observed to a colleague in 1902, as though begging for comparison, "so I now have carefully to guard myself against the extremists of both sides." In a gesture of herbal homage, Roosevelt had boxwood clippings from Lincoln's Springfield, Illinois, home planted at his own Long Island house at Oyster Bay.[4]

Lincoln's lengthening shadow took on a tangible quality for Roosevelt in the spruce style of John Hay, TR's first secretary of state. Not long out of Brown University, Hay had served loyally as Lincoln's private secretary, living in the White House; he later, with John Nicolay, crafted a generous ten-volume biography of the sainted president published to much acclaim in 1890. Hay became acquainted with Thee during the war years and, through the father, came to know the family. "I can see the laughing face of the young man become suddenly shy and a little self-conscious," Corinne remembered, "as my father said to my mother: 'Mittie, I want to present to you [someone] who in the future, I believe, will make his name well known in the United States.'" Soft-spoken, meticulously groomed with a Van Dyke beard, and (following an advantageous marriage to stout Clara Stone, heir to an Ohio railroad fortune) impeccably tailored, Hay moved steadily up the Republican ranks. For TR's 1905 swearing-in ceremony, he picked the perfect gift. "The night before the inauguration," Roosevelt wrote to a British friend, Hay "gave me a ring containing some of Lincoln's hair, cut from his head just after he was assassinated nearly forty years ago; and I wore the ring when I took my oath of office the next day."[5]

For Mittie, the torturous war years sapped both her spirit and her strength. Corinne said that her mother suffered from "delicate health" during this period and thus struggled "to enter into the active life of her husband and children." Bamie, however, understood Mittie's ailments to have external origins: "I know the Roosevelts and I should hate to have married into them at that time unless I had been one of them in thought. They think they are just, but they are hard in a way." One imagines Cornelius and his several sons, bolstered by the blunt superiority of wealth, casually denouncing southern secession over Sunday Manhattan meals, the odd dropping of Dutch phrases rendering still more extreme the alienating effect upon the lone belle in the room. Worried about her Confederate brothers and possibly the old manse in Roswell (looted by General William Sherman's seaward-marching federals), Mittie possibly wrestled with questions of guilt and identity, living peacefully among the enemies of her people.[6]

Coolly inattentive to time—"I never exactly keep my appointments"—Mittie exhibited as the years passed a propensity for truancy, finding it difficult, amid a host of intricate preparations, to escape the boudoir. This reserve complemented a hygienic fixation, resulting in multiple daily baths, one to clean and a second to rinse. Guests might be guided in her presence to a white-sheeted chair, while her outdoor dress—white muslin, so Bamie later recalled, with "dust coat [and] brown paper cuffs so that not a single speck of dust or smudge could touch her"—suggested an obsession.[7]

And perhaps it communicated still more clearly some quiet resistance on Mittie's part to New York, to the Union army, and to a way of life so deeply antithetical to the rhythms of her rural Georgia. Status-conscious Manhattan's late-nineteenth-century social and economic aspirations required a punctilious attention to efficiency beyond her care or capacity. Consequently, Thee's congenital energy, adeptness, and drive invariably introduced a note of resentment into their marriage. "I love you and wish to please you more than any one else in the whole world, and will do everything I can to please you that is not unreasonable," Mittie once wrote her husband, "... *don't be too hard upon me.*"⁸ The couple's four children, sensitive to ailments of various kinds, possibly internalized this parental divide, captive to pressures they could not as yet name.

3

The Invalid

In the fall of 1861, a few weeks after Thee's allotment duties called him away from the Roosevelts' East Twentieth Street brownstone, Mittie discerned a slight variation in behavior from their elder son, now three. "Teedie is the most affectionate and endearing little creature in his ways," she wrote her afield husband, "but begins to require his Papa's discipline rather sadly. He is brimming full of mischief and has to be watched all the time. . . . I have written this at night, being the only time unoccupied with the dear, troublesome little children deserted by their Papa."[1] This gentle rebuke—of both progeny and papa—anticipated a more general maternal concern for Teedie's well-being. Formerly a robust infant, he suddenly began to experience a swarm of minor if insistent ailments leading to a more serious struggle with asthma.

Watching the boy's health closely, Mittie wrote concernedly to Thee in November, "Teedie has a very bad cold"; the following month she reported in some exhaustion, "Teedie was very unwell last night [and] I was up with him six or seven times." The child's condition worried Thee, who described his son as "too much sick." The maladies varied from fever to nausea to viral infections. So common was the unwanted company of acute diarrhea that it lingered allusively—referred to as "cholera morbus"—in family correspondence. One morning the enfeebled minor complained to Mittie, "I have a toothache in my stomach." The asthma attacks, some lasting for days, were of a more serious nature, leaving the trembling child drenched in sweat and gasping for air. It seems clear that Roosevelt associated his struggling condition with Thee's unsought absence. "My really great father . . . he saved my life,"

TR wrote years later. "Handsome dandy that he was, the thought of him now and always has been a sense of comfort. I could breathe, I could sleep, when he had me in his arms. My father—he got me breath, he got me lungs, strength—life."[2]

Whether in the care of Thee or Mittie, Teedie spent numerous nights "propped up," so Corinne reported, "in bed or in a big chair." The illness seems to have reduced his appetite, and this thin-shanked child appeared pallid and worn. Contrary to Roosevelt mythology, which suggests that weight training and other trappings of physical culture made for Teedie a successful teen-years transition to health, his susceptibility to asthma drifted into adulthood, giving reason to think that allergies may have played a role. Coal dust and damp basement air and ever-present animal hair (the Roosevelts were partial to pets) circulated about the family home. All the children, in fact, suffered from one ailment or another. Corinne too showed symptoms of asthma, while Elliott succumbed to any number of sudden colds. In search of plausible causes, Thee presumed his children's infirmities emanated from the house itself. "While I hope a great deal from next summer," he wrote in early 1862 of a potential seasonal cure, "I cannot help feeling that there must be something about the furnace or something that prevents them all from being healthy."[3]

Heroic asthmatic narratives aside, it was Bamie, Teedie's favorite of his three siblings and, other than his second wife, his closest confidant, who endured the greatest health challenge among the Roosevelt children, suffering from a spinal defect. Family lore insinuated that a negligent nurse had dropped the then-infant, though it is more likely that Bamie's curved back derived from Pott's disease, a rare kind of tuberculosis that results in arthritis of the intervertebral joints.

Conspicuous in her condition—a typically acidic Henry Adams once inelegantly described Bamie, whom he knew socially, as "bent like a corkscrew"—she walked with a stooping gait (only lightly disguised with special shoes) and spent a good deal of her youth planted upon a sofa in the rear of the family home. She was often made to be in a "terrible" harness, so she later recalled. "Poor little thing," Thee wrote of his daughter at age seven. "I never think of Bamie without pain. It seems such a dreary life that is in store for her." Contradicting these paternal concerns, however, the late-blooming bambina's *vita* proved to be unusually full and eventful. Considering that, despite a nagging spine, Bamie assumed many family responsibilities from her distracted mother, later served for several decades as TR's valued sounding board, and surprised all by marrying at the age of forty a decade-older divorced U.S. Navy officer with whom she subsequently bore a son, one might find her resourceful response to illness even more remarkable than that of her famous brother.[4]

Despite his various maladies, Teedie was equipped, as Mittie knew only too well, with an abundance of bounce complemented by a furious curiosity. The publisher George Haven Putnam, a friend of Thee's, first met Roosevelt as a "bright-eyed boy of ten," who "gave full evidence of energy, but his physique was slight and frail. I remember being impressed at once with the fact that the boy wanted to know. He was putting his tentacles out into the universe." Testimonials of the "slight and frail" kind are common in TR lore—Corinne preferred "fragile," Mittie thought him "like one of these very pale azaleas," and Roosevelt himself later proposed "sickly, delicate"—though such assertions give little hint of the great physical change to come. There appears to be precious little resemblance to the lean-faced youth in the thick, fleshy president with notorious teeth chomping above a fluttering double chin.[5] The child seems to have been swallowed by the man.

Teedie's adolescent invalidism, combined with a striking intellectual inquisitiveness—called by one acquaintance "his almost abnormal literary and scientific tastes"—made him something of an isolate to the inessential outside world. Early on he began to collect insect and animal specimens, his bedroom a menagerie of butterflies, ladybugs, and spiders. At the age of seven he penned a minor-key epic, "The Forgoing Ant," inspired by a children's digest on natural history.[6] This engagement with books signaled a more general withdrawal into the nursery, conditioned by bouts of cholera morbus and the ever-present asthma. Self-absorbed, he felt secure within his family circle, the most dynamic and active of his siblings, the one eager if a bit awkward outside of the house, never having—being educated by a parade of tutors—to negotiate the capricious hierarchies formed in schoolyard struggles or to beg for the attention of his teachers.

In this glossy Roosevelt bubble, Thee proved to be by far Teedie's greatest influence, the man from whom he absorbed a decidedly Victorian worldview. "He would not tolerate in us children selfishness or cruelty, idleness, cowardice or untruthfulness," TR later recalled. "As we grew older he made us understand that the same standard of clean living was demanded for the boys as for the girls; that what was wrong in a woman could not be right in a man. With great love and patience, and the most understanding sympathy and consideration, he combined insistence on discipline." This uncompromising code left little room for nuance and, despite its virtues, could valorize in adulthood a rigidly conformist outlook. One associate noted that TR "abhorred, above all, suggestive speech [and] loose living," the latter sin presumably on display when a cousin strayed from convention in choosing a wife. "Have just received a letter telling me that Cornelius has distinguished himself by marrying a French actress!" he fumed while at Harvard. "He is a disgrace to the family—the vulgar brute."[7]

On a less pious note, the art of almsgiving also passed down from father to fils. Though connected to the old Roosevelt & Son hardware and banking empire, Thee, thanks to C.V.S.'s fortune, had turned his attention increasingly to philanthropic enterprises. Looking to engage in good works, he helped organize the New York Children's Aid Society in 1853 (caring for orphaned and abandoned youth) and the New York Orthopedic Dispensary in 1866 (medical treatment for the indigent—a bow to Bamie's condition), as well as the American Museum of Natural History (1869) and the Metropolitan Museum of Art (1870). Various other institutions and associations benefitted from his generosity. "My brother's great love for his humankind," Corinne wrote affectionately, "was a direct inheritance from the man who was one of the founders in his city of nearly every patriotic, humanitarian, and educational endeavor."[8]

It must have pained Thee, placed upon so high a pedestal, to suffer the abiding rebuke of his children's uncooperative constitutions. A great believer in the hygienic virtues of travel and activity, he bundled his begats in the late spring of 1869 and, along with Mittie, stormed Europe. An echo of the Old World's grand tour tradition, this American adaptation, practiced by countless Boston Brahmins, New York Knickerbockers, and industrialists of sundry extraction, promised a culture-gulping crusade through temples, cathedrals, and museums miscellaneous. On such elevating terms did a ten-year-old Teedie gamely take his asthma abroad.

4

Traveling Cure

As the Roosevelts prepared to take wing, America in 1869 showed unmistakable signs of moving beyond the old questions of slavery and sectionalism. The Grant administration got underway in Washington; a ceremonial "golden spike" driven by railroad magnate Leland Stanford in Promontory Summit, Utah, commemorated the completion of the Pacific Railroad (later renamed the Transcontinental Railroad); and the Wyoming territorial legislature granted women the right to vote. Elsewhere in 1869 a twenty-two-year-old former Western Union employee named Thomas Edison received his first patent for an electric vote recorder designed to help legislative bodies tally ballots. On the sporting page, the lavishly mustachioed Cincinnati Red Stockings became baseball's first fully professional team (ten men on salary), while Rutgers defeated Princeton 6 to 4 in the first college football game. Among the criminally inclined, a blue-eyed Jesse James and his older brother Frank robbed a small two-room brick bank in Gallatin, Missouri, leaving its star-crossed cashier, one Captain John Sheets, dead.

In Europe, the year yielded a number of classic novels—including Leo Tolstoy's *War and Peace*, Gustave Flaubert's *Sentimental Education*, and Jules Verne's *Twenty Thousand Leagues Under the Sea*, all of which appeared in serialized and other forms. The first edition of the (still extant) scientific journal *Nature* was published in London, while the Folies Trévise (later Bergère), a cabaret music hall, opened in Paris, becoming, with its catalog of songs, operettas, can-can dancers, and discreet nudity, a centerpiece in coming years of the Belle Époque. Among the governing class, Queen Victoria gave name to an entire era, Napoleon III ruled as emperor of the French, and Otto von Bismarck reigned as chancellor of the North German Confederation (prelude to the German Empire). The power of these potentates was enhanced by the quickening pace of technology, symbolized in 1869 by the completion of the Suez Canal and the beginning of the Brooklyn Bridge—monuments, beyond their operable functions, to a new mechanical age.

Thee presumed that his brood, hitherto wards of the nursery, might benefit from an itinerary of travel. "My father," Bamie believed, "was far ahead of the people of his period in his ideas concerning the health of his children. He felt that . . . we must have a great deal of life in the open air."[1] Unable through prescribed medicines or home remedies to come upon a cure for Teedie's ongoing asthma—at one point the poor child was made to smoke a cigar—Thee seemed to fall, perhaps a little desperately, upon the notion that junketing, the uprooting of routine, might finally shake his son free.

The trip may have suggested to its conductor a similar therapeutic for his wife. Now sixteen years into her marriage, Mittie seemed to be in a measured fade, idle, indolent, and possibly mourning the life she had left behind in Georgia. Her mother, Martha, had died in 1864 and was entombed in Brooklyn's Green-Wood Cemetery far from bucolic Bulloch Hall; her Confederate brothers, unable to garner federal pardons, lived an ocean away in England. Her genteel helplessness, indifference to appointments, and obsession with cleanliness had reduced her presence within the family unit to merely ornamental.

A quiet calculation almost certainly factored into Mittie's ineffable ills over the years. On one occasion she wrote that it was "good policy . . . to keep up the appearance of a cold" and embellished upon this in practice to include the random heart tremor, digestive infirmity, and assorted twinges and torments of enigmatic origin. In response to these complaints, she occasionally absented herself from home, convalescing and taking water cures. Whereas Teedie's invalidism struck the boy as an unwanted prison, his mother perhaps embraced her condition as the price of permission to retreat from the bustling Roosevelt routine. Having borne Thee a quartet of babies between 1855 and 1861, she, twenty-six at the time of her last pregnancy, ceased having children.[2]

A trip to Europe thus offered Mittie the vague promise of improved health, though more concretely the opportunity to reunite with her brothers. And so, on a warm May day in 1869 the Roosevelts boarded the *Scotia*, a built-for-speed British paddle steamer operated by the Cunard Line and headed, on its nine-day voyage, for Liverpool. The luxury ship offered only first-class accommodations, for "people of good family," as the Roosevelts thought of themselves. "While going to the docks I cried a great deal," Teedie wrote in his diary, and called it "verry hard parting" from family and friends. Perhaps most markedly he missed the company of Edith Carow (originally Quereau from the French Huguenot), a treasured neighbor living a few blocks south on East Fourteenth Street in a Union Square brownstone who was particularly close to Corinne but very much, since the age of three, familiar with the entire family. Edie's alcoholic father, an old compeer of Thee's, oversaw a failing shipping concern, and her proud New England mother could be excessively censorious. Clearly gravitating to the Roosevelt household for emotional support, Edie established a special relationship with Teedie. Both were uncommonly interested in books, and their contrasting personalities—he spontaneous, she more reserved—seemed to complement rather than clash. Too, they shared a memory of solemn historical proportions, occupying, along with Elliott, an open second-floor window in old C.V.S.'s mansion on a late-April day in 1865 as Lincoln's long funeral cortège passed by—Dr. Charles DeCosta Brown, a local dentist with some proficiency in the art of embalming, having "removed the dust that had settled on the face" before the remains' Manhattan arrival, so the *New York Times* reported.[3]

Docking in Liverpool, the Roosevelts paused for a ten-day Bulloch reunion during which Teedie accompanied his newly acquainted cousins to the beach, then took to the road. A quick stopover in Chatsworth prefaced a journey north to the Lake District, before the family headed into Scotland where they trooped about Abbotsford, the "castle-in-miniature" country home of Sir Walter Scott, whose widely read *Waverley* novels (1814–1831) popularized the tartan craze. Afterward they scooted up to Glasgow, a booming hub of shipbuilding and trade with a population of about half a million. From there the Roosevelts turned south, arriving by train at the cathedral city of York, where Mittie wrote to her sister Anna "how sad [Teedie] had been to part with Edith." She further found her studious son somewhat abstracted, flashing a "quiet patrician air with his large blue eyes not looking at anything present and asking some such question as 'Father, did Texas wish to annex itself to the United States?'" The party soon moved on to Oxford and from there to London, where, amid outings to the British Museum, Westminster Abbey, and the "quite pretty" Thames, Teedie battled a ferocious headache and contended once again with asthma.[4] The boy was thus taken south to Hastings in the hope that the Channel climate might prove salubrious.

Teedie's struggles, however, continued on the Continent. "He had to sit up in bed to breathe," Mittie reported to Anna of one particularly intense bout. "After taking a strong cup of black coffee the spasmodic part of the attack ceased and he slept.... Had the coffee not taken effect he would have gone on struggling through the night, and been a complete wreck the next morning, in which condition you have so often seen him." Following a tour of Amsterdam, Switzerland, and several German-speaking cities—including Munich, Dresden, and Berlin (where Teedie found a Jewish "Sinagauge ... verry interesting")—the family moved on to Belgium before spending six weeks in Paris, Marseilles, and Nice. As winter approached, they made for temperate northern Italy. Along the way a procession of physicians attended Teedie, who perhaps began to feel himself a burden. "Papa called us children bothers," he wrote, "and I had to drink medicine." Mittie's patience also seemed stretched. "I read till Mama came in," he remembered, "and I stroked her head and she felt my hands and nearly cried because they were feverish."[5]

Along the Riviera, Thee, the generous benefactor of New York City's indigent children, revealed a less sensitive side when encountering a group of mendicant Italians. "Papa brought two baskets of doughey cakes," Teedie recorded:

> We tossed the cakes to them and we fed them like chickens with small pieces of cake and like chickens they ate it. Mr. Stevens [another touring Anglo] kept guard with a whip with which he pretended to whip a small boy. We made them open their mouths and tossed cake into it. For a "Coup de Grace" ... we made the crowds ... give us three cheers for U.S.A. before we gave them cakes.[6]

Though Teedie, struck by the ubiquity of cassock-sporting clerics, occasionally played priest with Elliott, the human condition of the country made only a passing impression upon him; he was more moved by the "lovly scenery" of a smoldering Vesuvius, the "beautiful echo" inside the eleventh-century Pisa Cathedral, and the "verry verry old Frescos" in Bologna. When socializing, he mixed with the children of other Americans: "We all had tea together," he wrote of one encounter, "and then had a great play."[7]

The Roosevelts spent Christmas in Rome, where Teedie, baptized in the Madison Square Presbyterian Church, swore to a newfound friend while playing leapfrog on the Pincian Hill that he "didn't believe in popes—that no real American would." Still a stranger to his unformed feelings, the boy experienced a surprising comeuppance when an immaculately attired Pius IX suddenly appeared. Corinne, among the leapers, later recorded the ensuing episode:

> The Pope, who was in his sedan-chair carried by bearers in beautiful costumes, his benign face framed in white hair and the close cap which he wore, caught sight of the group of eager little children craning their necks to see him pass; and he smiled and put out one fragile, delicate hand toward us, and lo! the late scoffer [Teedie] . . . fell upon his knees and kissed the delicate hand, which for a brief moment was laid upon his curling hair.[8]

Teedie captured the improbable moment with an appealingly self-deflating candor in his quickly filling diary: "We saw the Pope and we walked along and he extended his hand to me and I kissed it!!! hem!! hem!!"[9]

In early March 1870, the Roosevelts returned to Paris for nearly two months of metropolitan wandering and relaxation. By May they were back in England and, after a year abroad, began their return voyage to America on the fourteenth. The tour brought Teedie into an everyday intimacy with his parents, whose independent personalities he began to selectively assimilate inside himself. Thee pushed his irregularly educated children to speak French, to plow through novel after novel, and to take note of the artistic glut to be gleaned at each stop. Always the next rail station loomed, with hours of ennui spent in transit leading to the new hostel, the inevitable castle, the latest cathedral. Mittie, by contrast, communicated to her son something less easy to describe, a kind of impetuosity, a permission to feel intensely about his environment. If Thee, eager to plant the family flag on anything "historical," "architectural," or "significant," swore by a slew of Baedeker guidebooks, she leaned toward a less constricted itinerary—the best part of the journey for her, after all, had been the Bulloch reunion.

For Teedie, however, his temperament still much in flux, this first time abroad scarcely impressed. "I cordially hated it, as did my younger brother and sister," he wrote in a memoir. "Practically all the enjoyment we had was in exploring any ruins or mountains when we could get away from our elders, and in playing in the different hotels. Our one desire was to get back to America, and we regarded Europe with the most ignorant chauvinism and contempt."[10]

Certainly, the Continent had failed to cure Teedie's omnibus of ailments, which persisted throughout the trip. And in some small anxiety, Thee proposed to his son a more active and independent approach to building a better body. The boy would have to do it for himself.

5

Father of the Man

Teedie's passage from sickly asthmatic to Mount Rushmore is the stuff of legend. In later years he seemed to regard the paraphernalia of a well-appointed gym as the weights and bars armaments upon which to wage a kind of holy war. "Having been a rather sickly and awkward boy," he remembered, "I was . . . at first both nervous and distrustful of my own prowess. I had to train myself painfully and laboriously not merely as regards my body but as regards my soul and spirit."[1] This mingling of the carnal with the consecrated suggested that muscle might bear some mystical witness to morality. The words "strong," "manly," and "clean" flicker signally through Roosevelt's writings. In the throes of physical culture—a regimen ranging from calisthenics to combat sports—he glimpsed the gates of salvation. Years before famously referencing the "strenuous life" as a remedy to sedentary urban modernity, he had begun to formulate its meaning as a marker of personal redemption.

By embracing a fresh masculine ideal, Roosevelt followed a broader cultural inclination. In the wake of the Civil War, the old arcadian idols of agrarianism and the open frontier gave way to the dull routine of a factory labor system that wedged workers into cramped city spaces, pinched by poverty and unable to practice social mobility. For those many schoolboy scholars weaned on Jefferson's warning against sweatshops—"While we have land to labour then, let us never wish to see our citizens occupied at a work-bench"—the idea of masculinity needed to be rethought, as its early-republic antecedents now seemed outdated and irreplicable.[2] One could hardly imagine another Washington crossing another Delaware, another Daniel Boone crossing another Cumberland Gap, or another Ulysses Grant plunging his blue battalions into Virginia's heavily wooded wilderness in pursuit of Robert E. Lee's elusive army.

Concerns about the future of work and identity, industry and empire, rather, gave some shape and substance to the meaning of maleness in Gilded Age America. This quiet anxiety revealed itself in various ways, hailing the gridiron heroics of college football players, informing the growing vogue of "muscular Christianity" (YMCA shorthand for health, sacrifice, and physical strength), and even altering the prevailing trend of presidential grooming. Between Lincoln and Theodore Roosevelt, all but two of the White House's ten occupants sported facial hair; the muttonchopped John Quincy Adams and Martin Van Buren, by contrast, were the only pre–Civil War executives who dared to whisker. "The whole generation is womanised," as Henry James described this unease in his 1886 novel *The Bostonians*, "the masculine tone is passing out of the world; it's a feminine, a nervous, hysterical, chattering, canting age, an age of hollow phrases and false delicacy and exaggerated solicitudes and coddled sensibilities, which if we don't soon look out, will usher in the reign of mediocrity, of the feeblest and flattest and the most pretentious that has ever been."[3]

Young Theodore's earliest embrace of the masculine ideal occurred in the blood-and-guts act of taxidermy, his interest fueled in part, so he said, by a richly illustrated "volume of a hopelessly unscientific kind . . . about mammals," and perhaps more viscerally by the unexpected sight of a dead seal resting on a crest of wood near a certain Broadway market that he happened to be haunting. "That seal," he later wrote, "filled me with every possible feeling of romance and adventure." He soon began to stockpile mice, spiders, and bat cadavers, complete with rudimentary classification and indexing. Collection led to dissection—at which point the pickle-ish odor of formaldehyde and arsenic lingered about the house—and then to the desire for more elaborate trophies.[4]

At the age of thirteen Theodore convinced his father to employ John G. Bell, "a tall, clean-shaven, white-haired old gentleman, as straight as an Indian," so Roosevelt later recalled, to teach him the art of animal body preservation and display. Bell had once joined the legendary naturalist John James Audubon, author of *The Birds of America* (1827–1838), on a journey to the Upper Missouri River in present-day

Montana. Going to Bell's "musty little shop," Theodore learned how to mount birds—snowy owls, Egyptian plovers, and the occasional spruce grouse—as well as prepare skins. He considered his largely self-tutored mentor "a very interesting man, an American of the before-the-war type . . . [who] had no scientific knowledge" but enlarged the field of scholarship by his discovery of any number of buntings, sparrows, and whippoorwills.[5]

That same year young Theodore received from Thee his first firearm, a double-barreled pinfire shotgun of French extraction, which he later remembered as "excellent . . . for a clumsy . . . boy." Shooting with friends at Dobbs Ferry along the Hudson River led Roosevelt to the revelation that he was nearsighted, and he soon began to wear glasses. "I had no idea how beautiful the world was," he wrote, "until I got those spectacles."[6] This passionate devotion to nature, hunting, science, and collecting began to dominate his adolescence. These preferences and activities were supplemented by a liberal education both formal—including French, Latin, and German tutorials—and less so; he read an incredible number of books on his own, driven by an astonishing curiosity that carried him through James Fenimore Cooper's historical romances of the American frontier, Henry Wadsworth Longfellow's poetic sequence "The Saga of King Olaf" (costarring the hammer-wielding Norse god the "mighty Thor"), and *The Nibelungenlied*, an anonymously written medieval epic poem of the vengeance-and-honor kind adapted by Richard Wagner in the opera cycle *Der Ring des Nibelungen*.[7]

Roosevelt's mental development found some parallel in the parental push to strengthen his frail body. Since returning from Europe, Thee had shuffled the boy about—from Saratoga's leafy forest trails in upstate New York to C.V.S.'s Oyster Bay summer estate—searching for some climatic answer to his son's ongoing asthma. Frustrated, he brought Theodore to Dr. Alphonso D. Rockwell, something of a celebrity physician who treated Astors and Vanderbilts "and had," so his *New York Times* obituary later stated, "five horses shot under him" while serving in the Civil War. Rockwell described his young patient as "a bright, precocious boy . . . by no means robust," and mechanically recommended "more exercise." This suggestion caught Thee's attention, for he thought that Bamie's curved back might also benefit from a structure of physical training. Accordingly, he turned a second-story room in the family's Manhattan house into a gymnasium crammed full of "every imaginable swing and bar and seesaw." He then is said, according to Corinne, who got the story from her mother, to have called his son aside: "Theodore, you have the mind but you have not the body, and without the help of the body the mind cannot go as far as it should. You must *make* your body."[8]

Thee's edict may have merged with a still stronger compulsion on the part of the boy to hold his own in a scrape or scuffle, and to identify with the valor he encountered in shelves of vivid histories and the carefully curated legends of family lore. He later wrote:

> Having been ... sickly ... with no natural bodily prowess, and having lived much at home, I was at first quite unable to hold my own when thrown into contact with other boys of rougher antecedents. I was nervous and timid. Yet from reading of the people I admired—ranging from the soldiers of Valley Forge, and Morgan's riflemen, to the heroes of my favorite stories—and from hearing of the feats performed by my Southern forefathers and kinsfolk, and from knowing my father, I felt a great admiration for men who were fearless and who could hold their own in the world, and I had a great desire to be like them.[9]

A deeply motivated Roosevelt thus began to build his broomstick body, faithful to Thee's admonition as well as to his own ambition to swap illness for strength. Possibly some invidious parental comparison further informed his commitment to the gymnasium. "Sickness is always a shame," Thee is reported to have warned his receptive son, "and often a sin." Such sermons put Mittie at a disadvantage, for her chronic if ambiguous bouts of stress, depression, and fatigue set her outside the robust world her eldest son now aimed to embrace. And so he began to widen, tighten, and concentrate his frame in an environment largely, so Corinne remembered, "ungovernessed and unmaided."[10]

This masculine resolution he maintained in a sweat-stained upstairs exercise room, as well as during several country house summers near Riverdale along the Hudson, and even abroad when Thee once more conducted his family across the Atlantic—the restless Continent-trotting Roosevelts were again on the move, and this time a more mature Teedie was determined to absorb the wonders of the ancient and modern worlds.

6

The Jackals of Damascus

The Roosevelts' second grand tour (1872–73), a marathon journey through Egypt, the Levant, and Europe, was born of multiple motives. Builders were noisily erecting a new Manhattan home for the family, Thee had agreed to serve as American commissioner to the Vienna World's Fair, and the prospect of medicinal mineral waters—spas for Bamie—and presumably superior German educations for her siblings beckoned. A Paris pit stop promised Mittie boutique hopping among the beau monde, while a centerpiece Nile cruise held out hope that a dry climate might yet rid Theodore of his nagging asthma. The fourteen-year-old, proud proprietor of the "Roosevelt Museum of Natural History" (otherwise known as his bedroom), looked forward to hunting, sightseeing, and specimen collecting on three continents.

Boarding the SS *Russia*, a smooth-running five-years-old Cunard vessel, the Roosevelts left America in late October 1872. Docking once more in Liverpool, the family, following a week with the Bullochs, made a quick two-day London pause that prefaced slightly more extended stays in Brussels, Bonn, Paris, Turin, and Bologna, after which they crossed the Mediterranean. "How I gazed on it!" Theodore exclaimed in a travel diary before the Port of Alexandria, gateway to a city of some 210,000 and redolent with history. "It was Egypt, the land of my dreams . . . a land that was old when Rome was bright, was old when Babylon was in its glory, was old when Troy was taken! It was a sight to awaken a thousand thoughts, and it did." Hiring a carriage to the Hotel Abbat, the family passed through a vibrant, noisy street scene that fully concentrated Teedie's attention—"I shall never forget that drive. On all sides were screaming Arabs, shouting Dragomen, shrieking donkey boys and braying donkeys." Scouting about the city, he felt a whisper of disappointment while gazing up at Cleopatra's Needle ("somehow it did not impress me so much," he said of the weathered fifteenth-century BCE obelisk), though Pompey's Pillar, a Roman triumphal column in honor of the emperor Diocletian, caused a distinct stir—"I *felt* a great deal but I *said* nothing. You can not express yourself on such an occasion."[1]

The Roosevelts journeyed from Alexandria by rail to Cairo, where they boarded the *Ibis*—a long, lateen-rigged, dahabeah houseboat—and commenced a slow six-hundred-mile excursion south to Aswan, a center for tourism once garrisoned by Romans soldiers. Along the way Theodore, like so many, fell under the spell of Karnak's incomparable temple complex, a creature of many monarchs' construction—"I never was impressed by anything so much," he wrote of its otherworldly ruins. "It was not beautiful only, it was grand, magnificent, and awe-inspiring. It seemed to take me back thousands of years, to the time of the Pharaohs."[2]

As the weeks and months passed Theodore "outgrew all his clothes," so Bamie later wrote, "and of course there was no replacing them on the Nile." Undeterred in his tight trousers, the boy spent his days hunting with Thee, blasting every unsuspecting bird within range of his new shotgun (a Christmas present). "I have had great enjoyment from the shooting here," he wrote his aunt Anna. "The largest bird I have yet killed is a Crane which I shot as it rose from a lagoon near Thebes." Thee called Teedie "a most enthusiastic sportsman," while the most enthusiastic sportsman presumed to have secured "between one and two hundred skins."[3] These included pigeons and plovers, bats and sand chats, among other specimens.

Along the way, a different kind of rare bird unexpectedly came within the Roosevelts' purview—the Transcendentalist Ralph Waldo Emerson, beak-nosed, "ungainly in build" (said the son of Nathaniel Hawthorne), and fading slowly into senility. Born in 1803, the year of the Louisiana Purchase, and a onetime occupant of the Old Manse, a Concord property built by his grandfather and overlooking the North Bridge where minutemen had traded shots with British Army Regulars on a chilly April morning in 1775, Emerson, like the serenely decaying pyramids, reeked of historical association. "My father, who never lost a chance of bringing into the lives of his children some worth-while memory,"

Corinne remembered, "took us all to see the old poet, and I often think with pleasure of the lovely smile, somewhat vacant, it is true, but very gentle, with which he received the little children of his fellow countryman."[4] Emerson's eldest daughter, Ellen, wrote to a correspondent of her delight in making the Roosevelts' acquaintance—one of whom, toothy but pleasing, made an indelible impression:

> By degrees we came to like this family very much, and as we returned from the tombs at Beni Hassan, Mrs. R. asked Father and me to come to lunch with them. We agreed but first went to our boat to get brushed. Almost before we were ready, the pretty little boat the Roosevelt children used was waiting alongside, and we were rowed over to the Abou Erdan by Theodore, whose round red cheeks, honest blue yes, and perfectly brilliant teeth make him a handsome boy, though plain. He rowed with a pair of sculls, and a sailor behind him with another, talking to us. . . . Oh how much I enjoyed that visit![5]

Having their fill of the Nile, the Roosevelts moved on to Palestine, Syria, and Turkey, visiting Jerusalem ("just what I expected it to be" if a little on the small side, sniffed a travel-weary Theodore) among other biblical pilgrimage spots, before turning toward Europe. Thee needed to be in Vienna for the exposition.[6]

During the trip back to the Continent, Theodore suffered a number of ailments, ranging from stomach troubles to seasickness to the inevitable asthma. It is interesting to note that the complaints began to build as the pith of the trip neared its end. While pegging birds in Egypt, hunting jackals near Damascus, and climbing about the Judean highlands, he appeared to be in robust health. It is conceivable that, though this indicated a very real respiratory condition, he also perhaps imagined himself something of a wounded hero, now at rest on his return.

At this point in their journey the Roosevelts split up. Thee headed to Vienna while Mittie and Bamie made for the gentrified spa towns of Carlsbad and Franzensbad in today's Czech Republic before migrating to more metropolitan European shopping cities. The younger children, Theodore (age fourteen), Elliott (thirteen), and Corinne (eleven) stayed for several months in Dresden with the Minkwitz family, whose patriarch sat in the national Reichstag; there they were expected to study French and German. The location further recommended itself because the widow of Mittie's half brother, the old Confederate Daniel Stuart Elliott, lived nearby with her two children. Thus could Lucinda "Lucy" Elliott offer some slight kin oversight in a foreign setting. A city of nearly two hundred thousand situated on the River Elbe, Dresden, capital of the Kingdom of Saxony and part of the German Empire, had enjoyed a long history of cultural and artistic prominence. Retaining much of its medieval charm, the city boasted splendid museums, including the Zwinger, a palatial baroque edifice crammed with Old Masters, and the Semperoper, a magnificent neo-Renaissance opera house known for premiering, among others, Wagner's revolutionary works.

Like countless would-be Teutonophiles (including Mark Twain, who wrote, "All bad foreigners went to German Heaven—couldn't talk and wished they had gone to the other place"), Theodore found the language of Gutenberg and Goethe, Bach and Beethoven rough sledding, plodding through his lessons with little enthusiasm. Though assuring Thee in correspondence of his "considerable" academic progress, he appears to have defined "academic" loosely, as when introducing the familiar "Roosevelt Museum" methodology (slaying and flaying) to his unamused hosts. "My scientific pursuits cause the family a good deal of consternation," he wrote Aunt Anna of the poor Minkwitzes. "My arsenic was confiscated and my mice thrown (with the tongs) out of the window." Apparently impervious to such concerns, he kept, perhaps secretly, his taxidermy tools at the ready. Elliott noted, some weeks after the mice and tongs incident, that his brother had managed to skin a hedgehog and then hung it outside a window to dry—only to be defeated by a late-night thunderstorm. "Teedie woke up for a minute, turned over and said . . . 'Oh, it is raining and my hedgehog will be all spoiled.'" But having made, so Elliott said, only "a faint effort to get out of bed," his brother instead "sunk back and went to sleep."[7]

Mittie visited Dresden in early August, concerned at "find[ing] Teedie still with asthmatic feelings." She assured Thee, who remained in Austria, "Nobody could regret to take [him] away from his German more than I do, but he was too unwell to study," before packing up all the children, including Lucy's son John, and journeying to the Engadin, a picturesque valley region in the eastern Swiss Alps known for its therapeutic high-altitude air. After two weeks Mittie made for Paris to improve her wardrobe and find furnishings for the new Manhattan home; her children, shepherded by their tutor, Fräulein Anna, returned to Dresden for a final and short season of study. Along with their lessons the boys took up boxing, the absent Thee, now making his way separately back to New York, having sent gloves from London. Mittie found this latest diversion hardly charming, writing her husband, "Teedie [calling himself "Skinny" in the ring] had a bloody nose and Ellie [a.k.a. "Swelly"] a knock on the head of which they were proud.... I think it a horrid amusement."[8] In late October Mittie and the children, along with Bamie, left the Continent and headed to Liverpool, returning to New York in early November.

Theodore's two extended journeys abroad beg the question of what they meant to the boy. He later described the second tour as particularly impactful: "This trip formed a really useful part of my education.... I was ... old enough to enjoy it thoroughly and profit by it." Of his presidential antecedents, only Thomas Jefferson, James Monroe, John Quincy Adams, and James Buchanan had enjoyed such sustained contact with the Continent prior to their tenures in office; all were American ministers in one European capital or another, though none strayed so far as Roosevelt, who wandered beyond the rote London-Paris route to Egypt and Asia Minor. The experience assuredly fired the boy's blooming imagination, offering a memory chain of enchantments to be revisited over the years. He now held vivid images of the ancient ruins, storied rivers, and capital cities that edged their way into his reckoning with the world.[9]

Back in America, the Roosevelts occupied a new town house in an area of the city the *New York Times* later compared to Paris's fashionable Rue de la Paix. Joining a northerly migration among Manhattan's posh, they encamped at 6 West Fifty-Seventh Street, a couple of blocks south of Central Park. As many as nine servants staffed the residence. "It seems like another landmark reached on my life's journey," a proud Thee wrote Mittie of their sumptuous new mansion, which featured expensive Persian rugs, oak beams on the ceiling, and fine Eastlake-style paneling throughout—a top-floor gymnasium crowned the structure. Russell Sturgis, a Maryland-born cofounder of the Metropolitan Museum of Art and architect of such Victorian Gothic creations as Yale University's Battell Chapel and the First Baptist Church of Tarrytown, designed the building.[10]

The following year (1874) Thee began renting a charming summer retreat, a quiet country residence near Oyster Bay, Long Island, approximately thirty miles east of Manhattan. Its spacious verandah and clean white columns begged a sentimental comparison to Mittie's dear Bulloch Hall. The family called it "Tranquility." The house sat about two miles from the site where Theodore would later build Sagamore Hill, his own Oyster Bay abode. Thee's lavish outlays occurred in the wake of C.V.S.'s recent death (1871). The old man had left his four sons a $10 million bequest—Thee's share came to $2.5 million, nearly $62 million in today's currency. A New York general laborer, by comparison, made about $12 per week in 1870, while a gas fitter earned $15, a carpenter $27, and a mason $30.[11]

There is a photo of Tranquility kept in the Library of Congress: Thee and Mittie are sitting at opposite ends of a chair-strewn colonnade as Corinne and Edith Carow relax on the lawn.[12] Theodore, preparing for college at the time, seemed, along with the rest of his family, to have assumed that he and Edith—Teedie and Edie—were to be someday betrothed. Nothing had been said, though it was easy to assume, given their long and close acquaintance, that friendship had at some imperceptible point become courtship.

Such affairs of the heart, however, would have to wait, for Theodore, intensely wrapped up in the business of being a Roosevelt, now ventured out on his own for the first time, departing New York for the uncertain virtues of college, adding to his intimacies as a son of Harvard.

7

College Brahmin

A jumble of boyhood illnesses conspired with protracted travel to complicate Theodore's conventional education. Prior to three congenial years with Arthur Cutler, a young Harvard graduate, spent preparing for college, he had made do with a slew of tutors, a brief stay at a neighboring East Twentieth Street private school run by one Professor McMullen, and the still earlier ministrations of a French governess—"a loved and valued 'mam'selle,'" so Roosevelt reported.[1] On certain subjects, say natural history and zoology, this maven of birds and taxidermy ranged far beyond his peers. When assigned topics to write on, however, he lost interest and tended to drift. One might say that his precollegiate education was ramshackle in the best sense. Eternally curious, Theodore read constantly, displayed a deep interest in nature, and absorbed the contrasting family customs of southern Bullochs and Dutch Roosevelts as prods to illuminating the past. Eager to succeed, he determined to achieve respectable grades at Harvard, though the college never came close to firing his imagination.

This was not all Harvard's fault. Cambridge's store of distinguished literary lions, supplemented by Greater Boston's surplus of casual genius, included such thrice-named eminences as Henry Wadsworth Longfellow, James Russell Lowell, Oliver Wendell Holmes, Ralph Waldo Emerson, and the historian Henry Brooks Adams. The perks of privilege—Roosevelt & Son could also claim a magic name—were undoubtedly at work when Theodore, only a few months into his first academic year, was invited to Adams's well-appointed Marlborough Street brownstone in the exclusive Back Bay. "After dinner we had some real Turkish coffee," he reported to Bamie. "The Doctor improves very much on acquaintance." Roosevelt occasionally encountered other specimens of the plumed professoriate, as when forging through William James's course on the anatomy and physiology of vertebrates; he remembered the section, in which he received a 79, as "extremely interesting," something of a rare admission, for he more generally thought Harvard's delivery of the sciences distressingly theoretical compared to his own freewheeling adventures in "formaldehyde and arsenic."[2]

Despite spending several years in the family gymnasium, the firm-bodied Theodore still struck a lean, consumptive pose. He stood, a few months before entering Harvard in the fall of 1876, five feet, eight inches, but weighed only 124 pounds with a narrow twenty-six-and-a-half-inch waist. (West Point cadets about this time averaged nearly 140 pounds.) Clearly eager to affect his own style, that of a Victorian dandy, Roosevelt arrived on campus with reddish side-whiskers, much to the amusement of some classmates. The college counted a student body of 820, of whom 232 were in Theodore's freshman class; fewer than a quarter of these were the products of public schools. Tuition was $150 for the academic year, with various other expenses—books, stationery, clothing, and so on—ranging from an estimated $499 ("Least" in the school's coding) to $1,365 ("Ample"). This latter category included certain amenities, "Servant" at $30 and "Societies" at $50, presumably beyond the reach of the least. The Harvard "President's Report for 1876–77," perhaps sensitive to complaints that the school scarcely offered an appropriate model for democratic education, insisted that "the considerations which affect [student expenditures] have little or nothing to do with the College." Among these considerations, however, was pedigree, and Harvard was intensely interested in filling its seats with the sons of New England's first families. Most undergraduates grew up no more than a hundred miles from Cambridge, thus replicating a hierarchy that one could find among both its faculty and its incestuous governance bodies, whose interchangeable patrician names—awash in Lowells and Lodges, Wadsworths, Cabots, and Quincys—read like a dusty American history primer.[3]

To some, the college bore a distinct resemblance to an exclusive club. Adams presumed a quiet conspiracy among its fathers to perpetuate "custom, social ties, convenience, and, above all, economy. . . . Any other education," he quipped, "would have required a serious effort." The Boston editor and man of letters Horace E. Scudder, a Williams

College graduate, deplored Harvard's sheltered indifference to the bustling world beyond its gilded gates, writing in the July 1876 *Scribner's Monthly* that the school fostered a "well-bred cynicism and arrogant coolness, which, in a young man, do[es] not be-token the healthiest, strongest character." Among this blessed Brahminocracy, he continued, "the divine fervor of enthusiasm is openly, or by implication, voted a vulgar thing."[4] Roosevelt, of course, had enthusiasm in spades. And into this polite society, along with his plover pelts and whiskers, he unapologetically arrived, an exuberant personality, a tanned Nile voyager among a choir of pale prep-school boys.

Before Theodore invaded Cambridge, Bamie, mindful of her brother's lingering asthma, scouted ahead for rooms, concerned that the first-floor lodgings in the Yard, the only space made available to him by the college, were on the damp side. She identified a pleasant second-story apartment roughly between Harvard Square and the Charles River at 16 (now 36) Winthrop Street. The redbrick residence, built in 1860, featured large windows that invited the sun, and Bamie, wanting Theodore to commence his studies in comfort and familiarity, brought from New York an array of his favorite relics, including a collection of knives and stuffed birds. "When I arrived here on Wednesday night," he wrote Mittie in late September, "I found a fire burning in the grate, and the room looking just as cosy and comfortable as it could look. . . . What would I have done without Bamie!" He expressed further an eagerness to "take breakfast at commons, where the food is very fair," though within a week had informed Mittie otherwise—"I am decidedly discontented with the food at Commons, I am going to join a table with some of the Boston men." Assuming the status of an honorary Brahmin, Roosevelt quickly took notice of the campus's high-born Bostonians, informing Corinne, "On this very account I have avoided being very intimate with the New York fellows."[5] True to himself, however, he balanced this exercise in snobbery by sharing his quickly cluttered rooms with snakes, a turtle, and any number of mounted skins.

During this freshman-year winter, Roosevelt wrote his parents, eager to "describe completely one day of college life." Choosing a Monday, he chronicled a prenoon routine of breakfast, friendship, and a recitation:

> At half past seven my scout [servant], having made the fire and blacked the boots calls me, and I get around to breakfast at eight.

Only a few of the boys are at breakfast, most having spent the night in Boston. Our quarters now are nice and sunny, and the room is prettily papered and ornamented. For breakfast we have tea or coffee, hot biscuits, toast, chops or beef steak, and buckwheat cakes. After breakfast I study till ten, when the mail arrives and is eagerly inspected. From eleven to twelve there is a latin recitation with a meek-eyed Professor, who calls me Mr.Ruseé-felt (hardly any one can get my name correctly, except as Rosy).[6]

From the Latin classroom Roosevelt broke at midday for physical activity: "Then I go over to the gymnasium, where I have a set-to with the gloves with 'General' Lister, the boxing master—for I am training to box among the lightweights in the approaching match for the championship of Harvard."[7] Having his fill exchanging leather, Theodore eased into a casually structured postmeridian:

Then comes lunch, at which all the boys are assembled in an obstreperously joyful condition; a state of mind which brings on a free fight, to the detriment of Harry Jackson, who, with a dutch cheese and some coffee cups is put under the table; which proceeding calls forth dire threats of expulsion from Mrs Morgan. Afterwards studying and recitations took up the time till halfpast four; as I was then going home, suddenly I heard "Hi, Ted! Catch!" and a base ball whizzed by me. Our two "babies," Bob Bacon and Arthur Hooper, were playing ball behind one of the buildings. So I stayed and watched them, until the ball went through a window and a proctor started out to inquire—when we abruptly separated. That evening I took dinner with Mr and Mrs Tudor, and had a very pleasant home-like time.[8]

Presumably Thee's connections ensured his son access to any number of proper Bostonians—the Tudor family having made a fortune in the international ice trade.

Beyond the classroom, Roosevelt maintained an active social and sport regimen at Harvard, a mixture of whist and wrestling, a combination of poetry and dance classes giving way to the pleasures of hiking and the inevitable dissecting of his beloved specimens. On Sundays he taught Bible study, clearly emulating his father's example. "There were many things I tried to do because he did them," Theodore later wrote to the journalist and fellow Crimson alum Edward Sandford Martin, "which I found afterwards were not in my line. For instance, I taught Sunday school all through college, but afterwards gave it up, just as on experiment I could not do the charitable work which he had done." Upon reflection, he continued, a deeply ingrained Victorian desire to do well framed his Cambridge days—and eased him into athletics as well. "My ordinary companions in college would I think have had a tendency to look down upon me for doing Sunday school work if I had not also been a corking boxer. . . . I went in for boxing and wrestling a good deal, and I really think that while this was partly because I liked them as sports, it was even more because I intended to be a middling decent fellow, and I did not intend that anyone should laugh at me with impunity because I was decent."[9]

This defensiveness suggests the extent to which Theodore struck his classmates as unconventional and thus ripe for well-intentioned—or otherwise—ribbing. "When it was not considered good form to move at more than a walk, Roosevelt was always running" across the Yard, a friend remembered. Accustomed to being in a classroom of one, he peppered his instructors with queries. One contemporary noted that "it was perfectly proper for a student to interrupt the lecture and ask questions, but Roosevelt had a tendency to keep it up and run it into the ground"; an impatient geology professor finally cut the young man off one day: "Now look here, Roosevelt, let me talk." Theodore's restraint from the common sum of small sins—"I do not find it nearly so hard as I expected not to drink and smoke," he wrote a little priggishly to Thee his first year—may also have made him a target.[10] On one occasion he engaged in a fistfight with another student, swinging wildly at friends who tried to separate the combatants.

More prosaically, Roosevelt embraced his class advantage at Harvard. Unlike most undergraduates, he kept a horse and carriage in Cambridge—and these possessions, along with tight-fitting trousers and finely tailored jackets, marked him as a "swell." His attention to the campus's pecking order is evident in a junior-year note to Bamie, in which he crowed that, though he ranked nineteenth in his class, "only one *gentleman* stands ahead of me." Most of the boys with superior scores were mere grinds, he meant, prodded by their comparative penury to toil for high grades. Others were aware to a fraction of where Roosevelt resided in the college's hierarchy. Thomas Perry, Newport-born, married to a

Cabot, and a writing instructor, described Theodore's work as "good," while allowing that it lacked a certain genteel polish: "In this class there were at least half a dozen who knew and loved the best things, and who wrote well. Roosevelt's writing was to the point, but did not have their air of cultivation."[11]

Academically, Theodore completed his first year at Harvard with a middling if respectable class ranking of 111. He struggled mightily in Greek (scraping by with a score of 58—a passing grade being 50), while doing particularly well in a course on German composition and translation (92) that did not challenge his wobbly oral proficiency in the language.[12] In all, and despite being knocked out for a month by measles in the winter, he averaged a 75 in seven courses. Maturity and increasing familiarity with the Harvard system raised his grades the next year to an average of 80—this, despite the unexpected and devastating death of his father.

8

These Terrible Three Days

During his first Harvard fall, Theodore wrote Thee a glowing note thick with boyish affection: "I do not think there is a fellow in College who has a family that love him as much as you all do me, and I am *sure* there is no one who has a Father who is also his best and most intimate friend, as you are mine."[1] Such endearments rolled easily from Roosevelt's collegiate pen. In correspondence he addressed Mittie with variations of "Darling Little Motherling," while "My Own Dear Bamie" and "Little Pet Pussie" (Corinne) received a torrent of warm letters from Cambridge. Unabashedly sentimental, he recalled late in life the casual joy that Thee particularly brought to his children's lives.

> We . . . adored him. We used to wait in the library in the evening until we could hear his key rattling in the latch of the front hall, and then rush out to greet him; and we would troop into his room while he was dressing, to stay there as long as we were permitted, eagerly examining anything which came out of his pockets which could be regarded as an attractive novelty. Every child has fixed in his memory various details which strike it as of grave importance. The trinkets he used to keep in a little box on his dressing-table we children always used to speak of as "treasures."[2]

Roosevelt, when himself a father in possession of certain pocket curios, cultivated a similar gladsome routine with his own inquisitive chicks.

In October of Theodore's sophomore year, President Rutherford B.

Hayes nominated Thee to serve as collector of the Port of New York—a vital post charged with receiving duties on foreign goods entering the country's busiest harbor. Its incumbent, the tall, chubby-faced Chester Arthur, four years from taking the presidential oath of office, received one of the highest incomes of any federal official. The nomination broke to the surface a brewing intraparty dispute between regular and reform Republicans over the question of patronage. Among the latter, Hayes, sensitive to mounting criticism that the GOP monopolized the spoils of office for their own, pushed Thee forward as an honest, independent philanthropist. Regular (or Old Guard) Republicans preferred the existing system of sinecures and were led by Senator Roscoe Conkling, "Lord Roscoe" some whispered before his imperious carriage and sense of self-importance. Thomas Nast, the outstanding editorial cartoonist of the century's second half, liked to caricature Conkling as a strutting peacock, though the politician's Mephistophelian beard suggested still other possibilities.

While Senate Republicans clashed over Thee's appointment, the would-be collector's health showed unmistakable signs of decline, soon to be diagnosed as inoperable bowel cancer. On December 16, 1877, the day the upper chamber, under Conkling's direction, rejected Thee's nomination 31–25, Theodore wrote to Bamie from Cambridge, "I am very uneasy about Father. Does the Doctor think it anything serious?" No doubt reflecting on Thee's former efforts to remedy his children's ailments with wandering cures, and kept innocent of the illness's rapid progress, he suggested "a travelling trip would be the best thing for him." Roosevelt arrived in Manhattan for the holidays, unaware of his father's dire situation; accordingly, after a twelve-day stay, he returned to college for the new semester. At this point, Thee, his dark mane turned white, his increasing discomfort unevenly medicated, so a distressed Elliott recorded, with a "chloroform sleep," commenced a rapid descent— severe peritonitis (inflammation of the tissue lining the abdomen's inner wall) had set in. Corinne watched in shock, writing to Edith near the end, "I have sat with him some seven hours. He slept most of it but at times was in fearful agony. O Edith, it is the most frightful thing to see the person you love best in the world in terrible pain and not to be able to do a thing to alleviate it."[3]

Back in his Winthrop Street apartment Theodore, shielded from the truth and presuming a remission in order—"Father seems much brighter"—recorded in a daybook shortly after the New Year Thee's private parting words: "After all I was the dearest of his children to him." He was thus unprepared upon receiving notice five weeks later to return home immediately. The cancer moved quickly, however, perhaps after all protecting the nineteen-year-old from the final scenes of a terrible death, which he missed by only a few hours. "Saturday February 9," he identified the black date in a diary. "My dear Father."[4]

Roosevelt described the period between Thee's death and burial as "these terrible three days." On the trip down from Cambridge he had suffered in "hideous suspense" from the abrupt summons, a blow that only intensified when he arrived home and "kissed the dear, dead face and realized [Father] would never again on this earth speak to me." In late February Thee's estate was divided, as per his will, among his heirs; Theodore received $8,000 a year (about $240,000 a year in today's currency), a sum he knowingly referred to as "comfortable although not rich."[5]

Roosevelt's diary entries in March reveal an unrelieved suffering, complicated by the need to complete Harvard's spring term, which had begun the day before Thee's burial. These bleak passages read in part: "Have been thinking about Father all the evening, have had a good square break down"; "Looking back on his life, it seems as if mine must be such a weak useless one in comparison"; and "Every now & then there are very bitter moments." One particular incantation appeared in various forms throughout the year, as it did in a clinging August clause: "I have been thinking a great deal of father." This aching sentiment, with its attendant *père-fils* comparisons, he never escaped entirely. "Do you know that at the end of my term here," he wrote a family friend during his presidency, "I shall be exactly the age father was when he died? Unconsciously, I always find I am trying to model myself with my children on the way he was with us."[6]

Though distraught over Thee's passing, Theodore completed a strong sophomore campaign at Harvard. He did best in German Composition and Exercises (96) and well in Elementary Botany (89) and Anglo-American Constitutional History (87), while barely scraping by in French (51). Home for the summer, he engaged in at least two possibly grief-related acts of violence, shooting a neighbor's insistent dog ("rolling it over with my revolver very neatly as it ran alongside the horse") and firing on a host of targets ranging, so he carelessly said, "from bottles or buoys to sharks and porpoises" while cruising Long Island Sound.[7]

Returning to Cambridge that fall, Theodore accepted an invitation to join the Porcellian Club, founded in 1791, so the most common version has it, when a student, harboring a swine in his room and fearing faculty intervention, arranged an impromptu midnight meal among friends that beckoned future fellowship of the side-dish-and-pork sort. "Pig Club" didn't quite strike the proper collegiate note, though the Latinate "Porcellian" (from "*porcus*") did the trick. Several Civil War–era notables—including the Boston abolitionists Wendell Phillips and Charles Sumner, as well as Rooney Lee (son of General Robert E.)—preceded Roosevelt into "the Porc," as did a crush of Cabots, Lowells, and Saltonstalls. Years later Theodore's distant cousin, the competitively sociable Franklin Roosevelt, was blackballed from the club, giving him, so his wife, Eleanor, inferred, a lingering "inferiority complex."[8]

A few weeks after joining the *porcus* caucus, Theodore wrote Bamie, "Of course, I am delighted to be in, and have great fun up there; there is a billiard table, magnificent library, punch-room &c, and my best friends are in it." Though entry into the Porc constituted for Roosevelt a kind of collegiate social pinnacle (when writing as president to Kaiser Wilhelm II of his eldest daughter's engagement, he let slip the bridegroom-to-be's coveted Porcellian pedigree), he also joined some dozen campus clubs including Hasty Pudding (the country's oldest theatrical organization), the rifle and glee clubs, and the school's Natural History Society, to which he contributed a learned manifesto "On the Gills of Crustaceans."[9]

Academically, however, Harvard disappointed Roosevelt. He thought its uncritical embrace of scientific objectivity a schoolboy's excuse to tangle with theorems and abstractions rather than life itself. "As soon as I left college," he wrote some years later, "I got into active politics and there I found that the 'economic man' of most textbooks simply did not exist, and that many of the textbooks which in college had been held up to me as susceptible of immediate application to the practical facts of life were of no use when thus applied—exactly as neither Plato's *Republic* nor More's *Utopia* is of practical value as regards specific acts of legislation whether at Albany or Washington."[10]

Early in his collegiate career, Roosevelt had thought to become an ornithologist, his passion for birds (and bird shooting) now several years old. This never happened, of course, and there are mixed views as to why. Perhaps an academic career seemed to him—or his family—too steep a step down from the privileged life of a Roosevelt & Son legatee. It is difficult to envision his unusual energy occupied agreeably in department meetings, grading undergraduate exams, and having his research suffer the "revise and resubmit" syndrome of the peer review process. It is also conceivable that laboratory work—the chilly, antiseptic atmosphere of beakers, tongs, and test tubes—failed to stir his racing imagination. What, after all, could a closet of clean white lab coats mean to a young man who had recorded in his diary of watching warblers in Syria, tawny-hued kestrels hunting in Jerusalem, and a wake of "great black vultures" feeding in the Nile Delta? Roosevelt clearly craved to be in the field.[11]

He could, moreover, consider himself already a practicing ornithologist, having, along with his Harvard friend Harry Minot, put together a brief study, *The Summer Birds of the Adirondacks in Franklin County, N.Y.*, privately printed in 1877. "Written in the mountains," so Theodore noted, the small book cataloged with light annotation ninety-seven birds, beginning with Robin ("Moderately common. Sometimes found in the woods") and concluding with Herring Gull ("Rare"). As a naturalist, Roosevelt, if one might conjecture, wanted to be trooping about the teeming Galápagos Islands with Charles Darwin, exploring the vast Andes with Alexander von Humboldt, and searching the North American continent for elusive woolly mammoths with Lewis and Clark. Laboratory zoology paled by comparison. "In college I had determined to become a naturalist," he wrote a former classmate late in his presidency, "but I was perfectly clear that I was to be an out-of-doors fauna naturalist; and this my college professors united in declaring was an impossibility and that the only really scientific man with a career worth having was the scientific man who limited himself to work in the study with the microscope. After a while I . . . made up my mind that I should try some other career."[12]

It is perhaps not surprising, considering the intellectual climate of late-nineteenth-century America, that Harvard imparted upon Roosevelt an education trafficking in dressed-up notions of "Teutonic" supremacy. Nathaniel Southgate Shaler, in whose geology class he received his highest senior year mark (91), proved an especially influential mentor. Both an officer and a scholar, serving in the Union army and authoring a study of the Kentucky frontier, he appealed to Theodore's notions of a mentally alert and physically active man. The thickly bearded professor, born into a southern slaveholding family, also indulged in the casual scientific racism of his times. Writing on "The Negro Problem" (1884) in the popular *Atlantic Monthly*, Shaler proffered a host of inelegant observations. The formerly enslaved, he insisted, were better off in their bondage: "Every experiment of freeing blacks on this continent has in the end resulted in even worse conditions than slavery brought to them"; evolution worked against blacks: "They cannot as a race, for many generations, be brought to the level of our own people"; and race-mixing weakened civilization: "The halfbreeds are more inclined to vice and much shorter-lived, and are of weaker mental power."[13]

Some years later Frederick Ranlett, a Boston lawyer and Crimson alum, published "Theodore Roosevelt's College Rank and Studies" in the *Harvard Graduates' Magazine*. In the article he asked, in regard to mentors: "Is it a mere conceit to think that from the sturdy nature of Nathaniel Southgate Shaler, keen observer, good fighter, good friend, hater of shams, some strong and vital emanation of spirit may have passed into the character of Theodore Roosevelt?" Taking an interest in the essay, the president wrote to Ranlett from his Oyster Bay summer White House, "You are quite right as to the effect that Shaler produced upon me."[14]

Open to Shaler's influence, though more generally frustrated with Harvard's "scientific professors" who turned up their well-credentialed noses, so he said, at "the old school of faunal naturalists," Roosevelt left the career question hanging.[15] In other respects, however, he moved to bring a greater degree of permanence to his life—reaching for manhood, he thought it time to have his one great-and-forever affair of the heart.

Part II

SUNSET, SUNRISE

In a fortnight I shall go out West.
>Theodore Roosevelt, 1884

Eager to "hold my own in the rough and tumble":
Roosevelt in the New York State Assembly.

9

Alice Lee

The impression grew over the years that Theodore and Edith Carow shared an understanding. And that presumptive coupling caused certain tensions among certain interested parties. An anxious Corinne admired Edie immensely, considering herself less sophisticated, well read, and interesting. "The only person to whom I try to be faithful," she wrote in a diary at the age of fifteen, "is my dear Edith, and she thinks my letters stupid!" In idolizing Theodore, however, Corinne found her feelings for Carow challenged by accompanying strains of envy and competition. Her brother's exchanges with Edie proved equally complicated, though for other reasons. In August 1878, six months after Thee's death, he appears to have abruptly proposed to Edith at Tranquility, the family's rented summer house. Despite their long intimacy as neighbors, playmates, and friends—"mama showed me the portrait of Eidieth . . . and her face stired up in me homesickness and longings," he had written at the age of eleven while traveling abroad—she rejected the suit for reasons that remain obscure. A few years later Roosevelt said simply, "We both of us had, and I suppose have, tempers that were far from being the best."[1]

Perhaps Edith sensed that her supposed beau, only nineteen, had yet to recover from his beloved father's passing, asking for her hand in some not altogether complimentary attitude of grief and need. In any case, she said no. And so opened the door for his grief and need to alight on another. This is where Alice Lee comes in.

In October, fresh off the turbulence at Tranquility, Roosevelt, now a Harvard junior, accompanied Crimson classmate Dick Saltonstall (whom he described to Mittie as "a good sort of fellow—but painfully 'fresh'") to the latter's Chestnut Hill estate for a weekend. There he met Alice Lee, daughter of the prominent banker George Cabot Lee and friend of Dick's sister Rose. In proper Victorian fashion, Roosevelt's relationship with Alice, nearly three years his junior, began with a family-attended Sunday church service followed by a more intimate round of chestnut picking. Prior to meeting Alice, Roosevelt, despite a natural exuberance, had managed to avoid any semblance of falling victim to love at first sight. His affection for Edith had surfaced over several years and within the safe social context of their families and friends. He lacked, moreover, what one might call a romantic readiness, his greatest interest in females up to this time being his indulgent sisters, who took him uncritically and on his own terms. One Bostonian, a debutante of the late 1870s, remembered the young Roosevelt as "studious, ambitious, eccentric—not the sort to appeal at first." Boisterous and restless, plainspoken, and more of a hopper than a dancer, he could scarcely play the practiced gallant; one might still catch about him the faint scent of formaldehyde. His voluminous reading, wide travels, and mixing among the starry Cambridge college-ocracy give the impression of a developed presence, though his interactions with girls struck a distinctly less sophisticated, less confident note. According to one of his daughters, "he tended to hide his feelings about women."[2]

Alice (called "Sunshine") liked to laugh, relished social occasions, and enjoyed hiking and tennis. Tall, trim, and agreeably swan-necked, she had honey-colored hair, arresting light-gray eyes, and a small angled-up nose. Contemporaries called her "enchanting," "gay," and "exceptionally bright." Though attached to Edith the way a slightly oblivious boy might be attached to his mother, Roosevelt had never really invested deeply in the relationship, possibly not knowing how. He described Alice, by contrast, as "my first love." How much of this had to do with the previous several months' hardship is difficult to say. Had Thee lived, would Theodore so quickly have considered marriage? Did Edith's rejection lead to a rapid-rebound relationship? And did he apply pressure on himself, now an upperclassman, to firm up otherwise vague and indefinite plans for the future? Perhaps he simply felt a physical passion—"my first"—that moved him off the mark. "As long as I live," he told a cousin at this time, "I shall never forget how sweetly she looked, and how prettily she greeted me."[3]

Only a month after making Alice's acquaintance Roosevelt confided in a diary that he meant to marry the girl. But the girl wasn't so sure. The urgency of his appeal and the escalation of visits were flattering if perhaps excessive for Alice, accustomed to her own Chestnut Hill set. Unable to mask his innocence, he showed each emotion, determined to force the moment to bend his way. "I have been anxiously expecting a letter from you and Rose for the last two or three days," he wrote to her from Cambridge in early December, "but none has become." For good measure he advertised his aching availability: "I have been dexterously avoiding forming any engagements for Saturday." Five days later, in a more private plea, he beseeched his distant Dutch Reformed deity for the strength to remain true to his late father's example, doing "nothing I would have been ashamed to confess to him."[4]

For Roosevelt, questions of eros and occupation were naturally knitted together. At one time he had believed "I shall probably . . . pursue a scientific course," though his interest in Alice quickly quashed this—to be sure faint—possibility. Declaring himself "in love," rather, he wrote to a classmate of his desire to make "everything subordinate to winning her; so you can perhaps understand a change in my ideas as regards science," which, considering the years of training involved, would have been a dubious career track for people of their social prominence. Certainly, Sunshine shared none of his interest in animal biology. Once when the couple visited a zoo, so Roosevelt reported to Corinne, "I detected her wondering, from vague reminiscences of poodles, 'who had shaved the lions'—being otherwise unable to account for their manes."[5]

In Cambridge, Theodore completed a busy academic year while paying court to Alice. He took second in the school's lightweight boxing division, helped to organize a finance club (which invited Henry George, author of the immensely popular *Progress and Poverty*, a primer on economic inequality in Gilded Age America, to campus), and enjoyed a two-week winter hunting trip to Maine. His letters during this year are inevitably seasoned with some construction of ". . . went out to Chestnut Hill."[6]

Academically, Roosevelt managed his strongest semester, finishing with an 84 percent. His scores ranged from 97 in elementary zoology and 92 in geography to 60 in forensic science; he now ranked thirteenth in his class. He considered himself altogether quite fortunate. "I have had uncommonly good luck in everything this year," he wrote Corinne, "from studies to societies." In June, he proposed to Alice—who said no, though in a light and inoffensive way that made it clear he might pursue his suit when the summer ended and he returned to Cambridge.[7]

That fall Alice, now eighteen, came out in society. And though preoccupied with the rituals of debutantism—always having about her a bevy of bright friends—she agreed, accompanied by said bevy, to visit the Roosevelts in New York shortly after Christmas. There, on his own turf, Theodore played the consummate swain, showing her about town, frequenting parties, and, of course, "danc[ing] the old year out and drink[ing] the new year in." He found her presence "perfectly lovely ... and so natural." Having just come out, Alice agreed, apparently with a bit of coaxing, to put herself back in—consenting the following month, on her own turf, to marry Roosevelt. "At last everything is settled," he filled up a diary page, "but it seems impossible to realize. I am so happy that I dare not trust in my own happiness."[8]

One for endearments both playful and clichéd, Roosevelt, who occasionally addressed Mittie in correspondence as "Darling Muffie," now placed Alice on a pedestal. Certain labored refrains flit about his *lettres d'amour*; the identifiers "pretty," "pure," and "sweet" are reflexive fallbacks, while his intended's presence fairly glowed in a sequence of superlatives that included "little sunshine," "little sunbeam," and "my sunny faced darling." The noun "witch" and adverb "bewitchingly" also pop up, as when the freshly affianced TR informed a cousin, "The little witch led me a dance before she surrendered, I can tell you, and the last six months have been perfect agony. . . . How bewitchingly pretty she is!"[9]

With the wedding set for October 27, the groom's twenty-second birthday, Roosevelt completed his degree in the spring. He maintained as always an active club agenda, serving as Hasty Pudding's secretary, Porcellian's librarian, and the *Harvard Advocate*'s editor—the latter sheet subsequently to come into its own by printing the apprentice works of Wallace Stevens, T. S. Eliot, and E. E. Cummings. Academically he appears, with a 78 percent average, to have slacked off a bit. Nearly all his courses were electives, though only sections in advanced zoology and geology seem to have held his attention. Accordingly, his class rank slipped to a more than respectable 21 out of a graduating cohort of 161; balancing social occasions with days-on-end cramming sessions, he graduated magna cum laude.[10]

That summer Roosevelt happily circulated among Alice, friends, and family. Only the unwelcome return of an annoying illness—"laid up by a touch of cholera morbus. Very embarrassing for a lover, is'n't it? So unromantic, you know; suggestive of too much unripe fruit"—cast a shadow. After hiking about Maine in early July, he took a longer August holiday to the Midwest with Elliott, where the brothers experienced "good shooting" in Iowa. Praising "the farm people" of rural America as "intensely independent" and "pretty rough," Theodore, a Harvard boxing tough by way of a Manhattan brownstone, enjoyed tramping about the Corn Belt. "I do'n't wonder at their thinking us their equals," he wrote Bamie in the manner of one slumming, "for we are dressed about as badly as mortals could be, with our cropped heads, unshaven faces, dirty gray shirts, still dirtier yellow trowsers and cowhide boots; moreover, we can shoot as well as they can."[11]

Though proud of mixing among the natives, Theodore grew concerned with Elliott's drinking. "We have come back here after . . . hunting," he wrote Corinne from Chicago, and "Elliott revels in the change to civilization—and epicurean pleasures. As soon as we got here he took some ale to get the dust out of his throat; then a milkpunch because he was thirsty; a mint julep because it was hot; a brandy smash 'to keep the cold out of his stomach'; and then sherry and bitters to give him an appetite."[12]

As the years passed, the bitters-sipping Elliott could feel himself sliding behind his charismatic older brother. Afflicted, despite a regular gymnasium regimen, by seizures and fainting spells, he flashed signs of anxiety over his future. "What will I become when I am a man?" he had once written to Thee, expressing his apparently slender hope to be "as good as you, if it is in me. But it is hard." Unable to concentrate in school, he had been sent to chalky West Texas at the age of fifteen to hunt and toughen up. Instead, he fell into a funk, writing his father guiltily of "spending all your money" on a false cure. He never went to college. He did, however, inherit Thee's fine, strong looks, rode and shot better than Theodore, and was the more charming, socially adept, and sophisticated of the boys; many preferred his easy company to that of his intense sibling. Perhaps some quiet competition surfaced on the midwestern trip as when, so Theodore told Corinne, Elliott consumed his liquors and "marveled at my . . . roast beef and potatoes . . . appetite." At night, so the reforming asthmatic insisted, "*he* felt 'stuffy' . . . *I* did'n't."[13]

Theodore and Alice were married at the Brookline Unitarian Church in Massachusetts; a small throng of Manhattan politicos, including incoming Brooklyn (and future New York City) mayor Seth Low, were in attendance, a tribute to the groom's late and obviously still lamented father. A bit of New England royalty graced the ceremony as well, including old Amos Lawrence, a wealthy merchant/philanthropist who, in the 1850s, had helped finance John Brown's legal defense following the radical abolitionist's assault on a federal arsenal at Harpers Ferry, Virginia. A reception at the Lees' Chestnut Hill home gave way to a truncated honeymoon—Roosevelt was now in his first semester as a Columbia University law student—that was spent, after a wedding night in Springfield, at Tranquility. "Our intense happiness," he blushed before his diary, "is too sacred to be written about."[14]

Despite the suggestion of permanence, Theodore, the new groom, the budding esquire-to-be, lacked in fact a strong sense of what he might do in life. Though taking classes at Columbia, he found the prevailing "let the buyer beware" ethos emphasized at the school offensive. "Some of the teaching of the law books and of the classroom seemed to me to be against justice," he wrote in a memoir. "The *caveat emptor* side of the law, like the *caveat emptor* side of business, seemed to me repellent; it did not make for social fair dealing."[15] His career path as yet unclaimed, there seemed to be a well-intentioned conspiracy to push him quietly into Thee's place. Roosevelt found himself elected about this time to serve as a trustee of both the New York Infant Asylum and the Orthopedic Dispensary—administrative positions formerly held by his father.

On a similar if domestic note, Mittie expected Theodore to preside over Sunday meals, a ritual that emphasized both his growing stature and perhaps the family's desire that Jr. should more fully assume Sr.'s place. But these cut-and-paste anticipations were wishful exercises. Roosevelt proved too active, independent, and eccentric to be harnessed by the intentions of others. The impulsive proposal to Edith followed by the quick courtship of Alice might have been reactions to Thee's death—perhaps his wan resolution to study law was as well. As time soon showed, however, this young man was only beginning to discover what he could do.

10

The Scholar in Politics

The newlywed Roosevelts, following the groom's indifferent academic year at Columbia, honeymooned properly in Europe in 1881. The voyage, a ten-day passage to Queenstown (now Cobh), Ireland, on the White Star steamer *Celtic*, proved a perfect misery for the seasick Alice. Perhaps impatient with his cabinmate's mal de mer, Roosevelt complained of having to coax the invalid to peck about her plate "at every blessed meal she ate." The trip could have held few surprises for him, having already marched in childhood through any number of London museums, Berlin galleries, and Roman ruins. And yet one senses from his occasional references to Alice as "Baby" and "The Little Pink Wife" that Roosevelt enjoyed the role of guide. There is some indication, however, that the Pink one's resistance to socializing with Europeans—a clique of Bostonians accompanied the couple—caught his critical eye. "Alice resents it as an impertinence," he wrote Corinne from Paris, "if she is addressed in any language but english."[1]

The great event of the trip for him, in fact, proved to be a clockwork ascent up the famous Matterhorn, a nearly fifteen-thousand-foot Alpine peak straddling Switzerland and Italy. Despite its sudden vogue, the mountain had claimed numerous casualties since a party led by the British explorer Edward Whymper had first scratched its summit in 1865—four having died on that expedition in a rather gruesome fall. A confident Roosevelt wrote to Bamie of the mountain, "Accidents . . . are generally due either to rashness, or else to a combination of timidity and fatigue; a fairly hardy man, cautious but not cowardly, with good guides, has little to fear." Accompanied by two "good guides," he started off from tiny Zermatt, a Swiss resort, on August 3 at nine in the morning, reaching the Club Hut at six that evening. Erected by the Swiss Alpine Club in 1880, it contained more than a dozen beds to accommodate the increasing number of climbers. Commencing a little before 4:00 a.m. the following day, the men reached the top in about three hours—taking in "a most glorious sunrise." By early afternoon, a chuffed Roosevelt was back at Zermatt. He described the experience that day as "like going up and down enormous stairs on your hands and knees for nine hours." Though admitting to "excessively laborious" moments, he cavalierly swore to feeling "as fresh as ever" following a post-slope "cup of tea and . . . warm bath." Clearly testing himself ("I was anxious"), he tackled the mountain, so he told Bamie, "because it is reputed very difficult."[2]

In early October, the Roosevelts returned to the United States aboard the *Britannic*, at which point Theodore began a second year at Columbia Law School, before abruptly dropping out a few weeks later. Whether he nursed fancies of a Senate seat or some less elevated Washington or Albany situation is unclear. A Harvard friend, William Roscoe Thayer, later wrote of a conversation between the two late in their Cambridge days: "Roosevelt and I sat in the window-seat [in Holworthy Hall] overlooking the College Yard and . . . discussed what we intended to do after graduation. 'I am going to try to help the cause of better government in New York City; I don't know exactly how,' said Theodore. I recall, still, looking hard at him with an eager, inquisitive look and saying to myself, 'I wonder whether he is the real thing, or only the bundle of eccentricities which he appears.'"[3]

Shortly after quitting Columbia, Roosevelt began attending political meetings on nearby East Fifty-Ninth Street at Morton Hall, nerve center of the city's 21st District Republican Association, the party of his father. Hardly impressive, the hall, a second-floor walk-up ("barn-like," Theodore thought) acridly scented with cigar smoke, housed the dozen or so occasions each year when the ward's representatives—a predictable blend of ambitious businessmen and lawyers, a good many of Irish vintage—gathered to organize committees, executive councils, and primaries for the vote-getting machine that made their public careers possible. Strange that Roosevelt, blessed with an independent income and definitely not of the machine-mind kind, should join their company. Aware of what friends and family might think, he chose to make light of his membership at Morton, writing playfully to a former college classmate, "Too True! Too True! I have become a 'political hack,'" and, as if to make the effort look experimental, if not ephemeral, continued, "But do'n't think I am going to go into politics after this year, for I am not." A generous dollop of class difference motivated the remark. The Founding generation of Washington, Adams, and Jefferson might consider themselves members of an elite "natural aristocracy," though the rise of mass democracy made partisan loyalties a sine qua non for political advancement.[4] The derisory expression "Grantism," a reference to Ulysses Grant, president for much of the 1870s, seemed to encapsulate this arrangement, evoking an era of unprecedented corruption later described by the literary historian Vernon Parrington as "the Great Barbecue," conjuring up images of pliant politicians serving the choicest cuts of public lands to the lords of railroad, coal, and mining empires.

Presumably Harvard men—their money old, their connections impeccable—looked down upon such crass scrambling for sinecures. "When I began to make inquiries as to the whereabouts of the local Republican Association and the means of joining it," Roosevelt later wrote, "these men . . . laughed at me, and told me that politics were 'low'; that the organizations were not controlled by 'gentlemen'; that I would find them run by saloon-keepers, horse-car conductors, and the like, and not by men with any of whom I would come in contact outside; and, moreover, they assured me that the men I met would be rough and brutal and unpleasant to deal with."[5] But this only piqued Roosevelt's pride:

> I answered that if this were so it merely meant that the people I knew did not belong to the governing class, and that the other people did—and that I intended to be one of the governing class; that if they proved too hard-bit for me I supposed I would have to quit, but that I certainly would not quit until I had made the effort and found out whether I really was too weak to hold my own in the rough and tumble.[6]

Though used to socializing with any number of Astors and Chandlers, Vanderbilts and Van Rensselaers, Roosevelt now found himself in the random company of Smiths and O'Sullivans, Millers and Murphys. And Murrays too. Joe Murray, a seasoned politico in the 21st District, caught the dim whiff of political backlash as the autumn 1881 elections approached. A brewing clash within Republican ranks literally turned into a blood sport, with the party's Stalwarts faction favoring spoils-style patronage, while its moderate Half-Breeds (as in half Republican) bedmates leaned toward a merit system of dispensing government jobs. In September, shortly before the Roosevelts had returned from Europe, the borderline delusional Stalwart Charles Guiteau, believing himself unfairly passed up for a diplomatic post, assassinated the dark-horse president—and Half-Breeds favorite—James Garfield (two revolver shots; the one lodged in his abdomen proving, after several bedridden weeks, fatal). A shocked public, so Murray reasoned, would now react against politics as usual. And in the 21st District the usual was Assemblyman William Trimble.

Eager to nominate a fresh face, Murray turned to Roosevelt. Outfitted in immaculately cut clothing, gold-rimmed glasses, and matching watch fob—critics catcalled him "Jane-Dandy," "his Lordship," and "Oscar Wilde"—he seemed of a different breed. Indeed, his youth, naïveté, and connection to New York's deep-pocketed Knickerbocker elite made him, so Murray argued, an ideal candidate. Lining up the votes, he managed to get Roosevelt, only twenty-three, nominated on the first ballot. In a solidly Republican district, TR swept to an easy 3,490 to 1,989 victory over Dr. W. W. Strew, formerly medical superintendent of the New York City Lunatic Asylum on slender Blackwell's Island. "I was," Roosevelt rejoiced, "triumphantly elected."[7]

More than a statesman, he aspired as well to be a literary lion, and the same month that he captured his first public office he completed his first book, *The Naval War of 1812*, a study of the struggle between the United States and Britain for trade rights in the Napoleonic-era Atlantic. Roosevelt began the manuscript in the autumn of 1879, a period during which Alice had yet to make up her mind to accept his marriage proposal. Uncertain of her response and possibly finding himself, even while completing his senior year at Harvard, with time on his hands, he leaned toward action rather than reflection. The project, though in some respects an apprentice exercise, drew from Roosevelt a more fluid and focused style than the prosy sentiments he often unpacked for Alice. When writing about nature or war (and not himself), his paragraphs, at their best, were filled with tensity and movement.

Thanks to his various travels, Theodore knew certain parts and ports of the Atlantic—a major theater of combat between the Anglo-American peoples in 1812—fairly well. And while honeymooning, he took the manuscript to his Liverpool-based uncle Irvine Bulloch for a look-over and the benefit of his technical knowledge. He further, while in Britain, scoured the *Naval Chronicle* among other sources; in America he ferreted out various materials—including logbooks, diaries, and tonnage measurements—previously unexploited by writers. Much of this research was conducted at the Astor Library, a public repository located in the East Village; its impressive collection was consolidated with the Lenox Library in 1895 to become the New York Public Library.[8]

Perhaps Roosevelt dreamt of becoming a sort of American Macaulay. Thomas Babington Macaulay occupied fully the worlds of politics and literature, serving as (among other state posts) secretary of war early in the reign of Queen Victoria and penning, as if on the side, the dramatic, dogmatic, and supremely readable five-volume epic *The History of England* (1848). In Lord Macaulay's hands, the past revealed the superiority of Anglo-Saxon institutions, while teeming with a colorful cast of heroes and villains. Roosevelt, despite nodding to the historiography and employing a range of archival research, was interested in making his book a living document, one intended to guide contemporary American defense spending and strategy. He argued that while the U.S. Navy had managed decades earlier to eke out a tactical victory against Britain's thick forest of 130 ships of the line, it had long since been neglected by Congress. "To bring up our navy to the condition in which it stood in 1812 it would not be *necessary*," he insisted, "to spend any more money than at present; only instead of using it to patch up a hundred antiquated hulks, it should be employed in building half a dozen ships on the most effective model."[9]

A second prominent theme in the book involved its author's attention to race, a not uncommon consideration in an era informed by the industrial nations' conquests of Africa and much of Asia. Though recognizing that Britain's desperate struggle against Napoleon prompted its illegal impressment of U.S. sailors and ships—the then-neutral Americans trading at the time with both belligerents—he considered it tragic that the Anglo nations, ethnically alike, should be so divided. His remarks on the subject were informed, variously, by his education, his readings, and liberal doses of *Nibelungenlied*-style myth and lore:

On the New England coast the English blood was as pure as in any part of Britain; in New York and New Jersey it was mixed with that of the Dutch settlers—and the Dutch are by race nearer to the true old English of Alfred and Harold than are, for example, the thoroughly anglicized Welsh of Cornwall. Otherwise, the infusion of new blood into the English race on this side of the Atlantic has been chiefly from three sources—German, Irish, and Norse; and these . . . represent the elemental parts of the composite English stock in about the same proportions in which they were originally combined—mainly Teutonic, largely Celtic, and with a Scandinavian admixture.[10]

According to Roosevelt, the war constituted above all a kind of cousins' conflict. His debatable analysis thus hews perhaps more closely to the fashion of late-nineteenth-century Anglo-Saxonism than to the actual economic and ideological divisions that produced the struggle.

Roosevelt's research, if industrious, at times got the better of his story, leading to passages replete with tedium. He seemed particularly taken with technical detail. On the subject of British frigates, he let a tangle of numbers propel the narrative: "The *Phœbe*, carried 46 guns, 26 long 18's on the gun-deck and 32-pound carronades above. The 38-gun . . . *Macedonian*, carried 48 or 49 guns, long 18's below and 32-pound carronades above." He thought it further worth mentioning that "there was really less disparity between the force and rate of a 44 that carried 54 guns, than there was in a 38 that carried 49."[11] Elsewhere, however, the narrative moves briskly, giving the reader a vivid picture of naval combat. Roosevelt wrote effectively of the HMS *Shannon*'s 1813 capture of the USS *Chesapeake* off Boston Harbor following an intense fifteen-minute fight that resulted in some 250 combined casualties:

> All was confusion and dismay on board the *Chesapeake*. Lieutenant Ludlow had been mortally wounded and carried below; [Captain James] Lawrence himself, while standing on the quarter-deck, fatally conspicuous by his full-dress uniform and commanding stature, was shot down, as the vessels closed. . . . He fell dying, and was carried below, exclaiming: "Don't give up the ship." . . . At 6.02 Captain Broke stepped from the *Shannon*'s gangway rail on to the muzzle of the *Chesapeake*'s aftermost carronade, and thence over the bulwark on to her quarter-deck, followed by about 20 men. As

they came aboard ... almost the only man that made any resistance was the chaplain, Mr. Livermore, who advanced, firing his pistol at Broke, and in return nearly had his arm hewed off by a stroke from the latter's broad Toledo blade."[12]

In time, such picturesque expression—on war, hunting, politics, and more—combined with a rising political career to bring Roosevelt to the circulation-pushing center of newspaper and magazine editors' interest.

Much of *The Naval War of 1812*'s more searing criticism is reserved for Thomas Jefferson, an antipathy its author never shook. While president, Jefferson had sought to prevent war with Britain by placing an embargo on American goods—keeping U.S. ships off the high seas, he reasoned, would make them safe from predation. This tactic, accompanied by Jefferson's hesitancy to enlarge the nation's navy, earned Roosevelt's censure as "criminal folly."[13] More broadly, TR thought Jefferson abstract and intellectual, altogether lacking in the kind of martial qualities the nation had needed to combat England. His pantheon of greats, rather, included Washington, Jackson, and particularly Lincoln, men tried and tested by war. "Jefferson, though a man whose views and theories had a profound influence upon our national life," he observed, "was perhaps the most incapable Executive that ever filled the presidential chair; being almost purely a visionary, he was utterly unable to grapple with the slightest actual danger, and ... without the prudence to avoid war or the forethought to prepare for it, [his] Administration drifted helplessly into ... conflict." While harsh—Jefferson did sign legislation in 1802 establishing the United States Military Academy at West Point—this judgment has found allies. Dumas Malone, the dean of twentieth-century Jefferson studies, wrote in 1974, "It may now appear that [Jefferson] was slower than he should have been in recognizing how ruthless the rulers of the contending nations actually were—how indifferent to the rights of others and how inaccessible to reason. He may have sought more assurance and consideration than any neutral could hope to gain during such a war. Convinced that time was his young country's greatest need, he may have been over-disposed to procrastinate."[14]

Published by G. P. Putnam's Sons in the spring of 1882, *The Naval War of 1812* augured well for its young author, soon to supplement his private and political incomes with popular writing. A *Harper's* reviewer called the book "cool and impartial" before crowning it "the most intrepid account that has yet appeared of the naval actions of the war of 1812."[15] Several American colleges adopted it for classroom use, while multiple printings of the study appeared within a couple of years. Perhaps the most interesting feature of the work is how it so perfectly prefaced Roosevelt's push for a big navy in the imperial days of the 1890s and still later during his presidency. A partisan scholar, he could make the past a plaything of public policy. More immediately, the book aligned with Theodore's demonic resolve to ascend summit after summit. Only two years removed from Harvard, he had become a husband, author, and assemblyman; having made his body, he now determined to make a reputation.

11

Enter the Dude

In the day's diction, Roosevelt was a "dude," a grand dandy in bespoke suit and shiny trimmings, with a quick stride designed to catch the eye. The side-whiskers and peculiar vocal range, which could quaver between a conventional tenor and a completely unexpected falsetto, only added to the package's caprice. Though hardly a bohemian, he enjoyed playing the city slicker in buttoned-down Albany, carrying his conspicuous youth, Harvard pedigree, and reputation as a rising historian into the center of New York state politics.[1]

On a cold early-January day in 1882, Roosevelt arrived by train to occupy his place in the assembly. He quartered in one of the city's finest hotels, the Delavan House, a rambling five-story, four-hundred-room structure built in 1845 and covering an entire block. As one contemporary sourcebook noted, guests were favored with "all modern improvements . . . including safety passenger elevator, steam heat, electric lights . . . telegraph office, barber's shop, billiard rooms, etc." A French chef ruled over the facility's au courant kitchen.[2] The capitol building in which the legislature met seemed a monument-in-the-making to the nation's richest and most populous state, the latest U.S. census placing New York's 5 million easily ahead of second-best Pennsylvania's nearly 4.3 million. Begun in 1867, opened for business in 1880, and still unfinished upon Roosevelt's arrival, the labyrinthine white granite pile, a creature of no fewer than five architects, featured a mishmash of Romanesque, Renaissance, and Victorian styles. Some thought the capitol an object of architectural grandeur; others considered its "uniqueness" an eyesore—and a boondoggle to boot. Its $25 million price tag comes to nearly $1 billion in today's dollars.

Roosevelt, it might be remembered, was not the first of his family to grace the legislature. A granduncle, James Roosevelt, a loyalist of Tammany Hall (founded in 1789 and for many generations the main patronage machine of New York City Democrats), had served there in the 1830s and '40s.[3] Of course, much had changed since Uncle Jimmy's time. Then, questions of freedom, slavery, and states' rights had dominated public debate. Now, however, issues related to the country's expanding railroad regime, maturing manufacturing sector, and ripening financial system came to the fore. In all these sectors, New York could claim to be in the vanguard of a profound, contested, but above all modern process.

This was the rising (Empire) state Roosevelt now served. His initial entrance into the red-carpeted assembly, so one legislator remembered, begat a palpable buzz:

> Suddenly our eyes, and those of everybody on the floor, became glued on a young man who was coming in through the door. His hair was parted in the center, and he had sideburns. He wore a single eye-glass, with a gold chain over his ear. He had on a cutaway coat with one button at the top, and the ends of its tails almost reached the tops of his shoes. He carried a gold-headed cane in one hand, a silk hat in the other, and he walked in the bent-over fashion that was the style with the young men of his day. His trousers were as tight as a tailor could make them, and had a bell-shaped bottom to cover his shoes. "Who's the dude?" I asked another member, while the same question was being put in a dozen different parts of the hall.[4]

Roosevelt, being Roosevelt, proceeded over the next several weeks to introduce a slew of bills—ranging from bond reform to judicial workload to Manhattan's hygienically dicey water supply—that stood absolutely no chance of being taken up by the legislature. But the attention-grabbing maneuver underscored both his innate need for action and his high sense of self-regard: better a noble Quixote than a servile Sancho Panza pensioned at the public's expense. In reply, some of his colleagues thought this showy moralist merely a tight-trousered exhibitionist.

Roosevelt's dress, high-pitched declamations, and obnoxious energy—one unamused colleague thought he resembled "a Jack coming out of the box"—were new sights in the assembly. Eager to play up to the papers, he happily posed as a crusader, giving good copy in a self-appointed campaign to save the state from both the unscrupulous speculator extraordinaire Jay Gould (a "common thief") and the Democrats ("There is good and bad in each party, but while the bad largely predominates in yours," he baited the opposition, "it is the good which predominates in ours!"). A friendly observer and fellow assemblyman, Isaac Hunt, later noted that "in those days [Roosevelt] had no discretion at all. He was the most indiscreet guy I ever met."[5]

Despite such antics, Theodore won the grudging approval of Democratic New York governor (and future president) Grover Cleveland. Distinguished by an immense head, walrus mustache, and thick body (he was tagged "Uncle Jumbo" by cutups), Cleveland enjoyed a cordial relationship with Roosevelt, even ushering to success a civil service reform bill the latter had sponsored in an effort to dispel the odor emanating from the still-fermenting Stalwarts/Half-Breeds feud. "It was clear to me, even thus early," Cleveland later observed, "that he was looking to a public career, that he was studying political conditions with a care that I have never known any man to show, and that he was firmly convinced that he would some day reach prominence."[6] To succeed, however, Theodore would have to develop a far greater understanding of statecraft, finances, and society beyond the velvety cocoon of New York's comfortable leisure class, and that would take time.

Several pressing questions confronted late-nineteenth-century America, encapsulated in concerns over growing economic inequality. Capital and labor frequently clashed, and a rising wave of European immigration challenged the resources of the nation's cities; meanwhile concentrations of vast wealth in the Vanderbilt, Rockefeller, and Carnegie vein began to attract critical attention. The young Roosevelt seemed poorly positioned to grasp the underlying social and financial motives that made for such ferment, evident in the five hundred or so strikes and walkouts in the industrial North each year. Distanced by class, education, and outlook from the poor, he reflexively fell back upon a dated laissez-faire, cushioned slightly by his father's support for charitable organizations. True, he despised the new money, which seemed a law unto itself, though he had yet to absorb the pernicious impact of monopolization upon consumers and workers. "The worst foe of the poor man," he was quoted as saying in one New York paper, "is the labor leader who tries to teach him that he is a victim of conspiracy and injustice, when in reality he is merely working out his fate with blood and sweat as the immense majority of men who are worthy of the name always have done and always will have to do."[7] These social Darwinian sentiments were by no means exclusive to Roosevelt, but reflected rather a broader culture-wide custom. The turn in coming years toward a regulatory state model—the Progressive Era—would complete Theodore's post-Harvard education, embodied in his presidential efforts to offer Americans, so he said, a "square deal."

During assembly season, Roosevelt spent his weekends with Alice in Manhattan, the couple having purchased a West Forty-Fifth Street brownstone. She otherwise occupied her time with tennis and tea parties, shopping and chat. Theodore, the "indiscreet" Albany blade, played at home the dutiful husband; his diary at this time reeked of sugarplum sentiment: "Back again in my own lovely little home, with the sweetest and prettiest of all little wives . . . I can imagine nothing more happy in life than an evening spent in my cosy little sitting room, before a bright fire of soft coal, my books all around me, and playing backgammon with my own dainty mistress."[8]

In the political arena, by contrast, he could come on like a young lion. Future New York governor and 1916 Republican presidential candidate Charles Evans Hughes, a Columbia law student in the early 1880s, remembered Roosevelt's charisma and sociability: "It is impossible to give you the impression that was created by that original spirit in the Assembly at Albany. He was not there very long before everyone was impressed with his marked individuality. . . . [He] was a splendid breeze blowing through the legislative halls."[9]

And once those chambers recessed in the spring of 1883, Roosevelt made a sudden decision to go west. A happy captive to his impulses, he now sought the cowboy experience, a Manhattan dandy about to bring the term "dude ranch" into existence.

12

The Vanishing West

In early May 1883, at a meeting of the Free Trade Club, an ever-sociable Roosevelt was introduced to Commander Henry Honychurch Gorringe, a retired naval officer eager to meet *The Naval War of 1812*'s young author.[1] Having lately returned from the Trans-Mississippi West with the idea of establishing a hunting ranch for affluent easterners, Gorringe perhaps sensed a ready mark and proposed that Roosevelt try his hand hunting in the Dakota Territory's Badlands. The northernmost part of Jefferson's old Louisiana Purchase, the area, first organized in 1861, would subsequently be split into two states, both entering the Union in 1889.

Proprietor of an abandoned and not-quite-ready-for-guests army barracks by the Little Missouri River, Gorringe suggested that Roosevelt occupy the nearby Pyramid Park Hotel in the hamlet of Little Missouri (now Medora, North Dakota)—both postscripts of the Northern Pacific Railway. There, Gorringe continued, his new friend could find a saloon and shops, as well as hunting guides and all the game—bears and buffalo, elk and antelope—he might desire. Texas, East Coast, and foreign capital had established several ranches in the region and local boosters played up its prospects. In the fall of 1883, the *Dickinson Press*, located in present-day Stark County, North Dakota, touted the village of Little Missouri as "one of the most prosperous and rapidly growing towns along the line of the Northern Pacific. New buildings of every description are going up as fast as a large force of carpenters can do the work and an air of business and enterprise is apparent that would do honor to an older town.... Game of all kinds is plentiful in the surrounding country and it is becoming quite a resort for pleasure seekers and those who love the chase."[2] Sorely tempted by such big-sky testimony, and perhaps eager to even out the balance sheet of brotherly competition, Elliott having newly returned with a surplus of skins from a yearlong tiger and elephant hunting expedition in India, Roosevelt decided to go that fall.

But first he hoped to make progress on his new property, several dozen acres at Oyster Bay, the area redolent of summer house memories spent at Tranquility. Prospects of a growing family—Alice was now pregnant—may have prodded Theodore to contemplate a country residence in which he might play the provincial squire. He intended to call the estate "Leeholm," in Alice's honor. Having secured an architect, with construction to begin the following year, he boarded a train in early September for, so he wrote Bamie, "a hunting trip in Dacotah."[3] Alice, four months into her confinement, had to make do with her husband's characteristically effusive letters. "Sweetest little wife," he wrote in one, artlessly mixing the tender with the territorial, "I think all the time of my laughing, teazing, beauty, and how pretty she is, and how she goes to sleep in my arms, and I could almost cry I love you so. But I think the hunting will do me good. And I am anxious to kill some large game."[4]

Following a five-day train journey covering some 1,800 dusty miles over mainly flat ground, Roosevelt arrived at the Pyramid Park Hotel, just yards from the station house. There he met Lincoln Lang, an Irish-born sixteen-year-old whose Scottish father, Gregor, served as Gorringe's local agent. Years later, Lincoln wrote of the spry newcomer, who had greeted him with a typically emphatic "Dee-lighted!":

> I do not know if it was the direct, forceful manner of his speech, his sincere hearty grip, the open friendly gaze with which he regarded me, or something of all combined, that instantly reached for and numbered me among his friends.... Young and all, as I was, the consciousness was instantly borne in upon me of meeting a man different from any I had ever met before. Just where the difference lay, I could not have told, although in good time I would learn, but certain it is, right there and then, I fell for him strong.[5]

Roosevelt quickly embraced the prairie grasslands' mise-en-scène. "The charm of ranch life comes in its freedom," he wrote of his time on the Little Missouri, "and the vigorous, open-air existence it forces a man to lead." Accustomed to mediating life through literature—he once condemned Tolstoy's *The Kreutzer Sonata* as "erotic perversion" for trafficking in adultery—he said of the starkly beautiful landscape that now surrounded him, "When one is in the Bad Lands he feels as if they somehow *look* just exactly as Poe's tales and poems *sound*."[6]

A number of interests merged for Roosevelt during that first splendid season in the Dakotas. His love of nature, enthusiasm for hunting, and fashionable faith in evolutionary biology found various degrees of indulgence. The dwindling Indian presence on the plains further captured his attention. Some 350 miles to the west lay the Little Bighorn Battlefield where, just seven years earlier, some two thousand Lakota, Dakota, Arapaho, and Northern Cheyenne defeated the seven-hundred-strong U.S. 7th Cavalry Regiment under the command of Lieutenant Colonel George Armstrong Custer. But the Indian Wars were now coming to an end, superseded by the relentless encroachments of railroads and ranches. Though occasionally given to sacralizing the animal life of the West, Roosevelt spared less empathy for its native peoples who, he believed, in their resistance to prevailing property rights practices, were the inevitable casualties in the ancient contest between savagery and civilization. Shortly after returning from the Badlands he wrote unfeelingly on this subject:

> During the past century a good deal of sentimental nonsense has been talked about our taking the Indians' land. Now, I do not mean to say for a moment that gross wrong has not been done the Indians, both by Government and individuals, again and again. . . . But as regards taking the land, at least from the Western Indians, the simple truth is that the latter never had any real ownership in it at all.[7]

The economy of nature apparently patterned human improvement on Anglo-friendly terms that refused to recognize any other form of land tenure than its own. From the agreeable vantage of youth and inheritance, Roosevelt coldly wrote of the Dakotas' native peoples, "Let him, like . . . whites who will not work, perish from the face of the earth which he cumbers."[8]

Eager to hunt, Theodore hoped to bag a buffalo from the nearly extinct northern herd, once numbering about 1.5 million—casualties, like the Indians, of the railways and, more especially, of the sudden markets these lines opened for buffalo hides, meat, and bones, which triggered a mass killing in the 1870s. Shortly after arriving, Roosevelt, accompanied by Joe Ferris, a guide and native Canadian, headed south toward Little Cannonball Creek in search of game. For several hours under a hot sun, they encountered no prey, only "the brown, barren land" that congealed in a "dreary sameness." Finally they sighted in the distance "three black specks"—buffalo, which, considering the exhausted condition of their ponies, they proposed to creep up upon. Easing within firing range, Theodore managed a shot, which struck one of the beasts but failed to bring it down—all three lumbered off over a slight rise, their agitated tails now conspicuously aiming up.[9]

Roosevelt and Ferris decided to follow, thinking the wounded one might separate from the others. And so, for several miles they loped along, finally spotting the trio in a hollow. In the open, they cantered their horses toward the bulls, which then took off, initiating a chaotic chase in which the Manhattan dandy found himself in real difficulty. "When up within twenty feet [of a buffalo] I fired my rifle," Theodore later wrote, "but the darkness, and especially the violent, labored motion of my pony, made me miss; I tried to get in closer, when suddenly . . . the bull . . . charged me with lowered horns." At this point the frightened horse suddenly reared up, knocking Roosevelt's rifle against his forehead, producing a sizeable gash—"the blood," so he remembered, "poured into my eyes." The bull darted by, and Ferris vainly fired as it disappeared into the dark.[10]

This skirmish was followed by a few days of rain; unable to find the three—or any—bison, the men crossed into Montana, hoping their luck might change. And so it did. Riding along a ridge of shattered buttes, their horses suddenly began to violently sniff the air. Roosevelt, thinking either a bear or a buffalo near, slipped off his ride and ran along the valley. After nearly a hundred yards he spotted a bison casually feeding in a ravine. Raising his rifle, he "put the bullet," so he reported, "behind his shoulder. The wound was an almost immediately fatal one, yet with surprising agility for so large and heavy an animal, he bounded up the opposite side of the ravine, heedless of two more balls, both of which went into his flank and ranged forwards, and disappeared over the ridge at a lumbering gallop, the blood pouring from his mouth and nostrils."

Tracking the spattered trail, Roosevelt and Ferris found the bull dead a short distance away; they stripped the meat and made an "uncommonly good" meal for themselves.[11]

Elated, Theodore made a characteristically impulsive financial decision. Returning from the hunt, he wrote a check for $14,000, some $420,000 in today's dollars, for the primary interest in the nearby Chimney Butte Ranch (known also as the Maltese Cross Ranch) and thus, with the scratch of a pen, promptly entered the cattle industry. He had also recently invested $20,000 in G. P. Putnam's Sons, the publishing house that had released *The Naval War of 1812*. Considering Putnam's strong reputation and Roosevelt's growing stature as an author, this venture looked far more sound than sinking dollars into a business that he approached, one might say, from a romantic perspective. When trying to define the Badlands' pull upon his heart, TR fell upon cowpoke poetry: "It was a land of vast silent spaces, of lonely rivers, and of plains where the wild game stared at the passing horseman."[12]

Roosevelt returned from his buffalo hunt in late fall and shortly thereafter entrained for Albany to serve a third legislative term. Eager for advancement, he sought its speakership; considering that Republicans held large majorities in both houses of the assembly, it became apparent that whoever won the party's December nomination would claim the prize. Having announced his candidacy, Theodore fielded inquiries from curious colleagues. He emphasized to one Chemung County assemblyman his great disdain for boss politics: "I am a Republican, pure and simple, neither a 'half breed' nor a 'stalwart'; and certainly no man, nor yet any . . . clique, can do my thinking for me."[13] Come election day, however, boss politics determined the outcome as Titus Sheard—having been earlier promised the post if he could unseat the incumbent Democrat in his district—rather handily defeated Roosevelt, 42 to 30.

Generous with his challenger, Sheard offered Roosevelt his choice of panel appointments and the latter asked for and received the chairmanship of the Committee on Cities, a berth of some influence. Now into the new year, the late winter of 1884 found Theodore—fledgling rancher and reformer, novice investor and writer—filled with activity. A father-to-be, he remained in Albany working on several bills designed to reduce the power of the political machines. Professionally and domestically his situation seemed assured, secured by an attractive combination of youth, money, and magnetism. Strange, then, how this pretty world suddenly blew apart over a few painful days in February.

13

A Curse on This House

Since cornering his elusive buffalo and returning east, Roosevelt had devoted most of his time to assembly business, making for Manhattan, and his heavily pregnant wife, only irregularly. Presumably for her safety and his schedule, Theodore sublet the couple's home, moving Alice into Mittie's West Fifty-Seventh Street mansion. There, all seemed secure. Bamie served as a nurse-in-residence, Elliott lived close by, and Alice's parents, awaiting the happy day, were bunking at the fashionable Brunswick Hotel near Madison Square Park. A family doctor hovered attentively in attendance. Alice's expectant condition naturally caught everyone's eye, though Mittie's well-being warranted consideration as well; having taken to bed, she appeared to be afflicted by a persistent cold.

Roosevelt's letters to Alice in the weeks leading up to her delivery are warm if typically self-absorbed. He noted a triad of intrepid successes, ranging from politics ("In the House we had a most exciting debate on my Reform Charter bill, and I won a victory"), to boxing ("Today I sparred as usual; my teacher is a small man and in the set-to today I bloodied his nose by an upper cut, and knocked him out"), to showing off among the club and sport sort ("All the men were perfectly enchanted with . . . [my] hunting trophies").[1]

On Tuesday, February 12, Roosevelt, following a brief stay in the city, boarded an Albany-bound train and returned to the capital. There he received upon arrival a telegram from Alice, whose brave pose belied her anxiety: "I am feeling well tonight but am very much worried over . . . your little mother, her fever is still very high and the Dr is rather afraid of typhoid . . . I wish I could have my little new baby soon." Weighed down with assembly business and not particularly anxious—Mittie often complained of illness—he put the missive aside. The following day a more definitive communication arrived, announcing the birth of his daughter the previous evening though giving some light cause for concern. In a telegram that day to Dora Watkins, his childhood nurse, Roosevelt said of Alice's condition: "The mother only fairly well." Presuming fairly well to be well enough, he decided to stay in Albany, until later in the day when a second, urgent cable arrived calling him back home—Alice was dying from an undiagnosed kidney ailment, masked by her pregnancy, known as Bright's disease, though now called nephritis.[2]

Back in Manhattan a distraught Elliott, having encamped at West Fifty-Seventh Street and perhaps conflating Thee's suffering six years earlier with Alice and Mittie's sinking conditions, said to Corinne, "There is a curse on this house." Late that evening a supremely worried Theodore arrived at Grand Central Station and then raced to his family. There ensued several hours of fiendish suffering spilling over to the fourteenth—Valentine's Day. Mittie, cared for by Bamie on the ground floor, died at 3:00 a.m. of typhoid fever, possibly having ingested contaminated food or water. Eleven hours later, at 2:00 p.m., Alice, comatose on the third floor and attended by Corinne, also expired. Sometime that hellish day Roosevelt placed a large "X" in his diary, under which he theatrically wrote, "The light has gone out of my life."[3]

Alice and Mittie were buried together in a double funeral service at Green-Wood Cemetery in Brooklyn, a few blocks south of Prospect Park. Styled as a garden graveyard for urbanizing Manhattan, it counted a number of notable entombments—including *New-York Tribune* editor Horace Greeley, the famous Congregationalist clergyman Henry Ward Beecher, and electric telegraph inventor Samuel Morse; the notorious Tammany Hall patronage master, William "Boss" Tweed, also rested within its green rim. Roosevelt, in character, refused to linger over his misery. Days after the interment he returned to Albany, writing on February 21 to the German American Carl Schurz, formerly a senator, cabinet member, and Lincoln's ambassador to Spain: "Your words of kind sympathy were very welcome to me; and you can see I have taken up my work again; indeed I think I should go mad if I were not employed."[4]

Mittie's will left her eldest son $62,500, nearly $2 million in today's currency; other legacies were less easy to register. In time Roosevelt, rediscovering "the light ... of my life," remarried and started a second family, which became during his presidential years a point of great public interest, the younger children—cherubic to the press—keeping a veritable zoo in the White House. Bereft of her abettor, Alice all but vanished from memory; she appears not at all in her husband's 1913 memoir. Perhaps taking their cue from his silence, friends and the second Mrs. Roosevelt collectively asserted that dear Alice, a sweet if vacuous girl, a perennial child-bride, could hardly have kindled Theodore's vital personality and searching intellect. There is the suggestion in such uncharitable asides that her death came almost as a kind of convenience. But not for all. Her sharp-eyed (and sharper-tongued) daughter, also named Alice, wondered the length of her long life (1884–1980) over the mystery of that fateful fourteenth of February. "My father never told me anything about this," she once confessed to an interviewer. "In fact, he never ever mentioned my mother to me, which was absolutely wrong." She was left to ponder each year, rather, over the hushed-up circumstances of her tragic-by-association birthday—bonded always with her mother's and grandmother's death days: "The whole thing seems to have been a medical fiasco," she mused over that blighted mansion on Fifty-Seventh Street. "I have visions of everyone in long white nightgowns rushing hysterically between floors."[5]

Momentarily stunned, Theodore seemed at a loss how to proceed. "For joy or for sorrow my life has now been lived out," he supposed to his diary.[6] But given that within a few months he would play a leading role as a reform politician trying to get a reform Republican nominated for November's presidential contest, these words come off as wooden. Beyond the performative expression of grief and the deep bow to Victorian proprieties, there lay an abiding urge to move on. Roosevelt, the perennial "Jack coming out of the box," really had very little time for tragedy; he refused to sit still and would have considered deep mourning—other than the measured painful days he had experienced following Thee's passing—as fundamentally morbid if not a sign of weakness. Essentially, he lived in the moment, drawn invariably to the perpetual next event. Thee, in any case, had been the true love of his life.

In the spring of 1884, just weeks after Alice's death, he decided to alter his circumstances and, calling himself "tired and restless," resigned from the assembly. "I will not stay in public life unless I can do so on my own terms," he wrote to one newspaper editor, "and my ideal, whether lived up to or not is rather a high one." He discussed "going back into private for a few years," departing the East on occasional extended hunting trips to "the far West or in the Northern Woods," and more generally finding satisfaction in scholarly pursuits—"there will be plenty of work to do writing."[7] These abstract sentiments suggest withdrawal, a kind of retirement from the strenuous life soon to become the guiding star of Roosevelt's well-documented path to prominence. Only twenty-five and suddenly a widower, he scrambled to recover, to recoup, and to build himself up again. His presumed remedies—travel and literary labor—were patrician pursuits, certainly commensurate with his class, if not his emotional makeup. The excitement, competition, and sheer vanity of politics, rather, excited him more than he yet understood; Albany was but an opening act, and before the awful year expired, a presidential election gave him something fresh to fight for.

14

Picking Up the Pieces

Baby Alice, christened the day after her mother's February funeral, was quickly bundled off to live with her aunt Bamie. Her father, proceeding to Albany, put in motion the machinery by which both the "cursed" house (Mittie's mansion) and the West Forty-Fifth Street brownstone he had shared with Alice were quickly sold. These renunciations were countered by the building of another box. In early March Roosevelt decided to go ahead with Leeholm, the Oyster Bay estate—to be a shingle-style structure in the popular Queen Anne mode—now to double as a monument to his dead wife. He signed a contract to begin construction in early March; once again the ever-steady Bamie, while her brother played politics and nursed his hurt, watched over his affairs.

In April, though having decided to quit the assembly, Roosevelt attended the New York State Republican convention in Utica, one of five hundred delegates. He was determined, as part of an independent group, to support the presidential nomination of the silver-whiskered Vermont senator George F. Edmunds over both incumbent president Chester Arthur, an accidental—by way of assassination—executive lacking strong support within his party, and the formidable former Maine senator James G. Blaine, a spoilsman par excellence who adeptly employed patronage while extracting favors from any number of special interests, including the burgeoning railroad industry. Edmunds touted civil service reform, and this attracted Roosevelt, who disdained Blaine and considered Arthur a nonentity. Though a small unit at Utica, the seventy-some independents held the balance of power between the two larger camps and parlayed this perfectly, getting Arthur's supporters to shift to their side and thus carrying the contest for the Vermonter. For his efforts, Roosevelt earned a place in the coming Chicago national nominating convention as an at-large delegate.

Word of his success quickly circulated. His old pre-Harvard prep tutor, Arthur Cutler, looked on with pride at the independents' unexpected success. "Theodore's reputation is national and even to us who know him it is phenomenal," he wrote Bamie that spring. "Whatever the future may have in store for him, no man in the country has begun his public career more brilliantly." The *Philadelphia Press* concurred, insisting that "Theodore Roosevelt has won a brilliant victory by keen intuitions and resolute, swift act, which place him at the front of his party in the state." Another young politico, thirty-four-year-old Henry Cabot Lodge of Massachusetts, took note as well. In early May he wrote to Roosevelt suggesting they join forces at the convention to defeat Blaine. He may have reminded his new correspondent that they had met in passing some months earlier at Boston's St. Botolph Club on Newbury Street, a private men's social space interested in advancing the fine arts, just off the downtown's storied Common. Though willing to support Edmunds, Lodge hoped, along with many in the GOP, to see Abraham Lincoln's eldest son, Robert, then secretary of war, inheritor of an indelible name, and sporting a familiar beard, pursue the nomination. Lodge and Roosevelt agreed to partner in Chicago and fight for a reform candidate.[1]

Tall and thin with close-cropped light-brown hair, prominent blue eyes, and a period-piece beard, Lodge belonged to one of Boston's most distinguished clans. Bluff and exclusive by nature, he carried on in a clipped Harvard cadence, a bit puffed-up in his opinions and excessively proud of his heritage. "If Lodge says a thing he will do it," observed one *Saturday Evening Post* writer, "but if he will not do a thing he will [also] say so, and usually in a manner that will make the person who made the request an enemy for life. . . . He considers himself so far superior to the ordinary run of people that the mere addition of another enemy to his long string means nothing to him one way or the other." Pairing Lodge and Roosevelt is, on the surface, absurd. The former, dry and snobbish, had very little of the latter's easy bounce or bonhomie, and it is impossible to imagine the pompous Lodge shambling through the Badlands' shortgrass to hunt buffalo. At Harvard,

Lodge had written his dissertation, "Anglo-Saxon Land-Law," under Henry Adams's direction. A product of the same high Brahmin milieu that bred Lodge, Adams later described his protégé as "sometimes bitter, often genial, always intelligent." And in comparing Lodge and Roosevelt, Adams, himself something of a dry ironist who never took to the boyish Theodore, thought the former "the more interesting of the two." His compliments were often accompanied by caveats, however, as this one showed: "Roosevelts are born and never can be taught," he quipped, and wanly praised the less-impulsive Lodge as a "creature of teaching—Boston incarnate."[2]

Roosevelt arrived in Chicago on the last day of May. He and his reform allies faced a strong opposition—men who, over two decades, had burnished the Republican Party's brand for having saved the Union and facilitated the nation's rapid industrial development. Housed in the city's Interstate Exposition Hall, a kind of architectural phoenix put up in 1872, the year after the great Chicago Fire, the gathering bore evidence of the West's rising importance. Whereas the formerly dominant antebellum Democratic Party had held its first six conventions in Baltimore (1832–1852), the now-prevailing GOP held six of its first nine conventions in either Cincinnati or Chicago (1856–1888). The Exposition Hall, a glass and metal contraption—"huge," said Roosevelt—with dark ornamental domes fronting Michigan Avenue, resembled exhibition buildings in London and New York. Designed primarily for yearly displays of industrial manufactures, it also served as the initial home of the city's symphony orchestra.[3] Demolished in 1890, it gave way to the current Art Institute of Chicago.

Into this bustling environment stepped a preening Roosevelt, eager, as in his Harvard days, to make an entrance. Though having dispensed with the side-whiskers, this fashionable dude appeared, so New York's *Sun* reported, "wearing a clipper straw hat and carrying a natty cane." His peers, the paper continued, "expressed their surprise." The press seemed particularly infatuated with the boater cap—as its owner surely desired; the *New York Mail* called it a "nobby straw" while the *Boston Herald* supposed it "small" with "a straight rim dyed blue on the underside." More generally, these dailies, weeklies, and reviews seemed caught under a strange spell, unable to get enough of Roosevelt—his nose was "pugnacious," his manner "nervously forcible," and his aspect a combination of jittery and "jaunty."[4]

Walking into the Exposition Hall Roosevelt, housed at the neighboring Grand Pacific Hotel, would have noticed rows untold of neatly spaced cheap cane chairs facing a wooden stage and resting below tightly configured galleries that bathed in natural light from immense industrial windows.[5] A slew of rackety brass bands vied for attention. The building, both inside and out, abounded in flags; the party's recently martyred leaders, Lincoln and Garfield, were remembered in portraiture.

Roosevelt and Lodge, the latter bunking at the Leland Hotel on Michigan Avenue, proceeded, as young pups, to make the reformers' case for denying Blaine—"our greatest danger," Theodore privately decried—the nomination.[6] But this predictably came to naught when Blaine captured the contest on the fourth ballot with Edmunds trailing a distant third. "We found plenty of Anti-Blaine feeling," Lodge informed his journal, "but could make no combination on anyone and returned disheartened to New York." Roosevelt wrote Bamie in the same vein: "Well, the fight has been fought and lost, and moreover our defeat is an overwhelming rout." The question now facing the thwarted reformers was, would they support Blaine? Or put another way, did they wish to continue their political careers? They were welcome to keep either their principles or their seats at the Republican table, but certainly not both. This unpalatable understanding put Roosevelt in a foul mood as he discovered his conscience inconveniently clashing with his political aspirations. The day the convention ended he was cornered by a reporter from the *New York World* who wished to know if he planned to bolt the GOP. "Flashing with indignation" (so the paper said), TR parried with, "I decline to say anything about the action of the Convention. I have worked hard for Mr. Edmunds and he was my choice." When asked point-blank if he would support Blaine, he stonewalled: "It is a subject that I do not care to talk about." As if to wash his hands of the matter, he professed a sublime indifference to the coming campaign season: "I am going cattle-ranching in Dakota for the remainder of the summer and a part of the fall. What I shall do after that I cannot tell you."[7]

But for Roosevelt and Lodge, "bolt" became the season's ringing word, an albatross to be silently suffered. It uncomfortably shadowed them, much to their everlasting chagrin, as many of their social acquaintances and reform-minded friends watched their waffling with disdain. At heart pragmatic (and ambitious) men, they both knew that to break ranks meant instant and lasting ostracization—political death.

And so they opted for self-interest, something Lodge later called "the bitterest thing I ever had to do in my life." Making his way by train from Chicago up to the Badlands, Roosevelt gave a curt interview to a reporter from the *St. Paul Pioneer Press* aimed at putting the matter to rest: "I shall bolt the Convention by no means. I have no personal objections to Blaine."[8]

Their now-former friends in the reform fraternity refused to let this apostasy pass. Henry Lee, a cousin of Roosevelt's former father-in-law, George Lee, is said to have told a colleague, "As for Cabot Lodge, nobody's surprised at *him*; but you can tell that young whipper-snapper in New York from me that his independence was the only thing in him we cared for, and if he has gone back on that, we don't care to hear anything more about him." Collectively such men were known as Mugwumps—independent Republicans, often of New England extraction, who now crossed over to support the Democratic presidential nominee, Grover Cleveland. Typically educated men—Harvard president Charles Eliot, future Supreme Court justice Louis Brandeis, and the distinguished editor George William Curtis were in the bloc—they shamed, merely by their principled existence, those who held their blue noses for Blaine.[9]

As one of the nose-holders, Roosevelt, loathing the idea of ceding the ethical high ground, lashed out at his accusers. "Most of my friends seem surprised to find that I have not developed hoofs and horns," he wrote to Lodge that summer. "I have received shoals of letters, pathetic and abusive, to which I have replied with vivacity or ferocity, according to the circumstances of the case." In a further communication he fumed, "I get so angry with the 'mugwumps,'" and in still another he referred inelegantly to "those political and literary hermaphrodites the mugwumps."[10] In a memoir, Roosevelt, forgetting both his own early commitment to independent politics and that of his father, argued that Mugwumpery failed entirely in the practice of realpolitik:

> I had ... some exasperating experiences with the "silk stocking" reformer type ... the gentlemen who were very nice, very refined, who shook their heads over political corruption and discussed it in drawing-rooms ... but who were wholly unable to grapple with real men in real life. They were apt vociferously to demand "reform" as if it were some concrete substance, like cake, which could be handed

out at will, in tangible masses, if only the demand were urgent enough. These parlor reformers made up for inefficiency in action by zeal in criticizing; and they delighted in criticizing the men who really were doing the things which they said ought to be done, but which they lacked the sinewy power to do.[11]

These acerbic words, written nearly thirty years after the 1884 election, accented Roosevelt's still simmering anger. Above all, he recognized that in a very public way the independents had called his bluff, shown the limits of his political moralism, and then wagged a collective accusatory finger when he refused to do the decent thing and follow them into a genteel exile.

In the moment, however, his future seemed a very uncertain thing. Whisking away to the Badlands, he now wrestled with two recent and unexpected blows—Alice's death and the loss of his callow political illusions. His prospects, both personally and professionally, looked much different than they had only six months earlier when he was a respected assemblyman, sitting on important state committees, and going home on long Manhattan weekends. Clearly his aspirations ranged beyond an Albany sinecure and a slippered domestic bliss. He now made his second journey to the West, the tyro proprietor of the Maltese Cross Ranch, though otherwise unsure of his next move.

15

Cowboy Blues

Following Thee's death, a confused Roosevelt had rushed into activity, clubbing up at Harvard, pressing for a commitment from a cagey Edith Carow, and, when that clumsy bid backfired, marrying the more easily managed Alice Lee. In the difficult summer of 1884, however, he drifted about the distant Badlands, seemingly in search of a less conspicuous salve. Though a restless ranch proprietor, he fell otherwise into a ruminative mood, evident in a series of brooding passages published the following year in *Hunting Trips of a Ranchman*, his tourist's-eye ode to the nation's vanishing frontier. To wit:

> Nowhere, not even at sea, does a man feel more lonely than when riding over the far-reaching, seemingly never-ending plains ... their very vastness and loneliness and their melancholy monotony have a strong fascination for him. The landscape seems always the same, and after the traveler has plodded on for miles and miles he gets to feel as if the distance was indeed boundless. ... Nowhere else does one seem so far off from all mankind; the plains stretch out in death-like and measureless expanse, and as he journeys over them they will for many miles be lacking in all signs of life.[1]

Reflecting before columns of ghostly buttes ravaged by wind and water, he discerned a horizon both "unreal and strange."[2] Wishing for no immediate memories of the blasted circumstances he had just abandoned, Roosevelt fell into the rhythm of a herdsman's routine, a playacting exercise performed in an attitude of unspoken grief.

William Sewall, a skilled outdoorsman who had once served a then-undergraduate Roosevelt as a hunting guide in the winter Maine woods and now worked his patron's Maltese Cross Ranch, remembered this compromised summer: "Roosevelt was very melancholy at times, much down in spirits. He told me one day that he felt as if it did not make any difference what became of him—he had nothing to live for." When reminded of baby Alice back home, Roosevelt seemed curiously unresponsive, saying, "Her aunt can take care of her," before adding, "She would be just as well off without me." More than indulging his sorrow, he seemed uninterested in fatherhood, declining, in his several and long letters to Bamie, to ask about or even mention Alice. He wrote to her, rather, about the calm cadences of ranch life—the thirteen-hour days in the saddle, the occasional antelope hunt, and his dreams of amassing a congeries of cattle. "The country," he declared, appearing to find some peace, "has a curious, fantastic beauty of its own."[3]

Roosevelt's bovine investment had survived the winter well—only about 25 cows succumbed to wolves and weather, while more than 150 calves were born to take their places. Encouraged and with typical impulsivity, he purchased, only three days after arriving, another 1,000 cattle (the herd brought in from St. Paul) at a cost of $810,000 in today's dollars. His inheritance from Mittie helped to make this proper rancher's paradise a reality.[4]

The transaction spurred Roosevelt to alter his living arrangements. At present he occupied a durable one-and-a-half-story log cabin of ponderosa pine with a shingled roof and simple root cellar for storage. It contained a kitchen, living room, and bedroom with an upstairs loft. Seeking a still more remote spot—the Maltese Cross Ranch lay only a few miles from tiny Medora, conjured up by the Northern Pacific Railway's presence—he relocated about twenty-five miles north, establishing the Elkhorn Ranch. "There was virgin country," one of his farmhands later remembered, "silent places, and the still unspoiled sylvan atmosphere." At Elkhorn, Roosevelt later wrote, "I built [a] . . . long, low . . . house of hewn logs, with a veranda, and with, in addition to the other rooms, a bedroom for myself, and a sitting-room with a big fire-place. I got out a rocking-chair—I am very fond of rocking-chairs—and enough books to fill two or three shelves, and a rubber bathtub so that I could get a bath." He decorated this primitive cabin with bearskins and buffalo robes "of our own killing"; a mass of shed deer and elk antlers littered the porch. Aside from game, he and his men feasted on sugar, bacon, and canned tomatoes along with an assortment of jams and jellies. After domesticating several cows, they enjoyed milk as well.⁵

When not cattle-handling, Roosevelt engaged in long stretches of sustained hunting, ranging as far west as Fort McKinney in the Wyoming Territory near the Powder River, a sixteen-day journey. Reaching the Bighorn Range, he and his companion-guide, Bill Merrifield, a Canadian originally a little skeptical of his new associate's spectacles, abandoned their wagon, taking their pack ponies into the mountains. They hunted nearly every day on foot, donning moccasins and buckskin suits. "I came out after two weeks," Roosevelt reported to Bamie, having killed three grizzly bears, a half dozen elk, and various deer and grouse. The fishing good, he and Merrifield occasionally dined on trout. Though enjoying his days, Roosevelt was under few illusions that the "hunting life" could be sustained. He had encountered in Wyoming, so he informed Bamie, "a herd of a dozen parties either of English or Eastern amateurs, or of professional hunters."⁶

It was about this time that he began to show unease with the nation's increasingly urban and industrial aspect. From what source or situation, he wondered, would the pioneer virtues of old now arise? "For we ourselves, and the life that we lead," he wrote, one might say eulogistically, in *Hunting Trips of a Ranchman*, "will shortly pass away from the plains as completely as the red and white hunters who have vanished. . . . The free, open-air life of the ranchman, the pleasantest and healthiest life in America, is from its very nature ephemeral. The broad and boundless prairies have already been bounded and will soon be made narrow."⁷

Roosevelt returned east that fall to campaign for the Republican Party—and the ubiquitous Blaine. From mid-October to early November, he gave several speeches, most in his native New York. No doubt his former friends in the independent camp were amazed at this brazen effort, and at each stop Theodore felt compelled not merely to stump for the ticket but to defend his convenient change of heart. In a Malden, Massachusetts, address he acknowledged that "Mr. Blaine was nominated much against the wishes of many of us, against my wishes," before segueing to fair play—"but he was nominated . . . honorably"—and finishing with a little old-fashioned political hokum—"I for one am quite content to abide by the decision of the plain people." For his troubles, New York Republicans offered Roosevelt a congressional candidacy, which, eager to avoid a personal interest in the campaign (and possibly sensing defeat—Lodge subsequently lost his race to represent Massachusetts's 6th District)—he turned down. Come November, election results were mixed with Democrats retaining a majority in the House and Republicans keeping their slim supremacy in the Senate. Blaine lost a tight contest to Cleveland, who claimed all thirty-six of New York's electors with a razor-thin margin of 1,149 out of more than a million ballots. Shortly thereafter Roosevelt seemed intent on falling on his sword, though considering the studied drama in his diaries, letters, and books, he may have simply expressed an emotion of the moment when writing to Lodge, "I . . . do not believe that I shall ever be likely to come back into political life. . . . We have both of us . . . fought the losing fight grimly out to the end."[8]

Following the election, Theodore spent the winter months writing *Hunting Trips of a Ranchman*, published by G. P. Putnam's Sons. For publicity purposes it included a full-length portrait of its buckskin-suited author sporting shin-high soft moccasins and holding a Winchester rifle that drew attention to a cartridge belt doubling as a knife clasp; he stands a little stiffly before a backdrop of painted flora with clumps of assembled store-bought hay passing for verdure. His signature pince-nez glasses are nowhere to be seen. Dedicated to Elliott, the book came out in July 1885. Dropping the technical terminology oft employed in *The Naval War of 1812*, Roosevelt now opted for something a little lighter and sprightlier, its tone belying the difficult circumstances of the previous year. He stressed, rather, the strength of his young body, the virtues of hard work, and the awful beauty of the Badlands. "The free . . . life" of the plains he thought a tonic, as were the "occasions . . . when a man has to show his skill in shifting for himself."[9] One might almost forget that this proud Porcellian enjoyed his cowboy life part-time, or that he expected his ranch hands to call him "Mr. Roosevelt."

Reviewers thought highly of the book. A *New York Times* critic believed it would "take a leading position in the literature of the American sportsman" while a writer for London's *Spectator* called the study "bright and fresh and full of good reading." Roosevelt held the manuscript in high regard. A few years later, in 1891, at which point he had written no fewer than seven books, he told one correspondent that "the best . . . among them are *The Winning of the West*, and the *Hunting Trips of a Ranchman*."[10]

Several months prior to publication, Roosevelt returned to the Elkhorn Ranch, preparing for the punishing summer roundup—riding hundreds of miles, roping steers, and wrestling calves—to which he devoted slightly more than a month. "We are working pretty hard," he wrote Lodge in June. "Yesterday I was in the saddle at 2 A.M., and except for two very hasty meals, after each of which I took a fresh horse, did not stop working till 8:15 P.M.; and was up at half past three this morning. The eight-hour law does not apply to cowboys." Lincoln Lang credited his employer, whose body grew noticeably thicker and more muscular, with toughing it out alongside his crew: "After the novelty of the experience had worn off, I do not think he liked it any better than the rest, for at best it was grueling hard work, combined with the acme of personal discomfort." He thought Roosevelt displayed a "natural intensiveness."[11]

With visions of cowherd grandeur, Theodore completed his third significant purchase of cattle that summer, adding 1,500 head. In all, his (uninsured) investment in the industry came to a steep $85,000, about $2.7 million in today's currency.[12] On top of this he spent another $45,000 to build Leeholm, which, upon returning to New York, he decided, for his own unstated reasons, to name instead Sagamore Hill (a derivation of "sachem" or chief) in honor of the former Indian presence on the island. Perhaps this signaled an emancipation from the recent dark past. The twenty-three-room structure, commanding ninety-five acres of undulating woodland and adorned with a profusion of dormers, gables, and colored glass, featured a rocking-chair-friendly front piazza and no fewer than eight fireplaces.[13] The first floor, busy with bearskins and deer heads, took on the aspect of an exhibit, evoking nothing so much as young Teedie's "Roosevelt Museum of Natural History" all grown up. The residence otherwise quickly filled with books.

During the summer at Oyster Bay, Theodore spent time with Alice, now eighteen months old and under Bamie's doting care. In late August he returned to the Badlands by way of the Chicago Limited, apparently still uncertain, despite the recent lavish outlay on cattle, about his future. But within a few months this confusion lifted in the most agreeable way possible.

16

Back on Track

Edith Carow reentered Roosevelt's life in the fall of 1885, her once-secure social position now slipping. This private trial mirrored a broader upheaval in class status as industrial wealth had begun to edge out the older Brahmin and Knickerbocker families whose gilded pedigrees of preachers, statesmen, and educators no longer commanded compelling cultural respect. Born in Norwich, Connecticut, in 1861, Carow descended on her mother's side from the eighteenth-century Puritan divine Jonathan Edwards and could claim relation to various Pierponts, including a founder of Yale College; she counted the novelist Edith Wharton a distant cousin. The Carows, by contrast, had accrued a fortune in the Atlantic trade; Edie's grandfather, Isaac, a partner in the Kermit & Carow shipping line, once served as president of the New York Chamber of Commerce.[1]

This ancestral momentum petered out when Charles Carow, Edith's father, proved to be a poor capitalist. The fortunes of the family declined steadily, an inconvenient detail discovered upon Charles's alcohol-related death at the age of fifty-seven in the late winter of 1883. Pleading penury, Edith's mother, Gertrude, and younger sister, Emily, would later decamp for Italy. There they led a somewhat embittered existence, proud people squeezed out of their home and living in a style of conscripted exile. Unable to rise above their difficult circumstances, so one scholar has written, "They were an anchor on Edith's life."[2]

The connection between Carow and Roosevelt, forged in childhood, remained an aloof if living thing despite the former's rebuff of her would-be lover. Edith, who had gamely attended and "danced the soles off her shoes" at Theodore's wedding, occasionally saw him and Alice at Patriarch Balls, a subscription society event open only to New York's "best" families. She served in the spring of 1882 as one of Corinne's eight bridesmaids and, in an after-ceremony note to the newlywed, bid adieu to their shared youth: "I have kept realizing that you were leaving your old life behind, and if we live to be ninety years old we can never be two girls together again."[3]

In the autumn of 1885, some twenty months after Alice's death, Theodore, either by plan or chance, came upon Edith as she was leaving Bamie's Madison Avenue house. Attuned to Victorian proprieties and eager to remain loyal to the memory of his departed wife, he had maintained a cordial distance from Edith since becoming a widower. But this stoic if conspicuous grieving—the silent cowboy, the forlorn father—now collapsed rather completely. Within a matter of weeks, on November 17, the two had become secretly engaged—he offering, along with his love, a watch, a ring, and a fine pearl necklace. Presumptuously consigned by friends and family to a fast-approaching spinsterhood, Edith, practical and self-possessed with a cool façade, hinted to her beau of untapped intensity. "Now I do care about being pretty for you," she admitted, "with all the passion of a girl who has never loved before."[4]

More than a lover, Edith had always held out for Theodore, the boy and the man, the promise of maternal protection and affection. They had spent their juvenescence together, he sickly and spindly, she seemingly as much a part of his people as her own. Loyal, serious, and perhaps at the age of twenty-four giving off, in her unwed status, the assurance of fidelity to her earliest admirer, she now appeared to occupy the place so many had once thought her due. Still, a certain awkwardness shadowed the situation. Did a quick engagement dishonor Alice? Might remarriage injure TR's self-pride as a moralist? And what would his sisters, knowing Edith as a longtime friend from a fading family, think of her suddenly elevated status? Leaving these ambivalences to time, the intendeds kept their engagement clandestine for nearly a year.

Come spring 1886, Roosevelt returned to Dakota while Edith visited her mother and sister in Italy. In a typically Rooseveltian turn of events, he discovered one morning in late March that his ranch boat, a small, cheap conveyance used to cross the Little Missouri River, was missing and proceeded, with the aid of two hands ("tough, hardy, resolute fellows, quick as cats, strong as bears"), to hunt down the thieves. One gets the sense from Roosevelt's involved—and subsequently published—narrative of the several-day chase in "bitterly cold" weather that he enjoyed the adventure, which, of course, he could have avoided by simply building himself another $30 boat. Rather, he and his men quickly constructed a "flat-bottomed scow" and took off. For "to submit tamely and meekly to theft," Theodore contended, "is to invite almost certain repetition of the offense." To keep his mind occupied, he brought along a copy of Tolstoy's *Anna Karenina*.[5] On the afternoon of the third day, the party came upon the pilfered craft and located the thieves' camp. There they arrested "the German," so Roosevelt wrote, "whose weapons were on the ground," and awaited his confederates. These two men soon appeared, with rifles on their shoulders:

> When they were within twenty yards or so we straightened up from behind the bank, covering them with our cocked rifles, while I shouted to them to hold up their hands—an order that in such a case, in the West, a man is not apt to disregard if he thinks the giver is in earnest. . . . Finnigan hesitated for a second, his eyes fairly wolfish; then, as I walked up within a few paces, covering the center of his chest so as to avoid overshooting and repeating the command, he saw that he had no show, and, with an oath, let his rifle drop and held his hands up beside his head.[6]

Buoyed by the chase and the usual spring roundup involving thousands of cattle and sixty hard-riding men "in the saddle," Roosevelt stayed in Dakota until July, when he returned east, possibly chasing an appointed position on the New York Board of Health that never panned out. While in the city he made a quick circuit of friends and family, perhaps giving some light offense by leaving so abruptly. "I felt more melancholy than you would give your cold blooded brother credit for feeling when I said goodbye to my dearest sister," he wrote Bamie the following month from Medora. He asked about the "cunning little yellow headed baby Lee," and struck a paternal if remote pose: "Do kiss the little darling for me and tell her her father thinks of her and of you very often."[7]

He was further forced, in that Medora note, to tell Bamie of his impending wedding, word having leaked into the New York press. "I am engaged to Edith and before Christmas I shall . . . marry her," he wrote somewhat stiffly. "You are the first person to whom I have breathed a word on this subject." Boxed in by both propriety and the faint fear of Alice's unreconciled ghost, he seemed embarrassed and not a little confused: "I utterly disbelieve in and disapprove of second marriages; I have always considered that they argued weakness in a man's character. You could not reproach me one half as bitterly for my inconstancy and unfaithfulness as I reproach myself. Were I sure there was a heaven my one prayer would be I might never go there, lest I should meet those I loved on earth who are dead."[8]

That same busy autumn of 1886 Roosevelt unexpectedly found himself the Republican candidate for mayor of New York City, nominated just shy of his twenty-eighth birthday. While attending the party's August convention, he was cornered by a group of politicos who pressed him to make the race. Known as an independent in the GOP, TR was to be a sacrificial lamb. Abram Hewitt, a Tammany Democrat, looked the likely winner, and a third aspirant, Labor candidate Henry George, author, as noted, of the influential *Progress and Poverty*, had attracted the support of workers, socialists, and even some crossover Catholic Democrats. In any case, it had been fourteen years since a Republican had won a Manhattan mayoral contest. The state's GOP machine wanted a clean candidate while it regrouped and thought of the future, perhaps sensing that Roosevelt might draw independents and moderates back to the fold in time for a second Blaine nomination in 1888.

Lodge advised his young friend to refuse the dubious honor, but a clearly ambitious Theodore persisted, though candidly telling a friend from childhood, Fanny Smith Dana, "There is no chance of success," and "had the [party's] chances been better I would probably not have been asked." Roosevelt almost certainly relished the opportunity to hit the campaign circuit on his own behalf, to glory in the canvassing and stump for independent Republicanism. A nomination to govern the nation's largest city, moreover, promised to hasten his name far beyond the Hudson. "It cannot be denied that his candidacy is attractive in many respects and he is liable to get votes from many sources," the New York *Sun* noted. "It is not merely the chance of being elected Mayor that interests him. There are other offices he might prefer. To be in his youth the candidate for the first office in the first city of the U.S., and to poll a good vote for that office, is something more than empty honor.... He cannot be Mayor this year, but who knows what may happen in some other year? Congressman, Governor, Senator, President?"[9]

Mulling over his opponents, Roosevelt had no doubt he could run a respectable second, edging aside the radical George. How all this might impact his approaching wedding seems to have troubled him not. He and Edith planned to marry in England in December and then trek about Europe for three months, not spend their winter in Albany managing budget fights.

As things turned out, he—and she—had nothing to worry about, honeymoon-wise. Roosevelt suffered a great loss on election day, finishing an embarrassing third with 60,000 votes to Hewitt's 90,000 and George's 68,000. The party chieftains had been right all along: no Republican stood a chance that year. In a sporting telegraph sent the evening of the disaster, Theodore congratulated Lodge on his successful congressional race in Massachusetts—"Am more delighted than I can say"—while acknowledging of himself, "Am badly defeated. Worse even than I feared."[10]

Four days after the election, Roosevelt and Bamie sailed incognito aboard the transatlantic liner *Etruria* to England as "Mr. and Miss Merrifield"; Edith, already overseas with her mother and sister, would meet them in London. A charming Brit, Cecil Arthur Spring Rice ("Springy"), formerly a clerk in the Foreign Office and now a private secretary to future prime minister Lord Rosebery, saw through the façade and over the nine-day New York–to–Liverpool voyage developed a warm rapport with both Roosevelts. Tall and lithe with a long face and pasted-down hair, he was a natural raconteur, given to humor, and perhaps best known today for writing the patriotic hymn "I Vow to Thee My Country," used at the funeral of Winston Churchill, the wedding of Prince Charles and Lady Diana Spencer, and countless Remembrance (Poppy) Day services. Springy readily agreed to serve as his new friend's best man.

The ceremony, presided over by one Cannon Cammidge, took place on December 2 in the Anglican church of St. George's, Hanover Square, in central London. Only a handful of friends were present; Bamie sufficed as Edith's attendant. The groom nearly arrived late, engaging in an involved conversation, so Bamie recalled, "on the demography of the South Pacific" that began in her brother's Brown's Hotel digs and persisted in the hansom cab. The newlyweds promptly departed for the

Continent, Roosevelt's second European honeymoon in six years, taking in Florence, Sorrento, Milan, and Paris before returning to London and thence to America. Docking in late March 1887 and asked his plans by a reporter, Roosevelt, the recently defeated New York mayoral candidate, coolly replied, "I intend to divide my time between literature and ranching."[11]

While in Europe, Edith had insisted to Theodore that Alice, now three, live with them at Sagamore Hill and know her as "Mother." Only a few months earlier, in September of the previous year, Roosevelt had assured Bamie that she might remain Alice's primary parent: "As I have already told you, if you wish to you shall keep Baby Lee, I of course paying the expense." Now he was forced to go back on his word. For Alice the returns were decidedly cloudy. "My stepmother was terribly conscientious about me when they married," she told an interviewer many years later. "My father obviously didn't want the symbol of his infidelity around. His *two* infidelities, in fact: infidelity to my stepmother by marrying my mother first and to my mother by going back to my stepmother after she died. It was all so dreadfully Victorian and mixed up."[12]

Nine months after the wedding, on September 13, 1887, at two-fifteen in the morning, Edith gave birth to Theodore Roosevelt Jr. The delivery came "quickly and safely," the proud and no doubt relieved father reported, much pleased, as he put it, to have a "son and heir."[13] A great deal had changed for him over the previous year—marriage and two children at home, along with a disappointing if profile-lifting nomination for mayor of New York City. Filled increasingly with both purpose and possibility, his life now took on a fresh momentum.

Part III

SONG OF THE STRENUOUS LIFE

I always believe in going hard at everything.
            Theodore Roosevelt, 1901

Resplendent in Brooks Brothers: Roosevelt the Rough Rider.

17

The Historian

A year before remarrying, Roosevelt, surveying the fickle Dakota cow business, had written in *Hunting Trips of a Ranchman*, "The profits... are great; but the chances for loss are great also. A winter of unusual severity will work sad havoc among the young cattle." And true enough, while he idled about Europe with Edith, a punishing plains winter all but destroyed his rash investment. Deep blue snows began to fall in November, temperatures plunged to forty below zero by December, and a late-January blizzard blanketed the territory. Hungry cattle, chewing desperately on brittle sagebrush, died off in droves. "Everywhere monstrous snowdrifts were in evidence," Lincoln Lang remembered. "Except for an occasional partial let-up, while the northern furies were concentrating for a new drive, it was always snowing, blowing, and intensely cold." The March thaw revealed a mess of stiff-legged cow carcasses littering the frontier. Roosevelt's account books indicate that only 106 cattle were branded that spring, down from 475 the previous year. Stunned by the losses and suddenly an Oyster Bay begetter—"I have a small son now; and am settling down more and more to country life"—he casually dropped out of the cattle business.[1] Though occasionally going back for hunting trips, he sold the Elkhorn Ranch in 1898; after making a quick, nostalgic presidential stop in 1903, he never again returned.

Despite his early if admittedly uneven political push, Roosevelt thought his future might now flower as a historian. "I shall probably never be in politics again," he told a colleague in January 1888, noting both a concern lest the GOP "get into the habit of becoming a mere party of reaction," and a more personal interest in making a living by the pen—"My literary work occupies a good deal of my time; and I have on the whole done fairly well at it; I should like to write some book that would really take rank as in the very first class."[2] A homilizer at heart, Roosevelt determined to acquaint readers with their heroic pioneer past, inspiring the present industrial-age generation, sadly slackened by its many amenities, to commit itself to renewed toil and effort. Theodore's historical imagination, clearly swayed by his time in the rugged West, trafficked romantically in the opinion that frontier peoples were the truest Americans—ethnically mixed, spiritually varied, and Manifest Destiny's inevitable offspring.

One rollicking if tendentious biography (*Life of Thomas Hart Benton*, 1886) and a brash stab in the history-as-epic genre (*The Winning of the West*, four volumes, 1889–1896) were produced during this period. The former assayed with real brio the life of Benton, or "Old Bullion," a Missouri senator known for backing antebellum expansion across the frontier, a theme Roosevelt readily exploited in his book for contemporary purposes. America, after all, was on the move. Seven new states had entered the Union between 1876 and 1890, prefacing the country's emerging commitment to fashioning an overseas empire. A simmering crisis in the distant Pacific (1887–1889) between the United States, Great Britain, and Germany for control of the Samoan Islands pointed to both the perils and the possibilities of collecting colonies. In a letter touting the virtues of remaining in Samoa, Roosevelt, in full spread-eagle mode, declared it further "a great misfortune that we have not annexed Hawaii; gone on with our navy, and started an inter-oceanic canal at Nicaragua."[3]

The Benton book allowed its author ample room to defend the blooming jingo agenda. Critical of "recent historians" who had condemned the antebellum tilt toward Manifest Destiny as merely a ruse "to acquire lands out of which to carve new slave-holding states," Roosevelt insisted that many of the pioneers responded to a higher calling, "the chief among them being the fact that Westerners honestly believed themselves to be indeed . . . the heirs of the earth . . . and were prepared to struggle stoutly for the immediate possession of their heritage." The book received mainly favorable reviews, though one notice in the *Nation* detected a disturbing "strain of blood and iron [and] muscular Christianity minus the Christian part in the author's philosophy of civilization."[4]

The Winning of the West marked Roosevelt's high point as a popular historian. Always an intense and rapid worker, he came to financial terms with G. P. Putnam's Sons in March 1888 and turned in the first two volumes of the study only thirteen months later. "I realize perfectly," he wrote George H. Putnam, "that my chance of making a permanent literary reputation depends on how I do this big work."[5] As a researcher he broke fresh ground, unearthing unpublished manuscripts, referencing uncited letters, and quoted from pioneer diaries. Despite the sheen of archival analysis, however, his history lacked the depth, detachment, and interpretive power evident in the works of the period's best past-masters. These men included Henry Adams (author of a nine-volume history of the Jefferson and Madison administration built, in part, upon European-housed documents), John Hay and John Nicolay (biographers, as noted, of a sprawling study of Lincoln), and the old Boston Brahmin Francis Parkman, a gifted stylist whose classic seven-volume history of France and England in North America set a high bar for frontier sagas. Roosevelt felt a particular affinity for Parkman, another Harvard man who had trooped about the West, and to whom he affectionately dedicated *Winning*. In assaying the victory of Protestant/constitutional/Anglo-Saxon Britain over Catholic/monarchical/Latin France in the Seven Years' War (1756–1763), Parkman provided Roosevelt with a template to draft his own paean to the peoples of a rising West.

A clash of ethnicities runs throughout *Winning*, a recipe evident in the book's opening three chapters, entitled "The Spread of the English-Speaking Peoples," "The French of the Ohio Valley," and "The Appalachian [Indian] Confederacies." He assigned to the restless Anglos and Celts a special role in the Darwinian scramble to the top. "There have been many other races that at one time or another had their great periods of race expansion," he wrote, "but there has never been another whose expansion has been either so broad or so rapid." Inserting both himself and his readers into the narrative, he called the frontier's native peoples "our main opponents" and elevated the hunter into something of a mythical figure "swayed by gusts of stormy passion" and driven by "the love of freedom." Above all, the backwoodsmen constituted the truest of Americans as "they were . . . the best fitted to conquer the wilderness and hold it against all comers."[6]

For Roosevelt, pride of place went to the migrating Scotch Irish who had fled British oppression, gained a toehold in Pennsylvania, and then moved down the Appalachians. "Mingled with the descendants of many other races," he touted the Celtic contribution in a flow of purple prose, "they . . . formed the kernel of the distinctively and intensely American stock who were the pioneers of our people in their march westward, the vanguard of the army of fighting settlers, who, with axe and rifle, won their way from the Alleghenies to the Rio Grande and the Pacific."[7] By downgrading the historical importance of the northern Puritans and southern planters, he dismissed by association the modern Mugwump (a Puritan by another name), while conveniently lessening the stain of slavery, whose practitioners were presumably men of local scope rather than robust continentalists. The logic of his argument reserves the highest degree of "Americanness" for those engaged in the presumed pathfinder process of serial uprooting, fighting, and embedding—perhaps a curious claim for a many-generation Manhattanite to make.

The manuscript's popularity owed not a little to its galloping pace; Roosevelt clearly knew how to make a paragraph move. In his vivid description of a British officer's death at the Battle of Kings Mountain in the Revolutionary-era South Carolina upcountry, one can fairly smell the acrid white smoke rising from the tight patriot line: "As he rode full speed against a part of Sevier's men . . . he became a fair mark for the vengeful backwoods riflemen. Several of them fired together and he fell suddenly from his horse, pierced by half a dozen bullets almost at the same instant. The gallant British leader was dead, while his foot yet hung in the stirrup."[8]

More than a new-world triumph, the Revolution constituted but one front in the victory of English speakers globally, including much of India, Africa, and Australia. "This is not foreign to American history," Roosevelt argued in a classic amalgam of Darwinism and destiny. "The vast movement by which this continent was conquered and peopled cannot be rightly understood if considered solely by itself. It was the crowning and greatest achievement of a series of mighty movements, and it must be taken in connection with them. Its true significance will be lost unless we grasp, however roughly, the past race-history of the nations who took part therein."[9]

Aching to claim some honorary or vicarious backwoods bond, Roosevelt fairly begged to be considered a kind of Daniel Boone II. "For a number of years," he wrote of the inconsecutive months he had spent bossing Badlands ranch hands and reading Jane Austen, "I . . . lived and worked like any other frontiersman." In branding cattle, hunting for food, and policing a small farmstead (nabbing, that is, the sneak thieves who stole his boat), "we," so he swore, did "exactly . . . as did the pioneers who had a hundred years previously . . . built their log-cabins beside the Kentucky or in the valleys of the Great Smokies."[10] These sentimental words, bordering on bathos, are more generally indicative of Roosevelt's desire to personalize the past, control the narrative, and place himself, finally, in the center of its story.

The Winning of the West proved to be both a critical and a popular success. Praising its "remarkable dramatic and narrative power," the *New-York Tribune* thought the book soon to "take its place with the most valuable and indispensable works in the library of American history."[11] A bestseller, it struck a resonant chord with readers perhaps eager to embrace a preindustrial portrait of their country. Parkman's epic prepared the ground for Roosevelt's work, as did William Prescott's *History of the Conquest of Mexico* (1843), John Lothrop Motley's *The Rise of the Dutch Republic* (1856), and perhaps most notably George Bancroft's ten-volume *History of the United States of America, from the Discovery of the American Continent* (1854–1878). All these literary-minded men, including Roosevelt, attended Harvard, evidence of the East's near monopoly on portraying the past.

TR also shared with Parkman and company the conviction that historians, though attentive to ferreting out archival treasures, were at heart artists. Bereft of inspiration, no author, he believed, could expect to draw a sizeable audience or influence. "It certainly adds to one's pleasure to have read history and to appreciate the picturesque," he wrote a correspondent in 1906 while on a presidential trip to observe construction on the Panama Canal. "When on Wednesday we approached the coast and the jungle-covered mountains loomed clearer and clearer until we could see the surf beating on the shores . . . I kept thinking of the four centuries of wild and bloody romance, mixed with abject squalor and suffering, which made up the history of the Isthmus."[12]

Some six years later, in 1912, Roosevelt delivered an address titled "History as Literature" before the American Historical Association (AHA) in Boston in which he attacked the presumably bland and bloodless accounts of the past advanced by a fact-gathering professoriate—his audience of academics, in other words. Appealing to the ancient Greeks and Romans, he emphasized the power of poetry and mythology, chastised a mere scientific approach ("It is a shallow criticism to assert that imagination tends to inaccuracy"), and thought scholars should take sides ("The greatest historian [is] also . . . a great moralist").[13] In a separate communication to the distinguished British author and statesman George Otto Trevelyan, possibly a model for the young Roosevelt who hoped to master both worlds, he denounced the AHA as "a preposterous little organization" that prized narrow studies on esoteric subjects. Its members, he argued:

> . . . solemnly believed that if there were only enough of them, and that if they only collected enough facts of all kinds and sorts, there would cease to be any need hereafter for great writers, great thinkers. . . . They have done much real harm in preventing the development of students who might have a large grasp of what history should really be. They represent what is in itself the excellent revolt against superficiality and lack of research, but they have grown into the opposite and equally noxious belief that research is all in all, that accumulation of facts is everything.[14]

The big wheel of western studies, Frederick Jackson Turner, an academic historian best known for his essay "The Significance of the Frontier in American History" (1893), offered mixed opinions of Roosevelt's *Winning* and thus, more generally, its author's drawn-to-drama approach. The two men were friendly correspondents, exchanging a handful of letters having to do with their shared enthusiasm for the nation's borderlands. When reviewing the fourth book for the *American Historical Review*, Turner insisted that "Mr. Roosevelt has done a real service to our history in his volumes of the West. He has rescued a whole movement in American development from the hands of unskillful annalists; he has made use of widely scattered original sources, not heretofore exploited; and with graphic vigor he has portrayed the advance of the pioneer into the wastes of the continent."[15] Several years later, however, Turner privately offered to one correspondent a rather circumspect assessment of Roosevelt the historian:

> [He] was more concerned with *men* than with *institutions*, and especially with the strenuous life, and more particularly, the fight-

ing of the frontier.... While the epic period of the West fascinated Roosevelt... I was trying to see it as a whole—on the institutional, social, economic, and political side, its effects upon the nation as a whole, and I saw that there was a persistent pervasive influence in American life, which did not get its full attention from those who... approached the West as fighting ground."[16]

Turner, in other words, believed that Roosevelt, despite his dim appraisal of the professoriate, practiced his own highly selective rendering of the frontier—one replete with hunters and backwoodsmen, Indians and makeshift soldiers, though largely innocent of the politicians, businessmen, and missionaries, among others, who also shaped a rising Trans-Appalachian civilization.

In truth, Roosevelt's relationship with the West nestled very near to mythology. He thought it the most "American" of places, giving vent to a fierce warrior spirit that subdued both the British and the Indians. He believed himself part of this epochal promenade in its late bison-hunting days. "I owe more than I can ever express to the West," he once wrote in a memoir. "It was a fine, healthy life... it taught a man self-reliance, hardihood, and the value of instant decision—in short, the virtues that ought to come from life in the open country."[17] In weighing such words, it should be remembered that Roosevelt came to the range as a hunter looking for trophies, a gentleman cowhand with smart boots and a ranch house filled with a small library. His most intense involvement in Dakota was during widower years, bookended by Alice's death and Edith's arrival. Remarriage, the brutal winter that savaged his cow colony, and *Winning*'s success shrank his human connection with the region. Though it continued to conceptually inform and feed certain emotional needs, it ceased to live for him as a place of real people. A herdsman no more, he sought still another kind of frontier, and in 1888 reentered the political fray.

18

Washington Entrée

As an independent Republican and sworn enemy of the spoils system, Roosevelt sympathized with efforts to block partisan appointments to civil service jobs. Such blatant patronage had long informed the machine-style politics that emerged in the 1830s during the reign of Andrew Jackson and lived on after the Civil War. But this practice of boodle, graft, and gravy became increasingly difficult to defend. The Geological Survey, created in 1879 (assessing the mineral potential of the West), and the Interstate Commerce Commission, in 1887 (regulating the railroad industry), were but two of the distinctly technical government agencies that contradicted Jackson's old claim that "the duties of all public officers are . . . so plain and simple that men . . . may readily qualify themselves for their performance." It became apparent, rather, that some specialized bureaus required professional expertise. Thus did Congress pass the Pendleton Act (1883) in an effort to replace the sinecured with the skilled. It introduced a merit system complete with competitive exams and made it illegal to fire or demote federal employees for political reasons. It further created the United States Civil Service Commission, a three-person panel charged with policing the system.[1] This is the body Roosevelt joined in the spring of 1889.

The act empowering the commission contained real limitations. Though there were about 132,000 federal employees, far exceeding the 20,000 in Jackson's day, fewer than 14,000 fell under its rather limited purview; the bulk of these, aside from positions in Washington, D.C., clustered in the country's customhouses and in its larger post offices.[2] Though fashionably popular following a series of high-profile scandals including the Crédit Mobilier (a company created by the Union Pacific to inflate railroad construction costs paid with public monies) and the Whiskey Ring (a group of distillers and distributers who bribed Treasury officials to evade taxes), the Pendleton measure received scant support. Spoils politics still ruled Congress; presidents were indifferent to its success and cabinet members, including, importantly, the postmaster general, were often cordially unresponsive to the Civil Service Commission.

Among several of the act's better-heeled defenders, however—marginalized northeastern Republicans from ancient patrician families—the attack on cronyism reflected a desire to eradicate the power of partisan machines. This reaction to a ripening milieu of urbanization, Irish immigration, and Tammany Hall sway is one that Roosevelt selectively shared. "We of New York," he told a correspondent in 1884, "have lived for the past few years under the rule of an oligarchy composed of demagogues, office-holders and corrupt party wirepullers. We have been under the rule of an aristocracy composed of the worst instead of the best element."[3]

His route to the Civil Service Commission commenced with a presidential election. The 1888 contest pitted incumbent Grover Cleveland against the Republican challenger and former Indiana senator Benjamin Harrison: stocky, stubby-legged, and called "the Human Iceberg" behind his back. The campaign's principal point of contention, tariff reform—Cleveland sought to lower rates while Harrison, with the backing of the industrial class, championed protection—hardly rallied Roosevelt. "I really take very little interest in what people regard as the main issue," he wrote Bamie in August. "There are fifty questions of more lasting importance"; among these he included "the civil service." In the same note he called Harrison, with neither commentary nor enthusiasm, "a very good man"; having already bent his knee before Blaine, he understood that only party regularity could further his fledgling political career.[4]

Doing his part, Roosevelt spent several days in September aboard a rickety railcar campaigning in Michigan, Illinois, and Minnesota—"a trifle wearing" he confided to Spring Rice.[5] The following month he turned thirty, and on November 6 Harrison claimed a victory in the Electoral College (233 to 168), while Cleveland captured a slim plurality in the popular vote (48.6 percent to 47.8 percent). Though hostile to spoils politics, Theodore thought he had earned a place in the new administration. Knowing of his desire to be appointed assistant secretary of state, Lodge and the portly Maine congressman Thomas Reed pressed Harrison for the post, though this proved a nonstarter as incoming secretary of state Blaine could hardly have looked upon Roosevelt with favor. Setting aside personal differences, Blaine, writing "confidentially" to Lodge's wife, Anna (her husband's diplomatic go-between), offered a more compelling—and devastatingly accurate—reason to chase another candidate.

> My real trouble in regard to Mr. Roosevelt is that I fear he lacks the repose and patient endurance required in an Assistant Secretary. Mr. Roosevelt is amazingly quick in apprehension. Is there not danger that he might be too quick in execution? I do somehow fear that my sleep at Augusta or Bar Harbor would not be quite so easy and refreshing if so brilliant and aggressive a man had hold of the helm. Matters are constantly occurring which require the most thoughtful concentration and the most stubborn inaction. Do *you* think that Mr. T.R.'s temperament would give guaranty of that course?[6]

Undaunted, Roosevelt continued to seek, as much as his nimble dignity allowed, a position in the government; one weary Harrison advisor thought him as "persistent as a mosquito on a summer night" and suggested appointment on the low-paying Civil Service Commission ($3,500 per annum) possibly as a way of putting him in a corner. Of course, Theodore accepted.[7]

Though the post looked less than promising—by this late date the civil service debate had become stale—Roosevelt almost certainly recognized that his future in national politics, the only politics that he cared to play, meant a Washington situation rather than performing before small-town careerists in the Albany assembly. In the nation's capital, rather, he could forge important friendships, have his name before the president and influential congressional leaders, and, more important, come to know the restless federal city as a place where he might one day wield real power. Only eight years earlier he had walked into the 21st District Republican Association at Morton Hall and begun to learn the finer points of practical politics. He hoped now to repeat that educative process on a larger stage.

In its brief history, the commission had become known as a quiet spot for salary-drawing bureaucrats to drowse. Mainly, these paper-pushers oversaw the mass of civil service exams administered around the country; occasionally they might investigate accusations of fraud on the tests, though their powers were limited to merely apprising higher-ups of the small sins they had discovered. Roosevelt's two colleagues on the commission, Hugh Thompson and Charles Lyman, were studies in contrast. The former, an ex–Confederate officer and governor of South Carolina, struck Roosevelt as altogether more competent than the latter, a former Union army officer from Connecticut. "Thank Heaven I have Thompson for a colleague," he wrote Lodge. "Lyman is a good, honest, hardworking man, very familiar with the law; but he is also the most intolerably slow of all the men who ever adored red tape." He subsequently downgraded Lyman to Lodge as "utterly useless."[8]

Roosevelt arrived in Washington near the middle of May 1889, occupying an office in the west wing of the tall-columned neoclassical City Hall building on Judiciary Square facing Indiana Avenue. Within days of moving in, Theodore ("We are overwhelmed with work," he gloated to one reformer) had already put his impress on the commission. Knowing New York well, of course, he conducted a quick investigation late that same month on civil service exams held in the U.S. Custom House quartered in the Merchants' Exchange Building on Wall Street, discovering evidence of cheating—questions leaked to candidates. "I 'went it strong' into the Custom House people," he wrote enthusiastically to Bamie, "and did some pretty good work; I think it will have an excellent effect, and in addition there is some personal satisfaction to me in having shown that I did not intend to have the Commission remain a mere board of head clerks."[9]

Having exercised a small but headline-worthy success, Roosevelt quickly initiated a more promising attack on political plunder—the nation's mail system. The plenitude of post office jobs meant a mountain of patronage, and the new commissioner, eager to enlist reform-minded newspaper editors in this particular crusade, now sought maximum public interest by making a big splash. With the aid of informants, he exposed evidence of corruption, auctioned jobs, and fudged exam scores, on a lightning-fast midwestern circuit that began in Indianapolis, Harrison's hometown and certain to catch the president's surprised eye. "We had only a week's trip but we stirred things up well," Roosevelt wrote Lodge upon his return. The *Chicago Morning News* concurred, observing that "one of the conspicuous successes of President Harrison's administration is the Hon. Teddy Roosevelt. . . . He has made various spoilsmen of his party as mad as hornets, and he seems to be glad of it."[10] Postmaster General John Wanamaker, among the mad, or at least the puzzled, could scarcely understand the young commissioner's motives, a confusion to be repeated over the years among any number of entrenched Republicans who liked the system just fine.

Urbane, cordial, and clean-shaven, Wanamaker, a Philadelphia fixture, diplomatically settled in for a long if mostly quiet civil war with Roosevelt. Impresario of Wanamaker's, one of the country's first department stores, he had made a large fortune and essentially patronaged himself into the president's cabinet. Though Roosevelt's friends thought a head-rolling revolution at hand—"They chose the wrong man," Spring Rice predicted. "He obeys the law and enforces it. There is a scream for his removal in consequence. He is having a fine time and going strong"—Theodore, in fact, made little headway against Wanamaker's empire. The postmaster, with Harrison's placid complicity, continued to cram the nation's post offices with loyal Republicans, while largely gumming up the commission's efforts to intervene. Predictably, the would-be crusader grew frustrated with both Harrison and, more generally, the structural restraints upon his circumstances. "I do wish the President would give me a little active, even if only verbal encouragement," he wrote Lodge. "It is dead weight to stagger under, without a particle of sympathy from any one of our leaders."[11]

Socially, Roosevelt took immediately to Washington, moving his family into a residence on Jefferson Place a few blocks north of the Executive Mansion, and enjoying with Edith a several-evenings-a-week routine of dinners and entertainments. He formed during this period two friendships of varying consequence with older men—John Hay and Henry Adams—whom he knew, as noted, if only slightly in youth, the first as his father's friend, the second as a Harvard professor and one-night Cambridge dinner companion. Close confidants, Hay and Adams built adjoining mansions across the street from Lafayette Park and seemed, considering their respective ties to the Lincoln administration and the Adams political dynasty, to hold all American history, which they wrote of in abundance, in their aging hands. Roosevelt was entranced. Hay, a sometime poet and novelist with inherited in-law money, had taken a turn as assistant secretary of state. The petite, bald, and Van Dyke–bearded Adams remained aloof from formal politics, employing his days as a kind of intellectual-at-large predicting the coming Armageddon of a world driven increasingly by an unconscionable industrial regime.

Within this exclusive society salad one should include Lodge, a congressman and less accomplished gentleman historian. The closeness of this quartet is worth noting and may be gleaned in a busy Roosevelt to Spring Rice letter saying in part, "Henry Adams is exactly the same as ever; we dine with him tomorrow night. John Hay still has for his idols [the devil] James G. Blaine and [the angel] Henry James Jr—a combination which indicates a wide range of appreciation. Cabot is in great form, and I begin to think there really is some chance of his making the Senatorship." The foursome's intimacy, however, should not be overstated. Hay and Adams were of an older generation, kept a cordial (or in Adams's case contemptuous) distance from the whirligig of professional boss politics, and enjoyed a financial independence that permitted enviable degrees of freedom. Their wry, dry, and ironic temperaments, moreover, clashed with the earnest Roosevelt's constant go and glow—TR once complained to Lodge of their "satirical cynicism" and "lack . . . in robustness of fiber."[12]

Aside from his commission salary, Theodore continued to draw from a family trust, received money from the Boston Lees for Alice's needs, and earned income through his writing. In 1892 the estate of Edith's recently deceased uncle, John Carow, left her $1,200 per annum, about $40,000 in today's dollars. But keeping two houses with a growing brood proved a challenge, one typically borne by Edith, who maintained the family budget instead of her distracted husband. Expenses during the commission years included a swarm of cooks, coachmen, gardeners, and laundresses; the Roosevelts paid about $300 per year for coal and wood, between $350 and $550 for doctors' bills, and $250 for property taxes on Sagamore Hill. Electricians in Cincinnati, to offer some comparison, earned on average $915 a year.[13]

Recurrent pleas by an economizing Edith took on an added urgency during this Washington period when the Roosevelt family increased by three: Kermit (1889), Ethel (1891), and Archie (1894). Their births conspired with an uncooperative bathroom scale to make TR feel the burden of years. Though confronted with weight gain, a consequence of overeating and too many hours in the office, he expected Edith, whom he liked to see, so he said, in "very pretty and dainty... white summer clothes," to maintain a trim figure; he "prefers me thin," she told a relative. Several years later, when criticizing one of his sons (a ten-year-old Quentin, the youngest) before the family "because," so TR grumbled, "I thought he was fat and inert and ate too much," Edith, in a stage whisper to Alice and Ethel, said that this Sagamore Hill sire resembled nothing so much as "the father guinea pig that wanted to eat his little ones!"[14] Such pressures and expectations Roosevelt could hardly contain; by turns loving and demanding, he set a high bar for those in his sights—including his struggling brother, Elliott.

19

Elliott's Story

Elliott, "Dear old Nell" to his overbearing older brother, struck numerous intimates as the most amiable, athletic, and physically attractive of his siblings. Less bookish though delightfully sociable, he seemed in youth destined for some impending glory. "Perhaps he was nothing so aggressive or so forceful a man as Theodore," remembered one acquaintance, "but if personal popularity could have bestowed public honours on any man there was nothing beyond the reach of Elliott Roosevelt." Despite such rosy promise, Nell's prospects casually unraveled in adolescence when he began to suffer from seizure-like symptoms—variously diagnosed as nerves, night terrors, headaches, and hysteria—thought to have been brought on by stress. The sources of his struggles remain elusive. Perhaps he suffered from epilepsy, or buckled under the pressure of his father's ever-present expectations, or experienced a confusing and possibly culturally verboten sexual coming-out. Whatever the foundation of his affliction, he turned, while still in his teens, to alcohol, which he later chased with laudanum and morphine. This destructive recourse to self-remedy became a point of hushed observation and no little concern among his kin. "Conversation about Uncle Ellie and his problems was frequent when I was young," Alice later reported. "I could tell because it would stop when I entered the room."[1]

In 1883, at the age of twenty-three, Elliott married New York socialite Anna Rebecca Hall, whose family kept an estate in Tivoli some thirty miles north of Poughkeepsie along the Hudson River. Ellie and Annie had three children, the eldest, Anna Eleanor, to become the longest-serving and most distinguished First Lady in the country's history.

Unable to stick in business—withdrawing from positions in real estate, banking, and brokerage—Elliott built a country residence on Long Island, dubbed "Half Way Nirvana," and indulged in a steady diet of spirits-fueled parties. "I do hate his Hempstead life," a reproving Theodore wrote Bamie in the summer of 1888. "I do'n't know whether he could get along without the excitement now, but it is certainly very unhealthy, and it leads to nothing."[2]

Perhaps unwilling to engage with his family's, or at least his brother's, disapproval (aside from condemning Nell's drinking, Theodore criticized Anna as vacuous, ornamental, and a poor influence), and having checked himself out of a Michigan sanitarium, Elliott took his family to Europe in 1890. There, in Paris, a pregnant Anna, facing a daunting winter and perhaps aware of her husband's affair with an American named Mrs. Florence Bagley Sherman, prevailed upon Bamie to come to the Continent and convince Elliott to seek additional treatment. At this point Elliott's situation began to implode. Back in New York, Theodore received a powder-keg communication from a law firm representing Katy Mann, a servant in Elliott's fashionable East Thirties Manhattan brownstone, who was soon, the note stated, to bear his child. Theodore blanched at this unwelcome news, which he called a "hideous revelation" and Nell a "flagrant man-swine." As Alice noted of her father, "He believed rather strongly in certain elementary principles and moral values. He could be quite tough about mistresses and illegitimate babies and all that." His Victorian sensibilities offended, TR seemed eager to orchestrate a break between Elliott and Anna, who, so he imperiously wrote Bamie, "ought not to have any more children, and those she has should be brought up away from him."[3]

In February 1891, Nell checked into the Marien Grund Sanctuary at Graz, Austria, for three months. While he was there, Bamie, under Theodore's orders, confronted him with Katy Mann's accusation, which included a threat to bring a paternity suit unless he provided $10,000, (about $330,000 in today's currency) for the support of their son, Elliott Roosevelt Mann. Elliott denied Katy's allegation and Theodore now took his side ("Of course she is lying"), though Mann's determination to pursue litigation, armed, so she insisted, with incriminating love letters from Elliott, threatened a public scandal.[4] In something of a quiet panic, Elliott left Austria and returned to Paris, where he acquired yet another American mistress, a Mrs. Evans.

Meanwhile, Theodore and an uncle, James King Gracie, Mittie's brother-in-law, had hired a specialist, an "expert in likeness," to examine young Elliott Mann; he declared the infant unquestionably a Roosevelt. Theodore then counseled his brother to pay for child support and in a June 7 letter to Bamie advised her in minute detail to bring Anna and the children home—leaving Elliott to rot on the Continent if necessary:

> Anna must be made to understand that it is both maudlin and criminal—I am choosing my words with scientific exactness—to continue living with Elliott.... Do everything to persuade her to come home at once, unless ... better still, he will come too. Once here I'll guarantee to see that he is shut up.... Make up your mind to one dreadful scene. Use this letter if you like.... Do not care an atom for his threats of going off alone. Let him go.... What happens to him is of purely minor importance now.[5]

Elliott continued to insist upon his innocence, but Theodore refused to be drawn in. "However the suit went," he wrote Nell on the fourteenth, "it would create a great scandal; and much would be dragged out that we are very desirous of keeping from the public." He pointedly referred to Elliott's taste for "liquor or opiates."[6]

The redoubtable Bamie returned to America with Anna and the three children, while Nell checked into an inebriate asylum near Paris. In August Theodore, moving to protect the financial future of Elliott's family—a portfolio of stocks, bonds, and real estate amounting to some $6 million in today's dollars—applied for a writ in lunacy to have his brother declared insane. This move made the case public, and the New York *Sun* duly reported of "a Commission appointed by Justice O'Brien of the [state] Supreme Court to enquire into the mental condition of Elliott Roosevelt, with a view to having a committee appointed to care for his person and for his estate. The application was made by his brother ... [who] avers in the papers in the case that the mental faculties of his brother have been failing him for nearly two years ... [and that he] became violent and on three occasions threatened to take his own life. He had to be placed in surveillance. Mr. Roosevelt says he is 'unable to say how far the result is due to indulgence in drink or other excesses.'"[7] Elliott, an ocean away, rallied and fought the writ while certifying physicians disagreed on his condition.

That autumn the stress of the situation possibly caught up with Theodore, who took ill with a serious case of bronchitis. In January 1892 he determined to take matters into his own hands, sailing to Europe and confronting Elliott. "Won!" he wrote Bamie on the twenty-first, and crowed that their brother had "surrendered completely, and was utterly broken." Meaning that in return for Theodore's dropping the insanity suit, Nell had agreed to place two-thirds of his property in a trust for Anna and their children. Elliott further consented to return to America and check into the Keeley Institute, opened in 1879 and catering to the treatment of alcoholics, in Dwight, Illinois.[8] He was thereafter quietly exiled to rural Abingdon, Virginia, where Corinne's husband, Douglas Robinson, was developing a mining tract.

Though Theodore had bragged to Bamie of the great victory won in Paris, Elliott's despondent mistress, Mrs. Evans, thought TR a common bully. She wrote in a diary the day her overmatched beau left for America:

> This morning, with his silk hat, his overcoat, gloves and cigar, E. came to my room to say goodbye. It is all over.... Now my love was swallowed up in pity—for he looks so bruised, so beaten down by the past week with his brother. How could they treat so generous and noble a man as they have. He is more noble a figure in my eyes, with all his confessed faults, than either his wife or brother.[9]

Back in the States, Elliott's situation quickly unraveled. In December Anna, only twenty-nine, died of diphtheria, and five months later his oldest and namesake son succumbed to scarlet fever. Shattered and humiliated—barred as he was from Anna's deathbed—he consumed each day large quantities of brandy, anisette, and green mint. "He can't be helped, and he must simply be let go his own gait," Theodore wrote Bamie, adding, in what he no doubt considered a pragmatic aside, "Poor fellow! if only he could have died instead of Anna!" This wish, half met, succeeded not quite two years later, in August 1894, when the convalescent—consuming by this point several bottles of champagne a day—suffered a fatal seizure in his Manhattan apartment soon after a suicide attempt. Having his way, Theodore could now play the benign patriarch: "There is one great comfort I already feel," he wrote Corinne. "I only need to have pleasant thoughts of Elliott now. He is just the gallant, generous, manly boy and young man whom everyone loved."[10]

Nine months after Elliott's death, Roosevelt returned to Manhattan with his family. After six years in Washington as a civil service commissioner he sought, at an ambitious thirty-six, still higher political office, but this required reconnecting with New York's all-important power brokers.

20

The Top Cop

In the spring of 1895, after the Republicans had won City Hall, Roosevelt assumed the presidency of the four-member Board of New York City Police Commissioners. Initiating the appointment, he had prevailed upon Lemuel Quigg, an Empire State journalist, congressman, and political fixer, to get the ball rolling. "I hated to leave Washington," he wrote Bamie, "for I love the life . . . but . . . I am nearly through what I can do here; and this is a good way of leaving a position which I greatly like but which I do not wish permanently to retain, and I think it a good thing to be definitely identified with my city once more." In fact, Theodore had wanted very badly the previous fall to make a second run for mayor of Gotham. Edith's objection—she dreaded an expensive race involving family money with victory no sure thing—had nixed the idea. His sense of regret could only have amplified when the reform-minded Republican William Lafayette Strong claimed the prize. "The last four weeks, ever since I decided not to run, have been pretty bitter ones for me," he confided to Lodge that autumn. "I would literally have given my right arm to have made the race, win or lose. It was the one golden chance." He revealed further a minor rupture on the domestic front: "You may guess that these weeks have not been particularly pleasant ones. . . . At the time, with Edith feeling as intensely as she did, I did not see how I could well go in; though I have grown to feel more and more that in this instance I should have gone counter to her wishes and made the race anyhow. . . . I should have realized that she *could* not see the matter as it really was, or realize my feelings."[1] Shortly thereafter, Strong appointed Roosevelt to the Police Commission.

Though politely commending his friend's return to New York, Lodge considered Theodore a coming man and thought his future lay in Washington. About this time he wrote the incoming commissioner, one can only say clairvoyantly, as much: "I am under no delusion about you. You have won a following, a big one and great reputation. You only need to use these advantages politically—in party matters you can force the machine to give you what you want. . . . You are too dangerous and too strong for them to fight you profitably."[2]

Roosevelt's office was located at 300 Mulberry Street just north of Houston, near a neighborhood later to be christened Little Italy. One commissioner had sardonically called the functional if architecturally unremarkable four-story stone and brick building, erected in 1862, "that antique and shabby palace, that sepulcher of reputations, that tomb of character, that morgue of political ambition."[3] Almost immediately into his tenure Roosevelt went to war with the Dublin-born Thomas Byrnes, chief of the New York City Police. A Civil War veteran, career policeman, and talented self-promoter with a national reputation—having popularized the relentless "third degree" of questioning suspects—Byrnes enjoyed an estimable reputation. A series of detective fiction books written in the late 1880s featuring "Inspector Barnes" (*The Great Bank Robbery*, *A Tragic Mystery*, and others) written by Julian Hawthorne, son of a more serious novelist, traded upon his celebrity; the ubiquitous chief subsequently appeared more than a century later in Caleb Carr's 1994 bestseller, *The Alienist*.

Roosevelt quickly took against Byrnes, learning through the grapevine of his susceptibility to bribes, cooperative relationship with organized crime, and shakedowns of local grocers, haberdasheries, bars, and brothels. "No man intimately acquainted with both the lower and the humbler sides of New York life . . . can realize how far this corruption extended," Roosevelt later informed the *Atlantic Monthly*'s influential readership. "The policeman, the ward politician, the liquor seller, and the criminal alternately preyed on one another and helped one another to prey on the general public." Sizing up the situation during his first weeks on the job, he wrote to Lodge, "I am going to be absorbed in the work here and under a terrific strain; I have got to move against the scandals in this Department, if my work is to be at all thorough."[4]

Roosevelt quickly identified a plan of attack—cutting the head off the proverbial snake. "I think I shall move against Byrnes at once," he confided to a colleague just weeks into his term. "I thoroughly distrust him, and cannot do any thorough work while he remains." The inevitable end came abruptly. Within ten days Byrnes, facing a full investigation by the commission into his professional conduct, doubtlessly to include a fine-tooth combing into how he had made a staggering $350,000 through stock tips from well-placed Wall Street contacts, resigned—the bitter pill sweetened with a full pension.[5]

Roosevelt next moved to investigate the force's performance and productivity via a highly publicized round of night patrols, in which he surreptitiously walked the beat to see if his men were occupied at their posts. The tactic was pure Roosevelt—efficient, effective, and more than a little self-aggrandizing; the press, as he predicted, loved it. "We have a real Police Commissioner," cackled an amused editor for Joseph Pulitzer's *New York World*, the nation's largest-circulation newspaper. "His name is Theodore Roosevelt. His teeth are big and white; his eyes are small and piercing; his voice is rasping . . . his heart is full of reform . . . and he is at work now teaching the force that it is paid to work." Accompanied by Jacob Riis, a Danish American muckraking journalist interested in the urban impoverished and author of the tenement-life exposé *How the Other Half Lives* (1890), Roosevelt, eager to discover "exactly what the men were doing," made a number of nocturnal sweeps around the several blocks proximate to Mulberry Street and the broader East Side. At first, he often failed to see even a single officer, though word of his tactics quickly—to the great amusement of New Yorkers—got the attention of his astonished force. "These midnight rambles are great fun," he wrote Bamie with typical enthusiasm. "My whole work brings me in contact with every class of people in New York, as no other work possibly could; and I get a glimpse of the real life of the swarming millions."[6] He thought the spot checks productive even though each sequence cost him forty consecutive hours without sleep.

Roosevelt's next donnybrook, a self-appointed mission to uphold the state's Sunday Excise Law, passed in 1857 and reaffirmed by the assembly in 1892, met with what could only be called mixed results. Largely a cosmetic commandment variously observed by upstaters and aggressively ignored in the city, the rule caught the new reform-minded commissioner's eye. In his crusade against police force corruption, Roosevelt identified the flouting of this particular statute as a particular sin. Officers accepted bribes from saloons for ignoring the law, and this cankered the reputation of all cops. He hoped to hinder, moreover, the liquor cartel's connection to Democratic Tammany Hall. To put Roosevelt's campaign into perspective, it should be remembered that there were more than ten thousand saloons in Manhattan, that all classes in the city would resent enforcement—from beer-swilling day laborers to champagne-sipping dandies—and that a fair amount of liquor revenue, about $6 million in today's dollars, circulated through Gotham on the Sabbath. In June, shortly after forcing Byrnes out, Roosevelt informed his officers that they would henceforth firmly enforce Sunday saloon closings. When challenged by the press on what looked like a surely quixotic misadventure in policing public morality, he flashed before the *Sun* a blinkered if steely determination: "I do not deal with public sentiment. I deal with the law."[7]

On Sunday, June 23, the police started shutting down the city's saloons and a slew of people, some quite highly placed, took no little umbrage. Playing to the media, Democratic senator David B. Hill damned the "notoriety-seeking Police Commissioners" and singled Roosevelt out for, so he said, "indulging in a champagne dinner at the Union League Club" while denying thirsty workingmen their leisure-day due. Theodore conceded to Bamie the difficulty he suddenly faced—"I have now run up against an ugly snag"—though it looked to a great many that this trouble-seeking commissioner, only two months on the job, had gone out of his way to pick a fight for righteousness. And it is true that he felt very much on the side of the angels. "The country Republicans and all the decent church-going Republicans are very strongly in my favor," he argued, while "the Platt machine people, especially in this City, are on the verge of open war with me." The head of said machine, the balding, bewhiskered Thomas Platt, known as "the Easy Boss" for his deft handling of GOP policymaking in the state, cordially came to hate Roosevelt's flaming disregard for party regularity. Roosevelt returned the sentiment in kind, calling this practiced wire-puller's influence "simply poisonous."[8] The two would have ample opportunity over the next few years to clash, the state and the GOP hardly able to contain their contrasting styles, temperaments, and tactics.

Invariably, the press followed the Sunday saloon fight with great interest. The *New York World* tagged Roosevelt "a little tin Czar" for choosing the laws he wished to respect. Many of the city's statutes, after all, including those decreeing no fishing from docks on Sundays, no entering a moving streetcar, and no kite flying in certain neighborhoods, were mercifully unenforced. To others, Roosevelt's crackdown looked anything but arbitrary. He was accused of courting rural New Yorkers, temperance crusaders, and Protestant churches by abusing Tammany Hall, Manhattan's working class, and, invariably, immigrants. Naturally this public moralist, weaned on a diet of Darwinian platitudes, resented any insinuation that social class—or simple snobbery—influenced his decision to go after the saloons. And when the *Staats-Zeitung*, New York's leading German-language newspaper, raised such concerns, Roosevelt privately lashed back, insisting to one correspondent, "When [it] says that I hit mainly the poor man, [it] is . . . guilty of deliberate falsehood. The same is true in its statement that I openly favor class legislation." To Carl Schurz, critical of the Sabbath ban, he argued that "the poor man who is prevented from getting drunk on Sunday is benefited by our course."[9] As with his recent struggle to control Elliott's (and Elliott's children's) future, Roosevelt reserved right for himself.

By August, following several weeks of dry Sundays, tensions in the city were fraying with no relief in sight. On the fifth, a dubious-looking package addressed to Roosevelt appeared at the post office, which a cautious clerk opened to discover a letter bomb. "There is much hostility," the letter's would-be recipient conceded to Lodge, but hastened to accentuate, perhaps a little defensively, the "surprising support from quarters that I did not expect." Belying these brave words, however, the party bosses were intensely interested in the ill-starred campaign's impact on the coming full elections. A clearly concerned Theodore bustled about the island, speaking to various Republican groups, attempting to explain the police board's liquor policy; some of these organizations did their best to distance themselves from "the police czar," including the GOP's County Committee, which held a late-October meeting in Carnegie Hall. "Of course," Roosevelt said to Lodge of this gathering, "I was excluded."[10]

On election day, Tammany claimed a big victory in the city, all but dealing a death blow to the blue laws; the provoked German American vote had made the difference. Republicans were victorious in rural and upstate areas, however, and maintained control of the statehouse in Albany. But power, as everyone knew, emanated from Manhattan, and nothing could disguise the trouncing Theodore took in his hometown. "The political outlook," he confirmed to Bamie days after the election, "is rather discouraging." And yet Roosevelt proved, as Lodge had suggested, "too dangerous and too strong" for the Platt machine to move against. Many New Yorkers, rather, were taken by his energy, integrity, and growing reputation as a reformer. Bram Stoker, an Irish theater manager and journalist soon to publish the gothic horror novel *Dracula*, first met TR at a literary dinner about this time and confided to a diary that his new acquaintance "must be President some day. A man you can't cajole, can't frighten, can't buy."[11]

Roosevelt spent much of the next year in a fight with Andrew D. Parker, a fellow commissioner, over the allotment of promotions. The two quickly developed a deep enmity. Partisanship factored into their feud as Parker insisted that half of the highest-placed positions go to Democrats, an overture that Roosevelt, pleading "best man for the job," refused to entertain. Parker further castigated Roosevelt's autocratic ways ("Think's he's the whole board") and believed, correctly, that his nemesis regarded the cop job as a means to a more powerful political position. But as president of the board Roosevelt held the high ground and, moving with typical speed, began the process of having Parker dismissed from the commission on the somewhat piddling charge of having missed several of the board's meetings. "Mr. Parker has been an unfaithful public servant," TR told the *New York Times*, "and in my opinion he should be removed." For good measure, he accused his colleague of "treachery and double-dealing." After a lavishly covered investigation and trial—at which further charges, including a failure to investigate citizens' complaints, were leveled—Mayor Strong, in March of the following year (1897), discharged Parker from office. In a separate statement appearing in the *New York Journal*, Strong more ecumenically condemned the morale-lowering disruption in policing brought about by the fracas—implicitly rebuking both men: "Instead of Harmony, controversy and bitter feeling arose, with the result that upon matters of importance [the] action of the Board was hindered." Putting a more positive spin on events, TR blithely told the same paper in the same edition, "The removal of Mr. Parker will at once solve all the difficulties . . . and enable us to go on successfully."[12]

But Roosevelt had no plans "to go on" in New York. The following month, rather, he returned to Washington as assistant secretary of the navy, a reward for his work the previous autumn campaigning for the newly inaugurated president William McKinley. Thickly built with deep-set eyes and bushy brows, the former governor was the fifth Ohio-born candidate to win the office since the late 1860s. When dressed in de rigueur business black, this thin-lipped, pale-skinned, unsmiling man looked the very caricature of a small-town funeral director. Acknowledging, to Lodge, "I have [had] a somewhat stormy career" on Mulberry Street, Roosevelt happily resigned. He left little impress on the inscrutable city, impervious in its stubborn plentitude to one-note crusaders. Hardly inconsequential, however, his two years on the Police Commission made him a more assured and polished public official. He gave countless speeches, dealt adeptly with the press, and demonstrated an eagerness for taking on large jobs. These lessons, along with a growing reputation as a law-and-order Republican, he now took back to Washington.

21

In the Navy

Roosevelt actually cared little for a McKinley candidacy, initially leaning toward House Speaker Thomas Reed of Maine to tote the party's pennon. Pudgy-faced, triple-chinned, and weighing more than three hundred pounds ("I love fish balls dearly," he confessed to a diary, "but as they make me fat I ought to give them up"), the savvy Reed mastered the art of lower-chamber leadership, controlling committee assignments, rewarding loyalty, and becoming its most influential presiding officer since the clever Henry Clay in the 1820s.[1] Occasionally lampooned by Democrats as "Czar Reed," he lingered on the periphery of a literary-minded Washington social group that included Roosevelt along with Hay and Adams. To a budding number of would-be imperialists, moreover, his interest in building up the navy seemed consistent with the main trends of post–Civil War expansion that would bring American power to the Pacific.

McKinley, by contrast, firmly committed to Blaine in 1884, struck Theodore as a mere machine politician, agreeable to the whims of stronger men. "It will be a great misfortune to have McKinley nominated," he wrote Lodge, and confided to Bamie, "McKinley . . . I utterly distrust." He feared, perhaps above all, that the governor lacked the requisite moxie to take on the welling opposition of Democrats and Populists (agrarian reformers hostile to Wall Street), who had fused in 1896 over the explosive proposal to enlarge the nation's money supply by coining silver dollars. Broadly speaking, southern and western debtors, damaged by the recent Panic of 1893, wished to inflate currency, while creditors, typified by the GOP-backed East Coast financial aristocracy, wanted to maintain the monetary status quo, the single-metal—gold—system. Taking the side of respectability, Roosevelt condemned the "silly fools" who dared attack "sound money" with silver.[2]

In mid-June 1896 the Republicans assembled in St. Louis, whose "unique geographical advantages" and "ease of access from all points of the United States," so the party's *Official Proceedings* puffed, argued in its favor. The convention collected in a temporary wooden structure—essentially a big barn erected in sixty days—after the original site, the Exposition and Music Hall, one of the country's first electric-lit buildings, failed to remodel its seating in a timely fashion. When it came time to choose a nominee in this elaborate shed, McKinley bested the badly outmaneuvered Reed on the first ballot 661.5 to 84.5. Sensing imminent doom, Reed's wife, Susan, had futilely implored Lodge to "make a brave fight." A political realist despite the romantic veneer, Roosevelt quickly fell in line, telling Bamie on the twentieth, "I am pretty well satisfied with the outcome at St. Louis," and now referred to McKinley as "an upright and honorable man, of very considerable ability." He did retain certain reservations, however: "He is not a strong man ... and unless he is well backed I should feel rather uneasy about him in a serious crisis." Roosevelt thought the party plank—favoring the gold standard, the acquisition of Hawaii, and a canal across Central America—"excellent."[3]

In the November general election McKinley faced former Nebraska congressman William Jennings Bryan, a free-silver Democrat endorsed by the Populist Party. Known variously as "the Boy Orator," "the Great Commoner," and "the Silver Knight," the thirty-six-year-old Bryan, two years Roosevelt's junior, campaigned on the Chicago platform hammered out in the party's July convention. These commitments included the coinage of free silver, a call for stricter controls of industry, and a reduction of corporate-friendly high tariffs that, so Bryanites complained, "enriched the few at the expense of the many." The political battle of 1896, in other words, reflected a still broader class struggle.

McKinley's campaign manager, "Dollar Mark" Hanna, a wealthy Cleveland businessman turned political kingmaker who had attended high school with John D. Rockefeller, recognized that Roosevelt, an eastern dude with Dakota connections, could make a strong appeal for the party in the West—the heart of Populism. Accordingly, the GOP sent the old buffalo hunter on a three-week barnstorming tour across the Mississippi. TR thought the prospects for victory trending up, writing to Lodge in September, "The wage-earners are drifting our way and the revolt among the farmers is shrinking rather than spreading. In... the extreme West of North Dakota the sentiment was for gold among the small ranchmen and they will give McKinley two to one majority there." Though conceding "the situation in the West generally has been one of great danger," he believed the progress "our way was very perceptible." The campaigning burnished not only McKinley's candidacy but also Roosevelt's growing reputation. People began to refer to him as "Teddy" (a wordplay he loathed), the press found him excellent copy—as when he recklessly compared the pacifist Bryan to "the leaders of the Terror" in Revolutionary France—and he began to circulate among the party's aging Civil War gentry, sharing a stage with Abraham Lincoln's son Robert in Chicago.[4]

Despite Roosevelt's optimism that "the tide" of western voters had begun to inch "our way," most of the West went for Bryan. McKinley did, however, capture majorities in both the Electoral College (271–176) and the popular vote (51.1 percent to 47.7 percent); his victory in North Dakota, moreover, suggested Theodore's effectiveness on the hustings. Republicans further maintained control of both the House and the Senate, thus giving the party a clean congressional sweep. With the incoming GOP administration replacing the outgoing Cleveland regime, a flock of appointment-wishing worthies, having campaigned for the winning side, now demanded their share—and this cluster included Roosevelt.

Above all, Theodore coveted the post of navy secretary, believing the country's security and prosperity hinged, as he had noted in his first book, on a strong and technologically advanced fleet. Lodge pushed on his behalf, visiting McKinley in the president-elect's hometown of Canton, Ohio, where, during a long discussion on several subjects, he brought up the cabinet position. On December 2 Lodge informed Roosevelt of what had transpired. McKinley had opened on an empty pleasantry—"He spoke of you with great regard for your character and your services and he would like to have you in Washington"—before raising a concern that anyone familiar with Roosevelt's reputation for impatience might have: "I hope he has no preconceived plans which he would wish to drive through the moment he got in." Lodge assured McKinley that he "need not give himself the slightest uneasiness on that score."[5]

Roosevelt responded to Lodge in a casually belligerent tone that, if anything, gave credence to McKinley's concerns. "I do hope he will take a strong stand both about Hawaii and Cuba," he wrote of the mounting pressure in the United States to annex the Hawaiian Islands and topple the wobbly Spanish colonial regime in Havana. "I do not think a war with Spain would be serious enough to cause much strain on the country."[6]

Before deciding on Roosevelt, however, McKinley had to consider the feelings of the powerful Platt. And this meant that Roosevelt, hated "like poison" by the Easy Boss, now had to play nice. Understanding Platt's concern over patronage at the growing Brooklyn Navy Yard, he wrote Lodge on December 9: "Of course I should not go into the Department to make war upon Platt, and so far as I had any influence, I would not allow the patronage to be used for any such purpose." A week later he met with the "exceedingly polite" Easy Boss, though failing to get the backing he so badly wanted. Platt, rather, had his own agenda. Eager to cap his career in the U.S. Senate, he was opposed in the looming GOP caucus by Joseph Choate, a popular reform Republican who had supported Roosevelt's initial run for the assembly in 1881. At the time a grateful TR had written to Choate, "I owe both my nomination and election more to you than to any other one man." Platt now wanted Theodore to show his hand. And this TR did by refusing to give speeches on Choate's behalf.[7] On January 14, 1897, the Easy Boss crushed Choate on the first ballot 142–7; five days later, Platt defeated the incumbent Democrat David B. Hill in the state assembly to take the seat.

Roosevelt, still serving as police commissioner, stewed through the winter, engaged in the campaign to oust Parker, while a host of allies lobbied on his behalf. These included the reliable Hay and Reed as well as a new entity, Maria Storer, a Cincinnati-stationed patron of fine arts and wife of former congressman Bellamy Storer. Making her own pilgrimage to Canton, she asked that the navy post might go to her young friend—but McKinley hesitated. A midwesterner largely lacking imperial aspirations, he had no taste for war, either overseas or in the capital. "I am afraid he is too pugnacious," the president-elect said to Storer of Roosevelt. "I want peace and I am told that your friend Theodore is always getting into rows with everybody." Storer's Queen City neighbor Judge William Howard Taft, a former solicitor general in Washington who had occasionally taken morning walks with Roosevelt when the latter served on the Civil Service Commission, also recommended his appointment. McKinley trod carefully: "The truth is, Will," he said, "Roosevelt is always in such a state of mind."[8]

At last, in early February, McKinley selected former Massachusetts congressman John D. Long. The choice infuriated Lodge, by now the master of Bay State politics, though apparently unable, like Platt, to control patronage in his own backyard. Moreover, Lodge's relations with the "ponderous and slow-moving" Long, a gradualist on the question of fleet expansion, were cool as he, Lodge, headed a bloc of big-navy Yankees. One of their number, Stephen M. Weld, a wealthy Greater Boston cotton broker whose company operated branches in India and Japan, had written a colleague in January, "Long has not been, and I do not think is now, in a mental and physical condition to fill this place.... He is not the sort of man who should represent New England. We need a man who would stand up and fight for his opinions, and who would be a staff for our President to lean upon, and who would give his administration vigor and back-bone."[9]

Long's appointment strengthened Lodge's hand to now demand Roosevelt for the navy's second slot. It was clear to McKinley that a suitable place at the table needed to be made for TR, a coming force among a younger faction in the party who wished to see the GOP continue to champion industrial development while also embracing the country's role as a rising imperial power. Importantly, Platt, convinced Theodore could do him no harm as Long's underling, and wishing him out of New York, gave his blessing to the new president, and McKinley made the nomination on April 6, 1897. "I am now Assistant Secretary of the Navy," Roosevelt wrote Spring Rice on the twenty-eighth. "Cabot Lodge plus... a few others got me in." Playing nice, he called Long "a perfect dear."[10]

Within two months Long no doubt realized the bleakly comedic misalliance he now presided over, a case of the senior-member small-navy cautionary and the junior-member big-navy belligerent. Preaching preparedness, and burning for a fleet of shiny new battleships, Roosevelt made his case in a ructious June 2 address at the Naval War College in Newport, Rhode Island. Eager to dispel concerns that enlarging the country's armed services meant unchecked militarism, he opened by emphasizing the nation's presumably peaceful nature—"In this country there is not the slightest danger of an overdevelopment of warlike spirit"—before commencing with a steady epigrammatic attack on passivity: "Preparation for war is the surest guarantee of peace"; "Peace, like freedom, is not a gift that tarries long in the hands of cowards"; "Peace is a goddess only when she comes with sword girt on thigh." He further condemned the new mass consumerism, the tempting fruit of industrialization that threatened to replace the martial with the material—"A rich nation which is slothful, timid, or unwieldy is an easy prey for any people which still retains those most valuable of all qualities, the soldierly virtues."[11]

Warming to the topic, Roosevelt engaged in rhetorical half-truths and shaky historical analogies, as when he insisted that "the men who to-day protest against a navy . . . are close kin to the men who, when the Southern States seceded, wished to let the Union be disrupted in peace rather than restored through the grim agony of armed conflict." He further grasped for the mantle of humanitarian when arguing that the "Armenian butcheries" perpetrated by the declining Ottoman Empire under the reign of Sultan Abdul Hamid II—between 100,000 and 300,000 killed from 1894 to 1897—were abetted by the "tame submission" of pacifists. Naturally he made several references to the War of 1812, his hobbyhorse, insisting that "then, as now," the nation's safety hinged on its determination to produce "a formidable fighting navy."[12]

This backward glance, however, gave way to more contemporary concerns. "The change in military conditions in modern times" brought about by technological advances, he argued, now made it impossible to maintain a safe existence behind the historic security of two blue oceans. "Our interests are as great in the Pacific as in the Atlantic," he declared, anticipating the coming American Century, in "Hawaii . . . as in the West Indies."[13] Protecting the snug American shore, he concluded, meant extending that seaboard to a satellite of distant islands, rich in commerce, safe in arms.

The responses in the press were mainly positive, offering some indication of public opinion. "Well done, nobly spoken!" sang the *Washington Post*, while the New York *Sun* called the speech "manly, patriotic, intelligent and convincing." The anti-imperialist *Harper's*, by contrast, thought it rather "bellicose," and Long quietly objected—"He didn't like the address I made to the War College at Newport the other day," Roosevelt told a correspondent.[14] But the naysayers were neutralized. In less than a year, the United States would invade Cuba as part of a largely seaborne war with Spain. At that point the Newport sermon seemed oracular, evidence of its author's uncanny ability to read the times, shape the debate, and occupy the critical seat of action. Hardly alone, he belonged to a circle of men eager to push American power outward, to win the country's place in a world seemingly supine before Anglo-Saxon energies, economies, and navies.

22

By Jingo

Movement toward an American empire followed an unprecedented expansion of population and power. Between 1860 and 1900 the number of U.S. citizens more than doubled to 76 million, an average increase of some 24 percent each ten-year census, a figure never since replicated. By 1900 the country, its vintage seaboard ancestry still with living memories of ancient revolutionaries in the family, lagged demographically behind only the Qing, British, and Russian Empires. On the financial front, eastern capital endorsed an astonishing industrial boom. What Google, Apple, and Amazon have meant to our own century's tech economy, the Union Pacific Railroad, Standard Oil, and AT&T brought to the nineteenth-century operations of transportation, energy, and communications. These enterprises, along with budding monopolies in finance (J.P. Morgan & Co.) and infrastructure (Carnegie Steel), generated tremendous, if glaringly stratified, wealth that altered evermore America's relations with itself and the world.

Now back in Washington, Roosevelt partnered with Lodge to promote a shared big-navy vision. They were informally joined in this project by two historians, Captain Alfred Thayer Mahan and Brooks Adams (Henry's brother), both of whom offered intellectual heft in the crusade to dragoon Congress into building battleships. All but Mahan were agents of old America and old money. Perhaps this is why they collectively touted expansion principally for purposes of prestige and security rather than economic advantage. "Our people are neither cravens nor weaklings," Roosevelt maintained, "and we face the future high of heart and confident of soul eager to do the great work of a great world power."[1]

For a few brief years this group constituted a distinct social circle, dining together, discussing books, reading the congressional tea leaves, and honing a shared geopolitical vision. Their bond occasionally led to more intimate connections. In 1889 the bachelor Brooks, forty-one and heeding his dying mother's wish that he marry, had wed Evelyn Davis, sister of Lodge's wife, Nannie.

As a clique, these jingoes (a term first bandied about British pubs a generation earlier when saluting an aggressive foreign policy) were deeply disappointed in the condition of U.S. diplomacy. In 1893 a group of American-born sugar planters and missionaries had led a coup against Queen Lili'uokalani's Hawaiian kingdom. The opinion of one State Department official, who floridly insisted that "the Hawaiian pear is now fully ripe and this is the golden hour for the United States to pluck it," was shared by many. But not the one whose opinion mattered most, then-president Grover Cleveland. Condemning the insurrection as illegal, he demanded the queen's restoration and withdrew a treaty from the Senate calling for Hawaii's seizure. "I . . . regard the proposed annexation of these islands as not only opposed to our national policy," he asserted, "but as a perversion of our national mission."[2]

In May 1897, having just occupied his naval office, Roosevelt wrote a blistering note to Mahan, condemning the former president's action as "a colossal crime." He further ticked off a list of itemized ambitions he dearly wished his nation to undertake. These included gobbling up Hawaii ("If I had my way we would annex those islands yesterday"), bringing Cuba into the American sphere ("Until we definitely turn Spain out . . . we will always be menaced by trouble there"), and identifying prospects for future pocketing ("We should acquire the Danish Islands"). If the almighty British Empire had a problem with any of these plans, he continued, it would be only too easy to make it see reason: "I do not fear England; Canada, is a hostage for her good behavior." He indulged in added speculation of the "we should build" kind—as in, "we should build the Nicaraguan canal" and "we should build a dozen new battleships"—before catching his breath and reminding Mahan, "This letter must be strictly private. I speak to you with the greatest freedom."[3] What is remarkable about this note is less its author's habitual bumptiousness than the fact that much of what it called for rather quickly came to pass.

His correspondent, Captain Mahan, had written one of the more important books of the period, *The Influence of Sea Power upon History: 1660–1783*, a study of fleet warfare published in 1890. Tall, trim, and balding with a rakish goatee, Mahan had grown up an army brat, his father teaching military strategy at West Point. After attending a private school in Maryland and spending two years at Columbia College, he graduated from the Naval Academy in 1859. Unlike Roosevelt's dashing uncle Irvine, Mahan saw little action during the Civil War, his participation in the successful November 1861 amphibious assault at Port Royal, South Carolina, a notable exception. Described as "bookish," he served for thirty-four years in the navy and preferred outdated square-rigged sailing vessels—"In a stiff breeze . . . there is a wild sort of delight"—to modern, smoky steamships; he had little love for active sea duty and preferred lecturing at the Naval War College.[4]

Big ideas were in vogue during the century's second half. Darwinism dominated scientific thought, Marxism emphasized class struggle as the motor of history, and Freudianism was emerging in the nascent field of psychoanalysis. All were in some sense informed by the liberal, industrial, democratic age building since the 1760s in Manchester factories and Revolutionary Parisian parlors. Like most popular theories (*Influence of Sea Power* was quickly translated into several languages), Mahan's contained a simple maxim: a nation could only attain power by maintaining a large navy. The progress of England, a small island entity until its imperial turn, runs as a leitmotif throughout the text. Attentive to intellectual trends, Mahan further embedded in the study an evolutionary twist with rising (Britain—think victory at Trafalgar) and declining (Spain—think doomed armada) kingdoms engaged in the great struggle "to secure to one's own people a disproportionate share of . . . growth and prosperity."[5] Though on the surface a densely constructed analysis of European naval combat in the dawning era of international wars, Mahan's work might just as easily be approached as a prologue to a fresh age of American aspirations.

What did the European experience have to teach the United States? And how had recent technological innovations impacted the contest for global supremacy? In the age of steam, far-flung colonies were required to provide the precious fueling stations so essential to modern navies. "The necessity of renewing coal," Mahan wrote, "makes the cruiser of the present day even more dependent than of old on his port."[6] This meant that Americans would have to venture to distant islands and archipelagoes in search of raw materials and harbors from which to extend their markets and military presence. Though a practical argument, it proposed a radical reconfiguration of the nation's identity. For generations Americans had celebrated their republican genesis in a great revolutionary struggle against the mighty John Bull. Could the country maintain its promise as a new-world beacon for the global oppressed—"the last best hope of earth," Lincoln had indelibly put it—if it now proposed to drop anchor and colonize other peoples?

These weighty issues seemed to elude Roosevelt, a master of prettifying realpolitik in any number of "duty" and "destiny" dialects. Penning a fawning five-page review of Mahan's tome in the *Atlantic Monthly*, he peddled superlatives, calling *Influence of Sea Power* "the best and most important, and also by far the most interesting, book on naval history." Artless, excited, and eager to spread the word, Roosevelt amply editorialized: "Our greatest need is the need of a fighting-fleet"; "Passive defense . . . is always a most dangerous expedient"; "We need a large navy."[7] The romantic age of naval improvisation had come to an end; investment, efficiency, and long-range strategy, his review stressed, were now the means by which great nations ruled the waves.

Much impressed, Roosevelt wrote to Mahan after reading the book over two engrossed days ("busy as I am"). He thought it an excellent advertisement for the indispensability of a modern navy and welcomed its appearance in the coming struggle with pinchpenny senators and economy-minded representatives. "I wish the . . . book," he told the good captain, "could be placed where it could be read by the navy's foes, especially in congress."[8] Proper forts were needed, he knew, along with heavy coastal guns, bases of supply, and superior training to maintain a fleet commensurate with the country's growing ambitions.

Roosevelt found a second court theorist in Brooks Adams, whose 1895 study *The Law of Civilization and Decay* offered an outline of Western history and economic development that aligned with concerns among conservatives that the emerging industrial order—capitalism, mass immigration, popular democracy—threatened to upend traditional America. One might suggest that Adams detailed, unwittingly or not, the "decay" of his famous family; having once given the nation presidents, it now lingered on the rough edges of a robber baron republic. Like Roosevelt, Brooks despised the emerging financial regime, finding it "without aspiration or imagination," and championed instead the old warrior class, a military caste that had produced in recent centuries "the ideal statesman," from Sir Thomas Cromwell to Frederick the Great to William III to George Washington.[9] The passing of power from the martial to the moneyed constituted a tragedy in the eyes of an entire tier of grieving Brahmins and Knickerbockers, country house legatees of a dying way of life.

In certain passages, Brooks melded a fashionable evolutionism with an unseemly anti-Semitism, as when arguing that in a competitive environment, "nature begins to sift the economic minds themselves, culling a favoured aristocracy of the craftiest and the subtlest types; choosing, for example, the Armenian in Byzantium, the Marwari in India, and the Jew in London."[10] Who might challenge this predatory money-class? And how were Americans to maintain their fighting trim? It is with these questions that Adams's and Mahan's claims could be said to converge; the former diagnosed the problem of modernity and the latter offered an emancipatory antidote—machine-age manifest destiny through a big navy, colonies, and the occasional war to promote tone.

When Roosevelt returned to Washington in the spring of 1897, he often luncheoned with Brooks. Both were Porcellians (one wonders if they wore the club's green pig-studded necktie advertising affiliation), rode about the capital together on thoroughbred horses, and engaged in involved weltpolitik discussions of the armchair-general kind. Along with Lodge they formed a distinct club of theorist, soldier, and lawmaker.[11] In a remarkable communication about this time, Adams counseled Roosevelt to grasp for power and tame the capitalists who sapped the country of its old virtues:

> The whole world, as I look at the future and the present, seems to me to be rotting. The one hope for us, the one chance to escape from our slavery even for a year, is war, war which shall bring down the British empire. . . . I have watched your career with deep interest. . . . You are an adventurer and you have but one thing to sell—your sword. You can . . . fight when and where you are sent, just as every soldier must in a commercial age, or you can lie and rot. Capital will not employ you if you have a conscience, a heart, patriotism, honesty, or self-respect. . . . Wall Street is a hard master. It only wants men who it can buy and own.[12]

Roosevelt, to be sure, never accepted Adams's views uncritically. He knew him to be a bundle of nerves, a temperamental exaggeration ever portending some distant and reckoning doom. After Brooks half-seriously called himself "a free silver man" in the Populist fight against the gold bugs, Roosevelt complained to Lodge that Adams's "theories are beautiful, but in practice they mean a simple dishonesty." In a slightly lengthier diagnosis, he wrote Spring Rice, "The trouble is largely that his mind is a little unhinged. All his thoughts show extraordinary intellectual and literary dishonesty; but I don't think it is due to moral shortcomings. I think it really is the fact that he isn't quite straight in his head."[13]

At heart an intellectual magpie, Roosevelt took what he needed from both Adams and Mahan, building a case for a big navy, embracing the evolutionary contest for supremacy, and pining to lift the soldier above the stockbroker. Such stray musings, the fodder of small-circulation reviews and after-dinner chat, perhaps seemed untethered from the main lines of approved national policy. But a decades-long swell in American power gave increasing respect to such assessments. Men like Roosevelt articulated the concerns of a small class of adventurers in the late 1890s, a cadre eager to assemble the strength of the industrial state for purposes of national greatness. They had their suspicions and premonitions neatly arranged in the scientific apparatus of historical "laws," prophets at pains to move their country forward, toward the glories of war.

23

And the War Came

Resettling in Washington, Roosevelt became a fixture at the Metropolitan Club, a private H Street outfit founded in 1863 whose stated interest in furthering "literary, mutual improvement, and social purposes" scarcely obscured a more concrete desire by power to luncheon with power. At any given meal the navy's new assistant secretary might count himself among a cluster of cabinet officers, media moguls, and the occasional Vanderbilt or du Pont; in the succeeding century Franklin Roosevelt and John F. Kennedy graced its elegantly marbled spaces, as did slightly lower-placed luminaries including Robert McNamara and Henry Kissinger. The talk among members that spring of 1897 drifted invariably to the idea of American empire. Uneasy reports of newly industrialized Japan's interest in the Pacific provoked concern, as when Theodore, only four days on the job, wrote McKinley, bypassing Long completely, that the torpedo-laden Japanese cruiser *Naniwa Kan* and the USS *Philadelphia* ("not quite so swift and . . . she has no torpedoes") were both in Oahu. "The Japanese Navy," he reminded the president, "is an efficient fighting navy."[1]

That late summer, Long and his family spent three weeks at their Buckfield, Maine, retreat. "We have never enjoyed the farm so much," the secretary wrote at the time. "The clear, inspiring air, the cool days, the beautiful hills and landscape, the absolute rest and retirement." Back in Washington, Acting Secretary Roosevelt immediately sprang into action, forming committees, purchasing naval supplies, and monitoring the progress of various programs. Much of this blur appeared nebulous and without prescription other than what Roosevelt thought he might be haphazardly accomplishing, or getting away with, in a few frenzied weeks. A supportive New York *Sun*, however, discerned a definite outline, contending that the decks "were cleared for action" and "in the absence of... Long" Roosevelt "has the whole Navy bordering on a war footing."[2] When Long returned from vacation Theodore fairly pounced on his boss, insisting on the need for no fewer than a half dozen battleships as part of a broader fleet modernization.

This impulse for imperial adventure quickly focused on an old object: America's lingering quest for Cuba. In the 1820s Thomas Jefferson had written James Monroe of having "looked upon [it] as the most interesting addition which could ever be made to our system of States," while antebellum presidents James Polk and Franklin Pierce tried without success to purchase the island from Spain.[3] Since then a series of liberation movements in Cuba—the Ten Years' War (1868–1878), the Little War (1879–1880), and the War of Independence (1895–1898)—had enticed a growing number of jingoes to demand that their government fulfill its evident destiny and vanquish at last the continent's last vestiges of old-world colonialism.

The year 1898 opened with an antigovernment riot in Havana, promising a prolonged clash between colonized and colonizer that threatened U.S.-owned sugar and mining interests on the island. The flamboyant yellow journalism in America, typified by William Randolph Hearst's *New York Journal* and Joseph Pulitzer's *New York World*, turned the struggle into a moral drama of the freedom-versus-tyranny kind. This trope played well and penetrated deep into the country. The *Dubuque Times*, for one, demanded the prompt "annihilation of the Spanish dogs."[4] The upheaval in Havana and the U.S. consul general's fears for the lives of Americans there prompted McKinley, facing criticism from Democrats and the press, to send a warship to Cuba, a not unusual occurrence between the two neighbors. This required Spain's permission, which was given by Madrid as welcome evidence that the two nations remained at peace with their respective ports open. Thus, on January 25 the armor-plated battleship USS *Maine*, commissioned in 1895 and possessed of four 10-inch Mark II guns that could fire a 500-pound shell to a range of 20,000 yards, dropped anchor in Havana Harbor.

Undeceived by "ports open" courtesies, Roosevelt imagined war to be imminent and desperately wanted to be in on the action. Long thought him theatrical, self-absorbed, and a superfluous gasbag:

Mr. Roosevelt came in, shut the door, and began his usual emphatic and dead-in-earnest manner. After referring sensibly to two or three matters of business, he told me that, in case of war with Spain, he intends to abandon everything and go to the front. He bores me with plans of naval and military movement, and the necessity of having some scheme of attack arranged for instant execution in case of an emergency. By tomorrow morning, he will have got half a dozen heads of bureaus together and have spoiled twenty pages of good writing paper, and lain awake half the night.[5]

That no front yet existed hardly gave the impatient assistant secretary pause. Chock-full of Metropolitan Club expansionist chatter, sensitive to the deep historical "laws" that put Spain in the wrong, and perhaps above all equipped with an adventurer's knowing understanding of the moment's prevailing possibilities, he seemed certain of war's nigh arrival.

At 9:40 p.m. on February 15, the *Maine*, most of its crew sleeping or resting, exploded and sank—there were a shocking 260 fatalities from a crew of 355. Opinion split on the cause of the blast, a critical consideration since only Spanish perfidy could lead to war. "My own judgment," Long wrote in a diary the day after the detonation, "is . . . that it was the result of an accident, such as every ship of war, with the tremendously high and powerful explosives which we now have on board, is liable to suffer." Lieutenant Philip Alger, a professor of mathematics at the Naval Academy and an expert on ordnance, agreed, circulating a bulletin a few days later that suggested a sudden fire in the ship's coal bunkers likely caused the disaster. Hot for action, Roosevelt chafed at such sobriety. "Don't you think it inadvisable for Prof. Alger to express opinions in this way?" he wrote Captain Charles O'Neil, chief of the Bureau of Ordnance. "Mr. Alger . . . tak[ing] the Spanish side . . . cannot possibly know anything about the accident," he continued, before grasping at straws: "All the best men in the department agree that, whether probable or not, it certainly is *possible* that the ship was blown up by a mine which might, or might not, have been towed under her."[6]

Public opinion initially leaned Long and O'Neil's way, toward a suspicion that the explosion constituted an unfortunate accident. It made little sense that Spain, fully aware of its precarious position, would bait the

United States by permitting the ship to dock in Havana only to blow it up. The consensus for some decades now is that a spontaneous fire likely ignited the ammunition stock. But a mess of tensions—from the yellow press to the jingoes to the long-held desire of establishing a protectorate over Cuba—pushed in the direction of blaming Spain. Three days after the *Maine* went down, an official U.S. Naval Court of Inquiry opened an investigation. Roosevelt had little doubt what had happened in the harbor. The ship, he wrote to one correspondent, "was sunk by an act of dirty treachery." He feared, however, that government officials lacking the fighting spirit might spoil the moment and "officially it will go down as an accident."[7]

Roosevelt no doubt had Long in mind among those likely to take a pacific line. Complaining of insomnia and lethargy, the older man shuffled around the Navy Department in the days following the blast, perhaps feeling the mounting pressure of the moment. Early on the afternoon of February 25 he exited his office for the rest of the day, leaving Roosevelt in charge. The extent to which the latter cherished his occasional acting secretary role might be gleaned from an embarrassingly transparent note he had written a vacationing Long the previous summer: "I hope you are having a very pleasant time, and if things go on as they are now there isn't the slightest earthly reason for you to come back for six weeks more."[8] Now, Roosevelt didn't need six weeks. He quickly fired off a fateful cablegram to Admiral George Dewey, commander of the Asiatic Squadron and currently inspecting the U.S. fleet in Hong Kong. An old naval hand, Dewey, with close-cropped white hair and impeccably pressed dress, had served in Admiral David Farragut's famous flotilla that captured New Orleans from the Confederates in the spring of 1862. He received the following:

> ORDER THE SQUADRON, EXCEPT THE *MONOCACY*, TO HONG KONG. KEEP FULL OF COAL. IN THE EVENT OF DECLARATION OF WAR WITH SPAIN, YOUR DUTY WILL BE TO SEE THAT THE SPANISH SQUADRON DOES NOT LEAVE THE ASIATIC COAST, AND THEN OFFENSIVE OPERATIONS IN PHILIPPINE ISLANDS. KEEP *OLYMPIA* UNTIL FURTHER ORDERS.[9]

Before the day's end, Roosevelt further put U.S. squadron commanders about the globe on alert and scared up tremendous reserves of ammunition.

Long returned the next day, annoyed at his second's initiative. "I find that Roosevelt, in his precipitate way, has come very near causing more of an explosion than happened to the Maine," he wrote in a journal. "He has gone at things like a bull in a china shop."[10]

One can make too much of Roosevelt's cable, imputing a dashing decision fashioned by a young comer counter to the inertia of a dozy bureaucracy. The navy had first planned for a possible attack on the Philippines in 1895 as tensions in Cuba increased; the following year the Office of Naval Intelligence recommended that, in the event of war, Manila be besieged, and in 1897 more war gaming concluded that the United States should support rebels on the islands in order to give American policymakers "a controlling voice" in any postcolonial future.[11] So rooted and familiar was this strategy that Long, despite denouncing Roosevelt's bull-like antics, did not rescind his directives. When war did come in April, these plans—to which Roosevelt contributed but did not initiate—were put into play, and on the early morning of May 1, with the famous order to the USS *Olympia*'s captain, "You may fire when ready, Gridley," Dewey's technologically superior Asiatic Squadron proceeded to destroy the seven-ship Spanish Pacific Squadron.

Before that happened, the court of inquiry had reported to McKinley on March 20 its ruling that the *Maine* was destroyed by a submarine mine. A little more than a week later this became public news, and though the court accused no nation of being responsible for the alleged device, public opinion—"Remember the Maine! To Hell with Spain!"—moved decisively toward war.

Despite such flag waving, Roosevelt worried that amity might yet prevail. "What the Administration will ultimately do I do'n't know," he complained to Bamie. "McKinley is bent on peace, I fear."[12] Putting in long hours at the Navy Department, he had little time that long winter for his growing family and ill wife. His sixth and final child, Quentin, was born in November 1897 and Edith, the following month, came down with influenza. Watched over by a trained nurse, her condition worsened in January with a near-constant fever; the following month she noticed "a swelling in her abdomen." A specialist from Johns Hopkins, Sir William Osler, was brought in and declared the patient "crucially ill"—he recommended surgery to deal with an abscess in the psoas muscle. Roosevelt, spouting off about "a lot of perfectly incompetent doctors," demurred until continued pain, fever, and a second medical opinion confirming the original diagnosis forced his hand in early March, about the time Dewey's fleet concentrated in Hong Kong. "Of course it was a severe operation," he wrote Bamie on the seventh, "and her convalescence may be a matter of months"; two weeks later he informed Brooks Adams, "She is crawling back to life." With an ailing spouse and a nation about to go to war, Roosevelt had no reservations regarding where his deepest loyalties lay. "I would have turned from my wife's deathbed," he later told an aide, "to have answered that call."[13]

On April 23, three days after signing a joint congressional resolution demanding Spain's withdrawal from Cuba and authorizing the use of military force to that effect, McKinley called for 125,000 volunteers to bolster the much smaller 30,000-soldier regular army. This order, possibly a nod to the country's storied minutemen tradition (and perhaps an amalgam of cost-consciousness, isolationism, and concern that "a standing force," as Madison had put it in *The Federalist Papers*, constituted a necessary if "dangerous" element), provided for the organization of three volunteer cavalry regiments, "to be composed exclusively of frontiersmen possessing special qualifications as horsemen and marksmen." Moving quickly, Roosevelt resigned his naval position on May 6, five days after Dewey's victory at Manila Bay.[14]

From a distant Constantinople, the drifting Henry Adams, a droll gossip for all his proper Brahmin training, thought Theodore's behavior inexplicable. "Is his wife dead?" he wrote to a correspondent. "Has he quarreled with everybody? Is he quite mad?" Long displayed a similar astonishment, presuming his eager assistant, guaranteed a field command through connections, barmy: "He has lost his head to this unutterable folly of deserting the post where he is of most service and running off to ride a horse and, probably, brush mosquitoes from his neck on the Florida sands. His heart is right, and he means well, but it is one of those cases of ... vain-glory." Pausing for a moment, however, Long acknowledged that given the right set of unexpected circumstances, the remarkably charmed Roosevelt might just luck his way into a legend: "And yet, how absurd all this will sound if, by some turn of fortune, he should accomplish some great thing and strike a very high mark."[15]

Secretary of War Russell Alger (no relation to Philip Alger) offered Roosevelt command of the 1st U.S. Volunteer Cavalry. Pleading inexperience, Roosevelt wisely suggested instead his Washington friend Colonel Leonard Wood, a doctor (McKinley's physician), soldier, and military administrator who had earned the Medal of Honor during the campaign to capture Geronimo, a prominent Bedonkohe Apache leader, in the last years of the Indian Wars. When Wood agreed, Theodore happily accepted a lieutenant colonel commission.

Long familiar with Roosevelt's capacity for commanding the stage, the *New York Press* was fooled not a bit by gradations in rank; Colonel Wood, it contended, "is lost sight of entirely in the effulgence of Teethadore."[16] Of practical necessity, Roosevelt brought eleven extra pairs of eyeglasses sewn into his wide-brimmed—with one side fashionably pinned up—slouch hats. Eager to shine for his star turn, he ordered a smart khaki-colored officer's uniform from Brooks Brothers with bright-yellow trim on the cuffs and collar; his low-heeled boots were handmade. As at Cambridge and Albany, he aimed to make an entrance.

24

Rough Rider

On May 15, 1898, Roosevelt arrived in San Antonio, Texas, to train his sun-bronzed soldiers. Hailing from the Southwest, these men were presumed by the War Department to be sufficiently seasoned to cope with a humid Cuban summer. Though officially designated the 1st United States Volunteer Cavalry, it quickly acquired a new nom de guerre, the euphonic "Rough Riders." "At first we fought against the use of the term," Roosevelt later wrote, "but to no purpose. . . . [and] we adopted the term ourselves." Wanting badly to be in the fight, he left nothing to chance, firing off a communication to McKinley on the twenty-fifth following only a few days of rudimentary exercise and drill: "We are ready now to leave at any moment, and we earnestly hope we will be put into Cuba with the very first troops; the sooner the better; at any rate, we do want to see active service against the enemy." He described his force to Lodge as a "typical American regiment. . . . Three fourths of our men have at one time or another been cowboys or else are small stockmen; certainly two thirds have fathers who fought on one side or the other in the civil war."[1]

Despite its western inflection, the thousand-strong division included several men from the East, "almost all graduates of Harvard, Yale, Princeton, etc.," Theodore took note. Added to this human stew were Native Americans and Hispanics alongside Irish, Italians, and Jews. Collectively the force embodied the era's melting-pot enthusiasm for a mingled American type—with the Ivy apex presumably providing poise. In line with the day's customary racial codes, blacks and Asian volunteers were not accepted into the regiment. Apparently the only

African American to accompany it to Cuba was, so Roosevelt noted in a memoir, "my colored body-servant, Marshall, the most faithful and loyal of men."[2]

In late May the Rough Riders entrained for Tampa, then a sleepy town of 5,500. Enjoying the privileges of a gentleman's war, Roosevelt met Edith in the comfortable Tampa Bay Hotel for three nights. Describing for his children the more primitive digs occupied by his men, he wrote, "We were very tired and very dirty when we arrived. . . . Our camp is on a great flat, on sandy soil without a tree, though round about are pines and palmettos."[3] These connections with home raise the question of Roosevelt's sense of responsibility. As noted, a host of colleagues and acquaintances were dumbfounded by his decision to make for Cuba. This enveloping self-centeredness—what might a widowed Edith do with five children and a stepdaughter, the eldest only fourteen?—played to type.

To be fair, however, Roosevelt was by no means the only aspiring politician eager to burnish his reputation in war. The 1896 Democratic presidential candidate, Williams Jennings Bryan, an anti-imperialist anxious to separate Spain from its Havana mandate, also showed up in the blistering Florida sun, having recruited a two-thousand-man regiment for the Nebraska National Guard. Planted in Jacksonville's Camp Cuba Libre, it sat and sat. Lacking Roosevelt's impeccable connections, Colonel Bryan and his pink-faced Cornhuskers never got to Cuba.

The situation in Tampa offered evidence of the country's relative unpreparedness to send an army overseas. Some thirty thousand troops milled about the inevitable scrub and sand pine a good ten miles from the pier with only a single rail track available to put this mass of tan-clad humanity on boats. "No words could describe to you the confusion and lack of system and the general mismanagement of affairs here," Roosevelt complained to Lodge. Valuing this direct line to Washington, he used it to the full—"Do, old man, try to see that the expedition is no longer deferred."[4]

In fact, it was just about to launch, though Theodore learned on June 6 that Major General William Shafter, old, obese, and suffering from gout, had decided that due to transport limitations only 560 Rough Riders were to make the voyage; they would go without their horses, though the officers might keep theirs. "We would rather crawl on all fours," a barely bothered Roosevelt wrote Bamie, "than not go." At midmonth, the American flotilla—16,000 men—took off, its (now inappropriately named) Rough Riders quotient camping on the decks of the USS *Yucatán*, one of forty-eight ships steaming in three complementing columns, the black-hulled transports highlighting the gray-framed warships. In the evenings—the slow-moving journey took six days—bands played a miscellany of songs, from the patriotic ("The Star-Spangled Banner") to the sentimental ("The Girl I Left Behind Me"). Catching sight of the "high barren-looking" Cuban mountains, Roosevelt thought of Montana, and one has the impression that nothing in this supposedly alien environment took him particularly by surprise, so long had he imagined himself intended for some shade of guns-and-horses glory. "It is a great historical expedition," he wrote with reverence to Corinne, "and I thrill to feel that I am part of it."[5]

The *Yucatán* docked at Daiquirí (for which the sweet rum-based cocktail is supposedly named), a dozen miles east of Santiago. Founded by Spanish conquistadors in 1515 and the jumping-off point of Hernán Cortés's Aztec Empire–conquering expedition to Mexico, Santiago now contained a dilapidated ironworks amid a host of shelters, shacks, and lean-tos. The landing, conducted to the strains of "There'll Be a Hot Time in the Old Town Tonight," proved easy, as no shots, other than jittery American salvos, were fired; among the few casualties was one of Roosevelt's two horses, Rain-in-the-Face, drowned in a botched disembarkment effort. He would ride into battle, rather, on top of Little Texas, a recently purchased four-year-old chestnut gelding.[6] The U.S. force's orders were to move inland and take Santiago, its environs a thick green screen of high hills filled with Spanish defenses. The most daunting of these obstacles, a heavily fortified ridge just outside the city known as San Juan Heights, threatened to impede the American advance until either dysentery or diplomacy could, so the Spanish military on the island hoped, bring the invasion to an end.

On the twenty-fourth Roosevelt and his men got their first taste of combat at the Battle of Las Guásimas, a rearguard effort by Spanish forces to slow Major General "Fighting Joe" Wheeler's advancing columns. A small-framed Georgia-born commander with a West Point education, Wheeler had fought in the Confederate cavalry at Chickamauga before giving ground to Sherman's scorched-earth March to the Sea. Now determined to lay siege to Santiago, he ordered a force, including the 1st Volunteer and 1st and 10th Regular Cavalries—the latter consisting of black horsemen known as buffalo soldiers—to assault the enemy's position at Las Guásimas. The Americans had about 1,760 men facing 1,500, though they would be entering difficult terrain filled with Spanish snipers using smokeless powder to avoid detection. Following the two-hour fight, both sides claimed a qualified victory. The Spanish inflicted more casualties (27 killed/52 wounded) than they took (7 killed/14 wounded) and momentarily halted the American advance. Offering a slightly different version, the *New York Times*, under the page-one heading

SERIOUS BATTLE NEAR SANTIAGO
ROOSEVELT'S ROUGH RIDERS IN
THE FIRST ENGAGEMENT

reported that "the Spaniards opened fire from the thick brush and had every advantage of numbers and position; but [US] troops drove them back from the start, stormed the block-house around which they made the final stand, and sent them scattering over the mountains."[7]

Involved in the thick of the fighting, Roosevelt reported to Corinne the following day, "One man was killed as he stood beside a tree with me. Another bullet went through a tree behind which I stood and filled my eyes with bark.... The fire was very hot at one or two points where the men around me went down like ninepins." A silk-stocking warrior, he included in the same note a request for certain essential toiletries and comforts. "My bag has never turned up, like most of our baggage, and it is very doubtful if it ever does turn up, and I have nothing with me," he complained, "no soap, toothbrush, razor, brandy, medicine chest, socks or underclothes." Might Corinne appeal to her husband ("ask Douglas") to send the articles by express to Tampa? "I shan't be very comfortable," he grumbled, "until I get them."[8]

From Las Guásimas, the 1st Volunteer Cavalry assumed over the next six days a support role behind regiments of regular army troops. Then, on the seventh day, July 1, "the sky cloudless, the air soft and balmy," reported one officer, they reached San Juan Heights. Early in the morning the Americans began an artillery barrage, which invited the Spanish to reply in kind—one of its shells exploded near Roosevelt; a fragment of shrapnel danced across his wrist "but did not," so he reported, "even break the skin."[9] When the cannonading ceased the Rough Riders were deployed, behind a regular army brigade, about a half mile from San

Juan Hill to await further orders. There they incurred steady fire from German-made Mauser rifles, taking imperfect shelter behind whatever flora and natural embankments they could find. By noon, a little more than three hours into the fight, Roosevelt could see American forces slowly making their way up San Juan Hill.

With orders to support the regular cavalry, Roosevelt did something a little different. "I had come to the conclusion that it was silly to stay in the valley firing at the hills, because that was really where we were most exposed," he later wrote. Confronting a regular army officer, he asked why the man's force did not advance—and learned it had no orders to do so. Roosevelt volunteered to give the command, but "there was naturally," he dryly noted, "a little reluctance." Instead, he moved his own "grinning men" forward. On this day he seemed at perfect ease. "I had not enjoyed the Guásimas fight at all," he observed, "because I had been so uncertain as to what I ought to do. But the San Juan fight was entirely different.... We could see [the Spanish] and I knew exactly how to proceed." Riding up and down his massing line, barking out orders, he seemed to have willed himself and these circumstances to a moment of inevitable crisis and release: "I waved my hat, and we went up the hill with a rush."[10]

Under heavy fire, Roosevelt's force joined the 3rd and 10th Cavalry regiments—the latter of whose officers included John "Black Jack" Pershing—in an assault on Kettle Hill, part of the broader battle for the San Juan Heights. "Some of our troops," Pershing later observed, "had pushed forward to aid the Rough Riders in the capture of this position, where white troops and black, Regulars and Volunteers, fought shoulder-to-shoulder." About forty yards from the top, Roosevelt, coming upon a wire fence, jumped off Little Texas and ran up the grassy rise with other soldiers toward the enemy's trenches. Near the summit he fired at two Spaniards, killing the second, who "doubled up," so he later reported, "like a Jackrabbit." When accused by critics two years later of shooting a Spanish soldier in the back, he told a colleague, "I [aimed at] the left breast, as he brought down his rifle, still smoking, he having fired at me." In all, 90 of the 450 Rough Riders who saw action that day were either killed or wounded. Roosevelt, relatively untouched, gloried in the engagement, perhaps surprised that his otherworldly luck had held once again. "I commanded the regiment, and led it victoriously in a hard fought battle," he wrote Lodge on July 10, not mentioning other

U.S. forces involved in the contest. "I never expected to come through! I am as strong as a bull moose."[11]

If a bit peremptory in monopolizing victory (note the three "I's" in the three sentences just quoted), Colonel Roosevelt—having quickly received promotion—did show an impressive coolness during the Heights campaign. His force contributed to the Spanish retreat from Kettle Hill, and then quickly supported the regular troops assaulting San Juan Hill. Flush with victory, he called the charge "the great day of my life."[12]

Two weeks of general unpleasantry followed as the siege of Santiago left the Americans dealing with dysentery, malaria, and Spanish artillery. In correspondence with Lodge, Roosevelt lingered over several subjects during this period, from his desire to be awarded the Congressional Medal of Honor ("naturally I should like to have it"), to his insistence on a dictated peace ("It will be a great misfortune to accept less than unconditional surrender"), to his complaint about a certain senior officer ("Gen. Shafter is tacking and veering"). And then the situation suddenly changed. The Spanish surrendered Santiago on the seventeenth and, amid a yellow fever scare, Roosevelt's Rough Riders, among several other regiments, sailed out of the city's harbor on August 8 after fewer than fifty days in Cuba. Hostilities ended on the twelfth and the combatants met in Paris that December to sign a peace treaty. John Hay, serving in London as ambassador to the Court of St. James's, captured the high-spirited mood of the past few months when writing to Theodore, "It has been a splendid little war." A clearly calculating Lodge could see his friend's horizons widen considerably. "You have won for yourself a high place already as one of the popular heroes of the war," he exclaimed, perhaps wondering if the charge up Kettle Hill might, like the pivotal battles of Trenton (Washington), New Orleans (Jackson), and Vicksburg (Grant), make the boy colonel—still under forty, but old enough to be president—a reckoning force in the nation's political future.[13]

Leaving nothing to chance, Roosevelt wanted his war impressions on record, and within a few months Charles Scribner's Sons published *The Rough Riders*, a brash, self-serving adventure story colorfully plotted and briskly paced. Reminiscent of his childhood European traveling diary, the Colonel reached occasionally for the elegiac: "We knew not whither we were bound, nor what we were to do; but we believed that the nearing future held for us many chances of death and hardship." Though generous to his men and many of his fellow officers, to whom the work is dedicated, the study invariably put its author at the seat of a far larger story—the emergence of an overseas American empire. The humorist Finley Peter Dunne, creator of the nationally syndicated "Mr. Dooley" sketches featuring the everyman proprietor of a South Side Chicago Irish pub, "quoted" in cartoonish thick immigrant accent certain star-turn passages from the book, including the epic charge: "I sint th' ar-my home an'attackted San Juan hill. Ar-rmed on'y with a small thirty-two which I used in th' West to shoot th' fleet prairie-dog.... They has been some discussion as to who was th' first man to r-reach th/ summit iv San Juan hill. . . . I will say, f'r th' binifit iv posterity, that I was th' on'y man I see. An' I had a tilliscope." A deadpan Dooley concluded with some friendly advice: "If I was him I'd call th' book Alone in Cubia." To his credit, a game Roosevelt wrote Dunne, "I regret to state that my family and intimate friends are delighted with your review," and invited the writer to visit Oyster Bay on his next trip east.[14]

With hindsight we know that the struggle with Spain casually established a pattern for wars of choice in the American Century—perhaps an inadvertent addendum to Roosevelt's notion that each generation needed to rebel, as he once wrote, from "a life of that peace which springs merely from lack either of desire or of power to strive after great things." *The Rough Riders*, a great popular success, played to this theme, touting the blue-suited troops' self-reliance, the "high resolve and fiery desire" burning in their eyes, and its author's assurances that their proud "widows and orphans" would be "taken care of." In such patriotic passages, the fruit of only 137 days of military service, Roosevelt helped to popularize the "splendid little war" legend, whose influence other leaders, in more difficult circumstances, would continue to feel. In April 1961, immediately after the disastrous Bay of Pigs invasion, another Cuban incursion, this one by U.S.-backed exiles from the revolutionary Castro regime, a defensive John F. Kennedy, himself a war hero, sounded positively Rooseveltian in a speech to the American Society of News Editors: "The complacent, the self-indulgent, the soft-societies are about to be swept away with the debris of history. Only the strong, only the industrious, only the determined, only the courageous, only the visionary who determine the real nature of our struggle can survive." The Vietnam War awaited.[15]

Part IV

PREACHER TO PULPIT

He really believes he is the American flag.
                John Jay Chapman, author and critic, 1898

Reform governor Roosevelt.

25

Turns to Gold

Following a precautionary five-day post-Cuba quarantine at Camp Wikoff on Long Island's eastern edge, Roosevelt, suddenly the most celebrated man in America, was the object of intense political interest. The fall 1898 elections were approaching, and New York Republicans doubted the prospects of incumbent governor Frank Black, a long-faced former newspaper editor supported by the Thomas Platt camp though under heavy criticism for using taxpayer dollars on a projected expansion of the nearly seventy-five-year-old Erie Canal, whose commercial heyday lay in the dim pre-transcontinental-railroad 1850s. Some papers called the plan a boondoggle. Thinning with age, stoop-shouldered, and the waning master of the state's GOP, Platt held a weak hand. If he continued to back Black, the Democrats might win in a cakewalk, but he loathed Roosevelt, the obvious war hero antidote, for his earlier police commissioner crusading.[1]

The aforementioned GOP troubleshooter Lemuel Quigg, friendly to both principals, received Platt's resigned permission to sound Roosevelt out. The latter, promising to treat the machine with no undue umbrage, received its grudging assent. Quigg later revealed that considerations far beyond Albany factored into Platt's hostility toward the newly minted Colonel. He "was still unwilling to bring your name before the convention . . . because, in his heart of hearts, he had opposed the Spanish War," he wrote Roosevelt in 1913. "He often talked to me, when I was urging your nomination, of the expensive responsibilities which would result to the United States from your success in the Philippines and Cuba, and he held you personally as much responsible for our declaration of war with Spain as the destruction of our battleship in Havana Harbor." Moreover, Platt knew well the power of the state's gubernatorial seat—since 1868, three of its occupants (Horatio Seymour, Samuel Tilden, and Grover Cleveland) had secured presidential nominations. "I remember him saying to me," Quigg continued, that if Roosevelt "'becomes Governor of New York, sooner or later, with his personality, he will have to be a candidate for President of the United States . . . I am afraid to start that thing going.'"[2]

Lodge, on the other hand, was only too eager to embellish Roosevelt's record. As summer segued into fall he called upon McKinley to support Theodore's Kettle Hill heroics with a Medal of Honor (officially recommended by Wood), though also, so he wrote the president, "in view of the immense importance of the New York election." But there were a couple of snags. First, McKinley refused to take the bait. In early August while still in Santiago, Roosevelt had signed, along with seven other officers, a grandstanding round-robin letter that made its way into the press. Insisting "the army is disabled by malarial fever to the extent that its efficiency is destroyed," these men demanded that their forces "should be at once taken out of the island of Cuba." It is possible that McKinley thought this unusual appeal to public opinion a dangerous precedent not to be encouraged. Second, and more important, the War Department pointed out that Wood was not an eyewitness to Roosevelt's actions at Kettle Hill, while other accounts were vague. Incensed, Roosevelt actively lobbied for the award, complaining to Lodge, "I am entitled . . . and I want it. . . . If I didn't earn it, then no commissioned officer can ever earn it." Disposed to throw a tantrum, he described himself as feeling "rather ugly on this medal of honor business" and thought "the President and War Department may as well understand it." The following year a board of officers, reviewing the case, determined that he had performed his duty, "and nothing more." Nearly a century later in 1997, involvement from some in Congress, along with TR's great-grandson Tweed Roosevelt, caused the Department of the Army to reappraise the Colonel's claim. It found that Roosevelt's "bravery in battle did not rise to the level that would justify the Medal of Honor and, indeed, it did not rise to the level of men who fought in that engagement." Subsequent congressional pressure, however, overturned this decision, and in 2001, in the last days of the Clinton presidency, Roosevelt posthumously received the award.[3]

Despite this unseemly prizefight, Theodore floated through a supremely charmed 1898. Rejecting the advice of family and friends, he had resigned his secure seat in the Navy Department, then become a national hero, and finally forced a grudging Platt to put him in line for a future presidential run. No wonder he wrote to Columbia University president Seth Low in late August, "I am just letting events take their course."[4] At this pleasant point, however, he encountered an unexpected hiccup—a case of too many nominations.

John Jay Chapman, a writer, Porcellian, and son of a New York Stock Exchange president, had maneuvered over the late summer to get Roosevelt, so he thought, to be the Independent Republican faction's gubernatorial candidate. A reformer with a distinguished pedigree—a grandmother worked with the abolitionist William Lloyd Garrison; the first chief justice of the United States, John Jay, resided a little higher up the family tree—he hatched a plan of faintly Machiavellian proportions. Reasoning that the GOP needed Roosevelt no matter what, he proposed to quickly bestow the nomination upon the Colonel, leaving Platt's machine with no choice but to *second* that action. This, Chapman believed, would then free Roosevelt from the machine and raise inestimably the profile of the good government types in New York, if not around the country. Filled with stardust dreams, he approached Roosevelt in August, *prior* to Quigg's own Oyster Bay pilgrimage. According to Chapman, the Colonel said yes to the plan.

And so, on September 10, the Independents announced "our reasons for nominating him" in the sympathetic *New-York Tribune*: "We think that the evils of our public life can be traced to the exclusive control over nominations by the party bosses and their creatures. While Roosevelt is a party man, he is one in whom the masses of the people of both parties feel a confidence amounting to devotion, and who in his person represents reform." Though flattered, Theodore knew that he could not formally align himself with the party's Independents, who had just referred to his major supporters, the GOP's string-pullers, as "the evils of our public life." He had swallowed Blaine for much less gain in 1884 and would do more swallowing now. Numbers mattered, and Platt's machine controlled seven hundred of the delegates (out of a total of nearly a thousand) who would cast votes at the Saratoga convention later that month. There really was only one path forward, and Roosevelt, shortly after "an entirely satisfactory talk" with Platt, wrote Lodge with a studied nonchalance on the nineteenth, "Apparently, I am going to be nominated."⁵

Chapman's grand plan had collapsed, overturning his errant hopes and breaking his boyish heart. "I never before . . . have felt that glorious touch of hero-worship," he wrote of visiting the Colonel at Oyster Bay, and, when accused of "being in love with him," could only reply, "Indeed I was." Prone to strong impulses—while in college, after assaulting a supposed rival for a young lady's affections, he contritely thrust his left hand in a coal fire, occasioning its amputation—he took Roosevelt's rejection hard.⁶

In a note to his second wife, the heiress Elizabeth Astor Winthrop Chanler, Chapman brooded. "He did commit [to] us and let us go ahead. Each man judges him with a different shade of meaning. I see in him only a very muddleheaded and at the same time pigheaded young man, who needs to be shoved right at the crucial point." These heated emotions never quite cooled. In a private memorandum written in 1919, months after Roosevelt's death, Chapman revisited the long-ago nomination fracas: "But Roosevelt never afterwards told the truth about the episode. He persuaded himself that he hadn't understood my original proposition—whereas he had understood it; only events had caused him to change his mind as to the expediency of it." Playing to win, the Colonel had sided with the machine. Not wishing to sully his reform reputation, however, and angling for maximum support, he wrote "with great reluctance" to Chapman just days before the convention, "I do not see how I can accept the independent nomination and keep good faith with the other men on my ticket," before opportunistically adding, "I should greatly like the aid of the Independents." Observing Roosevelt's delicate dance with GOP regulars and their in-party critics, Henry Adams winked to a friend over the nimble gyrations of the dexterous "dear Teddy, who can follow the hounds as well as run with the hares."⁷

The race, however, wasn't quite over just yet. Fighting for renomination, Black refused to go quietly, pointing out, with documents provided to his campaign by Tammany Hall, that the Colonel had a residency requirement problem. The previous year his property taxes in Oyster Bay had doubled and he had smoothly transferred his legal address to Bamie's Manhattan town house, but this property too came under a heavy tariff assessment and, on the advice of the less than vigilant Uncle Jimmy Roosevelt, Theodore declared Washington, D.C., his legal residence. According to the New York Constitution, however, gubernatorial candidates were required to have been in "continuous" habitation in the state for at least five years prior to their election.[8]

Into this mess, at the behest of party strategists, stepped Elihu Root, charged with finding a way to make Roosevelt's residency problem disappear. A brilliant corporate lawyer possessed, so TR's sister Corinne later recalled, of a "pregnant wit, and quiet, brilliant sarcasm," Root was an indispensable fixture in Progressive Era American governance, later heading both the War and State departments; for his advocacy of arbitration agreements in the Western Hemisphere, he earned the 1912 Nobel Peace Prize.[9] Before collecting these laurels, however, he went to work in September 1898 making Roosevelt a clean candidate.

Facing a sea of dark-suited Republicans at the party's Saratoga convention, Root explained the many ways one might interpret the word "residence," and accompanied this, so he later quipped, "with a lot of ballyhoo" and extraneous detail that left his audience appropriately mystified. The *Cortland Democrat*, while avoiding the word "lie," declared foul: "Now the question is, when did Mr. Roosevelt tell the truth—when he said he resided in Washington, or when in order to be eligible as Governor, he said it was all a mistake and he has resided in New York all the time?" But the convention, eager to back a winner, sustained Root's legalese, and Roosevelt was free to wrest the nomination from Black, which he did in a 753 to 218 pasting. At this point the now-official candidate discreetly paid $1,050 (about $40,000 in today's dollars) in New York City back taxes. In the 1930s Root confided to a biographer, "Roosevelt was a youngster. He didn't know much about business or business affairs. He got caught in a little inconsistency of an affidavit about his tax. . . . I went all over it and came to the conclusion that it was all right. It was a question of using the word 'residence' in one of several senses."[10]

Root indirectly captured in this communication an important side of Roosevelt's remarkable personal appeal. An inexperienced politician, he survived both the tax and Independent nomination hurdles, either of which could have hamstrung his candidacy. But voters seemed to regard these obstacles as proof of Roosevelt's distance from daily corruption. Yes, he might be led astray by Uncle Jimmy's poor advice or have his candidacy taken on resignedly by the Easy Boss, yet these things merely accentuated his presumed virtue. As a novice officer, his champions may have added, he had stormed the San Juan Heights—and now proposed, in a sense, to do the same thing in New York politics. This rare narrative proved, among a plurality of voters, just enough. Watching Roosevelt on the campaign hustings, a former member of the state assembly wrote to a colleague, "He spoke about ten minutes—The speech was nothing, but the man's presence was everything, it was electrical, magnetic—I looked at the faces of hundreds and saw only pleasure and satisfaction—when the train moved away scores of men and women ran after the train waving hats and handkerchiefs and cheering trying to keep him in sight as long as possible."[11] On November 8, 1898, less than two weeks after turning forty, Roosevelt captured a closely fought gubernatorial race over the Democrat Augustus Van Wyck, formerly on the Superior Court in Brooklyn, by fewer than 18,000 votes out of more than 1.3 million cast.

Confident in his abilities—"I am going to make a pretty decent Governor," he gushed—Roosevelt and his large family moved into the Executive Mansion in Albany. Though a comfortable Eagle Street residence, it seemed to suffer in its rambling Queen Anne confusion from a kind of Gilded Age architectural inferiority. The Colonel found it "painfully suggestive of that kind of elegance which one sees in a swell Chicago hotel or in the board room of the directors of some big railways."[12] Giving the house a personal touch, Roosevelt had a gymnasium put in.

Pairing TR with Platt to chart the path for state politics proved to be a beautiful disaster. The two men simply did not understand each other, but rather condescended to caricatures of the boy-reformer-versus-the-cynical-kingpin kind. Expressing caution, the Easy Boss had confessed to the incoming governor his apprehension that a too-literal commitment to reform might scare away some of the party's biggest benefactors: "I had heard that you were a little loose on the relations of capital and labor, on trusts and combinations . . . on those numerous questions affecting the security of earnings and the right of a man to run his own business in his own way."[13]

As if to confirm the Easy Boss's fears, Governor Roosevelt quickly ambled into an intraparty fight by supporting the Ford Franchise Tax Bill, named after its sponsor, the reform Republican state senator and economist John Ford. Some of New York's major utility and transportation companies—water, bridges, tunnels, elevated subways—received generous advantages from the state, including low to no taxes, and GOP progressives sought to end this practice. Roosevelt supported them, concerned that the capitalists were turning workers into radicals. "One of the reasons why I am so anxious to see corporations pay their full share of the taxes," he wrote John Daniel Crimmins, a prominent Manhattan philanthropist, "is because I want to prevent any just discontent becoming a factor in the socialistic movement." Platt, however, jumped to just the opposite conclusion, writing to Roosevelt in early May 1899, "To my very great surprise, you did a thing which has caused the business community of New York to wonder how far the notions of Populism, as laid down in Kansas and Nebraska, have taken hold upon the Republican party of the State of New York." He further accused the governor of "entertain[ing] various *altruistic* ideas" that required "very profound consideration" before becoming law. Two days later, Roosevelt replied to the Easy Boss, smartly sticking to politics: "In the long run ... we should be beaten, and badly beaten, if we took the attitude of saying that corporations should not, when they receive great benefits and make a great deal of money, pay their share of the public burdens." Before the month's end the governor signed the bill in an extra session of the legislature—over, so Roosevelt told Lodge, Platt's "bitter" and "frantic" opposition.[14]

Despite crossing swords with the machine on the franchise bill and several other issues—Roosevelt signed legislation strengthening the eight-hour work law among state employees, updated factory inspection regulations, and improved tenement shop conditions—he proved to be a shrewd political fighter, understanding the all-important art of picking his battles. As he explained to Henry Loewenthal, managing editor of the *New York Times*, some months after the franchise scuffle:

> My strength has consisted very largely in the fact that I have never begun a fight save with extreme caution; that by constant consultation I have kept the Machine, without which I was powerless, on my side, save in the two or three exceptional cases where I could make the issue so clean-cut that I could rally the great sentiment of the people behind me; and that I have not weakened myself by making unsuccessful fights. Two or three failures on my part would have made me very nearly powerless.[15]

Careful though he might be, Roosevelt still put a discernible crimp in the off-the-books barter system of corporate payments for political services advanced by Platt. Though the governor's powers were on balance limited when measured beside the efficient machine, he still presented an obstacle of sorts, a consideration that many Republicans resented having to consider.

And so they considered promoting him out of New York.

26

Kicked Upstairs

With McKinley running for reelection in 1900, Roosevelt looked ahead, strategically eyeing the party's 1904 nomination as his route to the White House. But this raised the tricky question of what he might do in the interlude. He could seek a second gubernatorial term, of course, though that would mean more opportunities to clash with Platt and, in any case, would only take him through 1902, with a couple of dangling years to fill. He preferred returning to Washington as secretary of war and cringed before the suggestion that he consider the vice presidency, a portfolio without power occupied in recent years by a swarm of Gilded Age seat warmers—including William Wheeler, Thomas Hendricks, and Levi Morton. Lodge, however, more attuned to the prevailing party winds, began to nudge Roosevelt in the summer of 1899 to think seriously about this third option. The Colonel hedged—"I confess I should like a position with more work in it"—and offered only the vaguest assurance that "I should feel like taking any honorable position that offered itself."[1] That August, McKinley selected Root to head the War Department, and the number of honorable positions now narrowed. At this point Roosevelt admitted, perhaps a little desperately and probably without Edith's enthusiasm, to an interest in becoming governor-general of the Philippines, a controversial American appendage following the extraction of Spain's colonial regime.

In November the vice presidency question gained momentum when incumbent Garret Hobart, an influential New Jersey political insider, died of a lingering heart disease. Considering that one-quarter of all veeps (dating back to 1789) had now expired in harness (six out of twenty-four), Roosevelt's desire for a less somnolent situation takes on multiple meanings. But there were those, beyond Lodge, who wished to make him part of the executive team. As a young war hero, a reform governor, and an eastern patrician popular in the West, he offered an attractive balance to the business-first Republicanism embodied by McKinley.

Some, however, preferred the capable Root, who, like Roosevelt, resided in New York, a significant consideration as the state's electoral votes had gone to the winning candidate in every national campaign since 1880. But with the situation in both Cuba (now a U.S. protectorate moving toward a qualified independence slated for 1902) and the Philippines uncertain, Root was disinclined to leave the war office. As the calendar year ended, Roosevelt, with no clear path, prudently resolved to keep his options open.

Lodge did not make this easy. In a late–January 1900 meeting with McKinley, he openly endorsed Roosevelt for the vice presidency, an office, as all knew, controlled by party higher-ups at summer nominating conventions. "He is evidently perfectly content," Lodge subsequently reported back, "to have you on the ticket with him." Perhaps, above all, Cabot had intended the conversation to wake Roosevelt up: "If you do not take the Vice-Presidency New York will have lost it. This Platt does not want to have happen, and the attitude of the organization, which has now come around to desire you to take it, is something to be considered." He dressed up this appeal with suitable caveats and compliments—"I am not going to urge you one way or the other"; "I have great confidence in your instinct"—before closing on an insinuating note: "I think the Vice Presidency the better road to the future, as well as the safer one."[2]

Hedging and clearly angling for more time, Roosevelt pled economy for his uncharacteristic hesitancy: "As Governor, I am comparatively well paid, having not only a salary but a house which is practically kept up during the winter... but great pressure would come upon me if I went in as Vice-President. I could only live simply."[3] Certainly Washington entertained on a grander scale than Albany, though one can rather easily imagine Roosevelt dropping Albany in a heartbeat to charge up another hill, even if he had to buy another Brooks Brothers uniform to do so.

The would-be candidate carefully maneuvered through the winter of 1900, consistently emoting his lack of interest in running as McKinley's number two, though never making the kind of Shermanesque statement—"I will not accept if nominated and will not serve if elected," William T. Sherman had said in 1884 of a possible presidential bid—that would close the door. Aware that the Platt machine and "all the big-monied interests" wanted him out of New York, he seemed to oscillate between pride and anger. In correspondence he painted himself as something of a lone crusader (alone in Albany . . .) fighting the corporations who "think the best thing to do is to put me in the Vice-Presidency." There is truth here, though perhaps a half-truth. For while Platt most certainly wanted Roosevelt in Washington, so did Lodge, his greatest political ally. The governor knew that, without having to ask, he might count on the New York machine to boost his chances, even while keeping a qualified distance from its Wall Street wing, still fuming over the franchise tax. It seems safe to say that Roosevelt, despite the "comparatively well paid" post he now held, wanted a higher-profile placement in 1900 as the elections (if victorious, which looked likely) promised. But he had to be a candidate for *something*. Accordingly, he never positively refused to consider the vice presidency, understanding that his popularity kept him within reach of a convention draft. Henry Adams, for one, could see the parts coming together. "Of all the new phenomena," he wrote a friend about this time, "Teddy Roosevelt is the queerest, for he has become a serious fact . . . [and] will stand in for the V.P."[4]

How right Adams was. By the spring, Roosevelt had agreed to serve as a delegate at the June Republican National Convention in Philadelphia, which, so Lodge knew, could lead to only one outcome. "If you go to that Convention," he wrote Roosevelt on April 16, "you will be nominated, as the situation looks today, and if you are nominated . . . you will be unable to refuse." Playing both sides, the noncandidate candidate replied the following day, "I believe that I would be looked upon as rather a coward if I didn't go." Sensing that his many rhetorical refusals to entertain the idea of running as McKinley's second might now lead to charges of hypocrisy, he reminded Lodge, "I did *not* say that I would not under any circumstances accept the vice-presidency." This line he practiced later that month when telling New York *Sun* editor Paul Dana, "I have refrained from saying that under no circumstances would I take the [office], simply because if it were vital for me to help the ticket by going on, I would feel that the situation was changed."[5]

Among those who looked critically upon a Roosevelt candidacy was Edith, accustomed to reading politics with a skeptical eye. Three weeks before the convention, Alton B. Parker, a Democrat, chief justice of New York's Court of Appeals, and later to be Roosevelt's opponent for the presidency in 1904, dined at the Executive Mansion in Albany. After soup, he dared to say aloud in Edith's presence what so many Republicans had been saying for months—"You will see your husband unanimously nominated for the office of Vice-President"—only to be instantly contradicted by the state's First Lady who called him a "disagreeable thing."[6]

On June 15 Roosevelt arrived in Philadelphia. He moved freely, agreeably through hotel lobbies, shook innumerable hands, and wore a wide-rimmed army hat quickly christened "an acceptance hat" by attendees. He never ceased holding court with reporters. McKinley's manager, Senator Mark Hanna, so eager to thrust Roosevelt onto the campaign hustings in 1896, now watched the growing Rough Rider wave with alarm. Perhaps Hanna could feel his hold on the delegates slipping, or possibly he saw in Roosevelt a genuine danger to the party, as a well-intentioned but erratic reformer who threatened the generation-long recipe—rapid industrialization and machine politics—sacred to GOP success. Twenty-one years older than Roosevelt, Hanna had amassed a fortune in several business enterprises including coal, steel, and railroads. Thick-jowled, big-eared, and possessed, so a biographer noted, of "clear bright brown eyes" suggesting "a searching quality," he had hoped to nip any stray veep blooms in the bud. "Governor Roosevelt will not be nominated for Vice President, and has not been discussed in that connection by Party leaders, or those who might speak for the administration," he had told the *Cincinnati Enquirer* in early May.[7]

The Colonel knew quite well where he stood with both Hanna and McKinley. "The President in a cold-blooded way has always rather liked me, or at least has admired certain qualities in me," he had written confidentially to friends earlier that year. "There are certain bits of work he would be delighted to have me do. But at bottom neither he nor Hanna (although I really like both) sympathize with my feelings or feel comfortable about me, because they cannot understand what it is that makes me act in certain ways at certain times, and therefore think me indiscreet and overimpulsive."[8] Roosevelt had, of course, run into orthodoxy before. The Harvard dudes had wondered at his casual idiosyncrasies, the bright young belles found his intense interest in dissection off-putting, and the Platt machine squinted at his well-petted independence.

The convention, held in the Exposition Auditorium just south of the University of Pennsylvania, opened on the nineteenth. Staying at the Hotel Walton near Center City, Hanna had for the previous two days anxiously attempted to persuade McKinley, via long-distance telephone to Washington, to announce his preference for vice president. But this McKinley refused. As one of his aides evenly told an incredulous Hanna, "The choice of the convention will be his choice; he has no advice to give." Upset and feeling momentum moving against him, Hanna is reported to have said of Roosevelt before a group of southern Republicans, "Don't any of you realize that there's only one life between that madman and the Presidency?"[9] Hanna had formerly enjoyed the reputation of kingmaker, but McKinley's loud silence gave him no clout to contest the Roosevelt movement. He looked weak and he knew it. On June 21 TR was nominated, capturing every vote cast (925), a single delegate, the modest Roosevelt, having modestly abstained.

And then he went to work. Throughout the late summer and fall he campaigned nearly continuously, traveling more than twenty thousand miles in twenty-four states, and giving hundreds of set speeches attacking Bryan, nominated again by the Democrats, as a radical silverite who threatened the country's sound money policies. According to the *New York Times*, Roosevelt, now lovingly caricatured with enormous teeth and perpetual pince-nez, addressed some 3 million people during the canvass. "Tis Tiddy alone that's running," cracked Finley Peter Dunne in the *Chicago Journal*, "and he ain't running, he's galloping." The candidate's charisma translated especially well in the West, where the newspapers blared, "RANGE GREETS ROOSEVELT," "WYOMING IS STIRRED UP," "ENTHUSIASM AROUSED IN UTAH."[10]

Come November, with a booming economy and a "splendid little war" on its résumé, the GOP retained the presidency and both congressional houses. Roosevelt's presence on the ticket helped the party collect more states and electoral votes (28 and 292) than it had four years earlier (23 and 271). Washington, Utah, Wyoming, South Dakota, Nebraska, and Kansas all flipped from Democrat to Republican, almost certainly leaning more Rough Rider than McKinley. The outcome only stoked

Hanna's concerns—"Your *duty* to the country," he wrote the president, "is to *live* for four years from next March."[11]

Both flushed and exhausted with victory—"At present I have over a thousand letters and telegrams to answer"—the vice president–elect finished his gubernatorial tenure and on January 7, 1901, went to Colorado for an extended hunting trip. Returning late the following month, he soon after embarked for Washington and, on March 4, took the oath of his new office. The morning of the ceremony proved a true joy. An agreeable flock of family and friends met at Bamie's Washington home (Roosevelt having brought to her husband, William Sheffield Cowles, a freshly claimed mountain lion skin) for morning breakfast and champagne to celebrate the day. They boarded carriages to the Capitol and from there walked to the Senate Chamber for the swearing-in ritual. McKinley's more elaborate outdoor East Portico ceremony and speech followed as the central event; a fugitive shower of late-winter sleet greeted the new century's first inauguration.[12]

And then a restless Roosevelt suddenly had a considerable amount of time on his hands. He spent the next four months mainly at Oyster Bay, amid his books, family, and correspondence; two western hunting trips brought, one suspects, welcome relief to this enforced domestic rhythm. After three hectic but satisfying years, a period during which he clambered consecutively from national hero to governor to vice president, the world must have seemed to him now a very quiet place.

27

Keys to the Kingdom

Less than a month into an impassive vice presidency, a fidgety Roosevelt itched to move beyond the office. "I intend studying law with a view to seeing if I cannot go into practice as a lawyer when my term . . . comes to an end," he wrote Leonard Wood in late March. "I have always thought I might end as a professor of history," he continued in a daydreaming vein, before calling his own bluff—"but if possible I should prefer a more active life." And so, the weeks rolled on into the late summer. With time to spare, Roosevelt visited the Pan-American Exposition in Buffalo and attended a quarter-centennial celebration of Colorado statehood during which, so he reported to Lodge, "I have been greatly astonished at the feeling displayed for me, not only in Colorado and Kansas, but in Missouri and even in Illinois." He further kept abreast of literary affairs, writing to an old Harvard friend, the popular author of western fiction Owen Wister (best known for *The Virginian*, a cowboy saga with the enduring line: "When you call me that, smile!"), to attack Frank Norris's recently published *The Octopus*, a class-conscious novel depicting the manipulation of freight rates to create monopolies (octopi) and based on an actual conflict between San Joaquin farmers and the Southern Pacific Railroad. Reading, so he said, "like the ravings . . . [of] Bryan," the book, a study of corporate corruption, struck this particular Oyster Bay patrician as "so very hysterical and exaggerated."[1]

On September 6 Roosevelt was supping at the Vermont Fish and Game League luncheon on Lake Champlain's Isle La Motte. Shortly after 4:00 p.m., he received an urgent phone call informing him that McKinley, making his own tour of the Pan-American Exposition, had been shot minutes earlier while shaking hands in a receiving line. The vice president's party quickly raced to Buffalo. To their relief, they found, so they thought, a mending McKinley—"The President," Roosevelt wrote to Bamie on the seventh, "is coming along splendidly." The only wrinkle, so he told Lodge, was that the surgeons' good work "thereby saved the life of [the] assailant," Leon Czolgosz, a slender, blue-eyed, and round-faced twenty-eight-year-old anarchist born in Michigan to Polish immigrants. Roosevelt referred to him in correspondence as "the dog." Concealing a .32-caliber revolver in a handkerchief, Czolgosz, with a Bach cantata playing in the background, fired two bullets into the president from close range in the exposition's Temple of Music. One of the projectiles, as physicians would discover in a few days, did irreparable damage to McKinley's stomach, liver, and pancreas. Explaining himself, Czolgosz told police, "I don't believe one man should have so much service and another man should have none."[2]

With the president apparently healing—"the patient stood the operation well," the *New York Times* reported—Roosevelt left Buffalo on the tenth to join his family in the Adirondacks. About this time Henry Adams wrote John Hay from Stockholm, "If the President recovers, he will be politically very strong." Unable to harness an impetuous thought, he further noted, as though speaking for an entire class of queasy Brahmins, "Then, curiously, behind all, in my mind, in all our minds, silent and awful . . . flies the thought of Teddy's luck!" A prominent representative of the business class weighed in with equal interest. Assuring the nation in a stream of staccato sentences that "the financial situation is absolutely good. There is nothing to derange it. The banks will take care of that. You need not worry about it," J. P. Morgan—an octopod in his own right—flexed the power of the country's tendriling investment system. The money men, he seemed to have little doubt, were the republic's real sources of power and authority.[3]

And then McKinley began to sink. On September 13, 320 miles to the east, Roosevelt, in company with a small Adirondacks climbing party having just hiked up Mount Marcy, received several concerning telegrams, the most germane being:

> THE PRESIDENT APPEARS TO BE DYING AND MEMBERS OF THE CABINET IN BUFFALO THINK YOU SHOULD LOSE NO TIME IN COMING[4]

Gangrene had set in. Within a matter of hours, at 2:15 a.m. the following morning, McKinley, the last president to have served in the Civil War, had died. Roosevelt arrived in Buffalo early that afternoon, his train met by a dozen mounted police officers along with Ansley Wilcox, an acquaintance and New York political insider, who took the as yet uninaugurated president to his Delaware Avenue house for a proposed hasty repast, which Roosevelt waved off. Rather, in borrowed dress clothes, top hat, and satin tie, he went a mile down the avenue to Milburn House, home of John Milburn, the horrified head of the exposition's board of directors, to view the slain president's body—something an in-progress autopsy prevented. Instead, he met with a gathering of McKinley's—now his—cabinet in the parlor (Secretary of State Hay remained in Washington). Elihu Root suggested an immediate swearing-in, though Roosevelt paused, preferring to take the oath at Wilcox's mansion, a stately residence with the distinct advantage of not containing a dead president in its upstairs. And so there, in Ansley Wilcox's library, at about three o'clock, Root formally asked "Mr. Vice-President" on behalf of the cabinet to take the oath. Roosevelt replied, "Mr. Secretary, I will take the oath," and, perhaps feeling that the grave moment called for a little august extemporizing, added, "In this hour of deep and terrible National bereavement, I wish to state that it shall be my aim to continue, absolutely without variance, the policy of President McKinley, for the peace and prosperity and honor of our beloved country." At this point, federal judge John Hazel approached Roosevelt, standing in front of a bay window, and administered the oath. "At the last moment," so Wilcox later noted, "the newspaper men, who were eager for admission, were all let in, but were prohibited from taking photographs."[5]

There followed an impromptu cabinet meeting in which Roosevelt got all to agree to remain in their posts for the time being, a much-needed sign of continuity. Later that afternoon Hanna arrived in a carriage, visibly shocked at the death of a friend as well as a president, his relationship with McKinley going back some twenty years. He now extended Roosevelt a formal, cold hand, muttering something to the effect that his support for the new administration depended on its fealty to the mandate won in the previous year's election. Roosevelt, in other words, ruled in a dead man's shadow.[6]

Two days later, on a brilliantly sunny day, McKinley's black-draped funeral train made its way to Washington. Wanting family when he arrived, Roosevelt telegraphed Corinne, who later remembered:

> [He] told us that as Mrs. Roosevelt was attending to last important matters at Sagamore, she could not be with him the day he moved into the White House, and that he was very anxious that not only my sister and her husband, but that we [including Corinne's spouse] also should dine with him the first night that he slept in the old mansion.... As we sat around the table he turned and said: "Do you realize that this is the birthday of our father?... I have realized it as I signed various papers all day long, and I feel that it is a good omen that I begin my duties in this house on this day."[7]

Later that week Edith and the younger children arrived at the White House, uncertain of their strange new surroundings, which were conspicuously ornamented in a haze of black mourning bunting and public grief. "I suppose in a short time I shall adjust myself," Edith wrote to her sister, Emily, "but the horror of it hangs over me and I am never without fear for Theodore. The secret service men follow him everywhere." She did allow, however, that the presidential salary ($50,000 ever since the Grant administration, some $1.8 million in today's dollars) meant that for a hardworking home economist with six children, "life will be far easier than that of the Vice President's wife. For one thing I shall not have to count the pennies."[8]

Being with family buoyed Roosevelt's spirits, and retaining Lodge as a confidant helped as well. Under different circumstances this might have proven awkward, as the Massachusetts senator had formerly occupied the implied senior position in their now-seventeen-year friendship. But Cabot had never coveted a White House residency, having made his place in the Senate a seat of real power. The alliance meant much to Roosevelt who, at forty-two, was then and remains the nation's youngest occupant of the executive office. "It is a dreadful thing coming into the Presidency this way," he wrote Lodge on the twenty-third, "but it would be a far worse thing to be morbid about it. Here is the task, and I have got to do it to the best of my ability; and that is all there is about it."[9]

28

Shifting American Scene

McKinley's murder conformed to a broader pattern of political violence among modernity's malcontents. Over a twenty-year period (1881–1901) the Russian, French, Spanish, Austrian, and Italian heads of state were, like the American president, assassinated by anarchists. A host of historical forces—liberalism, industrialism, and secularism—had combined to fundamentally reorient the relationship between rulers and ruled. In the United States, dissent from systemic economic inequality could be glimpsed in the long Populist crusade against the "money power," while calls for reforming the democratic process found traction in proposed legislation providing for women's suffrage, the direct election of U.S. senators, and direct voter participation in primary races. Reform mayors and governors—including Cleveland's Tom Johnson, Detroit's Hazen Pingree, and Wisconsin's Robert La Follette—gave institutional voices to increasingly strident calls for state regulation over railroads and utilities, all part of a growing movement toward limiting industrial consolidation in an anxious age of monopolization.

"The Average American," so the popular magazine *Current Literature* declared in 1901, was predominantly of "the Anglo-Saxon strain" and more precisely "is a man five feet eight inches in height . . . and a weight of 150 pounds. His family consists of one wife and three children, a fourth child having died in infancy. His age is thirty-seven years, and he expects to live thirty years longer. . . . His home is near Columbus, Ind. . . . The house is of two stories, containing seven rooms." The average American consumed about twenty pounds of tobacco a year along with "seven and a half gallons of spirits and wine, not less than seventy-five gallons of beer." Typically Protestant, he seldom attended church though insisted that his children be regularly marched off to Sunday school. A little averse to technology and sensitive to expenses, he preferred mailing letters to sending telegrams.[1]

Most Americans, apropos our Indiana man, lived in the northern states; throughout the country 60 percent resided in areas of fewer than 2,500, but that percentage was shifting and within twenty years a plurality would live in urban areas. Between 1880 and 1900 the combined populations of New York, Chicago, Detroit, Pittsburgh, and Buffalo more than doubled from 2.8 million to more than 6 million. Agricultural laborers, working on 5.7 million farms, still constituted the largest single bloc of employees, though some 10 million were occupied in various manufacturing positions. Industry, in fact, now ruled the economic roost. By 1900 the value of machined products amounted to more than $13 billion, far outstripping the $4.7 billion coming from cropping. Such flux occasioned great disparities of material well-being. During the 1896 campaign, supporters had cheered McKinley as the "advance agent of prosperity," a prophecy borne out, to be sure, for certain groups, though in 1904 roughly 10 million Americans lived in poverty amid this selective plenty.[2]

The perils of stratification were evident in overlapping capital-versus-labor, Anglo-versus-immigrant, and rural-versus-urban confrontations; the country's freshly acquired island colonies called into question the nation's very identity—republic or empire? These tensions, predicated on the existence of fixed and unequal classes, threatened to upend older notions of American mobility popularized in the colonial era by Benjamin Franklin ("early to bed and early to rise, makes a man healthy, wealthy, and wise") and more recently recognized in the rags-to-riches juvenilia of Horatio Alger, author of formulaic young-adult novels—*Luck and Pluck*, *Strive and Succeed*, *Bound to Rise*, and so on—featuring impoverished boys working toward maturity and middle-class security.

The inability of the emerging industrial system to meet such promises resulted in a series of violent confrontations between workers and bosses. Chicago's Haymarket Riot (1886), beginning as a peaceful rally for an eight-hour workday, resulted in eleven deaths and scores of injuries; the Battle of Homestead (1892) pitted the Carnegie Steel Company against its picketing employees; the 1894 Pullman railroad strike, commencing in Chicago but spreading through the country, did not end until then-president Cleveland deployed thousands of U.S. marshals and twelve thousand army troops to quell the work stoppage. These efforts on the part of laborers to organize constituted the urban equivalent of Populism's questioning of corporatism. Both movements were rooted in the Panic of 1873, a sharp economic downturn leading to a quarter century of economic uncertainty for workers that overlapped the more widely felt Panic of 1893, a four-year depression that affected every aspect of the economy.

The severity of commercial conditions touched popular angst at an unprecedented level, increasingly informing the reactions of middle-class consumers. Several corruption-exposing periodicals (*Collier's Weekly*, *McClure's Magazine*, *Munsey's Magazine*) addressed these concerns with a stable of reform-minded journalists reporting on fraudulent advertising, ineffective patent medicines, and adulterated foods, as well as poverty, prostitution, and child labor. Larger exposés on illegal price rigging, most notably Ida Tarbell's slashing *The History of the Standard Oil Company*—"Mr. Rockefeller has systemically played with loaded dice"—were also in vogue. Roosevelt was mixed-minded about these efforts. Though often dismissive of the business class for cheating workers—"The capitalist," he wrote in a memoir, "is an unworthy citizen who pays the efficient man no more than he has been content to pay the average man . . . and effort should be made by the Government to check and punish him"—he nevertheless saw in the urban reformers the seeds of socialism. Applying an epithet to an entire class of crusading print protestors and borrowing from John Bunyan's 1678 Christian allegory *The Pilgrim's Progress*, he denounced in a 1906 speech "the man with the muck-rake, the man who could look no way but downward . . . who was offered a celestial crown for his muck-rake . . . but continued to rake to himself the filth of the floor."[3]

Looking askance at both the socialist and the capitalist, Roosevelt believed his country could have the benefits of a powerful industrial economy alongside an active central government responsive to a growing urban, middle-class constituency's concerns. Like so many well-born, he loathed the industrial lords who presumably cared only for making dollars. He perhaps contrasted this "vulgar" new money with his own impeccably pedigreed old money. His friends and acquaintances were other historians and patricians (Lodge and the Adamses of the Brahmin brand, Hay coming in through an indelible connection to Lincoln); he corresponded with artists and writers (Augustus Saint-Gaudens, John La Farge, and Edith Wharton) and, alerted by his son Kermit to the talents of Edwin Arlington Robinson, secured the impoverished poet a sinecure at the New York Customs Office. Though TR valued his Dakota and Rough Rider experiences, these were cowboy and soldier sidelines, the impulsive callings of a rich man at play—recall how quickly he left Cuba when boredom set in. At heart, Roosevelt's progressivism stemmed from a conservative desire to see the old elite maintain authority rather than defer to a rising robber-baronocracy.

Great changes in foreign policy further complicated the American scene in 1901. With the abrupt acquisition of the Philippines archipelago and the Hawaiian Islands, the United States suddenly became a fledgling Pacific power, positioned in competition with Japan and Russia, among other nations, for commercial advantage in Asia. The country's anti-imperialists, a diverse group including Andrew Carnegie, the Chicago social worker Jane Addams, and former Massachusetts senator George Boutwell, had denounced this precipitous embrace of empire. It threatened, so they argued, to push America into the whirlwind of international politics, to lead the nation into future wars, and to contradict its proud history as a former colony that had rebelled against its own oppressive overseas master. Much of this opposition had dissipated after the election of 1900, though it continued to inform public opinion, and Roosevelt, deeply annoyed at those who questioned the fruits of the Spanish-American War (calling them "unhung traitors, and ... liars, slanderers and scandalmongers to boot"), hoped to attack it for political capital. "I should like to keep this anti-imperialist issue to the fore in the congressional campaign," he wrote Lodge in the summer of 1902, "for if it is made the main issue we can certainly beat the Democrats out of their boots."[4]

When reviewing America's prospects on the threshold of a fresh era, one ineffable element seemed perhaps to hover above all others: Roosevelt's auspicious timing—"Teddy's luck!" as Adams had it. Assuming the reins of government at the precise moment when his style of leadership, cautiously progressive and globally focused, met the culture halfway, TR spoke on behalf of a rising generation. For more than thirty years, since the peace of Appomattox, the nation had tilted toward conservative congressional control and conventional isolationism, even as industrial development rapidly altered the republic's character. These inconsistencies quickly came to the fore in the new century, along with older problems posed by the country's never-reconciled relationship with race.

29

The Dinner

The day McKinley died, Roosevelt had written a brief note to the educator, orator, and influential black leader Booker T. Washington, canceling, with "deep regret," his planned visit to Washington's Tuskegee Institute, a vocational school for African Americans in Alabama. The new president, however, urgently wished to discuss patronage appointments in the South—"I must see you as soon as possible"—and seventeen days later, on October 1, 1901, the two men convened at the White House. "After discussing many matters," Washington reported, Roosevelt "finally agreed to appoint a certain white man, whose name had been discussed, to an important judicial position." Washington then went to Mississippi on a speaking tour, only to find, upon his return to the capital on the sixteenth, an invitation to dine that evening with the president, members of his family, and Colorado mine owner and casual TR hunting partner Philip B. Stewart. "We talked at considerable length concerning plans about the South," Washington remembered of his after-supper exchange with Roosevelt.[1]

In effect, two kinds of presidents met that evening. Washington spoke, in certain respects, for the "sovereign nation" of Africans in America; and he registered no less as a symbol of the social mobility mantra upon which the country staked its special provenance.[2] Born into slavery, Washington preached the Emersonian song of self-reliance, defying the post-Reconstruction Jim Crowism that distinguished the New (from plantation to apartheid) South. Medium-complexioned with penetrating light-gray eyes, Washington was a stocky five feet, nine inches, carrying a few extra pounds from the constant travel and work he endured. Like Roosevelt, he read constantly, corresponded widely, and called newspaper reporters by their first names. As much as any American, he embodied the rising-people theme preached reflexively in pulpits and textbooks—and at Tuskegee. Roosevelt found him an excellent judge of men and counted on his help with the appointments of southern Republicans. This was a particularly important project for the new president as he knew that the Dixie GOP's loyalty still leaned toward the party's Hanna branch, and without allies controlling appointments and patronage, he might fail to secure the 1904 nomination. TR was well aware that Chester Arthur, the last president brought to office by an assassin, had been unable to win over enough Republican delegates to remain in power.

Roosevelt respected Washington, though he held otherwise conventionally negative views toward blacks. The informal influence of his antebellum maternal Georgia roots ("my mother . . . was a sweet, gracious, beautiful Southern Woman . . . entirely 'unreconstructed' to the day of her death") combined with a more systemic education in the dominant social Darwinism of the day to reinforce his adherence to existing color-line codes. On questions of politics and employment, Roosevelt doubted the wisdom of the black franchise and saw little place for the race above domestic and menial labor. "Now as to the Negroes!" he once wrote Owen Wister, while in the White House, "I entirely agree with you that . . . they are altogether inferior to the whites." And at the 1905 Lincoln Dinner of the New York Republican Club, he further claimed that "all reflecting men of both races are united in feeling that race purity must be maintained."[3] To be sure, Roosevelt held out hope for black advancement, though in a very abstract if not absentminded way, insisting that if evolutionary theory were correct the formerly enslaved in America might, through efficacious contact with white civilization, catch up in a century or three.

On the evening in question Washington arrived at eight, entering the north door of the White House and joining Stewart in the Blue Room before being ushered into the State Dining Room; everyone wore formal dress. African American labor had helped to build the Executive Mansion (1792–1800) and enslaved men and women had worked inside the dwelling and on its grounds during much of the early republic. Among them were three teenagers—Ursula, Edith, and Frances—Jefferson had brought from his Monticello home to learn the art of cookery from chef

Honoré Julien; Ursula's baby boy, Asnet, was the first of a dozen children born in the White House. Black leaders had also frequented the residence, perhaps most memorably in 1863 when Lincoln and Frederick Douglass discussed issues relating to race during the Civil War. The latter remembered the president "seated . . . in a low armchair . . . surrounded by a large number of documents" and several secretaries. "Though I was not entirely satisfied with his views," Douglass wrote, "I was . . . well satisfied with the man." Other exchanges in other fashions followed, as in 1878 when the Natchez-born Marie Selika Williams, a coloratura soprano (the "Queen of Staccato") performed Verdi's "Ernani involami" before a White House audience in the Green Room.[4] But the Roosevelt-Washington tête-à-tête was the first time a president had *entertained* an African American in "the People's Mansion."

This distinction left little impression on Washington himself. "My surprise can be imagined when, two or three days afterward, the whole press, North and South, was filled with despatches and editorials relating to my dinner with the President," he later observed. Many of these commentaries were predictably condemnatory. "When Mr. Roosevelt sits down to dinner with a Negro," the *Times-Democrat* of New Orleans complained, "he declares that the Negro is the social equal of the white man"; Memphis's *Commercial Appeal* insisted that "no Southern woman with proper self-respect would now accept an invitation to the White House"; while the *Richmond News* said, "He has destroyed the kindly, warm regard and personal affection for him which were growing up fast in the South." Considering that the Democrats owned Dixie and the region had last gone Republican in 1872 while still under military occupation—and would not flip to the GOP until nearly a century later (Nixon's "southern strategy")—one is inclined to question the fastness of the growing.[5] Perhaps uncertain of his action, Roosevelt is said to have sought informal counsel. A week after the supper, the president, among several honorary degree recipients at Yale's bicentennial celebration, approached Mark Twain, himself to be "gowned and hooded for baptism." Known to dip occasionally into apocrypha, Twain later wrote in a memoir:

> The President asked me if I thought he was right in inviting Booker Washington to lunch [sic] at the White House. I judged by his tone that he was worried and troubled and sorry about that showy adven-

ture, and wanted a little word of comfort and approval. I said it was a private citizen's privilege to invite whom he pleased to his table, but that perhaps a president's liberties were more limited. . . . I didn't tell him all I thought about it—we never do that. . . . Privately, I thought it a president's duty to refrain from offending the nation merely to advertise himself and make noise.[6]

That Roosevelt would have thought much of what Twain, a prominent anti-imperialist, had to say is doubtful. Just three months prior to the New Haven conclave he had referred to the celebrated *Huckleberry Finn* author as one of "our prize idiots."[7]

Though castigated by the South's press and political class—"social equality with the negro means decadence and damnation," South Carolina's lieutenant governor said of the supper—the president had not sought to make a race statement. "There was no disposition on . . . Mr. Roosevelt's part," Washington argued, "to attack any custom in the South." Rather, TR thought principally of patronage and his chances of winning election in his own right. Senator Hanna, the GOP's national chairman, stood in his way. In 1896 Hanna had secured the party's nomination for McKinley by backing the "lily-white" faction of southern delegates against the old biracial "black-and-tan" bloc empowered during Reconstruction. These Dixie delegates, no matter their pigmentation, were important only for securing nominations since the solid South, as noted, mechanically went Democrat in national elections. With Washington's assistance, Roosevelt reversed Hanna's strategy by offering patronage to the black-and-tans as well as to conservative Gold Democrats who repudiated their party's swing toward Bryanism and the free-silver crusade. Nearly two-thirds of federal appointments in select southern states would now go to Roosevelt supporters.[8]

Days after the dinner controversy broke, the president vigorously defended himself in correspondence, writing to the New York congressman and former Harvard football coach Lucius Littauer, "As to the Booker T. Washington incident, I had not thought whatever of anything save of having a chance of showing some little respect to a man whom I cordially esteem as a good citizen and good American." Less than a week later, in a heated letter to his onetime classmate (and future Massachusetts governor) Curtis Guild, he lashed out: "The idiot or vicious Bourbon [i.e., hopelessly reactionary, like aristocratic France's dying

Bourbon Dynasty] element of the South is crazy because I have had Booker T. Washington to dine. I shall have him to dine just as often as I please." In fact, he never so pleased again. Rather, within a few years he had altered his opinion appreciably. "I am not satisfied," he wrote Wister in 1906, "that I acted wisely in . . . the Booker Washington dinner."[9]

Though often regarded as a sui generis occasion, the supper more broadly demonstrated Roosevelt's ability to capture the public's attention. Whether as a Rough Rider, governor, or president, he offered the papers excellent copy, knew the media value of his attractive young family, and understood the significance of his charisma. Though off to a rocky start in the autumn of 1901, he quickly identified a popular crusade with which to make his name, marching off to take on the massive money power.

30

Playing Monopoly

In his first annual message to Congress—December 1901—Roosevelt addressed a series of concerns and challenges facing the nation. He commenced with a deep bow to McKinley's memory, perhaps troweling it on a bit thick when saying that the respected if reserved Ohioan "was the most widely loved man in all the United States." Mention of the slain president offered Roosevelt the opportunity to damn terrorists and insurgents—"All mankind should band against the anarchist"—and call for immigration restriction on "all persons who are of a low moral tendency or of unsavory reputation." He similarly suggested that anyone coming into the country with designs on staying should offer up "proper proof of ... enough money to insure a decent start under American conditions." One wonders what those many indebted farmers of free-silver stripe made of such a pay-to-play proposition. The message segued to the nation's new empire. Hawaii, Roosevelt supposed, was best "develop[ed] ... on the traditional American lines"; Cuba, "the beautiful Queen of the Antilles," he thought just fine, but conceded that "our problem is larger" in the Philippines.[1]

More provocatively, however, the message raised the unpleasant question of monopolization in the American economy. In several deft passages Roosevelt spoke as directly and critically of class division in the country as any president had since Andrew Jackson tendered his scorching 1832 veto message explaining why he killed a bill to extend the life of the powerful (a "monster" in Old Hickory's words) federally authorized second Bank of the United States. Be it an early-nineteenth-century depository controlled by financial elites or early-twentieth-century trusts dominated by a handful of oligarchs, the problems of bigness, fairness, and opportunity confronted both men.

Conceding the certain virtues wrought by the captains of industry—the building up of commerce, expansion of the railways, and rise in living standards—Roosevelt insisted they had "on the whole done great good." And then he went on the attack. "There is a widespread conviction in the minds of the American people," he argued, "that the great corporations known as trusts are ... hurtful to the general welfare." When one of the all too periodic panics inevitably ensued, he continued, "the capitalist may be shorn of his luxuries; but the wage-worker may be deprived of even bare necessities." In the past, he maintained, "old laws, and old customs" tended to intervene against such stark discrepancies in wealth, though considering recent trends in industrial development, these guide rails "are no longer sufficient." Accordingly, he now made the case for more active government intervention in order that "combination and concentration should be, not prohibited, but supervised and within reasonable limits controlled." The system suffered from "real and grave" sins, he observed, before concluding that "a resolute and practical effort must be made to correct these evils."[2]

And correct them, he intended to do. Within weeks of addressing Congress, Roosevelt announced his intent to bust, under the 1890 Sherman Antitrust Act, the Northern Securities Company, a railroad monopoly formed in 1901 and capitalized at some $14 billion in today's currency. It controlled the Great Northern and Northern Pacific lines, along with other associated tracks. James J. Hill, the Canadian American railway tycoon, formed the company along with J. P. Morgan and E. H. Harriman. This massive consolidation concerned Roosevelt. It gave a handful of private citizens immense power over the nation's economy, brought millions of workers in supporting sectors such as farming, timber, and mining under the purview of distant New York money men, and provided increased impetus behind the building momentum of "Morganization"—leviathan-like industrial consolidation brought about by a few financiers who were disposed to choke off competition. Quoted only a few months earlier in the *New York World* muttering imperiously, "I owe the public nothing," the somber-suited Morgan, rotund and bulbous-nosed (said, because of acne rosacea, to resemble a purple cauliflower), embodied for many the villainy of the super-rich.[3]

Playing his cards close to the vest, Roosevelt casually inquired of Hanna at a working breakfast on February 18, "What do you think about the Northern Securities Company?" The senator, a great friend (and shareholder) of the railway, blessed the venture as "the best thing."[4] Only forty-eight hours later the government, under the aegis of Roosevelt's capable attorney general, Philander Knox, a McKinley appointment and prominent corporate lawyer with a deceptively placid bearing ("Sleepy Phil"), brought suit against Hill's railway empire—no other cabinet members were consulted. An alarmed Morgan and several of his officers arrived in the capital on the twenty-first to dine with a group of prominent politicians and industrialists. The following day, bidden by Roosevelt, the anxious titan appeared at the White House for a morning meeting with the president and Knox. According to *New-York Commercial Advertiser* editor Joseph Bucklin Bishop, a Roosevelt confidant since the latter's crusading Police Commission days, it was a rough meeting for Morgan. He later wrote in a fawning authorized biography:

> Mr. Morgan protested against the President's conduct in acting without letting him know of his purpose in advance. The President replied: "That is just what we did not want to do." "If we have done anything wrong," said Mr. Morgan, "send your man (meaning the Attorney General) to my man (naming one of his lawyers) and they can fix it up." "That can't be done," said the President. "We don't want to fix it up," added Mr. Knox, "we want to stop it." Then Mr. Morgan asked: "Are you going to attack my other interests, the Steel Trust and the others?" "Certainly not," replied the President, "unless we find out that in any case they have done something that we regard as wrong."[5]

Following the impromptu summit, Roosevelt observed to Knox that Morgan's cavalier attitude mirrored perfectly the Wall Street perspective—"Mr. Morgan could not help regarding me as a big rival operator, who either intended to ruin all his interests or else could be induced to come to an agreement to ruin none."[6] The financier, he concluded, showed no poetry, honor, or imagination, but rather practiced the inevitable "fix it up" shortcut common to men who put dollars above all.

Morgan might have thought he had a right to a more generous reception from Roosevelt, whom he had supported in the 1898 gubernatorial campaign to the tune of a quiet $10,000 donation, about $365,000 in today's currency. Two years later, after capturing the vice presidency, Theodore, trying his hand at diplomacy, had organized a dinner for Morgan at Manhattan's swank Union League Club. "It represents an effort on my part to become a conservative man, in touch with the influential classes," he told Root, tongue only partly in cheek, "and I think I deserve encouragement."[7] Morgan, moreover, the astute financier of railroads, steel syndicates, and coal companies, could claim to be an indispensable architect of American modernization, power, and prestige. That his tactics and strategies produced great concern among farmers, wage earners, and other small-scale producers in the country, however, seemed to escape him. These groups, historically on the side of laissez-faire, now wished for the central state to step in and tame the trusts.

Following his February meeting with Morgan, Roosevelt withdrew from an active role in the Northern Securities case, as the legal process took its course. Knox filed the formal complaint in March (Morgan publicly listed among the defendants) and the case concluded in the Supreme Court two years later. There, a 5–4 majority sustained an earlier circuit court ruling that Morgan, Harriman, and Hill's railroad consortium violated the Sherman Antitrust Act. Though a sliver of a decision, the public and the press thought it a resounding victory for democracy. "Even Morgan no longer rules the earth," the *Literary Digest* proclaimed, while New York's *Evening Post* perhaps too optimistically declared that "the most far-reaching benefit of the decision is the vindication of national control." Some questioned, however, Roosevelt's apparent willingness to enlarge the executive office's scope to take on the barons—and saw him, not Morgan, as the republic's real threat. "Imagine the Demagogue as President, armed with all the legitimate power of an office grown greater than man had dreamed was possible," pondered the *New York World*. "He is Everything. He is Power. He is Patronage. He is Privilege."[8]

And he also knew how to hold a grudge. In July 1902, with the Northern Securities case just beginning to circulate through the bar, Associate Justice Horace Gray of Massachusetts, terminally ill, resigned from the Supreme Court. Wanting the Bay State to retain the seat, Lodge argued for the appointment of Oliver Wendell Holmes Jr., tall, thin, and lantern-jawed with radiant light-blue eyes and a silvering handlebar mustache. An impeccable Brahmin (his namesake father, a poet and doctor, had popularized the term in an 1860 *Atlantic Monthly* article on the old New England gentry), thrice-wounded Civil War veteran, and since 1899 chief justice of the Massachusetts Supreme Court, Holmes thoroughly impressed Roosevelt. The president, in a July 10 communication to Lodge, noted particularly the jurist's habit of keeping a prudent distance from the capitalists:

> The labor decisions which have been criticized by some of the big railroad men and other members of large corporations constitute to my mind a strong point in Judge Holmes' favor. The ablest lawyers and greatest judges are men whose past has naturally brought them into close relationship with the wealthiest and most powerful clients, and I am glad when I can find a judge who has been able to preserve his aloofness of mind so as to keep his broad humanity of feeling and his sympathy for the class from which he has not drawn his clients.[9]

Roosevelt did, however, retain a single reservation. "Now I should like to know that Judge Holmes was in entire sympathy with our views," he told Lodge, "before I would feel justified in appointing him." Assurances forthcoming, the appointment followed a few weeks later.[10]

But Holmes's minority dissent in the Northern Securities case soured his relations with Roosevelt. Prior to the court's decision the President had written to his eldest son, Ted, "Judge Holmes . . . is a great jurist and constructive statesman and one of the most interesting men I have ever met." Afterward he complained to Lodge, "Holmes should have been an ideal man on the bench. As a matter of fact he has been a bitter disappointment."[11]

Years later, in the winter of 1921, Holmes's thoughts returned to the old battle over Morgan's empire. "It broke up our incipient friendship," he wrote an English colleague of the president's reaction, "as he looked on my dissent to the *Northern Securities* case as a political departure (or, I suspect, more truly, couldn't forgive anyone who stood in his way). We talked freely later but it never was the same after that, and if he had not been restrained by [a] friend, I am told that he would have made a fool of himself and would have excluded me from the White House. . . . I never cared a damn whether I went there or not."[12]

Roosevelt's record as an anti-monopolist is mixed. Believing himself capable of discerning a "good trust" (say, United States Steel) from a "bad trust" (say, Standard Oil), he recognized how a conspicuous case—à la Northern Securities—might put the public at ease and place the corporations on warning without him having to do much axe wielding. Appearances meant something, and the cyclonic Roosevelt, with several cooperative newspaper editors in his pocket, seized the sobriquet "trustbuster" for his administration's initiation of more than forty antitrust suits in seven and a half years. The succeeding Taft administration, by contrast, though filing nearly a hundred suits in but a single term, never earned such accolades.

Attentive to his legacy, Roosevelt wrote to an aide, "The Northern Securities suit is one of the great achievements of my administration."[13] Eager to burnish his credentials, the new president looked for signal successes both at home and abroad. His rapid path to the White House, he knew, had stemmed from the Spanish-American War, and trouble in any part of the country's emerging empire might cast doubt on that conflict.

31

Bred of Empire

For three years the Philippine-American War (1899–1902) devastated the archipelago and called into question McKinley's sunny assertion that the U.S. mission amounted to a blessing of "benevolent assimilation." In practice this meant facilitating the Filipino transition to civil rule—from Catholic, Latin colonialism, its sponsors insisted, to Protestant, English liberties—while maintaining the islands as a military asset to open the elusive China market dominated at the time by Japan and a handful of European nations. During the conflict, Roosevelt repeatedly stressed that should the Philippine people "desire independence they shall have it," though such promises came with the caveat that "of course there is always the possibility that they may themselves behave in such a fashion as to put it off indefinitely."[1]

Anti-imperialist sentiment in the United States condemned the war, seeing a cruel irony in the country's assuming a Pacific empire after so loudly denouncing Spain's subjugation of Cuba. South Dakota's first senator, Silver Republican Richard Pettigrew, wrote contemptuously to McKinley, "The blood of . . . boys sacrificed in that contest must be laid at the door of your administration, and that impartial history must place you among the most dishonored of rulers in all time."[2] Though fighting, primarily of the guerrilla kind, would continue, U.S. military success against the Filipino Army in 1899 at the Battle of Manila, led by Major General Arthur MacArthur Jr., was followed by the establishment in 1900 of a commission to organize a civilian government in the Philippines. William Howard Taft, a federal judge and dean of the University of Cincinnati law school, was summoned by McKinley to the

White House, so he thought, to be offered a recently vacated Supreme Court seat, but instead found himself on a boat to Manila. The following year he became governor-general of the Philippines. In company with McKinley and Secretary of War Root, he oversaw the Philippine theater prior to Roosevelt's presidency.

Throughout the conflict the press printed stories, often based on letters written by astonished soldiers to their families, of American misconduct. Evidence of water torture and mutilation, arson and indiscriminate killing, were brought to light, much to the embarrassment of both the military and the McKinley administration. While the army of the Philippine Republic sustained about twenty thousand casualties, the number of civilians killed reached into the hundreds of thousands, most of these due to war-related disease and famine. Among a minority of Americans, Mark Twain felt ashamed. "I have seen," he told a *New York Herald* reporter in October 1900, "that we do not intend to free, but to subjugate the people of the Philippines. We have gone there to conquer, not to redeem."[3]

Roosevelt assumed the presidency nearly a year before the official end of the war in June 1902. In its wake he faced sharp questions regarding atrocities and worried that they—both the questions and the atrocities—might threaten his path to the nomination in 1904. As this debate took shape, he crossed swords with Nelson A. Miles, the last commanding general of the U.S. Army, a position formerly held by George Washington and Ulysses S. Grant, among others. An old warhorse in his early sixties, Miles had won the Medal of Honor for courage at the Civil War Battle of Chancellorsville and later fought in the last Indian Wars. In the latter conflict his subordinates had perpetrated, without his permission, the killing of Hunkpapa leader Sitting Bull and the subsequent massacre of at least 250 Lakota people (against 25 army dead) near Wounded Knee Creek on the Pine Ridge Reservation in South Dakota in December 1890. During the Spanish-American War, Miles had led the successful invasion of Puerto Rico.

Eyeing the White House, Miles, so Roosevelt contended, had wanted to challenge McKinley for the Republican nomination in 1900 and had invited the hero of Kettle Hill to be his running mate. "His estimate of the political situation," Theodore later wrote to Root in confidence, "was utterly fatuous." Roosevelt and Miles openly clashed in late 1901 when the latter, possibly appealing to the anti-imperialist vote in the hope of running as a Democrat in 1904, was suspected of leaking sensitive Philippine War documents to congressmen and newspapers. Privately, the new president denounced "these utterly baseless slanders against the army," and more publicly dressed down the general at a White House reception in December. "Mr. Roosevelt," so the *Army and Navy Register* observed, "approached General Miles in a manner which, without exaggeration, may be described as savage."[4]

Three months later, in March 1902, Miles spoke to the former Kentucky congressman and Louisville *Courier-Journal* editor Henry Watterson, a Democrat eager to make Roosevelt a single-term president. The interview quickly shaded toward conspiracy and cover-up, the general alleging that army atrocities in the Philippines were being concealed. Taking up his pen, an angry Roosevelt wrote to Miles, "I do not like the clear implication ... that brutalities have been committed by our troops in the Philippines," before reminding him that "in the Wounded Knee fight the troops under your command killed squaws and children as well as unarmed Indians." He followed this up with two seething letters to Root, lashing out at Miles while defending the army's—and thus his administration's—record: "The warfare in the Philippines has been conducted by our troops with very great leniency." Shortly thereafter he wrote to a friendly journalist from the New York *Evening Post*, "General Miles' usefulness is at an end and he must go."[5]

And indeed, the following year Miles was gone—though not because of Roosevelt's wrath, but for having reached the mandatory retirement age of sixty-four. Were he a younger man, he would in any case have fallen afoul of the General Staff Act of 1903, initiated by Root in response to the slow mobilization of U.S. forces against Spain and the drift among nations to follow the goose-stepping German model of a well-coordinated general staff. A rotating—no more than four years—chief of staff now replaced the commanding general position filled for nearly eight years by Miles.

While Roosevelt scuffled with this plumed and sashed nemesis, the Senate Committee on the Philippines, established in December 1899 to oversee administration in the archipelago, had begun referring questions of U.S. atrocities to the upper chamber's Foreign Relations Committee, chaired by Lodge. In the spring of 1902, this body was charged with reviewing multiple accusations from military personnel regarding incidences of torture and executions. Damaging testimony quickly came to light in the genocide trial of Marine Corps major Littleton Waller; following the ambush of U.S. troops at the Battle of Balangiga in September 1901, he had been tasked by Brigadier General Jacob H. Smith with subduing the civilian population on the island of Samar in the Eastern Visayas. As a result, 2,000 to 2,500 Filipinos were killed. "I want no prisoners," Smith told him. "I wish you to kill and burn, the more you kill and burn the better it will please me. I want all persons killed who are capable of bearing arms in actual hostilities against the United States." When asked by Waller to be more precise on the age limit for killings and executions, Smith replied, "Ten years." Thinking this order immoral, Waller cautioned one Captain Porter, "I've had instructions to kill everyone over ten years old. But we are not making war on women and children, only on men capable of bearing arms. Keep that in mind no matter what other orders you receive." Waller was later tried for murder in ordering the executions without trial of eleven Filipinos. A court-martial board acquitted the accused officer, deemed the "Butcher of Samar" in some American newspapers.[6]

In April Smith confessed—leading to his court-martial and conviction—to having ordered the slaughter, an outrage that Roosevelt had known about for months and, along with Root and Taft, had kept quiet, believing the military could more quickly end the insurrection if allowed to conduct a campaign against the Philippine Republic without questions from a probing free press. One might say that the four most important Republicans of the period 1901 to 1912—Roosevelt, Lodge, Root, and Taft—fought vigorously, cohesively, to protect their party's and their own reputations by concealing or shielding testimony outlining American atrocities in the archipelago. Collectively they had little faith in the future of self-government on the islands. Taft called the Filipinos "magnificent liars" who were a century away from "realiz[ing] . . . Anglo-Saxon liberty," while Lodge doubted the wisdom of home rule. "That we must try the experiment sooner or later I have no doubt," he wrote Roosevelt in July, "but I do feel that it is of the utmost importance to move very slowly. In all history no Asiatic people have established a representative government until Japan tried it, and their experiment has not been a very brilliant success." That same month Roosevelt told the prominent theologian Lyman Abbott that he had little hesitancy in carrying out "our plain duty to the people's suffering from barbarism by removing barbarism." A little indignant at having to endure the slings and arrows of the anti-imperialists, he wanted a bit of gratitude instead. "I question if any three peoples have ever owed more to another nation than the Filipinos, Cubans and Porto Ricans owe us for what we have done during the last three years."[7]

By this time, the summer of 1902, critics of America's new empire were running out of steam. Lodge's committee had brought to light numerous atrocities carried out against American soldiers—including drownings, roastings, and dismemberments—while Roosevelt employed the patriotic Fourth of July holiday to issue a proclamation declaring the cessation of hostilities in the Philippines, except in "the country inhabited by the Moro tribes." These Muslim peoples to the south, descended from Malayans, Indians, and Arabs, held out until 1913 when defeated at the Battle of Bud Bagsak by an American force led by General John Pershing.

Importantly, that same July Congress passed the Philippine Organic Act, which provided for the appurtenances of self-rule—including the establishment of the Philippine Assembly and an independent judiciary—while lodging the preponderance of power in Taft's Philippine Commission. The public seemed eager to move on. For Roosevelt, having seen America's three-year Pacific war to a successful conclusion and taken on the Northern Securities trust, his capacity for the presidency seemed beyond question. He might have hoped for a quiet end to a demanding year; instead, he got a coal strike that threatened the winter's fuel supply.

32

King Coal

While Roosevelt seethed over General Miles and the anti-imperialists, a strike in eastern Pennsylvania's rugged anthracite region began attracting national attention. The area—on former Susquehannock Indian lands and site of a coal economy since the 1770s—had drawn a steady wave of Welsh, Irish, English, and German immigrants following the Civil War, along with smaller concentrations of Polish, Ukrainian, Hungarian, Slovak, and Italian peoples. Some 800,000 now lived there. The strike began in May 1902 with employees asking for increased wages (stuck on $560 per annum, $20,000 in today's dollars), decreased hours, and, most odious to quarry owners, recognition of the United Mine Workers of America (UMWA) as the authorized agent to bargain on their behalf.[1] When, after several weeks of futile negotiations, these conditions went unmet, 147,000 men walked off their jobs. In past work stoppages, public opinion had reflexively backed capital, but in the altered climate of what was coming to be known as progressive reform, the miners received a more sympathetic hearing. Who, an increasing number of Americans began to ask, were a few distant titans to control the fuel and heating needs of millions?

Throughout the spring, Roosevelt watched with growing concern as the two sides maneuvered without reaching a resolution; at this time, he saw no opportunity to intervene in a thus far peaceful disagreement. Negotiating for the miners, UMWA president John Mitchell, a young, second-generation Irish immigrant, orphaned at the age of six, proved a pragmatic, resourceful advocate for labor. He counseled arbitration, appeared willing to negotiate on the question of union recognition, and kept crews of pump men in the mines to prevent flooding. Philadelphia and Reading Railroad president George Baer, thickly goateed with hooded eyes fronting an even expression, spoke for the mine owners. An arrogant paternalism clouded his judgment, and in certain on-high asides—"The rights and interests of the laboring man will be protected and cared for, not by the labor agitators, but by the Christian men to whom God in His infinite wisdom has given the control of the property interests of the country"—he appeared stuck in the receding nineteenth century.[2]

Inevitably, violence carried out by both sides began to overtake the coalfield communities. These clashes included several murders, various riots, and the occasional wrecked train, blown-up bridge, or other form of property damage. Governor William Stone sent state troops to mill about the region with a shoot-to-kill pledge against provocateurs. By late summer, Roosevelt, with an eye on the barren negotiations, the coming fall elections, and the looming winter calendar, turned to Philander Knox, asking his attorney general, "What is the reason we cannot proceed against the coal operators as being engaged in a trust? I ask because it is a question continually being asked of me."[3] Knox replied that the Supreme Court would never countenance such a move (the Northern Securities case had yet to be adjudicated), though the president perhaps considered primarily the possibility of his own intervention.

Days later, Roosevelt began a two-week New England swing on behalf of GOP candidates in which he gave several speeches critical of unreflective capitalism. "The great corporations which we have grown to speak of rather loosely as trusts are the creatures of the State," he told a crowd in Providence, Rhode Island, "and the State not only has the right to control them, but it is in duty bound to control them wherever the need of such control is shown. There is clearly a need of supervision . . . wherever, as in our own country at the present time, business corporations become so very powerful alike for beneficent work and for work that is not always beneficent."[4] This kind of Rooseveltian finger-wagging raised concerns among some Republicans, though the public reacted positively and this no doubt convinced TR to continue making control of the corporations a campaign theme for a party unaccustomed to doing so.

And then suddenly, on September 3, in Pittsfield, Massachusetts, the president nearly lost his life. Following a morning speech in the city's Park Square, Roosevelt was joined in a four-horse open barouche by his secretary George Cortelyou, Governor Winthrop Crane, and the Scottish-born William Craig, a rather large secret service officer who, while in the Royal Horse Guards of the British Army, had protected Queen Victoria. As the presidential carriage moved through town, a speeding trolley conveying Pittsfield Electric Street Railway officials keen to meet Roosevelt rounded a curve and smashed it to pieces. Craig, present in Buffalo the previous year at McKinley's assassination, was crushed by the trolley, the first secret service agent to die while protecting a president (Leslie Coffelt, mortally wounded by three bullets while defending Truman against an assault in front of Blair House in Washington, D.C., in 1950, being the only other).[5]

The crash threw Roosevelt out of the carriage onto his front. His face, lips, and clothing were by turns bruised, cut, and covered in mud. The enraged president had to be restrained from attacking the streetcar driver, Euclid Madden, who later pled guilty to manslaughter and served six months in jail. Despite his furious reaction, Roosevelt was in bad shape. Though offering a sporting reply to a professionally concerned King Edward VII—"My hurts were trivial"—and determined to campaign in the Midwest, he soon discovered the debilitating extent of his injuries. While in Indianapolis on the twenty-third, his throbbing left leg became too painful for him to continue. Physicians discovered an abscess and immediately operated, draining the laceration to prevent blood poisoning; given a local anesthetic, the famous patient chatted happily through the operation. Two days earlier Henry Adams, following Roosevelt's travails in the press, had written to a confidant that the idea of his good friend John Hay assuming the executive office (with the country bereft of a vice president, the secretary of state stood next in line) "caused me to grin at the ways of men . . . and Teddies," though he acknowledged the seemingly indestructible nature of the gentleman Rough Rider—"I could not quite seem to grapple with the idea of Theodore's becoming a serious corpse."[6]

Though consigned for the time being to a wheelchair, Roosevelt, having heard from eastern governors and mayors of impending trouble should the coal strike continue into the winter, moved in early October to reach a resolution. Asserting a presidential prerogative, he wrote to Mitchell, the miners' representative, on the first, "The failure of the coal supply . . . has become a matter of vital concern to the whole nation." Two days later Roosevelt and Knox, insisting on arbitration, met with Mitchell, other UMWA representatives, and the presidents and chairmen of three railroads, including Baer. Addressing the group, the president, his mending leg conspicuously propped up, opened by articulating what he called the Square Deal, a critique of plutocracy and its tendency to smother opportunity among the working class. "I wish to call your attention," he said, "to the fact that there are three parties affected by the situation in the anthracite trade—the operators, the miners, and the general public. I speak for neither the operators nor the miners, but for the general public."[7]

Baer was upset at the presidential invitation to meet. He wanted no part of arbitration and seemed intent on sabotaging the proceedings by snubbing Mitchell, whom he indecorously called "a criminal" leading a band of "mutineers." The attempt to reach a solution at this point accordingly failed. "What my next move will be I cannot yet say," Roosevelt wrote Mark Hanna later that day. "I feel most strongly that the attitude of the operators is one which accentuates the need of the Government having some power of supervision and regulation over such corporations." Infuriated by the "wooden-headed obstinacy and stupidity" he encountered from the capital side of the table, he said of Baer, "If it weren't for the high office I hold, I would have chucked him out of that window."[8]

Though frustrated, Roosevelt managed to accomplish more than he perhaps realized. Unlike previous presidents who at times had sent in soldiers to put down striking workers, he treated the union's representatives with respect as proper partners in the bargaining process. Hardly pro-union, he believed, rather, that the corporations were radicalizing public opinion, carelessly cutting their own throats by adopting, so he told Hanna, "a fairly hopeless attitude" that, if unchecked, would bring about "grave disaster."[9] Moving aggressively, he confided to a few high-placed officials, including Governor Strong, that in the name of maintaining public order he was prepared to send troops into Pennsylvania to operate the mines. With this provocative news rippling through Washington, the Indiana Republican representative James Watson met with Roosevelt to discuss the anthracite issue. According to the congressman:

> I asked the President what he intended to do provided he could not either coax them into arbitration or force them into it, to which he

replied with his characteristic vehemence: "I am President of the United States, I am the Commander in chief of the Army, I will seize the mines by military force, I will operate them by military power. I will give the people coal."[10]

When queried by Watson about the Constitution and the problem of seizing private property without due process of law, Roosevelt refused to flinch. "The Constitution was made for the people"—he stopped and faced the congressman—"and not the people for the Constitution."[11]

Days later, Roosevelt's threat bore fruit. Root, meeting with the ubiquitous J. P. Morgan on October 11, explained that the miners were willing to go back immediately if the operators agreed to arbitration by a five-person commission (subsequently enlarged to seven). A target of the administration in the ongoing Northern Securities case, Pierpont pressed Baer and his colleagues to agree to mediation. Apparently the big stick worked in domestic as well as foreign affairs.

One hurdle, however, still had to be overcome. The mine operators refused to countenance the idea of a "labor man" on the commission, and this seemed for a few days a possible deal-breaker; but they made room at last for an "eminent sociologist" among the seven and left it to Roosevelt to choose. He duly appointed Edgar E. Clark, head of the railway conductors' union and formerly, following a stint taking classes at Williams College, a brakeman on the Denver and Rio Grande Western Railroad. "To my intense relief," the president wrote Governor Crane, "this utter absurdity" of passing Clark off as an academic "was received."[12] The owners knew, of course, about Clark's labor background, and perhaps considered this appointment their inevitable compromise, as long as it did not look like they were giving in to the workers.

On October 23 the strike ended, the men returned to the mines, and the commission—including a Roman Catholic bishop, a brigadier-general, and a retired coal operator—went to work. It toured the coal communities in question, accumulated data on the cost of living, and took the testimonies of hundreds of people. Clarence Darrow, later to become one of the century's most famous lawyers for defending the Chicago teenage killers Nathan Leopold and Richard Loeb and for battling William Jennings Bryan in the Scopes Monkey Trial, gave the closing argument for the miners. Baer, delivering the operators' summation, remained tone-deaf: "These men don't suffer," he said of the workers, "why, hell, half of them don't even speak English."[13]

The following March the commission sent its report to Roosevelt. The settlement included concessions for both sides—the miners received a 10 percent pay increase and saw their workday reduced to nine hours, with an arrangement of arbitration for future disputes; the operators were pleased that the UMWA did not receive formal recognition and that the report strongly condemned strike-associated violence.

By establishing a commission and convincing the operators to abide by its decision, Roosevelt, pushed along by the progressive tide, managed a significant feat. The old ideology of American workers as autonomous and free to bargain individually for the value of their sweat and skills remained a holdover from an agrarian era, even as the industrial age with its massive factory force rendered such quaint creeds obsolete. Owners had continued to assert a classical liberal heritage of "free" markets and opportunity, even as competition-crushing monopolies came to predominate. Between roughly 1900 and 1935, however, classical liberalism evolved into New Deal liberalism, and Roosevelt's Square Deal played a significant role in this process. Under the president's direction, labor joined industry—and consumers—as a vital interest with a seat at the nation's negotiating table. The anthracite strike further stressed the government's new status as a broker, operating in the name of the people and no longer willing to sit on the sidelines while capital and labor periodically went to war.

Roosevelt understood, as few of his predecessors had, the potential of the presidency to affect public policy. "The strike certainly would not have been settled," he wrote one correspondent, "if I had not interfered."[14] By his actions TR garnered considerable popular support, in turn altering the balance of power in Washington. Congress had since the Civil War tended to dominate the nation's policymaking. The election of nonentities (Hayes and Harrison), the assassinations of three executives (Lincoln, Garfield, and McKinley), and the inability of any president after 1876 to complete consecutive terms all served to sustain Capitol Hill's hegemony. Only a little more than a year into his presidency, however, Roosevelt had augmented his office's stature, initiating a trend that has yet to end.

Part V

CULT OF CHARISMA

Theodore is never sober, only he is drunk with himself and not with rum.

                          Henry Adams, 1902

Roosevelt in the White House:
"I have enjoyed every moment of this so-called arduous and exacting task."

33

A Gentleman's Place

The Roosevelt White House, filled with children, trembled with energy. In 1901 when the family moved in, they ranged in age from seventeen-year-old Alice to a not-quite-four Quentin, high-spirited and known as his mother's "fine bad little boy." A generation had passed since Abram, Irvin, and Mollie Garfield briefly graced 1600 Pennsylvania Avenue during their father's six-month tenure in office (truncated by Charles Guiteau's whistling bullets), after which the building had long lacked for adolescent zest. The Roosevelts, by contrast, completely took over the house and grounds. The upstairs bedrooms were crammed with offspring; the lawns housed ducks, dogs, and cats along with more exotic animalia including Algonquin the pony, Maude the pig, and a blue macaw named Eli Yale in honor of the university's primary benefactor.[1] Considering this lively occupancy, it seems fitting that the residence's official name shifted early in Roosevelt's tenancy, from the slightly forbidding Executive Mansion to the less formal White House, a rechristening emphasized in all subsequent invitation cards and letterheads. An indefatigably social creature, the president liberally entertained, holding a plenitude of parties and receptions, dances and dinners. Always, though often to Edith's chagrin, generous with accommodations, he spent much of his salary on sumptuous Pennsylvania Avenue gatherings, chatting up politicians, newspapermen, writers, and artists.

With nearly equal interest, Roosevelt embraced the possibilities of neighboring Rock Creek Park, a hiking and riding enclave just north of the city. The nation's third national park, its nearly 1,800 acres acted like a magnet upon Roosevelt, who often practiced some manner of bullying or cajoling in convincing others to troop along—sun, snow, or slush—in his rambunctious wake. The *Washington Post* reporter Henry Litchfield West remembered that the president "occasionally invited foreign ambassadors to accompany him," apparently conceding little to age, fitness, or footwear. After one "merry chase up and down hill," the would-be Olympian-in-chief laughingly described a rather helpless member of a forced march as "very soft! very soft!"[2]

Among the higher-placed dragooned, ambassador Sir Mortimer Durand, a po-faced veteran of the British Raj come to represent the king's empire in Washington, left a memoir selectively laced with humiliation. Rumored to be an excellent rider with an interest in cricket, he failed to see the point in treating a metropolitan park as a jungle gym. His reflection offers a window into Roosevelt's forty-year childhood:

> We drove out to the Rock Creek . . . and [the President] then plunged down the *khud* [ravine] and made me struggle through bushes and over rocks for two hours and a half, at an impossible speed, till I was so done that I could hardly stand. His great delight is rock climbing, which is my weak-point. I disgraced myself completely, and my arms and shoulders are still stiff with dragging myself up by roots and ledges. At one place I fairly stuck, and could not get over the top till he caught me by the collar and hauled at me. He is certainly a "strenuous" man all through. He was dripping with sweat, his clothes frayed by the rocks and bushes and covered with dirt, but he was happy as a school-boy. We talked chiefly about war and shooting. . . . He did almost all the talking, to my great relief, for I had no breath to spare.[3]

Another companion, Jean Jules Jusserand, longtime French ambassador to the U.S. (1902–1924), a scholar, author, and heir to a wealthy Lyonnais family fortune, observed in a memoir that "what the President called a walk was a run"; curious onlookers, he continued, drawn to the recreating Roosevelt, "alighted from their carriages and followed us a distance." If pursued too closely the former Rough Rider might approach his admirers and, with a tip of the cap and cordial bow, "ask . . . them kindly to desist."[4]

Though the presidential mansion was redolent of historical suggestion—Jefferson had planned the Lewis and Clark expedition within its walls, Dolley Madison fled ("And now, dear sister, I must leave this house") with a portrait of George Washington before the invading British, and Lincoln had signed the Emancipation Proclamation in his second-floor office following three hours of New Year's Day handshaking—the century-old structure, first occupied in 1800 by John and Abigail Adams, looked every bit its age. Designed to house the head of state for a small agrarian republic, it now served as the nerve center of a sprawling industrial nation. As a space for entertaining foreign and domestic dignitaries, and accommodating the executive office, it had become shabbily inadequate, more creaky hotel than hive of empire. The upper floors presented a crazy quilt of inharmonious alterations over the decades, while the basement emitted a butcher shop scent mingled with the unmistakable fetor of a Potomac fish market. Alice Roosevelt, one of the inhabitants, described the house as "really rather ugly.... I have memories of hideous dark rooms and of Tiffany glass." The place contained, she continued, "acres of... overwrought gilt furniture.... It was what could only be described as late Grant and early Pullman."[5]

The building's many inadequacies compelled Congress, in June 1902, to appropriate $475,000 ($16.7 million in today's money) to retain the distinguished New York architectural firm McKim, Mead & White to renovate the space.[6] Their work included the beautiful old Pennsylvania Station (1910–1963) in Midtown Manhattan, the Beaux-Arts Brooklyn Museum, and the main campus of Columbia University. Eager to return the structure to its classic simplicity, Charles McKim, egg-headed with pinned-back ears and piercing eyes, took the lead in working with the Roosevelts to purge the house of its unhappy hodgepodge of Victorian-era cushions and drapes, yellowing wallpaper, and tumescent furniture.

The president had proposed to keep his family in the mansion during renovations, while outsourcing his office a mile or so northwest on Massachusetts Avenue to the recently completed Townsend House. Within days of beginning construction, however, this brave plan collapsed in a thick cloud of plaster powder. "The house is torn to pieces," McKim noted of the hullabaloo. "Bedlam let loose does not compare with it." Accordingly, the Roosevelts took alternate digs at Jackson Place, a modest brick and stone row residence on Lafayette Square, prior to a prudent summer decampment to Oyster Bay.[7]

Returning on October 1 to what was supposed to be a finished White House, Roosevelt discovered instead a vast work in progress; the East and West Wings remained in triage while the grounds were a mess of pockets and craters. Delighted with the improvements to this point, he offered no complaints. Edith, by contrast, arriving in D.C. three days after her husband, looked with trepidation upon the chaos, a confusion of glaring white rooms lacking portraits and drapes, furniture, and flooring. The December social season neared and, assuring the First Lady a finished home, interior decorating companies from Boston (A. H. Davenport & Co., outfitter of James J. Hill's Minneapolis house, so yes, the president and his Northern Securities nemesis employed the same decorator) and New York (Herter Brothers, having done up the White House's Red Room during Grant's tenure) worked furiously over the next eight weeks to complete the décor.[8]

With the Roosevelts pinched at Jackson Place, either Edith or her husband was daily in contact with the contractors to press for progress. They were able to move in on November 4. As one historian notes, "Each of the seven bedrooms had its own bath, gleaming with white ceramic tile and shining with nickel plate"; fireplaces gave a cozy feel to these spaces while push-button devices signaling downstairs maids and footmen struck a more modern note. Alice claimed a room in the east hall, while her brothers and Ethel colonized the north side. A sitting room, ostensibly for Edith and situated beside her and Theodore's bedchamber, became a de facto family room, a place to share holidays, birthday parties, and more common day-to-day exchanges.[9]

On December 18 the renovations were finally completed, to mixed reviews. The new space, its once-simple Federal-style interior now decked out in imperial Georgian, appeared to those familiar with the old structure to be reaching for a finely wrought grandiosity. "The President," novelist Henry James sighed, "is distinctly tending—or trying—to make a 'court,'" while Henry Adams, whose forebears had lived in the White House and who had first trod its antebellum halls as a child in 1850, concurred. Given a personal tour in January 1903, he wrote to one confidant, "The house . . . is now quite a gentleman's place, mostly done in white, and where the safe white is abandoned for red and green velvet, less successful. The state dining-room in oak is charming. Theodore innocently delights in its space which dwarfs him. . . . Mrs. Roosevelt, I say, accepts the state-rooms with even more pleasure than Theodore does, and looks less lost in them, although she too needs a crown."[10]

More than merely refurbishing the existing structure, the upgrade carried out under Roosevelt literally extended the White House, tacking on the West Wing. A necessary innovation, it housed the nearly three dozen clerks, secretaries, and messengers required to make the executive branch operate efficiently. Just south of the addition, Roosevelt had a tennis court installed; an energetic if clumsy athlete, he loved playing doubles with his Tennis Cabinet, a rotating roster of aides, officials, and friends both old and new. Ambassador Jusserand, future secretary of war Henry Stimson, and former Yale All-American football player Pudge Heffelfinger were among the racket swingers.

Roosevelt used his new office intermittently, typically engaging in paperwork and staying in touch with his staff. He often held meetings in the White House proper and, when deviating from this, occasionally heard complaints from congressmen used to being welcomed to the president's home, rather than being shunted off to an adjoining office complex. Roosevelt continued to keep a study on the second floor of the residence, a room that received the bright south sun and accommodated a desk given by Queen Victoria to President Hayes carved from the HMS *Resolute*, a three-masted Arctic discovery ship trapped in ice in 1854 and recovered the following year by the American whaler *George Henry* outside of Baffin Bay. John F. Kennedy became the first president to use this desk in the West Wing.[11]

Built on the former site of horse stables and greenhouses—Kim's passion for a clean look overrode Edith's desire to keep an economizing nursery for White House events—the West Wing would undergo substantial changes. In 1909 Taft doubled its size (never among the svelte Tennis Cabinet clique, he shed few tears over the court's removal) and had the initial presidential Oval Office put in. A fire did considerable damage to this area during Herbert Hoover's administration, the first major blaze on the grounds since the War of 1812, resulting in its rebuilding, this time with air conditioning. Facing still more space constraints, Franklin Roosevelt later oversaw another significant renovation; the alterations included a set of subterranean offices. Today, most of the president's staff roosts across the street from the West Wing in the French Second Empire–style Eisenhower Executive Office Building, initiated during the Grant administration and completed in 1888.

The Roosevelts were pleased with their life in Washington, and the renovations only added to this satisfaction. In a letter to his eldest son, the president offered a glimpse into their genial routine:

Life is lovely here. The country is beautiful and I do not think that any two people ever got more enjoyment out of the White House than Mother and I. We love the House itself without and within, for its associations, for its stateliness and its simplicity. We love the garden. And we like Washington. We almost always take our breakfast on the south portico now [it being late May] . . . then we stroll about the garden for fifteen or twenty minutes looking at the flowers and the fountain and admiring the trees. Then I work until between four and five, usually having some official people to lunch—now a couple of Senators, now a couple of Ambassadors, now a literary man, now a capitalist or a labor leader, or a scientist, or a big-game hunter. If Mother wants to ride, we then spend a couple of hours on horseback.[12]

Invariably, these simple pleasures had their limits. Writing to yet another son, Kermit, Roosevelt allowed, "Lovely tho the White House is, it is not home; and Sagamore Hill is."[13]

Along with monitoring the Executive Mansion's extensive renovations, recuperating from leg surgery, and mediating the anthracite strike, Roosevelt observed with obvious interest the fall congressional elections. These proved entirely satisfying for the president as the GOP, in power and thus prone to lose seats in off-year balloting, enlarged its membership in both the House (198 to 206) and Senate (55 to 57). Even when accounting for the fact that the 1900 census increased the number of representatives, these results spoke of the party's popularity. Perhaps most gratifying to Roosevelt, the West—Bryan country and the cradle of the free-silver crusade—returned roughly a hundred thousand more votes for GOP candidates than it had in 1898. "I am well contented," Roosevelt wrote to a cousin, "with the elections."[14]

The campaign season having concluded, Roosevelt entrained for Smedes, Mississippi, about seventy-five miles northwest of Jackson, on what proved to be a disappointing hunting trip. On the morning of November 14, the president and his guide followed on horseback a pack of yapping dogs on the trail of a bear. After milling about for a few hours, they gave up and tramped back to camp. There they heard horns, and an approaching messenger declared their bear to be cornered some ten miles away. Racing to the site, Roosevelt discovered a scrawny, bloodied black bear tied to a willow tree. Though legend would long have it that

TR pardoned the creature—an epic replayed in the Thanksgiving ritual (since the tenure of George H. W. Bush) of offering the official Broad Breasted White turkey absolution—in fact, he merely refused to shoot the poor animal before riding off with an official injunction to "put it out of its misery." Another hunter quickly thrust a knife into the bear. "I have just had a most unsatisfactory experience," Roosevelt wrote of the hunt to a Colorado politician.[15]

Others, however, happily cashed in on the lavishly reported episode. The *Washington Post* cartoonist Clifford Berryman (of "Remember the Maine" fame) showed a compassionate Roosevelt "Drawing the Line in Mississippi" before a big-eared bear cub. The caricature inspired Morris Michtom, a Brooklyn candy shop owner, to manufacture a moppet-esque bear doll, which he sent to the president. Receiving Roosevelt's permission to use his name, Michtom began to mass-produce, to brisk sales, "Teddy's bears."

Their ubiquity bore evidence of the president's waxing status, a calculus registerable in ways both traditional (off-year elections) and novel (toy sales). Concluding a remarkably eventful early-presidential tenure, Roosevelt looked now, in the coming year, to tour much of the country, to engage with the electorate and register the depth of his impressive popularity. Seeking a sympathetic reception, the old Rough Rider entrained into the interior, pushing toward the Pacific.

34

Into the Heart

In the spring of 1903, following the conclusion of a special congressional session, Roosevelt commenced what came to be known as the Great Loop Tour, a twenty-five-state circuit through much of the western United States. In all, he traveled fourteen thousand miles and delivered more than 250 speeches, some being mere pit stops addressing starstruck assemblies lining a dusty railroad route, or, as in the case of one Des Moines audience, a crammed high school.[1] He left Washington the first week of April and returned the first week of June. Eager to emphasize the virtues of conservation, the president occupied sixteen agreeable days ambling about Yellowstone National Park, unwilling, though sorely tempted by the large number of roaming elk, to engage in a hunt on a federal reserve that might have resulted in negative publicity. He spent three additional days camping in Yosemite with the acclaimed Scottish-born naturalist John Muir, who looked, with a seven-inch beard tickling his chest, every bit the eco-mystic his "John of the Mountains" moniker suggested; the two posed reverently for an iconic photograph at majestic Glacier Point. Along the route, groups of former Rough Riders showed up at various stations to meet their old colonel, while elderly Civil War veterans, some in faded blue uniforms, strained to hear this latest president pontificate.

In the early republic, Washington, Monroe, and Jackson had conducted rather arduous presidential tours. These were largely horse-and-carriage affairs over often indifferent roads in unpredictable weather. Hardly vacations, these excursions were meant to advance certain aims and agendas. Astride a great white charger whenever entering a town (often accompanied by local militia), an image-conscious Washington strove to rally support for the new federal Constitution in the face of long-standing state loyalties. More generally, he gave to thousands of farmers, merchants, and homemakers a passing glimpse of the powdered hair, broad shoulders, and large straight nose haphazardly captured in illustrations innumerable. Monroe's 1817 and 1819 goodwill tours also sought to stress national unity, an imperative following the War of 1812, which had divided the country along sectional lines. Jackson's spring 1833 tour through New England and the mid-Atlantic states was similarly choreographed, coming directly after the president had quashed South Carolina's efforts to annul a federal tariff law in the name of states' rights. Many nationalists in Greater Boston now greeted the heretofore detested Jackson—a Tennessee slaveholder associated with certain small-government tendencies—with (mostly) open arms.

The pace of presidential tours picked up after the Civil War. Andrew Johnson, eager to sell his pro-southern vision of Reconstruction, made a disastrous 1866 "swing around the circle" during which professional hecklers hounded his every stop. Rutherford B. Hayes (bringing along William Tecumseh Sherman for star power) endured a seventy-one-day Great Western Tour in 1880. Grover Cleveland took a briefer three-week five-thousand-mile Goodwill Tour in 1887 that carried him as far south as Montgomery, as far west as Omaha, and as far north as St. Paul. Cleveland's successor, Benjamin Harrison, a former Union army general, made a nine-thousand-mile southern circuit in the spring of 1891; striking an ecumenical pose among white crowds, he told a gathering at El Paso that the war had "brought blessings to the victors and vanquished."[2]

As the latest executive on wheels, Roosevelt traveled decidedly in style aboard six railcars, two reserved for luggage. The posh presidential compartment—*Elysian*—sported mahogany furniture, tiled bathrooms, and a private kitchen commanded by a chef. Eager to block off boredom on the long evening stretches, Roosevelt brought along dozens of books.[3] Though having already made up his mind to run for a full term the following year, he refused to engage in an elaborate campaign tour. He shook all hands, met countless small-town Democratic chieftains along with their GOP compeers, and uttered nary a partisan line. Even so, the West tempted Republicans as a region ripe for the picking. Since the Civil War a solid South trafficking in Lost Cause hagiography and a (less solid) North fashioning its own iconography à la the apotheosis of Lincoln were the two major parties' sectional strongholds. But the West remained in play. In 1900 McKinley and his Rough Rider protégé had made serious inroads into what had been, only four years earlier, a Bryan free-silver bastion. Perhaps in traversing the Trans-Mississippi on an elaborate and hotly covered celebration of Americana by way of the Continental Divide, Roosevelt meant to capture the public's imagination, banishing the residue of Bryanism to the old Confederate states while seeing if the cult of Teddy might forge a fresh consensus in cowboy land.

Moving through the Upper Midwest and into the Great Plains, Roosevelt talked in very general terms about the tensions between capital and labor in America, and of the nation's new identity as a budding imperial power. He spoke from the back of his train (left hand gripping a steel support, right hand gesticulating for emphasis), as well as on stages and, in more impromptu moments, atop chairs and tables. He enunciated in a clipped, patrician accent pitched in a surprisingly (to audiences) high and not terribly tuneful key. When reading from a script he could fall into a rhythmic, singsongy cadence; he preferred a long "no" ("noo") and rolling, hard, and occasionally alliterative p's ("**pe**ople," "**p**ur**p**ose," "**p**ros**p**er"). Growing thicker of finger, jowl, and midriff since his not-so-distant Rough Rider turn, he sometimes complained of the sedentary life of the desk jockey. Aside from the added pounds, audiences would have noticed the encroachment of salt in his formerly pepper mustache and perhaps a soupçon of silver around his perpetually tanned temples.

Entering the Badlands, where he had graduated from eastern dude to (pretend) western ranchman, Roosevelt indulged in the tour's sole sentimental journey. Fittingly, his train pulled up at tiny Medora, where he had arrived twenty summers ago to hunt, as he had said at the time, "in Dacotah."[4] He now shook hands, spoke briefly, and engaged in a few minutes of awkward chat, the distance in circumstances between the locals and their once-young hero having only grown over the years.

Exiting Montana on April 8, Roosevelt's locomotive descended into the northwestern corner of Wyoming, arriving at Yellowstone, the nation's first national park (1872). Reading, horseback riding, and calling on Old Faithful occupied the president during his two-week respite. Taking up his official duties again, TR moved east on what he called a "very hard and rather monotonous" journey through Nebraska and Iowa into Missouri. Along the route he gave dozens of addresses before cheering crowds, and though, so he told John Hay, "I admired the thrift and indeed the beauty both of the country and the towns," he acknowledged that this sea of sodbusters and second-generation pioneers, garnished in their ocher-colored calicos and indifferently fitting sack coats, at last blended together—"I could not to save my neck differentiate one town from another or one crowd from another." The presidential party continued on, looping back and heading west again into Kansas, where he shared a Sunday service songbook with "two very nice little girls . . . their brown sunburned . . . arms and faces had been scrubbed till they almost shone," before rolling into Colorado on a clear morning. To his minor embarrassment the state's governor and a small congress of Rough Rider emeriti greeted him at the first rail stop with a cooked breakfast at the ready. "It seemed absurd," he wrote to a colleague, "to get off and eat at the tail end of a chuck wagon in a top hat and a frock coat."[5] But of course he did.

After scooting through the "waterless desert country" of New Mexico, the President crossed into Arizona, making the obligatory stop at the Grand Canyon, a formation "wonderful and beautiful beyond description," so he wrote his daughter Ethel. In slightly more prosaic language, he told Hay of touring the canyon "with an assorted collection of Rough Riders, most of them with homicidal pasts," an overstated but not entirely untrue allusion to the difficulties some of his former soldiers had faced upon returning home from the war. Evoking his Egyptian journals and European diaries, penned in youth and dotted with occasionally self-conscious strains of poetry, Roosevelt now reached for something suitably elegiac, writing that the canyon "is beautiful and terrible and unearthly. It made me feel as if I were gazing at a sunset of strange and awful splendor."[6]

From Arizona Roosevelt journeyed to Los Angeles, arriving on May 8, and finding Southern California a "wonderful paradise—a veritable hotbed of fruits and flowers." Eager to appraise the state's preeminent educational facilities, he visited both the University of California at Berkeley ("the greatest") and, days later, Stanford University ("singularly beautiful in architecture and surroundings"). Greeted in San Francisco by sixty thousand shrieking schoolchildren lined up along the city's main streets and avenues, he was regaled with a "bellowing hospitality and passed," so he said, "three wild days." From the city's board of trade, he received a gold goblet to go along with the greater haul of vases, tankards, medals, figurines, canes, and drinking cups—as well as a plump badger ("Josiah") from a young Kansas girl—accumulated on the trip. At Yosemite he experienced the "solemn temple of the giant sequoias" with Muir, the two sharing a sudden snowstorm in a thick grove of silver fir. "Camping with the President was a memorable experience," a smitten Muir later wrote to friends. "I fairly fell in love with him."[7]

Continuing north, Roosevelt met a throng—150,000 strong—in Portland, Oregon, before sailing the Puget Sound to Seattle, a Pacific boomtown whose population of 80,000 would more than triple over the next decade. The president's prediction to Hay, however—"I suppose our children will see . . . Seattle containing a million inhabitants"—has yet to materialize, the 2020 census finding 737,000 in the Emerald City. He described the Northwest more generally as redolent of England's wet coastal climate yet producing a distinctly novel American character type: "I think [they] . . . will be different—will in the end represent a new type on this continent."[8]

The casual wonders of the trip left a deep impression on TR. He remembered the old Kansas man, a Civil War veteran, who told him that "forty years ago today I was in Chancellorsville"; he noted how "many of the leading men in Utah," despite their Mormon "ages of faith," also revealed a "most materialistic common sense"; and he thoroughly enjoyed the various regional buffets of pies and cakes, meats and creams, breads and butters—the results of which could be glimpsed in a seventeen-pound weight gain. He endured countless renditions of "Hail to the Chief" accompanied by a seemingly endless quota of compliments, hands, and second helpings, all of which he politely took, shook, and too seldom forsook.[9]

Though the canned addresses Roosevelt delivered on tour tended to traffic in banalities—dealing, so the *Wisconsin State Journal* yawned, in "decency, with common sense, and useful, plain strong living"—they could not mask the president's evident pride in recognizing the power of his office. He knew both the value and responsibility of putting on a good show. "At each stop there were the usual audiences of grizzled, bearded, elderly men," he wrote Hay, "of smooth-faced, shy, hulking young men; of older women either faded and dragged or exceedingly brisk and capable; and of robust, healthy, high-spirited girls. Most of these people habitually led rather gray lives, and they came in to see the President much as they would have come in to see a circus. It was something to talk over and remember and tell their children."[10]

On August 12, just three days after writing these reflections to Hay, Roosevelt learned that the Colombian Senate had unanimously rejected a treaty negotiated earlier that year by the secretary of state giving the United States authorization to build a canal through the Colombian province of Panama. Over the next three months Roosevelt chafed, intrigued, and made the canal a top priority. Coming home from his western tour "feeling pretty well tired," so he told daughter Alice, he now moved alertly, methodically, through the fall, eager to be the hidden hand of revolution.[11]

35

Taking Panama

Roosevelt's interest in Panama predated his presidency. In 1898, following the war in Cuba, Secretary of State Hay, operating under McKinley's auspices, undertook negotiations with Great Britain to conclude a new canal pact. The old Clayton-Bulwer Treaty of 1850, intended to lessen tensions between the two countries, had committed its signatories to each gaining the consent of the other prior to constructing an interoceanic waterway in Central America, and further guaranteed this artery would be unfortified and open to all shipping on a neutral basis. And then other things—the Crimean War, the U.S Civil War, the Scramble for Africa, and so on—preoccupied both nations. France, on the other hand, noting the recent completion of Egypt's Suez Canal, moved in 1881 to build its sister waterway in the Colombian province of Panama. This proved a fool's errand of epic proportions. Engineering challenges, a debilitating climate, and a strikingly high death rate among workers doomed the project—but only for the time being. For in June 1902 the United States, now a two-ocean power, purchased French interests in Panama for $40 million, about $1.4 billion in today's dollars. In effect, the act authorized the president to reach an accord with Colombia for a canal route.

But what of John Bull's consent? Two years earlier in February 1900, John Hay, an Anglophile enamored of British manners, politics, and friendships (the latter "will be a pleasure and advantage to me the rest of my life," he wrote as a young man), had concluded a treaty with his English other, Sir Julian Pauncefote, giving the United States the right to build and control a canal across the Central American isthmus. The waterway was to be neutral and without fortifications, holdovers of the 1850 pact. But these clauses, tied to a fading freedom-of-the-seas philosophy, caused a real kerfuffle among Washington's jingoes. Lodge and Roosevelt were in the forefront of its critics—"I do not approve of the ... treaty," the latter wrote—and under Cabot's leadership it died in the Senate.[1] Obliged to renegotiate, Hay conducted a second pact with Pauncefote that November. The British, though not liking the American insistence on studding the canal with military installations (implied, not stated in the treaty), went along, deeply involved at the time in the deeply unpopular Boer War.

With the treaty now in hand and Congress having anted up the necessary cash to conduct discussions with Colombia, Roosevelt paused for a moment. "Why cannot we buy the Panama isthmus outright," he wrote Hay, "instead of leasing it?" Told that the Colombian constitution presented difficulties on this front, he slipped into the kind of robber-baron-ese he detested when coming from the blunt tongues of financial titans: "I think they would change their constitution if we offered enough."[2] Instead, the United States entered into talks, and five months later, in January 1903, the Hay-Herrán Treaty was concluded, giving America a renewable lease of ninety-nine years to erect and operate a canal across the Panamanian isthmus for an initial $10 million disbursement followed by annual payments of $250,000.

And then months went by with the Colombian Senate debating but not consenting to the treaty. On June 8, at Roosevelt's insistence, Hay sent fresh directives—a mixture of truths, half-truths, and bluster—to the U.S. minister in Bogotá, Arthur Beaupre:

> The Colombian government apparently does not appreciate the gravity of the situation. The canal negotiations were initiated by Colombia, and ... with slight modifications, were finally accepted by us. In virtue of this agreement our congress reversed its previous judgement [to build a canal in Nicaragua] and decided upon the Panama rout. If Colombia should now reject the treaty or unduly delay its ratification, the friendly understanding between the two countries would be so seriously compromised that action might be undertaken by the congress next winter which every friend of Colombia might regret.[3]

Five days later Roosevelt informally discussed the treaty situation with the New York attorney William Cromwell, a prominent canal lobbyist paid handsomely (to the tune of $800,000) for his efforts.[4] The president was resolved, he told his guest, to build the waterway, even if that meant, should Colombia kill the treaty, backing the long-simmering Panamanian separatist movement, part of the political instability that had dogged the country throughout the nineteenth century. The following day the *New York World* fairly screamed:

> NEW REPUBLIC MAY ARISE TO GRANT CANAL
> The State of Panama Ready to Secede
> If the Treaty is rejected by the Colombian Congress[5]

Other papers in New York and Washington quickly picked up the story. A not-so-gentle momentum had begun to take hold.

Meanwhile, Colombian president José Manuel Marroquín, a philosopher, scholar, and poet before falling into politics, had insisted upon the treaty's passage. His senate, however, was unwilling to go along, and in July the U.S. State Department received an informal communication from Bogotá suggesting that an increase in the rights fee to build the canal (from the $10 million stipulated in the Hay-Herrán Treaty to $15 million) and a separate rights transferal tax might do the trick. An irritated Roosevelt informed Hay to let "those contemptible little creatures" know "they are jeopardizing things and imperiling their own future."[6]

And then nearly a month passed before, on August 12, Ambassador Beaupre notified the State Department of the Colombian Senate's now-official demand for the additional dollars. Hay's American sources in Bogotá explained that a strong antitreaty sentiment had swept the country, perhaps prompting the Senate's hawkish response. Two days later the president declared his displeasure through an agent, Illinois senator Shelby Cullom, who, in his Lincoln-looking Shenandoah beard, had luncheoned at Oyster Bay. The following day impressions of their conversation supplied by the senator appeared in the *New York Herald*, no doubt with Roosevelt's permission if not insistence. When asked if Bogotá's failure to confirm the Hay-Herrán pact would kill the canal idea, Cullom barely blinked. "We might make another treaty," he said, "not with Colombia, but with Panama." When reminded that Panama was not a nation, he smoothly batted this concern aside: "Intimations have been made that there is great discontent on the Isthmus over the action of the Congress of the central government, and Panama might break away and set up a government which we could treat with." Might the United States, the *Herald* naturally wished to know, encourage such an uprising? Commencing with a definitive "No" that segued into a less than definitive "I suppose not," Cullom concluded with what amounted to an ultimatum: "But this country wants to build that canal and build it now."[7]

This sentiment became the psalm of the day as Panamanian independence appeared to be merely a matter of time. In a personal letter to Hay on September 15, Roosevelt expressed his eagerness "in some shape or way to interfere when it becomes necessary so as to secure the Panama route without further dealing with the foolish and homicidal corruptionists in Bogotá."[8] To be sure, the situation in Panama had long leaned toward revolt. Having broken from Spain in 1821, it joined the Republic of Gran Colombia, a state comprising much of northern South America and southern Central America. This union dissolved in 1831 and, aside from a short-lived republic in 1840–41, Panama, though separated by highlands related to the Andean system, remained a part of Colombia. Over the years dozens of riots and insurrections rippled through the isthmus; on several occasions, the United States supported Bogotá by obstructing rebel operations in the area of the Panamanian railroad. Colombia now seemed to Roosevelt maddeningly ungrateful.

In mid-October two agents sent by the president to monitor conditions in Panama—posing as English sightseers—returned to Washington. They informed Roosevelt of a coming revolution, probably within the next few weeks. Several days later the USS *Dixie*, an auxiliary cruiser used primarily as a training ship, steamed quietly toward Cuba, laden with a battalion of marines. Other craft, including the *Boston*, *Wyoming*, and *Marblehead*, also began to move within range of Panama. Working behind the scenes, a Parisian-born engineer, soldier, and adventurer named Philippe Bunau-Varilla drafted a Panamanian constitution, organized (on paper) the prospective country's military, and gave assurances as to the security of its as yet nonexistent treasury. His wife stitched its presumptive national flag, subsequently rejected by the revolutionaries, who preferred an indigenous design. A longtime lobbyist for the Panamanian route and an agent for the failed French company that stood to make a profit by selling its canal rights to the United States, Bunau-Varilla worked from the Waldorf-Astoria in New York, playing to the press, lining up congressional support, and arranging funds to facilitate American intervention. "At every turn of my steps it seemed as if I were accompanied by a protecting divinity," he later wrote of his uncanny career. "Every time I was in need of a man he appeared." In the fall of 1903 that man, of course, was Theodore Roosevelt.[9]

On November 2, with U.S. ships in place and a battalion of Panamanian soldiers and several hundred firemen and railroad workers at the ready, Roosevelt cabled Admiral John Hubbard, an old South Berwick, Maine, sea dog commanding the USS *Nashville* off the Panamanian isthmus: "Prevent landing of any armed force with hostile intent . . . at any point within 50 miles of Panama. Government force reported approaching [Colón] in vessels. Prevent their landing, if in your judgement the landing would precipitate a conflict."[10]

The following day the revolution began, the go having been given by Bunau-Varilla and his New York associates. It required both time and protection, which the U.S. Navy capably provided. The Panamanian revolutionaries claimed independence on the fourth, on which day Roosevelt casually wrote his eldest son, Theodore, "Just at present I am attending to the Panama business." Offering the American argument, he accused Colombia of having "behaved infamously about the treaty for the building of the Panama Canal; and I do not intend in the police work that I will have to do in connection with the new insurrection any longer to do for her work which is not merely profitless but brings no gratitude." He did allow, "There will be some lively times in carrying out this policy." The following day the *Dixie* docked in Colón with several hundred marines for insurance, though no fighting ensued. On the sixth Hay cabled Felix Ehrman, the U.S. vice consul in Panama, to enter, "when you are satisfied that a de facto government, republican in form . . . has been established," into relations with the new state as a pretext to American recognition.[11] In Bogotá, Beaupre simultaneously delivered to the Colombian government a communication from Hay asserting Roosevelt's right to police the Panamanian isthmus:

> The people of Panama having, by an apparently unanimous movement, dissolved their political connection with the republic of Colombia and resumed their independence, and having adopted a government of their own . . . with which the government of the United States of America has entered into relations, the president

of the United States . . . holds that he is bound not merely by treaty obligations, but by the interests of civilization, to see that the peaceful traffic of the world across the isthmus of Panama shall no longer be disturbed by a constant succession of unnecessary and wasteful civil wars.[12]

Nearly four months later, in late February 1904, with the Panamanian constitution approved and the election of Manuel Amador Guerrero as the country's first president, the Hay-Bunau-Varilla Treaty, signed two weeks after the revolution, went before the U.S. Senate. Giving the Colossus of the North "all the rights, power and authority within the [canal] zone" along with "a monopoly for the construction, maintenance, and operation" of the waterway, the pact tilted far in Washington's direction. Indeed, the phrases "The United States has the right . . . ," "The Republic of Panama grants the United States . . . ," and "The Republic of Panama shall permit . . ." litter the text. The Senate, with some Democratic opposition, passed the treaty 66 to 14.[13]

Though the canal could now go forward, it came at a cost. For many Hispanic countries Roosevelt's unwillingness to respect Colombia's sovereignty smacked of Yankee hypocrisy. "By refusing to allow Colombia to uphold her . . . rights over a territory where she held dominion for eighty years," a subsequent U.S. minister to Colombia, James Du Bois, informed Secretary of State Philander Knox in 1912, "the friendship of nearly a century [with the U.S.] disappeared, the indignation of every Colombian, and millions of other Latin-Americans, was aroused and is still most intensely active. The confidence and trust in the justice and fairness of the United States, so long manifested, has completely vanished, and the maleficent influence of this condition is permeating public opinion in all Latin-American countries."[14]

During his presidency, Roosevelt denied having had anything to do with the revolution. "The administration behaved throughout not only with good faith," he wrote a colleague in the fall of 1904, "but with extraordinary patience and large generosity toward those with whom it dealt." In a communication to Colombian president Rafael Reyes the following year, he offered a shamelessly brazen assessment of U.S. actions: "This country, so far from wronging Colombia, made every possible effort to persuade Colombia to allow herself to be benefited. I cannot seem by remaining quiet to countenance for one moment the idea that this country did anything but show a spirit not merely of justice but of generosity in its dealings with Colombia."[15]

Once out of office, however, Roosevelt tendered sharper remarks on the subject. "I have always felt that the one thing for which I deserved most credit in my entire Administration," he told his successor, William Howard Taft, in December 1910, "was my action in seizing the psychological moment to get complete control of Panama." Three months later, delivering a Charter Day address at the University of California at Berkeley, he unpacked a more public and no doubt therapeutic confession of the heart. Outfitted in an academic cap and gown and facing an audience of eight thousand at the campus's Greek Theatre (its stage to be later graced by the Grateful Dead, Jimi Hendrix, and the Doors), Roosevelt reveled in self-congratulation: "I am interested in the Panama Canal because I started it. If I had followed traditional conservative methods I should have submitted a dignified state paper of probably 200 pages to the Congress and the debate would have been going on yet, but *I took the Canal Zone* and let Congress debate, and while the debate goes on the Canal does also."[16] A spray of applause and audible snickering accompanied this repartee.

Such open boasting did little to appease Colombia, eager to seek redress for the loss of its Panamanian province. Finally in 1914, under President Woodrow Wilson's direction, the United States negotiated a treaty with Colombia that apologized for America's role in the 1903 revolution and paid Bogotá nearly $1 billion in today's dollars for its recognition of Panama's independence. An irate Roosevelt believed the compensation "a purely malevolent attempt to blacken [my] Administration."[17] His Senate friends, Lodge leading the charge, kept the treaty bottled up until it was ratified in 1921, on condition that a "sincere regret" clause be expunged. The discovery of oil deposits in the region, a reason to make nice with Colombia, no doubt facilitated this GOP reversal of policy.

The old gunboat diplomacy, moreover, seemed a very dangerous, clumsy, and counterproductive tool during the era of the First World War. With the Wilson administration seeking, amid the collapse of several European empires, to attain global leadership under the League of Nations rubric, acts of flagrant aggression were no longer the thing. "It is absolutely essential for the peoples of the world to realize that they can never have international peace and order if they permit their representatives to sanction the unmoral practices of the past," one presidential advisor wrote Wilson in 1918. "Every large nation, as you know has been guilty.... Roosevelt's rape of Panama brings it closely home."[18]

These after-the-fact reckonings, however, addressed a different day. The Senate's ratification of the Hay-Bunau-Varilla Treaty, rather, gave to Roosevelt a string of successes that endeared him to much of the electorate, enamored of his Napoleonic swagger and evangelical call for America's "higher right" to build a canal where France had failed. On such congenial terms, Roosevelt fairly bounced into the race for reelection.

36

Atop the GOP

In the late winter of 1902, the *Washington Times* published a large front-page photograph of an almost smiling Mark Hanna with an accompanying caption—"THE MAN OF THE HOUR"—that segued into shameless praise: "No man in this country has developed more rapidly within the last half dozen years.... Today he is bigger than politics and politicians." Thus, the paper begged the impression that this "remarkably able" Ohio kingmaker stood ready to claim the next Republican nomination. Despite Roosevelt's popularity, there were solid reasons for such speculation. Aside from steering the GOP to victory in the last two national elections, Hanna both embodied the growing influence of big business in America and controlled a bevy of precious convention delegates. But did the senator, tired and taxed by ill health, want the nomination? He would be sixty-seven in 1904, and only the thin, long-nosed William Henry Harrison was older upon taking the oath of office—and he promptly died after serving a scant thirty-two days. Hanna, moreover, could feel progressivism's pulse beating through the country and knew some voters viewed his connections to the corporate class with suspicion. Would they be eager to trade the young, charismatic Roosevelt for an Old Guard grandee keen to stand pat on the trust question, among others? Perhaps he merely wished to keep his options open, though Hanna's insistence to a colleague in August 1902 that "I am not a candidate and will not be a candidate" might reflect his considered opinion of the prevailing political winds.[1]

This disavowal hardly meant, however, that Hanna wished to be maneuvered into supporting Roosevelt, or any other candidate, prior to the 1904 Republican convention. Perhaps, as with McKinley, he might yet play the roles of counselor and kingmaker. But this was not to be. Rather, his Ohio rival, fellow Republican senator Joseph Foraker—whose patronage requests from the McKinley administration had pended upon Hanna's approval—moved in May 1903 to embarrass his colleague. Word began to circulate that at the upcoming Republican state convention in Columbus a Foraker-backed resolution recommending Roosevelt's reelection would be proposed. It appeared that Hanna must either agree or make an awkward and public break with the president. Hanna hoped to maintain his independence and, in a strained, ambiguous telegram, told Roosevelt so on the twenty-third: "The issue that has been forced upon me in the matter of our State Convention this year indorsing you for the Republican nomination next year has come in a way which makes it necessary for me to oppose such a resolution. When you know all the facts, I am sure that you will approve my course." No facts were forthcoming. Not to be out-marshaled, Roosevelt made it all but impossible for Hanna to wriggle out of this tight trap. "I have not asked any man for his support," he replied on the twenty-fifth. "I have had nothing whatever to do with raising this issue. Inasmuch as it has been raised of course those who favor my administration and my nomination will favor endorsing both and those who do not will oppose." What could Hanna do? "In view of the sentiment expressed," he telegrammed Roosevelt the following day, "I shall not oppose the indorsement of your administration and candidacy by our State Convention."[2]

A week later the Ohio GOP rallied in Columbus and went wild for TR—"He is a fighter; a man of action; he does things, and he does them well," shouted one Cuyahoga County delegate before the assembly. After announcing the party's commitment to renominating Hanna for the Senate, Foraker moved on to the "more serious . . . duty" of Roosevelt's reelection, which caused an eruption of applause. "We are all agreed"—he waited for a slight cessation from the audience—"that next year [Roosevelt] is to be our candidate."[3]

In a note to Lodge that touched upon the Columbus convention, Roosevelt thought it likely that Hanna, if not angling for the White House, had desired the kind of influence he formerly enjoyed with McKinley and sought to make the new president his "suppliant." Wanting neither Hanna nor his Wall Street connections to sap his strength, Roosevelt, tired, he said, of "shilly-shallying," had used Foraker's ploy to force the senator's hand: "I . . . made up my mind that it was better to have a fight in the open at once than to run the risk of being knifed secretly." In fact, Hanna's fighting days were now over. Less than a year after the convention tussle, on February 15, 1904, he died of typhoid fever; Roosevelt had slipped quietly into the unconscious senator's house about three hours before the end to pay his respects.[4]

Four months after Hanna's passing, GOP delegates convened in the Chicago Coliseum, a large indoor arena erected in 1899 on South Wabash Avenue (less than a mile west of Soldier Field), which subsequently housed every GOP nominating gathering between 1904 and 1920. The arena sported an arched, skylit roof and sat sixteen thousand; to this day it has hosted more nominating conventions than any other building. Though a cautious consensus ensued, the party seemed a bit at odds with itself, both paying tribute to the past with portraits and orations made to the memories of Old Guard favorites Hanna and McKinley, yet unanimously selecting Roosevelt, the champion of GOP progressives, to lead the fall charge. This dissonance between factions would remain a feature of the party's institutional DNA; reminiscent of the earlier Stalwarts-versus-Half-Breeds tussle, it anticipated the moderate Nelson Rockefeller (northeastern)–versus–Barry Goldwater (Sunbelt) struggle in 1964, and the still-longer contest for ideological supremacy between liberal and conservative Republicans in the twenty-first century.

The convention also chose Roosevelt's running mate, Indiana senator Charles Fairbanks, a former McKinley advisor amenable to the Old Guard. Possessed of a bristling mustache, goatee, and conspicuous comb-over, he looked quiet, reliable, and even a bit boring—a perfect foil, in other words, to the live wire heading the ticket.

The Democrats, having twice been trounced with the old silverite Bryan and looking for their own staid and tame candidate, chose Alton B. Parker of the New York Court of Appeals—safe on the gold standard. Any faith that the industrial barons might abandon the GOP, however, was misplaced. "I hope Roosevelt will win," Andrew Carnegie observed during the campaign. "I am convinced that Republican rule is best for the country."[5] And much of the country seemed inclined to agree. With the coal strike settled, the Philippine War concluded, and the Panama Canal treaty safely ratified, Roosevelt could point to a portfolio of vigorous executive actions. Complaints by Democrats that the president practiced imperialism abroad or that the nation's economic prosperity privileged a small elite failed to move a compelling portion of the electorate.

One aspect of the canvassing, however, bothered TR—the large contributions flooding into his campaign from Wall Street, presumably his bête noire. Even with Bryanism relegated by Democrats to the back row, and the noun "trustbuster" beginning to enter the lexicon, the business elite reflexively embraced the GOP, the presumed protector of industrial development. Northern Securities scars aside, J. P. Morgan eagerly enough slid a cool $150,000 (about $5.1 million in today's dollars) into the Roosevelt campaign coffers, while the New York Life, Equitable, and Mutual insurance companies combined to deposit $100,000, a sum matched by Henry Clay Frick, former chairman of the Carnegie Steel Company.[6] When Rockefeller's Standard Oil empire also dropped in a few dollops, however, these proved a few dollars too many.

Sensitive to being pegged a tool of the business class, the president insisted in a flurry of late-October "confidential" telegrams and memorandums to his campaign manager George Cortelyou that Rockefeller's munificence be returned:

> I have just been informed that the Standard Oil people have contributed one hundred thousand dollars to our campaign. . . . The big business corporations have a tremendous stake in the welfare of this country. They know that this welfare can only be secured through the continuance in power of the republican party; and if they subscribe for the purpose of securing such national welfare, and with no thought of personal favors to them, why they are acting as is entirely proper; but we cannot under any circumstances afford to take a contribution which can be even improperly construed as putting us under an improper obligation, and in view of my past relation with the Standard Oil Company [TR had rhetorically attacked the firm and his Justice Department would file an antitrust suit in 1906] I fear that such a construction will be put upon receiving any aid from them.[7]

Roosevelt, in other words, framed the question in such a way that he might retain his self-image as an "independent" while simultaneously accepting donations from the industrialists. He would accept *nearly* the whole loaf (steel, securities, insurance, and so on) instead of the whole (oil) and call it a sacrifice. In the event, the thrifty Cortelyou never actually got around to returning the money.

In some desperation, Democrats latched on to the Wall Street theme and Parker spent the late days of the campaign in a swing around New Jersey and New York insisting that Morgan and company "hope to control the election." His blood up, as it had been when the Mugwumps questioned his convenient fidelity to Blaine, Roosevelt called the accusation "false" in a prepared statement that emphasized his crusader credentials in the Northern Securities case. And then the parties waited for election day. Over the preceding few months, the president had handicapped his chances, with surprisingly little precision. In a July note to Lodge he thought Wisconsin and West Virginia "in . . . peril," though he ended up taking each with ease (63 percent and 55 percent, respectively); in October he told Leonard Wood that "we shall win by rather a small majority" and listed for Kermit "the following states as doubtful," including New York, Rhode Island, Delaware, Indiana, Colorado, Montana, and Nevada—all of which he won handily. Perhaps the thrill of the fight clouded his judgment, though it might be that, enjoying competition, he puffed up his outmatched opponent, eager for yet another charge up yet another hill.[8]

To the English writer Rudyard Kipling—Roosevelt read *The Jungle Book* to his children, though he once called its author "a cad" for criticisms of America—the president privately identified a host of enemies just waiting to snatch the crown from his head. These nemeses included the anti-imperialists ("jack fools"), trusts ("I have alienated some of the big representatives"), and trade unions ("a muss"). Of course, the industrialists were mainly in support of his candidacy and organized labor had applauded his work in the anthracite strike. That his concerns were not altogether concerning might be inferred from the fact that he spent a good bit of his time in late October reading for pleasure. Five days before the November balloting, he wrote Kermit of making his way through the British historian Thomas Babington Macaulay's tomes and perusing Dickens's picaresque *Martin Chuzzlewit* and fat legal thriller *Bleak House*.[9]

The contest went to Roosevelt in a landslide. His 56.4 percent of the popular vote constituted the highest percentage claimed by a candidate in nearly a century, exceeding those of Jackson, Lincoln, and Grant, among others. The president further captured more states (thirty-two) and electoral votes (332) than any prior candidate. "Have swept the country," he sent a Western Union telegraph to Lodge hours after the balloting ended, "by majorities which astound me."[10] Making more history, Roosevelt became the first "accidental" president (via a predecessor's death) to win the office in his own right. John Tyler, Millard Fillmore, Andrew Johnson, and Chester Arthur never claimed such mandates. He seems, moreover, to have established a trend, for after him Calvin Coolidge, Harry Truman, and Lyndon Johnson (succeeding, respectively, Warren Harding, Franklin Roosevelt, and John Kennedy) were returned to the White House by voters.

Corinne Roosevelt Robinson met her brother at Newark, New Jersey, on election day, after he had cast his ballot at Oyster Bay. Comfortably planted in a private drawing-room car, she rode with him as far south as Philadelphia, listening as "he opened his heart to me." Having seized the public's imagination, he now ached to enter a select pantheon of public servants: "He . . . told me," so Corinne recalled, "that he had never wanted anything in his life quite as much as the outward and visible sign of his country's approval."[11]

And having that, a grateful Roosevelt impulsively wanted to demonstrate his fealty to the Cincinnatus model—associated with Lucius Quinctius Cincinnatus, a military leader of the early Roman Republic who voluntarily gave up power and returned to his estate. As Washington had resigned his commission following the American Revolution and later refused to stand for a third presidential term, so Roosevelt now reached for posterity, promising before a group of election night reporters never to accept another nomination for the executive office. He considered the three and a half years he served following McKinley's assassination as good as a full four. Though this gesture garnered much press attention, and caught his aghast daughter Alice off guard, McKinley had made a similar declaration in 1901, and all seven of the men who had served two terms in the presidency had abided, with little fanfare, by the informal injunction not to reach for a third, although Grant had been open to the possibility. In any case, the British statesman John Morley, visiting the White House at the time of Roosevelt's announcement, thought the declaration dubious:

> I asked him whether, if he retired in this way after four years, when he would only be 50 years old, he would not find life rather tame.

He gave me several reasons to justify his self-denying ordinance, and then he said, "And to tell you the truth, a man who has had eight years as President has not got much left in him." I don't suppose the strain of managing the Congress at Washington for eight years is a quarter of the strain of managing the House of Commons for twenty.[12]

Morley's skepticism, shared by many, provoked from Roosevelt reiterations of his election night pledge over the next four years—one he would come to regret.

TR's second inauguration took place on March 4 amid a thin gray filter of snow occasionally leavened by shards of sunlight. A crowd swarmed below a platform assembled on the East Front of the Capitol, watching as the nation's eighth chief justice, a sterling-haired Melville Fuller, administered the presidential oath of office. The previous day John Hay had bequeathed to Roosevelt a rare and auspicious gift, a precious relic from a somber occasion in 1865. "The hair in this ring is from the head of Abraham Lincoln," he wrote. "Dr. Taft cut it off the night of the assassination, and I got it from his son. . . . Please wear it to-morrow; you are one of the men who most thoroughly understand and appreciate Lincoln."[13] After a quick six-minute address, Roosevelt returned to the White House for a large luncheon while a parade of West Point cadets, Naval Academy midshipmen, and the inevitable train of Rough Riders proceeded along Pennsylvania Avenue—the relaxed president taking much of it in. Flickering motion pictures from the day show a reviewing stand thick with Edwardian fashion, including women in a variety of millinery creations, tailored suits, and trained skirts; the men, in contrast, looked depressingly identical in matching bowlers and black woolen coats.

One of the more striking outcomes of the 1904 elections was the emergence of a robust progressive strain in the GOP. Interested in checking the power of the trusts, lowering tariff rates, and seeing more regulation in the name of consumer safety, these nascent crusaders would soon clash with their Old Guard brethren. Among the more strident of their kind stood Wisconsin senator Robert ("Battling Bob") La Follette, a pompadoured reformer hot for railroad regulation. Though Roosevelt sympathized with aspects of the progressive agenda at this time—considering himself, as always, an independent and adept at managing competing interests—he thought trusts inevitable and even beneficial if properly placed under regulatory purview. Over the next few years this progressive–Old Guard quarrel became a prominent feature in GOP politics, a collision of interests Roosevelt mediated unevenly.

Days after the inauguration TR, standing in for his late brother Elliott, gave away his orphaned niece Eleanor in marriage to her distant cousin, Franklin Roosevelt. The date (March 17) and location (Manhattan) were concessions to a busy president's schedule, which included attending the city's St. Patrick's Day parade and delivering speeches before and following the 3:30 p.m. ceremony. The police presence around Roosevelt became overwhelming, leaving the bride, in white satin with point lace veil, court train, and pearl collar, to complain that "irate guests could not get into the [East Seventy-Sixth Street] house until after the ceremony was over!" Camping out in the library near the buffet table, Roosevelt basked before a fawning audience. Most of the guests, Eleanor later remembered, "were far more interested in . . . being able to see and listen to the President—and in a very short time we were standing alone!"[14]

Watching the scene unfold, Alice Roosevelt perhaps made a mental note that emerged some years later as her brightest bon mot: "My father always wanted to be the corpse at every funeral, the bride at every wedding, and the baby at every christening." Seemingly omnipotent, Roosevelt had stared down both Wall Street's money men and Colombia's government, imposed his will on Pennsylvania's coal kings, and lent a hand (and several ships) to Panama's revolutionaries. By turns belligerent, pragmatic, and generally effective, he strode a stage larger than even the American scene. With a keen geopolitical interest, he watched a mounting conflict in the East between Czarist Russia and the Empire of Japan. Apropos Alice's aphorism, he longed as well to be the arbiter of every clash between the world's major powers.

37

When Goliaths Go to War

In 1899 and again in 1900 Secretary of State John Hay, responding to U.S. commercial interests, issued consecutive circulars known collectively as the Open Door policy, calling for equal privileges among nations trading in China. Watching Russia, France, Germany, Japan, and Great Britain gobble up coastal concessions from the ailing Qing dynasty, the McKinley administration feared both a monopolization of this massive market—a population of 400 million, larger than the major European countries combined—and the unpalatable prospect of China fragmenting into economic colonies. These notes had no legal standing and Hay did not ask for replies. Although officials in London, Berlin, Paris, and elsewhere gestured sympathetically to the Open Door principle, in practice it had little effect.

By 1902 Hay had come to focus on Russia's aggressive incursion into Manchuria, sending diplomatic notes to St. Petersburg complaining of its opportunistic hold on the region. Roosevelt stewed over what to do. "I have not the slightest objection to the Russians knowing that I feel thoroughly aroused and irritated at their conduct in Manchuria," he told Hay, and discussed the possibility of "going to an extreme in the matter." Sensitive to the boundaries imposed upon him by the American public's lack of interest in Asia, Hay knew he held a weak hand, telling Roosevelt that "any scheme of concerted action with England and Japan . . . [is] out of the question." Over the previous few years, St. Petersburg's influence in China had increased appreciably. Following the Sino-Japanese War (1894–95), Russia joined Germany and France (the Triple Intervention) in coercing the victorious Meiji emperor's army out of the Liaodong Peninsula—only, in 1898, to provocatively acquire from China a twenty-five-year lease of the same; in 1903 Russia completed the South Manchurian Railway, and the following year Russian cars began to operate on the Circum-Baikal line, part of the nearly six-thousand-mile Siberian Railroad (later called the Trans-Siberian) connecting Moscow to Vladivostok. Unwilling to cede hegemony over the region to the czar's government, Japan carried off a surprise torpedo boat attack on the Russian Pacific Fleet at Port Arthur at the southern tip of the Liaodong in February 1904, thus commencing hostilities between the two rivals in a contest for predominance in East Asia. Roosevelt and his secretary of war Elihu Root were strongly pro-Japanese, the latter describing Tokyo's government, modeled in part along lines of Western modernization, as a "liberal and progressive constitutional Empire." Roosevelt thought it fitting that Japan be given a free hand in Korea, traditionally China's sphere of influence, but respect the Open Door in a future Russian-free Manchuria. "I was thoroughly well pleased with the Japanese victory," he wrote his eldest son shortly after the Port Arthur assault, "for Japan is playing our game."[1]

Over the next year a stalemate ensued. Japanese victories, most notably at Mukden in southern Manchuria, were countered by Russian insistence that its massive army and repositioned Baltic Fleet—the ships currently sailing eighteen thousand nautical miles through choppy seas around South Africa to reach Asia—would reset the earlier reversals. This prospect held little appeal for the president. "To judge from the Russians' attitude at present," he wrote Hay in late August, "if they were victorious they would be so intolerable as to force us to take action." He further complained to Lodge, "The Russians . . . are utterly insincere and treacherous; they have no conception of truth, no willingness to look facts in the face, no regard for others . . . [and] no knowledge of their own strength or weakness." The Japanese, by contrast, struck TR as a kind of England of the Orient, a winner in the civilizational sweepstakes, having dispensed with China and now appearing quite capable of handling Russia. "What wonderful people the Japanese are!" he gushed to Cecil Spring Rice, though otherwise confessing to an underlying unease that made him question the West's future in the East: "I wish I were certain that the Japanese down at bottom did not lump Russians, English, Americans, Germans, all of us, simply as white devils inferior to themselves . . . and to be treated politely only so long as would enable the Japanese to take advantage of our various national jealousies, and beat us in turn."[2]

John Hay, by contrast, his health in decline, his appetite for life compromised by personal tragedy, had lost interest in the war. In the spring of 1901, his twenty-four-year-old son, Del, possibly falling asleep on a stifling evening while sitting on a windowsill, had dropped to his death in front of the New Haven House hotel in Connecticut. The loss "of our boy made my wife and me old," he wrote a friend three years later, "at once and for the rest of our lives. There is no mitigation of grief—it grows worse with the slow exasperation of years." In a manner of medicating, Hay spent long stretches of time at his Lake Sunapee, New Hampshire, retreat. Reconciled to his fate, he wrote a colleague in England, "I have great doubts whether this tenement of clay which I inhabit will hold together." While Roosevelt kept an eye on international affairs, Hay slipped off to Europe in the spring of 1905 for treatment of his ailing heart. There he met up with Henry Adams, who wrote to Elizabeth Cameron, a confidant of both men, that Hay should have resigned years ago rather than serve at the pleasure of a boy president: "Theodore is his own Cabinet, and especially likes to play with foreign kings. Hay has had no choice but to hold the hats and look on. He had better go out, now that his excuse is good."[3] Twenty-nine days later, Hay died from a coronary thrombosis at Lake Sunapee.

Watching the standstill Russo-Japanese War from afar, Roosevelt determined to play peacemaker, a variation of the Square Deal abroad. As the leader of the only major nation without sizeable concessions in China, he hoped to assume the role of honest broker. Rather than nudging capital and labor to the table, he now sent word to Lloyd Griscom, the boyish-looking American minister to Japan, to gauge Tokyo's interest in outside mediation. Similar signals were offered up in St. Petersburg. Neither overture made an immediate impact, however, as neither of the belligerents wanted to appear eager for peace, though both were secretly communicating just such a desire to intermediaries, chiefly France. And then in late May 1905 the Russian Baltic Fleet, having finally made its way to the Tsushima Strait, a channel between Korea and Japan, suffered an epic defeat, losing six battleships among twenty-one other craft sunk or captured. The Japanese sacrificed a mere three torpedo boats. Possibly the most consequential sea battle since Trafalgar—Roosevelt called it "a slaughter rather than a fight"—it convinced the Russians to take up the American president's prompt to engage in arbitration. The previous month Ambassador Takahira, the Japanese minister in Washington, had already given word to former Philippines governor-general William Howard Taft, Root's replacement as war secretary, that Japan might welcome U.S. mediation. "It is not unlikely," he observed, "that the friendly good offices of some Power might be necessary."[4]

Roosevelt, wolf and bear hunting in Texas, Oklahoma, and Colorado ("this was unalloyed pleasure," he told his son Kermit), quickly replied to Taft: "I emphatically agree with the Japanese view that there should be direct negotiations on all terms of peace." He thought further that Japan should have "control over Korea," retain Port Arthur, and operate the southern Manchurian rail system. As for two other items on Tokyo's wish list—a heavy indemnity from Russia to pay for the war and the loss of Sakhalin, Russia's largest island and part of the Japanese archipelago—Roosevelt hesitated, telling Taft, "I am not yet prepared to express myself definitely."[5] He conveyed to his English friend George Otto Trevelyan more concrete reservations about Japan:

> Just at present they feel rather puffed up over their strength. Even if they are ultimately victorious I think it would have paid them better to have made peace after Mukden without extorting a money indemnity from the Russians, for a few months war would eat up whatever they would get in the end by way of indemnity.[6]

Still, he assured Spring Rice that he hoped "to lend some assistance to Japan in the present war in which I think she is right."[7]

Following the Russian disaster at Tsushima, the Japanese government let it be known that intervention on the part of President Roosevelt would be welcomed. He now knew that Tokyo's war machine had peaked and had no way of matching Russia's vast reserve of manpower. TR next instructed the U.S. ambassador to Russia, George von Lengerke Meyer, a Boston businessman of German descent, to nudge Czar Nicholas II into negotiations with Japan. On June 5 he sent a dispatch to Meyer saying in the main, "The President speaks with the most earnest and sincere desire to advise what is best for Russia," this "best" being for St. Petersburg to recognize "that the present contest is absolutely hopeless" and to consent to "discuss the whole peace question" with Japan.[8]

The following day the ambassador took a private train to Tsarskoye

Selo (now Pushkin), fifteen miles south of St. Petersburg and a residence of the Russian imperial family. At 2:00 p.m. he was ushered into the czar's study at the Catherine Palace. There Meyer delicately harped upon the need for peace—"it was of the utmost importance that war should cease"—and the social unrest the conflict had aroused in a potentially revolutionary Russia. He then tendered Roosevelt's mediation plan, "nothing being made public," he assured, "until Japan agrees." Nicholas allowed that his third cousin Kaiser Wilhelm II of Germany also favored a resolution. And then an awkward silence ensued. Finally the czar, though "convinced," so he told Meyer, "that . . . his people did not desire peace at any price and would support him in continuing the war," nevertheless consented—"if it will be absolutely secret as to my decision, should Japan decline"—to "the President's proposition," which the president proffered the very next day.[9]

While the details of when and where to hold the peace talks were ironed out, Roosevelt basked in the glory of his achievement. "Mr. Roosevelt's success has amazed everybody," the London *Morning Post* huzzahed. "He has displayed not only diplomatic abilities of the very highest order, but also great tact, great foresight, and finesse really extraordinary." Not without reason did Roosevelt confide to Kermit of having "by the exercise of a good deal of tact and judgment" brought the belligerent powers, eager for amity but impeded by pride, anxiety, and doubt, to the peace table.[10]

Playing his own secretary of state in the wake of Hay's final illness, Roosevelt hoped to entice Elihu Root, who had returned to a lucrative New York legal practice following his stint heading the War Department, to rejoin the cabinet. Noting Clara Root's disdain for Washington society, however, he thought her husband unlikely to quit their new Upper East Side address—a handsome Georgian structure erected by the firm of Carrère and Hastings, architects of the New York Public Library. "I should greatly like to have him able to deal with . . . this peace conference matter this summer," he wrote to Taft on July 3, "although I doubt if he accepts." Only three days later, however, he drafted another "Dear Will" note with the relieved opening line, "Root accepted and was glad to come in."[11]

Roosevelt, once so firmly in Japan's corner, began, in the stunning three months (March–May 1905) that produced the victories at Mukden and the Tsushima Strait, to regard the Meiji government's military as an emerging threat to American interests. He marveled at Japan's efficiency and élan, though worried over its recent successes in China and Manchuria. Agreeable to its entrée into the league of great nations—"While I am President," he told Griscom, "Japan . . . will be treated just exactly like the English, Germans, French or other civilized peoples"—he nevertheless gave considerable thought to how America might fight it in the future: "I think our objective should be the Japanese fleet." But in the guise of the honest broker, he looked now to be the peacemaker who maintained a balance of power in the region. "I should be sorry to see Russia driven out of East Asia," he wrote Whitelaw Reid, U.S. ambassador to the United Kingdom, shortly after the Baltic Fleet's decisive defeat, "and driven out she surely will be if the war goes on."[12]

38

Peace in the East

Before negotiations could begin, Russia and Japan skirmished over where to hold their summit, Russia preferring Paris and Japan opting for Chefoo (present-day Yantai, China). Roosevelt recommended The Hague, though Meiji officials, perhaps mindful of how France, Germany, and Russia—the Triple Intervention—had worked in concert following the Sino-Japanese War to return the Liaodong Peninsula to China, rejected a European site. The Russians suggested Washington and, when Roosevelt expressed concern over the capital city's summer heat, Japan agreed more generally to an American location. Among cooler climes, Portland, Maine, and Atlantic City, New Jersey, volunteered to act as hosts. Seeking a less-trafficked environment, Roosevelt ultimately proposed, with certain reserve, Portsmouth, New Hampshire, a modest-sized seaport city of ten thousand. He appeared, so the *New York Times* reported, slightly concerned that "the smart set in the resorts would fete the Russian delegates because they were white, and neglect the Japanese." A more concerning anti-Asian sentiment was then coiling about California, whose state legislature, stunned by Russia's string of losses, had recently passed a resolution condemning immigration from the East. "The Japanese Invasion, The Problem of the Hour," squawked the *San Francisco Chronicle*, while the Battle of Mukden raged. Appalled by the enmity coming out of the Far West, Roosevelt had told Griscom to quietly inform "the Japanese Government . . . that the . . . American people at large have not the slightest sympathy with the outrageous agitation against the Japanese in certain small sections along the Pacific slope."[1]

In July 1905, the president, leaving nothing to chance, sent an eighty-three-member diplomatic delegation to Tokyo, a "goodwill cruise" designed, in light of the recent victories by Japan and the United States' new Pacific acquisitions, to hash out agreements on spheres of influence in Korea, Manchuria, and the Philippines. Secretary of War Taft headed the mission, accompanied by several senators and nearly a dozen congressmen eager, on their return voyage, to tour greater Manila. The undoubted star of the show, however, was Alice Roosevelt—twenty-one, expensively appareled, and delightfully irreverent. Photographers were naturally drawn to the physically contrasting sinewy First Daughter (a.k.a. "Princess Alice") and the rotund Taft. To the surprise of many the two proved decidedly companionable on the trip, attached as if by compact to the same powerful patron. Playing a lightly avuncular role, "Mr. Taft," so Alice later wrote of a Hawaiian stopover, thoughtfully pleaded with the accompanying paparazzi "not to take photographs of me in my bathing suit."[2]

Following a ten-day voyage, the delegation's ship, auspiciously named *Manchuria*, docked in Yokohama, whence the party quickly made for Tokyo. There in the capital city, Taft and Prime Minister Katsura Tarō met on July 27, producing a confidential agreement—not a treaty and thus not bound to be brought before the Senate—on the two nations' potentially conflicting colonial agendas, essentially recognizing both Japan's right in making Korea a protectorate and America's fiat in the Philippines. Taft wired the content of this informal colloquy to Roosevelt, who replied on the thirty-first from Oyster Bay, "Your conversation with Count Katsura absolutely correct in every respect." He thought the Hermit Kingdom could absorb Japanese migration, believed the Philippines more secure from Japan's Imperial Navy, and supposed that Japan might now be less inclined to pursue a punitive peace with Russia. While Taft engaged in diplomacy, Alice was received by Japanese aristocracy, sat near the Meiji emperor during a luncheon, and collected a raft of gifts including an exquisite lacquer box, an embroidered screen, and a piece of gold cloth delicately stitched with white chrysanthemums. Reflecting on the quantity and quality of plunder, she later wrote, "I was a frankly unashamed pig." As in America, the Japanese people were captivated by the president's daughter, who, of all his children, most nearly approximated his charisma, appetite for enjoyment, and social verve. "Alice," so one of the wives of the delegation later remembered, "*was* the party."[3]

Back in America, Russia and Japan's plenipotentiaries finalized their respective plans for the Portsmouth peace conference. Sergei Witte, a tall, thickly built promotor of Russian industrialization, and Baron Roman Rosen, a longtime member of the Russian Foreign Asiatic Department, would head negotiations for the czar's government, while Ambassador Takahira Kogorō, serving on and off in the United States since 1879, and Baron Komura Jutarō, one of the first Japanese students at Harvard, led the Nippon mission. Roosevelt briefly met the delegations, separately, at his home at Sagamore Hill, where he remained during the negotiations. His infatuation with Japan—and poor opinion of the Russians—only grew because of these casual tête-à-têtes. "I cannot say that I liked him," he wrote confidentially to one correspondent of Witte, "for I thought his bragging and bluster not only foolish but shockingly vulgar when compared with the gentlemanly self-respecting self-restraint of the Japanese."[4]

During their meeting chez Roosevelt, Takahira and Komura produced their wish list. Russia was expected to pay a large indemnity (China having coughed up more than 16 million pounds of silver to end the Sino-Japanese War), recognize Japanese control of Korea, withdraw its military presence in Manchuria, and hand over both the Liaodong Peninsula and Sakhalin Island. The late-arriving Russians—Witte had toured much of Manhattan, seeing the stock market, visiting Tammany Hall, and meeting with Slavic immigrant communities—checked in next.[5] Armed with a sacrosanct letter from the czar, the delegation indicated Russia's acceptance of Korea as a virtual Japanese colony and its intention to transfer, with China's assent, its rights in the Liaodong Peninsula. It would never, however, pay an indemnity. Witte, unimpressed with Sagamore Hill, which he put on par with the small summer houses occupied by Muscovite landowners, insisted that Russia remained a military behemoth and that should the war continue, its latent strength and manpower would come increasingly into play.

The following day, August 5, the two delegations met at Oyster Bay aboard the *Mayflower*, the presidential steam yacht used from TR to Coolidge; a former navy ship built in 1896, it later served as a patrol craft for the Israeli navy before being decommissioned and broken up in 1955. Decked out in frock coats and top hats, the rival envoys met Roosevelt in turn. They were then formally introduced to each other and invited to mingle ("exchanging meaningless phrases and remarks on the weather," one of them remembered) before a cold buffet lunch and a champagne toast from Roosevelt offering "my most earnest hope and prayer . . . that a just and lasting peace may speedily be concluded."[6]

Three days later, the *Mayflower* arrived at the Portsmouth Naval Shipyard in Kittery, Maine, a small New England town of 2,800 just across the Piscataqua River from Portsmouth, New Hampshire. Opened in 1800, the yard had built nearly two dozen ships for the Union navy during the Civil War, though its fortunes—and importance—had since flagged. Negotiations were to take place here, on the second floor of Building 86, a recently erected warehouse swiftly converted into negotiation rooms. "On the whole the furnishing is simple but comfortable," Witte's secretary later noted. "Electric fans, producing a strong current of air, are fastened to brackets in the wall. Next to the Envoy's room there are smaller rooms for Secretaries and Attachés. The Japanese quarters are similar to ours. Evidently the State Department has tried to do its best." Altogether, he thought his hosts quite accommodating: "One cannot help admiring the contrast of the American surroundings and ours especially as compared to the poor premises of the Russian Foreign Office."[7]

The delegates were shuttled to the majestic four-story Hotel Wentworth in New Castle, two miles from Portsmouth. Built in 1874, the spacious Second Empire–style resort, accommodating up to four hundred guests, hosted the cream of East Coast society. Tennis courts, putting greens, and a bathing pond drew the active. "The attendance consists," so one of the Russians lightly complained, perhaps thinking of Paris, "of American maids, mulattos, and bell boys, who never come when rung for, and who invariably give unintelligible answers." Witte found the cooking inedible and dined frugally on bread and vegetables, though he did take to the billiards room; the Japanese were only moderately more pleased with the cuisine, but gamely tried to be agreeable guests.[8]

For more than three weeks in August, the two sides inched toward ending the war. Early on Russia dug in as Witte, under the oversight of both royal authority and a proud war faction in St. Petersburg, refused to pay an indemnity or yield Sakhalin. Disappointed at the Russian attitude and concerned by signals indicating that Britain and France were angling to play a role in the peace process, Roosevelt telegrammed Portsmouth, insisting that Rosen speak with him the next day at Sagamore Hill. There TR outlined, noting Japan's willingness to take only southern Sakhalin, a possible way to break the impasse: in return for having the northern half of the island restored, Russia would "pay a substantial sum for this surrender of territory by the Japanese and for the return of the Russian prisoners."[9] This amounted, of course, to a scaled-down indemnity, but Moscow could call it something else. Not entirely trusting Rosen to see that this proposal reached St. Petersburg, TR cabled the plan to Meyer to present to the czar.

At the same time, the president leaned on an old acquaintance, Kaneko Kentarō, a Harvard alum—overlapping Roosevelt's time in Cambridge, though the two did not meet until later—born into a samurai family. After lecturing at the University of Tokyo, Kaneko had embarked on a career in legal studies, government work, and diplomacy; at one time he sat in the House of Peers, the upper chamber of the Imperial Diet. During the Russo-Japanese War he served as a special envoy to the United States, giving speeches and publishing editorials accentuating Tokyo's version of events. Roosevelt, noting Japan's demand for a payment in restitution of $6 million ($206 million in today's dollars), informed Kaneko that it would likely prolong the war and undermine the respect his country had earned in defeating Russia on the field of battle:

> I . . . strongly advise Japan not to continue the fight for a money indemnity. If she does, then I believe that there will be a considerable shifting of public opinion against her. I do not believe that this public opinion will have any very tangible effect, but still it should not be disregarded. Moreover, I do not believe that the Japanese nation would achieve its ends if it continued the war simply on the question of the indemnity. I think that Russia will refuse to pay and that the general sentiment of the civilized world will back her in refusing to pay the great amount asked, or anything like such an amount.[10]

Taxed by both sides' intransigence, Roosevelt wrote to Kermit on the twenty-fifth, "I am having my hair turned gray by dealing with the Russian and Japanese peace negotiators."[11]

Finally, on August 29, Witte offered what he described as Russia's final proposal on the major questions—no indemnity and Japan could keep southern Sakhalin if it gave up its claim to the island's northern half. Russia further agreed to evacuate Manchuria and recognize Japanese rule in Korea. "Absolute silence reigned for a few seconds," noted one of the participants. "Witte, as usual, kept tearing up the paper that was lying beside him. Rosen smoked his cigarette. The Japanese continued to be enigmatic. As last Komura, in a well-controlled voice, said that the Japanese Government, having for its aim the restoration of peace and the bringing of the negotiations to a successful conclusion, expressed its consent.... This was the decisive movement of the negotiations." One week later, before a mess of pens, paper, and sealing wax, the two sides signed the Treaty of Portsmouth at the Navy Yard conference hall. As one of the Russians noted of his unexpected tutorial in American capitalism, "All this stationery had been given by different firms desirous of advertising their goods."[12]

Conducting a kind of personal diplomacy in both the Caribbean and East Asia, Roosevelt approached the zenith of his presidency in the autumn of 1905. This momentum could hardly persist. The vagaries of partisanship, the inevitable lessening of power for an executive who had already announced his impending retirement, and festering resentment between the GOP's progressive and Old Guard wings were realities Roosevelt now faced. A year after the Portsmouth Peace Conference, for which he was awarded the Nobel Peace Prize in 1906, he could feel the momentum of American politics in motion. Reflecting on his chain of successes, he wrote with some wariness to a friend, "It is about time for the swinging of the pendulum."[13]

Part VI

DRAMATIS REX

While President I have *been* President, emphatically.
Theodore Roosevelt, 1908

A natural campaigner, Roosevelt embraced the
bully pulpit as a form of political theater.

39

Roosevelt and the Regulatory State

In the autumn of 1905, fresh off the diplomatic triumph of Portsmouth, Roosevelt reengaged with the progressive crusade. The long-simmering question of railroad rate competition and fair pricing flared up, galvanizing an increasingly educated, consumer-oriented public, and thus drew in turn the attention of reform-minded congressmen. Though conceding "that these railroad men are not . . . exceptional villains," Roosevelt thought they often showed a "swinish indifference" in their dealings with "the people." He explained to one railway executive, Frederic Delano of the Wabash line (Franklin Roosevelt's uncle), "If we do not get some form of government regulation we shall be faced with a most unpleasant movement either for government ownership of the railroads, or else for legislation against corporations." He preferred, he assured Delano, regulation over ownership, the latter of which he thought would "be of a drastic and damaging character."[1]

Railroads had since the 1850s become the dominant feature in the American economy. No fewer than five transcontinental lines, built with the aid of government land grants, coupled the East and West Coasts. These enterprises and their innumerable arteries were part of a simultaneous process of expansion and consolidation that produced great efficiencies, though often through monopolistic practices that tamped down competition. As a result, Congress created the Interstate Commerce Commission (ICC) in 1887, a regulatory agency designed to produce equitable railroad rates. Three years later it passed the Sherman

Antitrust Act and, in 1903, the popular Elkins Act, which authorized the ICC to end the practice of rebates, in which major industries could force railroads to give them sharply reduced prices on pain—considering the nation's overbuilt, ultracompetitive rail network—of taking their business elsewhere. And yet none of these responses to the trusts' growing power proved satisfactory. "We are at this moment facing a new conflict in this country, the importance of which we are only just beginning to perceive," observed the muckraking journalist Ray Stannard Baker. "It lies between two great parties, one a progressive party seeking to give the government more power in business affairs, the other a conservative party striving to retain all the power possible in private hands. . . . And the crux of the new conflict in this case, recognized by both sides, is the Railroad rate."[2]

Roosevelt hit the rate question hard in his December 1905 annual message to Congress. While granting the great industrial barons their due ("exceptional men"), he more generally raised concern that they might "use their energies not in ways that are for the common good." In such cases, he continued, it seemed perfectly appropriate that the central government, "which represents the people as a whole," be given the power to contend with corporate malfeasance. He noted further that the Founders "provided especially that the regulation of interstate commerce should come within the sphere of the General Government," and that, in light of the more recent and "enormous development of great business agencies, usually corporate in form," such central state oversight was needed now more than ever. Specifically, he called for legislation empowering Congress to establish a maximum railroad rate, calling it "essential to any scheme of real reform."[3]

The president's message put GOP conservatives in both chambers on edge. The Old Guard, already made uneasy by the growing number of progressive Republicans, felt the principles of free market capitalism under direct assault from one of their own. This was the Roosevelt whom Boss Platt had wanted to kick upstairs to the vice presidency and out of New York's gubernatorial chair, the Roosevelt that Mark Hanna had thought a proud cowboy, too independent of party czars. Believing that the industrialists were blindly inviting a socialist response to existing economic inequality, TR leaned, as he had in the Northern Securities case and the anthracite strike, in the direction of the country's producers and consumers. The vast wealth and power accumulated by a handful of private individuals—a concern raised in the 1790s by Jeffersonians critical of a powerful Alexander Hamilton–backed national bank and by Jacksonians a generation later during the Bank War—now threatened to create a rich men's republic beyond the purview of the people.

Roosevelt's congressional message conformed to a broader push among GOP progressives authorizing the ICC to establish rail rates. On December 19 Iowa's junior senator and ICC member Jonathan Dolliver, whose walrus mustache, neatly parted dark hair, and corpulent trunk made him TR's near double, introduced legislation to do so. He further cooperated with Iowa representative William Hepburn—cordial, well respected, and a gifted debater—who introduced the bill in the House, which, on February 8, overwhelmingly supported it with only seven nays. A confident Dolliver liked its chances in the upper chamber, writing to a colleague, "It is now up to the Senate to beat it if they can. I do not think they can." In fact, Rhode Island senator Nelson Aldrich, the *obstructus maximus* of the Old Guard (and John D. Rockefeller Jr.'s father-in-law), briefly blocked Dolliver's efforts to report the bill before the Senate. Instead, leadership for moving the bill fell to Dolliver's commission colleague Benjamin Tillman, a one-eyed South Carolina Democrat willing to "cross the aisle" and hoping to bring twenty-six Democratic colleagues with him. Known as "Pitchfork Ben" for his combative rhetoric, this old southern Populist seemed an unlikely ally of the president—in fact, they rather detested each other. Following Roosevelt's White House dinner with Booker T. Washington, Tillman, a defender of lynch law, raged that "the action of President Roosevelt in entertaining" Washington "will necessitate our killing a thousand" blacks "in the South before they will learn their place again." Roosevelt retorted that the senator's racial tic came through in "very violent and foolish and wicked talk."[4] And yet on the question of railroad reform this southern neo-Jeffersonian and his patrician opposite from New York found enough common ground to form a tenuous alliance.

Tillman reported the Hepburn Bill to the Senate on February 26 for debate. It bogged down in March, and by April a concerned Roosevelt hoped to woo a select group of Old Guard Republicans—including both Lodge and his former attorney general, now Pennsylvania senator, Philander Knox—to see the legislation pass. Just weeks earlier the crusading journalist David Graham Phillips had published "The Treason of the Senate," a withering exposé of large campaign contributions from big business—singling Aldrich out—in the family magazine *Cosmopolitan*. Sensing an opportunity, Roosevelt, though probably agreeing with much of "Treason"'s critique, defended the Old Guard, a bloc of some two dozen. On April 14 he delivered a speech at the cornerstone laying of the House Office Building, in which he denounced Phillips—"Hysterical sensationalism is the poorest weapon wherewith to fight for lasting righteousness"—though this did nothing to bring in GOP votes on the Hepburn Bill. The legislation's success ultimately hinged, rather, on giving the courts authority to rule on cases that resulted from the act. The Old Guard pressed for this Allison amendment as a way to hedge against the ICC's ability to set rates. With Tillman unable to come up with enough Democratic votes, Roosevelt embraced this compromise and, in the face of disappointment among progressives, declared victory. The bill, he dubiously wrote a Milwaukee reformer, "contains practically exactly what I have both originally and always since asked for."[5] In late May it passed the Senate and, following a congressional conference with House colleagues, became law.

Though a qualified achievement, the Hepburn Act constituted one of the major pieces of legislation to emerge from Congress since Reconstruction. Hardly a one-trick pony, the act captured a broader cultural mood, evident in the way that Congress passed, during the same contentious 1906 legislative session, a second major piece of consumer protection, the Pure Food and Drug Act.

Much of the energy behind this statute's passage was provided by the writer Upton Sinclair's disturbing novel *The Jungle*, a lacerating portrayal of the Chicago meatpacking industry filled with stark social realism—and plenty of blood. Agile, angular, and vaguely cadaverous (he favored a diet of vegetables and nuts), the blue-eyed Sinclair spent several weeks in 1904 working in South Side packing houses gathering material, which first appeared over several months in *The Appeal to Reason*, a socialist newspaper. Its success—spotlighting the meat industry's unsanitary working conditions—eventuated a broader publication by Doubleday, Page, eager to take advantage of an approaching Senate debate on a pure-food bill. Sinclair's work addressed the plight of immigrant communities living in a kind of industrial peasantry along the shores of Lake Michigan, though his graphic descriptions of the casual carnage involved in turning millions of sheep, pigs, and cows into factory-to-table fare more viscerally captured the public's imagination. "The men upon the floor were going about their work," he wrote in one passage. "Neither squeals of hogs nor tears of visitors made any difference to them; one by one they hooked up the hogs, and one by one with a swift stroke they slit their throats. There was a long line of hogs, with squeals and life-blood ebbing away together; until at last each started again, and vanished with a splash into a huge vat of boiling water." Sinclair later observed that while "aim[ing] at the public's heart," he had "hit it in the stomach."[6]

One of those queasy readers, Indiana senator Albert Beveridge, a leading progressive, sent a copy to Roosevelt. On March 15, amid the Hepburn Bill struggle, TR wrote to Sinclair having perused, so he said, "if not all, yet a good deal of your book." He opened by accusing *The Jungle* of "preach[ing] socialism," though also granted that "in the long run radical action must be taken to do away with the effects of arrogant and selfish greed on the part of the capitalist." To his old Harvard friend Owen Wister, however, the president complained of the book's one-sidedness: "Sinclair . . . portrays the results of the present capitalistic system in Chicago as on one uniform level of hideous horror. Now . . . there is much need for reform; but I do not think [*The Jungle* has] . . . really produced a healthy effect."[7]

Perhaps having had his fill of the controversial novel, which ends in a revolutionary "CHICAGO WILL BE OURS!," he asked Attorney General William Moody, four days after corresponding with Sinclair, if an article written by the nation's most famous socialist, Eugene Debs, "The Growth of Socialism," might be censored. "Is it possible to proceed against Debs and the proprietor of this paper criminally?" he inquired, before requesting that the Post Office Department stop its further circulation "if we can legally keep it out." Personal feelings possibly edged into the equation. "The railroad corporations have provided Mr. Roosevelt with the most luxurious special trains," Debs had tersely written of this alleged progressive, "sumptuously furnished and abundantly stocked, *free of charge*."[8]

Momentum had been building for some time to regulate the nation's food supply. Industrialization made Americans less reliant on local milk, meats, fruits, and vegetables. Preservatives and refrigeration allowed for out-of-season edibles, and a growing number of people wanted to know just what (formaldehyde?) they were putting into their bodies. A similar cry against quack medicines took hold. Accordingly, the House (240–17) and Senate (63–4) rather handily passed the Pure Food and Drug Act, sending the bill to Roosevelt to sign on June 30, 1906. "It has been a great session," he told a correspondent, regarding the legislation in rail, meat inspection, and drug oversight as signal achievements of his presidency. "Taken together," he noted, they "mark a noteworthy advance in the policy of securing Federal supervision and control over corporations."[9]

Among the accolades, this season of superlatives marked a more private milestone for Roosevelt. A father for nearly half of his forty-seven years, he observed with interest the progress of his growing children, as did much of the country. And while the Hepburn debate began to heat up in February, he prepared to send his eldest off in the Washington wedding of the year.

40

Alice in White

Given a stage as the president's eldest offspring, Alice struggled with her role in the Roosevelt circle, often feeling more errant than intimate. Her father addressed this awkward situation awkwardly, silently eliding his first marriage, a double denial given Alice's natural interest in her long-gone mother. A fermenting resentment masked outright anger, her rebellion taking the form of a quiet war on strenuous life pieties. She pointedly indulged in expensive clothing, questionable friendships, and forbidden cigarettes; she called herself a pagan, mocked sentimentality, and was occasionally cruel; the media followed her closely. These minor mutinies won her the regard, even if scolding, of the one man whose fleeting attentions she craved. "Father doesn't care for me," she confessed to a diary while in her late teens. "That is to say, one eighth as much as he does for the other children. It is perfectly true that he doesn't, and, Lord, why *should* he. We are not in the least congenial. . . . Why *should* he pay any attention to me or things that I live for, except to look upon them with disapproval."[1]

Unable to share her father's fading Victorian proprieties and frustrated at having to swim upstream as a lesser, so she supposed, appendage in a house filled with half and step connections, Alice, anointed with an easy if mercurial charm and a strong personality, captured a sizeable slice of the public imagination. Dresses in "Alice Blue" came into custom, while the French chocolate company Guérin-Boutron mass-produced her visage, with rouged cheeks and impervious expression, on a card seamed inside a candy bar. "The family were always telling me," she later observed, "'Beware of publicity!' And there was publicity hitting me in the face every day. It was unbelievable!" This notoriety only deepened her sense of displacement. "I was accused of *courting* publicity," she wrote. "I destroyed a savage letter on the subject from my father, because I was so furious with him. There was he, one of the greatest experts in publicity there ever was, accusing me of trying to steal his limelight." Struggling to make sense of her conflicting feelings, she fell upon a bleak meter in her tortured journal: "No hope for Alice."[2]

Her situation as a kind of Oyster Bay other stemmed in part from financial independence. Two Lee trusts, bringing in a combined $10,000 a year ($360,000 in today's dollars), made their beneficiary a law unto herself. Alice's hard-to-pin temperament, late hours, and noon breakfasts were irritants to her father, who hardly knew what to do with this restless proto flapper. "Sister continues to lead the life of social excitement," he wrote Ted Jr. during the family's early White House residency, "which is I think all right for a girl to lead for a year or two, but which upon my word I do not regard as healthy from the standpoint of permanence." Roosevelt recognized, however, the value of having a celebrity daughter who delighted the press. Certainly, her State Department–approved addition to the Asia-bound Taft mission—"Alice in Wonderland," "Alice Enjoying the Surf in Hawaii," the papers played along—suggested as much.[3]

Below the surface of this insouciance lay more complicated feelings. Unable to reconcile with her imperfectly presented birth mother—"the impression I finally gleaned from others about her was that she was charming and frivolous and rather hideously Dickensian"—she engaged in an ongoing war of nerves with her stepmother, whose earnestness and inner reserve only accentuated the distance between the two. The genuine closeness of the family meant, moreover, that all the Roosevelts were ripe to bear the brunt of Alice's reliably wounding judgments. From the safety of years, Ethel called her older sister "a hellion... capable of doing almost anything to anyone at any time... what wickedry she might commit next was felt almost constantly by almost all the family." Alice's studied derision appears to have come principally from wanting far more than she could ever expect to receive from her father, a busy man with a second family. She noted with pleasure in a memoir his lively after-supper readings of British ballads, sentimental tales, and Longfellow's "Saga of King Olaf," before leading his tiny troops in an off-key suite of Civil War songs. She described rainy-day games of hide-

and-seek in the many-roomed Sagamore Hill as "the pleasantest and most scary" of childhood enchantments. She felt this closeness taper, however, when her father became president. His time was taken up, so she wrote, by "members of the Cabinet, Senators, and extraneous others.... We were hardly ever alone."[4]

Not long after her debut in 1901, Alice enjoyed the attentions of several beaux, including Edward Carpenter, a career army officer, and J. Van Ness Philips, of an old Knickerbocker family, both of whom proposed marriage. These associations were often turbulent—"I really have a... temper," she faithfully remarked after an argument with Carpenter—and "the Princess," perhaps feeling pressured, denied their overlapping and no doubt competitive suits with a glancing diary entry: "It's very foolish." Nursing insecurity, she fretted over money troubles (a taste for lavish outlays exceeded even the generous Lee trusts) and thought herself unattractive and sulky compared to other women. Marriage struck her as the most plausible path forward. "I swear to literally angle for an enormously rich man," she said, a little tongue-in-cheek, at the advanced age of eighteen.[5] The following year she met Nicholas Longworth.

A freshman congressman from an old Cincinnati first family, Nick, nearly fifteen years Alice's senior, had the charm, financial security, and budding political career that attracted her immediately. His people, successful in law, real estate, and viniculture, spent their long summers among Newport's seasonal gentry before decamping for Europe. Proud, polished, and civic-minded, they were among the Queen City's leading patrons of the arts; Nick himself was an accomplished violinist. A little portly and prematurely bald, he struck Alice as mature and experienced compared to the young blades typically on her trail. Easygoing and nonjudgmental, a heavy drinker and womanizer, he offered a contrast to her famous father, whose conventional probity she so conspicuously pushed aside. And yet in wanting to be with Nick, Alice could clearly see, so she acknowledged, "a father complex coming out." Pleased that his rambunctious daughter should pair off with an older man, Roosevelt seemed at least vaguely aware of a slight doppelgänger effect: "Longworth is a good fellow," he told one correspondent. "He is a Harvard man, like myself, was on the varsity crew, [and] was a member of my club, the Porcellian."[6]

Nick and Alice were acquainted during Washington's 1903 social season, though he initially fell hard for her bewitching sometime companion Countess Marguerite ("Maggie") Cassini, daughter of the Russian ambassador to the United States and a perfect social butterfly. The countess considered herself "almost ambassadress," and Roosevelt, amused from a distance, called her "Anna Karenina." Dark-complexioned, flirtatious, and followed by whispers of improper amours—"I suppose a triangle makes always more exciting speculation then a duo," she recalled of the Alice-Nick-Maggie ménage—the countess reveled in the mysteries of her questionable reputation. Perhaps for effect, she kept a powder puff nestled in her décolletage, which rose above an impossibly slim waist. Nick sent the countess long-stemmed roses, mooned about their living in a cozy "red brick house in Cincinnati," and apparently, so the almost ambassadress told Alice, unsuccessfully proposed on a sleighing party to Chevy Chase. It began to dawn on Alice at this time that Nick's laid-back manner came with certain expectations that he too not be judged, either for his drinking or his Don Juan deportment. "I don't think he should have been as nice to me as he has been," she confided to a diary, before finding her way to the usual self-abasement: "Oh why am I such a desperate pill."[7]

Despite this rocky start, Alice and Nick maintained contact, and she, if doubtful of his intentions—"the liar said he loved me"—visited Cincinnati in June 1905, apparently impressing all, even Mother Longworth. "Everybody was crazy about you," he wrote after the stay. "It was a beautiful world when you were here." Now secretly engaged—"Nick when he was kissing and feeling me did an evil thing . . . but it was my fault. I have let him do so much"—they accompanied that summer's Taft mission to Asia, fêted agreeably about the Pacific. For Alice, the impending nuptials represented both change and consistency. "One of the reasons I married was because I felt I had to get away from the White House and my family," she later noted. "I wanted a place of my own." And yet in marrying Nick she obviously hoped to remain in Washington where, despite a feigned indifference, she thrived on the political energy, gossip, and theater the city offered. Remarkably, she would remain there, sometimes referred to as "the other Washington Monument," until her death at the age of ninety-six in 1980. "She knew," said a front-page *New York Times* obituary, "every president from Benjamin Harrison to Gerald Ford."[8]

A few months after returning from Asia, Alice and Nick announced their plans to marry. The press coverage of the affianced First Daughter only intensified during this period, drawing increased attention to her appearances at various capital city luncheons, suppers, and dances. Certain tabloid courtesies remained in place; while the media might note Alice's occasional shopping trips to Manhattan, it refrained from commenting on her purchases. She delighted in the attention—and the crush of engagement gifts suddenly arriving through the mails, each one carefully cataloged in a scrapbook. Preparing for a White House wedding, Theodore and Edith worked with a member of the State Department when putting together a guest list; one thousand invitations were eventually sent out. On the morning of the ceremony, February 17, 1906, the city police and secret service were out in force helping the guests to navigate three separate entrances into the White House. Some arrived in carriages, while most, ensembled in suits and plumes, silks and furs, walked on the city's streets to the ceremony, the sidewalks being choked with onlookers.[9]

All the guests were shepherded into the huge and newly remodeled East Room, the space Abigail Adams once used for hanging out her family's wash and where Lincoln's body had lain in state; the press huddled together in the long, marble-columned Cross Hall. Before a swarm of friends, government officials, and the occasional nod to the past—this group included Nellie Grant Sartoris, the last East Room bride (1874), alas now divorced—Roosevelt, in a formal dark coat and pants contrasted with a stiff white vest and tucked-in tie, gave the bride away promptly at noon. Henry Yates Satterlee, the first Episcopal bishop of Washington, performed the service. Alice, "the nation's bride," wore, so one White House historian tells us, "a luxurious dress of white satin trimmed in lace handed down by her mother . . . and her grandmother. The dress was low waisted, with large bows on the short sleeves. A wreath of orange blossoms held the veil, which covered the long train. The diamond necklace she wore was her wedding present from the groom. Her large bouquet had depleted the supply of orchids in Washington, accounting for the absence of the usual orchid corsages among the ladies." Following the ceremony Alice's cousin, Franklin Roosevelt, organized her white and silver brocade train; photos of the couple and their families were then taken, after which much of this private party repaired to a dining room for dessert and dancing. President Roosevelt and the First Lady, still on duty, anchored a receiving line in the Blue Room, briskly bidding adieu to several hundred well-wishers, gently hustled along by aides.[10]

Slipping out of the White House shortly after the ceremony, Nick and Alice spent three weeks in Cuba, an oddly unromantic pilgrimage to the bride's father's most sacred shrine dressed up as a honeymoon. "We trod the old Rough Rider trail up San Juan Hill," Alice later wrote. "I don't know what I had expected, possibly a tropic jungle stretching out interminably. All I know is that the reality was quite different from the Spanish War scenes of my imagination." Disappointed, and perhaps self-consciously deflating her colonel father's heroics, she added, "The scenes of the military operations of 1898 seemed on as small a scale as the war itself had been." With more zest, she took rather quickly to "a sort of punch called a daiquiri."[11]

After a brief Washington interlude in which Alice discovered she knew nothing of running a household—"I still tremble when I think of her face to face with the practical details of life," Edith sighed—the couple committed in June to a more conventional European holiday. Their itinerary, packed with kings, queens, and kaisers, made for an exhausting summer, one laden with bridal treasure. The bounty included a gold snuffbox courtesy of Edward VII ("I still have it," she insisted several decades later), an exquisite Gobelin tapestry given by the French government, and a divine bracelet and diamonds from the House of Hohenzollern. Not all gifts made the grade. Alice found a mosaic table from the king of Italy, for one, "rather hideous."[12] These and other tributes—China's dowager empress gave bolts of beautiful brocade fabrics—conformed to the "Alice in Plunderland" sobriquet first earned the previous year while in Asia.

With his daughter married and his administration humming, Roosevelt suddenly found himself caught up in one of the more difficult challenges of his presidency. While the burgeoning progressive movement captured the public's imagination, more deeply rooted questions about race remained unresolved.

41

Brownsville

In late July, while Alice "did" Europe, black soldiers from the 25th United States Infantry Regiment arrived in Fort Brown, a military post on the outskirts of Brownsville, Texas (population six thousand), across the Rio Grande from Matamoros, Mexico. Many of these men were unaccustomed to the state's Jim Crow customs and laws. Following threats, curses, and apparently incidences of physical intimidation and assault, tensions between the locals and the racially segregated unit quickly came to a head. A white woman, unable to ascertain the perpetrator, reported being attacked "near her front door" on the evening of August 12; late the following night a brief shooting spree in Brownsville resulted in the death of Frank Natus, a bartender, and the wounding of a police officer. Though darkness prevented positive identification, several residents claimed to have seen up to fifteen black soldiers running through the streets with guns. Fort Brown's white commanding officer, Major Charles Penrose, had instituted a curfew that night and, while shots were being fired in the town, made a call to arms and found all soldiers present or accounted for. Nevertheless, on the fourteenth the city formed a "Citizens' Committee," which operated under the assumption that men from the regiment had terrorized their community. "You know the object of this meeting," one of the accusers stated at the time. "We know that this outrage was committed by negro soldiers. We want any information that will lead to a discovery of who did it."[1]

After a minimal (and nonbinding) investigation had turned up a soldier's cap and dozens of rifle shell casings, the committee, unable to tell the U.S. Army how to conduct its affairs, telegraphed Roosevelt on

August 15, beseeching his aid: "Our condition, Mr. President, is this: Our women and children are terrorized and our men are practically under constant alarm and watchfulness. No community can stand this strain for more than a few days. We look to you for relief; we ask you to have the troops at once removed from Fort Brown and replaced by white soldiers."[2] Penrose, unable to explain the shell casings and supposing it possible that the alleged miscreants had dashed back to the camp when hearing a bugle calling them to arms, now reluctantly sided with the town. The following day, Roosevelt ordered an investigation to be conducted by Major Augustus P. Blocksom, a career army officer who had engaged in campaigns against the Apache and later the Sioux, received a wound at San Juan Hill, and served more recently in the Philippine War. For the time being the soldiers were to remain in Brownsville.

Following a second appeal from the Citizens' Committee, however, he changed his mind, and on the twentieth ordered the unit to nearby Fort Ringgold, and then, fearing this might only incite a white mob, to the more remote Fort Reno in the Oklahoma Territory. Twelve black soldiers, suspected of being responsible for the melee, remained in Texas, confined at Fort Sam Houston in San Antonio. Nine days later Blocksom, largely accepting Penrose's version of events, insisted that the rioters were indeed soldiers from the 25th Infantry. In what should have been a sober moment for Roosevelt, however, Blocksom acknowledged that there were no positive identifications. Frustrated at his failure to attain the names of the men he believed had participated in the shoot-up, Blocksom insisted that the soldiers schemed to protect these identities. He recommended that those unwilling to offer assistance in this matter be summarily discharged from the service, even while acknowledging the increasing difficulties of defending Jim Crow in the new century. "The colored soldier is much more aggressive in his attitude on the social equality question," his report noted, "than he used to be."[3]

TR's personal views on black Americans were typical of those of his class and background. He abhorred the raw racism of a Ben Tillman while embracing the more genteel scientific Anglo-Saxonism preached in certain academic pulpits. Following his controversial White House supper with Booker T. Washington five years earlier, the president had largely steered clear of crossing public opinion on the race question.[4]

But now he would have to act. In September a San Antonio grand jury, unable to positively identify any of the dozen soldiers suspected of involvement in the Brownsville raid, returned no indictments. That same month, in a fractious Atlanta—marinating in racial tensions brought about by changes in jobs, housing, and political power—a race riot broke out when African American men were accused of raping several white women. From this pretext came two days of massive violence in which more than twenty-five blacks were shot, beaten, stabbed, and hanged. Roosevelt unhesitatingly conflated the two clashes in the South in a transparently one-sided fashion. He condemned, in a communication with a North Carolina editor, "the grave and evil fact that the negroes too often band together to shelter their own criminals, which action had an undoubted effect in helping to precipitate the hideous Atlanta race riots."[5]

Eager to conclude the Brownsville case, the president appointed Brigadier General Ernest A. Garlington, inspector general of the army, a native South Carolinian, and son of a Confederate state militia officer, to oversee fresh interviews in Texas and Oklahoma with members of the 25th Infantry. Roosevelt informed Garlington, "If the guilty parties cannot be discovered, the President approves [Blocksom's] recommendation that the whole three companies implicated in this atrocious outrage should be dismissed and the men forever debarred from re-enlisting in the Army or Navy of the United States." A month later, in late October, Garlington's report arrived at the War Department. Noting that the soldiers interviewed at Fort Sam Houston "assumed a wooden, stolid look," and that they further "admitted" to being aware "of the discrimination" practiced by whites in Brownsville, he thought them guilty. After spending parts of two days questioning soldiers individually and in small groups but failing to turn up any witnesses, he then proceeded to Fort Reno where he conducted further interviews. "I . . . could discover absolutely nothing," he wrote, "that would throw any light on the affair." Unable to turn up hard evidence, he succumbed to stereotyping, blaming "the secretive nature of the race" for the soldiers' silence. "I recommend," he concluded, "that orders be issued as soon as practicable discharging, without honor, every man in Companies B, C, and D of the Twenty-Fifth infantry." Without apology or an overly fastidious concern for justice, he noted further, "In making this recommendation I recognize the fact that a number of men who have no direct knowledge as to the identity of the men . . . who actually fired the shots . . . will incur this extreme penalty." American citizens, he shrugged, "must feel assured that the men wearing the uniform of the Army are their protectors, and not midnight assassins."[6]

Just days after Garlington's report docked in, with off-year elections a week away, Roosevelt invited Booker T. Washington to the White House, informing him that the Fort Brown unit was soon to be dismissed from duty. Stating the obvious, Washington stressed the fundamental unfairness that men identified by no one as having broken any laws and condemned largely based on shell casings discharged from clean—that is to say, apparently unfired—weapons should be drummed out of the service. He further told the President that his actions constituted "a great blunder" made "all the more regrettable" by "waiting until . . . the day after election before putting the order into effect."[7]

Garlington's report failed, however, to convince several important constituencies, including pockets of the press and some in Congress. "Not a particle of evidence" condemned the men, the *New York Times* insisted; rather, each investigation operated under the assumption of black guilt. Ohio senator Joseph Foraker concurred, noting in a memoir, "When I read and analyzed the testimony on which the President acted, I saw at once that it was flimsy, unreliable and insufficient and untruthful." More openly, Foraker decided to take Roosevelt on. Topped with a snowy crop of thinning hair above a bushy mustache, the senator entertained executive office aspirations. Popular among the business class, he disagreed with Roosevelt on railroad regulation and seemed to think that the Republican Old Guard might support him as a small "p" progressive in 1908. A veteran of the Union army, he considered himself a liberal on the race question and backed the character of the men in the 25th Infantry, calling them "orderly, well behaved, well disciplined and well drilled." His detailed criticisms of the earlier investigations— "General Andrew S. Burt, who commanded the regiment for ten years, testified that they were all worthy to be believed on their oaths"—began to burrow under Roosevelt's skin.[8]

Hoping to put the Brownsville affair and Atlanta riot to rest, the president sought to strike an ecumenical pose in his sixth annual message to Congress, delivered in early December. Balancing, so he presumed, "Every colored man should realize that the worst enemy of his race is the negro criminal," with "The members of the white race . . . should understand that every lynching represents by just so much a loosening of the bands of civilization," he then advanced a standard of collective guilt upon blacks in cases of rape that did not apply to whites: "It should be felt as in the highest degree an offense against the whole country, and against the colored race in particular, for a colored man to fail to help the officers of the law in hunting down with all possible earnestness and zeal every such infamous offender." This editorializing sentence obviously indicted the soldiers at Fort Brown, who, so TR believed, had hindered the government's investigation. He made this connection still more explicit when insisting, "The respectable colored people must learn not to harbor their criminals, but to assist the officers in bringing them to justice." And it was this silent complicity, he further argued, that "provokes such atrocious offenses as the one at Atlanta." The "two races," he concluded, in a less than ecumenical rallying cry, must make common cause against "criminals of color."[9]

Roosevelt's words infuriated certain parties, including the prominent black weekly the *New York Age* ("the President made a great mistake") and the U.S. Senate, which, under Foraker's prodding, requested from Secretary of War Taft documents relating to the affair. Though still supporting the main findings of the report, Roosevelt, sensitive to the telling shots of the opposition, flashed a sliver of doubt in a December communication to Taft: "A careful study ... of Major Blocksom's report ... leaves me uncertain whether or not the officers of the three colored companies who took part in the murderous riot at Brownsville are or are not blamable. I should like a thoro investigation and report on this matter." Five days after drafting this note, Roosevelt learned of his having been awarded the Nobel Peace Prize, for, so the Norwegian statesman Gunnar Knudsen observed on behalf of the Nobel Committee, his "happy role in bringing to an end the bloody war recently waged between two of the world's great powers, Japan and Russia."[10] Given the juxtaposition between the lofty sentiments expressed by the committee and those questioning the president's sense of justice at home, the timing of the tribute catches several shades of irony.

Hardly pausing, however, Roosevelt pushed back against the Senate, issuing a communication to that chamber on December 19 defending his actions. Arguing, despite the failure of multiple investigations to identify the men allegedly involved in the raid, that Blocksom's report had produced "scores of eyewitnesses," TR proceeded to dip into the picaresque, depicting scenes of dusky soldiers "leap[ing] over the wall from the barracks" on their way to terrorizing the town. Sensitive to critics who noted that lynch law seldom resulted in criminal charges but rather facilitated the kind of conspiracy of silence so loudly condemned by the president in the Brownsville case, Roosevelt swore his commitment to fairness: "I should take instant advantage of any opportunity whereby I could bring to justice a mob of lynchers." There were 714 lynchings during Roosevelt's presidency.[11]

Undeterred, the Senate moved forward with its slow-paced investigation. The black press advanced more swiftly, prevailing upon the president to reconsider his insistence on shared guilt for the soldiers. "You have acted impulsively and doggedly," so an editorial in the *Horizon*, a monthly magazine edited by W. E. B. Du Bois, claimed. "You have convicted them . . . [but] their guilt is today unproven. You know it is unproven. . . . The nation is watching you. The black millions are waiting. Theodore Roosevelt, are you an honest man? If so, speak."[12] And playing off the progressive mood, the *Washington Bee* offered a protest in verse:

> O President! O can it be!
> That within yourself you feel
> You are giving to the innocent
> What you have termed "square deal"![13]

Unamused, Roosevelt used the annual dinner of the Gridiron Club, held in January 1907 at the New Willard Hotel in downtown D.C. (in whose lobby Martin Luther King Jr. would decades later put the finishing touches on his "I Have a Dream" speech), to lash out at Foraker. A membership-only association founded in 1885 by Washington journalists, it featured a good-natured roasting of the president before allowing him to reply, presumably in an equally teasing tone. Instead, Roosevelt, before a crowd of more than two hundred, defended his railroad and regulation record ("with the utmost vigor," said one attendee), before focusing on the Brownsville case, in which he rejected the Senate's right to judge his actions. Given the opportunity to reply, Foraker offered a gracious, evenhanded rebuttal that upheld the upper chamber's right to look into the matter without bowing before "preachments" emanating "from the White House."[14]

Incensed by this velvet rebuke and aware of the rapt audience's lean toward his handsome, well-spoken critic, Roosevelt, "his face... as red as the stripes on the flag," so one observer noted, lost control; once Foraker sat down, he quickly bolted, "like a 'jack-out-of-the-box,'" to reclaim the floor. Declaring that some of the soldiers "were bloody butchers" and "ought to be hung," he high-handedly maintained that the Senate had no right to investigate his conduct in the affair: "It is my business and the business of nobody else." And should the Senate, he continued, "pass a resolution to reinstate these men, I will veto it; if they pass it over my veto, I will pay no attention to it. I welcome impeachment." This rare display of poor social manners on Roosevelt's part hardly helped his case. "According to my judgment," so Missouri congressman Champ Clark, a witness to the fracas, later remarked, "the sympathy of the majority of the audience was with the Senator."[15]

Several weeks after the dinner, Roosevelt wrote of Foraker to Ray Stannard Baker, one of his favorite journalists, "He, as I am personally inclined to believe, championed the cause of the colored troops merely as an incident in his campaign against me because of our fundamental disagreement on the question of the control of corporations." Eager for revenge, the president directed that future Republican Party patronage in Ohio be handled by Taft rather than the senator. Isolated by Roosevelt and attacked in the press for his cozy accommodation to big business, Foraker, seeking reelection in 1908, failed to win his party's caucus, which went to Theodore Burton, a man more congenial to the president. "Compared to the importance of defeating Foraker," TR privately observed, "it was of no consequence at all what particular man was chosen to succeed him."[16] Foraker never held another public office.

The following year, in March 1908, the Senate Committee on Military Affairs determined by a 9–4 vote that Roosevelt was justified in dismissing the soldiers of the 25th Infantry. Neither then nor since has conclusive evidence demonstrated the culpability of any man in the unit—but 167 soldiers were unjustly discharged. The Brownsville affair is not mentioned in Roosevelt's autobiography.[17]

In 1972 the army, prodded by the work of scholars, themselves perhaps prompted by the momentum of the civil rights movement, declared the soldiers innocent, and President Richard Nixon pardoned these men and changed their discharges to "honorable." Only two members of the 25th Infantry were still alive at the time.

The issue of race in progressive America, brought forcefully before the nation in the Brownsville case, extended beyond native shores, of course, touching the imperial outposts of the new empire. Cuba, so accommodating in making Roosevelt's reputation, now presumed to tarnish his reign. This "strange republic" to the south, only a few years freed of its Spanish masters, remained unreconciled to America's protectorate role.

1.

Theodore Roosevelt Sr. (Thee), a seventh-generation Dutch New Yorker, businessman, and philanthropist, "the best man I ever knew," his namesake son once said.

2.

TR's mother, Martha (Mittie) Bulloch, a Georgia belle whose brothers supported the Confederacy. A contemporary described her as "very beautiful, with black fine hair."

3.

Theodore (Teedie), whose youth was clouded by bouts of asthma. "He gave evidence of energy," one family friend noted, "but his physique was slight and frail."

4.

A re-creation of the East 20th Street brownstone where Roosevelt was born. TR lived on this site with his family for fourteen years.

5.

A six-year-old Theodore and his younger brother Elliott watch Lincoln's funeral procession from the sun-filled second-story window of their grandfather's Union Square house.

6.

The Roosevelts twice traveled abroad. This group portrait, taken in Egypt, shows Mittie and Thee sitting third and fourth from the left in the back, with their children, Bamie, Corinne, Elliott, and Theodore (with clasped hands) seated on the floor.

7.

Tranquility, the Roosevelts' Oyster Bay summer house. Mittie and Thee occupy the veranda, and Edith Carow (later to become TR's second wife) and Corinne are on the lawn.

8.

At Harvard, TR, middle row, third from the left, joined the exclusive Porcellian Club and "was 'higher' with wine than ever before."

9.

Despite his graduating magna cum laude, Harvard failed to fire Roosevelt's imagination. Interested in studying nature in the field, he chafed under professors who stressed laboratory work.

10.

Alice Hathaway Lee, daughter of a prominent Boston banker, was TR's first wife. Perhaps a little uncertain of the "studious, ambitious, eccentric" Roosevelt, she rejected his initial proposal.

11.

Roosevelt toured Europe on his honeymoon. In Switzerland, accompanied by guides, he climbed the Matterhorn. Returning to tea and a warm bath, he declared himself "fresh as ever."

12.

In the early 1880s Roosevelt went hunting in the Dakota Territory and purchased the Chimney Butte Ranch. He once occupied this log cabin near Medora, North Dakota.

13.

Sagamore Hill, the twenty-three-room Queen Anne–style box Roosevelt had built at Oyster Bay. During his presidency it served as the summer White House.

14.

Edith Carow Roosevelt, TR's second wife and First Lady of the United States. The two met as children and shared a love of literature.

15.

A private person, Edith served as an informal advisor to her husband; contemporaries thought her often a better judge of people than the president.

16.

The trophy room at Sagamore Hill included bison heads, elephant tusks, and animal skins. "Lovely tho the White House is," Roosevelt wrote one of his sons, "it is not home; and Sagamore Hill is."

17.

Lt. Col. Roosevelt in San Antonio, Texas, recruiting and training the 1st U.S. Volunteer Cavalry (soon named the Rough Riders) for service in the Spanish-American War.

18.

Roosevelt and the Rough Riders following the Battle of San Juan Hill in Santiago de Cuba. "San Juan," TR wrote, "was the great day of my life."

19.

Three years after the war's end, Roosevelt was president of the United States, then and still the youngest man ever to have been elected the nation's chief executive.

20.

A caricaturist's dream, Roosevelt's prominent teeth, quick smile, and rimless pince-nez glasses begged satire.

21.

The Roosevelts: Quentin, TR, Theodore Jr., Archie, Alice, Kermit, Edith, and Ethel. Like their father, the children brought an unprecedented youth and energy to the White House.

22.

Roosevelt once dined with Booker T. Washington in the White House. Many were upset that the president had entertained an African American in the Executive Mansion.

23.

Roosevelt running a steam shovel at Culebra Cut, Panama Canal. He was the first sitting president to travel abroad.

24.

"The speech was nothing," said one observer of Roosevelt's charisma on the campaign trail, "but the man's presence was everything."

25.

Late in his presidency Roosevelt sent the "Great White Fleet" of U.S. Navy battleships around the world. Emphasizing both American goodwill and readiness for war, the journey captured the world's attention.

26.

Roosevelt and his "Tennis Cabinet" on the White House lawn. The group, dragooned or otherwise, included a treasury official, the French ambassador, and the secretary of the Navy.

27.

Alice's White House wedding to Congressman Nicholas Longworth. TR hoped the marriage might tame his high-spirited daughter. "Sister continues to lead the life of social excitement," he once complained to Ted Jr., "which upon my word I do not regard as healthy."

28.

Alice as a child with her aunt Bamie. Never knowing her mother, who died two days after her birth, Alice felt an outsider growing up with half siblings. "Father doesn't care for me . . . as much as he does for the other children."

29.

Alice lived until 1980, well into her nineties. Long situated in the nation's capital, she was sometimes referred to as "the other Washington Monument."

30.

Following his presidency, Roosevelt, accompanied by his son Kermit, hunted in Africa for a year, trying to put American politics behind him.

31.

Although his expedition killed over five hundred animals, TR insisted it had exercised restraint. "We did not kill a tenth nor a hundredth part of what we might have killed had we been willing."

32.

Roosevelt with Chief Forester Gifford Pinchot, who shared TR's progressive politics and urged him to run again for the presidency.

33.

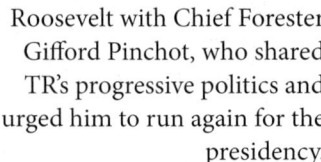

Blocked by the Republican Party's "Old Guard," Roosevelt formed the Progressive (also known as Bull Moose) Party, finishing second in the general election of 1912 behind the Democrat Woodrow Wilson.

34.

Roosevelt and Cândido Rondon (right) holding a jaguar skin during the Brazilian expedition where they mapped the mysterious Rio da Dúvida ("River of Doubt"). Brushing aside health concerns, TR said, "It's my last chance to be a boy!"

35.

During the Great War, Roosevelt grew to loathe Woodrow Wilson, who initially pursued a policy of neutrality. "I think he enjoyed his hate of Wilson," one journalist observed, "he expressed it so well; he indulged it so completely."

36.

Condemning opposition to America's war effort, TR thought "any man" who expressed sympathy for Germany should be "arrested and either shot, hung, or imprisoned for life."

37.

Roosevelt died two months after the war ended. His flag-draped casket is carried into Christ Church (Episcopal), Oyster Bay.

38.

Procession to the grave. "Death had to take him sleeping," said Vice President Thomas Marshall, "for if Roosevelt had been awake, there would have been a fight."

42

Cuban Encore

The United States' occupation of Cuba (1906–1909) might be read as a rider to an earlier (1902) crisis in Venezuela when Caracas defaulted on millions of dollars in bonds to European nations. Knowing the Germans, British, and French might take advantage of the situation to insert their influence, if not military, into the hemisphere, Roosevelt had sent a fleet to the Caribbean and proposed arbitration. Not wishing for a repeat performance, he advanced in the spring of 1904 what became known as the Roosevelt Corollary to the Monroe Doctrine. At a dinner of the Cuban Society of New York, commemorating the second anniversary of the island's "independence," Elihu Root, at the time a private citizen, read a letter from Roosevelt. "If a nation shows that it knows how to act with decency in industrial and political matters, if it keeps order and pays its obligations," the president's words filled the room, "then it need fear no interference from the United States." But should America determine that "a general loosening of the ties of a civilized society" had occurred—i.e., if the Latin republics got behind on their debt payments to the usual Euro/American suspects—then "intervention by some civilized nation"—i.e., the United States—would likely follow. The Caribbean big stick, in other words, had just gotten a little bigger.[1]

Though some criticized this latest show of gunboat diplomacy— the *New York World* called it "a flagrant exhibition of jingoism"—the corollary quickly jelled into a permanent feature of U.S. policy.[2] The impressive growth of the U.S. Navy under Roosevelt made such policing possible. In 1900 the United States possessed 8 battleships, 13 cruisers, and 18 torpedo boats, among 133 active craft. Eight years later, at the end of Roosevelt's presidency, it possessed 25 battleships, 27 cruisers, and 33 torpedo boats, among 180 active craft.[3]

In Cuba, many of the rebels formerly opposed to Spanish control were dismayed at the revolution's results. The end of direct U.S. rule in 1902 had failed to produce a robust republic. Jobs, property, and privilege, rather, were gobbled up by Americans and Europeans with the cooperation of a compliant government in Havana headed by the country's first president, Tomás Estrada Palma. Resentment boiled over following the elections of December 1905 when Palma's Moderate Party claimed a victory replete with allegations of voter fraud. Some 150,000 faked names were discovered on the electoral rolls, and supporters of the opposition Liberal Party were sacked from their positions in the civil service sector. The ensuing Cuban uprising carried out by opponents of the Palma government put the United States in an unexpected, unwelcome position. It had assumed with the 1903 Platt Amendment (passed in the Senate and subsequently integrated into the Cuban constitution) the right to intervene in Cuba's domestic and foreign affairs in order to guarantee the island's independence—presumably from European powers. But what would it do if revolutionaries *inside* Cuba posed a threat to the existing order? "Suppose they have an election," one U.S. senator had speculated. "One party or the other will be defeated. The party that is out is apt to complain, and with this kind of a provision, it seems to me ... by making trouble and creating difficulties, they would make a condition that would lead to an intervention of the United States."[4] This is precisely the situation America faced in 1906.

Concerned for his regime's future, Palma on September 8 requested assistance from the U.S. Navy. Eager to avoid being drawn into a potential civil war, Roosevelt briefly hedged. "In Cuba," he wrote a friend on the ninth (the day Palma suspended the constitution), "what I have dreaded has come to pass in the shape of a revolt or revolution." Three days later he all but called for an invasion, telegramming Assistant Secretary of State Robert Bacon from Oyster Bay, "Hurry instructions to Navy Department to send at once ... ships to Havana. ... We should have a large force of marines ... at the earliest possible moment on any vessels able to carry them." Bacon not only lined up these assets but also ordered Havana's occupation. Roosevelt, perhaps forgetting his own subordinate initiative in 1898 when commanding Dewey to ready his Asiatic Squadron in Hong Kong as a preface to attacking Spanish ships at Manila Bay, was not amused. "You had no business to direct the landing of those troops without specific authority from here," he dressed Bacon down. "Remember that unless you are directed otherwise from here the forces are only to be used to protect American life and property."[5]

The deployment of six thousand U.S. troops throughout the island, accompanied by Secretary of War Taft and Bacon serving as troubleshooters, caused some in the Senate to hesitate. Foraker, just about to become Roosevelt's adversary in the still unspooling Brownsville affair, informed the president that the U.S.'s treaty with Cuba called for *congressional approval* prior to sending in soldiers. TR flicked off this criticism as the merest of irritants. "I am sure you will agree with me that it would not have been wise to summon Congress to consider the situation in Cuba, which was changing from week to week and almost from day to day." He assured the Ohio senator that the upper chamber would, after the soldiers did their soldiering, play a role in deciding "as to what policy we shall permanently follow."[6]

The day after Roosevelt sent this communication, on September 28, the seventy-one-year-old Palma and the rest of Cuba's executive branch resigned; Taft, a seasoned colonial hand by way of Manila, now quickly established a provisional government. The president wanted to avoid the impression that the United States sought to subjugate the island. "Have directed the State Department," he telegrammed Taft on the twenty-ninth, "to continue Cuban foreign relations, consuls and ministers as if no change had occurred." The Cuban flag continued to fly over government buildings. Two days later, TR confessed to Henry Cabot Lodge the delicacy of intervening in the uprising with America's fall elections looming—he wished to avoid a GOP backlash: "Of course in what I have done, while my prime aim has been to follow the right policy from the standpoint of the permanent interests of both Cuba and the United States, I have also endeavored so to act to prevent hurt to the party pending the present election."[7] This letter appears in the second volume of *Selections from the Correspondence of Theodore Roosevelt and Henry Cabot Lodge* (1925), though with the "pending the present election" passage excised.

Taft returned to Washington in October, leaving Charles Magoon, a Nebraska lawyer serving as U.S. minister to Panama, to head the provisional government. Thus began a three-year occupation, lasting until February 1909, just before Roosevelt's term expired the following month.

Throughout these autumn machinations, the president remained engaged in an exasperating conflict at home, fuming over San Francisco's efforts to segregate both Asian immigrants and Asian Americans. The link between a trio of problems confronting his administration in 1906—the Brownsville affair, the Cuban uprising, and anti-Asian sentiment on the West Coast—was a troubling response to race. Roosevelt shared in these shortcomings. Even when touting the Havana government's independence and the provisional nature of the U.S. occupation, he scarcely took this Latin republic seriously, peopled as it was, so he observed to his son Kermit, by "those ridiculous dagos."[8]

43

Genuine Race Feeling

On October 11, just as Roosevelt welcomed the quieting of the Cuban uprising, the San Francisco Board of Education passed a resolution relegating all Japanese, Chinese, and Korean students to the Oriental Public School, established in 1859 and located in the heart of Chinatown. This provocation conformed to a broader if uneven policy of excluding Asian peoples, particularly strong along the West Coast. Tokyo's newfound prominence in the wake of the Russo-Japanese War contributed to the rise in Anglo anxiety. Aside from recognizing the vulnerability of its recent Pacific possessions, U.S. officials were frustrated that commercial restrictions in Manchuria effectively kept their tradesmen at bay. Californians, on the other hand, were deeply concerned with the prospects of increased Asian immigration. In 1880 there were only some 150 Japanese (mainly studying at colleges and universities) living in the United States, and in the 1890s fresh arrivals rarely rose above 2,000 a year. The 1898 acquisition of the Hawaiian Islands, however, meant that the archipelago's Japanese workers, many on sugarcane and pineapple plantations, were eligible to enter the U.S. without passports. And in 1904 nearly 8,000 did. Alarm of the "yellow peril" and "Asian hordes" kind informed public opinion in places like San Francisco.[1] Building on the earlier Chinese Exclusion Act (1882), critics began to rally for the restriction of further Japanese immigration while also proposing to segregate housing, schools, and restaurants.

The 1906 San Francisco earthquake heightened race tensions as Japanese merchants established businesses in formerly all-white areas. Certain Anglo groups—as well as organized labor—responded with boycotts, intimidation, and violence. By late summer Tokyo newspapers were reporting of the ill treatment of Japanese in the city, an insult only intensified by the Board of Education's controversial decision. Proud of its emergence as a great power, the Japanese government looked with some welling resentment at this calculated humiliation. On October 25, it reminded Washington that the board's action violated an 1894 treaty between the two countries agreeing to "equal rights with Americans for Japanese residents in the United States." It further noted that continued abuses would be met with a boycott on American goods.

That same day, Roosevelt received a letter from an old friend, William Sturgis Bigelow ("Billy Big"). Son of a prominent Boston physician, educated at Harvard, and medically trained in Europe under Louis Pasteur, Bigelow, prematurely bald with a neatly clipped beard and, so one contemporary observed, an "indescribably clean" look, had at the age of thirty-two happily abandoned his native New England to live for several years in Japan. Attracted to the East as an antidote to the modern industrial West, he collected Japanese art and studied Buddhism. "They don't care—broadly speaking—what is done to them as long as it does not seem to be done to them as Japanese," he now told the president. "On this they are touchy. For California—or Congress—to legislate against them on the ground that they are Mongolians is just as if they should legislate against us on the ground that we are Germans—or negroes."[2]

Secretary of State Root shared Bigelow's concern, knowing that the U.S. trade position in Asia hinged decisively on its relationship with Japan. In a confidential note to a colleague, he described the San Francisco school board's "indefensible" decision to segregate students as an "exhibition of . . . provincial and uninstructed narrowness and prejudice" that only served to embarrass the country abroad. Dismayed that both the nation's trade and its global reputation should be imperiled "by the action of a few ignorant . . . men," he sent a soothing dispatch to the Japanese government, backed by a communication from Roosevelt to his acquaintance Kaneko Kentarō, who was now serving in Tokyo on an advisory council to the emperor. "It is so purely local," TR insisted of the school board's edict, "that we never heard of it here in Washington until we got dispatches from Tokyo speaking of the trouble it had caused in Japan." To this polite fiction he added a promise to employ "all the power I have under the Constitution to protect the rights of the Japanese who are here, and I shall deal with the subject at length in my message to Congress."[3]

That address, delivered on December 4, somewhat patronizingly praised the Japanese for having "won in a single generation the right to stand abreast of the foremost and most enlightened peoples of Europe and America." And having accomplished this, Japan had earned "the right to treatment on a basis of full and frank equality." Roosevelt called efforts to segregate Japanese students from the San Francisco schools "a wicked absurdity," insisting "we have as much to learn from Japan as Japan has to learn from us." He spoke further of the need to maintain good trade relations with Asia and called for laws that might enable the president, "acting for the United States Government," to "enforce the rights of aliens under treaties." Predictably, much of California and a cluster of southern Democrats denounced this probing appeal as a threat to states' rights.[4]

Over the winter both Roosevelt and Root began to appreciate that the San Francisco board's decision had far more to do with immigration than with education. This suggested a possible quid pro quo in which a repeal of the school order would be met with a reduction of Japanese labor entering the country. Accordingly, Roosevelt did something in character, which is to say unconventional—he invited both the Board of Education and San Francisco mayor Eugene Schmitz (sent to San Quentin State Prison a few months later having been found guilty of extortion and bribery) to Washington. And so, this compromised crew (some on the board were implicated with Schmitz on charges of graft) entrained across the country, reaching the capital on February 8, 1907. The president, unable in a federal republic to tell a local school board what to do, found himself in the unusual position of trying to persuade his guests that by segregating Japanese students, they risked plunging the country into a dangerous international incident, perhaps even war.

Root had been working behind the scenes and received from Japan assurance that if the school ban was rescinded it would sharply limit the number of exit permits to "skilled or unskilled laborers" seeking to enter America. Tokyo further promised to issue passports only to merchants, tourists, and students, along with the wives, children, and parents of existing Japanese workers in the United States. Emigration to Hawaii, the gateway to mainland America, was suspended. This informal arrangement quickly came to be known as the Gentlemen's Agreement. Pressed by Roosevelt, Root, and Taft, the San Francisco delegation, following six days of negotiations, withdrew its prohibition against Japanese students—sensing that Californians would likely regard them as heroes for catalyzing the newly reduced admittance quotas. This is precisely the view taken by the *San Francisco Chronicle*. "As a result of the school trouble," it maintained, "the cause of exclusion has been put forward to a point which its most ardent advocates could not have dreamed reaching in so short a time."[5] The potential crisis had come to an end.

Negotiations conducted during the winter of 1907 brought Japanese immigration down dramatically. Between 1909 and 1924, the year the Asian Exclusion Act superseded the Gentlemen's Agreement, there was a net gain of only 8,681 Japanese. Roosevelt recognized both the inherent unfairness of segregating West Coast schools—though he said little about discrimination in southern schools—and the troubling role of skin color intolerance in America. "Their whole attitude is very bad," he wrote Kermit, of the San Francisco school board. "But I have to face facts and one fact is that, save as between gentlemen of the two nationalities, there is a strong and bitter antipathy to the Japanese on the Pacific slope—the antipathy having been primarily due to labor competition, but complicated by genuine race feeling."[6]

In a communication to British foreign secretary Sir Edward Grey around this time, Roosevelt expressed concern for America's fledgling Pacific empire. "It is possible," he supposed, "that Japan hopes ultimately to seize the Philippines." He knew that "in the event of war we should be operating far from our base." Defusing tensions related to immigration and "industrial competition," he added, was critical to keeping the peace, though this, he had little doubt, would do little good without the threat of force. With naval appropriations rising during his first term, from $85 million per year to $188 million, the United States maintained a fleet second (nearly) to none. Tonnage figures for 1907 indicate that while trailing far behind Britain's 1,633,116, its 611,616 ticked above France (609,079), Germany (529,032), and Japan (374,701).[7] This big navy boom aligned comfortably with the president's intent to move forward in the new century as an international player in an arena of rising and receding powers. Pondering over a host of issues related to this vision—the country's new Pacific holdings, the security of the Western Hemisphere, and the canal being built in Panama—Roosevelt determined to make a statement on America's burgeoning military capacity certain to capture the world's attention.

44

A Ship in Every Port

In the wake of the Gentlemen's Agreement, Roosevelt worried over the future of Japanese-U.S. relations. From the low chatter of back channels, he thought it likely that a pro-war party in Tokyo, made tipsy by the Imperial Navy's recent victories against two Russian fleets, might now seek to dominate the western Pacific by eradicating American influence in the region. Naturally any evidence of the Meiji government's military preparedness, including the November 1906 launch of the heavily armed semi-dreadnought *Satsuma*, the first battleship built in Japan, caught the president's eye. Consequently, the following June, a few months after the San Francisco Board of Education affair, he requested from the Joint Army and Navy Board—later reorganized during World War II as the Joint Chiefs of Staff—its views on positioning U.S. naval ships. Most of the American navy docked on the East Coast, as it had since the country's founding. It seemed increasingly evident to TR, however, that a substantial investment in West Coast bases was now overdue. The following month, in reply to his probe, Rear Admiral Henry Newman Manney argued against sending the fleet to the Pacific.[1] Such a provocation, he feared, might bring on a war.

A few days after receiving the report, Roosevelt rejected the rear admiral's recommendation, telling Assistant Secretary of the Navy Truman Handy Newberry, "I am struck by its extreme folly." He argued that, far from antagonizing Tokyo, the best time to make a fleet move was in a time of peace. If, he huffed, the United States chose to preserve the maritime status quo, "we should abandon every position of ours in the Pacific Ocean that is not conterminous with our own territory." In a more abrupt appraisal made the same day, Roosevelt fired off a private communication to Bamie's husband, Rear Admiral William Sheffield Cowles: "Is Admiral Manney a lunatic! He has sent me some thoughts on the Japanese which really would do discredit to an out-patient of Bedlam."[2]

Dismissing Manney's report, the president followed his own lead. "My... judgment is that the only thing that will prevent war is the Japanese feeling that we shall not be beaten," he wrote Root, "and this feeling we can only excite by keeping and making our navy efficient in the highest degree." And so, in the name of discovering inevitable shortcomings "in coaling, repairing and the like," he thought it "high time that we should get our whole battle fleet on a practice voyage to the Pacific."[3]

During this same summer, Roosevelt called a group of senior naval officers to Oyster Bay. There, during a ninety-minute discussion, he laid out a plan of action: repositioning defense guns in the Philippines, establishing a coaling station at Subic Bay (seventy-five miles west of Manila), and sending several armed cruisers to the West Coast. He further agreed to a recommendation from Admiral George Dewey, the Navy Department's highest-ranking officer on the Joint Board, that the United States transfer its battleships to the Pacific on a training exercise. How many of these behemoths did the president presume to move? the question naturally arose. All that were ready, he said—a student of Alfred Mahan, he refused to divide the fleet. Hardly a novel idea, the notion of sending ships to the West Coast had been bandied about for at least a couple of years, in connection with Japan's ascendency. "I had been doing my best to be polite to the Japanese," Roosevelt later told a British friend in 1911, "and had finally become uncomfortably conscious of a very, very slight undertone of veiled truculence in their communications in connection with things that happened on the Pacific Slope; and I finally made up my mind that they thought I was afraid of them." Wanting to dispel this notion, he continued, "I definitely came to the conclusion that... it was time for a showdown."[4]

For Roosevelt, the redeployment of the battleships—he still had said nothing publicly about globetrotting the fleet, though confided to Lodge on July 10 of his intent to direct "a practice cruise around the world"—offered several advantages. He thought it equally a matter of floating diplomacy, of technical industry, and of testing the fleet's battleworthiness. Perhaps more than any of these, the voyage offered a conspicuous projection of national power that aligned with TR's innate joy in pomp and ceremony; at heart he remained the Harvard dude "deelighted" to capture the campus's attention with a one-horse carriage. The world, he knew, would pay attention to this imposing procession tilling the waves, a glorious coming-out party announcing the United States' new role in the wake of the Spanish-American War.[5]

Naval courtesy calls were not uncommon among the Great Powers. Typically employed to recognize the birthdays of royals as well as other national holidays, these exercises sometimes took on more serious aspects. A French fleet visiting the Russian port city of Kronstadt in 1891 anticipated a treaty of alliance between the two nations signed three years later. In 1902 Prussia's Prince Henry, the kaiser's brother, arrived in New York aboard the bedizened imperial yacht *Hohenzollern*, where he met with a "ponderous salute" of booming guns when visiting the battleship USS *Illinois*, docked off Governor's Island.[6] During this well-publicized trip an elaborately hatted Alice Roosevelt christened, with a bottle of champagne before a crowd of two thousand and accompanying brass bands, the American-built *Meteor*, a schooner-rigged yacht commissioned by the kaiser. The German prince bestowed a shower of pink roses upon the American princess.

On August 23, 1907, a little more than a month after apprising Lodge of the impending "cruise around the world," Roosevelt told the public something a little different, merely announcing that some dozen battleships were to dip below South America and steam to San Francisco. The return voyage, he claimed, remained as yet undetermined. The East Coast press, as might be expected, denounced the plan, carping about the cost, the defenselessness of their own fair cities, and the implied shift in power and priorities from New York to California. Eugene Hale of Maine, chairman of the Senate Committee on Naval Affairs, fumed that Congress would refuse to allocate the money necessary to fund the cruise. The president replied that he had money enough in the naval budget to put the warships in the Pacific, and there they would stay unless Congress coughed up enough cash to bring them back. Privately, to German minister Hermann Speck von Sternburg, Roosevelt called Hale a "physical coward," and told Lodge that the Maine senator exhibited all "the heroism of the average New York financier." Sure of his ground, he seemed to be reaching for a scepter when declaring of this uneven contest with a hesitant upper chamber, "I am Commander-in-Chief, and my decision is absolute in the matter."[7]

That the cruise's architects aspired to capture the international community's imagination might be inferred from the fact that, aside from being the largest convoy of battleships to circle the globe, it would do so in style: the ships' hulls were painted a flagrant white, easily distinguished from miles away. Referred to variously in the press as the Battle Fleet or the Atlantic Fleet, the moniker Great White Fleet did not take hold for several more years, but then became indelible. Though on a training and peace trip, the caravan made a point of carrying enough gray paint—just in case—to bring the vessels to a fighting trim. If pretty, this ivory armada could hardly claim to be cutting-edge. The previous year the Royal Navy had boasted the launch of the HMS *Dreadnought*, which, with increased firepower (an "all-big-gun ship") and speed (propelled by new steam turbines), prefaced an entire generation of technologically advanced battleships. The American navy, by contrast, was still decidedly pre-dreadnought.[8]

On December 16, 1907, at Hampton Roads, Virginia, thousands of observers and onlookers buzzed under a bright morning sun, excited to watch the argosy embark. Only forty-five years earlier the historic Battle of Hampton Roads, the first combat between ironclad ships—the USS *Monitor* and CSS *Virginia*—had forever marked this watery spot in American military history. Now the wide blue channel signified a further development in naval technology, the put-to-sea point of the Great White Fleet, a steel-and-steam colossus in tune with the era's industrial-imperial incline. With the USS *Connecticut* leading the squadron of sixteen ships to sea, cannons thundered and bands played while Roosevelt, aboard the presidential yacht *Mayflower*, absorbed the scene with unimpeded pride, his top hat in the endless act of gratuitous doffing. He chose this last-minute moment to inform Rear Admiral Robley ("Fighting Bob") Evans, charged with taking the fleet to San Francisco, that the squadron would in fact circumnavigate the globe. He could perhaps feel that day the culmination of his abiding big-navy dreams. "In my own judgment the most important service that I rendered to peace," he later wrote, "was the voyage of the battle fleet around the world."[9]

The ships—eighteen participated over the course of the cruise—were worth some $100 million (about $3.2 billion in today's currency); they carried thirteen thousand men along with several million pounds of beef and equally enormous quantities of potatoes, pickles, vegetables, and jams. The foreign press watched these proceedings with great interest. Britain's *Sunday Observer* flatly called the launch "a profound mistake," while the *Novoe Vremya* (*New Times*) in Russia, taking the Rooseveltian line, thought the fleet offered "the best guarantee of peace, by checking the elation of the Oriental nations." In Japan, the influential *Jiji Shimpō* (*Current Events*) genially expressed the hope that the ships "will be given a most cordial reception worthy of the special friendship between Japan and the United States."[10]

Plowing south, the flotilla arrived in Rio de Janeiro on January 12, 1908, escorted into the city's harbor by a Brazilian warship and cheered by several hundreds of thousands of people spilling across the waterfront—the first of many such immense receptions. On February 7 it stopped at the isolated Punta Arenas, Chile, a sheep farmers' paradise located on the Strait of Magellan, to take on coal. The fleet completed the passage through the fabled strait in twenty-two hours at well-paced four-hundred-yard intervals before emerging on the Pacific side. A week and some 1,800 miles later, the squadron sheltered at Valparaíso, seventy miles west of Santiago, basking in a friendly ovation from several hundreds of thousands massed along the littoral and accompanying peaks. "The whole scene," Evans wrote, "was most beautiful and impressive."[11]

Steaming north, the fleet reached Magdalena Bay (Baja California) on March 12. After taking on provisions, it anchored at San Diego on April 10, part of a four-day festival in a city honored to receive its first port of call—"Greatest . . . Display in the History of the American Navy," the local *Evening Tribune* shouted with obvious pride. The following month it reached San Francisco for an extended stay, greeted by a million spectators packed along the piers and hills; it had thus far covered 14,556 miles in just under five months. Recognizing the arrival's symbolism, a writer for the *New York Herald* wondered about the prospects of a Pacific century, observing that the country's base of power now "seemed to tip westward." After several weeks, on July 7, the armada returned to action, reaching Hawaii in nine days. From there it steamed on to Auckland, New Zealand, its longest single port-to-port journey of the cruise (3,870 miles), which it accomplished in just over a fortnight. The receptions the fleet received in its next ports of call, in Sydney and Melbourne, surpassed even the earlier South America outpourings. Clearly "yellow peril" concerns mixed with less anxious emotions in Oceania. "We are unfeignedly glad that America has invaded the Pacific," one Down Under broadsheet stated. "It is a move that cannot help but lessen our danger of Asiatic aggression and strengthen the grounds of our national security." The Melbourne *Age*, noting the "amazing advance of Japan into the rank of a first class Power," was pleased to see "our American cousins . . . mak[ing] a bid to recapture for the Anglo-Saxon blood the naval predominancy in the Pacific which Britain lately relinquished."[12]

After spending nearly a month in Australia—sufficiently attractive that the number of "unaccounted" U.S. sailors exceeded a hundred—and a week in Manila, the squadron steamed for nine days to Yokohama, arriving on October 18 to a tumultuous welcome that the *New York Herald* described as "unbounded and unprecedented." Children sang American songs, fireworks burst above the morning fog, and a raucous crowd larger than in San Francisco greeted the visitors. The next day several of the armada's highest-ranking officers entrained to Tokyo for a week of parties, luncheons, and an audience with the emperor. Determined, in light of lingering popular discontent over the San Francisco school segregation policy, that the enlisted men cause no trouble on shore leave, only a small number were permitted liberty. Presumably such restraints prompted a common complaint voiced by a sailor aboard the USS *Ohio*, who lamented the lack of female company: "If only some arrangement might be made by which we could occasionally see and talk to some of the fair sex, life would not be so stupid."[13]

Despite lingering tensions and mediated exchanges, the *Herald* noted that with an outpouring of sustained goodwill, "Japan has captured the American fleet. That captivity is wonderfully agreeable to every officer and man." From Washington, Roosevelt rejoiced in the reception, seeing it as part of a broader strategy of asserting U.S. power in the Pacific. "My policy of constant friendliness and courtesy toward Japan," he maintained a few weeks after the ships left Tokyo Bay, "coupled with sending the fleet around the world, has borne good results!"[14]

Departing Yokohama on October 25, a Second Squadron—half the fleet—arrived in Amoy (Xiamen) along China's southeast coast on the twenty-ninth for a brief six-day stay. Initially invited by the Chinese government to visit Chefoo (Yantai) near Manchuria, policymakers in Washington thought such a call might be misread as an American attempt to assert the Open Door and suggested another port. The First Squadron went on to Manila, joined by its sister fleet a week later for target practice and reprovisioning. On December 1 this full lineup began the long trek home.[15] Over the next eighty-three days it made brief stops in Ceylon, Suez, and Gibraltar, before returning to the Chesapeake Bay on February 22, 1909. It averaged 150 miles per day during this last leg; in all, over fourteen months, it had steamed some 45,000 miles.

Though touted by Roosevelt as an excellent way to gauge the battleships' preparedness for war, the cruise was in that respect compromised. It smartly passed through the Strait of Magellan during the Southern Hemisphere's mild summer; yet it could hardly hope to control the calendar in the event of a Pacific war. Furthermore, the lack of available fueling stations forced the fleet to rely on both U.S. and foreign-owned colliers—coal-laden cargo ships—to keep it afloat. And while the long journey gave every indication of the ships' steamability on an extended cruise, it would be a stretch to say it measured their ability to engage in battle.[16]

But for Roosevelt this parade-like procession over the ocean signified something more than could be measured by mere war planners and their bean-counting acolytes. It proposed, rather, a strategic rethinking of U.S. naval defense policy, which had always been Atlantic- and Caribbean-oriented. The president hardly initiated such a course, but instead responded to the radically altered balance of Pacific power. The manner of his response, however, was distinctly Rooseveltian, a striking gesture certain to capture the world's attention.

At home the cruise, though regarded generally as a triumph, also encountered a hail of criticism. It cost too much, its critics insisted, exposed the fleet to damage from the elements, and might even egg on a war with Japan. One southern newspaper had proposed impeachment charges to prevent the voyage. Roosevelt, always a lightning rod, regarded the Great White Fleet as a diplomatic triumph that bore his distinct philosophy of statecraft. "It was the best example that I know of," he later wrote one correspondent, "'of speaking softly and carrying a big stick.'" It proved further to be his last masterstroke as chief executive. His White House tenancy now waning, opponents, both inside and out of the GOP, considered themselves increasingly free to disagree with the president, whose final eighteen months in office were largely devoid of progressive achievements. This was a frustrating period for Roosevelt, inauspiciously triggered by a three-week financial panic in the autumn of 1907, only months after he had publicly assailed, before a largely skeptical Congress, "a spirit of greed" enveloping America.[17]

45

Panic Attack

Roosevelt's relationship with the business community rarely rose above mutual suspicion, seasoned with occasional caricature and contempt. "The average trader has a hallucination," so one publication observed in early 1907, "that the President hates Wall Street and would destroy it if he could." Celebrated by some as a trustbuster for instructing the Justice Department to go after the Northern Securities Company, Roosevelt, though concerned that the corporatization of America threatened to overturn the strenuous life, also recognized that powerful nations with large navies required a sufficiently modern economic base. He thus seemed puzzled when assailed as an enemy of the industrialists. "It is difficult for me to understand," he wrote the American banker Jacob Schiff, head of the multinational investment firm Kuhn, Loeb & Co., "why there should be this belief in Wall Street that I am a wild-eyed revolutionist." And yet in that same note he employed certain holier-than-thou clauses—"I cannot condone wrong"; "I wish to do everything in my power to aid every *honest* businessman"—that made the capitalists cringe.[1]

On March 11, 1907, J. P. Morgan, "at the request of many businessmen," so the financier told a reporter at the *Washington Star*, met with Roosevelt in Washington to discuss the current economic climate. The heads of several railroads had grown concerned that low freight rates, legislated by certain statehouses in conjunction with the newly enacted Hepburn Act, were driving down the value of railroad securities. Morgan appealed to the president "to allay the public anxiety as to the relations between the railroads and the government."[2] Three days later, as if to confirm the business class's apprehension over what this buster of trusts might do next, the stock market went into a deep swoon—known as "the rich man's panic"—losing one-quarter of its value and followed by the collapse of several major businesses. Roosevelt's former personal secretary and troubleshooter extraordinaire George Cortelyou, now heading the Treasury Department, acted quickly, transferring more than $10 million in government funds to shore up the battered reserves of several New York banks. The slide was checked, but a broader sense of economic uncertainty prevailed.

The business community remained on edge that summer when a federal judge for the Northern District of Illinois, Kenesaw Mountain Landis (later made commissioner of baseball by embarrassed owners following the Black Sox scandal that threw the 1919 World Series), levied a massive fine of nearly $1 billion in today's dollars on the Standard Oil Company for accepting freight rebates from the Chicago & Alton Railroad in violation of the Elkins Act. Rockefeller's empire, so the *New York Times* declared, "received a severe shock that appeared capable of destroying the entire organization." But Rockefeller's barbed comment at the time, "Judge Landis will be dead a long time before this fine is paid," was borne out when a U.S. circuit court of appeals sitting in Chicago unanimously quashed the penalty. One of the three judges, Peter Grosscup, "scathingly arraigned the lower court," so a news story noted, "for virtually convicting a corporation that had never been indicted or tried." In this unsettled environment some among the industrial elite, feeling targeted by the president and watching the stock market sink, thought their Pennsylvania Avenue antagonist emotionally erratic and looking to lodge power in his own hands.[3] A few of them, with real malice, whispered that this moderate imbiber was after all a secret drinker.

And so matters meandered into October when, with Roosevelt hunting in Louisiana—"It was not until the twelfth day of steady hunting that I got my bear"—a failed attempt by the United Copper Company to corner the market resulted in a panic that knocked out the venerable Knickerbocker Trust Company, one of the country's largest banks.[4] Fear gripped the financial community as the sequential implosions of satellite businesses and brokerage houses caused the New York Stock Exchange to drop 50 percent from its previous-year peak. Roosevelt hastened back to Washington on the twenty-third to find the country's credit system paralyzed.

After conferring with Root and Assistant Secretary of State Robert Bacon, men with Wall Street ties, the president, eager to bolster the business community, okayed a transfer of nearly $70 million (about $2.2 billion today) to several New York City banks. On their own initiative, a handful of the country's most conspicuous tycoons—Morgan, Harriman, and Rockefeller among them—were simultaneously providing large sums and securities to stem the panic. A pledge of $25 million by a group of Manhattan bankers on the twenty-fourth managed to keep the stock exchange open; that same afternoon, with both federal and private contributions weighing in, prices began to rebound. The following day a relieved and grateful Roosevelt publicly commended "those conservative and substantial businessmen who in this crisis have acted with such wisdom and public spirit." He may sheepishly have felt exposed by the notion that while these titans were trying to keep the banks solvent, he had been out of town chasing a bear.[5]

But the crisis, if momentarily averted, spilled over into a second week. The underwriting firm of Moore and Schley was overleveraged, having secured huge loans to purchase six million shares of the Tennessee Coal, Iron and Railroad Company (TCI)—at one time the country's second-largest steel producer—that it could no longer service.

Its impending insolvency, coming hard on the heels of the Knickerbocker Trust crash, threatened to cause a cascade of bank failures. Seeing a path forward, Morgan proposed to the "Coke King" Henry Clay Frick and Elbert Gary, a corporate officer instrumental in the creation of industrial monopolies (and namesake of Gary, Indiana), that they organize through United States Steel the purchase of TCI and thus bail out Moore and Schley. But this raised the question of monopolization. The backers of this bold proposal, therefore, sought presidential and Justice Department approval before acting. But they would have to move quickly.[6]

On November 5 Frick and Gary arrived for an intimate White House breakfast with Roosevelt, during which the financiers convinced their perhaps too trusting host that, for the country's financial stability, U.S. Steel must be given a free hand to obtain TCI. In a letter to Attorney General Charles Bonaparte later that day, the president argued that his millionaire guests' request was sacrificial, for "as a mere business transaction they do not care to purchase the stock." They now proposed, rather, to save the wobbly financial situation, and TR, a romantic, an outdoorsman, and a gentleman cowboy, found nothing in his repertoire or Rough Rider bromides to critically assess the financial magicians who now proposed to make the worrisomely declining Dow tick up into safe territory. He told Bonaparte:

> They feel that it is immensely to their interest, as to the interest of every responsible businessman, to try to prevent a panic and general industrial smashup at this time, and that they are willing to go into this transaction, which they would not otherwise go into, because it seems the opinion of those best fitted to express judgment in New York that it will be an important factor in preventing a break that might be ruinous; and that this has been urged upon them by the combination of the most responsible bankers in New York who are now thus engaged in endeavoring to save the situation.[7]

To be sure, the purchase played an important role in righting the precarious financial situation, but did it give too much to the financiers? Was the price paid by U.S. Steel for TCI a bit too bargain-basement? Such inconvenient questions came up when Roosevelt's successor, William Howard Taft, gave the Justice Department permission in 1911 to bring suit to dissolve U.S. Steel, partly on the grounds of its acquisition of TCI. In a 1913 memoir, Roosevelt categorically defended his decision to let the deal go through—"The action was emphatically for the general good"—and noted his successor's apparent inconsistency—"While Mr. Taft was a member of my cabinet . . . he never protested against, and as far as I knew approved of my action."[8] No doubt Roosevelt was sincere, though his intervention in the TCI transaction demonstrated certain limits on his leadership. Staring down Congress to keep the Great White Fleet circling the earth was one thing, but conducting personal diplomacy with financiers on financial issues proved to be a competency beyond his ken.

Too often Roosevelt resorted to such informal means of dealing with corporations, parading as the big-stick-wielding arbiter who knew the difference between a good trust and a bad. But this cavalier approach relied upon private agreements that might be difficult to police and were susceptible to the vagaries of prevailing political or economic winds. Though it won over millions of consumers and gave Roosevelt the reputation of a presidential crusader smashing monopolies and promoting competition, it also provoked anxiety among a business elite equally attuned to the headlines.

The Panic of 1907 fits into a broader history of American finance. Congressional efforts to create national depositories to provide a more stable currency and credit system—the first (1791–1811) and second (1816–1836) Banks of the United States—were attacked by critics for creating a "money power" prone to corrupt the republic; neither survived its twenty-year charter. In place of this arrangement, Congress adopted the Independent Treasury structure in 1846, empowering the Treasury Department to do the government's banking (moving public funds out of private banks) while operating independently of the commercial financial system. This arrangement was amended somewhat during the Civil War when a spate of banking acts—the fighting proved incredibly expensive—passed through Congress. The Treasury's oversight was limited, however, as the Panics of 1873, 1893, and 1907 attested. The latter crisis led to the Federal Reserve Act of 1913, which created a structure of finance somewhat akin to the old Bank of the United States and is the system we retain today.

Roosevelt's role in challenging Wall Street's power was largely a bully pulpit affair, with rhetoric exceeding action. But his words did resonate, and they made him, in the eyes of some, an erratic manager of the American economy. "The course which I have taken in dealing with the big corporations is the only course compatible with the real welfare of the Republic, I am certain," he wrote to a British friend in December 1907. "It has not caused the panic, but it may have brought it on a little sooner than otherwise and have accentuated it for the moment." The fallout over the president's intervention would be more than merely political. "The Reaction against Roosevelt, socially, is violent," Henry Adams, a sometime White House dinner guest, informed a colleague that same month, "and, like all Presidents, he will probably find himself, in his last year, a severely dethroned king."[9]

These words proved prophetic. Entering a final full calendar year in office, his power slipping by the day while the GOP's congressional Old Guard opted out of the progressive crusade, Roosevelt stewed. Lashing out in a private communication—"Congress has not given me nearly all the legislation I should have had"—he opened 1908 with a loud protest, a public complaint denouncing his unheroic Capitol Hill critics.[10]

46

Thunder from On High

In December 1907, with the October panic still ripe in mind, Roosevelt sent his annual presidential message to Congress. Studded with reform initiatives, it made a broad call for state regulation over what its author considered a too-little-chaperoned corporate class. "Only the National Government," he contended, "can in thoroughgoing fashion exercise the needed control." This required no "extension of Federal authority," he continued, arguing that "such authority already exists under the Constitution in amplest and most far-reaching form." Met with a splendid indifference, the message carried little weight among legislators. George W. Perkins, a partner in J. P. Morgan & Co., noted that "the feeling at the Capitol against anything and everything the President wants, is very bitter," while Speaker of the House Joe Cannon quipped, in a typically vinegary aside, "That fellow at the other end of the Avenue wants everything, from the birth of Christ to the death of the devil."[1] The moral high-handedness Cannon detected in Roosevelt's rhetoric served as an unsatisfying substitute for real power.

And so—during the height of the Washington social season, while beginning to formally engineer the nomination of his handpicked successor, William Howard Taft, and trying, so he wrote a correspondent, "to get some exercise riding or walking every day"—he drafted yet another message to both chambers. The December communication was constitutionally prescribed (the president "shall from time to time give to the Congress Information of the State of the Union"), but what Roosevelt now proposed was a more personal proclamation, laced with occasional wrath and eager to identify the enemy. "I am worked up to my limit," he wrote Kermit on January 27, "having just been carefully preparing a message to Congress in which I intend to draw the issue as sharply as I well can between the men of predatory wealth and the administration." Wholly invested in the struggle, he swore to his son, "I believe in these principles with all my soul."[2]

These principles—rooted in the idea of consumer protection against corporate fiat—he thought under siege. Wall Street, now challenged by a spreading spirit of reform, sought, so he maintained in the January message, to marshal its enormous resources for the buying of courts, senators, and state legislatures. America seemed on the verge of becoming a rich man's republic. "From the railroad-rate law to the pure-food law," he defended the Square Deal, "every measure for honesty in business that has been passed during the last six years has been opposed by these men on its passage and in its administration with every resource that bitter and unscrupulous craft could suggest and the command of almost unlimited money secure."[3] In light of Congress's unwillingness to pursue his progressive agenda any further, Roosevelt took the first step in this searing document to break from political convention by railing against his own party in an election year.

The message-cum-manifesto indulged in both score-settling and name-calling, a therapeutic text for a proud man unused to being ignored. The epithets "law-defying wealth," "predatory wealth," and "corrupt men of vast wealth" served as bully pulpit put-downs meant to expose the corporations' plans "to rob the people." Roosevelt called for greater government oversight of capital-labor relations as well as "a certain measure of control over the physical operation of railways." No doubt more than a few of his Capitol Hill antagonists saw the specter of socialism lurking in such auspicious sentences. And yet it was precisely the fear of unchecked business board rule—the destruction of unions, competition, and consumer protections—that Roosevelt feared would ultimately raise a revolutionary response from the left. In striving to control the trusts, he argued, "we seek . . . to avoid the vindictive and dreadful radicalism which, if left uncontrolled, it is certain in the end to arouse."[4]

He further cited problems with the country's courts, viewed increasingly by the public, he feared, as extensions of a free market economy in which justice was yet another commodity to be bought and sold to the highest bidder. "A judge who on the bench bows down before a corporation," he declared, "performs an even worse service to the body politic than the legislator or executive who goes wrong." In closing, he quoted from Lincoln's eloquent second inaugural address—"as God gives us to see the right, let us strive on to finish the work we are in"—thus connecting the ancient fight against the southern plantocracy to the present campaign against the northern plutocracy.[5]

Those unsympathetic to the message dismissed the president's remarks as evidence of mental atrophy, the fledgling science of psychoanalysis beginning to filter into the public consciousness. "I am compelled to say," so Syracuse University chancellor James Roscoe Day tsk-tsked, that "much of it reads like the ravings of a disordered mind." The New York papers waxed equally clinical, with the *Times* referring to Roosevelt's "delusion that those who disagree with him and who oppose him are criminals banded together in a conspiracy," while the *Sun* maintained that "any person skilled in psychologic indications" would be concerned when reflecting "that the hand which penned this message is the same hand which directs the American Navy." Charleston's *News and Courier* snatched up the "disordered mind" motif, observing that "it is altogether the craziest of his many public utterances, without form or void. Evidently the strain of his place is telling on him, and for himself, as well as for the country, it is a blessed thing that he will soon be relieved from his official responsibilities." The *Hartford Times*, favoring something a little less condemnatory, settled for "tirade," while the *St. Louis Globe-Democrat* preferred "ill timed and ill tempered."

Democrats and progressive Republicans, by contrast, lauded the address. Oregon senator Jonathan Bourne Jr. called it "the greatest message ever written by a President of the United States," while Robert La Follette thought it "the strongest state paper of the Roosevelt administration."[6] William Jennings Bryan, making a run for his third Democratic Party presidential nomination, also commended the document:

> It is a brave message and needed at this time. All friends of reform have reason to rejoice that the President has used his high position to call attention to the wrongs that need to be remedied. He has discovered the running sore in our national life. He has pointed out the corrupting influences that flow from predatory wealth, and from the monopolistic enterprises which have given unearned riches to the few who, by controlling the great industries of the nation, have levied tribute upon the whole country.[7]

More important, Roosevelt's message had given direction to the public's progressive mood. It could not be read, Cleveland's *Plain Dealer* professed, "without feeling that the head of the nation has the heart of the common man and the courage of a brave one." The *Philadelphia Press* credited the president with a preacher's knack for inspiring "a great moral awakening of the deeper convictions and conscience of the American people," while the *St. Paul Pioneer Press* somewhat emphatically said that Roosevelt "has flayed the hypocrisy and deceit of those who have sought to mislead the public by misrepresentations of his policy, and left them standing in disgusting nakedness before the country."[8]

Such exercises in heroic editorializing could only have contributed to the stray Caesarism beguiling Roosevelt. That spring, once Congress had adjourned, he told a colleague that the GOP's popularity was "due to my hold, and the hold the policies I championed had, upon the people." The following month he wrote to the British statesman George Otto Trevelyan that "a great many honest people in this country who lead hard lives" manage to "avoid envy and hatred and despair" because of their "faith in me and in the principles I preach."[9] These words hardly sound like the valedictory of a self-imposed exile.

Part VII

AFTER THE MAGIC

We have a very, very erratic comet now sweeping across our horizon.
                                            Woodrow Wilson, 1912

Roosevelt in a self-imposed African exile—
the calm before a stormy return to politics.

47

Successor Politics

When pondering his imminent retirement, Roosevelt identified both Root and Taft as possible heirs to the throne. Physically, the contenders constituted a study in contrasts. The former was lean with somber brown eyes, close-cropped graying hair, and matching mustache; while the latter was heavy with a jiggling chin, pomaded chestnut tresses, and a hirsute handlebar above the upper lip. Both had trained in law but taken different paths. Taft had sat for nearly eight years on the U.S. Court of Appeals for the Sixth Circuit, while Root went into private practice, making a small fortune representing banks, railroads, and trusts before joining the McKinley administration in 1899. Fiercely competent, Root, equipped, so one biographer has noted, with "an extraordinary talent for finding workable solutions to technical and complex problems," succeeded by sheer acumen where mere mortals tumbled.[1] Respected, esteemed, and considered a genuine Washington wise man—a designation that eluded the less strongly defined Taft—he struck some in the GOP as the party's next leader. But Roosevelt thought not.

"There is too much opposition to him on account of his corporate connections," he told Oscar Davis, the *New York Times*'s Washington correspondent, in 1908. "I would rather see Elihu Root in the White House than any other man now possible. I have told several men recently that I would walk on my hands and knees from the White House to the Capitol to see Root made President. But I know it cannot be done. He couldn't be elected." Root later insisted that he had decided in 1904, the year he passed up the Republican nomination for New York governor, not to aim for a White House occupancy. "I could have had the nomination by acclamation . . . with the idea that it would put me into line for the Presidency," he wrote *Utica Press* editor George Dunham in 1912. "I had then to determine what I wanted to do with the rest of my life; whether I was willing to sacrifice my independence of thought and expression and action, my family life, my privacy, my tastes, for the chance of the Presidency. I concluded I was not willing to do that, not because the chance did not seem to be a good one but because I was not willing to pay the price."[2] These "I could have" asides are conceivable if not altogether convincing. For Root would go on to claim a Senate seat and polled the second-most votes on the second ballot of the 1916 Republican presidential nomination that eventually went to New York governor Charles Evans Hughes. What he lacked in 1908 was Roosevelt's push.

Other aspirants were lacking it as well, including Hughes, Speaker of the House Joe Cannon, and Senator Foraker. How ironic, then, that the one who did win his favor, Taft, really didn't want the prize, preferring appointment as chief justice to the Supreme Court, having already turned down two offers by Roosevelt to submit his name for open associate justice positions.

Taft's ambitious wife, Helen (Nellie) Herron Taft, however, much preferred the presidency for her husband. Born into a distinguished Cincinnati family—her jurist father attended Miami University with Benjamin Harrison and formed a law partnership with Rutherford B. Hayes—she enjoyed a particularly memorable trip to Washington at the age of seventeen, staying for a week ("it was a very important event") in the Hayes White House. Now, as part of team Taft, she kept abreast of the city's fluid pecking order. Following a long discussion with Roosevelt in the spring of 1906, Will Taft wrote to Nellie, "He was full of the Presidency and wanted to talk about chances. . . . He thinks I am the one to take his mantle and that now I would be nominated." What he didn't know was that Roosevelt had offered a more qualified appraisal about this time to Chicago newspaper publisher H. H. Kohlsaat: "Root would make the best President, but Taft the best candidate."[3]

Leaving nothing to chance, Roosevelt advanced Will's suit whenever the opportunity arose. In early 1908 he identified Hughes, marked by cold blue eyes, thick eyebrows, and a Garibaldi beard, as the choice of "the men" in the GOP "most hostile to me." Though conceding the governor to be "a fairly good man," TR thought him "inordinately conceited" and possessed of a humorless personality, styling him "the bearded iceberg." An adept public servant—he would go on to serve as secretary of state in the Harding and Coolidge administrations and twice sit, the latter occasion as chief justice, on the U.S. Supreme Court—Hughes maintained respectful if never warm relations with Roosevelt. Recognizing Hughes's real appeal, however, the president wrote with some concern to Kermit in late January, with the Republican National Convention only five months away, "Hughes is not knee-high to Taft in any way, but he has the kind of quality which is apt to win out in conventions as against a man of bold, generous type like Taft, who looks out too little for his own interests."[4]

Taking it upon himself to escort Taft across the finish line, Roosevelt sought to eliminate Hughes from contention. After learning that "the iceberg" was to offer a major address on national policy issues before the New York Republican Club on January 31 (a coming-out party for the would-be candidate), Roosevelt cannily released his fiery special message to Congress on the same day, thereby dominating the news cycle and relegating Hughes's speech to the back pages of the nation's newspapers. "If Hughes is going to play the game," TR crowed, "he must learn the tricks."[5]

Though near the nomination, Taft was now saddled with two incompatible patrons: Roosevelt and Nellie, each of whom wanted the credit for guiding the candidate to victory. The president needed to feel, as always, that his influence predominated, while the capable Nellie, denied a political career because of her gender, was determined to see Will reach the White House. She suspected Roosevelt of secretly planning to set aside his third-term phobia and using her husband as a stalking horse before elbowing himself into the race. She never trusted TR. Inevitably friction surfaced between the two with the rotund Taft wedged uncomfortably in the center. Accused by Nellie of political promiscuity, Roosevelt wrote to Will in late 1906,

> Mrs. Taft could not have told you that I said I might probably have to support Hughes for the Presidency. I do not think there is one chance in a thousand of it. What I said to her was that you must not be too entirely aloof because if you were it might dishearten your supporters and put us all in such shape that some man like Hughes, or more probably some man from the West, would turn up with so

much popular sentiment behind him that there would be no course open but to support him.

Drawing attention to Nellie's deliberate (to his mind) misinterpretation, he declared, "I was careful to make the statement with every kind of proviso."[6]

Though soon to retire, Roosevelt remained the dominant figure in the GOP and his endorsement meant everything. Progressive Republicans looked upon Taft as the president's chosen heir, while the Old Guard accepted him as the best way to make their party boss vacate the White House as promised. On no other grounds is it likely that these disparate constituencies would have united on Taft.

With this tenuous consensus in place, the GOP convention opened on June 16 at the Chicago Coliseum. Both Roosevelt and Taft, per custom, were absent, remaining in Washington and kept informed of the hoopla via telegraph. With the weather oscillating between mild and "infernally hot," the four-day gathering hammered out its platform, snoozed through a slow-moving queue of gesticulating speakers, and chewed on the question of a nominee. Henry Cabot Lodge served as chairman of the convention, with orders from Roosevelt to halt any effort on the part of riotous delegates to hoist the Rough Rider atop another ticket. Pictures of the president, however, were conspicuous throughout the arena, and at one point a forty-seven-minute demonstration erupted from the twelve thousand partisans when Lodge called Roosevelt "the best abused and most popular man in the United States." Waves of "Four more years!" competed with chants of "We want Teddy!" for supremacy. An overjoyed Alice, attending her first convention, called the rocking arena "a gallery performance."[7]

Taft's subsequent selection (taking 527 of the 702 votes) met with a muted approval compared to the outburst reserved for Roosevelt. Much to Nellie's chagrin, the delegates gave their new standard-bearer an ovation of only twenty-five minutes. A month later and a time zone behind, their opponents gathered in Denver, the first nominating convention held in the West, and chose, for the third time, William Jennings Bryan—the Boy Orator aging, but still the star of the party. One important item in its platform, a plank attacking "the partnership which has existed between corporations of the country and the Republican party," echoed certain of the choicer sentiments in Roosevelt's special January message to Congress.[8] And perhaps this overlap, along with Taft's nomination, proved fitting. No matter the coalition, candidate, or cause, Roosevelt continued, even in a grudging retreat, to dominate the nation's political headlines.

48

Regime Change

Safely nominated, Taft awkwardly attempted to both embrace and forsake his powerful patron. "The chief function of the next administration in my judgment is distinct from . . . that which has been performed by President Roosevelt," he told the press a few weeks after the GOP convention. But he then expressed, in the next breath, a desire "to complete the perfect machinery" already in place. This mixed messaging came increasingly to inform Taft's exchanges with the outgoing president. Though chipper and congenial, he wanted to be his own politician, and perhaps underestimated the looming reach of Roosevelt's shadow. The latter, a war hero and hunter, author and Nobel laureate, strode the American scene a man in full, equally comfortable discussing Tolstoy, dining with kings, or sharing coffee with cowboys. Taft, by contrast, a creature of public appointments, had never won an election, never captured the public's imagination, and fancied an occasional midday nap. Henry Adams once uncharitably referred to him as "a fat mush."[1]

A slight souring of mood became evident during the campaign when Roosevelt, returning from an extended Oyster Bay summer in late September, anticipated canvassing the country for Taft, an activity that might double, one suspects, as something of an extended (and parade-filled) parting. But Taft never asked. Unable to restrain himself, the president peppered his would-be successor with a blizzard of "you shoulds" and "why don't yous"—as in: "You should put yourself prominently and emphatically into this campaign"; "You should take the most aggressive kind of attitude toward Bryan"; "Why don't you in your speech point out the fact that . . ." Possessed of America's most famous teeth, he further advised the candidate to "let the audience see you smile *always*." Twice in correspondence TR suggested that Taft find a more democratic sport than golf. "I am convinced that the prominence that has been given to your ... playing has not been wise," he declared. "I have received literally hundreds of letters from the West protesting about it." A clumsy but energetic proponent of net play, Roosevelt cushioned this criticism by telling Taft, "I never let any friends advertise my tennis, and never let a photo of me in tennis costume appear."[2]

Such nagging asides failed to appreciate that Taft's views on assuming the executive office—and sidelining his golf game among other sacrifices—were complicated. Considering his distaste for crowds, campaigning, and public speaking, his tart description of the 1908 campaign as "one of the most uncomfortable four months of my life" doubles as a prophecy for a troubled presidency.[3] If not exactly lazy, he liked his leisure and enjoyed card games, conversations with friends, and a quiet home life. The son of a distinguished public figure—his father, Alphonso, had served in Grant's cabinet as both secretary of war and attorney general—he felt pressure to succeed, and this no doubt played a role in his struggles with weight, a condition unleavened by Nellie's prodding aspirations. Taft's older half brother Charles, owner of the Philadelphia Phillies baseball team, a former congressman, and married to a pig-iron heiress, helped finance Will's political career. Everywhere he turned, powerful personalities were telling him what to do.

On the other side of the political divide, the Democratic Party, bereft of a presidential campaign victory since Grover Cleveland in 1892, looked with optimism upon the coming election. The recent financial panic belied the GOP's claim of fostering economic prosperity, while drawing unflattering attention to its Wall Street ties. Democrats, by contrast, appealed to progressives by calling for an end to plutocracy, a sentiment captured in Bryan's quasi-Populist campaign slogan, "Shall the People Rule?" It was Roosevelt's absence from the ticket, however, that put the balloting, so many prognosticators said, in play. "This election," one reporter observed, "is not going to be an open-and-shut affair."[4]

And yet it was. Not only did Taft overwhelm Bryan in the Electoral College (321–162), but Republicans retained control of both congressional houses. Though an impressive victory, Taft's 51.6 percent of the popular vote paled beside his predecessor's 56.4 percent in 1904, and he lost a trio of formerly Rough Rider western states: Nevada, Colorado, and Nebraska. His healthy popular-vote lead against Bryan (1.2 million) fell far short of Roosevelt's 2.5 million margin against Alton Parker. TR's congratulatory telegram to Taft coaxed a warm if slightly obsequious reply: "It is your administration that the victory approves." Others slid credit in still another direction. As Root, for one, wrote to Whitelaw Reid in late November, "It was a vote more against Bryan than for Taft."[5]

Wanting to leave his stamp on the White House, Roosevelt proceeded in the weeks after the election to make certain cosmetic changes in the residence, notably replacing two stone carvings of lions on the limestone mantel in the State Dining Room with bison. "They make a much more characteristic and American decoration," he explained to an architect from McKim, Mead & White, the firm that had refurbished the White House in 1902. Eyeing the dying calendar, he added, "It will have to be speedily done." And once done, Roosevelt hoped to see the White House survive as something of a monument to his reign. On December 19 he wrote the architect Cass Gilbert (soon to be known for Manhattan's neo-Gothic Woolworth Building, the world's tallest skyscraper upon its completion in 1913):

> Now that I am about to leave office there is something I should like to say thru you to the American Institute of Architects. During my incumbency of the Presidency the White House, under Mr. McKim's direction, was restored to the beauty, dignity and simplicity of its original plan. It is now, without and within, literally the ideal house for the head of a great democratic republic. It should be a matter of pride and honorable obligation to the whole Nation to prevent its being in any way marred. If I had it in my power as I leave office, I should like to leave as a legacy to you, and to the American Institute of Architects, the duty of preserving a perpetual "eye of guardianship" over the White House to see that it is kept unchanged and unmarred from this time on.[6]

Perhaps, in paying tribute to America's clean-columned Federal style (c. 1750–1830), he hoped to see a neo-Federal chic forever attached to his name.

He would not, however, have history's stage all to himself. During that same winter he read with mounting irritation the recently issued

Letters of John Hay and Extracts from Diary. Astonished that their author dared consider himself a mover of recent American foreign policy, he struck back in a private, late-January communication to Lodge. Though selectively generous—"Hay was a man of remarkable ability"— he more generally thought his former cabinet colleague an effete intellectual, good with words and manners, but hardly a top-shelf statesman: "He was not a great Secretary of State." Reserving for himself the lion's share of credit for running the State Department, he observed further, "The biggest matters... such as the Portsmouth peace, the acquisition of Panama, and sending the fleet around the world, I managed without consultation with anyone; for when a matter is of capital importance, it is well to have it handled by one man only."[7]

In a far more public venue, his final annual message to Congress, Roosevelt embellished on the "one man only" theme. Frustrated with the Old Guard and its conservative partners in the judiciary, he now called for a philosopher king to save representative government from the people's alleged representatives:

> The danger to American democracy lies not in the least in the concentration of administrative power in responsible and accountable hands. It lies in having the power insufficiently concentrated, so that no one can be held responsible to the people for its use. Concentrated power is palpable, visible, responsible, easily reached, quickly held to account. Power scattered through many administrators, many legislators, many men who work behind and through legislators and administrators, is impalpable, is unseen, is irresponsible, can not be reached, can not be held to account. Democracy is in peril wherever the administration of political power is scattered, among a variety of men who work in secret, whose very names are unknown to the common people. It is not in peril from any man who derives authority from the people, who exercises it in sight of the people, and who is from time to time to give an account of its exercise to the people.[8]

Having sufficiently offended Capitol Hill, Roosevelt next went after the business class, expressing his hope in the message that laborers "shall own a far greater share than at present of the wealth they produce," though without saying exactly how. But this bully pulpit postscript constituted less a précis of crisp policy proposals than a rebuke of a Congress he had come close to holding in contempt.[9]

Other and more satisfying resolutions awaited the outgoing president. Per his custom, he opened the White House on New Year's Day to an impossibly long line of well-wishers, briskly, mechanically shaking some 8,500 hands in the process. As was her wont, Edith stood beside her husband, strategically holding a bouquet of orchids as a buffer to would-be graspers and claspers. The following month the Great White Fleet returned to Hampton Roads, and Roosevelt, boarding the just-anchored USS *Connecticut* and standing atop a 12-inch gun turret, addressed a tightly packed crowd of sailors and officers. "You've done the trick," he bellowed out. "Other nations may do as you have done, but they will follow you."[10]

This presumed end of Roosevelt's public career drew a mixed reaction from Washingtonians. Supreme Court associate justice Oliver Wendell Holmes Jr. supposed that the time had come for fresh leadership. "The present incumbents [of the White House] are very sad, I think," he wrote an English friend in late February. "I shall miss them personally a good deal, but I can't help thinking it is well of the country to have a change." Henry Adams, however, bored with mere politics, lamented his neighbor's imminent exit: "Theodore Roosevelt too is going off; another great loss to me," he wrote a colleague. "He kept us amused. Whatever charges his enemies made against him, they never included that of dullness."[11]

In this pre-inauguration period, relations between the Roosevelts and Tafts cooled. The former had thoroughly enjoyed the White House and perhaps unconsciously considered it their own. The five children had spent much of their young lives in the historic building; Alice, of course, married there. Nellie Taft may have intuited such proprietorship, and recognized that Washington society, if not the country at large, was likely to find any Roosevelt replacement a dull blade. On December 11 Edith gave her successor a tour of the residence (a first in First Lady history), with an acerbic Alice in tow. After their guest had left, the younger woman, suddenly affecting bulging eyes and a hidden chin, mimed what she uncharitably called Nellie's "hippopotamus face." The night before the inauguration, the Tafts were White House guests for an intimate dinner with the Roosevelts, though Edith's evident melancholy and Nellie's unease caused Will to refer to the occasion four years later as "that funeral."[12]

In line with her rejection of Taftism, Alice delighted when a heavy inauguration day snow turned Washington "into loathsome slush." By summoning a storm, it seemed that the gods were protesting Taft's ascendancy—"I knew there would be a blizzard when I went out," Roosevelt quipped.[13] At ten that morning he and his successor, both in top hats, left the White House in an enclosed horse-drawn carriage flanked by security personnel; ten inches of snow had piled up on either side of Pennsylvania Avenue. Ebullient to the end, Roosevelt occasionally lowered his window to wave to the crowds threading the way. At the Capitol building, the outgoing president signed several bills passed the previous evening before joining Taft for the noon swearing-in ceremony, held in the Senate Chamber due to the tempest. Afterward he took another carriage to Union Station, followed by a great throng. There he met Edith and, after a weather-induced delay of two hours, headed to New York, the Roosevelt presidency now over.

His record during these years yielded real if measured achievements. The Elkins, Hepburn, and Pure Food and Drug Acts stand among his greatest victories, while his push for a big navy reflected the controversial realities of America's imperial aspirations. Not unlike Jefferson, who had called for his country to create "an empire of liberty" different from European colonialism, Roosevelt believed that America's new overseas possessions would be run benevolently on behalf of the Filipinos, Panamanians, and Cubans it now presumed to tutor. In turn, they were expected, in sight of an ever-looming big stick, to contribute coaling stations, consumer markets, and raw materials to help feed and police the American Century.

More persuasively, Roosevelt embodied, for an agitated nation challenged by unreflective industrialization, a progressive agenda geared toward the public good. Legions of supporters saw him as fundamentally fair, evenhanded, and on their side. They delighted in his rhetorical assaults on the "malefactors of great wealth." He fed off this adulation and knew that in its absence he would discover in himself a great void. "When you see me quoted in the press as welcoming the rest I will have after [leaving office] take no stock in it," he had written Bryan, "for I have enjoyed every moment of this so-called arduous and exacting task." And on March 10, just a week after Taft's investiture, he confided to his old friend Spring Rice, "Of course, I would like to have stayed on as President—any strong man would."[14]

Sensing the frustrations of being a king without a country, he had decided months prior to Taft's presidency to remove himself from America. In the wake of his first wife's death, he had disappeared into the Dakota Territory; he now proposed to take his guns and misgivings even farther into "the wild," in search of an elusive peace he had yet to find.

49

African Exile

Dreams of a long seasonal safari had teased Roosevelt during his late scrapes with the congressional Old Guard. "A year hence I shall leave the Presidency," he wrote to the British soldier/hunter John Henry Patterson in March 1908, "and, while I cannot now decide what I shall do, it is possible that I might be able to make a trip to Africa." He sheepishly acknowledged that "for ten years I have led a busy, sedentary life" in politics and "shall be in no trim for the hardest kind of explorers' work," though the boy in him, the one who long ago, on a dreamy Nile excursion with his family, had shot bird after bird after bird, stressed an intense desire to "get into a game country" and take the measure of the land. "I am no butcher," he assured Patterson as if to assure himself, "but I would like to *see* plenty of game, and fill a few head."[1]

Several weeks later he addressed a similar communication to yet another British sportsman, Edward Buxton, author of *Two African Trips with Notes and Suggestions on Big Game Preservation in Africa* (1902). As though preparing a list for the local meat-merchant, Roosevelt identified the particular prey he preferred: "I should ... like to try for one bull elephant.... If I get a chance I should *like* to kill one giraffe, one eland, one gnu, [and] one buffalo." He queried Buxton about the need for a "special license" to engage in big game hunting, though promised to be disciplined in his stalking. "I know I need not tell you that I shall do nothing in the nature of butchery, and unless they are actually needed for food shall shoot simply one head of each species."[2]

That summer, following Taft's nomination, Roosevelt sat down with the journalist Ray Stannard Baker to discuss his future. Looking uncharacteristically tired, he repeated a variation of "Well, I'm through now. I've done my work," and expressed an interest in leaving the country for an extended period. He wanted to avoid, so he explained, being asked repeatedly his opinion of the new administration: "If I talk, people will say that I am interfering where I have no right to interfere. If I refuse to talk, they will say that my silence is disapproval."[3] He mentioned further a desire to avoid emulating Ulysses S. Grant's exhausting postpresidential world tour (1877–1879), in which the retired general seemed intent to meet every crowned, bejeweled, and otherwise ermined eminence on three continents. He sought, so he assured Baker, solitude.

It ran through the minds of a handful of New England academics, however, that Roosevelt might be enticed to assume yet another presidency—Harvard University's. In the autumn of 1908 the holder of that high office, Charles William Eliot, announced his impending retirement following a forty-year tenure. Roosevelt was a Harvard man, of course, had authored several respected historical works, and had the support of some key faculty, including his former teacher William James. But reality intervened. One of the university's overseers, Henry Lee Higginson, founder of the Boston Symphony Orchestra, could hardly imagine the spry Roosevelt bobbing about the groves of academe. "I do not believe that he could give up the very large field in which he has lived and be happy in a quiet, studious atmosphere of Yankee scholars," he observed. "Next, we need a man of judgment, and is judgment to be found coupled with such enormous energy?" Harvard never tendered an offer.[4]

Only fifty with four children under the age of twenty, Roosevelt took care to scare up funding for his African exodus. Collaterally, he worried about drawing bad press from critics who might conflate "hunting" with "slaughter," and sought to frame this elaborate safari as an exercise in scholarly discovery. Accordingly, while still president, he had approached the Smithsonian Museum promising to pay "every penny of my own expenses," though pointing out that in return for financing field naturalists, taxidermists, and a small army of baggers, boxers, and shippers, the museum could expect "the specimens I collect." In sum, he swore, "I give the Government much of value." Though initially wary of subsidizing what some Americans might see as a sportsman's long holiday, the Smithsonian eventually came around to TR's opinion.[5]

Eager to avoid having to explain himself before a Congress that might be interested in the museum's use of taxpayer dollars, Roosevelt prevailed upon the Smithsonian to establish a private fund of $30,000 to meet his needs. His secretary of commerce and labor, Oscar Straus, anted up $5,000—as did other friends and government officials, including Robert Bacon, a onetime J. P. Morgan official intimately involved in the creation of U.S. Steel. Another titan, Andrew Carnegie, eager to enlist Roosevelt in the cause of putting an end to war (the Carnegie Endowment for International Peace, formed in 1910), kicked in $2,750. Roosevelt further arranged with his primary publisher, Charles Scribner's Sons, to draft articles of his African adventures for the house's monthly magazine. His rather princely $50,000 compensation, about $1.6 million in today's dollars, and a generous 20 percent royalty rate for the pieces' republication as a book, ensured that the safari would be, at the least, a financial success.[6]

One of our best-read presidents, Roosevelt brought a crush of books on the journey. This "pigskin library," bound in leather for protection, included Dickens's *Pickwick Papers*, Shelley's poems, and Twain's *Tom Sawyer*, as well as Euripides, the Bible, Dante, and Poe. He once noted his "trick" for "reading over and over again books for which [I] really care." Roosevelt's nineteen-year-old son, Kermit, the most contemplative of his siblings and Edith's favorite, joined the safari as official photographer, taking a leave from Harvard.[7]

On March 23, not quite three weeks since Taft had moved into the White House, Roosevelt's expedition boarded the steamer *Hamburg* at the pier in Hoboken. The former president, now preferring to be addressed as "Colonel," befitting his military rank, endured the salutations and serenades of several hundred who watched his ship move the following morning onto the ocean. Hours earlier he had met with a small embarrassment that embodied one of his chief reasons for leaving. An exuberant if too-familiar Hobokenite had patted him on the back while brashly stating, "You'll be the next President of the United States, Colonel. That's what you will be." A mannerly Roosevelt smiled, waved, and offered an amiable "Hush!" in a stage whisper.[8]

Others were clearly eager to see the Colonel gone. Old Tom Platt, now in his seventies, confined to a wheelchair, and no longer a prime mover in Empire State politics, seemed to wish a malign fate on Roosevelt, whose public career, so improbable just a decade earlier, had now entered the history books. "There are a great many people who do not think Mr. Roosevelt will ever return from Africa alive," he purred to a reporter's query. "Many who have undertaken the same trip have been stricken by disease or killed by accident." No calamities occurred, however, on the voyage over. Roosevelt traveled in some decided luxury, rather, enjoying a suite that included two bedrooms and baths at the bargain rate (the Hamburg-Amerika Line happy with his patronage) of $600, about $19,000 today.[9] The hunting party arrived in Naples on April 4 and took the *Admiral* to Mombasa in British East Africa (Kenya). Over the next year the group, in various iterations, moved up the continent, to the Belgian Congo, Anglo-Egyptian Sudan, and finally to Cairo.

Hardly had they arrived when Roosevelt realized a quick infusion of cash was needed; apparently taking 260 natives on safari had crimped his budget. He told Charles Walcott, secretary of the Smithsonian, that if it failed to "make arrangements for the extra money needed" by August 1, "the scientific people will have to go home and the scientific expedition [will] come to an end." The hunting, of course, would not be interrupted: "My son and I will continue the trip on our own account." He estimated an extra $30,000 would save the trip for, so he vaingloriously said, "science in America." Sensing that there might be need for a plan B, he wrote Carnegie of his genteel penury: "Now my dear Sir, I know the multitude of demands made upon you, and it may very well be that it is out of the question for you to give such a sum," but what, after all, could compare with "rendering a great service to science." Walcott, though a little leery about the Smithsonian expedition becoming the Carnegie expedition, agreed to accept $20,000 from the retired industrialist, which he hoped to return with money raised elsewhere.[10]

The Colonel's caravan moved into the interior, making between fourteen and twenty-three miles per day. Game was abundant, and Roosevelt quickly accumulated all the specimens he had promised the Smithsonian. This did not prevent the occasional promiscuous shooting, as when, in a fumbling effort to bring down a single submerged bull hippo, the quick-triggered Colonel happened to kill a number of cows, an embarrassment he squared by insisting that after all it meant meat for the locals. Going far beyond the number of trophies he expected to entrust to science, Roosevelt rationalized his killing spree as, depending on the day, a matter of population control, a matter of mercy, or a matter of preventing big game from running riot in local villages. Only the taxidermists were busier. "Kermit's and my rifles have tended to get ahead of the ... resources of the naturalists," he wrote Corinne, after a busy three days in the bush that brought in three rhinoceroses and several kinds of buck. In a popular memoir of these adventures that appeared the following year—*African Game Trails: An Account of the African Wanderings of an American Hunter-Naturalist*—Roosevelt assured readers that temptation met resistance: "We were in hunting-grounds practically as good as any that have ever existed, but we did not kill a tenth nor a hundredth part of what we might have killed had we been willing."[11]

They were, however, willing to kill plenty. Before the expedition broke up the following March at Khartoum, Roosevelt and Kermit alone had shot more than five hundred animals, including eleven elephants, twenty rhinoceroses, nine giraffes, seventeen lions, eight hippopotamuses, nearly two hundred antelope, and dozens of gazelles and zebras, among other faunae. A far greater surplus of specimens—nearly 4,000 mammals and 2,700 birds—was shipped to the Smithsonian. The Bronx Zoo, the California Academy of Sciences, and the National Zoo in Washington also found their collections enhanced.[12]

Drafting more than a dozen articles for *Scribner's* kept the Colonel busy in his safari off-hours. Colorful exercises, they aimed to bring readers to the grassy savanna. "Right in front of me," he wrote of one hunt, "there appeared, from behind the bushes which had first screened him from my eyes, the tawny, galloping form of a big maneless lion. Crack! the Winchester spoke." There appeared the odd dollop of sportsman sagacity as well: "Under certain circumstances a lion may be easily killed, whereas a rhino would be a dangerous foe."[13]

When otherwise unoccupied, Roosevelt listened to random rumblings from America that Taft, falling under Old Guard influence, had failed to further the progressive agenda. Lodge warned him in correspondence to be careful what he said to the press. "You will be met at Khartoum by eight or ten newspaper correspondents," he sized up the scenario. "Some of them will be very hostile to Taft and will try to rouse your indignation against him by what they say. They will all try to get you to say things. I think it is of the first importance that you should say absolutely nothing about American politics before you get home."[14] Root also wrote to the Colonel, offering an obligatory homage that prefaced a plea to give Taft a chance:

> Of course we have missed you immensely & not only your personal friends but the people of the country generally seem to find your

return the most interesting thing on the horizon. The change has been a good deal like that from an automobile to a [horse-drawn] cab. Taft is big & good natured & easy going & lets things drift considerably. That is sometimes a good thing but not always. He is making a good president & will I think win his way into public confidence but he has not yet altogether arrived. I think he will. He deserves to.[15]

These softly placed suggestions revealed an underlying uncertainty about what Roosevelt might do, a question that confused even those of closer acquaintance. "I am getting more and more puzzled," Theodore Jr. said, expressing a common equivocalness, "at what attitude father will take when he gets home."[16] But home, for the moment, would have to wait. The not-quite-year in Africa anticipated a racing two-month tour of Europe, still another reprieve from the pressures of American politics that awaited the pince-nezed hunter-historian-philanthropist-naturalist, who had sworn upon the graves of nearly a dozen dropped elephants that his palmy political days were done.

50

Storming Europe

In the summer of 1908, with his White House residency down to a few final months, Roosevelt had written a British acquaintance of his distaste for European pomp and protocol: "I have not the slightest desire to meet [the kaiser] when I am thru with the Presidency.... In fact, I should go nearly crazy if I were obliged to make numbers of formal visits to people of merely titular interest."[1] And yet the Colonel's plans for a modest post-Africa jaunt on the Continent—social calls to old confidants spiced with a handful of lectures at Oxford, Berlin, and the Sorbonne—had evolved into something approaching a grand tour. Agreeing to meet a king or three led invariably to summiting with any number of emperors and aristocrats, politicians and press lords. Reunited with Edith and Ethel in mid-March in Khartoum, capital of Anglo-Egyptian Sudan, the party proceeded nearly six hundred miles on a northbound train to Wadi Halfa and from there, aboard the steamer *Ibis*, down the Nile to Cairo, stopping along the way to see Karnak's ancient ruins, which Roosevelt had first glimpsed as a boy.

Amid the travel, splendor, and boredom, the Colonel received about this time a flaming communication from Gifford Pinchot, a Roosevelt friend, Tennis Cabinet intimate, and dedicated conservationist appointed by the then-president to serve as the United States Forest Service's first chief, or forester. Regarded by critics as a bit of a fanatic (the "Sir Galahad of the Woodlands" sobriquet captured his knight-errant quality), he served as a self-appointed keeper of the progressive faith while Roosevelt roamed the tawny African hills. Pinchot—his French grandfather, Cyril Constantine Désiré Pinchot, a soldier under

Napoleon, emigrated to the United States in 1816—counted congressmen on his mother's side and money aplenty from his father's successful interior furnishings business. Tall with a bushy mustache and prominent chin, Pinchot navigated through New England's incestuous academic establishment, matriculating from Phillips Exeter to Yale, where he joined the exclusive Skull and Bones society. He now warned Roosevelt that the Old Guard was on the march. "We have fallen back down the hill you have led us up," he insisted, "and there is a general belief that the special interests are once more in substantial control of both Congress and the Administration." He refused to attack Taft head-on but attributed to him "a most surprising weakness and indecision." Instead of embracing the progressive mantle, the new president had gravitated toward GOP-approved "Trust attorneys and other Reactionaries," and thus placed "party solidarity above the public welfare." But rest assured, Pinchot promised the Colonel, "the hold of your policies on the plain people is stronger than ever."[2]

Rather than blame Taft, Pinchot criticized Interior Secretary Richard Ballinger, who had revoked executive protection of certain lands, including hydroelectric and coal development sites in Alaska.[3] Conservation, of course, had been a very near and dear point of policy for TR. Roosevelt thought nature the key to reclaiming the American character in an urban age and had created during his presidency more than fifty wildlife refuges, five national parks, and eighteen national monuments, including the Grand Canyon, Devil's Tower in Wyoming, and Mount Olympus in Washington State.

Opinions on opening pristine forests, waterways, and mineral-rich acreage for commercial development were split. Muckrakers pointed out that a few major corporations were getting fat off the public lands; on the other side of the environmental divide, Colorado's National Domain League and Spokane's Western Conservation League railed against "Federal tenantry," which they equated with eastern control over western resources. Accusing Ballinger of cooperating with industrialists to make public properties available for private profiteering, Pinchot leaked material from his office that appeared in two *Collier's Weekly* articles in November 1909. Apparently pining for martyrdom, he further denounced Ballinger, his boss, as an enemy of conservation in a combustible letter that an ally, Iowa senator Jonathan Dolliver, read to the upper chamber; the note additionally acknowledged that he, Pinchot, had supplied the press with confidential material exposing the secretary's cozy relations with those corporations desirous of western land concessions. Taft, who even before this storm had privately described Pinchot as "a radical and a crank," had no alternative but to fire the forester, which he did in January 1910, just months before Roosevelt concluded his safari and moved on to Europe.[4]

Where Pinchot awaited him. And there, in a charming villa near Porto Maurizio in Italy, site of a brief Roosevelt family vacation, he devoted the better part of the day of April 11 to unpacking the GOP's current muddle. "One of the best and most satisfactory talks I ever had," he recorded in his diary. Presumably this conversation included, beyond damning Ballingerism, also condemning the controversial Payne-Aldrich tariff (1909), a paean to corporate protectionism supported in the Northeast, receiving mixed reviews in the Midwest, but strongly opposed in the South and West. This victory for Old Guardism's industrialist benefactors was ratified by Taft's support—he supposed it would stimulate the economy—and turned into a political hot potato. GOP progressives took the opportunity to jump off the Taft bandwagon and look for another leader; like Pinchot, they badly wanted a certain Rough Rider to reenter the ring.[5]

Amid these distant American rumblings, Roosevelt plunged into a teeming season of European high society. He met Pope Pius X and King Victor Emmanuel III in Rome, while Vienna's ancient Hofburg Palace served as a ridiculously elegant space for a thirty-five-minute conversation (in French) with Emperor Franz Joseph I. Conducted by a Capuchin monk, Roosevelt laid wreaths in the Habsburg tombs for an empress and a crown prince. In felt hat and colonel's coat, he next journeyed to Budapest, greeted, despite a steady rain, by several thousand. Accompanied by Kermit, he toured the parliamentary buildings and held a press conference at his lodging in the Hotel Hungaria. The usual palace tour and prime minister pop-in transpired the following day before Roosevelt headed for Paris, arriving on April 21.[6]

There the Colonel visited Napoleon's tomb in the Hôtel des Invalides; dined at the regal Élysée Palace, residence of the Republic's presidents; and met—as a participant of authorial, constitutional, and natural history repute—with the French Academy. Receptions, luncheons, and an opera night followed.[7] Exiting Paris, the Colonel and family sojourned around the Continent, being presented to Holland's Queen Wilhelmina and Belgium's King Albert, among a hodgepodge of interchangeable aristocrats. In Oslo's National Theater, facing an audience of nearly two thousand—including King Haakon VII and Queen Maud of Norway, one of Queen Victoria's forty-two grandchildren—he delivered a belated Nobel address. All was protocol and politeness during these gatherings, though the genial veneer seemed tested a week later in Berlin where Roosevelt suspected a subtle resentment of American strength. Writing to an English correspondent, he offered the following observations:

> It was evident that, next to England, America was very unpopular in Germany. The upper classes, stiff, domineering, formal, with the organized army, the organized bureaucracy, the organized industry of their great, highly civilized and admirably administered country behind them, regard America with dislike. . . . They felt that we were entirely unorganized, that we had no business to be formidable rivals at all in view of our loose democratic governmental methods, and that it was exasperating to feel that our great territory, great national resources, and strength of individual initiative enabled us in spite of our manifold shortcomings to be formidable industrial rivals of Germany.[8]

Roosevelt further believed that his volunteer service in the Spanish-American War offended Prussian sensibilities, personifying an "irregular" route to military success. At heart, he thought these martinets knew not what to make of an outsize adventurer, and this accounted, so he supposed, for the fact that only hundreds, rather than thousands (as elsewhere in Europe), greeted him at German railways.

On May 6, the title-rich Edward VII—King of the United Kingdom of Great Britain and Ireland and the British Dominions, and Emperor of India—suffering from severe bronchitis, having long smoked dozens of cigarettes and cigars a day, died at Buckingham Palace. A mob of European heads of state raced to London for the funeral, and so did Roosevelt, implored by Taft to act as a "special ambassador" for the United States. Thus, the title-rich special ambassador—colonel, ex-president, former governor, erstwhile Rough Rider, and past Porcellian—arrived at London's Victoria Station on the sixteenth, and four days later, amid the largest gathering ever of European royalty, many of whose titles would not survive the impending Great War, joined the cortège moving from

Westminster Hall to Windsor Castle for the interment. An astounding three to five million mourners blanketed their passage through the city. The *Daily Mail* called Roosevelt "the great American" and noted how he stoically sat "like granite... in his carriage" during the solemn processioning.[9] With these formalities concluded, the Colonel enjoyed an additional three weeks in London, seeing and staying with old friends, and meeting the occasional American abroad, including his daughter Alice, sumptuously attired, provocative in speech, and clearly comfortable in the profession of socialite. All of this gently grated on her father, no doubt to the delight of the "Princess."

Ensconced in a tasteful Chesterfield Street town house with Alice and Edith, Roosevelt received a crush of well-wishers, including Cecil Spring Rice, Arthur Conan Doyle, and Rudyard Kipling. He accepted an honorary degree from Cambridge (whose students naturally conjured up a Teddy bear to hail their august guest) and delivered the Romanes Lecture at Oxford, the first American to do so. Inaugurated in 1892 and held at the university's Christopher Wren–designed Sheldonian Theatre, the lecture can be on any subject in the areas, broadly speaking, of art, science, and literature. Prior to Roosevelt, William Gladstone, Thomas Huxley, and Lord Curzon had graced its dais; those following the Colonel have included Winston Churchill, Saul Bellow, Iris Murdoch, and Hillary Clinton. Roosevelt, garbed in an impressive scholarly robe, unlimbered a nearly thirteen-thousand-word address ("Biological Analogies in History") that waxed a little mystical in its efforts to penetrate the workings of human societies. "We agreed to mark the lecture 'Beta Minus,'" quipped the archbishop of York following the performance, adding, "While we felt the lecture was not a very great contribution to science, we were sure that the lecturer was a very great man."[10]

Others thought so as well. "Roosevelt has turned us all upside down," Spring Rice gushed. "He has enjoyed himself hugely and I must say, by the side of our statesmen, looks a little bit taller, bigger and stronger." The accuracy of these elevating words might be inferred from the Colonel's difficulty remembering the names of the generic aristocrats who crossed his path in London. He described one such plumed nonentity as "a tall, shambling young man in a light blue uniform, whose card proclaimed him to be the Prince of Cumberland, or Prince Somebody of Cumberland, I forget which." Monarchy, by contrast, eagerly embraced its live-wire guest. Watching this onetime Dakota cattle rancher effortlessly charm the blue bloods (one thinks of Benjamin Franklin in pre-Revolutionary Paris), the eminent jurist Sir Frederick Pollock wrote Oliver Wendell Holmes Jr. in some amazement, "Is not Roosevelt's quasi-royal progress extraordinary?"[11]

Though pleased with his London triumph—"I thoroughly enjoyed my stay"—the Colonel looked forward to returning home, telling Lodge, "I am really fagged out." He sailed from Southampton on June 10 aboard the luxurious SS *Kaiserin Auguste Victoria*, where awaiting him atop a listing mountain of ship's mail was a poignant, pitiable letter from Taft written two weeks earlier. Opening with "It is now a year and three months since I assumed office and I have had a hard time," the communication revealed a decent, self-deprecating, if slightly out-of-his-depth president unable to master the art of Pennsylvania Avenue politics. "I have been conscientiously trying to carry out your policies, but my method of doing so has not worked smoothly," he allowed, before revealing that Nellie had suffered a stroke—"a nervous collapse," he called it—that impaired her speech and right-side limbs. With assistance, she continued to function selectively as First Lady, though her husband did acknowledge, "Mrs. Taft is not an easy patient and any attempt to control her only increased the nervous strain." One wonders to what extent Taft felt abandoned by his two strongest supporters to face the brewing feud between progressive and Old Guard Republicans. Alluding to the unpopular Payne-Aldrich tariff, he confessed to Roosevelt that "the fight to . . . comply with party promises has been a hard one," and castigated the reformers in his coalition who "have probably furnished ammunition enough to the press and the public to make a Democratic House" in the coming autumn elections.[12]

Arriving in New York on June 18, the Colonel received a furiously enthusiastic reception. "Every craft in the harbor, decked with banners and blowing whistles, was taking part in the welcome," his soon-to-be daughter-in-law, Eleanor Alexander (Mrs. Theodore Roosevelt Jr.) remembered the day. "When we landed at the Battery there were great crowds, tumultuous cheering, speeches, and a parade of horse-drawn carriages." Dozens of aging Rough Riders brought a western flavor to the affair.[13] Making his way uptown through the ticker tape, Roosevelt was met with unceasing shouts of "Teddy!" pierced by the random "Our next president!" The *Pittsburgh Leader* called the outburst a "deification," while the *Colorado Springs Gazette* puzzled over the "power which

Mr. Roosevelt now holds."[14] Much of the country had apparently forgotten that it already had a president.

While still in London, Roosevelt had received an invitation from Taft to visit the White House upon his return. This he cordially put off, uncertain of his plans, so he told his successor, "until I reach Oyster Bay, and find something about what work is in store for me." Now back home, he pocketed a second summons from the president, but this too he postponed, no doubt wanting to discover more about the political condition of the country before publicly committing himself to sitting down with Taft, who would surely relish the positive publicity. "My dear Mr. President, your invitation to the White House touches me greatly," he wrote with affected jocularity, before begging off with an awkward "but I don't think it well for an ex-President to go to the White House . . . except when he cannot help it."[15] He gave not the vaguest hint of when he might next see Taft.

That same unsettled spring, Roosevelt wrote to Lodge of his disappointment in the new administration for having too tamely aligned itself with the Old Guard. "It seems to me that Taft, Cannon, and Aldrich and the others have totally misestimated the character of the movement which we now have to face in American life." He further confessed the errancy of backing Taft in the first place. "I . . . had to admit to myself that deep down underneath I had all along known he was wrong," and, sounding a little like a worked-up Napoleon returning from his Elban exile to chase Louis XVIII out of Paris: "I went out of the country and gave him the fullest possible chance to work out his own salvation."[16] Clearly a rupture was coming.

51

Lay of the Land

Roosevelt's return corresponded with the refusal of progressive politics to fade away, and the fate of both the man and the movement were to be inextricably linked over the next two years through the momentous election of 1912. "Is this not the logical time," suggested a heretical *Kansas City Star*, hitherto orthodox Republican but now asking readers "to look forward to a new party... dedicated to the square deal and led by Theodore Roosevelt?" In the western states a score of Rough Rider clubs spontaneously arose in support of their conquering hero. The Colonel played coy. "I most emphatically desire that I shall not be put in the position of having to run for the Presidency," he wrote Lodge, clearly lingering over such a possibility. "I might even be able to *guide* this movement, but I should be wholly unable to *stop* it, even if I were to try." He spilled a small ocean of ink throughout the spring and summer in private epistles, airing such concerns, letting his chosen know that he felt used by the GOP, which coveted his popularity for campaigning purposes but governed against his values. "I have played my part," he observed to one, "and I have the very strongest objection to having to play any further."[1]

Certainly he could expect little pity from his nominal colleagues. These politicians would note that Roosevelt had foisted Taft upon them and that if the new president proved, as the Colonel inferred, unable to stand up to Senate conservatives, well, he had only himself to blame. But Roosevelt knew his worth and resented the party upper echelon's welcoming his association with the Republican brand while ignoring his policy proposals. "It is unfair to me to have me suffer for the distrust which others have earned," he wrote one correspondent, "and for which I am in no way responsible."[2]

Progressivism's quickening influence might be measured in the highbrow popularity of Herbert Croly's *The Promise of American Life* (1909). Dapper, professorial, and a little bohemian, Croly helped to forge the modern public intellectual profession. Later to cofound the *New Republic*, he sought to fashion a modern form of liberalism, capable of advancing industrialization without promoting industrial oligarchy. The book, playing off a familiar Founding Fathers dichotomy, advocated Hamiltonian means (strong government) to achieve Jeffersonian ends (democracy). Big business had radically transformed the nation over the past few decades and only a powerful federal presence could serve as a counterbalance to preserve the people's rights. Croly favored increasing state centralization, what he called a "New Nationalism," and considered Roosevelt, whose special address to Congress two years earlier had asked for much the same, its champion. "The whole tendency of his programme," he argued, "is to give a democratic meaning and purpose to the Hamiltonian tradition and method."[3]

Croly's influential book portrayed the Colonel as a progressive crusader on the right side of history, though Roosevelt scarcely needed anyone to project his opinions. Even before steaming to Africa, he had agreed to serve as a special contributing editor on the *Outlook*, a leading weekly magazine focusing on social and political issues. Paid handsomely ($385,000 in today's dollars) for roughly an article each month, TR enjoyed the additional perk of a three-room suite in downtown Manhattan, no doubt more of a convenient meeting space for a busy ex-president than a writer's sanctuary.[4]

Roosevelt spent most of his summer at Sagamore Hill, ruminating on Taft and, by association, his own cloudy political future. An attitude of grievance inevitably crept into his conversations and correspondence. One point of contention arose over appointments. Despite telling Roosevelt, in a weak or perhaps merely careless moment, that he planned to leave his predecessor's deputies in office, Taft had replaced several of these men, including ambassador to France Henry White ("a grave misfortune," the Colonel groused) and an old TR friend, Newton Dexter North, director of the U.S. Census ("I can't understand why North was taken out").[5] Though it was certainly Taft's prerogative to control patronage, the removals had the power to produce a wrinkle or even a rift should Roosevelt let it be known he was offended. And this seemed a real possibility as several of the new administration's critics found their way to Oyster Bay to sit and sup and carefully unpack their register of resentments.

Finally, in late June, Roosevelt and Taft arranged to meet. Visiting Lodge in Nahant, a quaint peninsula town in Massachusetts, TR could hardly avoid his successor, installed for the summer at nearby Beverly in a fourteen-room classic white-clapboard cottage near the ocean. Accompanied by Lodge, Roosevelt motored to the residence, though neither of the principals seemed particularly interested in rekindling their old intimacy; they were, it was noticed, never left alone during the call. Taft awkwardly persisted in referring to Roosevelt as "Mr. President," though the other openly protested. The hovering press, lined up outside the estate's gates, received word, naturally, that the reunion had been "delightful."[6]

Back in New York, Roosevelt received more than a thousand speaking requests, most coming from Republican constituencies eyeing the impending autumn elections. "The ultra-Taft people have been bent on making me come out for Taft in a way which would, in the first place, represent insincerity on my part," he complained to an English friend, "and in the next place, would simply cause me to lose all my hold on my supporters." Lodge had gingerly tried to cajole the Colonel into a show of partisan rapport—"All I want you to do and all I meant to suggest was that you should make it clear by one or two speeches that you desired the success of the Republican Party"—though when TR decided to favor the campaign trail, he did so for his own reasons, among them the opportunity to rehash his controversial 1908 special message to Congress before captive audiences. And so, in late August, he commenced a three-week swing through sixteen western states, the heart of progressive politics, where he hammered away at the corporations, and the courts who failed to keep them in line.[7]

A newspaper extract from a stop in Omaha gives some indication of what transpired: "The city is decorated in American flags—not bunting, because the reception committee frowned upon this as being tawdry. Guests invited to the luncheon have been advised that it will not be necessary to wear frock coats and silk hats." The Colonel shook hands with all the visitors while a democratic "first come, first served" protocol prevailed in the convention hall where he spoke. No seats were reserved, and a mingling of "cowboys and Rough Riders" circulated among the throng.⁸

The campaign's most vital address came at Osawatomie, Kansas, a little town (2,500) sixty miles southwest of Kansas City, and site of an infamous armed 1856 engagement between proslavery "Border Ruffians" and antislavery Free-Staters commanded by John Brown, later to be hanged for his failed raid on a federal arsenal at Harpers Ferry, Virginia. At a ceremony commemorating Brown (whom Roosevelt privately loathed, calling him a "bloody-minded fanatic"), the former president inserted, apropos Croly, the New Nationalism theme into the campaign, abandoning Old Guard dogma and canvassing instead for GOP progressives, insurgents, and, no doubt, himself. In a series of detonating sentences, he called for extending government oversight of corporations, a graduated income tax, regulation of child labor, and a workers' compensation act for federal employees. By putting the rights of people above those of property, TR confirmed the view of conservative Aldrich and Cannon Republicans that he pursued an unprecedented agenda of government activism. Even Roosevelt acknowledged that he had moved beyond the old policies of his presidency. "When I say that I am for the square deal [now]," he told the thirty thousand gathered at Osawatomie, "I mean not merely that I stand for fair play under the present rules of the game, but that I stand for having those rules changed so as to work for a more substantial equality of opportunity."⁹

The address further advanced the idea of expanding presidential authority. It was simply too easy, Roosevelt maintained, for the plutocrats to solicit senators, representatives, and even the country's courts for hire. "This New Nationalism regards the executive power as the steward of the public welfare," he insisted. "It demands of the judiciary that it shall be interested primarily in human welfare rather than in property, just as it demands that the representative body shall represent all the people rather than any one class or section of the people."¹⁰ Western audiences loved this populistic rhetoric, while many in the East grew concerned.

Lodge, in the latter camp, knew the Osawatomie speech might spell trouble for the party and quickly, but carefully, addressed its author in a note marked "personal." Easing into the topic—"People were startled, naturally, by what you said at the John Brown Celebration"—he assured TR of his own fidelity—"I was not startled, because I had talked over all those questions with you so often." No doubt "the enemy" were eager to portray the address as incendiary, Lodge continued, but "the utterances were not extreme and only a presentation of the policies you have been advocating for some time." He did, however, disagree with Roosevelt on the question of whether the judiciary favored the industrial class:

> When I see you I shall want to have a full talk in regard to this matter of court decisions, about which I admit I am very conservative. I think respect for the law is of the utmost importance. The courts are charged with the duty of saying what the law is, not what it ought to be, and I think that to encourage resistance to the decisions of the courts tends to lead to a disregard of the law.[11]

With no silver lining in sight, he strained to end on a positive note: "I am very glad that you spoke in approval of the President's action on the tariff board."[12]

Like Lodge, Taft was stunned by Roosevelt's new attitude on the courts, writing his brother Charles in some cold fury:

> He has attacked the Supreme Court, which came like a bolt out of a clear sky, and which has aroused great indignation throughout the country on the part of the conservatives. His tour through the West has been one continual ovation, and his speeches have been the same old kind—attacking corporations, corruption in politics, and setting forth his own views and his own actions as instances of proper conduct with reference to the wicked powers of evil in the Republic.[13]

He found Roosevelt's speeches "fuller of the ego now than they ever were," but loath to alienate the party's insurgents so close to the elections, he decided "to sit tight and let him talk." Beyond that day, however, Taft seemed to intuit the unwanted war that awaited him. "It looks a little bit," he told Charles, "as if he were hunting reason for criticizing me and justifying his attitude toward me."[14]

The New York *Evening Post* expressed similar concerns over the former president's recent speeches. A front-page story—"ROOSEVELT IGNORED TAFT"—breathlessly reported that "followers of the political game unanimously point out that Mr. Roosevelt has not yet given the country any definite understanding of his attitude toward the Taft administration and Taft." A more detailed page-six analysis rang with an uncanny clairvoyance:

> [The Colonel] put forth his views with the tone of the chief of a great party, and as a summons to a great political struggle, yet he never once mentioned the party to which he is supposed to belong . . . nor referred in the remotest way to the President to whom he sent a telegram last year pledging "loyalty." What are we to make of this? Are we to infer that Mr. Roosevelt proposes to found and head a new party? . . . Is this [Osawatomie] speech to be taken as a bold bid for the Presidency in 1912?[15]

Sapped by division, the GOP, already accused of lagging behind the progressive curve, limped into the autumn elections.

But Roosevelt did some limping too. Proclaiming himself unable to support a conservative New York gubernatorial nominee, he attended the state's late-September Republican convention in Saratoga where, unsurprisingly, the delegates elected him chairman. "We have beaten the reactionary machine," he bragged following the selection of a mild progressive—former U.S. attorney Henry L. Stimson, known for prosecuting antitrust cases—to run for governor.[16] But this momentary assertion of power soured on November 8 when, in what everyone knew to be a likely Democratic year, Stimson lost decisively to the wealthy businessman John Dix, 48 percent to 43 percent. It was the first time a Democratic governor had been elected since 1891.

As New York went, so went the nation; Democrats captured control of the House for the first time since 1894, while picking up seven Senate and six gubernatorial seats. Republicans quickly apportioned blame for this electoral disaster. The New York *Sun*, an organ of business conservatism, attacked TR, its day-after-the-debacle front page blaring "ROOSEVELT IS REJECTED" and "ROOSEVELT CAMPAIGN GOES TO WRECK." But such attacks scarcely fazed the proud former president, never one to give defeat its due. "My own belief is that if I had not made the fight, first at Saratoga and then in the campaign," he wrote Theodore Jr. on November 11, "we should have been beaten by from two to three hundred thousand majority; but of course I shall not say a word of this in public, for nobody cares a rap for 'might have beens,' and all that the public look at is the fact that I did make the fight and was badly beaten. In New York State the hatred of me amounted to a mania."[17]

That same day he wrote Arthur Lee, a longtime English friend, giving his version of the gathering storm within the GOP. He depicted himself as straddling the sane if narrowing center between radical wings:

> This year I was fighting with one hand tied behind me. I could not conscientiously give Taft an unreserved endorsement, and the failure to do so alienated thousands of people—although if I had done so, I should have alienated tens of scores of thousands. On the other hand, the wild extremists were bitter because I did not attack Taft outright, and were discontented because I refused to break with Root and Lodge. The situation was really impossible.

Predicting "probabl[e] defeat in 1912" under Taft, he now claimed to be looking toward 1916, whence the party might "endeavor to reorganize under really capable and sanely progressive leadership."[18] But could he wait that long?

Taft, even more than Roosevelt, registered the depths of the November disaster. "It was not only a landslide," he moaned to Secretary of State Philander Knox, "but a tidal wave and holocaust all rolled into one general cataclysm."[19] The election of progressive Democratic governors (including former Princeton president Woodrow Wilson), the selection of the first socialist congressman in U.S. history (the Austrian American Victor Berger of Milwaukee), and the drubbing of Republican gubernatorial candidate Warren G. Harding (collecting only 40 percent of the vote) in Taft's native Ohio, all pointed to grave trouble ahead for both the administration and the party.

Roosevelt, by contrast, saw only opportunity for those on the proper side of the progressive crusade. "I think the chances are a hundred to one that I never shall be President again—perhaps a thousand to one," he wrote to the beloved Kansas newspaper editor William Allen White (variously dubbed "the Sage of Emporia" and "the Spokesman for Middle America") on December 12, only to close with a rather conspicuous caveat: "But however improbable, it is possible that circumstances might arise when it would be unpatriotic of me, when it would represent going back on my principles and my friends, to refuse to be President."[20] And no one had ever accused Roosevelt of being unpatriotic.

52

Widening Divide

One could argue equally for the Colonel's post-safari prudence or imprudence. A sizeable section of the electorate clearly wished to see progressivism continue and chafed, as did he, against the Old Guard's inertia. Taking a long view, we know that the movement had yet to peak, ultimately ushering in a Democratic president, Wilson, who had promised to govern in its name. And yet Roosevelt, now two years out of office and unevenly advised, knew perhaps less about the state of the Republican base than he presumed. Met with raucous receptions while campaigning in the pro-reform West hardly helped him to grasp the political mood in the more conservative East. His communications to Lodge ("I entirely agree with you"), Root ("I perfectly reveled in your letter"), and Taft ("I am sincerely obliged to you") at this time were cordial and careful, for he knew that a widening divide separated them.[1] Still unsure of how to proceed, but so very eager to return to the ring, he mistook popularity for power; how, after all, could a man who had just outshone a procession of European kings fail to reclaim his place among a clique of mere politicians?

Others were moving more confidently toward an open break with their Republican colleagues. In January 1911, Robert La Follette announced the formation of the National Progressive Republican League, which included several of his Senate colleagues, six governors, and various influential journalists including *Chicago Tribune* publisher Medill McCormick. These men contended that the Old Guard had broken faith with the American people, who had presumed that Taft would govern in the guise of his predecessor, something the then-candidate had said repeatedly while campaigning. La Follette asked Roosevelt to join the league, though the Colonel cannily resisted—"I think that we wish to be careful not to seem to be dictating to good people who may not be quite as far advanced as we are"—sensing that it operated as a screen for the Wisconsinite's presidential ambitions. He had, moreover, never warmed to La Follette, privately calling him a "half zealot and half self-seeking demagogue," and could not see how splitting the GOP would defeat the Democrats in 1912.[2] Better, he seemed to believe at this time, to let the Old Guard lead the party into a second disastrous defeat, at which time he himself might then be recalled in 1916 to reclaim the White House.

Moreover, TR looked askance at the league's platform, which went light on conservation and corporate regulation, opting instead to stress direct-democracy reforms including the controversial trio of initiative (citizens bypassing their legislature to introduce new laws), referendum (voters striking down legislature-approved laws), and recall (the removal of public officials from office).[3] These indices of popular democracy sounded a little too populistic for Roosevelt, whose New Nationalism stressed a powerful executive—top-down reform, not bottom-up.

Undeterred by Roosevelt's caution, La Follette, eager to assume command of the growing insurgency, announced his candidacy for the Republican nomination in June. This threw off the Colonel's calculus. He had thought himself capable of suffering through another electoral cycle on the sidelines, but Battling Bob now threatened to beat him off the mark and steal a march, perhaps even the presidency. More immediately, Roosevelt understood that he would be asked to publicly take sides in a Taft–versus–La Follette contest, and though not a candidate himself, he had no desire to burnish the bona fides of either. Building a personal narrative of discontent in 1910, he had argued that the Old Guard represented a reactionary force in American politics; now, in 1911, he dismissed La Follette for leaning too far left. As he wrote William Allen White:

> The chief debit against him is that so far he has not been willing to denounce as fearlessly evil when it appears in the multitude as when it appears in the few. Very rich men have many sins to their credit; corporations have done much that is evil. But so have labor

unions, and the professional Socialists of the Debs . . . type, that is, the Socialist who in practice is really an Anarchist, is quite as serious a foe to this country as the most conscienceless scoundrel of wealth in Wall Street.[4]

Dimly seeing a path forward, Roosevelt began to regard himself as the nominee of the golden mean.

TR did much of his musing from a well-appointed Fourth Avenue office. There he wrote essays and reviews, received guests, and more generally opined about the state of the nation. He supplemented this lucrative literary work with the publication of *African Game Trails*, a big seller for Scribners that brought its author an initial royalty of some $910,000 in today's dollars. Slipping easily into his practiced popular-adventure prose, Roosevelt regaled readers with tales of "the monstrous river-horse [a hippo] snorting and plunging beside the boat; the giraffe looking over the tree tops at the nearing horseman . . . [and] the snarling leopard and coiled python with their lethal beauty." Trafficking in the exotic, he wrote of bright flowers and "dark-skinned races," of hunting elephants on Mount Kenya and camping on the banks of the White Nile at Lado Enclave in search of rhinos. In command of this rousing narrative, he seemed to have control over little else. And to a few longtime Roosevelt observers, the Colonel, holding court in a Manhattan office suite, looked faintly lost, bereft of formal authority and unable to comfortably reconcile his mass popularity with the constraints of a republican constitution. "He is a sort of president-regent," Ray Stannard Baker wrote following a visit to *Outlook* headquarters. "In some ways he possesses more power than the president, for he is essentially the real leader of the people. And yet he really has no power at all. . . . Somehow I felt, as I sat there today, that his work had passed its apex; that he could not return to his former power. There was a lack, somewhere, of his old grip on things. The movement has gone beyond him."[5]

Perhaps this very concern was what moved Roosevelt to make yet another western tour in the spring. Accompanied by Edith, he planned to see their son Archie, now seventeen, at the Evans School in Mesa, Arizona, where he'd landed after being expelled from exclusive Groton for making critical remarks about the institution's headmaster. Made to feel vaguely deficient in the Roosevelt hothouse for his academic struggles—both parents tutored the boy with varying degrees of success—Archie later wrote, "I suppose that subconsciously I realized I was a misfit." After the Arizona pit stop, which included appearing at the heavily attended dedication of the Theodore Roosevelt Dam, the former First Couple visited Theodore Jr.—struggling a bit, following the obligatory Harvard turn, to carve out a business career—and his pregnant wife, Eleanor, in San Francisco; the Colonel's first grandchild (Grace) arrived in August.[6]

That autumn TR, though still denying interest in the nomination, inevitably moved toward the same. His comments regarding Taft were increasingly aggressive if not openly critical. "I do not pretend to say that I like Taft," he wrote in a private note, "or approve of him, or enjoy supporting him." No doubt the ubiquity of "Roosevelt clubs" in the western and midwestern states bolstered his attitude. Though playing reluctant, he fed the building momentum with a steady diet of pungent *Outlook* articles that endeavored to both define and direct the progressive agenda. In one editorial—"The Trusts, the People, and the Square Deal"—he claimed to have "always believed that it would . . . be necessary to give the National Government complete power over the organization and capitalization of all business concerns engaged in inter-State commerce." The existing antitrust laws had failed to protect consumers, he continued, as a combination of "insincere politicians" and the "Wall Street Crowd" successfully managed matters to their own ends. Adhering to the powerful-executive argument, the Colonel insisted upon the government's right in the modern age to "control [corporations] in such fashion as amply to safeguard the interests of the whole public."[7]

In this and other articles the natural combatant in Roosevelt emerged, though he was not yet prepared to take on the Old Guard. "Taft will get the nomination; sure!" he wrote Theodore Jr., while adding, "Gifford Pinchot is a dear, but he is a fanatic." And yet he seemed eager to talk up the possibility of nomination, to stir interest and thus support. "I very emphatically feel that to me personally to be nominated in 1912 would be a calamity," he told Benjamin Lindsey, a Colorado progressive, before adding the obligatory "unless . . ." followed by the inevitable appeal to the public: ". . . the bulk of the people wanted a given job done, and for their own sakes, and not mine, wanted me to do the job."[8]

And so he marched into a new year, a noncandidate eager to be claimed by the people.

53

The Battle Begins

The year 1912 opened for Roosevelt on an equivocal note. La Follette, having emerged as a national progressive leader, appeared eager to take on Taft, and even if unsuccessful he could lay claim to the reform mantle moving forward. That would leave the Colonel, despite his enormous popularity, on the outside of this Republican Party infighting. But in January, with the primary season looming, a measure of clarity began to emerge within the insurgent cause—to La Follette's cost. For on the sixteenth, a Roosevelt National Committee formed in Chicago, establishing a presence in the city's Congress Plaza Hotel, erected in 1893 for the World's Columbian Exposition and a favored destination of transiting power brokers. The committee's existence overlapped the private pleas of several governors urging the Colonel to contest Taft for the nomination. One of them, Michigan's Chase Salmon Osborn, delivered an address that month criticizing La Follette and pressing Roosevelt to reclaim his hold on the GOP.[1]

On the eighteenth the Colonel, having recently informed Bamie, "I believe the flurry in favor of my nomination has spent its force," now wrote Osborn from his *Outlook* office, laying out a plausible path to the candidacy. Working himself into a fighter's lather—"It is impossible for me much longer to remain silent"—he suggested "having you and Governor Glasscock [of West Virginia], Governor Stubbs of Kansas . . . and Governor Bass of New Hampshire, write me a letter to which I could answer. . . . The letter . . . might simply briefly state the writer's belief that the people of his State, or their States . . . desire to have me run for the Presidency, and to know whether in such a case I would refuse the nomination." Shunning any suggestion of self-interest, he bowed deeply before the pleas of vox populi—"I want to make it very clear that I am honestly desirous of considering the matter solely from the standpoint of the public interest, and not in the least from my own standpoint." And should "the plain people ... the people as a whole desire me," he continued, "I would feel in honor bound to do so." He signed off with an urgent adieu: "What do you think of the plan?"[2]

Osborn and the handful of governors he covenanted with were absolutely thrilled. Seven of them signed a private round-robin letter to Roosevelt dated February 10 asking him to seek the Republican Party's nomination. The states these men represented—Michigan, Missouri, Kansas, New Hampshire, Nebraska, Wyoming, and Vermont—give a sense of the rural rather than urban style of progressivism that cleaved so loyally to the Colonel. The governors, operating, Stubbs said, in an "unofficial but active committee," released for public consumption at this time a ringing statement: "A principle is of no avail without a man: a cause is lost without a leader. In Theodore Roosevelt we believe the principle has the man and the cause the leader. It is our opinion that this is the sentiment of the majority of the people of the United States."[3] Nearly every piece was now in place for Roosevelt to take the stage.

Before he confronted Taft, however, there remained another possible impediment to the nomination—La Follette. The Wisconsin senator had met TR, then serving in the Civil Service Commission, as a young congressman in the early 1890s and "thought him an unusually able and energetic man." La Follette's good opinion tapered during TR's presidency when he came to regard the famed trustbuster as a mere paper tiger indulging in "rhetorical radicalism" that "filled the air with noise and smoke." Such "cannonading," La Follette argued, made Roosevelt a successful politician but it hardly yielded strong progressive leadership.[4]

Thinking himself the rightful lion of reform Republicanism, La Follette resented Roosevelt's coy game of claiming in correspondence no interest in the nomination, while refusing to say so publicly. But "as soon as my candidacy began to take on proportions that looked like success," the senator later observed, "there was what seemed to me to be unmistakable evidence of his doing everything in his power to block it, excepting to come out openly against me." Unable to stem Roosevelt's momentum, La Follette suddenly came undone. On February 2, he delivered a disastrous address at the Periodical Publishers Association in Philadelphia. Exhausted from a grueling speaking schedule, worried over a sick daughter, and no doubt troubled by Roosevelt's loud silence on the candidate question, he seemed to flirt with a breakdown, giving a rambling, angry, and often incoherent speech that sealed his fate. "Respectful attention gave way at the end of an hour to confusion," the Philadelphia *Evening Bulletin* observed, "and at the end of two hours the confusion took on the proportion of an uproar, composed largely of demands from various parts of the big banquet hall that the Senator from Wisconsin 'sit down.'" Malicious rumors and reports suggested that La Follette had frothed at the mouth or was drunk; Donald Seitz, the evening's toastmaster, said afterward of the senator, "He has simply wiped himself off the map."[5] Progressives considered themselves now free to openly cleave to the Colonel's standard.

With the governors' endorsement released, Roosevelt had only to pick his moment to declare for the GOP prize. But first, in a communication dated the twelfth, Root attempted to deter TR. Genuinely fond of his former boss, though equally skeptical of the progressive movement, he hoped to prevent a break within Republican ranks:

> It seems to me that those who ask you to make a declaration are asking you . . . to incur the considerable probability of being defeated for the nomination, or, if successful in that, of being defeated in the election, and that the consequences to your future, to your power of leadership in the interests of the causes which you have at heart, and to your position in history, would be so injurious that . . . no number of friends have any right to ask such a sacrifice.[6]

This appeal to posterity held little charm for Roosevelt. Living always and intensely in the moment, he hardly cared what the history books might make of his latest crusade—indeed, he would write its history himself.

Accordingly, the Colonel rolled into Columbus to deliver the most controversial speech of his career, "A Charter of Democracy," before the Ohio Constitutional Convention, then debating several progressive amendments, including an eight-hour workday for public employees and a workmen's compensation program. Several thousand had gathered on the grounds of the statehouse to catch a glimpse of Roosevelt. "Suffragists, a whole body of them," so New York's *Sun* reported, "had entered the hall in the earlier hours of the morning and filled up the first row of the ladies' gallery, where they waved at the Colonel." Moving beyond garden-variety progressivism—"I believe in providing for direct nominations by the people"; "I believe in the election of United States Senators by direct vote"—Roosevelt resurrected the spirit of the Osawatomie address, calling for the public to police the judiciary. Noting how some state courts mechanically rejected workmen's compensation suits, he gave grounds for their—the justices—removal: "Either the recall will have to be adopted or else it will have to be made much easier than it now is to get rid, not merely of a bad judge, but of a judge who, however virtuous, has grown so out of touch with social needs and facts that he is unfit longer to render good service on the bench." And even a fit magistrate might make the occasional unsound ruling, at which time, TR continued, "the people should have the right to recall that decision if they think it wrong." One should not, he cautioned, "make a fetish of a judge."[7]

For those who regarded the country's courts as wisely placed beyond popular power by the checks-and-balances-minded Framers, the notion of judicial recall struck at the heart of responsible government. Under the stark header "NO LONGER A REPUBLICAN," the *New York Times* reported of Roosevelt's address, "From beginning to end there is not a Republican doctrine or profession of faith in [it], but there is throughout a bold and defiant renunciation of the principles of that party." Reflecting on the address some years later, Alice noted that it "gave his opponents the angle from which to attack him as a dangerous radical, and really distressed many of his most sincere friends and supporters." Among the latter, Lodge was perhaps the most long-standing. "I never thought that any situation could arise which would have made me so miserably unhappy as I have been during the past week," he wrote Roosevelt on the twenty-eighth. "I found myself confronted with the fact that I was opposed to your policies declared at Columbus with great force in regard to changes in our Constitution and principles of government as I understand them. . . . I knew of course that you and I differed on some of these points," he closed, "but I had not realized that the difference was so wide." In a separate communication to his old friend Brooks Adams, Lodge observed, "It does not seem as if he had grasped or mastered his subject and as if he dealt with it lightly, as if he did not realize that his propositions, which he evidently had not worked out, struck at the very roots of all government."[8]

An ardent TR supporter, the bald Brooks had already, "as an old friend of yours," tendered his best advice to Roosevelt: "Try and get some thoroughly competent constitutional and economic lawyer, if you know such a one, to advise you always before you speak." Root, still another venerable confidant, expressed "regret" at Roosevelt's new-found radicalism. More than a momentary pose, however, he thought it addressed a deeper need in TR to dominate at any cost. He wrote Edward Martin, longtime editorialist for *Life* magazine and cofounder of the *Harvard Lampoon*:

> He is essentially a fighter and when he gets into a fight he is completely dominated by the desire to destroy his adversary. He instinctively lays hold of every weapon which can be used for that end. Accordingly, he is saying a lot of things and taking a lot of positions which are inspired by the desire to win. I have no doubt he thinks he believes what he says, but he doesn't. He has merely picked up certain popular ideas which were at hand as one might pick up a poker or chair with which to strike.[9]

Voters, of course, could be drawn to fighters, and the Colonel had once again captured the public's imagination. At the Cleveland train station, returning home from Columbus, he responded to a reporter's question about his political future with a typically Rooseveltian "My hat is in the ring . . . the fight is on and I am stripped to the buff." Arriving in Boston on February 25, he formally replied to the progressive governors by announcing his candidacy. The hat-in-the-ring theme took off, rippling through the newspapers and into popular culture. Roosevelt recycled it on occasion, while New Jersey governor and Democratic presidential aspirant Woodrow Wilson also made use of the meme. In Kansas City to give a brief address to the Grain Dealers Association, he was asked by reporters to respond to Roosevelt's hat-in-the-ring declaration. "Well, so is mine," the former Princeton professor said, "and my head is in it."[10] The popular ragtime composer Egbert Van Alstyne and lyricist Harry Williams commemorated

Roosevelt's phrase with a C major campaign song whose paint-by-numbers lyrics include:

> This certain old fellow who looks very young,
> Said fool with my hat and you're going to be stung!
> You may not believe it but I'm here to say,
> I put the first oyster in Old Oyster Bay.
> ... I haven't a bull dog, I haven't a hound
> So Wall Street is kicking my hat all around.
> My hat's in the ring, my hat's in the ring,
> It's bound all around with an old woolen string;
> I'm filled with delight, I'm ready to fight.[11]

Thus commenced a brief if vigorous trafficking in hat/ring pins, buttons, and posters.

Hours after Roosevelt announced his intention to challenge Taft for the nomination, the president received word, while dining at the White House, of the battle he now faced. "I told you so four years ago," Nellie scolded her already chastened husband, resurrecting her claims that TR would invariably seek another term, "and you would not believe me." In no mood for "I told you sos," Taft bit back: "I know you did, dear, and I think you are perfectly happy now. You would have preferred the Colonel to come out against me than to you been wrong yourself."[12] Over the next two weeks Roosevelt campaign headquarters popped up in Washington, New York, and Chicago. These gave guidance to numerous branch offices in dozens of states, many progressive-minded, though others undoubtedly leaned more toward the man than the movement.

And yet history could be said, despite any number of hats and rings, to side with Taft. Since the party's birth in the 1850s, nearly every Republican president seeking reelection had been renominated.[13] Though Roosevelt was undeniably the more popular candidate, only thirteen states held primaries. Elsewhere delegates to the party's nominating convention would be selected by state caucuses and conventions under the control of party bosses.

The primaries ran from March into early June and yielded impressive Roosevelt majorities. The Colonel claimed 278 delegates along with wins in several major states including Illinois, Pennsylvania, and

New Jersey. Taft, suffering the embarrassment of losing his native Ohio, trailed badly with 48, while La Follette finished with 36. Still dominant among many rank-and-file Republicans, Roosevelt captured more than 1.1 million votes, a slightly greater sum than Taft's (768,000) and La Follette's (327,000) combined.[14]

And this rattled Taft, accentuating his limitations as a national leader. TR inspired, spoke of destiny, and made people passionate. He caused things to happen, cared little for custom, and thoroughly enjoyed wielding power. Taft, by contrast, approached the presidency with real diffidence, never mastered the practice of melding disparate constituencies, and failed to unite his party's feuding regular and progressive wings. Though a frequent vacationer, he complained of having little time to vacation. "There is no question that my brother was a very poor politician," Horace Taft later observed. "He loathed the arts of that trade and when, of necessity, he had to practice them, he was very clumsy." Recognizing his limits, the president made no apologies. When signing Edward Douglass White's commission in 1910 to serve as the nation's ninth chief justice of the Supreme Court, he said, or sighed, "There is nothing I would have loved more than being Chief Justice of the United States. I cannot help seeing the irony in the fact that I, who desired that office so much, should now be signing the commission of another man."[15]

In late April, watching the primary returns ticking Roosevelt's way, Taft spoke at the Boston Arena. "I am here to reply to an old and true friend," he said, eager to dispel the Colonel's claims that party regulars were plotting to steal the nomination from the former president. "I do not want to fight Theodore Roosevelt, but sometimes a man in a corner fights. I am going to fight." He then produced several personal letters written over the past year or so from a sociable Roosevelt innocuously praising Taft; more damagingly, these communications also showed that their author had since attacked his successor in public for things he had praised him for in private. The New York *Evening Post* subsequently called the letters an indictment "of Roosevelt's personal character."[16] Taft, with the passion of a wannabe chief justice, further assailed TR's recent criticisms of the nation's courts:

> One who so lightly regards constitutional principles and especially the independence of the judiciary, one who is so naturally impatient

of legal restraints and of due legal procedure and who has so misunderstood what liberty regulated by law is could not safely be entrusted with successive Presidential terms. I say this sorrowfully, but I say it with the full conviction of its truth.[17]

Taft also brought up the third-term bugaboo, insisting that Roosevelt threatened to "violate our most useful and necessary governmental tradition" by disrespecting the precedent established by Washington and honored by his successors.[18] Again he inferred that the Colonel cared little about constitutional norms, always regarding his own interests as more urgent.

To be fair, Taft's inclination to be a passive president largely hewed to tradition. We might thus align him with the largely forgotten Gilded Age presidents, and even those not-so-roaring-1920s executives Warren G. Harding and Calvin Coolidge. But it is also true that the times caught up with Taft. Eager for reform, Americans had voted for Roosevelt to do such work—and thought they had done the same in 1908, believing Taft would carry on his predecessor's polices; this trend now worked in Wilson's favor.

Uncomfortably cornered by Roosevelt, the primaries, and the prospects of mounting a massive campaign for a second term he could easily have done without, Taft finally found a reason to fight. He would defend the party against the Colonel's radicalism and keep him from claiming its history, mantle, and brand as his own. In early 1912 he told his military aide Archibald Butt (soon to perish in the April sinking of the British liner *Titanic*), "I fear things are going to become very bitter before long. But, Archie, I am going to defeat him in the Convention. He may defeat me for reelection, and he probably will, but I think I will defeat him in the Convention."[19] Still party leader, still supported by the Old Guard, Taft knew his importance to those powerful men within the GOP who feared Roosevelt's return. He counted on the machine when failed by the people.

54

Armageddon Arrives

In May, during Roosevelt's dominant run through the primary season, Taft had asked Root for a public statement that might shine an unkindly light upon TR's presidency. To his credit, Root held back. Caught between the ambitions of two old friends, he confined his thoughts to private correspondence. "I am in favor of your nomination," he wrote Taft on the fifth. "When, however, we come to questions as between the two administrations, and questions of Theodore's personal right or wrong conduct during his administration, and comparisons between his course and yours, the fact cannot be ignored that I was a member of his administration." Unwilling to lay himself open "to the charge of betraying confidence and disloyalty," he opted to remain on the sideline of this unseemly GOP spat. "I hope that you will pull through," he closed. "I believe you will."[1]

The following month Republicans prepared to swoop into Chicago, site of the party's fifteenth quadrennial national convention. Many delegates, appointed in state races, were contested, and both the Taft and Roosevelt camps demanded them as their due. On June 1 the president received a communication from Clarence Kelsey, founder and presiding officer of the Title Guarantee and Trust Company (specializing in mortgage sales), and an old friend from their Yale days. It smelled a little of desperation: "It seems that the fate of the Republican Party now rests in the hands of the National Committee and that if it handles the case [of disputed delegates] with courage and determination it can save the day. It should not mince matters or temporize with Roosevelt or his claims but should summarily throw out all his contests and force him out of the convention." Clearly accusations of unfairness would follow, but Kelsey thought the alternative unacceptable: "No matter how much he howls or the press howls, or how unjudicial the Committee is accused of being, it should take the consequences and with certainty and speed install your delegates and take control of the convention. The giving of some of the delegates to him and giving him a chance to fight on the floor of the convention to win over enough to give him a majority, will betray the party into his hands." Having split the GOP, the Colonel should be obliged, Kelsey concluded, to "form a new party and fight as an independent" rather than claim for himself the legacies associated with Lincoln, postwar prosperity, and overseas expansion—"a good will and history [which] he has betrayed."[2]

Taft replied to Kelsey on the fourth with the confidence of a man who, as both party leader and in the bosses' good graces, knew the convention's ultimate outcome. "Never fear, old man, we are going to fight and, believe me, we are going to win." Leaving nothing to chance, Taft successfully recommended Root as convention chairman.[3]

Days before that assembly collected, the Republican National Committee (RNC), several of its members serving at Taft's pleasure, gathered to discuss the claims, challenges, and counterchallenges of 254 contested delegates, nearly half of the 540 necessary for the nomination. Clearly many of these would-be representatives, on both sides, were fraudulent, though Roosevelt, as usual, reserved right for himself. "They will have to steal the delegates outright in order to prevent my nomination," he wrote a colleague on the eve of the RNC's delegate review, "and if the stealing is flagrant no one can tell what the result may be." He seemed eminently open to a showdown that would take his case out of the party and to the people. And this appeared increasingly likely when the committee awarded the preponderance of the contested cases (235) to Taft. Roosevelt learned of this decision at Oyster Bay via a long-distance telephone, which he never quite reconciled to having in his house; an unreconstructed Victorian on the technology front, he also preferred horse-drawn carriages to automobiles and waited until 1914 to electrify Sagamore Hill. The seething Colonel, trembling between "theft," "scandal," and "stole," boomed in private correspondence, "I have absolutely no affiliations with any party," before packing up much of his family and speeding toward Chicago, greeted at LaSalle Street Station by fifty thousand ear-piercing enthusiasts. The city's *Tribune* sided with the aggrieved Roosevelt in a screaming "THOU SHALL NOT STEAL!" headline condemning the Old Guard's "steamroller" strategy of doling out delegates.[4]

Roosevelt's mere presence in Chicago constituted an open appeal of the RNC's actions, an entreaty based on both his commanding performance in the primaries and his insistence on the public's preference, indeed demand, for progressive reform. Essentially, he argued that the Republican hierarchy should defer to the wishes of Republican voters, that the people's choice prevail over the party's. And perhaps he imagined that his cult of popularity might conjure a situation, a scenario, or even a threat that could not be ignored by the bland bosses. Everywhere he went—in Egypt, Europe, and now Chicago—it seemed that crowds clamored to be in his hypnotic presence. "People packed the windows and lined the roofs and the elevated tracks and were so thick in the streets we could hardly move in the procession," Theodore's cousin Nicholas Roosevelt wrote of their Windy City arrival. "Everyone was howling with delight, and cries of 'Teddy!' filled the air. At the cross streets, as far as we could see to either side, or back or forward, people were wedged in like pins. Everyone cheered. Everyone screamed. Everyone was hurled along in the irresistible force of the delighted mob."[5]

Amid this surge and swell, however, the former president never acknowledged that the rules by which he would ultimately be beaten in 1912 were the same rules he had used in 1904 to outmaneuver Mark Hanna, and again in 1908 to push Taft upon the Old Guard. No longer controlling the levers of power, he furiously played the populist, the people's champion, warrior, and white knight.

The evening before the convention opened at the Chicago Coliseum, Roosevelt addressed a crowd of six thousand in the Chicago Auditorium, a still-standing Romanesque structure designed by Henry Hobson Richardson of Boston's Trinity Church fame. Introduced by Idaho senator William Borah (later Alice Roosevelt Longworth's nearly two-decades-older lover and the father of her only child, Paulina, born in 1925), Roosevelt took the dais before a hail of wild applause. He opened on a soldierly note—"we are standing... we are fighting"— and told the audience that his defeat in the delegate brawl constituted a misfortune for all Americans: "If we condone political theft... our civilization itself cannot endure." He then attacked Taft ("the accepted representative of the bosses"), portrayed himself as indispensable ("if I had not made the . . . fight it would have completely broken down"), and referred to regular Republicans as "our enemies." Understanding that his only hope lay in a popular revolt against politics-as-usual, Roosevelt, the man who had refused to abandon the "corrupt" Blaine in 1884, who had made peace enough with the GOP to get the New York senate and vice presidential nominations that led to his White House tenure, now angled for open war against his former benefactors. Raising his besotted audience to a fever pitch, he closed on a note that reached for the heavens: "We fight in honorable fashion for the good of mankind; fearless of the future; unheeding of our individual fates; with unflinching hearts and undimmed eyes; we stand at Armageddon, and we battle for the Lord!"[6]

The Auditorium address begged the question: Did Roosevelt presume to bolt the convention? This prospect caused more than a few progressive Republicans, pondering the possible end of their political careers—"fearless of the future"?—to waver. The Illinois delegation, strongly for Roosevelt during the primary season, now paused, as did several other states that TR had thought firm. Of all the potentially compromised, perhaps none was more disturbed by the Armageddon address than Alice's congressman husband. On the ballot for what promised to be a tight reelection bid in an unusual political year, Nick Longworth, representing Ohio's 1st Congressional District—Taft's Cincinnati—counted the current president a political ally. Though not unsympathetic to his father-in-law's progressivism, Longworth needed the apparatus of party machinery if he hoped to win in November. He stayed regular.

On June 22, the convention's final day, the states doled out their delegate counts, a perfunctory exercise, though one still possessed of color and contrast as progressive Republicans—and a shouting Alice—defied the Taft majority with chants of "We want Teddy!" During the proceedings, Henry Allen, a Kansas newspaper czar, read before the entire convention a statement from Roosevelt filled with anger, resentment, and moral righteousness. "A clear majority of the delegates honestly elected to this convention were chosen by the people to nominate me," he insisted, reserving for himself the right to define both "clear majority" and "honestly." His megalomania at this point knew no bounds: "The

Convention as now composed," he declared, "has no claim to represent the voters of the Republican Party." In this short manifesto he used the term "fraud" or "fraudulent" seven times, an accusation interspersed with appeals for "Roosevelt delegates" to "decline to vote on any matter before the Convention." He seemed content to burn the GOP to the ground. After many hours, near 9:30 p.m., Taft was officially renominated, and this precipitated the mass bolt that the aggrieved Colonel had all but demanded, as 344 delegates stalked out of the Coliseum and into the dark Chicago streets.[7]

That same evening, many of these same delegates were marched in a body to a rump Roosevelt convention at Orchestra Hall, about a mile north of the Coliseum on South Michigan Avenue. There, among his faithful, Roosevelt, in full roar, asked the dissenting delegates to go back to their home districts, discern "the sentiment of the people," and then return to Chicago to choose progressive candidates and a reform platform.[8] Though willing, so he said, to support any nominee, the Colonel—and everyone in the building—knew the only possible outcome of a fresh convention.

Despite the obvious fact that the progressive bolt all but gave the presidency to the Democratic nominee—determined the following month to be New Jersey governor Woodrow Wilson—the mood among many regular Republicans appeared to be relief that at least Roosevelt had at last been driven from the party. Extending his "admiration for and appreciation of your services in Chicago," Supreme Court chief justice White lauded Root in a June 24 letter for "the discharge of your duty" when "it seemed we were possibly near a great crisis."[9]

As the summer drew on, Taft simmered over the ugly political fight he had desperately wished to avoid. Frustrated, he called Roosevelt a "honeyfugler" for breaking his promise to retire; he thought him further, so he wrote Alice's sister-in-law Annie Longworth Wallingford (hitting a little close to home), "the greatest menace to our institutions that we have had in a long time—indeed I don't remember one in our history so dangerous and so powerful." The following month he said to Nellie of his unwanted rival: "I look upon him as I look upon a freak, almost, in the zoological garden, a kind of animal not often found. So far as personal relations with him are concerned, they don't exist—I do not have any feeling one way or the other."[10]

Taft no doubt grasped both the anxious pitch of Roosevelt's new politics and the by turns brooding, theatrical, and conceited quality upon which it rested. Hemmed in by a long-standing partisan tradition that refused to elevate mavericks, TR ached to make the inspiring speech, fight in the next war, or defuse the ever-rising crisis. At this point in his remarkable life, he could live no other way.

55

The Lord's Candidate

In early July Roosevelt wrote "in strict confidence" to a colleague that "the Democrats will probably win if they nominate a progressive," which they did in choosing Wilson. Surveying a thinning field of options, the Colonel anxiously adopted a southern strategy, trying to woo white voters from the Democratic Party. He proposed dropping a long-standing policy among Republicans to court the region's blacks, which, since the end of Reconstruction, had yielded the GOP precious little in Dixie. In one stroke he presumed to create, as an aide said, "two white parties in the South," his own alongside the Democrats, and by proxy punish black Republicans for siding with Taft at the convention. "There is not and cannot be in the Southern States," Roosevelt contended, "a party based upon the negro vote and under negro leadership or the leadership of white men who derive their power solely from negroes."[1] Playing upon old Confederate sympathies, he hoped to win support among southerners who agreed with him on containing the great Yankee capitalists and now knew him to be safe on race.

But this cordial nod and bob before Jim Crow encountered quick resistance. On the eve of the new Progressive Party's convention, rival white and black delegations from four Deep South states vied for seating at the assembly, causing a momentary stasis. All the would-be deputies were hot for Roosevelt, of course, though it was now incumbent upon the Colonel to determine, at least in such contested cases, the Progressive state slates. He chose to do so in an open letter to the journalist Julian Harris, son of Joel Chandler Harris, the Georgia-born author, as noted earlier, of the Uncle Remus stories. Cleaving to a raft of self-serving platitudes, Roosevelt stressed the reform cause's color-blindness ("We have made the Progressive issue a moral, not a racial issue"), doubted the wisdom of black participation in governance ("The progress that has been made among the negroes of the South during these forty-five years has not been made as a result of political effort"), and seemed eager to ignore completely questions of racial justice ("It is unwise to revive bitterness by dwelling on the errors and shortcomings of the past"). Though welcoming certified northern "colored delegates" to the convention, he suggested that their southern brethren defer "to the best white men" in Dixie.[2]

G. B. Ellis, a black Chicago Republican, considered Roosevelt's letter and "lily white" policy a betrayal of a long loyal constituency: "We've been with the Colonel because we expected fair play. If we don't get it the Colonel don't get our votes." New York's *Evening Post* affirmed this view in the page-one headline "NEGRO ISSUE A BLUNDER: Exclusion Rudely Jars Running of Roosevelt's Convention," while Booker T. Washington, advising the present administration on race issues, discouraged a colleague's endorsement of Roosevelt and likely voted for Taft in the general election.[3]

The Progressive convention opened on August 5 in the Chicago Coliseum, where Republicans had earlier nominated Taft. Occupying his old haunt, the Congress Plaza Hotel, Roosevelt held court as a king-in-waiting with no contested delegates to prevent his coronation. Having fought fruitlessly for months to smite the wicked Old Guard, his devotees now came together in a fellowship of the virtuous, unshackled, so they presumed, from the constraints of mere politics and eager to reach for a progressive millennium. California senator Hiram Johnson, chosen as Roosevelt's running mate, gravely stated that "our work is holy work," while the strains of "Onward, Christian Soldiers" and "Battle Hymn of the Republic" sporadically blared throughout the assembly "with much fervor." An amused *New York Times* described the convention as "a Methodist camp meeting" in disguise, an observation echoed in Edith Roosevelt's contention that it resembled "a great religious meeting with deep seriousness beneath all the enthusiasm."[4]

Though one East Coast newspaper dismissed the assembly as "crusaders" and thought the Harvard-educated Colonel oddly out of place in their presence, the caucus leaned toward educated and economically secure supporters, many of whom had never participated in organized politics and, in their innocence and earnestness, opposed any accommodation with politics-as-usual. These men and a striking number of women—Chicago settlement activist Jane Addams seconded Roosevelt's nomination at the convention—turned out in droves to back TR. With some two thousand delegates, nearly twice as many as the Republicans had fielded for Taft, the Progressives, proud of their break with the politicians, represented the professional white American middle class. Professors, social workers, and clergy were among their number, as well as small-town businessmen, local journalists, and a distinct circle of suffragists.[5] Remembering the agrarian movements of the populist past, filled with "farmers who had failed, lawyers and doctors who were not orthodox, teachers who could not make the grade," William Allen White saw something completely different among the scrubbed reformers collecting in Chicago:

> Here were the successful middle-class country-town citizens, the farmer whose barn was painted, the well paid railroad engineer, and the country editor. It was a well dressed crowd. . . . Judging the delegates by their clothes, I figured that there was not a man or woman on the floor who was making less than two thousand a year, and not one, on the other hand, who was topping ten thousand. Proletarian and plutocrat were absent.[6]

All came to proclaim for Roosevelt, who, following an opening prayer and the singing of "America" by the entire convention, gave his acceptance speech before several thousand a little before 1:00 p.m. on the sixth. Emerging from a stairway that led up to a platform, he faced a thick din of noise punctuated by shouts of "We want Teddy!"; bright-red banners dominated the floor. "The first six or eight minutes of the applause was genuine and spontaneous," one observer noted, "and then devises were employed to keep it alive." The Colonel greeted Grand Army of the Republic veterans on the dais, urged on the delegates' sustained ovation, and, grabbing one of the banners, proceeded in full peacock mode to wave ebulliently before the crowd while women from the California delegation spontaneously ambled up the platform to shake his hand. There followed a raspy group sing-along of "John Brown's Body" before, nearly an hour after TR first appeared, convention chairman Albert Beveridge gaveled the assembly to order.[7]

Roosevelt then proceeded to deliver what he called a "confession of faith," laying out his platform with the rare confidence of a politician who is bigger than his party. He stressed the right to recall judicial decisions at both the state and federal level, touted the need to make the process of altering the Constitution easier, and called for, in the name of "social . . . justice," a national commission to regulate "all the great industrial concerns engaged in interstate business." For two hours Roosevelt held the audience's attention, not really breaking fresh ground but offering iterations of New Nationalism orthodoxy, all the while denouncing the existing partisan system as dominated by "two old parties . . . with no soul," and insisting that the progressive movement embraced a "cause . . . based on eternal principles of righteousness." Apparently these precepts included the need for a big navy, a personal passion the worked-up orator slipped into the address, much to the chagrin of the more pacifist-minded among his latest political allies. Ending on a crowd-pleasing note, the Colonel repeated his famous line of impending apocalypse uttered at the Republican convention just seven weeks earlier: "To you who gird yourself for this great new fight in the never-ending warfare for the good of humankind, I say in closing . . . we stand at Armageddon, and we battle for the Lord!"[8]

The eminently caricaturable Colonel, he of the cheeky teeth and perennial pince-nez, adopted yet another persona that busy political summer. Having already given his good name to a brisk business in toy bears, he now declared himself before the press to be feeling as strong, entering the campaign season, as a "bull moose." The papers immediately ran with the image, and the *New York Times* casually pushed "Progressive Party" to the side when describing the bolters as belonging to "Mr. Roosevelt's Bull Moose Party." Variations inevitably ensued, including those prone to a playful Moosevelt-ian theme. These included a splendid Edward Windsor Kemble drawing in *Harper's Weekly* of a smiling bull moose sporting an unmistakable Roosevelt face (choppers and eyeglasses galore) as a bandaged and bruised GOP elephant observed to a skeptical Democratic donkey, "Suffering snakes, how Theodore has changed." Getting into the spirit, the *New York Evening World* and *Washington Herald* printed up the mix list for the "Bull Moose Cocktail," featuring vermouth, dry gin, orange bitters, and a "dash of brandy."[9]

In the frenzied course of this moose-apalooza, Henry Adams looked askance at the Colonel's rising cult with its oddly evangelical undertone. "And now comes our Theodore!" he wrote in September to the art historian Bernard Berenson. "He preaches that the other people are all wicked . . . but he will save you"; for he who "believes in Theodore," Adams winced, "all will be well."[10] This condemnation by Brahmin Boston existed, however, as an outlier to the broader interest building about the coming election. During the antebellum period several presidential canvasses were held—in 1824, 1848, 1856, and 1860—in which at least three candidates received at least 10 percent of the popular vote. But sectionalism's post–Civil War decline and the strengthening of partisan ties had tended to narrow national races to a choice of two.[11] The abrupt Bull Moose phenomenon now smashed like a wrecking ball through this consensus. And Roosevelt, the president who had once refused a precedent-breaking third term, now sought to make, as a third-party candidate, still another kind of electoral history.

56

The Last Hurrah

Roosevelt faced in Woodrow Wilson a lifelong academic lately gone into the political game. Formerly a professor of history at the newly established Bryn Mawr College on the Philadelphia Main Line, Wilson had moved on to Wesleyan University in central Connecticut, where he also served as an assistant coach of the Cardinals football team. Two years later, he accepted the Chair of Jurisprudence and Political Economy at Princeton, where he built a reputation as a scholar and public speaker. Respected across the campus community, Wilson was appointed president of the university in 1902, achieving success in reorganizing the school's curriculum and establishing a preceptorial system. He fell afoul of alumni, however, when attempting to dismantle the informal off-campus eating clubs that had first emerged in the 1850s, dominated the institution's social life, and snobbishly left one-third of each class bereft of membership. At Princeton, the deep-pocketed snobs proved more powerful than their president.[1] Wilson suffered a second defeat in 1909 when his bid to locate a graduate school building on the main campus collapsed after a wealthy donor made a gift to the campaign conditional on the structure's placement elsewhere.

In a period when university presidents could command both national and international attention—Charles Eliot elevated Harvard from its social club trappings into an institution of world renown; Columbia's Nicholas "Miraculous" Murray Butler won the Nobel Peace Prize for efforts to strengthen international law and was Taft's 1912 running mate; Michigan's James B. Angell found time during his long Ann Arbor tenure to serve as U.S. minister to China and Turkey—Wilson became a hot political commodity in New Jersey. With a reputation as a collegiate reformer and public intellectual, he piqued the interest of the state's Democratic Party, then riding a protracted losing streak in gubernatorial elections. Offered the nomination in early 1910, Wilson, walking away from "the pleasantest country club in America" (as F. Scott Fitzgerald tagged Princeton), accepted and, in a Democratic year, easily won. "The question of my nomination for the governorship," he said at the time, already envisioning a White House run, "is the mere preliminary of a plan to nominate me in 1912 for the presidency."[2]

Possessed of a long, horsey face accentuated by a projecting jaw, bad teeth, and large ears, Wilson, in his glasses and Princeton gown, connoted "academic," at least in the public's slightly skewed perception of the scholar in politics. A southerner by birth—his earliest memory as a child in Augusta, Georgia, was learning of Lincoln's election—he offered a moderate progressivism palatable to those who rejected Roosevelt's more radical judicial-recall rhetoric. In tune with the culture, he promised to rein in the corporations by strengthening the nation's existing antitrust laws, rather than by empowering the presidency as TR wished. His views on women's suffrage and black enfranchisement were something less than progressive, which is to say they were agreeable to most Americans. On the reform front, Wilson's record in New Jersey— he signed a major workmen's compensation statute and helped to push through a bill that required primaries for elective office, thus curtailing the power of the state's political bosses—played well in the press. A clearly charmed *New York Times* called him "a sound Democrat, progressive in every sense, but a conservative in respect to the foundational principles of the Constitution of this Government."[3] He was presumed, in other words, to be liberal-minded, but not too liberal-minded.

Taft, by comparison, lacked both Roosevelt's charisma and Wilson's freshness on the political stage. Adopting a de rigueur progressivism, he touted his administration's record taking down trusts, including the recently disassembled Standard Oil. He sided with Wilson in calling for Congress to deal with the issue of monopoly through established legislation, but had precious little ideological wiggle room to connect with voters eager to experiment with a New Nationalism–style approach to regulating the corporate state. His trio of opponents were far less constrained. Eugene Debs and the Socialist Party, sounding a little like the Populists of old, called in their platform for "the collective ownership and democratic management" of major American industries, while Roosevelt and Wilson were able to promise the public more regulation than Taft, hemmed in by the Old Guard's unwillingness to go on the road to Armageddon. Indeed, in affirming its "intention to uphold at all times the authority and integrity of the Courts," the GOP simultaneously held the line on judicial power while advertising its difficulties escaping Roosevelt's long shadow.[4]

Of his two major adversaries, Roosevelt knew Wilson to be the more potent. Certainly, the GOP split all but guaranteed a Democratic president, but even beyond electoral map realities, the former Princetonian challenged the Colonel's control of the political spotlight. In the Taft camp, Archie Butt admitted Wilson's appeal, which he saw as an attraction of contrasting parts: "The governor is ... handsome in a cold, intellectual kind of way, yet magnetic too, which seldom goes with that precise type." Roosevelt had for some years recognized Wilson as a stimulating public thinker, leading to an occasional correspondence between them. Pleased with Wilson's patriotic "Ideals of America" essay appearing in the December 1902 *Atlantic Monthly*, he wrote its author, "Is there any chance of your getting down to Washington to spend a night with me at the White House this winter? There are many things I would like to talk over with you." Now, nearly a decade later, the two men were vying for the same prize, and Wilson had the advantage of novelty. The public could project upon him in a way it no longer could Roosevelt, an entertaining, fascinating, but all too familiar face, now fifteen years in the public eye, ever since that "crowded hour" on a green hill in Cuba. Though two years TR's senior, Wilson was the political colt in this partisan struggle.[5]

Perhaps it is not surprising, considering the messy divorce within the GOP, that the campaign took on an unusually sour quality. "I stopped reading the accounts of the bitter political contest," Nellie Taft later recalled, "because I found that the opposition newspapers made so much more impression on me than those that were friendly to my husband." She found herself "in a state of constant rage."[6] Roosevelt spent September barnstorming about the country; images of the corpulent former president thrusting his thick index finger at the audience to accentuate a point while a pool of reporters furiously committed to paper his every utterance made for good copy. After a brief Oyster Bay respite in early October, he embarked on a campaign in the Midwest, howling himself into an inflamed throat. Some events were canceled, though he gave several speeches in Chicago and Racine, Wisconsin, and on the fourteenth went on from there to Milwaukee.

Finishing an 8:00 p.m. meal at the Hotel Gilpatrick on Third Street, a stone-clad structure embellished by a corner turret, Roosevelt and an entourage of six (including a bodyguard and a security man) proceeded to exit the building. Getting into an open-air automobile, the Colonel gestured toward the accompanying crowd when suddenly John Schrank, a short, stocky, thirty-six-year-old former saloonkeeper standing five feet away, fired a .38-caliber bullet from a Colt revolver that ripped through Roosevelt's steel eyeglass case before entering and exiting the single-folded fifty-page speech he had prepared to deliver—"Progressive Cause Greater Than Any Individual"—and lodging in his chest. "He pinked me," the surprised Colonel muttered. Though unarmed at that moment, TR apparently did on occasion keep "a good-sized pistol" in his hip pocket, as Harvard president Charles Eliot once noted: "When I asked if he habitually carried a revolver, he replied, 'Yes, when I am going into public places. I should have some chance of shooting the assassin before he could shoot me.'"[7]

By this time TR's handlers, including Elbert Martin, a stenographer and former football player, had disarmed and brought the unresisting Schrank to the ground. Earlier in Saginaw, Michigan, Martin had picked up a man who pushed too close to Roosevelt and slammed him into a gutter; now he had Schrank in a half nelson and, with his knee pinioned upon the would-be assassin's spine, seemed intent on breaking his back. "Don't hurt him," Roosevelt shouted, "bring him here. I want to look at him." Handing Schrank's gun to the Colonel, Martin pulled the man up so that Roosevelt could gaze into his troubled eyes.[8]

Several police officers had now arrived, and the cry "The Colonel's shot!" brought Dr. Scurry Terrell, a Texas throat specialist engaged for the campaign, who insisted that his famous patient be transported to a hospital. But TR refused to go and demanded that his car make for the Milwaukee Auditorium (now Miller High Life Theatre). "After the bullet I had no real pain," he explained. "The wound felt hot." While the former president's party was transported "slowly through the crowded streets," so one witness noted, "the people constantly cheer[ed] . . . as they recognized the Colonel. Word of the attempt on his life had not yet reached them, and they behaved only as such crowds do on political occasions."

Once inside the auditorium, in a small room behind the stage, Roosevelt submitted to a quick examination by Terrell, who discovered a lightly bleeding wound just under the right nipple. "It's all right, Doctor," the Colonel said, "there's no perforation" of the lung. "I don't get any pain from this breathing."[9] Since he emitted no blood from the mouth and seemed content to apply a handkerchief to what appeared to be a flesh wound (the bullet had actually settled in a chest muscle), Roosevelt was allowed, as if he could be stopped, to deliver his address. And when he appeared on the stage ten thousand voices erupted.

Though informed of the Colonel's condition, the audience seemed to presume his assailant had missed, for how else could he now be standing before them? Waiting for the cheering to subside, Roosevelt explained what had transpired before adding, with the practiced pause of a circus showman, "But it takes more than that to kill a bull moose!" and unbuttoned his vest to reveal the stigmata-like bloodstains on his shirt. He then proceeded with his speech. After about thirty-five minutes, "he began," a member of his entourage remembered, "to be obviously somewhat unsteady on his feet, and we were afraid he would pitch forward off the stage. So we had a few good strong men take places as near the stage as they could get and directly in front of him." After forty-five minutes TR announced "I will speak fifteen minutes more"—only to continue for nearly an hour. Perhaps the flaming exhibitionist in him wished to indulge a kind of martyrdom in the round.[10]

Roosevelt was transported to Milwaukee's Johnston Emergency Hospital, a twenty-four-bed facility, where his wound was x-rayed and dressed. He was then taken to Chicago's Mercy Hospital, at which a small company of thoracic specialists decided to leave the bullet in place, where it remained for the rest of his life. The following day a distraught Edith and Alice arrived in Chicago. The latter, obviously proud of her indomitable father's determination to keep to his speech—"It was so exactly what he would do"—thought he looked "surprisingly well, though obviously uncomfortable." Surveying the wound, Edith described it as "about the size of a dime" and surrounded by a discolored mass of black-and-blue muscles.[11] Both Taft and Wilson issued statements of sympathy and briefly suspended their campaigns.

Schrank, Bavarian-born, orphaned not long after arriving in America at the age of nine, and prone to religious enthusiasms, claimed that William McKinley's ghost had appeared to him on multiple occasions, demanding that he "avenge my death" and identifying Roosevelt as his assassin. Schrank also expressed concern that a third Roosevelt term would destabilize the republic and set off another civil war. In September he had purchased a revolver and begun to shadow the Colonel's campaign in the South. At Chattanooga, so he said, "I was near enough to shoot him," but didn't "because it was a new thing to me. I didn't just exactly have courage enough to do it." In court on November 13, just a month after "pinking" the Colonel, Schrank pled guilty, adding, "I did not intend to kill the citizen Roosevelt. I intended to kill Roosevelt, the third termer." On the twenty-second a group of five alienists (as psychiatrists were then called) delivered their opinion that, due to "suffering from insane delusions," their patient would be "unable to confer intelligently with counsel or to conduct his defense." Judge August Backus accordingly committed Schrank to an asylum near Oshkosh, Wisconsin, where he remained until his death in 1943.[12]

Back on the campaign trail, Wilson, coming from a southern states' rights tradition, drew a sharp distinction between his "New Freedom"—stressing the breakup of trusts as necessary to counter monopolization—and Roosevelt's "New Nationalism"—accepting industrial oligarchy as inevitable, though policing it with government regulation. Ever the professor, he wanted the election to come down to a contest of ideas but knew that the Colonel's support transcended such "New" this and that nomenclature. "Do not be too confident of the result," he had written to Mary Allen Hulbert, a friend and trusted confidant several weeks before the election. "I feel that Roosevelt's strength is altogether incalculable. The contest is between him and me, not between Taft and me." In sharp and illuminating strokes, he proceeded to handicap the race as a question of personalities, in which the iconic Colonel held the high ground: "He appeals to their imagination; I do not. He is a real, vivid person, whom they have seen and shouted themselves hoarse over and voted for, millions strong; I am a vague, conjectural personality, more made up of opinions and academic prepossession than of human traits and red corpuscles. We shall see what will happen!"[13]

What happened was that come November, the Democrats triumphed spectacularly, claiming a mandate of historical proportions comparable to their sweeping House, Senate, and presidential victories in 1852 and 1892. Iowa, Maine, New Hampshire, Ohio, and Rhode Island went against the GOP in a presidential race for the first time ever, in a period encompassing fifteen elections. Wilson took a commanding 435 electoral votes to Roosevelt's 88 and Taft's 8, the fewest ever by a Republican, though later matched by a hapless Alf Landon, overwhelmed in Franklin Roosevelt's 1936 reelection juggernaut. Debs did not carry a state. This was only the second time in American history that a third-party candidate finished in the top two, the other being in 1860 when the Democratic Party split over sectional issues and the Southern Democratic candidate, John Breckinridge, trailed only Lincoln.

The popular vote percentages in 1912 were closer than the Electoral College tally, with Wilson capturing 41.8 percent, Roosevelt 27.4 percent, Taft 23.2 percent, and Debs 6.0 percent. The country's appetite for reform might be measured in Debs's relative success as the Socialist candidate. Not only did he more than double his percentage of the popular vote from 1908, but he outpolled the incumbent Taft in seven states including Florida, where he received more votes than both Taft and Roosevelt. The Colonel, by contrast, might be said to have underperformed—traditionally strong in the Mountain West states, the old Rough Rider and Dakota cowpoke finished behind both Wilson and Taft in several of these contests. Coast to coast, he carried only six states.

On the evening of November 5, as the election returns revealed a GOP catastrophe, Roosevelt's old boss from 1898, John D. Long, formerly secretary of the navy and now retired to a quiet Massachusetts law practice, wrote with some bitterness in his diary: "Republican had smashed the Republican party for this year & solely because, like a boy that won't play unless he is captain, he did not get the nomination." That same day, Roosevelt too mused uneasily over the contest and the electorate's unheroic, to his mind, attitude. "I had expected defeat, but I had expected that we would make a better showing," he allowed to an English acquaintance. "We had all the money, all the newspapers and all the political machinery against us and, above all, we had the habit of thought of the immense mass of dull unimaginative men who simply vote according to the party symbol."[14]

Among those luckless incumbents buried below the Democratic wave was Nicholas Longworth, who stayed true to Taft while his wife stuck by her father. Two days before the balloting, Alice anxiously reflected upon the contest's damage to her marriage: "Nick and I had a tremendous row after lunch on account of me not being for him, not 'standing by' him, and I am so hurt and angry. . . . Of course [I] earnestly desire his success—but we are surely drifting decidedly far apart." Nick lost an excruciatingly close race—by ninety-seven votes—and called for a recount that, after nearly a week, merely repeated the result. Considering that the Progressive candidate in the contest, one Millard Andrew, came in third with more than five thousand ballots, and that Progressive votes tended to come out of Republican hides, it seems highly likely that the Colonel's decision to mount a third-party bid cost his son-in-law the election. Or perhaps Alice did? She later noted that her public appearance with Progressive vice presidential candidate Hiram Johnson in Nick's congressional district surely counted for something—"I figured I was worth at least [ninety-seven] votes in Cincinnati." Here was evidence yet again that TR remained for her, as he did for his sisters, Bamie and Corinne, the most important man in her life.[15]

In the election's sobering wake, Roosevelt could sense the permanence of his exile—and so could Edith. "The disappointment," she wrote Kermit in mid-December, "went deeper than he admits to himself." It seems that among the GOP faithful, only Taft could be said to have come out all right. True, the (expected) defeat stung, but within a year of leaving the presidency he had shed nearly a hundred pounds—and kept them off for the rest of his life, the last nine years of which he served contentedly as chief justice of the Supreme Court.[16]

But what now for Roosevelt? Only fifty-four and unwilling to retire in any conventional sense, he remained in the grips of an inner drive to dominate. A year after Wilson's victory, he left the country for a jungle expedition in the Amazon, shades of his long African withdrawal following Taft's victory in 1908. In both instances he returned determined to impose his way, his will, upon American politics.

Part VIII

QUICKER THAN THE ROSE

In the nature of things we must die soon anyhow—and we have warmed both hands before the fire of life.
>Theodore Roosevelt, 1918

A suddenly frail Roosevelt in the final year of a strenuous life.

57

The Wages of Doubt

Unable to reclaim the White House, Roosevelt medicated by writing a memoir, reliving the glories of youth, the rapid amble up the political ladder, and the pleasures of a big-stick presidency. He says next to nothing about the recent Bull Moose campaign. The book, rather, comprises various tropes—it traffics in the homiletic arts, segues into boosterism, and lands always near the neighborhood of vindication. Cloaked in Victorian reserve, it offers a too-constrained impression of its emphatic subject, and contemporary readers will discover far more of the Colonel's inner life by perusing his published letters and diaries. One would never know from *Theodore Roosevelt: An Autobiography* that its author had slipped into a prolonged depression following his father's death, was once married to the ill-fated Alice Lee, or threatened to have his troubled brother, Elliott, declared insane. Roosevelt regarded such revelations as morbid and stayed on the sunny side of war, politics, and self-justification. And even on these constrained terms he is attentively selective. His financial failure in "cowboy land" and controversial censure of Brownsville's black soldiers are quietly elided; Lincoln's name pops up in the book more often than Taft's. "The hardest task I have is to keep my temper," TR wrote Lodge in February 1913 of the manuscript's progress, "and not speak of certain people."[1] All too often, however, he spoke too little even of himself, remaining elusive in full sight.

Roosevelt finished the memoir in October 1913, eager to push on to his next major project. He had accepted an invitation to deliver a series of lectures in Argentina and Brazil that November, followed by an Amazon River cruise. His assent, however, prompted Brazilian president Hermes da Fonseca to suggest a hunting trip into the country's little-known interior. The adventure appealed to Roosevelt immensely. "I have to go," he insisted. "It's my last chance to be a boy!" Such man-versus-nature expeditions were au courant at the time. In 1909 the Peary-Henson party (very nearly) reached the North Pole, while the Norwegian explorer Roald Amundsen arrived at the South Pole in December 1911. This industrial-age conquest of the world's last "lost spaces" offered the illusion, not so unlike ranching in Dakota, of going back in time and experiencing life in more immediate and less mediated terms. Theodore's son Kermit, employed by the Anglo-Brazilian Iron Company as a supervisor on bridge construction, agreed—shades of Africa again—to accompany his father (and a rather large retinue of guides, naturalists, and natives) into the jungle. "Yesterday mother gave me another long talk about father, and . . . I must look after him," he wrote one intimate. "She's dreadfully worried about him, and there's nothing for me to do but go."[2]

As on the earlier safari, Roosevelt received substantial sponsorship, this time promising specimens to the American Museum of Natural History on Manhattan's Upper West Side. And once again, he negotiated an advantageous deal for the publication of his lectures and adventures. The *Outlook* paid $5,000 for a series of local color articles, while Scribners ponied up $15,000 for a book. His appearance fees in Brazil, Argentina, and—added to the itinerary—Chile came to an additional $10,000. After expenses, he estimated a net profit of $20,000, about $600,000 in today's dollars. Roosevelt's companions on the journey included Father John Augustine Zahm, a former University of Notre Dame administrator, charismatic South American explorer, and author of *Following the Conquistadores: Up the Orinoco and Down the Magdalena* (1910), a purple-prose exercise to the Colonel's liking. The two men shared a love of Dante. The naturalist George Cherrie, lithe but muscular with leathered skin and a perpetual tan, had just returned from a long trip abroad when the American Museum invited him to join the expedition to Brazil, though neglecting to name its celebrity leader. Relaxing "at my home among the green Vermont hills," he later recalled, "my enthusiasm did not break bonds." Days later, however, while attending a conference in New York, he discovered Roosevelt's role in the affair and immediately agreed to go.[3]

The surveyor and military officer Cândido Rondon, whom the Colonel met upon arriving in Rio de Janeiro, proved to be by far the excursion's most important addition. Formerly assigned by Brazil's telegraph commission to the far-flung interior towns of the Mato Grosso ("Thick Bush"), the dark-skinned Rondon, resplendent in gleaming leather boots and a trim officer's uniform that cloaked an erect carriage, had a wealth of experience negotiating the country's jungles, waterfalls, cliffs, and canyons; he counted on his mother's side descent from the Terena and Bororo indigenous peoples. His pairing with Roosevelt was a case of like finding like. As one commentator has written:

> Rondon's life was . . . incredible, so full of colorful incidents. . . . As the only Brazilian to have a state named after him (Rondônia, along the Bolivian border), Rondon is hardly unknown. By the end of his long life, he had traveled more than 25,000 miles—equivalent to the circumference of the earth—exploring and mapping uncharted territory. He had helped overthrow an emperor; prevented at least one Latin American war; suppressed domestic rebellions; become "the largest single contributor of specimens to the National Museum in Rio de Janeiro"; created the Indian Protection Service, which earned him a nomination for the Nobel Peace Prize; established his country's first national parks; and refused an invitation to become a military dictator.[4]

During one of his many surveys, Rondon had come upon the headwaters of a mysterious, uncharted waterway, what he called the Rio da Dúvida—the River of Doubt. As Cherrie later noted, "Before sailing and during the voyage we discussed many routes that we might follow through Brazil, but not until we had reached Rio de Janeiro was it definitely settled where we were to go. . . . During a conference with Brazil's minister of Foreign Affairs, that official volunteered the cooperation of his government in the exploration of this unknown river. The idea appealed to Colonel Roosevelt's imagination, and he immediately accepted the offer."[5]

The expedition promised Brazil's leaders an opportunity to advertise the country's barely tapped interior resources, mineral exploitation and vast rubber tree forests among them. The potential for European and American investment and perhaps migration further made the Colonel's trek into the Amazon basin a real coup. That he would most likely turn his travels into a best-selling book only enhanced the venture's appeal. In return, the government provided an impressive company of human capital—army officers, guards, porters, field specialists, and so on. Roosevelt came prepared as well, bringing with him a small mountain of supplies including, just in case, the instrument of a quick and lethal end. "I have always made it a practice on such trips," he confided to a favorite journalist, "to take a bottle of morphine with me. Because one never knows what is going to happen, and I did not mean to be caught by some accident where I should have to die a lingering death."[6]

Along with linguistic challenges—Roosevelt and the Portuguese-speaking Rondon communicated in French, neither proficient in the other's mother tongue—a host of differences distinguished the intrepid Americans and their Brazilian partners. Rondon led a highly trained team in the field, including a zoologist, a botanist, and a geologist. Cherrie to the contrary, most of the Colonel's party consisted of men with little or no experience in the kind of dense tropic wilderness they now faced. This discrepancy became immediately evident when the expedition first dined. The Americans brought an impressive pantry of goods, sweets, and spices that advertised nothing so much as their inexperience. The lean Rondon, looking at the plump Roosevelt, knew that their trip would likely involve long stretches on meager rations, and that tinned foods, rather than chocolate bars, would prove the best complement to whatever game they might bag along the way.

Commencing in Cáceres, a tiny spot along the Paraguay River, the expedition moved in December to Tapirapuã, holding the headwaters of the River of Doubt, where a large cache of bird and mammal skulls and skins were accumulated and sent back to the coast to be taken to New York. The caravan, now a smaller party, proceeded on, kept company by the loud sounds of bright macaws, howling monkeys, and the occasional toucan. Playing the missionary, Zahm, much to Rondon's disgust, insisted on being carried about in a chair by the local Parecís Indians. The Colonel would have none of this and promptly banished the eccentric cleric to Tapirapuã. "Father Zahm . . . showed him[self] so completely incompetent and selfish," Kermit wrote home, "that he got on everyone's nerves, and then he tried a couple of things that made it easy to send him back."[7]

In February, heavy rains slowed the explorers' advance north to José Bonifácio, resulting in the decision to relinquish their tents and unwieldy Canadian canoes. Out of the forest appeared bands of Nhambiquaras, first contacted in the 1770s and, so Rondon estimated, having once encountered these peoples on his passage through their territory to extend telegraph lines, numbering some ten thousand. They carried long bows and arrows, their septums and upper lips pierced with quills. Rondon carefully posted guards, though the two groups made cordial contact—one photo shows Roosevelt seated and writing in a notebook supported on one crossed leg while several interested natives mill about, one's bare bum innocently brushing against the Colonel's dark leather boots. Reaching the River of Doubt on the twenty-seventh, the expedition initially moved at a gruelingly slow place, inundated by tropical showers, consumed by insects, and idled by rapids requiring frequent portaging. Amid the boils, heat, and mosquitoes, Roosevelt played the proper gentleman, maintaining a small library including Goethe and Schiller along, so he noted, with "a steady course of Gibbon, [and] . . . a volume of Arsène Lupin." Attentive to hygiene, he bathed and swam each day in the unfolding river "although in it," he later observed, "we caught piranhas."[8]

On March 14, after nearly three weeks on their watery route, tragedy struck when Kermit, impatiently disregarding Rondon's order to remain on land until an investigating party could determine the extent and volatility of an approaching rapid, led a group in a small canoe onto the water. Quickly caught in a whirlpool, their craft capsized, and they lost a man—Simplicio. The elder Roosevelt and Rondon seemed to silently agree not to pursue the matter. The Colonel glancingly mentions the calamity in his book *Through the Brazilian Wilderness*—"Poor Simplicio must have been pulled under at once, and his life beaten out on the boulders beneath the racing torrent"—without details. His strongest emotion appeared to be relief: "Kermit was a great comfort and help to me on the trip; but the fear of some fatal accident befalling him was always a nightmare to me. He was to be married as soon as the trip was over; and it did not seem to me that I could bear to bring bad tidings to his betrothed and to his mother." The drowned man, by contrast, could be quickly mourned, paid for, and put away: "Simplicio was unmarried. Later we sent to his mother all the money that would have been his had he lived."[9]

Its ranks depleted, the expedition looked more generally to be slightly imperiled. Having surrendered several canoes, tents, and other supplies while making maddeningly little progress moving down the Dúvida, they now discovered Rondon's dog, Lobo, felled by two arrows whose sharp points told Rondon they belonged not to the Nhambiquaras, but possibly to a people who had never encountered whites. Their provisions all but depleted, the voyagers fed increasingly off the land. Roosevelt dined on his first brown woolly monkey stew, a diet supplemented by pineapples, wild beans, toucans, and parrots—the latter, he noted, "were very good." Jungle cuisine notwithstanding, the "mass attacks" from malaria-carrying mosquitoes and several varieties of aggressive flies made their days, Cherrie recalled, miserable: "In all my thirty years' experience in South American work, on the Amazon, the Orinoco, the Magdalena, and many other . . . insect-infested regions, I have never been in a locality where there were, day and night, such swarms." Roosevelt took to wearing socks on his hands and wrapped a towel about his head and neck. Termites and carregadores ants ate a hole in one of his shoes, destroyed a handkerchief, and munched liberally, so he said, on "my drawers."[10]

On March 27 the Colonel, while joining others in trying to correct an "upset canoe," cut his right leg on a rock, the same limb he had injured in a streetcar accident and had surgically treated while president. He acquired a visible limp that drew attention from neighboring vultures. "I now had a sharp attack of fever," he further reported, and though attended by a physician, his health seemed on the verge of giving out. Hiking with Cherrie on the thirtieth, he grew exhausted, causing Kermit to confide in his diary, "Worried a lot about father's heart." Matters worsened in early April when a murder took place. One morning the conspicuously well-fed Julio de Lima, punished several times as a food thief, received a rebuke from Paixão-Paishon—"a huge negro," Roosevelt wrote, "a corporal and acting sergeant in the engineer corps"—for stealing dried meat. Shortly thereafter, just outside of camp, de Lima shot and killed his accuser before disappearing into the jungle.[11]

The following day Roosevelt's fever spiked, and he slipped into unconsciousness with periods of delirium. He "was out of his head," Kermit later noted, remembering how his afflicted father recited Coleridge ("In Xanadu did Kubla Khan a stately pleasure-dome decree . . .") before "talking at random." At one point Cherrie, greatly concerned, wrote in his daybook, "I don't believe he can live through the night." Approaching at this delicate stage a particularly narrow canyon on the river, some in the party advised abandoning their canoes and setting off on foot through the forest—the portaging, they insisted, simply took too much time. Gathering Cherrie and Kermit, the Colonel asked to be left behind: "Boys, I realize that some of us are not going to finish this journey. I know that I am only a burden to the rest of you . . . I will stop here."[12] Of course, they refused this desperate request.

Treated with quinine, Roosevelt's temperature lessened, and after a few days the ragged expedition continued down the river, only to suddenly encounter a desperate de Lima, standing behind a group of trees and insisting on his right to surrender and be rescued. Rondon, in the lead craft, remained silent and kept moving and Roosevelt, trailing behind, did the same. Down to nineteen undernourished men, the Colonel later explained, he "had no intention of taking the murderer aboard, to the jeopardy of the other members of the party." At their next stop, Rondon sent two "expert woodsmen" to bring de Lima back, but they never found him.[13]

By the second week of April the sequence of forbidding rapids abated, and the expedition began to make good time. On the fourteenth it happened upon "civilization"—a wooden signpost with the initials "J. A.," indicating the claim of a rubber tapper, and nearby a group of fishermen, the party's first contact with other humans in seven weeks. Two days later Roosevelt, obviously in great discomfort, submitted to a primitive riverbank operation on his festering leg performed by José Cajazeira, the expedition's capable physician. With no anesthetic at hand, a stoic Roosevelt watched as Cajazeira cut into his thigh, draining an abscess filled with blood and a concentration of fetid pus. On April 26 the expedition came to a more or less official end when it reached a supply post at the confluence with the Aripuanã River. The next day, following a prolonged separation ceremony outlining the expedition's findings, the group broke up. Following medical treatment in Manaus, the Colonel, having taxied down the Amazon on a cargo craft, boarded the British steamship *Aidan* at Belém and commenced the final leg of his journey to New York.

On the surface, the grueling odyssey into Brazil had been a conspicuous success. Some 2,500 birds and 500 mammals, along with a surfeit of insects and fish, many fresh to science, were collected for the American Museum of Natural History. And forthwith several hundred miles of a formerly uncharted water artery through the Mato Grosso could now be mapped with some precision. A second journey to the river in the late 1920s led by the British explorer George Miller Dyott confirmed the—to some, still disputed—findings of 1914. The Dúvida, by this time, was now officially known as the Rio Roosevelt.

Its namesake, perhaps having made a Faustian bargain, returned to America physically diminished. Most noticeably he had lost fifty-five pounds, though the weight would quickly return to the Colonel, whose daily breakfasts alone included liberal quantities of meats, pancakes, and potatoes washed down with cup after cup of sweetened coffee. More permanently, he felt the effect of infection for the rest of his days. "At 56 I never should have undertaken that South American trip," he told the journalist Henry Stoddard. "It just put the jungle fever into me when I was too old to fight it." A year after the excursion, TR's old college friend Charles Washburn reported seeing "evidence for the first time that this mighty human dynamo is working with a somewhat diminished energy." TR had just returned from shooting moose in Quebec Province. "He told me," Washburn wrote, "that it was his last hunting trip."[14]

With no other mountains, moose, or rivers to conquer, and increasingly unequal to the effort, Roosevelt returned to Oyster Bay in the spring of 1914. Four years earlier, having safaried in Africa, he had come home and promptly crossed swords with the Republican Old Guard, a move that struck some as an erratic response to boredom dressed up as duty. He now set his sights on Woodrow Wilson and, in the second half of the year, the Great War that had suddenly engulfed the world.

58

Wilson's Washington

During the Mexican Revolution (1910–1920), an extended struggle that toppled President Porfirio Díaz's decades-long autocratic rule and left a power vacuum among competing factions, U.S. troops were positioned along the southern border. In a break with Taft's efforts employing economic suasion—loans to Latin republics to further foreign policy goals—Wilson argued that idealism should inform American statecraft. As the former college professor primly told a British diplomat, "I am going to teach the South American republics to elect good men." Skeptics hooted that Wilson had merely replaced dollar diplomacy with missionary diplomacy. After Díaz's fall a democratically elected government led by Francisco Madero briefly held power, until a coup by rebels murdered Madero and his vice president in late February 1913, just days before Wilson's inauguration, and made Victoriano Huerta, another general in the Latin strongman mien, president. The Wilson administration refused to recognize this new regime, which the president referred to as "a government of butchers." He insisted, rather, that Mexico hold democratic elections.[1]

The following year in April, the Tampico Affair—nine U.S. Navy sailors on shore to obtain supplies were briefly detained by Mexican soldiers—overlapped with news of the impending arrival of a weapons-laden German steamer, the *Ypiranga*, making for Veracruz. The ordnance, some of it originating from the Remington Company in the United States, was in fact being sourced by a Russian arms dealer and an American financier, John Wesley De Kay, who had large interests in Mexico. The shipment violated an arms embargo Wilson had imposed on Huerta's government the previous August, and on the morning of April 21, several vessels from the U.S. Atlantic Fleet, including the battleships *Florida* and *Utah*, along with attendant marines and navy sailors, began to seize control of the city's waterfront. By evening six thousand American soldiers were ashore and the Battle of Veracruz, fought over two days and resulting in more than two hundred Mexican deaths and nineteen American casualties, had become the occupation of Veracruz.²

This operation contributed to the ongoing instability inside Mexico—Huerta's regime soon fell, giving way to a civil war—and from Oyster Bay Roosevelt lingered over the prospects of a Rough Rider redux. "I believe that in case of a serious war, I should ask permission to raise a division of cavalry, composed of nine regiments, such as I had in the Spanish war," he wrote one correspondent. The Colonel ultimately held back, uncertain that playing a modern conquistador promised sufficient glory: "I am very doubtful . . . whether I should go into a mere war with Mexico, and I certainly would not go into it if I do not know whether it was to be war or peace."³

That fall, Roosevelt's attention turned to an altogether novel crisis, the onset of the Great War, as well as to a more familiar calendar occurrence, the November elections, in whose service he canvassed for Progressive candidates in several southern, eastern, and midwestern states. The fire of 1912 had burned out, however, and he remained more or less committed to the GOP, for only in its favor would he have any prospect of future political influence. The war, by contrast, riveted TR completely. He had long envisioned a coming conflict, as when writing in 1901, "Germany is the great growing power, and both her faults and her virtues, at least of the superficial kind, are so different from ours, and her ambitions in extra-European matters are so great, that she may clash with us." In other respects, he had turned a tin ear to circumstances on the Continent. "No better bit of governmental work has been done in Europe than the work of the Austrians in governing Bosnia and Herzegovina," he insisted, some five years before the young Bosnian revolutionary Gavrilo Princip, part of a secret pan-Serb society, assassinated the heir to the Austro-Hungarian throne and set the world on fire.⁴

From the war's onset Roosevelt criticized the kaiser's government, condemning its violation of neutral rights ("It does not seem to me that any adequate defense can be made for Germany's [invasion of] Belgium") and dreading the geopolitical shift should the Second Reich and its satellites triumph: "Do you not believe that if Germany won in this war, smashed the English Fleet and destroyed the British Empire, within a year or two she would insist upon taking the dominant position in South and Central America," he wrote Hugo Münsterberg, a Harvard professor by way of West Prussia. "I believe so. Indeed, I know so."[5]

On the other hand, he feared that a German defeat would allow Russia to move into Europe while removing a potential U.S. ally in containing Japanese expansion. The current composition of American leadership—the peace-minded William Jennings Bryan now headed the State Department—hardly cushioned his concerns. "It is not a good thing," he wrote an English friend on August 1, 1914, the day Germany declared war on Russia, "for a country to have a professional yodeler, a human trombone like Mr. Bryan as Secretary of State, nor a college president with an astute and shifty mind . . . and no real knowledge or wisdom concerning internal and international affairs as head of the nation." Name-calling aside, the Colonel did have reason to question Wilson's limited credentials in the field of foreign relations. Roosevelt, by contrast, had made several trips to Europe, including recently (June 1914) while attending his son Kermit's Madrid wedding to the Baltimore-born Belle Willard, daughter of the U.S. ambassador to Spain. More broadly, the breadth of his transnational experiences ranged far beyond that of the former Princeton president. He had fought in an overseas war and circulated comfortably among the Continent's royalty; he enjoyed personal relationships (including several decades-long friendships) with well-placed Englishmen and had won the Nobel Peace Prize for mediating the Russo-Japanese War. Dismayed that the nation should now find itself led by "yodelers," and no doubt ruing his misfortune to have served seven years in the White House without a global war to sink his splendid teeth into, Roosevelt engaged in kibitzing. "In international affairs," he observed to a colleague, "Wilson is almost as much of a prize jackass as Bryan."[6]

In the autumn of 1914, the Colonel bit his tongue on the campaign trail, having promised anxious Progressives not to condemn Wilson's pacifism, a real concern considering the many German Americans the party hoped to court. Rather, in a late-September *Outlook* essay, Roosevelt, perhaps thinking of the triumphant Treaty of Portsmouth, counseled the country to "stand ready to act as an instrument for the achievement of a just peace if or when the opportunity arises."[7] In subsequent essays, though still emphasizing the importance of American neutrality, he began to sharply attack both Wilson and Bryan for the nation's lack of military preparedness. That November Progressive candidates were soundly defeated, claiming about half the number of 1912 votes and losing every gubernatorial contest entered other than popular incumbent Hiram Johnson's comfortable victory in California. The party's already meager presence in the House of Representatives shrank from ten to six seats. Democrats, riding Wilson's early record as a New Freedom reformer—lowering the tariff, revising the nation's banking structure via the Federal Reserve Act, and signing antitrust legislation that banned a host of anticompetitive practices—maintained control of both congressional houses, though the GOP picked up dozens of lower chamber seats.

Following the elections, Roosevelt, increasingly tired, too heavy, and possibly depressed over his inability to dominate public opinion, professed to be leaning toward retirement. In a letter to Rear Admiral Presley Marion Rixey, his personal presidential physician, he admitted to a host of nagging ailments:

> As for me, my dear doctor, I am practically through. I am not a man like you who keeps his youth almost to the end; and I am now pretty nearly done out. I would not say this except to my old friend . . . because it is rather poor business to speak about one's personal ailments; but the trouble is that I have rheumatism or gout and things of that kind to a degree that makes it impossible for me to take very much exercise.

Making no apologies for nearly dying in the Amazon ("I am more pleased than I can say that I was able to take the . . . trip. I knew it would be my last thing of the kind"), he shrugged off Rixey's suggestion that either fate or the nation still had plans for this suddenly old man: "I was pleased but amused, my dear fellow, at your saying that I had work to do in the future. I have none. The Kaleidoscope has been shaken."[8]

One wonders if even Roosevelt, his health concerns aside, believed that. He had in fact just signed a lucrative three-year contract ($25,000 per annum, or $750,000 per in today's dollars) to write for the monthly *Metropolitan Magazine*. He planned, so he told Lodge in December, to use this print platform to flay the Wilson administration. "Nothing irritated me more last summer than the attitude of my own [Progressive] friends and also of the Republicans toward Wilson's foreign policy especially in Mexico. My own friends and supporters besought me not to touch him.... I told [them] that as I was doing what I could for them this fall I should not make an attack which they thought would hurt them but that after election I should smite the administration with a heavy hand."[9] He now proceeded to smite.

In January 1915 Scribners published the Colonel's condemnatory *America and the World War*, a hastily assembled attack on Wilson's "policy of national unpreparedness." Calling Germany's violation of Belgian neutrality in order to attack France "a crime," he insisted "in the strongest way" that the administration should "have interfered" to the extent of delivering "at least . . . a most emphatic diplomatic protest." Thereafter followed a cloud of contempt. Wilson is "much applauded by . . . the professional pacifists," engages in "a foreign policy of . . . prattling feebleness," and responds to his critics "with a cheap sneer." Bryan was also ripe for ridicule, displaying in his "prince of peace" permutation the second-rate "emotionalism of the professional orator."[10] Reaching for familiar themes, Roosevelt insisted that the navy be strengthened, thought too many risk-averse politicians failed to embody the strenuous life ideal, and likened the administration's resistance to beefing up the military to James Buchanan's appeasement of southern fire-eaters in the fateful secession winter of 1860–61. Roosevelt had always wanted to play the role of Lincoln.

Edgy and armed with no greater influence than the occasional byline, TR paced through an uncomfortable winter. Though favoring England—"I have unequivocally expressed my sympathies with the Allies"—he condemned Britain's unusually restrictive naval blockade of Germany, which included the stopping and inspecting of neutral American vessels heading to the Continent. "I think Great Britain . . . has done things to our ships that ought not to have been done," he informed Sir Edward Grey, His Majesty's secretary of state for foreign affairs, in late January, and wrote an old friend, the dapper British journalist and *Spectator* editor John St. Loe Strachey, the following month, "England has acted pretty roughly as regards the rights of neutrals. . . . I cannot accept your view." Eager to engage with the distant fighting, the Colonel opened sleepy Sagamore Hill to a host of pro-war military and political advisors that upset the rhythms of rural Long Island life. "He likes the house full of Tom, Dick and Harry," an exhausted Edith protested to Kermit, "and I can't quite keep up with the pace." Her other sons, Ted, Archie, and Quentin had recently enrolled in a military training camp in upstate Plattsburgh run by Major General Leonard Wood, Roosevelt's nominal superior in the long-ago Cuban campaign.[11]

The Colonel's public stumping for war preparedness marked the end of his domestic reform crusade phase, while all but dissolving his relationship with the Progressives—many of whom, like Jane Addams, belonged to the camp of "professional pacifists." Though one might regard Roosevelt's reflexive embrace of martial glory as merely emotional, it might be remembered that, as a young man, he had produced a work of scholarship that anticipated the choices America faced in 1915. Drawing on "the old lesson" that a "well-officered, and well-trained force" was indispensable to success, he had argued in *The Naval War of 1812* that "it is true economy to have the regular force prepared beforehand, without waiting until we have been forced to prepare it by . . . disasters." Jefferson's ineffectual efforts employing a skeletal marine defense to combat British aggression on the seas in the years leading up to the conflict were summarily dismissed in that work as "painfully ludicrous."[12]

And now a century later, Roosevelt argued that the country unwisely resisted the inevitable need for U.S. intervention in Europe. "At best this war will be a stalemate for the Allies unless America gets into it," he told a favored *New York Evening Mail* editor. "For us the question to determine is whether we will get into this war with the Allies cooperating with us, or go into a later war against Germany without help from the Allies. Wilson ought to see that we must make a choice." With access to *Metropolitan Magazine*'s large readership, Roosevelt settled down to the task of making the president see the light.

59

Rumors of War

The May 7, 1915, torpedoing of the British ocean liner RMS *Lusitania* by an Imperial German Navy U-boat eleven miles off the Irish coast, en route from New York to Liverpool, escalated pressure on Wilson to confront the challenge of American neutrality. Of the nearly 2,000 passengers and crew, 1,198 perished in the attack, including 128 Americans. Questions over whether the ship, a veteran of more than two hundred trans-Atlantic crossings, constituted a legitimate military target were subsequently raised, and it was later disclosed that the craft carried on this fated journey artillery fuses, shell casings, and machine gun ammunition. Wilson's response, demanding that Germany immediately cease assaults on ships carrying citizens of neutral countries, fell miles shy of a seething Roosevelt's desire for revenge. "The murder of the . . . men, women and children on the *Lusitania* is due, solely, to Wilson's abject cowardice," he wrote his son Archie, but neither the president nor Bryan, he continued, will "go to war unless they are kicked into it." His anger extended beyond the administration, however, highlighting the Colonel's increasing disappointment in "the hyphenated Americans," the "solid flubdub," and the "pacifist vote," and still more generally "every man who has not got in him both the sterner virtues and the power of seeking after an ideal."[1] Disgusted with Wilson's apparent popularity, Roosevelt began to doubt the so-called virtues of democracy.

Going public, TR peppered his *Metropolitan* essays with sharp attacks on the president, whose insistence that "there is such a thing as a man being too proud to fight" merely begged his contempt. Rather, he wrote, "the duty of a leader is to lead; and it is a dreadful thing that any man chosen to lead his fellow countrymen should himself show, not merely so profound a lack of patriotism, but such misunderstanding of patriotism, as to be willing to say in a great crisis what . . . Wilson thus said at the time of the sinking of the *Lusitania*." That August, following an address on the drill plain at the U.S. Military Instruction Camp at Plattsburgh, Roosevelt provocatively raised before reporters the question of Wilson's legitimacy: "I wish to make one comment on the statement so frequently made that we must stand by the President. I heartily subscribe to this on condition and only on condition that it is followed by the statement so long as the President stands by the country." Three days later Wilson wrote of the nettlesome Colonel to his fiancée Edith Bolling Galt (his wife, Ellen, having died of Bright's disease the previous August), "He is too common a nuisance to bother our minds about and the best way to vanquish him is to take no notice of him whatever. . . . Bless your dear heart, how I love you for getting so furious with T.R. for his assault on me! I could almost warm my hands at those flaming hot sentences in your letter of Thursday morning!"[2]

The Colonel, though himself engaged to Edith the year after Alice's death, apparently thought little of Wilson's presidential dip into the dating pool. "The worthy gentleman's motto seems to be," he wrote to one correspondent, "'My wife is dead! Long live my wife.'"[3]

Despite Roosevelt's concerns that "every soft creature" in the country wished for nothing more than "pleasure or ease," momentum for military preparedness picked up in 1916 when it became apparent that the European powers were settling in for a long war. Discussions over compulsory service, an enlarged navy, and new munitions plants, however, vied that political year with the looming presidential election. The Colonel recognized that whatever attenuated power he now piloted came from his hold over a tight knot of reformers within the GOP. "Of course, it is possible that the Republicans will win without any assistance from the Progressives at all," he wrote Lodge on the edge of the new year. "But on the assumption that there is need of trying to unite all the anti-Wilson forces into a coherent whole, I hope that the Republicans will take action such as will render it possible for the Progressives to go in with them. Unless there is a really vital national crisis I do not intend to separate myself from my Progressive supporters."[4]

Neither did they intend to separate from him. While cruising the Caribbean in February on a six-week vacation with Edith, he learned via cablegram that Progressives planned to advance his candidacy in several states. From Port of Spain, Trinidad, Roosevelt issued a forswearing statement "declining to be a candidate in the primaries" and further promising "I will not enter into any fight for the nomination." Of course, this surface reserve left the door open to a nomination by acclamation, something he seemed receptive to, if the people were sufficiently willing to do as he said: "It would be a mistake to nominate me unless the country has in its mood something of the heroic." Playing the destiny card, he compared the present situation to those of the American Revolution and the Civil War—"one of those rare times which come only at long intervals in a nation's history" and call upon uncommon leadership. The *New York Times* rightly declared the statement "a Bid for [the] Presidency."[5]

Returning to Oyster Bay in March, Roosevelt knew many in the GOP were preparing to support Charles Evans Hughes, the former New York governor now sitting as a Taft appointment on the Supreme Court. A mild progressive while in Albany, increasing the power of public utility regulation and placing limits on political donations by corporations, he seemed capable of bridging the gap between the party's reform and conservative wings. Temperamentally disinclined to run for the office, Hughes hated campaigning and wholly lacked Roosevelt's charisma. Eager to see if he might somehow supplant this presumptive frontrunner, the Colonel attended a small luncheon summit on May 31 at the Park Avenue home of his old Harvard friend Robert Bacon. The principals included Leonard Wood (quietly nursing his own executive office aspirations), Henry Cabot Lodge, and Elihu Root, the latter of whom Roosevelt had accused of turning traitor at the 1912 Republican convention ("What an awful set of crooks they were at Chicago!").[6] Bacon seemed to have mixed motives, preparing the way for Roosevelt to rejoin the party while also abetting Root's presidential candidacy, which was announced a week later on April 7. In a scene worthy of Shakespeare—a gathering of White House rivals tinged with accusations of past betrayal—only a shared contempt of Wilson could bring them together.

That June, Hughes garnered the Republican nomination on the third ballot while Roosevelt, a "noncandidate," peaked in fifth place on the second roll call. Though disappointed in the decision ("Hughes—ugh!"), the Colonel telegrammed "THE CONFEREES OF THE PROGRESSIVE PARTY" from Oyster Bay on the tenth, the final day of the

GOP *and* Progressive conventions (the former meeting at the Chicago Coliseum, the latter in the Chicago Auditorium), to decline their nomination—though "I deeply appreciate your loyalty to me." Remarkably, Roosevelt suggested that the party run the conservative Lodge, a man, he abstractly said, of "wide experience in public affairs," but whom no one had ever mistaken for being particularly progressive.[7] The reformers thought not and unenthusiastically adopted Hughes. Some, however, would cross over in November, seeking their Armageddon moment with Wilson, the peace candidate who "kept us out of war."

Roosevelt's reintegration into the Republican fold inevitably included a reckoning with Taft. In their first frosty meeting in nearly four years, the two had served as pallbearers at the April 1915 funeral for the literary historian Thomas Lounsbury. Now, during the 1916 campaign, while attending a Union League Club reception in Manhattan for Hughes, the Colonel reluctantly agreed to acknowledge Taft more formally. "I shall most certainly not seek him out at the Club," he told a journalist, but "if he comes up to me and wishes to shake hands, I shall shake hands."[8]

Amid this strange political year, Roosevelt looked as well to resurrect his military career. Since the U.S. occupation of Veracruz and the collapse of Huerta's government in 1914, no fewer than five presidents had tried to lead Mexico, the current head of state being Venustiano Carranza, a wealthy landowner and cagey politician who doubled as First Chief of the Constitutionalist Army. When he fell out with one of his finest generals, the tall, round-cheeked, and heavily mustached Francisco "Pancho" Villa, a sharecropper's son and former bandit, a bloody civil war ensued. Defeated between April and November 1915 by Carranza's forces at the battles of Celaya, Trinidad, and Agua Prieta, Villa, his army down to perhaps two hundred men, was on the run and felt betrayed by Wilson, who had recognized Carranza's regime and permitted his soldiers to cross into U.S. territory to attack the Villistas. Though he had once thought of Villa as a reformer in the Robin Hood mold and even expressed "entire confidence" in the revolutionary, Wilson could see that continued warfare undermined America's foothold in Mexico's mining, petroleum, and rubber industries.[9]

Incensed, Villa, now reduced to guerrilla warfare, sought to prompt a U.S. intervention in Mexico, hoping it would discredit Carranza's government. In January 1916 his band attacked a train near Santa Isabel in Chihuahua and killed sixteen American engineers who had entered the country from California (to open a mine) under a safe conduct assurance from the government. The following month the revolutionaries raided the border town of Columbus, New Mexico, which resulted in ten civilian deaths before the 13th Cavalry Regiment drove them out. With Carranza's wary consent, Wilson ordered the Punitive Expedition, a military operation led by General John J. Pershing charged with tracking down Villa's paramilitary force. For nearly a year, before U.S. entry into the First World War ended the mission, the Yankees penetrated 350 miles into Mexico, but never caught sight of the elusive Villa.

That July, Roosevelt wrote Secretary of War Newton Baker—whose placid smooth face, right-parted hair, and period pince-nez made him look a little like Wilson—requesting "permission to raise and command an infantry division," including "one motorcycle regiment with machine guns," for service in Mexico.[10] He proposed further that the War Department allow this force to assemble at Fort Sill in Oklahoma. Baker forwarded the request to Major General Henry P. McCain, the chief administrative officer of the U.S. Army, who assured the former president his petition would be considered most carefully should war break out with Mexico.

While Pershing searched for Villa, Roosevelt made an extended autumn campaign swing, touching several states between Maine and Arizona at the request of the Republican National Committee. On November 3, his disdain for Wilson reached new rhetorical heights in an incendiary address—"The Soul of the Nation"—delivered at New York's Cooper Union, site of a famous 1860 speech by Lincoln that made the single-term Illinois congressman a serious contender for the presidency. Glad to "speak in this historic building," the Colonel referenced the sixteenth president repeatedly, asking his audience "to compare this record of Lincoln's with the cynicism shown by Mr. Wilson." Warming to his subject, he made graphic, even ghoulish references to the *Lusitania*'s sinking, noting "the dead mothers with their dead babies" and the "scores" of corpses lying cool "in the Queenstown morgue." He then crudely referenced Shadow Lawn, a rambling fifty-two-room estate of dubious architectural taste in West Long Branch, New Jersey, that served as Wilson's summer White House in 1915 and 1916. "There should be shadows enough at Shadow Lawn; the Shadows of men, women, and children who have risen from the ooze of the ocean bottom and from graves in foreign lands; the shadows of the helpless whom Mr. Wilson did not dare protect lest he might have to face danger; the shadows of babies gasping pitifully as they sank under the waves."[11]

Four days later Americans went to the polls and, in a squeaker, Wilson was reelected by a 277 to 254 margin in the Electoral College. Several newspapers called the contest for Hughes early, but the returns from the West were strongly for Wilson, who won every state beyond the Mississippi River except four. A stunned Hughes refused for two weeks to concede. The Sagamore Hill perspective was fluently expressed by an irate Edith who protested that "another four years must pass with this vile and hypocritical charlatan at the head of the nation." Her husband, keen to cast a pox on all pretenders to the throne he had once owned, declared himself "very greatly relieved to be able to believe that the real fact was that the west fixed its eyes on Hughes' pussy-footing and lack of vision, and on the machine and reactionary support of him, and voted against him on these counts, and only incidentally for Wilson."[12] Obviously the Colonel retained the right, as he had so often over the years, to play independent.

Within weeks of the election, in late January, Berlin rescinded its Sussex Pledge of the previous year, in which it had agreed to give warning prior to sinking merchant and passenger ships and to provide for the safety of passengers and crews. Suffering under a tightening British blockade that resulted in a civilian death toll estimated at more than half a million, and counting on the kaiser's army to knock out the Allied forces before large concentrations of American troops could arrive on the Continent, Germany now announced the resumption of unrestricted submarine warfare. Three days later, the United States cut off diplomatic relations with Germany, and only a few hours after that the SS *Housatonic*, a nearly thirty-year-old American liner loaded with Texas wheat and sailing toward Liverpool, was sunk by a U-boat off the Isles of Scilly near the Cornish peninsula.

At this point, several dominoes began to fall. On February 27 Wilson asked Congress for authority to arm American merchant vessels, and four days later ordered the publication of a secret diplomatic communication—intercepted by British intelligence—issued from Berlin in January proposing a military pact between Germany and Mexico should the United States enter the war. The so-called Zimmermann note (after Arthur Zimmermann, the East Prussian–born state secretary of foreign affairs) included Germany's promise to see that Mexico reclaim Texas, Arizona, and New Mexico—all lost to Yankee cupidity in the 1830s and 1840s. "GERMANY SEEKS AN ALLIANCE AGAINST US," the *New York Times* trumpeted, and a sense of urgency began to envelop Capitol Hill. Wilson summoned Congress to meet in a special session on April 2, at which he announced the severing of diplomatic relations with Germany and requested a declaration of war: "We will not choose the path of submission."

Less than two weeks earlier, Roosevelt, his blood up, had accused Wilson in a public address of permitting "a war of murder upon us," negatively contrasting the present "empty gesture" policy emanating from Washington to "the days when this Republic prized manhood." But all had suddenly changed. Hot for combat, the Colonel now needed to make peace with, so he said, "the most wretched creature we have had in the Presidential chair," if he hoped to win a fresh division, saddle up for the Somme, and earn his spurs all over again.[13]

60

Forever Jingo

America's entry into the First World War revived an old reflex in Roosevelt, the desire to pack a kit and amble off to glory. In 1886, while serving on the Board of New York City Police Commissioners, he wrote then–secretary of war William Endicott of a plan to personally "raise some companies of horse riflemen" should the Apache uprising in Mexico call for a strong U.S. response; a dozen years later he stormed the San Juan Heights in Cuba, and in 1911 told President Taft, regarding yet another border concern with Mexico, that in the event of "a serious war . . . I would wish immediately to apply for permission" to fight. Now, as Germany loomed as the next great threat, he burned to put King Edward VII's showy funeral to shame: "As for myself, at this time I think I could do this country most good by dying in a reasonably honorable fashion, at the head of my division."[1] Driven by a congenital jingoism, he sensed, at the age of fifty-nine and long out of power, the onset of irrelevancy, to which he reacted with anger, indignation, and resentment. This practiced opponent of Old Guardism, this tribune of the progressive future, wanted nothing so much as to repeat the past.

Eager to claim "my division," he raced down to Washington in early April, bunking with Nick and Alice. A young Franklin Roosevelt, assistant secretary of the navy, was prevailed upon to clear a path for his distant relative, telling Secretary of War Baker that the Colonel happened to be in town and very much wished an audience with the president. Consequently, the elder Roosevelt arrived at the White House on the tenth and was escorted to the Green Room where he met with Wilson for twenty-five minutes, asking for his division. The president politely put off making a commitment, leaving Roosevelt afterward to play nice before a swarming press, whom he told, on the White House steps, that his long-standing criticism of Wilson's neutrality "was buried with the President's declaration of war." The New York Times, citing "the general opinion in Washington," optimistically said of the summit, "The result might well be a sweeping aside of party lines that would get the country solidly behind the Administration program."[2]

TR further held a series of meetings at the Longworths' stately Dupont Circle neighborhood town house, a fine Beaux-Arts box erected in 1881. His callers included Secretary Baker, French ambassador Jules Jusserand, and British ambassador Spring Rice. The Colonel must have felt, almost, as though he occupied the West Wing again. "I found the house filled with visitors on the first floor, most of them Senators and close friends of Colonel Roosevelt," Baker later reported. "The former President seemed to be in high spirits. He came out when I arrived and greeted me cordially, put his hand through my arm and took me upstairs to one of the bedrooms. He then described his hopes for leading a division in France."[3] Baker obligingly listened but refused to be drawn in and headed for the door.

The prospect of a "Roosevelt Division" left the administration cold. TR had insisted on the right to pick his officer corps, which would have put him in competition with the regular army. If he was allowed to assemble a force, moreover, other calls to do the same would inevitably come, thus compromising the professional military's recruiting. Skeptics were legion. After the war General Pershing, commander of the American Expeditionary Forces in France, directly questioned Roosevelt's skills and stamina when observing that the Colonel, still susceptible to Cuban fever (likely a recurring form of malaria) and further diminished physically in the punishing Amazon jungle, "was not in the best health and could not have withstood the hard work and exposure of the training camp and trenches."[4]

Roosevelt seemed to some extent aware of his limitations, and thought his chief contribution lay in inspiring the soldiery. "I would not have lasted long, probably even mild hardship would have been too much for me," he wrote Archie in the late summer of 1917, "but I would have lasted long enough to get a hundred thousand men in fighting mood, and in efficient shape to the front; and then I would have been entirely willing to have had 'nunc dimittis' [Song of Simeon] sung over me."[5]

Three days after meeting with Wilson, Roosevelt received a communication from Secretary Baker regarding "the subject of our conversation." In a mannered yet firm note, he told the former president, eager to rush to the front with a volunteer force, no.

> The War College Division earnestly recommends that no American troops be employed in active service in any European theater until after an adequate period of training, and that during this period all available trained officers and men in the Regular Army or National Guard be employed in training the new levees called into service. It should, therefore, be our policy at first to devote all our energies to raising troops in sufficient numbers to exert a substantial influence in a later stage of the war. Partially trained troops will be entirely unfit for such duty.[6]

Baker assured the Colonel that this decision was based on "purely military" considerations and he expressed little doubt that "there are . . . other ways" in which the former Rough Rider might enhance the Allied cause "apart from a military expedition." He then more pointedly observed that those likely destined for France would be among "the ablest and most experienced professional military men in our country. . . . I could not reconcile my mind to a recommendation which deprived our soldiers of the most experienced leadership available, in deference to any mere sentimental consideration."[7] Roosevelt, in other words, was for all his good intentions but a corpulent armchair general, a nineteenth-century bravo in a fading Brooks Brothers uniform.

Simmering at Oyster Bay, Roosevelt replied to Baker on the twenty-third, eager in a long fourteen-page communication to contradict the secretary at every turn. Out of official favor for years, he now relied upon ancient contacts offering questionable reconnaissance. He quoted to Baker the contents of a letter just received from his old friend James Bryce, lately British ambassador to the United States and homing in on eighty, pleading for an American presence on the Continent: "The moral effect of the appearance in the war line of an American force would be immense." Hotly defending his military record, Roosevelt bombarded Baker (amid a host of prickly "my dear sirs") with several references to his service in Cuba, a dubious strategy that could only have accentuated his reader's suspicion that the Colonel lived not a little in the past. Such phrases and allusions included: "In the Spanish War . . ."; "The regiment which I commanded in the Santiago campaign . . ."; "The great majority of men who were in my old regiment will eagerly come forward under me, in so far as they are yet fit." Indeed, TR invoked even the American Civil War on his side as when noting the success of cavalry under Confederate general Nathan Bedford Forrest. Though asking for a rather large favor, Roosevelt could not resist sticking a well-aimed thumb in Baker's official eye: "Our nation has not prepared in any adequate way during the last two and a half years to meet the crisis which now faces us." Rather, he continued, Wilson proposed to pay blood money ("billions of dollars") to the Allies "while we stay here in comfort and slowly proceed to train an army," to fight a war that might end before a single doughboy made it to the Continent.[8]

Baker replied on May 5, still courteous but still firm. "For obvious reasons," he wrote, "I cannot allow myself to be drawn into a discussion of your personal experience and qualifications." Rather than devoting precious resources to a "hastily summoned and unprofessional force," professional soldiers were preferred. Roosevelt countered on the eighth with a patronizing letter, littered with more and aggressive "my dear Mr. Secretarys", in which he quoted back to the no doubt exasperated cabinet official his own words—"You say . . ."; "You then describe . . ."; "Your next paragraph . . ."—before dismissing such concerns in a thick mist of logic chopping. Baker had earlier indicated (Roosevelt quoting selectively from their correspondence) that of course it would be a nice thing if an army could be trained quickly; these words were now pushed forward as evidence of the need for a volunteer force. Contradicting Baker at every turn, the note, perhaps therapeutic for its author, could only have antagonized its reader. Renewing his request "respectfully, but earnestly," TR submitted the names of men he wished to have serve under him—"civilian colonels . . . brigade commanders . . . certain junior officers"—for his nonexistent division.[9] Baker could only have sighed.

Having had his fill of underlings, Roosevelt, a day after writing Lodge, "It is imperatively necessary to expose [Wilson's] hypocrisy," drafted a succinct, single-paragraph letter to the hypocrite himself on May 18: "I respectfully ask permission immediately to raise two divisions for immediate service at the front." Wilson replied—twice. That same day, in the *New York Times*, a statement appeared from the president: "I shall not avail myself, at any rate at the present stage of the war ... to organize volunteer divisions." Though adding, "It would be very agreeable to me to pay Mr. Roosevelt this compliment and the Allies the compliment of sending to their aid one of our most distinguished public men," he proceeded to publicly impugn the Colonel's request: "Mr. Roosevelt told me, when I had the pleasure of seeing him a few weeks ago, that he would wish to have associated with him some of the most effective officers of the regular army. He named many of those whom he would desire to have designated for the service, and they were men who cannot possibly be spared from the too small force of officers at our command for the much more pressing and necessary duty of training regular troops to be put into the field in France and Belgium." The following day, in a private, single-sentence communication, Wilson informed Roosevelt, "I very much regret that I cannot comply with [your] request."[10]

Years later, Alice wrote in a memoir of her father's frustrating efforts to enter the war, "The division was the thing he wanted. He wanted that opportunity and it was a very bitter thing when it was refused." His aspirations blunted, the Colonel looked enviously upon the rising generation of combatants, and more specifically, to his several sons. "I don't care a continental whether they fight in Yankee uniforms or British uniforms or in their undershirts," he asserted, "so long as they're fighting. That's the main point—they are fighting." On June 20 Ted and Archie were attached, with the ranks, respectively, of major and second lieutenant, to Pershing's Paris headquarters, Roosevelt having made the request directly to Pershing. Kermit joined the British Army as an honorary captain, his father having implored Prime Minister David Lloyd George for this consideration, and was sent to the Mesopotamian (Iraq) theater as part of a machine gun corps before higher-ups, fearing for the young man's safety, moved him to a transport pool; he later transferred to the U.S. Army. In July Quentin, the youngest of the litter at nineteen and now, having dropped out of Harvard, a first lieutenant in the newly formed 1st Reserve Aero Squadron, shipped out for France. "It's rather up to us," he said about this time, "to practice what Father preaches." The urgency of Father's intent might be noted in a perfectly serious message that the Colonel forwarded some months later to an English friend: "How glad I would be if I could see Ted, Kermit, Archie, Quentin and [son-in-law] Dick all coming permanently home in a bunch, shy, say, three arms and two legs, evenly distributed among them!"[11] Perhaps reflecting upon his charmed rendezvous with danger—a shrapnel-grazed wrist in the Spanish-American War, surviving a would-be assassin's bullet in Milwaukee—he may have thought his boys equally immune.

Despite Wilson's reluctance to employ volunteer units overseas, some sentiment had built up for the Colonel's cause. Edward North Smith, a Watertown, New York, lawyer, wrote his close friend Secretary of State Robert Lansing on the importance of letting Roosevelt have his division. "I assume that if I had been in the President's position," he wrote in June, "I should have followed the advice of the army experts." And yet he thought it important to "see a little real American spirit aroused" of the "spread the eagle . . . [and] brass band" variety. "Don't let the boys go into this thing as a matter of drudgery," he counseled, thinking of Roosevelt's ability to enliven anything he touched, "but let them go into it as a matter of joy and a consciousness of devotion." Showing the note to Wilson, Lansing insisted that it "express[ed] a view which is gaining favor with many."[12]

And that included America's war-torn French allies. In May the *New York Times* had printed soon-to-be prime minister Georges Clemenceau's cable to Wilson backing the Colonel's desire to enter the fight. "There is in France," Clemenceau argued, "one name which sums up the beauty of American intervention. It is the name Roosevelt." Stringing together a slew of pretty words and phrases—"idealist," "prestige," "vital idealism"—he stressed TR's unmistakable magnetism. Perhaps he begged the point a little too much in a less than flattering comparison between the present and past presidents: "It is possible that your own mind, inclosed in its austere legal frontiers, which has been the source of so many noble actions, has failed to be impressed by the vital hold which personalities like Roosevelt have on popular imagination."[13]

Though Clemenceau's cable correctly emphasized the power of morale, it failed to register a more urgent reality: stressed over the war, unable to sleep well, and suffering various fevers and inflammations, TR was breaking down physically. In October, under Edith's orders, Roosevelt spent two weeks as a patient at Jack Cooper's health farm in Stamford, Connecticut. The Colonel, so the *New York Times* observed, "is understood to be a bit overworked and it is said he needs rest and certain physical exercises and treatments to restore him to his former vigor." Predictably, the celebrity patient found the regimen tedious in the extreme. "I have come down here for a fortnight to see if I couldn't get into somewhat better condition," he wrote Archie. "I lead a life of irksome monotony, and the exercises bore until I feel as if I should scream."[14]

Unhappily confined to the American shore, Roosevelt proposed a host of freedom-infringing actions in several *Metropolitan* and *Kansas City Star* war editorials. He demanded (as did many Americans) banning the German language; he believed that teachers should be made to sign loyalty oaths, that police officers should be empowered to break up crowds listening to speakers who questioned the war, and that conscientious objectors—including Quakers and Mennonites—should forfeit the right to vote. In one piece he wrote that "any man in the United States who at this time directly or indirectly expresses approval of or sympathy with Germany in . . . this war, should be arrested and either shot, hung, or imprisoned for life, according to the gravity of the offense." The president received most of this gratuitous acid. Among several *Star* attacks, one in particular—"Wilson . . . is engaged in the betrayal of democracy"—encapsulated his long and generally unedifying skirmish with the president. Noting the country's strict sedition laws, which made it a crime to criticize the government or the war effort (nearly a thousand people were imprisoned, including longtime presidential candidate Eugene Debs), the pro-war *North American Review* observed of Roosevelt, "He is aching to go somewhere, preferably to France, but why not to jail?" Writing to Wilson in late November, Harry Garfield, Williams College president and eldest son of President James Garfield, called Roosevelt "a dangerous leader . . . in the present emergency."[15]

Other well-placed voices agreed. "The United States at war is not a playground for ex-presidents to display their foolish egotism," argued *New York Journal* editor Arthur Brisbane; Missouri senator William Stone said, in a January 1918 speech, "The heart of this man is aflame with ambition, and he runs amuck." Using the same word to different ends, Wilson wrote in a private communication, "I really think the best way to treat Mr. Roosevelt is to take no notice of him. That breaks his heart."[16]

Now nine years out of the White House, Roosevelt remained captive to his diminishing energy and fierce pride; perhaps above all he harbored an enduring anger, aimed formerly at Taft and now at Wilson, but more generally against the unkind concoctions of time, change, and aging that threatened to still a strenuous life.

61

Mortal After All

The Colonel, accused by Senator Stone of confusing ambition for patriotism, suffered a severe health crisis that late winter, the first raw weeks of 1918. A day after having a painful abscess in his rectum lanced, he began, while puttering about his *Metropolitan* offices in Manhattan, to bleed. Going immediately to the Langdon Hotel on Fifth Avenue and Fifty-Sixth Street where he kept rooms, he changed clothes, intending to resume working, but instead passed out. A Midtown physician, called by TR's accompanying secretary, arrived at the suite, and sent the still-bleeding Roosevelt to Roosevelt Hospital (named for a great-uncle who founded the clinic in 1871), where the ailing former president remained for a difficult month, having a fistula removed and several abscesses treated. Official friends (King George V) and enemies (Wilson) along with those who had been both in and out of the Colonel's court (Taft) all sent regards to the big-name patient.[1]

"My old Brazilian trouble, both the fever and the abscesses recurred and I had to go under the knife," Roosevelt briefed Kermit of his condition. He wrote further of the wide concern his illness had aroused and in such a self-exonerating way as to reveal how deeply the horned and hoofed Wilson had gotten under his skin.

> I have taken a somewhat sardonic amusement in the real panic that affected a great many people when for a moment it looked as if I might not pull through. They have been bitterly against me for the last three and a half years and have denounced me beyond measure. But when they thought I might die they suddenly had an awful

feeling that maybe I represented what down at the bottom of their hearts they really believed to be right, and that although they have followed Wilson they knew also, down at the bottom of their hearts, that they did so only because he pandered to the basest side of their natures, and gave them an excuse for following the easy path that led away from effort and hardship and risk.[2]

The journalist Lincoln Steffens, a close observer and sometime dining companion of the Colonel, wrote knowingly in a 1931 memoir, "I think he enjoyed his hate of Wilson; he expressed it so well; he indulged it so completely."[3]

While convalescing that spring at Oyster Bay, Roosevelt continued to attack the president in the *Kansas City Star*. When not calling upon the administration to "acknowledge its dreadful failures" in prosecuting the war, he accused it of having brought the hard-pressed Entente powers—Britain, France, and Russia—"to the brink of destruction," and thus continued to flog the no-longer-germane unpreparedness theme. Two of the articles were so viscerally critical that his editor refused to run them. Only when the American army began to see combat did he see hope. "Thank Heaven that our sons and brothers are now to stand at Armageddon," he declared, falling back upon a favorite phrasing, offering a Father Theodore benediction to the boys about to face battle.[4]

"I've had my first real fight," Quentin wrote his mother in early July. "I was doubtful before—for I thought I might get cold feet, or something, but you don't. You get so excited that you forget everything except getting the other fellow." Days later, flying a French Nieuport 28, Quentin made his first kill, shooting down a German plane near Château-Thierry, a feat lavishly reported in the press. "Whatever now befalls Quentin," Roosevelt wrote his daughter Ethel, "he has now had his crowded hour, and his day of honor and triumph."[5] Hardly had this moment of family pride peaked when an ill-boding cable arrived from Pershing:

> Regret very much that your son, Lieutenant Quentin Roosevelt, reported as missing. On July 14 [Bastille Day], with a patrol of twelve planes, he left on a mission.... Seven enemy planes were sighted and attacked after which enemy planes returned and our planes broke off combat, returning to their base. Lieutenant Roosevelt did

not return. A member of the squadron reports seeing one of our planes fall out of the combat and into the clouds, and the French report an American plane seen descending.[6]

Pershing's cable appeared in newspapers around the country. And by the seventeenth it was clear that Quentin had been killed in aerial combat over Chamery. Two machine gun bullets fired by Sergeant Karl Thom, an ace who ended the war with twenty-seven victories, pierced his head; he was thrown from his plane on contact. Quentin's remains were buried by the Germans with full battlefield honors and the French government posthumously awarded him the Croix de Guerre with palm.

Lieutenant Edward Buford, an acquaintance of Quentin's and also reported missing on the same mission, later wrote his father of what transpired that black morning over Chamery:

> Four of us were out on an early patrol and we had just crossed the lines looking for Boche [French slang for Germans] observation machines, when we ran into seven Fokker Chasse planes. They had the altitude and the advantage of the sun on us. . . . The fight developed in a general free-for-all. I tried to keep an eye on all of our fellows but we were hopelessly separated and out-numbered nearly two to one. About a half a mile away I saw one of our planes [Quentin's] with three Boche on him, and he seemed to be having a pretty hard time with them.[7]

Medal of Honor recipient Eddie Rickenbacker, the most celebrated American fighter ace of the war with twenty-six kills, commanded the 94th Aero "Hat-in-the-Ring" Squadron for which Quentin flew. In a memoir, he warmly remembered his comrade as "gay, hearty and absolutely square in everything he said or did. . . . We loved him purely for his own natural self." Rickenbacker also reported that Quentin "was reckless to such a degree that his commanding officers had to caution him repeatedly about the senselessness of his lack of caution. His bravery was so notorious that we all knew he would either achieve some great spectacular success or be killed in the attempt." Back at Sagamore Hill, condolences poured in. Replying to one, Roosevelt stoically wrote of his sons, "They sailed from our shores over a year ago; their mother and I knew their temper and quality; and we did not expect to see all of them come back."[8]

Though slowed by ill health and saddened by Quentin's death, Roosevelt returned to the campaign trail that autumn, eager to erase Wilson's influence and perhaps revive his own improbable prospects for a presidential run in 1920. Indeed, Missouri governor Frederick Gardner had written to Wilson in September, encouraging him to seek a third term as "it is almost a certainty that . . . Roosevelt will be the Republican nominee." While canvassing about the country the Colonel put together a collection of his recent press writings for Scribners; the pieces merely repeated, with diminishing returns, his flagrant anger at Wilson. The book's title, *The Great Adventure*, gave a lively sheen to a somber text crammed with recriminations; and its dedication—"To all who in this war have paid with their bodies for their souls' desire"—somewhat peremptorily suggested that the conflict's young casualties were at one with the old Colonel's sentiments. In truth, he struggled to reconcile his stinging grief. "There is no use of my writing about Quentin," he told the novelist Edith Wharton, a longtime acquaintance, "for I should break down if I tried. His death is heartbreaking."[9]

On November 5, 1918, just six days before Germany and the Allied powers signed an armistice in a train carriage outside of Compiègne ending the war (nearly three thousand soldiers dying on the conflict's final day), Roosevelt voted at Oyster Bay, his ballot part of a nationwide turning away from the Democratic Party, which lost both houses of Congress. Writing to his long-standing epistolary friend Rudyard Kipling, the Colonel seemed to think that he had once more come to occupy the center of America's political universe: "I took a certain sardonic amusement in the fact that whereas four years ago, to put it mildly, my attitude was not popular, I was now the one man whom they insisted upon following and whose statements were taken as the platform." As if about to descend upon Europe and himself lead the impending peace negotiations, he further observed to Kipling, "In France . . . there is at least one public servant, Clemenceau, to whom I am much more closely knit than before the war, and with whom I can work in the heartiest accord."[10]

But he knew his health was now fast failing. Suffering throughout November—doctors variously diagnosed gout, rheumatism, lumbago, and other maladies—he spent much of the month stationary either in bed or sitting. Undaunted, he determined to undermine Wilson's Fourteen Points proposal for a postwar settlement—creation of a League of Nations, armament reduction, freedom of the seas, and so on. On December 10, three days before the president arrived aboard the USS *George Washington* in the French port city of Brest, Roosevelt, confined to a hospital bed, wrote a personal letter to British foreign secretary Arthur Balfour:

> The people voted a want of confidence, by returning to each House of Congress a majority of the Republican Party of which I am one of the leaders. That party stands for the unconditional surrender of Germany and for absolute loyalty to France and England in the peace negotiations. We do not believe in what we understand to be Mr. Wilson's interpretation of "the Freedom of the Seas."[11]

Roosevelt had every right, of course, to question Wilson's peace program, though his manner and method showed dubious if not duplicitous judgment. He wrote a little hysterically in the *Kansas City Star* that the proposal to reduce armaments "means that we are to scrap our army and navy," and he baitingly noted that the support of socialists, pacificists, and "hyphenated Americans" for the Fourteen Points (also endorsed at this time by most Democrats and a smaller number of Republicans) merely underlined its errancy.[12] Unsatisfied with a merely national audience, Roosevelt forwarded his thoughts to Prime Minister Lloyd George and France's Clemenceau.

It seemed clear as the year came to an end that TR planned a prolonged attack on Wilson's peace program. He identified its impractical open covenants clause—"diplomacy shall proceed always frankly and in the public view"—as indicative of an unserious approach to world affairs. "Let us dictate peace by the hammering of guns," he wrote Lodge, "and not chat about peace to the accompaniment of the clicking of typewriters."[13]

In choosing the men to make up his peace commission at Versailles, a defensive Wilson, stung by the November elections, decided to head the U.S. legation himself, thus breaking precedent by becoming both the first president to visit Europe while in office and the first to personally negotiate a major treaty. When Louisiana senator Joseph Ransdell suggested he make Roosevelt part of the commission, the president flatly refused, unwilling at this point to even use the name of his nemesis:

"I am afraid I cannot venture to act upon the advice of your letter... because it has been my unfortunate experience that the man you mention seeks to take charge of anything he has a part in, and to take charge in a way thoroughly disloyal to his associates."[14]

While Wilson met with a hero's reception in France, Roosevelt, his health worsening, his pain increasing, continued to bang out angry *Star* editorials. On January 3, 1919, he drafted a fresh attack on the League of Nations; it proved to be his last piece. Two days later, at Sagamore Hill, the Colonel, in great discomfort that showed in the exhaustion of his drawn face, dictated a few letters to Edith; friends stopped by, but were turned away. That evening, in need of assistance, he said to his longtime valet and bodyguard James Amos, "Don't you think I might go to bed now?" Just after midnight Edith withdrew to her own room, Theodore's nurse having already retired. The house grew quiet and Roosevelt's apartment dimly glowed from the light of an old lamp. Amos remained with him, sitting feet from the bed. About four in the morning the Colonel's breathing became irregular; it appeared to stop, but resumed, only and finally to cease. The nurse, alerted by Amos, summoned Edith, who, leaning over her husband, called out, "Theodore darling!" only to be met by an enveloping silence. "T. stopped breathing," she wrote in a diary. "Had had sweet, sound sleep."[15]

Roosevelt died of an embolism, a blocked artery of the lung. Hours after his passing, Archie, at Sagamore Hill recuperating from a war wound, cabled his brothers, both now in Germany, "The old Lion is dead."[16]

Lion casting a long shadow: Roosevelt and his four sons.

Coda: Patrimonies

> To feel that one has inspired a boy to conduct that has resulted in his death, has a pretty serious side for a father—and at the same time I would not have cared for my boys and they would not have cared for me if our relations had not been just along that line.
> Theodore Roosevelt, 1918

Roosevelt cherished both his family and his country, though neither quite fulfilled his exacting expectations. When a ten-year-old Theodore Jr. exhibited symptoms of stress, Dr. Alexander Lambert, a professor at Cornell Medical College, diagnosed the boy as straining under the gaze of a famous father. Roosevelt confessed, "It has been a great temptation to push him . . . to be all the things I would like to have been and wasn't," though he promised Lambert, "Hereafter, I shall never press Ted in either body or mind." But press he did. While attending the private Groton School, Ted, for health reasons, was warned off football, only to have his insistent father step in. "I have come to the conclusion that the danger of damage to Ted physically if he plays," he wrote the academy's rector, "is probably not so great as the danger to him morally if I forbade him to play." And should an injury occur, he continued, "I shall take all the responsibility of his being hurt."[1]

Ted's difficulties having a celebrity father continued at Harvard. The press periodically followed him about campus, exasperating Roosevelt. "I am inclined to tell him," TR complained to Harvard president Charles Eliot, "if he sees any men taking a photograph of him, to run up and smash the camera"—before asking Eliot, "I do not suppose you could interfere?" And when Ted ran into academic difficulties, the Colonel ran interference on his own, writing an assistant dean defending his son, but more generally reliving his own collegiate days. The note isn't long but contains twenty iterations of "I" with a liberal sprinkling of "me" and "my." Among them: "I went in for boxing and wrestling in the light-weight class"; "I got into the Porc. in my junior year"; and "I was the last man of the Phi Beta Kappa." Competition came naturally to Roosevelt, and that included a cross-generational rivalry with Ted. "He can outwalk and outrun me with ease, and perhaps could outswim me," he wrote one correspondent of his then-fifteen-year-old son, but added, "I could probably still beat him at boxing and wrestling." Reflecting on her cousin Ted's imposing inheritance, Eleanor Roosevelt believed that "the disadvantages of being a great man's son far outweigh the advantages. . . . He was always accused of imitating his father in speech, walk, and smile. . . . and found wanting."[2]

Though the oldest male and namesake, Ted hardly monopolized his father's attentions or expectations. Writing of his youngest daughter, Ethel, then sixteen, the Colonel noted "a tendency to be too nervous and excitable and to do too much"—words often applied in some variation to his own adolescent self. And Archie, the least academically inclined of the offspring, often posed a challenge. "He wants to enter the navy, and if I can get him an appointment to Annapolis and he is able to pass the entrance examinations, his career will be settled," TR informed a friend. "He is not at all a bright little boy," he observed of the thirteen-year-old. In the same letter, Roosevelt described Kermit as having "more genuine literary taste than any other of the children, being much like Edith in this way." Unfortunately, he continued, "I have been utterly unable to teach him to box" or "to make him care for shooting."[3]

Unsurprisingly, all the boys came to adopt a rather Rooseveltian sense of military duty, a tendency encouraged by their father, who pulled strings during the First World War to see them sent speedily to the front. When it appeared as though Quentin might more quickly get into aerial combat fighting for Canada, the Colonel inquired along such lines; similarly, he managed, as noted, to place Kermit with British forces. "The favor," Roosevelt told one British official at the time, "is that the boy shall have the chance to serve, and if necessary be killed in serving. It is the kind of favor I have secured for my three other sons." With all the boys in uniform, he told a trusted newspaper editor, "I'd rather none came back than one, able to go, had stayed at home." Quentin, of course, was killed in aerial combat; Ted, whose wife, Eleanor, told TR that her husband "has always worried for fear he would not be worthy of you," was gassed and wounded at Soissons; Archie suffered shrapnel injuries to the arm and knee so severe that he was discharged from the service with full disability. The elder Roosevelt accepted these blows with equanimity, writing to Rudyard Kipling shortly after the armistice, "Archie . . . will be crippled for a year or two and possibly permanently, but it won't interfere with his work. Ted . . . [is] still limping, but able to hold his job." The two accumulated a trunkful of medals including the Distinguished Service Cross, the Silver Star, and the Chevalier Légion d'honneur.[4]

During the Second World War all the living brothers again served. Archie, nearly fifty and having moved about the petroleum industry, secured from Franklin Roosevelt a lieutenant colonel's commission and fought in New Guinea, where he was seriously wounded by an enemy grenade, becoming the only American soldier ever to be medically discharged twice, in two separate wars, for the same injury, a shattered left kneecap. Ted, having trafficked perhaps a little too conspicuously in his father's path, serving as assistant secretary of the navy in the early 1920s and later as governor of Puerto Rico and governor-general of the Philippines, successfully petitioned the army to fight in World War II. Hampered by arthritis and forced to walk with a cane, he participated in both the North African and Italian campaigns before accompanying, in a jeep bearing the byname "Rough Rider," the first band of troops onto Utah Beach during the D-Day assault, the only general on the sand. A month later he died of heart failure at the age of fifty-six.

Kermit too had bobbed about in his father's considerable wake. Unsuccessful in business, he went on hunting and scientific expeditions reminiscent of his earlier travels with the Colonel to Africa and the Amazon. In 1925 he and Ted, sponsored by Chicago's Field Museum of Natural History, collected animal specimens in Asia; four years later they scoured parts of southwestern China looking for the legendary giant panda.[5] Kermit served in the late 1930s as vice president of the New York Zoological Society (today the Wildlife Conservation Society), an organization founded in 1895 by several affluent hunters, including TR. Suffering from depression and alcoholism, he received, with FDR's aid, a commission in 1942 as a major in the U.S. Army and, with his health clearly precarious, he worked as an intelligence officer in Alaska, presumably out of harm's reach. There, in June 1943, he killed himself with a gunshot to the head. Edith, who lived for five more years, was told her favorite child had died of heart disease.

In his later years, Archie, the only one of Roosevelt's four sons to survive the world wars, went on to form the Roosevelt & Cross brokerage house, joined the far-right John Birch Society, and, having had his fill of permissive postwar culture, compiled a trove of his father's less elegant utterances—"A perfectly stupid race can never rise to a very high plane; the negro, for instance, has been kept down as much by lack of intellectual development as by anything else"—in the meant-to-be-vindicatory 1968 book *Theodore Roosevelt on Race, Riots, Reds, Crime*.[6] He died in 1979, the last of Edith's biological children; four months later, in early 1980, his half sister, Alice, born the year the Washington Monument was completed, *Adventures of Huckleberry Finn* was published, and workers laid the cornerstone for the Statue of Liberty, died at the age of ninety-six.

Politically, the Colonel's closest kin is Franklin Delano Roosevelt. In a 1913 communication between the two following the latter's promotion to the Navy Department, TR wrote, "I was very much pleased that you were appointed as Assistant Secretary of the Navy. It is interesting to see that you are in another place [including the New York legislature] which I myself once held."[7] Over the next twenty years this list of overlaps grew to include vice presidential candidacies, the governorship of New York, membership on the Harvard Board of Overseers, and, of course, the presidency of the United States. During the Depression, FDR embraced this association, seeing the earlier progressive movement as a precursor to what his own administration sought to accomplish. "I think you are entirely accurate," he wrote one correspondent, "in comparing the fight in the Republican Party [in 1912] with the general principles and ideals of the New Deal." One of his advisors, future Supreme Court justice Felix Frankfurter, endorsed this view in a 1934 letter to FDR, complaining that the same conservative interests that had moved "against T.R. . . . are now expressing themselves so violently and so sanctimoniously against your policies."[8]

A second successor of sorts might be Donald Trump, who also challenged the country's democratic norms. Both presidents exhibited an enormous, inexhaustible self-regard, and considered themselves tribunes of the people, speaking for non-elites in opposition to evils—Old Guardism and the Deep State—confronting the republic. Their appeals contained a therapeutic strain for many Americans during periods of great economic and demographic change, unpredictable technological innovation, and growing inequality. Bigger than their parties, both developed cult-of-personality personas, as both progressive and MAGA Republicans leaned more toward the man than the partisan system with which their heroes selectively identified. When Taft captured most GOP delegates at the 1912 convention, Roosevelt, believing he represented "the real Republican party," claimed that the nomination had been "stolen" and bolted. Trump threatened an independent candidacy in early 2016, arguing that the "Republican Party establishment" had determined to keep his delegate total below the threshold needed for victory; four years later, when running for a second term, he too refused to concede defeat.[9]

Other overlaps between the two are suggestive. When criticizing legal decisions, each sometimes attacked the nation's courts, calling into question the judiciary's legitimacy; both remained, even in defeat, the dominant figure in the GOP and fed off public adulation, giving speeches laced with personal grievances before loyalists. Both men seemed intent, moreover, to use their personal popularity to challenge, if not overturn, the existing political framework; moderate Republicans considered them grave dangers to constitutional rule. Taft's insistence that Roosevelt was "the greatest menace to our institutions that we have had in a long time" might be paired with Mitt Romney's 2023 caution that Trump exhibited an "authoritarian" strain and was likely, if reelected, to attempt to "impose his will . . . on the judicial system, on the legislative branch and on the entire nation."[10]

Beyond the political arena, it seems fitting that Roosevelt made his name in the war against Spain, as though anticipating the series of U.S. interventions, occupations, and fighting in Asia that began with the Battle of Manila Bay. "Of course we will have trouble in the Philippines," TR wrote a colleague shortly after the islands were taken, "but there are worse things in National life than trouble. We are a very different people now," he added with sudden clarity, "both in our own estimation and in that of others, from what we were a year ago."[11]

Amid this immense change, Roosevelt's power to project the illusion of continuity fashioned his remarkable popularity. Ill at ease with the emerging corporate regime, this patrician, cowboy, and soldier both emblemized and sentimentalized a connection to a preindustrial past.

Though a big-navy enthusiast and father of the Great White Fleet, he salved the country's nostalgia for a fading frontier, even as imperialism's progress gave rise to an American Century. In a different time, he would have fought (with Sparta) in the Peloponnesian War, marched off to the Holy Land with medieval crusaders, or sailed a caravel over the blue Atlantic in search of a new world. Enframed within the contours of a modern democratic republic, he lived instead a political existence, contemptuous of the congressional Old Guard, eager to bring his people to Armageddon, and, finally, to embrace a life, so he once said, rich with "hard and dangerous endeavor."[12]

Acknowledgments

For access to unpublished materials, I'm grateful to Harvard University's Houghton and Widener Libraries, as well as the Library of Congress and the Theodore Roosevelt Center at Dickinson State University. Elizabethtown College provided a sabbatical leave giving this sometime writer time to write, while colleagues at the school's High Library processed various TR-related requests with courtesy and skill. My continued thanks to Chris Calhoun for excellent representation and to the outstanding team at Scribner, particularly my editor, Colin Harrison, and Emily Polson. Once again I find myself in debt to the expert copyediting of Mark LaFlaur and his team.

Notes

Letters: Theodore Roosevelt, *The Letters of Theodore Roosevelt*, vols. 1–8, ed. Elting E. Morison (Cambridge, MA: Harvard University Press, 1951–54).
Autobiography: Theodore Roosevelt, *Theodore Roosevelt: An Autobiography* (New York: Macmillan, 1913).

Introduction: *The Wide Horizon*

1. Nicholas Roosevelt, *Theodore Roosevelt: The Man as I Knew Him* (New York: Dodd, Mead, 1967), 6.
2. *Letters*, 6:1583, 6:1589; Theodore Roosevelt, *The Strenuous Life: Essays and Addresses* (New York: Century, 1902), 1.
3. *Autobiography*, 569; David E. Sanger, "From Trustbusters to Trust Trusters," *New York Times*, December 6, 1998.
4. *A Compilation of the Messages and Papers of the Presidents*, vol. 16 (New York: Bureau of National Literature, 1922), 6923.
5. Rubén Darío, "To Roosevelt," https://poets.org/poem/roosevelt.
6. *Letters*, 6:1491.
7. Nathan Miller, *Theodore Roosevelt: A Life* (New York: William Morrow, 1992), 123; James E. Amos, *Theodore Roosevelt: Hero to His Valet* (New York: John Day, 1927), 100–101.
8. *British Documents on Foreign Affairs: Reports and Papers from the Foreign Office Confidential Print. Series C; North American, 1837–1914*, vol. 12, ed. Kenneth Borne (Frederick, MD: University Publications of America, 1986), 49; H. G. Wells, *Experiment in Autobiography* (New York: Macmillan, 1934), 649; *Letters*, 1:60.
9. David A. Bell, *Men on Horseback: The Power of Charisma in the Age of Revolution* (New York: Farrar, Straus and Giroux, 2020), 5; H. H. Gerth and C. Wright Mills, eds., *From Max Weber: Essays in Sociology* (New York: Oxford University Press, 1946), 52–55.
10. Mrs. Winthrop Chanler [Margaret Terry Chanler], *Roman Spring* (Boston: Little, Brown, 1934), 195; R. W. B. Lewis, *Edith Wharton: A Biography* (New York: Harper & Row, 1975), 329; Stephen Gwynn, ed., *The Letters and Friendships of Sir Cecil Spring Rice*, vol. 1 (Boston: Houghton Mifflin, 1929), 346.
11. Frederick S. Wood, ed., *Roosevelt as We Knew Him: The Personal Recollections of One Hundred and Fifty of His Friends and Associates* (Philadelphia: John C. Winston, 1927), 102; Henry Adams, *The Education of Henry Adams* (Boston: Houghton Mifflin, 1918), 365.
12. *Autobiography*, 120.

13 Roosevelt, *The Strenuous Life*, 20; *Letters*, 5:590, 5:229.
14 Richard Hofstadter, *The American Political Tradition: And the Men Who Made It* (New York: Alfred A. Knopf, 1948), 206.
15 Mark De Wolfe Howe, ed., *Holmes-Pollock Letters: The Correspondence of Mr. Justice Holmes and Sir Frederick Pollock, 1874–1932*, vol. 2 (Cambridge, MA: Harvard University Press, 1941), 64.
16 *Letters*, 8:826, 6:1329.

1: North and South

1 *Chicago Tribune*, June 19, 1858; Abraham Lincoln, *Selected Speeches and Writings* (New York: Library of America, 1992), 131.
2 Carleton Putnam, *Theodore Roosevelt: The Formative Years, 1858–1886* (New York: Charles Scribner's Sons, 1958), 4; F. Scott Fitzgerald, *The Great Gatsby* (New York: Charles Scribner's Sons, 1925), 217.
3 Edmund Morris, *The Rise of Theodore Roosevelt* (New York: Modern Library, 2001), 4–7; Kathleen Dalton, *Theodore Roosevelt: A Strenuous Life* (New York: Alfred A. Knopf, 2002), 16.
4 Morris, *Rise of Theodore Roosevelt*, 5; Corinne Roosevelt Robinson, *My Brother Theodore Roosevelt* (New York: Charles Scribner's Sons, 1921), 3–7.
5 A. H. Millar, "The Scottish Ancestors of President Roosevelt," *Scottish Historical Review* (July 1904), 416–20; Putnam, *Theodore Roosevelt*, 8; Savannah Unit, Federal Writers' Project, Works Progress Administration of Georgia, "Mulberry Grove in Colonial Times," *Georgia Historical Quarterly* (September 1939), 247.
6 H. Niles, ed., *Principles and Acts of the American Revolution* (Baltimore: William Ogden Niles, 1822), 160.
7 Putnam, *Theodore Roosevelt*, 1.
8 Robinson, *My Brother Theodore Roosevelt*, 10, 12. For a sketch on slavery at Bulloch Hall see: https://web.archive.org/web/20080604073107/http://www.bulloch hall.org/permanentexhibits.asp.
9 Betty Boyd Caroli, *The Roosevelt Women* (New York: Basic Books, 1998), 30; David McCullough, *Mornings on Horseback* (New York: Simon & Schuster, 1981), 45; Blanche Wiesen Cook, *Eleanor Roosevelt*, vol. 1 (New York: Viking, 1992), 28; Joseph Bucklin Bishop, ed., *Theodore Roosevelt's Letters to His Children* (New York: Charles Scribner's Sons, 1919), 67.
10 Robinson, *My Brother Theodore Roosevelt*, 18; Putnam, *Theodore Roosevelt*, 3.
11 Robinson, *My Brother Theodore Roosevelt*, 13, 15.
12 Putnam, *Theodore Roosevelt*, 2.
13 Ibid., 15, 16.
14 Ibid., 16.
15 Ibid., 17.
16 Ibid., 18.
17 Morris, *Rise of Theodore Roosevelt*, 3; Dalton, *Theodore Roosevelt*, 23.

2: Casualties of War

1 McCullough, *Mornings on Horseback*, 57. Following Thee's death, a good friend, the businessman and philanthropist William E. Dodge Jr., glancingly wrote, "From

peculiar circumstances he was unable to volunteer for military service, as was his wish." *Theodore Roosevelt Senior: A Tribute: The Proceedings at a Meeting of the Union League Club New York City, February 14, 1878* (New York: Request, 1902), 16.
2 McCullough, *Mornings on Horseback*, 57; Putnam, *Theodore Roosevelt*, 47, 31.
3 *Theodore Roosevelt Senior*, 18; Morris, *Rise of Theodore Roosevelt*, 10.
4 Robinson, *My Brother Theodore Roosevelt*, 25; *Letters*, 4:1132; *Letters*, 3:343–44; Dalton, *Theodore Roosevelt*, 207.
5 Robinson, *My Brother Theodore Roosevelt*, 8; John Taliaferro, *All the Great Prizes: The Life of John Hay, from Lincoln to Roosevelt* (New York: Simon & Schuster, 2013), 258–59; *Letters*, 4:1133. The contrast between Hay's discreetness and Roosevelt's exuberance is evident in the reflections of the French ambassador J. J. Jusserand, who joined the men in Hay's well-appointed Lafayette Square home one evening: "Mr. Hay showed us after dinner some of the rarities of his library—the first volume published by Tennyson, the poet's own copy, with corrections in his hand; the autograph manuscript of Lincoln's Gettysburg address, and some proofs revised by him. . . . As the conversation passed to other subjects, President Roosevelt, still holding one of the precious printed sheets, shook it unconsciously but strenuously, to the unexpressed dismay of the owner, much too polite to show his feelings." J. J. Jusserand, *What Me Befell: The Reminiscences of J. J. Jusserand* (Boston: Houghton Mifflin, 1933), 240.
6 Robinson, *My Brother Theodore Roosevelt*, 18; Miller, *Theodore Roosevelt*, 35; Karl Schriftgiesser, *The Amazing Roosevelt Family, 1613–1942* (New York: Wilfred Funk, 1942), 175.
7 Putnam, *Theodore Roosevelt*, 52–53; Alice Roosevelt Longworth, *Crowded Hours: Reminiscences* (New York: Charles Scribner's Sons, 1933), 20. Corinne later acknowledged that Mittie's "mental suffering during the war must have been great." Robinson, *My Brother Theodore Roosevelt*, 21.
8 Dalton, *Theodore Roosevelt*, 22.

3: *The Invalid*

1 Putnam, *Theodore Roosevelt*, 24.
2 Ibid., 25; Morris, *Rise of Theodore Roosevelt*, 11; *The Autobiography of Lincoln Steffens*, vol. 1 (New York: Harcourt, Brace & World, 1931), 349–50.
3 Robinson, *My Brother Theodore Roosevelt*, 36; Dalton, *Theodore Roosevelt*, 35; Putnam, *Theodore Roosevelt*, 25.
4 J. C. Levenson et al., *The Letters of Henry Adams*, vol. 6 (Cambridge, MA: Belknap Press of Harvard University Press, 1988), 519; Lilian Rixey, *Bamie: Theodore Roosevelt's Remarkable Sister* (New York: David McKay, 1963), 4; McCullough, *Mornings on Horseback*, 34.
5 Wood, ed., *Roosevelt as We Knew Him*, 6; Robinson, *My Brother Theodore Roosevelt*, 1; Putnam, *Theodore Roosevelt*, 26; *Autobiography*, 17.
6 Robinson, *My Brother Theodore Roosevelt*, 94, 2.
7 *Autobiography*, 8; Wood, ed., *Roosevelt as We Knew Him*, 340; Morris, *Rise of Theodore Roosevelt*, 63.
8 Robinson, *My Brother Theodore Roosevelt*, 6, 3–4.

4: Traveling Cure

1. Rixey, *Bamie*, 6.
2. Dalton, *Theodore Roosevelt*, 23.
3. *Theodore Roosevelt's Diaries of Boyhood and Youth* (New York: Charles Scribner's Sons, 1928), 13.
4. Putnam, *Theodore Roosevelt*, 61, 62. Used to the Hudson, Teedie thought the Thames "a verry, verry small river or a large creek." *Theodore Roosevelt's Diaries*, 30.
5. Morris, *Rise of Theodore Roosevelt*, 25; *Theodore Roosevelt's Diaries*, 83; Putnam, *Theodore Roosevelt*, 65.
6. Morris, *Rise of Theodore Roosevelt*, 27.
7. *Theodore Roosevelt's Diaries*, 152, 134, 195, 160.
8. Robinson, *My Brother Theodore Roosevelt*, 46–47.
9. *Theodore Roosevelt's Diaries*, 173.
10. *Autobiography*, 17.

5: Father of the Man

1. *Autobiography*, 52. This quote comes from the 1922 edition.
2. Jefferson's concern regarding workers in factories comes from his 1785 book *Notes on the State of Virginia*.
3. Henry James, *The Bostonians* (New York: Macmillan, 1886), 333.
4. *Autobiography*, 17, 14; Putnam, *Theodore Roosevelt*, 30.
5. *Autobiography*, 22; Paul Russell Cutright, *Theodore Roosevelt: The Making of a Conservationist* (Urbana: University of Illinois Press, 1985), 31; Theodore Roosevelt, "My Life as a Naturalist," *American Museum Journal* (May 1918), 322–23.
6. *Autobiography*, 22.
7. Thomas G. Dyer, *Theodore Roosevelt and the Idea of Race* (Baton Rouge: Louisiana State University Press, 1980), 2.
8. A. D. Rockwell, *Rambling Recollections: An Autobiography* (New York: Paul B. Hoeber, 1920), 261; *New York Times*, April 13, 1933; Miller, *Theodore Roosevelt*, 45–46; Robinson, *My Brother Theodore Roosevelt*, 50.
9. *Autobiography*, 32.
10. Dalton, *Theodore Roosevelt*, 50; Robinson, *My Brother Theodore Roosevelt*, 50.

6: The Jackals of Damascus

1. *Theodore Roosevelt's Diaries*, 276, 277.
2. *Letters*, 1:6; *Theodore Roosevelt's Diaries*, 40.
3. Rixey, *Bamie*, 20; *Letters*, 1:7. A not uncommon Roosevelt diary entry for Christmas Eve reads in part: "My time today was fully occupied with skinning birds." *Theodore Roosevelt's Diaries*, 296.
4. Julian Hawthorne, *Hawthorne and His Circle* (New York: Harper & Brothers, 1903), 65; Robinson, *My Brother Theodore Roosevelt*, 63.
5. Edith E. W. Gregg, ed., *The Letters of Ellen Tucker Emerson*, vol. 2 (Kent, OH: Kent State University Press, 1982), 57.
6. *Theodore Roosevelt's Diaries*, 312.
7. J. R. LeMaster and James Wilson, eds., "The Awful German Language," in *The Mark

Twain Encyclopedia (New York: Garland, 1993), 57–58; Putnam, *Theodore Roosevelt*, 104, 105; *Letters*, 1:9.
8 Putnam, *Theodore Roosevelt*, 108, 110, 111.
9 *Autobiography*, 23, 17.
10 *New York Times*, October 30, 2005; Morris, *Rise of Theodore Roosevelt*, 48.
11 Edward Young, *Special Report on Immigration: Accompanying Information for Immigrants* (Washington: Government Printing Office, 1871), 209.
12 Mabel Potter Daggett, "Mrs. Roosevelt, the Woman in the Background," *The Delineator* (March 1909), 393.

7: College Brahmin

1 *Autobiography*, 17.
2 Cutright, *Theodore Roosevelt*, 104; Putnam, *Theodore Roosevelt*, 134; Henry Pringle, *Theodore Roosevelt: A Biography* (New York: Harcourt Brace Jovanovich, 1956), 27; *Letters*, 1:22, 1:25.
3 Miller, *Theodore Roosevelt*, 64; Putnam, *Theodore Roosevelt*, 129; Dalton, *Theodore Roosevelt*, 61; *Annual Reports of the President and Treasurer of Harvard College, 1876–77* (Cambridge, MA: Press of John Wilson & Son, 1878), 4, 8, 11, 12, 25, 27.
4 Adams, *Education of Henry Adams*, 44; Horace E. Scudder, "Harvard University," *Scribner's Monthly* (New York: Scribner, 1876), 355.
5 Rixey, *Bamie*, 26; *Letters*, 1:20; McCullough, *Mornings on Horseback*, 170.
6 *Letters*, 1:24.
7 Ibid.
8 Ibid.
9 Ibid., 2:1443–44.
10 Putnam, *Theodore Roosevelt*, 140; Philip M. Boffey, "Theodore Roosevelt at Harvard," *Harvard Crimson*, December 12, 1957, can be found at https://www.thecrimson.com/article/1957/12/12/theodore-roosevelt-at-harvard-pthe-crimson/; Dalton, *Theodore Roosevelt*, 63; *Letters from Theodore Roosevelt to Anna Roosevelt Cowles, 1870–1918* (New York: Charles Scribner's Sons, 1924), 13.
11 *Letters*, 1:42; Putnam, *Theodore Roosevelt*, 139. Italics added.
12 *Letters*, 1:25; Cutright, *Theodore Roosevelt*, 99.

8: These Terrible Three Days

1 *Letters*, 1:18.
2 *Autobiography*, 10.
3 *Letters*, 1:31; Putnam, *Theodore Roosevelt*, 148n82, 147.
4 *Theodore Roosevelt's Diaries*, 365; Dalton, *Theodore Roosevelt*, 68; Edward P. Kohn, ed., *A Most Glorious Ride: The Diaries of Theodore Roosevelt, 1877–1886* (Albany: State University of New York Press, 2015), 19.
5 Kohn, ed., *A Most Glorious Ride*, 19, 21.
6 *The Harvard University Catalogue, 1877–78* (Cambridge, MA: Press of John Wilson & Son, 1877), 7; Kohn, ed., *A Most Glorious Ride*, 21, 22, 45; *Letters*, 3:162.
7 *Letters*, 1:25; Kohn, ed., *A Most Glorious Ride*, 47.
8 "The Porcellian Club," *Harvard Crimson*, February 23, 1887; Philip M. Boffey, "Franklin Delano Roosevelt at Harvard," *Harvard Crimson*, December 12, 1957.

According to Corinne's grandson, the journalist Joseph Alsop, FDR had once remarked to a friend "that his worst disappointment as a young man was his non-election to the club his father and Theodore Roosevelt had belonged to at Harvard." Joseph Alsop, *FDR: A Centenary Remembrance* (New York: Viking Press, 1982), 36–37.

9   *Letters*, 1:35; McCullough, *Mornings on Horseback*, 215; Cutright, *Theodore Roosevelt*, 108.
10 *Letters*, 5:694–95.
11 *Theodore Roosevelt's Diaries*, 280.
12 *The Summer Birds of the Adirondacks in Franklin County, N.Y.*, Sagamore Hill National Historic Site, https://www.theodorerooseveltcenter.org/Research/Digital-Library/Record?libID=o284478; *Letters*, 5:694. Roosevelt's distrust of mere book learning is evident in a 1908 note to William Howard Taft on the United States Military Academy's curriculum: "It seems to me a very great misfortune to lay so much stress upon mathematics . . . at West Point and fail to have languages taught in accordance with the best modern conversational methods. . . . A man who learns a language by studying a book but cannot speak it, loses at least half the benefit obtainable." *Letters*, 6:903.
13 Nathaniel Shaler, "The Negro Problem," *Atlantic Monthly* (November 1884), 698, 703, 706; Dyer, *Theodore Roosevelt and the Idea of Race*, 108.
14 *Letters*, 5:694, 5:694n2.
15 *Letters*, 3:72.

9: Alice Lee

1   Sylvia Jukes Morris, *Edith Kermit Roosevelt: Portrait of a First Lady* (New York: Coward, McCann & Geoghegan, 1980), 49; *Theodore Roosevelt's Diaries*, 103; Lewis L. Gould, *Edith Kermit Roosevelt: Creating the Modern First Lady* (Lawrence: University Press of Kansas, 2013), 6. Roosevelt's eldest daughter, Alice, once observed of Edith, her stepmother, "She let it be known that my father had proposed to her before he met my mother." Michael Teague, *Mrs. L: Conversations with Alice Roosevelt Longworth* (Garden City, NY: Doubleday, 1981), 30.
2   *Letters*, 1:16; Edward F. O'Keefe, *The Loves of Theodore Roosevelt: The Women Who Created a President* (New York: Simon & Schuster, 2024), 73; Morris, *Rise of Theodore Roosevelt*, 78; Putnam, *Theodore Roosevelt*, 166; Teague, *Mrs. L*, 79.
3   Putnam, *Theodore Roosevelt*, 167, 168; Morris, *Rise of Theodore Roosevelt*, 80.
4   *Letters*, 1:36; Kohn, ed., *A Most Glorious Ride*, 62.
5   Kohn, ed., *A Most Glorious Ride*, 98; *Letters*, 1:43, 1:48. Alice perhaps grew tired of her husband's harping on the lion episode. Shortly after entertaining friends in their Manhattan home, he wrote her that one had "said . . . he had never seen any one look so pretty as you did when you were asking me not to tell the 'shaved lion' story." *Letters*, 1:64.
6   *Letters*, 1:37, 1:36.
7   Ibid., 1:25; Robinson, *My Brother Theodore Roosevelt*, 111.
8   Kohn, ed., *A Most Glorious Ride*, 118, 127.
9   Putnam, *Theodore Roosevelt*, 190; Morris, *Rise of Theodore Roosevelt*, 104.
10 *Letters*, 1:25; Cutright, *Theodore Roosevelt*, 130.
11 *Letters*, 1:45, 1:46.

12. Ibid., 1:46.
13. Cook, *Eleanor Roosevelt*, 33, 35; *Letters*, 1:46.
14. Kohn, ed., *A Most Glorious Ride*, 162.
15. *Autobiography*, 61.

10: *The Scholar in Politics*

1. Putnam, *Theodore Roosevelt*, 229; *Letters*, 1:48–49.
2. *Letters*, 1:49–50. The year before Roosevelt tackled the Matterhorn, Mark Twain had written up the Whymper expedition's deadly reckoning with the mountain—"one of the most memorable of all the Alpine catastrophes"—in his popular travel book *A Tramp Abroad* (Hartford, CT: American Publishing, 1880), 345.
3. William Roscoe Thayer, *Theodore Roosevelt: An Intimate Biography* (New York: Grosset & Dunlap, 1919), 21.
4. *Autobiography*, 63; *Letters*, 1:55. In an 1813 letter to Adams, Jefferson wrote, "I agree with you that there is a natural aristocracy among men. The grounds of this are virtue and talents.... There is also an artificial aristocracy founded on wealth and birth, without either virtue or talents.... May we not even say that that form of government is the best which provides the most effectually for a pure selection of these natural aristoi into the offices of government?" Lester J. Cappon, ed., *The Adams-Jefferson Letters: The Complete Correspondence Between Thomas Jefferson & Abigail & John Adams* (Chapel Hill: University of North Carolina Press, 1959), 388.
5. *Autobiography*, 63.
6. Ibid.
7. McCullough, *Mornings on Horseback*, 256; *New York Times*, November 20, 1879; *Autobiography*, 68. Blackwell's Island is now Roosevelt Island, named for Franklin.
8. Morris, *Rise of Theodore Roosevelt*, 121.
9. Theodore Roosevelt, *The Naval War of 1812: Or the History of the United States Navy During the Last War with Great Britain* (New York: G. P. Putnam's Sons, 1882), 135–36.
10. Ibid., 26. For an overview of the racial climate in America at this time, see Daniel Okrent's *The Guarded Gate: Bigotry, Eugenics, and the Law That Kept Two Generations of Jews, Italians, and Other European Immigrants Out of America* (New York: Scribner, 2019).
11. Roosevelt, *Naval War of 1812*, 55.
12. Ibid., 184–85.
13. The "criminal folly" claim appeared in the preface to the book's third edition.
14. Theodore Roosevelt, *The Naval War of 1812: Or the History of the United States Navy During the Last War with Great Britain*, 5th ed. (New York: G. P. Putnam's Sons, 1884), 455; Dumas Malone, *Jefferson the President: Second Term, 1805–1809* (Boston: Little, Brown, 1974), xix.
15. Miller, *Theodore Roosevelt*, 129.

11: *Enter the Dude*

1. McCullough, *Mornings on Horseback*, 256.
2. Carl Johnson, "The Delavan House," November 9, 2015, at *Hoxsie! The History of Albany, Schenectady, and Troy*, https://hoxsie.org/2015/11/09/the-delavan-house/.

3   Schriftgiesser, *The Amazing Roosevelt Family*, 217.
4   John Walsh, *Kansas City Star*, February 12, 1922, quoted in Morris, *Rise of Theodore Roosevelt*, 144.
5   Morris, *Rise of Theodore Roosevelt*, 153, 177, 175.
6   George Parker, *Recollections of Grover Cleveland* (New York: Century, 1909), 250.
7   Florence Peterson, *Strikes in the United States, 1880–1936* (Washington, DC: Government Printing Office, 1938), 29; *New York Star*, April 19, 1883.
8   Kohn, ed., *A Most Glorious Ride*, 221.
9   Hughes quoted in Putnam, *Theodore Roosevelt*, 275.

12: *The Vanishing West*

1   Ibid., 307–8.
2   Chester L. Brooks and Ray H. Mattison, *Theodore Roosevelt and the Dakota Badlands* (Washington, DC: National Park Service, 1958), 11, 13–14.
3   *Letters*, 1:62.
4   Carol Felsenthal, *Alice Roosevelt Longworth* (New York: G. P. Putnam's Sons, 1988), 28.
5   Lincoln A. Lang, *Ranching with Roosevelt* (Philadelphia: J. B. Lippincott, 1926), 102.
6   Theodore Roosevelt, *Hunting Trips of a Ranchman: Sketches of Sport on the Northern Cattle Plains* (New York: G. P. Putnam's Sons, 1885), 14, 12; *Letters*, 6:1081.
7   Roosevelt, *Hunting Trips of a Ranchman*, 18.
8   Ibid., 18–19.
9   Ibid., 160–61.
10 Ibid., 262–63.
11 Ibid., 268, 269.
12 Lang, *Ranching with Roosevelt*, 116; Putnam, *Theodore Roosevelt*, 337; *Autobiography*, 103.
13 *Letters*, 1:63.

13: *A Curse on This House*

1   Ibid., 1:65, 1:64.
2   Felsenthal, *Alice Roosevelt Longworth*, 29; *Letters*, 1:65.
3   Morris, *Rise of Theodore Roosevelt*, 229; Rixey, *Bamie*, 20; Kohn, ed., *A Most Glorious Ride*, 228.
4   *Letters*, 1:66.
5   Dalton, *Theodore Roosevelt*, 90; Teague, *Mrs. L*, 4, 3.
6   Kohn, ed., *A Most Glorious Ride*, 229.
7   *Letters*, 1:66–67.

14: *Picking Up the Pieces*

1   Morris, *Rise of Theodore Roosevelt*, 245, 818n35; John A. Garraty, *Henry Cabot Lodge: A Biography* (New York: Alfred A. Knopf, 1953), 76.
2   *Saturday Evening Post*, May 7, 1910, 16; Adams, *Education of Henry Adams*, 368, 367. For an insightful study of the Roosevelt-Lodge link, see Laurence Jurdem's *The Rough Rider and the Professor: Theodore Roosevelt, Henry Cabot Lodge, and the Friendship That Changed American History* (New York: Pegasus Books, 2023).

3 *Letters*, 1:72.
4 Putnam, *Theodore Roosevelt*, 430. A regular Republican at the convention described Roosevelt as "a rather dudish-looking boy with eyeglasses," while another complained, "He may have ability, but he also has an inexhaustible supply of insufferable dudism and conceit." Joseph Benson Foraker, *Notes of a Busy Life*, vol. 1 (Cincinnati: Stewart & Kidd, 1916), 168.
5 See the "Souvenir Programme: National Republican Convention" at https://www.lib.uchicago.edu/e/scrc/findingaids/view.php?eadid=ICU.SPCL.REPUBLICAN1888.
6 *Letters*, 1:68.
7 Garraty, *Henry Cabot Lodge*, 77; *Letters*, 1:70; *New York World*, June 7, 1884.
8 Putnam, *Theodore Roosevelt*, 465; Morris, *Rise of Theodore Roosevelt*, 259.
9 Owen Wister, *Roosevelt: The Story of a Friendship, 1880–1919* (New York: Macmillan, 1930), 26.
10 *Letters*, 1:75–76, 1:80, 1:122.
11 *Autobiography*, 96.

15: Cowboy Blues

1 Roosevelt, *Hunting Trips of a Ranchman*, 197.
2 Ibid.
3 William Wingate Sewall, *Bill Sewall's Story of T. R.* (New York: Harper & Brothers, 1919), 47; *Letters*, 1:74.
4 *Letters*, 1:73.
5 Lang, *Ranching with Roosevelt*, 167; *Autobiography*, 106–7.
6 *Letters*, 1:81–82.
7 Roosevelt, *Hunting Trips of a Ranchman*, 19.
8 *Boston Daily Advertiser*, October 21, 1884; *Letters*, 1:88.
9 Roosevelt, *Hunting Trips of a Ranchman*, 52, 68.
10 *New York Times*, July 13, 1885, and *The Spectator*, July 16, 1885, both cited in Putnam, *Theodore Roosevelt*, 519; *Letters*, 1:241.
11 *Letters*, 1:91; Lang, *Ranching with Roosevelt*, 185.
12 Morris, *Rise of Theodore Roosevelt*, 294.
13 Daggett, "Mrs. Roosevelt," 477.

16: Back on Track

1 Catherine Forslund, "Edith Kermit Carow Roosevelt: The Victorian Modern First Lady," in Katherine A. S. Sibley, *A Companion to First Ladies* (New York: Wiley Blackwell, 2016), 299, 305; Nicholas Roosevelt, *Theodore Roosevelt: The Man as I Knew Him*, 20.
2 Forslund, "Edith Kermit Carow Roosevelt," 300.
3 Jukes Morris, *Edith Kermit Roosevelt*, 64, 70.
4 Ibid., 81; Gould, *Edith Kermit Roosevelt*, 9.
5 Theodore Roosevelt, *Ranch Life and the Hunting-Trail* (New York: Century, 1888), 116, 115.
6 Ibid., 120.
7 *Selections from the Correspondence of Theodore Roosevelt and Henry Cabot Lodge,*

1884–1918, vol. 1 (New York: Charles Scribner's Sons, 1925), 41; *Letters from Theodore Roosevelt to Anna Roosevelt Cowles*, 86–87.

8 Morris, *Rise of Theodore Roosevelt*, 336. Roosevelt's "disapprov[al] of second marriages" continued to have a purchase on Victorian sensibilities into the twentieth century and may, in the struggle between Woodrow Wilson and Lodge over the Treaty of Versailles, have contributed to their mutual antipathy. A biographer writes, "Lodge's personal disapproval of Wilson was heightened by the President's marriage to Mrs. Norman Galt in December 1915. Many people were unreasonably shocked by this marriage, which followed the first Mrs. Wilson's death by scarcely sixteen months. Lodge was too well bred to give vent publicly to his own opinion, but he did not conceal it from his friends." Garraty, *Henry Cabot Lodge*, 321.

9 *Letters*, 1:113; *Sun* (New York, NY), October 26, 1886.

10 *Selections from the Correspondence of Theodore Roosevelt and Henry Cabot Lodge*, vol. 1, 50.

11 Daggett, "Mrs. Roosevelt," 476; Rixey, *Bamie*, 66; *New York Herald*, March 28, 1887. When prompted by the St. George's registry to list his occupation, Roosevelt indicated "Rancher."

12 Felsenthal, *Alice Roosevelt Longworth*, 35; Teague, *Mrs. L*, 36.

13 *Letters*, 1:132–33.

17: The Historian

1 Roosevelt, *Hunting Trips of a Ranchman*, 20; Lang, *Ranching with Roosevelt*, 245–46; Putnam, *Theodore Roosevelt*, 595; *Letters*, 1:136.

2 *Letters*, 1:135–36.

3 Ibid., 1:379.

4 Theodore Roosevelt, *Life of Thomas Hart Benton* (Boston: Houghton Mifflin, 1887), 40–41; *The Nation*, March 29, 1888.

5 *Letters*, 1:211.

6 Theodore Roosevelt, *The Winning of the West: An Account of the Exploration and Settlement of Our Country from the Alleghenies to the Pacific*, vol. 1 (New York: G. P. Putnam's Sons, 1889), 2, 57, 156.

7 Ibid., 119. An echo of Roosevelt's argument might be found in David Hackett Fischer's 1989 study *Albion's Seed*, in which Fischer contended that the Scotch Irish in America fashioned "libertarian ideas . . . profoundly different from notions of liberty that had been carried to Massachusetts, Virginia and Pennsylvania. . . . The backcountry idea of natural liberty was created by a complex interaction between the American environment and a European folk culture. It derived in large part from the British border country, where anarchic violence had long been a condition of life. The natural liberty of the borderers was an idea at once more radically libertarian, more strenuously hostile to ordering institutions than were the other cultures of British America." David Hackett Fischer, *Albion's Seed: Four British Folkways in America* (New York: Oxford University Press, 1989), 777.

8 Theodore Roosevelt, *The Winning of the West: An Account of the Exploration and Settlement of Our Country from the Alleghenies to the Pacific*, vol. 2 (New York: G. P. Putnam's Sons, 1889), 168.

9 Roosevelt, *The Winning of the West*, vol. 1, 8; David H. Burton, *Theodore Roosevelt: Confident Imperialist* (Philadelphia: University of Pennsylvania Press, 1968), 19.

10 Roosevelt, *The Winning of the West*, vol. 1, xv–xvi.
11 *New-York Tribune*, June 30, 1889.
12 Despite the time crunch, Roosevelt, with the considerable assistance of Lodge and Bamie as well as archivists and amanuenses, conducted impressive research for *Winning*. These troves included newspapers, unpublished letters, diaries, and manuscripts from repositories in Washington, D.C., Nashville, Louisville, Lexington (KY), Richmond, New York, and elsewhere. Harrison John Thornton, "Theodore Roosevelt," in William T. Hutchinson, ed., *The Marcus W. Jernegan Essays in American Historiography* (New York: Russell & Russell, 1937), 237; *Letters*, 5:496.
13 Roosevelt delivered the address as president of the AHA, which at this time counted among its ranks a number of nonacademics. George Bancroft (1886), the industrialist James Ford Rhodes (1899), and Charles Francis Adams Jr. (1901) of the distinguished Adams clan were gentlemen scholars who had preceded Roosevelt to the AHA presidency. Theodore Roosevelt, "History as Literature," https://www.historians.org/about-aha-and-membership/aha-history-and-archives/presidential-addresses/theodore-roosevelt.
14 *Letters*, 3:707–8.
15 *American Historical Review* (October 1896), 171.
16 Wilbur R. Jacobs, ed., *The Historical World of Frederick Jackson Turner: With Selections from His Correspondence* (New Haven, CT: Yale University Press, 1968), 60–61.
17 *Autobiography*, 132, 106.

18: Washington Entrée

1 *A Compilation of the Messages and Papers of the Presidents*, vol. 3 (New York: Bureau of National Literature, 1897), 1011–12; Richard D. White Jr., *Roosevelt the Reformer: Theodore Roosevelt as Civil Service Commissioner, 1889–1895* (Tuscaloosa: University of Alabama Press, 2003), 4.
2 White, *Roosevelt the Reformer*, 21.
3 *Letters*, 1:84–85.
4 Ibid., 1:146.
5 Ibid., 1:149.
6 Edward P. Crapol, *James G. Blaine: Architect of Empire* (Wilmington, DE: SR Books, 2000), 113; William Henry Harbaugh, *Power and Responsibility: The Life and Times of Theodore Roosevelt* (New York: Farrar, Straus and Cudahy, 1961), 74.
7 White, *Roosevelt the Reformer*, 10.
8 *Selections from the Correspondence of Theodore Roosevelt and Henry Cabot Lodge*, vol. 1, 92, 96.
9 *Letters*, 1:162; 1:163.
10 Ibid., 1:166; *Chicago Morning News*, June 26, 1889.
11 Gwynn, ed., *Letters and Friendships of Sir Cecil Spring Rice*, vol. 1, 101; *Letters*, 1:175.
12 *Letters*, 1:277; 6:1490.
13 White, *Roosevelt the Reformer*, 102–3; *History of Wages in the United States from Colonial Times to 1928* (Washington, DC: Government Printing Office, 1929), 166.
14 Gould, *Edith Kermit Roosevelt*, 80; *Letters*, 2:1451; *Letters*, 5:495; *Letters*, 5:860.

19: Elliott's Story

1. John S. Wise, *Recollections of Thirteen Presidents* (New York: Doubleday, Page, 1906), 241; Richard Zacks, *Island of Vice: Theodore Roosevelt's Doomed Quest to Clean Up Sin-Loving New York* (New York: Doubleday, 2012), 123; Cook, *Eleanor Roosevelt*, 34; Teague, *Mrs. L*, 151. Alice noted of her father's moral code: "Was it George V who is reported to have said about a peer arrested for homosexuality, 'I thought men like that shot themselves'? Well, Father was a bit like that." Teague, *Mrs. L*, 112, 79.
2. Raymond E. Spinzia, "Elliott Roosevelt, Sr.—A Spiral into Darkness," *The Freeholder* (Fall 2007), 2–4; *Letters*, 1:141.
3. Spinzia, "Elliott Roosevelt, Sr.," 5; Morris, *Rise of Theodore Roosevelt*, 439–40; Teague, *Mrs. L*, 112.
4. Morris, *Rise of Theodore Roosevelt*, 447.
5. Ibid., 448.
6. Ibid., 449.
7. Ibid., 452–53.
8. Spinzia, "Elliott Roosevelt, Sr.," 6.
9. Morris, *Rise of Theodore Roosevelt*, 457.
10. H. W. Brands, *T. R.: The Last Romantic* (New York: Basic Books, 1997), 259; *Letters*, 1:397.

20: The Top Cop

1. *Letters*, 1:442, 8:1433.
2. *Selections from the Correspondence of Theodore Roosevelt and Henry Cabot Lodge*, vol. 1, 178.
3. White, *Roosevelt the Reformer*, 152; *New York Times*, November 28, 1909.
4. Theodore Roosevelt, "Municipal Administration: The New York Police Force," *Atlantic Monthly* (September 1897); *Letters*, 1:457. Roosevelt's determination "to move against the scandals" is near to the British novelist Anthony Trollope's idea in *The Prime Minister* (1876) that "new brooms sweep clean; and official new brooms, I think, sweep cleaner than any other." It is the recently appointed functionary, after all, "who intends by fresh Herculean labour to cleanse the Augean stable," and that includes "the gentleman at the Home Office who means to reform the police." Anthony Trollope, *The Prime Minister* (Toronto: Belford Brothers, 1876), 68.
5. *Selections from the Correspondence of Theodore Roosevelt and Henry Cabot Lodge*, vol. 1, 144; *Letters*, 1:456n1.
6. Zacks, *Island of Vice*, 79–80; *Letters*, 1:462; *Letters from Theodore Roosevelt to Anna Roosevelt Cowles*, 158. In a memoir Roosevelt wrote, "The man who was closest to me throughout my two years in the Police Department was Jacob Riis." *Autobiography*, 185.
7. Morris, *Rise of Theodore Roosevelt*, 515–16; *Sun* (New York, NY), June 20, 1895. Roosevelt's personalization of the Sunday saloon shutdown is obvious in this brief statement in the *Sun*, in which he uses the word "I" sixteen times.
8. *New York Times*, July 12, 1895; *Letters*, 1:464, 1:466, 1:480.
9. Zacks, *Island of Vice*, 136–37; *Letters*, 1:473.
10. *Letters*, 1:475; *Selections from the Correspondence of Theodore Roosevelt and Henry Cabot Lodge*, vol. 1, 191.

11 *Letters from Theodore Roosevelt to Anna Roosevelt Cowles*, 162; Morris, *Rise of Theodore Roosevelt*, 532.
12 *Autobiography of Lincoln Steffens*, vol. 1, 258; *New York Times*, July 8, 1896; *New York Journal*, March 18, 1897.

21: *In the Navy*

1 James Grant, *Mr. Speaker!: The Life of and Times of Thomas B. Reed, the Man Who Broke the Filibuster* (New York: Simon & Schuster, 2011), 211.
2 Morris, *Rise of Theodore Roosevelt*, 558; *Letters*, 1:543, 1:474, 1:552.
3 *Official Proceedings of the Eleventh Republican National Convention* (Minneapolis: Charles W. Johnson, 1896), 19, 22; Grant, *Mr. Speaker!*, 341; *Letters from Theodore Roosevelt to Anna Roosevelt Cowles*, 182–83.
4 *Letters*, 1:560; James MacGregor Burns and Susan Dunn, *The Three Roosevelts: Patrician Leaders Who Transformed America* (New York: Atlantic Monthly Press, 2001), 46.
5 *Selections from the Correspondence of Theodore Roosevelt and Henry Cabot Lodge*, vol. 1, 241.
6 *Letters*, 1:567.
7 Miller, *Theodore Roosevelt*, 247; *Letters*, 1:570, 1:572; 1:55.
8 Howard K. Beale, *Theodore Roosevelt and the Rise of America to World Power* (Baltimore: Johns Hopkins Press, 1956), 55.
9 Wendell D. Garrett, "John Davis Long, Secretary of the Navy, 1897–1902: A Study in Changing Political Alignments," *New England Quarterly* (September 1958), 296, 294.
10 *Letters*, 1:604.
11 *Address of Hon. Theodore Roosevelt, Assistant Secretary of the Navy, Before the Naval War College, Newport, RI* (Washington, DC: Government Printing Office, 1897), 3, 4, 24, 5.
12 Ibid., 10, 6, 12.
13 Ibid., 13, 16; Burton, *Theodore Roosevelt*, 44.
14 Miller, *Theodore Roosevelt*, 255; *Letters*, 1:623.

22: *By Jingo*

1 Beale, *Theodore Roosevelt*, 38.
2 *Hawaiian Native Claims Settlement Act, Part I: Hearings Before the Subcommittee on Indian Affairs of the Committee on Interior and Insular Affairs, House of Representatives* (Washington, DC: Government Printing Office, 1975), 35; John Kane, *Between Virtue and Power: The Persistent Moral Dilemma of U.S. Foreign Policy* (New Haven, CT: Yale University Press, 2008), 125.
3 *Letters*, 1:607–8.
4 Kenneth Wimmel, *Theodore Roosevelt and the Great White Fleet: American Sea Power Comes of Age* (Washington, DC: Brassy's, 1998), 48–49; Philip A. Crowl, "Alfred Thayer Mahan: The Naval Historian," in Peter Paret, ed., *Makers of Modern Strategy: From Machiavelli to the Nuclear Age* (Princeton, NJ: Princeton University Press, 1986), 445.
5 A. T. Mahan, *The Influence of Sea Power Upon History, 1660–1783* (Boston: Little, Brown, 1890), 1.

6. Ibid., 31.
7. *Atlantic Monthly* (October 1890), 563, 567.
8. *Letters*, 1:221–22.
9. Brooks Adams, *The Law of Civilization and Decay* (London: Macmillan, 1896), 53, 352.
10. Ibid., 362.
11. Burton, *Theodore Roosevelt*, 96; Arthur F. Beringause, *Brooks Adams: A Biography* (New York: Alfred A. Knopf, 1955), 157.
12. Beringause, *Brooks Adams*, 208–9.
13. *Letters*, 1:557, 1:620.

23: *And the War Came*

1. The Metropolitan Club of the City of Washington, https://www.metroclub.com/About-The-Club.aspx; *Letters*, 1:601.
2. *The Journal of John D. Long*, ed. Margaret Long (Rindge, NH: Richard R. Smith, 1956), 211; *Sun* (New York, NY), August 23, 1897.
3. Jefferson to Monroe, October 24, 1823, at https://founders.archives.gov/documents/Jefferson/98-01-02-3827.
4. George C. Herring, *From Colony to Superpower: U.S. Foreign Relations Since 1776* (New York: Oxford University Press, 2008), 311.
5. *Journal of John D. Long*, 212–13.
6. Ibid., 215; *Letters*, 1:785–86.
7. *Letters*, 1:775.
8. Ibid., 1:651.
9. Jan R. Van Meter, *Tippecanoe and Tyler Too: Famous Slogans and Catchphrases in American History* (Chicago: University of Chicago Press, 2008), 134.
10. *Journal of John D. Long*, 216.
11. Lewis L. Gould, *The Presidency of William McKinley* (Lawrence: University Press of Kansas, 1980), 95.
12. *Letters*, 1:796.
13. Jukes Morris, *Edith Kermit Roosevelt*, 166–70; *Letters*, 1:790, 1:798; Gould, *Edith Kermit Roosevelt*, 18.
14. Clinton Rossiter, ed., *The Federalist Papers* (New York: Penguin Books, 1961), 257; John C. Rayburn, "The Rough Riders in San Antonio, 1898," *Arizona and the West* (Summer 1961), 113.
15. J. C. Levenson et al., eds., *The Letters of Henry Adams*, vol. 4 (Cambridge, MA: Belknap Press of Harvard University Press, 1988), 577; *Journal of John D. Long*, 224.
16. Morris, *Rise of Theodore Roosevelt*, 643.

24: *Rough Rider*

1. Theodore Roosevelt, *The Rough Riders* (New York: Charles Scribner's Sons, 1899), 7; *Letters*, 2:832–33.
2. *Letters*, 2:832; Gary Gerstle, *American Crucible: Race and Nation in the Twentieth Century* (Princeton, NJ: Princeton University Press, 2001), 27–28; Roosevelt, *The Rough Riders*, 60.
3. Bishop, ed., *Theodore Roosevelt's Letters to His Children*, 13.
4. *Letters*, 2:837–38.

5 Ibid., 1:836; Robinson, *My Brother Theodore Roosevelt*, 170–71.
6 Evan Thomas, *The War Lovers: Roosevelt, Lodge, Hearst, and the Rush to Empire, 1898* (New York: Little, Brown, 2010), 292. Little Texas survived the war and was brought to Oyster Bay, where he died in 1904 and was buried in the property's pet cemetery, along with so many Roosevelt animals.
7 *New York Times*, June 25, 1898.
8 *Letters*, 2:844.
9 John J. Pershing, *My Life Before the World War, 1860–1917: A Memoir* (Lexington: University of Kentucky Press, 2013), 112; *Autobiography*, 262.
10 *Autobiography*, 242; Roosevelt, *The Rough Riders*, 130.
11 Pershing, *My Life Before the World War*, 116; Sara Watts, *Rough Rider in the White House: Theodore Roosevelt and the Politics of Desire* (Chicago: University of Chicago Press, 2003), 164; Jukes Morris, *Edith Kermit Roosevelt*, 181; *Letters*, 2:851, 2:1387.
12 Morris, *Rise of Theodore Roosevelt*, 875n89.
13 *Letters*, 2:850; William Roscoe Thayer, *The Life and Letters of John Hay*, vol. 2 (Boston: Houghton Mifflin, 1915), 337; *Selections from the Correspondence of Theodore Roosevelt and Henry Cabot Lodge*, vol. 1, 319.
14 Roosevelt, *The Rough Riders*, 65; F. P. Dunne, "Mr. Dooley: He Reviews a Book," *Harper's Weekly*, November 25, 1899, 1195; *Letters*, 2:1099.
15 Mario R. DiNunzio, *Theodore Roosevelt: An American Mind, Selected Writings* (New York: Penguin Books, 1994), 184; Roosevelt, *The Rough Riders*, 80, 232; Robert Dallek, *An Unfinished Life: John F. Kennedy, 1917–1936* (Boston: Little, Brown, 2003), 373–74.

25: Turns to Gold

1 G. Wallace Chessman, *Governor Theodore Roosevelt: The Albany Apprenticeship, 1898–1900* (Cambridge, MA: Harvard University Press, 1965), 21.
2 Ibid., 22–23.
3 Pringle, *Theodore Roosevelt*, 144; *Letters*, 2:865; *Selections from the Correspondence of Theodore Roosevelt and Henry Cabot Lodge*, vol. 1, 366; Dwight S. Mears, *The Medal of Honor: The Evolution of America's Highest Military Decoration* (Lawrence: University Press of Kansas, 2018), 153.
4 *Letters*, 2:869.
5 Chessman, *Governor Theodore Roosevelt*, 37; *Letters*, 2:876.
6 "John Jay Chapman, Brief Life of a Neglected Critic: 1862–1933," in Mark Antony De Wolfe Howe, ed., *John Jay Chapman and His Letters* (Boston: Houghton Mifflin, 1937), 142; https://www.harvardmagazine.com/2001/01/john-jay-chapman.html.
7 *John Jay Chapman and His Letters*, 140, 143; *Letters*, 2:876–77; Levenson et al., eds., *Letters of Henry Adams*, vol. 4, 619.
8 Miller, *Theodore Roosevelt*, 317.
9 Robinson, *My Brother Theodore Roosevelt*, 228.
10 *Letters*, 2:878n1; Jeff Paine, "Things Elihu Root Did Not Explain About Theodore Roosevelt," https://jeffpaine.blogspot.com/2021/02/things-elihu-root-did-not-explain-about.html; Miller, *Theodore Roosevelt*, 318; Philip C. Jessup, *Elihu Root*, vol. 1 (New York: Dodd, Mead, 1938), 198–99.
11 Chessman, *Governor Theodore Roosevelt*, 62.
12 *Letters*, 2:918, 2:944.

13 Pringle, *Theodore Roosevelt*, 146.
14 *Letters*, 2:1000, 2:1005, 2:1017; Morris, *Rise of Theodore Roosevelt*, 736–37.
15 *Letters*, 2:1249.

26: Kicked Upstairs

1 Ibid., 2:1023.
2 *Selections from the Correspondence of Theodore Roosevelt and Henry Cabot Lodge*, vol. 1, 440–41.
3 *Letters*, 2:1153.
4 Ibid., 2:1166, 2:1256; Levenson et al., eds., *Letters of Henry Adams*, vol. 4, 702.
5 *Selections from the Correspondence of Theodore Roosevelt and Henry Cabot Lodge*, vol. 1, 459; *Letters*, 2:1264, 2:1269, 2:1278.
6 Wood, ed., *Roosevelt as We Knew Him*, 73.
7 Herbert Croly, *Marcus Alonzo Hanna: His Life and Work* (New York: Macmillan, 1912), 138; Joseph Benson Foraker, *Notes of a Busy Life*, vol. 2 (Cincinnati: Stewart & Kidd, 1916), 92.
8 *Letters*, 3:57.
9 Gould, *Presidency of Theodore Roosevelt*, 8.
10 Dalton, *Theodore Roosevelt*, 195, 192; Miller, *Theodore Roosevelt*, 344.
11 Paul Grondahl, *I Rose Like a Rocket: The Political Education of Theodore Roosevelt* (New York: Free Press, 2004), 356.
12 *Letters*, 2:1413; *Letters from Theodore Roosevelt to Anna Roosevelt Cowles*, 249.

27: Keys to the Kingdom

1 *Letters*, 3:31, 3:128–29, 3:127.
2 Ibid., 3:139, 3:142; John W. Tyler, *The Life of McKinley: Soldier, Statesman and President* (Philadelphia: P. W. Ziegler, 1901), 464.
3 *New York Times*, September 7, 1901; Levenson et al., eds., *Letters of Henry Adams*, vol. 5, 291; Jean Strouse, *Morgan: American Financier* (New York: Perennial, 1999), 435.
4 Edmund Morris, *Theodore Rex* (New York: Random House, 2001), 3.
5 Wood, ed., *Roosevelt as We Knew Him*, 91, 89.
6 Croly, *Marcus Alonzo Hanna*, 360–62.
7 Robinson, *My Brother Theodore Roosevelt*, 206.
8 *A Bully Father: Theodore Roosevelt's Letters to His Children*, ed. Joan Peterson Kerr (New York: Random House, 1995), 54; Gould, *Edith Kermit Roosevelt*, 27.
9 *Letters*, 3:150.

28: Shifting American Scene

1 Henry Gannett, "The Average American," *Current Literature* 31 (July–December 1901), 421.
2 Harold U. Faulkner, *The Decline of Laissez Faire, 1897–1917* (New York: Rinehart, 1951), 8, 21, 7.
3 Ida M. Tarbell, *The History of the Standard Oil Company*, vol. 2 (New York: McClure, Phillips, 1904), 288; *Autobiography*, 525; Gabriel Kolko, *The Triumph of Conserva-*

tism: A Reinterpretation of American History, 1900–1916 (New York: Free Press of Glencoe, 1963), 112. Quite likely the only president to reference *Pilgrim's Progress* in a speech, Roosevelt played upon Bunyan's description of "the man who prefers a muck-rake to a celestial crown" to tag the muckrakers as single-minded reformers who lost sight of the wider world. John Bunyan, *The Pilgrim's Progress* (London: J. Haddon, 1847), 167.

4 Robert L. Beisner, *Twelve Against Empire: The Anti-Imperialists, 1898–1900* (New York: McGraw-Hill, 1968), 237; *Selections from the Correspondence of Theodore Roosevelt and Henry Cabot Lodge*, vol. 1, 521.

29: The Dinner

1 *Letters*, 3:149; Booker T. Washington, *My Larger Education: Being Chapters from My Experience* (New York: Doubleday, Page, 1911), 174–75.
2 On Booker T. Washington's presidential overtones, see Ishmael Reed's "Booker vs. the Negro-Saxons," in his introduction to Washington's *Up from Slavery* (New York: Signet Classics, 2000), vii.
3 *Letters*, 5:226; Alfred Henry Lewis, ed., *A Compilation of the Messages and Speeches of Theodore Roosevelt, 1901–1905* (New York: Bureau of National Literature and Art, 1906), 564.
4 Lina Mann, "The Enslaved Household of President Thomas Jefferson," Rubenstein Center Scholarship, November 20, 2019, https://www.whitehousehistory.org/slavery-in-the-thomas-jefferson-white-house#:~:text=Despite%20his%20preference%20for%20white,White%20House%20Chef%20Honor%C3%A9%20Julien; Frederick Douglass, *The Life and Times of Frederick Douglass* (Hartford, CT: Park Publishing, 1882), 422–24.
5 Washington, *My Larger Education*, 176; Ann J. Lane, *The Brownsville Affair: National Crisis and Black Reaction* (Port Washington, NY: Kennikat Press, 1971), 134; George E. Mowry, *The Era of Theodore Roosevelt, 1900–1912* (New York: Harper & Brothers, 1958), 165; Morris, *Theodore Rex*, 55.
6 Benjamin Griffin and Harriet Elinor Smith, eds., *Autobiography of Mark Twain*, vol. 3 (Berkeley: University of California Press, 2015), 257. Remarking, in a different context, on Roosevelt's eagerness to "advertise himself," Twain insisted that the president was "just like Tom Sawyer . . . always showing off." Bernard DeVoto, ed., *Mark Twain in Eruption* (New York: Harper & Brothers, 1940), 49. A seasoned skeptic, Twain was immune to Roosevelt's magic, writing a friend in 1905, "Every time, in 25 years, that I have met Roosevelt the man, a wave of welcome has streaked through me with the hand-grip; but whenever (as a rule) I meet Roosevelt the statesman & politician I find him destitute of morals & not respectworthy." Harold K. Bush et al., eds., *The Letters of Mark Twain and Joseph Hopkins Twichell* (Athens: University of Georgia Press, 2017), 356.
7 *Letters*, 3:112. Later in his presidency, Roosevelt wrote his son Kermit that "Mark Twain, tho a real genius, who has done admirable work in his line, is a man . . . without any real historical knowledge." He did consider *Huckleberry Finn* a classic. *Letters*, 5:590.
8 Washington, *My Larger Education*, 179; Mowry, *Era of Theodore Roosevelt*, 166.
9 *New York Times*, October 19, 1901; *Letters*, 3:181, 3:184, 5:227.

30: *Playing Monopoly*

1. *A Compilation of the Messages and Papers of the Presidents*, vol. 15 (New York: Bureau of National Literature, 1922), 6641, 6644, 6651, 6660, 6661.
2. Ibid., 6645–48.
3. *New York World*, May 11, 1901; Dalton, *Theodore Roosevelt*, 224.
4. Albro Martin, *James J. Hill and the Opening of the Northwest* (New York: Oxford University Press, 1976), 514.
5. Joseph Bucklin Bishop, *Theodore Roosevelt and His Time*, vol. 1 (New York: Charles Scribner's Son's, 1920), 184.
6. Ibid., 185.
7. Strouse, *Morgan*, 436; *Letters*, 2:1450.
8. Mowry, *Era of Theodore Roosevelt*, 131; Morris, *Theodore Rex*, 316.
9. *Selections from the Correspondence of Theodore Roosevelt and Henry Cabot Lodge*, vol. 1, 517.
10. Ibid., 519.
11. *Letters*, 3:437, 5:396.
12. Howe, ed., *Holmes-Pollock Letters*, vol. 2, 63.
13. *Letters*, 4:886.

31: *Bred of Empire*

1. Gould, *Presidency of William McKinley*, 180; Oscar M. Alfonso, *Theodore Roosevelt and the Philippines, 1897–1909* (New York: Oriole Editions, 1974), 71–72.
2. Gould, *Presidency of William McKinley*, 184.
3. Morton N. Cohen, "Mark Twain and the Philippines: Containing an Unpublished Letter," *Journal of the Central Mississippi Valley American Studies Association* (Fall 1960), 25–28.
4. *Letters*, 3:241, 3:240; Morris, *Theodore Rex*, 79.
5. Morris, *Theodore Rex*, 97; *Letters*, 3:245, 3:247.
6. *Los Angeles Herald*, September 8, 1902; Stuart Creighton Miller, *Benevolent Assimilation: The American Conquest of the Philippines, 1899–1903* (New Haven, CT: Yale University Press, 1982), 220.
7. Alfonso, *Theodore Roosevelt and the Philippines*, 44–45; *Selections from the Correspondence of Theodore Roosevelt and Henry Cabot Lodge*, vol. 1, 520; *Letters*, 3:119.

32: *King Coal*

1. Miller, *Theodore Roosevelt*, 370.
2. W. J. Ghent, *Our Benevolent Feudalism* (New York: Macmillan, 1902), 27.
3. Morris, *Theodore Rex*, 152; *Letters*, 3:323.
4. Hermann Hagedorn, ed., *The Works of Theodore Roosevelt*, vol. 18 (New York: Charles Scribner's Sons, 1925), 77.
5. Leslie Landrigan, "The Pittsfield Streetcar Driver Who Nearly Killed Teddy Roosevelt," New England Historical Society, February 13, 2019, https://www.newenglandhistoricalsociety.com/the-pittsfield-streetcar-driver-who-nearly-killed-teddy-roosevelt/.
6. *Letters*, 3:325; Levenson et al., eds., *Letters of Henry Adams*, vol. 4, 407.

7 *Letters*, 3:334; *Report of the Bureau of Mines of the Department of Internal Affairs of Pennsylvania* (Harrisburg: Wm. Stanley Ray, State Printer of Pennsylvania, 1903), 35.
8 Miller, *Theodore Roosevelt*, 374; *Letters*, 3:337; William E. Leuchtenburg, *The American President: From Teddy Roosevelt to Bill Clinton* (New York: Oxford University Press, 2015), 35.
9 *Letters*, 3:338.
10 Wood, ed., *Roosevelt as We Knew Him*, 111–12.
11 Ibid., 112.
12 *Letters*, 3:366.
13 Leuchtenburg, *The American President*, 35.
14 *Letters*, 3:592.

33: *A Gentleman's Place*

1 "The Roosevelt Pets," National Park Service, Theodore Roosevelt Birthplace, last updated September 28, 2024, https://www.nps.gov/thrb/learn/historyculture/the-roosevelt-pets.htm.
2 Wood, ed., *Roosevelt as We Knew Him*, 297–98.
3 Sir Percy Sykes, *The Right Honorable Sir Mortimer Durand: A Biography* (London: Cassell, 1926), 275–76. Alice Roosevelt later recalled how she and her siblings were also made to "play" strenuously: "Oh, those perfectly awful endurance tests masquerading as games! They were rugged to a degree. Very good, I suppose, if one didn't cut oneself to pieces." Teague, *Mrs. L*, 42.
4 Jusserand, *What Me Befell: The Reminiscences of J. J. Jusserand*, 333.
5 Irving Brant, *James Madison: Commander in Chief, 1812–1836* (Indianapolis: Bobbs-Merrill, 1961), 303; Teague, *Mrs. L*, 63.
6 William Seale, *The President's House*, 2nd ed., vol. 2 (Washington, DC: White House Historical Association, 2008), 661.
7 Ibid., 669.
8 Ibid., 674, 676.
9 Ibid., 678–80.
10 Ignas K. Skrupskelis and Elizabeth M. Berkeley, eds., *The Correspondence of William James*, vol. 3 (Charlottesville: University of Virginia Press, 1994), 280; Levenson et al., eds., *Letters of Henry Adams*, vol. 4, 438.
11 Seale, *The President's House*, vol. 2, 690.
12 *Letters*, 4:807.
13 *Letters*, 5:688.
14 *Letters*, 3:373.
15 Ibid., 3:378; *Washington Post*, November 15, 1902.

34: *Into the Heart*

1 For Roosevelt's itinerary, see *New York Times*, March 16, 1903.
2 Edward Frantz, "A March of Triumph? Benjamin Harrison's Southern Tour and the Limits of Racial and Regional Reconciliation," *Indiana Magazine of History* (December 2004), 293–320.
3 Michael F. Blake, *Go West, Mr. President: Theodore Roosevelt's Great Loop Tour of 1903* (Helena, MT: Twodot, 2020), 3.

4   *Letters*, 1:62.
5   *Letters*, 3:554, 3:355.
6   Bishop, ed., *Theodore Roosevelt's Letters to His Children*, 45; *Letters*, 3:548, 3:557.
7   *Letters*, 3:557, 3:558, 3:476; Blake, *Go West, Mr. President*, 147; Muir's letter can be found at https://scholarlycommons.pacific.edu/muir-correspondence/2736/.
8   *Letters*, 3:558.
9   Ibid., 3:561.
10 Blake, *Go West, Mr. President*, 20; *Letters*, 3:550.
11 *Letters*, 3:483.

35: *Taking Panama*

1   Taliaferro, *All the Great Prizes*, 221; *Letters*, 3:64.
2   *Letters*, 3:318; Raúl Pérez, "A Colombian View of the Panama Canal Question," *North American Review* (July 1903), 64.
3   Morris, *Theodore Rex*, 240.
4   Stephen Kinzer, *Overthrow: America's Century of Regime Change from Hawaii to Iraq* (New York: Henry Holt, 2006), 58–59.
5   Morris, *Theodore Rex*, 242.
6   Ronald E. Powaski, *American Presidential Statecraft: From Isolationism to Internationalism* (New York: Palgrave Macmillan, 2017), 29.
7   Morris, *Theodore Rex*, 263; *New York Herald*, August 15, 1903.
8   *Letters*, 3:599.
9   Robert H. Ferrell, *American Diplomacy: A History* (New York: W. W. Norton, 1975), 402.
10 *The Story of Panama: Hearings on the Rainey Resolution Before the Committee on Foreign Affairs of the House of Representatives*, no. 4 (Washington, DC: Government Printing Office, 1912), 668.
11 *Letters*, 3:644; Francis Curtis, *The Republican Party: A History of Its Fifty Years' Existence and a Record of Its Measures and Leaders, 1854–1904*, vol. 2 (New York: G. P. Putnam's Sons, 1904), 449.
12 Curtis, *The Republican Party*, 449–50.
13 Norman J. Padelford, "American Rights in the Panama Canal," *American Journal of International Law* (July 1940), 416–42; Matthew Parker, *Panama Fever: The Epic Story of the Building of the Panama Canal* (New York: Anchor Books, 2007), 249.
14 Lars Schoultz, *Beneath the United States: A History of U.S. Policy Toward Latin America* (Cambridge, MA: Harvard University Press, 1998), 174.
15 *Letters*, 4:922, 4:1124.
16 *Letters*, 7:179; Robert A. Friedlander, "A Reassessment of Roosevelt's Role in the Panamanian Revolution of 1903," *Western Political Quarterly* (June 1961), 535–43; *New York Times*, March 24, 1911.
17 James T. Du Bois, *Ex-U.S. Minister to Colombia James T. Du Bois on Colombia's Claims and Rights* (no publisher identified, 1914), 8; *Letters*, 8:1414.
18 Arthur Link, ed., *The Papers of Woodrow Wilson*, vol. 48 (Princeton, NJ: Princeton University Press, 1985), 630.

36: Atop the GOP

1. *Washington Times*, March 15, 1902; Mowry, *Era of Theodore Roosevelt*, 172.
2. Croly, *Marcus Alonzo Hanna*, 424–26; *Letters*, 3:481.
3. *Report of the Proceedings of the Ohio Republican State Convention* (Columbus, OH: Allied Printing, 1903), 41, 29.
4. *Letters*, 3:482. Hanna was interred at Lake View Cemetery, something of a necropolis for Cleveland's Gilded Age grandees, including John D. Rockefeller, John Hay, and James Garfield.
5. Pringle, *Theodore Roosevelt*, 249.
6. Matthew Josephson, *The President Makers: The Culture of Politics and Leadership in an Age of Enlightenment, 1896–1919* (New York: Frederick Ungar, 1940), 167.
7. *Letters*, 4:995–96.
8. Morris, *Theodore Rex*, 362–63; *Selections from the Correspondence of Theodore Roosevelt and Henry Cabot Lodge, 1884–1918*, vol. 2 (New York: Charles Scribner's Sons, 1925), 89; *Letters*, 4:974, 4:994.
9. *Letters*, 1:286; *Letters*, 4:1007–8, 4:1014.
10. *Selections from the Correspondence of Theodore Roosevelt and Henry Cabot Lodge*, vol. 2, 107.
11. Robinson, *My Brother Theodore Roosevelt*, 217.
12. John Morley (Viscount Morley), *Recollections*, vol. 2 (New York: Macmillan, 1917), 168.
13. *Letters*, 4:1131n1.
14. Cook, *Eleanor Roosevelt*, 166–67.

37: When Goliaths Go to War

1. *Letters*, 3:520, 4:724; Charles E. Neu, *An Uncertain Friendship: Theodore Roosevelt and Japan, 1906–1909* (Cambridge, MA: Harvard University Press, 1967), 7, 18.
2. Raymond A. Esthus, *Theodore Roosevelt and Japan* (Seattle: University of Washington Press, 1966), 63; *Letters*, 4:913, 4:1204–5, 4:1085; Gwynn, ed., *Letters and Friendships of Sir Cecil Spring Rice*, vol. 1, 472.
3. Taliaferro, *All the Great Prizes*, 523, 534, 538. With typical Rooseveltian verve, the president failed to register the physical infirmities of others. "Hay writes me rather gloomy letters about himself," he told Root three weeks before his secretary of state's death, "but I think he is really better than he knows, and after the rest this summer will be able to take up the winter's work all right." *Letters*, 4:1172.
4. *Letters*, 4:1202; Tyler Dennett, "Roosevelt and the Russo-Japanese War" (dissertation, Johns Hopkins University, 1924), 175–76.
5. *Letters*, 4:1160, 4:1162–63.
6. Ibid., 4:1174.
7. Ibid., 4:1178.
8. Ibid., 4:1203–4.
9. M. A. De Wolfe Howe, *George Von Lengerke Meyer: His Life and Public Services* (New York: Dodd, Mead, 1920), 158; Eugene P. Trani, *The Treaty of Portsmouth: An Adventure in American Diplomacy* (Lexington: University of Kentucky Press, 1969), 59; *Letters*, 4:1223.
10. *Morning Post* (London), June 12, 1905, quoted in Trani, *Treaty of Portsmouth*, 61; *Letters*, 4:1210.

11. *Letters*, 4:1260, 4:1262; Mark Alan Hewitt et al., *Carrère & Hastings: Architects* (New York: Acanthus Press, 2006), 368.
12. *Letters*, 4:1274–75, 4:1206; Beale, *Theodore Roosevelt*, 265.

38: Peace in the East

1. *Letters*, 4:1225, 4:1274; Trani, *Treaty of Portsmouth*, 65; *New York Times*, July 7, 1905; Masuda Hajimu, "Rumors of War: Immigration Disputes and the Social Construction of American-Japanese Relations, 1905–1913," *Diplomatic History* (January 2009), 1–37.
2. Longworth, *Crowded Hours*, 77.
3. *Letters*, 4:1293; Longworth, *Crowded Hours*, 83; Kerr, ed., *A Bully Father*, 72.
4. *Letters*, 5:23.
5. Trani, *Treaty of Portsmouth*, 116.
6. J. J. Korostovetz, *Pre-War Diplomacy: The Russo-Japanese Problem* (London: British Periodicals, 1920), 34–36.
7. Ibid., 44; Neil P. Chatelain, "Union Naval Yards & Stations," https://civilwarnavy.com/union-naval-yards-stations/.
8. Korostovetz, *Pre-War Diplomacy*, 46; Trani, *Treaty of Portsmouth*, 126.
9. *Letters*, 4:1306.
10. Ibid., 4:1309.
11. Ibid., 4:1316–17.
12. Korostovetz, *Pre-War Diplomacy*, 108, 124.
13. *Letters*, 5:365.

39: Roosevelt and the Regulatory State

1. Ibid., 5:25, 5:83, 5:54.
2. Michael Wolraich, *Unreasonable Men: Theodore Roosevelt and the Republican Rebels Who Created Progressive Politics* (New York: St. Martin's Press, 2014), 48.
3. *Compilation of the Messages and Papers of the Presidents*, vol. 16, 6974–75, 6977.
4. Lewis L. Gould, *The Presidency of Theodore Roosevelt* (Lawrence: University Press of Kansas, 1991), 159–60; Dalton, *Theodore Roosevelt*, 216; *Letters*, 4:1072.
5. Theodore Roosevelt, "The Man with the Muck-Rake," *American Rhetoric*, Top 100 Speeches (last updated December 10, 2021), https://www.americanrhetoric.com/speeches/teddyrooseveltmuckrake.htm; Gould, *Presidency of Theodore Roosevelt*, 162; *Letters*, 5:260.
6. Upton Sinclair, *The Jungle* (New York: Doubleday, Page, 1906), 40; Kolko, *Triumph of Conservatism*, 103.
7. *Letters*, 5:178–79, 5:229.
8. *Letters*, 5:186; Eugene V. Debs, "The Growth of Socialism," *Appeal to Reason*, March 17, 1906.
9. *Letters*, 5:329, 5:328.

40: Alice in White

1. Stacy A. Rozek, "'The First Daughter of the Land': Alice Roosevelt as Presidential Celebrity, 1902–1906," *Presidential Studies Quarterly* (Winter 1989), 55–56.

2. Stacy A. Cordery, *Alice: Alice Roosevelt Longworth, from White House Princess to Washington Power Broker* (New York: Viking, 2007), 52, 69; Teague, *Mrs. L*, 70–72.
3. Miller, *Theodore Roosevelt*, 194; *Letters*, 3:408.
4. Teague, *Mrs. L*, 5; Felsenthal, *Alice Roosevelt Longworth*, 64; Longworth, *Crowded Hours*, 7, 53.
5. Cordery, *Alice*, 92–94, 101.
6. William J. Mann, *The Wars of the Roosevelts: The Ruthless Rise of America's Greatest Political Family* (New York: Harper, 2016), 175; *Letters*, 5:149.
7. Felsenthal, *Alice Roosevelt Longworth*, 65; Marguerite Cassini, *Never a Dull Moment: The Memoirs of Countess Marguerite Cassini* (New York: Harper & Brothers, 1956), 140, 199–200; Jukes Morris, *Edith Kermit Roosevelt*, 274.
8. Cordery, *Alice*, 110, 112; Teague, *Mrs. L*, 129; *New York Times*, February 21, 1980.
9. Seale, *The President's House*, vol. 2, 714, 715.
10. Ibid., 715, 716; Teague, *Mrs. L*, 123. "The nation's bride" quip comes from the *Washington Post*, February 18, 1906.
11. Teague, *Mrs. L*, 129; Longworth, *Crowded Hours*, 115.
12. Felsenthal, *Alice Roosevelt Longworth*, 108; Teague, *Mrs. L*, 128.

41: Brownsville

1. *Brownsville Daily Herald*, August 13, 1906; Lane, *The Brownsville Affair*, 19.
2. Ibid.
3. Morris, *Theodore Rex*, 455.
4. Ray Stannard Baker, *Following the Color Line: An Account of Negro Citizenship in the American Democracy* (New York: Doubleday, Page, 1908), 246.
5. *Letters*, 5:509.
6. *The United States Army and Navy Journal, and Gazette*, vol. 44 (New York: Evening Post Building, 1907), 343; *The Brownsville Affray. Report of the Inspector-General of the Army; Order of the President Discharging Enlisted Men of Companies B, C, and D, Twenty-Fifth Infantry; Messages of the President to the Senate; and Majority and Minority Reports of the Senate Committee on Military Affairs* (Washington, DC: Government Printing Office, 1908), 4, 5, 7. The 25th Infantry's A Company was on a separate assignment in August and thus not stationed at Fort Brown.
7. Louis R. Harlan, *Booker T. Washington: The Wizard of Tuskegee, 1901–1915* (New York: Oxford University Press, 1983), 310.
8. Morris, *Theodore Rex*, 471; Foraker, *Notes of a Busy Life*, vol. 2, 234, 277.
9. *Compilation of the Messages and Papers of the Presidents*, vol. 16, 7030–31.
10. *Letters*, 5:521; https://www.nobelprize.org/prizes/peace/1906/roosevelt/facts/.
11. Theodore Roosevelt, *Presidential Addresses and State Papers*, vol. 5 (New York: Review of Reviews, 1910), 1064, 1066, 1079; William L. Ziglar, "The Decline of Lynching in America," *International Social Science Review* (Winter 1988), 15.
12. Lane, *The Brownsville Affair*, 128.
13. Ibid., 133.
14. Gould, *Presidency of Theodore Roosevelt*, 242; Champ Clark, *My Quarter Century of American Politics* (Harper & Brothers, 1920), 445.
15. Clark, *My Quarter Century of American Politics*, 442–46.
16. *Letters*, 5:634, 6:1455. "It was the personality of the man that chiefly attracted me," Baker wrote of meeting TR in the late 1890s, remembering in particular his

"concentration of purpose" and that he was reading "a book on the Sioux Indians." Doris Kearns Goodwin, *The Bully Pulpit: Theodore Roosevelt, William Howard Taft, and the Golden Age of Journalism* (New York: Simon & Schuster, 2013), 231–32.
17 Miller, *Theodore Roosevelt*, 465.

42: *Cuban Encore*

1 *Letters*, 4:801.
2 Ibid., n2.
3 "U.S. Ship Force Levels, 1886–Present," Naval History and Heritage Command (last updated November 17, 2017), https://www.history.navy.mil/research/histories/ship-histories/us-ship-force-levels.html.
4 Ada Ferrer, *Cuba: An American History* (New York: Scribner, 2021), 201–2.
5 *Letters*, 5:401, 5:408–9.
6 Ibid., 5:430.
7 Ibid., 5:435, 5:436.
8 Ibid., 5:465.

43: *Genuine Race Feeling*

1 Esthus, *Theodore Roosevelt and Japan*, 128; Neu, *An Uncertain Friendship*, 22.
2 T. J. Jackson Lears, *No Place of Grace: Antimodernism and the Transformation of American Culture, 1880–1920* (New York: Pantheon Books, 1981), 226; Mrs. Winthrop Chanler [Margaret Terry Chanler], *Autumn in the Valley* (Boston: Little, Brown, 1936), 24–25. Quote from Bigelow to TR comes from Murakata Akiko, "Theodore Roosevelt and William Sturgis Bigelow: The Story of a Friendship," *Harvard Library Bulletin* (January 1975), 99–100.
3 Neu, *An Uncertain Friendship*, 35; *Letters*, 5:473.
4 *Compilation of the Messages and Papers of the Presidents*, vol. 16, 7054–55.
5 Neu, *An Uncertain Friendship*, 179, 74, 70.
6 Esthus, *Theodore Roosevelt and Japan*, 149.
7 *Letters*, 5:528–29; Neu, *An Uncertain Friendship*, 91; *Senate Documents*, 60th Congress, 1st Session, no. 100, 587–88, as quoted in Thomas A. Bailey, "The World Cruise of the American Battleship Fleet, 1907–1909," *Pacific Historical Review* (December 1932), 403n69.

44: *A Ship in Every Port*

1 Wimmel, *Theodore Roosevelt and the Great White Fleet*, 220.
2 *Letters*, 5:725–26; https://www.theodorerooseveltcenter.org/Research/Digital-Library/Record/ImageViewer?libID=o199856.
3 *Letters*, 5:725.
4 Ibid., 7:393.
5 *Selections from the Correspondence of Theodore Roosevelt and Henry Cabot Lodge*, vol. 2, 274.
6 *Los Angeles Times*, February 24, 1902.
7 *Letters*, 5:720, 5:779; Wimmel, *Theodore Roosevelt and the Great White Fleet*, 223.

8. Wimmel, *Theodore Roosevelt and the Great White Fleet*, xii, xiii, xv. The first American dreadnoughts were commissioned in 1910—the USS *South Carolina* and the USS *Michigan*.
9. Jim Rasenberger, *America, 1908: The Dawn of Flight, the Race to the Pole, the Invention of the Model T, and the Making of a Modern Nation* (New York: Scribner, 2007), 41; *Autobiography*, 592.
10. Rasenberger, *America, 1908*, 41; James R. Reckner, *Teddy Roosevelt's Great White Fleet* (Annapolis: Naval Institute Press, 1988), 24.
11. Wimmel, *Theodore Roosevelt and the Great White Fleet*, 225, 227.
12. Rasenberger, *America, 1908*, 128; *San Diego Evening Tribune*, April 14, 1908; Wimmel, *Theodore Roosevelt and the Great White Fleet*, 229, 230, 236, 239; Bailey, "The World Cruise of the American Battleship Fleet," 411.
13. Reckner, *Teddy Roosevelt's Great White Fleet*, 102, 114; Rasenberger, *America, 1908*, 243, 48.
14. Wimmel, *Theodore Roosevelt and the Great White Fleet*, 242–43; *Letters*, 6:1432.
15. Wimmel, *Theodore Roosevelt and the Great White Fleet*, 241.
16. Ibid., 241.
17. *Letters*, 8:1018; *A Compilation of the Messages and Papers of the Presidents*, vol. 16, 7034.

45: Panic Attack

1. "Wall Street and the President," *World's Work* 13 (April 1907): 8708; Gould, *Presidency of Theodore Roosevelt*, 246; *Letters*, 5:631, emphasis added.
2. *Letters*, 5:617n1.
3. "Standard Oil Fined $29,240,000 in 1907; Landis Decision on Charges of Illegal Rebates Was Reversed 2 Years Later," *New York Times*, May 24, 1937, https://www.nytimes.com/1937/05/24/archives/standard-oil-fined-29240000-in-1907-landis-decision-on-charges-of.html.; https://www.upi.com/Archives/1908/07/22/US-appeals-court-overturns-29-million-fine-imposed-on-Standard-Oil/4117018313149/; Ron Chernow, *Titan: The Life of John D. Rockefeller, Sr.* (New York: Random House, 1998), 542; Robert F. Bruner and Sean Carr, *The Panic of 1907: Lessons Learned from the Market's Perfect Storm* (Hoboken, NJ: John Wiley & Sons, 2007), 32.
4. *Letters*, 5:821.
5. Gould, *Presidency of Theodore Roosevelt*, 248; Morris, *Theodore Rex*, 499. A few weeks before the panic, Roosevelt had privately denounced the bankers for the stormy 1907 economy—he included in this criticism a couple of the men he would publicly thank in October for helping the country pull out of the panic. "The utter recklessness of the financial world, and the worse than recklessness of its most eminent leaders, the Rockefellers, Harrimans, and the like," he wrote Columbia University president Nicholas Murray Butler on September 20, "rendered this absolutely inevitable." *Letters*, 5:797.
6. *Letters*, 5:830n1; Gould, *Presidency of Theodore Roosevelt*, 248.
7. *Letters*, 5:831.
8. *Autobiography*, 481, 606.
9. *Letters*, 6:875; Levenson et al., *Letters of Henry Adams*, vol. 6, 94.
10. *Letters*, 6:1044.

46: Thunder from On High

1 *A Compilation of the Messages and Papers of the Presidents*, vol. 16, 7074; Gould, *Presidency of Theodore Roosevelt*, 276–77.
2 *The Outlook*, January–April 1913, vol. 103 (New York: Outlook, 1913), 670; *Letters*, 6:916.
3 *Letters*, 6:1583.
4 Ibid., 6:1576–87.
5 Ibid., 6:1586, 6:1591.
6 *Current Literature* 44, no. 3 (March 1908), 231, 236, 237.
7 Ibid., 237.
8 Ibid., 237.
9 *Letters*, 6:1036; 6:1088.

47: Successor Politics

1 Richard W. Leopold, *Elihu Root and the Conservative Tradition* (Boston: Little, Brown, 1954), 6.
2 Oscar King Davis, *Released for Publication: Some Inside Political History of Theodore Roosevelt and His Times, 1898–1918* (Boston: Houghton Mifflin, 1925), 54; Jessup, *Elihu Root*, vol. 1, 427–28. In the summer of 1906 Roosevelt had confided to University of California president Benjamin Wheeler, "My own belief is that Root, if elected President, would carry on the contest very much as . . . I would; but I do not believe we can persuade people that this would be the case." *Letters*, 5:329.
3 Mrs. William Howard Taft [Helen Herron Taft], *Recollections of Full Years* (New York: Dodd, Mead, 1914), 6; Jessup, *Elihu Root*, vol. 1, 123.
4 *Letters*, 6:916.
5 Mark Sullivan, *Our Times: The United States, 1900–1925*, vol. 4 (New York: Scribner's Sons, 1932), 304n22.
6 *Letters*, 5:486.
7 "Observations of a Straggler," *The Voter: A Monthly Magazine of Politics* (July 1908), 30; Morris, *Theodore Rex*, 525; Longworth, *Crowded Hours*, 150.
8 Michael Kazin, *A Godly Hero: The Life of William Jennings Bryan* (New York: Alfred A. Knopf, 2006), 154.

48: Regime Change

1 *New York Times*, July 29, 1908; Ernest Samuels, *Henry Adams: The Major Phase* (Cambridge, MA: Belknap Press of Harvard University Press, 1964), 461.
2 *Letters*, 6:1209, 6:1247, 6:1248, 6:1231, 6:1234, 6:1235.
3 Mowry, *Era of Theodore Roosevelt*, 233.
4 Gould, *Presidency of Theodore Roosevelt*, 286.
5 Carl Sferrazza Anthony, *Nellie Taft: The Unconventional First Lady of the Ragtime Era* (New York: William Morrow, 2005), 19; Mowry, *Era of Theodore Roosevelt*, 231.
6 *Letters*, 6:1430, 6:1431.
7 Ibid., 6:1490, 6:1498.
8 *A Compilation of the Messages and Papers of the Presidents*, vol. 16, 7205.
9 Ibid.

10 Daggett, "Mrs. Roosevelt," 394; Mark Albertson, *U.S.S. Connecticut: Constitution State Battleship* (Mustang, OK: Tate, 2007), 65–66.
11 Levenson et al., *Letters of Henry Adams*, vol. 6, 199.
12 Anthony, *Nellie Taft*, 221; Josephson, *President Makers*, 281.
13 Longworth, *Crowded Hours*, 165; Gould, *Presidency of Theodore Roosevelt*, 297.
14 Dalton, *Theodore Roosevelt*, 344; Gwynn, ed., *Letters and Friendships of Sir Cecil Spring Rice*, vol. 1, 240.

49: African Exile

1 *Letters*, 6:978–79.
2 Ibid., 6:1034.
3 Wood, ed., *Roosevelt as We Knew Him*, 210–11.
4 Pringle, *Theodore Roosevelt*, 345.
5 *Letters*, 6:1413.
6 Patricia O'Toole, *When Trumpets Call: Theodore Roosevelt After the White House* (New York: Simon & Schuster, 2005), 19; Edmund Morris, *Colonel Roosevelt* (New York: Random House, 2010), 11.
7 Robinson, *My Brother Theodore Roosevelt*, 251–53; *Letters*, 5:137.
8 *New York Times*, March 23, 1909.
9 Pringle, *Theodore Roosevelt*, 358; O'Toole, *When Trumpets Call*, 34.
10 *Letters*, 7:14–15; O'Toole, *When Trumpets Call*, 64.
11 *Letters*, 7:16; Theodore Roosevelt, *African Game Trails: An Account of the African Wanderings of an American Hunter-Naturalist* (London: John Murray, 1910), 459.
12 Smithsonian African Expedition (1909), Smithsonian Libraries and Archives, https://www.si.edu/object/auth_exp_fbr_EACE0006; Miller, *Theodore Roosevelt*, 499; Dalton, *Theodore Roosevelt*, 358.
13 Roosevelt, *African Game Trails*, 72, 63.
14 *Selections from the Correspondence of Theodore Roosevelt and Henry Cabot Lodge*, vol. 2, 357.
15 Philip C. Jessup, *Elihu Root*, vol. 2 (New York: Dodd, Mead, 1938), 161.
16 Lewis L. Gould, *Four Hats in the Ring: The 1912 Election and the Birth of Modern American Politics* (Lawrence: University Press of Kansas, 2008), 12.

50: Storming Europe

1 *Letters*, 6:1089.
2 Mowry, *Era of Theodore Roosevelt*, 250; Gifford Pinchot, *Breaking New Ground* (New York: Harcourt, Brace, 1947), 498–500.
3 Mowry, *Era of Theodore Roosevelt*, 251. Offering a point of comparison between the Roosevelt and Taft administrations' conservation records, Pinchot had addressed the House of Representatives' Committee on Agriculture in February 1910: "In 1901 there were 2,300 permits for grazing. Last year there were 27,000. In 1901 there were no special-use permits. Last year there were 5,000. In 1901 there were no permits for crossing forests with stock. Last year there were 2,000.... Of timber sales in 1901 there were 31. This year [1909] there were 5,000." *Congressional Record: Containing the Proceedings and Debates of the Sixty-First Congress, Second Session*, vol. 45 (Washington, DC: Government Printing Office, 1910), 1336.

4 Mowry, *Era of Theodore Roosevelt*, 254.
5 *Letters*, 7:51n3.
6 Frederick E. Drinker and Jay Henry Mowbray, *Theodore Roosevelt: His Life and Work* (Washington, DC: National Publishing, 1919), 318; Zoltan Peterecz, "The Visit of the Most Popular American of the Day: Theodore Roosevelt in Hungary," *Hungarian Studies* (2014), 244–45, http://real.mtak.hu/39006/1/hstud.28.2014.2.3.pdf.
7 Drinker and Mowbray, *Theodore Roosevelt*, 321–23.
8 *Letters*, 7:391.
9 Pringle, *Theodore Roosevelt*, 370.
10 Miller, *Theodore Roosevelt*, 511.
11 Ibid., 510; *Letters*, 7:409; Mark De Wolfe Howe, ed., *Holmes-Pollock Letters: The Correspondence of Mr. Justice Holmes and Sir Frederick Pollock, 1874–1932*, vol. 1 (Cambridge, MA: Harvard University Press, 1941), 164.
12 *Letters*, 7:415, 7:86; Henry F. Pringle, *The Life and Times of William Howard Taft*, vol. 1 (New York: Farrar & Rinehart, 1939), 543–44.
13 Eleanor B. Roosevelt, *Day Before Yesterday: The Reminiscences of Mrs. Theodore Roosevelt, Jr.* (New York: Doubleday, 1959), 49.
14 Morris, *Colonel Roosevelt*, 85, 88.
15 *Letters*, 7:89, 7:93.
16 Ibid., 7:80.

51: Lay of the Land

1 Morris, *Colonel Roosevelt*, 94; *Letters*, 7:73–74.
2 *Letters*, 7:73.
3 Herbert Croly, *The Promise of American Life* (New York: Macmillan, 1912), 169. Croly tapped into a long-standing approach to reckoning with American development pitting Hamiltonians (northern, nationalistic, industrial) against Jeffersonians (southern, states' rights, agrarian). Perhaps the most lucid statement of this dichotomy appeared in the first volume of literary historian Vernon Parrington's *Main Currents in American Thought*. One finds in the book's table of contents: "Alexander Hamilton—The Leviathan State: Representative of conservative interests. A master of finance . . . the rule of the strong. Undemocratic. . . . Statesman of the rising capitalism," as well as "Thomas Jefferson—Agrarian Democrat . . . a philosophy of decentralization. Belief in the excellence of an agrarian economy . . . fear of cities and industrialism. . . . Faith in the common people." Vernon Louis Parrington, *Main Currents in American Thought: An Interpretation of American Literature from the Beginnings to 1920*, vol. 1 (New York: Harcourt, Brace, 1927), xv, xvi.
4 Miller, *Theodore Roosevelt*, 490.
5 *Letters*, 7:23.
6 Stephen P. Hall, "The Taft Summer White House," Beverly Historical Society (page last updated on July 23, 2003), https://bevhistsoc.tripod.com/thestory.htm.
7 *Letters*, 7:103; *Selections from the Correspondence of Theodore Roosevelt and Henry Cabot Lodge*, vol. 2, 375.
8 *Evening Post* (New York, NY), September 1, 1910.
9 *Letters*, 7:193; Theodore Roosevelt, *The New Nationalism* (New York: Outlook, 1910), 11–12.
10 Ibid., 28.

11 *Selections from the Correspondence of Theodore Roosevelt and Henry Cabot Lodge*, vol. 2, 388–90.
12 Ibid., 390.
13 Henry F. Pringle, *The Life and Times of William Howard Taft*, vol. 2 (New York: Farrar & Rinehart, 1939), 573.
14 Ibid.
15 *Evening Post* (New York, NY), September 1, 1910.
16 O'Toole, *When Trumpets Call*, 111.
17 *Sun* (New York, NY), November 9, 1910; *Letters*, 7:159.
18 *Letters*, 7:163.
19 *Taft and Roosevelt: The Intimate Letters of Archie Butt, Military Aide*, vol. 2 (Garden City, NY: Doubleday, Doran, 1930), 556.
20 *Letters*, 7:182.

52: Widening Divide

1 Ibid., 7:205, 7:484, 7:203.
2 William B. Murphy, "The National Progressive Republican League and the Elusive Quest for Progressive Unity," *Journal of the Gilded Age and Progressive Era* (October 2009), 531; *Letters*, 7:201; 7:532; John Milton Cooper Jr., *The Warrior and the Priest: Woodrow Wilson and Theodore Roosevelt* (Cambridge, MA: Belknap Press of Harvard University Press, 1983), 152–53.
3 Murphy, "The National Progressive Republican League," 529.
4 *Letters*, 7:418.
5 Roosevelt, *African Game Trails*, x–xi; Morris, *Colonel Roosevelt*, 129.
6 Dalton, *Theodore Roosevelt*, 373.
7 *Letters*, 7:345; Theodore Roosevelt, "The Trusts, the People, and the Square Deal," *The Outlook* (November 18, 1911), 649, 652. Roosevelt's insistence at this time that politicians partnered with the business class to steer the reform movement was an argument more fully explored in the 1960s by New Left historians. The major statement is Gabriel Kolko's 1963 study *The Triumph of Conservatism*.
8 *Letters*, 7:293, 7:336, 7:450–51. Despite calling Pinchot a "fanatic" and, in the same note, "an extremist," he wrote to Pinchot in 1916, "I had intended . . . if elected President in 1912 to make you Secretary of State." *Letters*, 8:1089.

53: The Battle Begins

1 Robert M. Warner, *Chase Salmon Osborn, 1860–1949* (Ann Arbor: University of Michigan, 1960), 21.
2 *Letters from Theodore Roosevelt to Anna Roosevelt Cowles*, 298; *Letters*, 7:485.
3 Andrew C. Pavord, "The Gamble for Power: Theodore Roosevelt's Decision to Run for the Presidency in 1912," *Presidential Studies Quarterly* (Summer 1996), 642.
4 Robert M. La Follette, *La Follette's Autobiography: A Personal Narrative of Political Experiences* (Madison, WI: Robert M. La Follette, 1913), 95, 478–79.
5 Ibid., 545; Sydney M. Milkis, *Theodore Roosevelt, the Progressive Party, and the Transformation of American Democracy* (Lawrence: University Press of Kansas, 2009), 52; Nancy C. Unger, *Fighting Bob La Follette: The Righteous Reformer* (Chapel Hill: University of North Carolina Press, 2000), 206.

6. Morris, *Colonel Roosevelt*, 167.
7. *Sun* (New York, NY), February 22, 1912; Theodore Roosevelt, "A Charter of Democracy" (Washington, DC: Government Printing Office, 1919), 11, 14.
8. *New York Times*, February 22, 1912; Longworth, *Crowded Hours*, 186–87; *Selections from the Correspondence of Theodore Roosevelt and Henry Cabot Lodge*, vol. 2, 423–24; Beringause, *Brooks Adams*, 343.
9. Beringause, *Brooks Adams*, 343–44; Jessup, *Elihu Root*, vol. 2, 180.
10. Sullivan, *Our Times*, vol. 4, 477; Arthur S. Link, ed., *The Papers of Woodrow Wilson*, vol. 24 (Princeton, NJ: Princeton University Press, 1977), 185.
11. "My hat's in the ring," see Gregory A. Wynn Theodore Roosevelt Collection at the Theodore Roosevelt Digital Library, Dickinson State University, https://www.theodorerooseveltcenter.org/Research/Digital-Library/Record?libID=o287794.
12. Anthony, *Nellie Taft*, 331.
13. Lincoln, Grant, Harrison, McKinley, and Roosevelt were all renominated; Hayes did not pursue a second term. Arthur, who came to the presidency due to Garfield's death, pined unsuccessfully for his own nomination. Grant was receptive to a third term in 1880, after having retired four years earlier; he led early in the party's convention balloting before Garfield claimed the prize.
14. Gould, *Four Hats in the Ring*, 65.
15. Paolo E. Coletta, *The Presidency of William Howard Taft* (Lawrence: University Press of Kansas, 1973), 261; Jeffrey Rosen, *William Howard Taft* (New York: Times Books, 2018), 10. On Taft's personality, Alice Roosevelt Longworth wrote of their 1905 trip to Asia: "He was never out of temper, possibly he was just a little too good humored. I never had the least awe of him. I always felt that I could 'get away with' whatever it was he objected to." Longworth, *Crowded Hours*, 69.
16. Jessup, *Elihu Root*, vol. 2, 181; *Evening Post* (New York, NY), April 26, 1912.
17. *Sun* (New York, NY), April 26, 1912.
18. *New York Times*, April 26, 1912.
19. *The Intimate Letters of Archie Butt, Military Aide*, vol. 2, 814.

54: *Armageddon Arrives*

1. Root to Taft, May 5, 1912, Series 7, Reel 455, William Howard Taft Papers, Library of Congress, Washington, DC.
2. Kelsey to Taft, June 1, 1912, Series 7, Reel 455, William Howard Taft Papers.
3. Taft to "My Dear Kels," June 4, 1912, Series 8, Reel 513; Root to Taft, May 5, 1912, Series 7, Reel 455, both in William Howard Taft Papers.
4. *Letters*, 7:553, 7:561–62.
5. Morris, *Colonel Roosevelt*, 195.
6. Hermann Hagedorn, ed., *The Works of Theodore Roosevelt*, vol. 19 (New York: Charles Scribner's Sons, 1925), 285–317.
7. *Letters*, 7:562–63.
8. Ibid., 7:563n1.
9. Jessup, *Elihu Root*, vol. 2, 204.
10. Taft to Mrs. Buckner R. Wallingford [Annie Rives Longworth Wallingford], July 17, 1912, Series 8, Reel 513, William Howard Taft Papers; Coletta, *Presidency of William Howard Taft*, 242.

NOTES

55: The Lord's Candidate

1. *Letters*, 7:568; Gould, *Four Hats in the Ring*, 134; Davis, *Released for Publication*, 317.
2. *Letters*, 7:586, 7:588, 7:587, 7:590.
3. Gould, *Four Hats in the Ring*, 136; *Evening Post* (New York, NY), August 6, 1912; Harlan, *Booker T. Washington*, 353–54.
4. *Evening Post* (New York, NY), August 6, 1912; *New York Times*, August 6, 1912; Gould, *Edith Kermit Roosevelt*, 124.
5. Cooper, *Warrior and the Priest*, 189. Roosevelt had come a little grudgingly to accept the idea of women voting. In the fall of 1908, he had written to Harriet Taylor Upton, an Ohio activist and daughter of a Republican congressman, "Personally I believe in woman's suffrage, but I am not an enthusiastic advocate of it because I do not regard it as a very important matter. I am unable to see that there has been any special improvement in the position of women in those States in the West that have adopted woman suffrage, as compared with those States adjoining them that have not adopted it. I do not think that giving the women suffrage will produce any marked improvement in the condition of women." He noted that his sisters, Bamie and Corinne, "are strongly against it," though conceded "my wife favors it," with the qualifier "but not very strongly." *Letters*, 6:1341.
6. *The Autobiography of William Allen White* (New York: Macmillan, 1946), 483.
7. *Evening Post* (New York, NY), August 6, 1912.
8. *Address by Theodore Roosevelt Before the Convention of the National Progressive Party in Chicago, August 1912*, in Theodore Roosevelt Birthplace National Historic Site Collection, Theodore Roosevelt Digital Library, Dickinson State University, https://www.theodorerooseveltcenter.org/Research/Digital-Library/Record?libID=o284876.
9. *New York Times*, June 27, 1912; Coletta, *Presidency of William Howard Taft*, 241; https://elementalmixology.blog/2015/03/23/drink-of-the-day-the-bull-moose-cocktail-2/.
10. Levenson et al., *Letters of Henry Adams*, vol. 6, 557.
11. The closest a third-party candidate came after 1860 to claiming 10 percent of the popular vote in a presidential election was in 1892, when the Populist and former congressman James B. Weaver, an Iowa homesteader from frontier days, captured 8.5 percent.

56: The Last Hurrah

1. On Wilson's career at Princeton see chapters 3–5 in John Milton Cooper Jr.'s *Woodrow Wilson: A Biography* (New York: Alfred A. Knopf, 2009).
2. F. Scott Fitzgerald, *This Side of Paradise* (New York: Charles Scribner's Sons, 1920), 40; John Morton Blum, *Woodrow Wilson and the Politics of Morality* (Boston: Little, Brown, 1956), 41.
3. Milkis, *Theodore Roosevelt*, 134.
4. http://sageamericanhistory.net/progressive/docs/SocialistPlat1912.htm; https://www.presidency.ucsb.edu/documents/republican-party-platform-1912.
5. *The Intimate Letters of Archie Butt, Military Aide*, vol. 2, 744; *Letters*, 3:391.

6 Herron Taft, *Recollections of Full Years*, 392.
7 Stan Gores, "The Attempted Assassination of Teddy Roosevelt," *Wisconsin Magazine of History* (Summer 1970), 269–77; Wood, ed., *Roosevelt as We Knew Him*, 101.
8 *Letters*, 7:705; Davis, *Released for Publication*, 374–76. Roosevelt told the French ambassador to the United States, Jean Jules Jusserand, that he "frequently received . . . letters" of a threatening nature—and that some were sent as well to his daughter Alice and his eldest son, only a teenager. Jusserand, *What Me Befell*, 240.
9 Davis, *Released for Publication*, 378–80; *Letters*, 7:705.
10 Davis, *Released for Publication*, 380–85.
11 Longworth, *Crowded Hours*, 216; Jukes Morris, *Edith Kermit Roosevelt*, 387; O'Keefe, *The Loves of Theodore Roosevelt*, 329.
12 Oliver E. Remey et al., *The Attempted Assassination of Ex-President Theodore Roosevelt* (Milwaukee, WI: Progressive Publishing, 1912), 93, 176, 101, 212; O'Toole, *When Trumpets Call*, 439n234.
13 Arthur S. Link, ed., *The Papers of Woodrow Wilson*, vol. 25 (Princeton, NJ: Princeton University Press, 1978), 55–56.
14 *Journal of John D. Long*, 330; *Letters*, 7:633.
15 Cordery, *Alice*, 235; Felsenthal, *Alice Roosevelt Longworth*, 131; Jean Vanden Heuvel, "The Sharpest Wit in Washington," *Saturday Evening Post*, December 4, 1965. The 1st Ohio Congressional District seat lost by Longworth had last gone to a Democrat in the 1880s. Longworth reclaimed the seat in the next (1914) election cycle and held it until his death in 1931.
16 Dalton, *Theodore Roosevelt*, 408; O'Toole, *When Trumpets Call*, 237.

57: The Wages of Doubt

1 *Selections from the Correspondence of Theodore Roosevelt and Henry Cabot Lodge*, vol. 2, 434.
2 Miller, *Theodore Roosevelt*, 535; Candice Millard, *The River of Doubt: Theodore Roosevelt's Darkest Journey* (New York: Anchor Books, 2005), 69. Decades after the Peary-Henson expedition, it was discovered that, due to navigational errors, the party probably fell a few miles shy of the pole. Roosevelt told a friend that the South American trip provided a needed respite from the Bull Moosers. "I shall be glad to be out of the country for one reason," he wrote Arthur Lee in July, "and that is the Progressive Party. The temptation is for the Progressives always to lie down on me, and in the unlikely event of the party continuing to exist, it has got to learn to walk alone." *Letters*, 7:741.
3 Morris, *Colonel Roosevelt*, 295; George K. Cherrie, *Dark Trails: Adventures of a Naturalist* (New York: G. P. Putnam's Sons, 1930), 247. On Roosevelt's relationship with Zahm, see Joseph R. Ornig, *My Last Chance to Be a Boy: Theodore Roosevelt's South American Expedition of 1913–1914* (Baton Rouge: Louisiana State University Press, 1994), 4–7. The American Museum of Natural History, to which Roosevelt provided specimens, put up an equestrian statue of the Colonel in 1939, placed at the building's entrance. The mounted Roosevelt is joined by two walking figures—a Native American and an African American, representing, so said the statue's sculptor James Earle Fraser (designer of

the 1913–1938 Indian head/buffalo head nickel), the continents of Africa and North America. By the late twentieth century, criticism of the piece as racist and advocating white supremacy began to circulate. These critiques were renewed in the wake of the 2020 murder of George Floyd by a Minneapolis police officer. In 2022 the museum, with the support of Theodore Roosevelt IV, the former president's great-grandson and a museum trustee, removed the statue.

4 Benjamin Moser, "The Cost of Order and Progress," *New York Review of Books*, November 23, 2023, 18. On the Roosevelt-Rondon expedition, see Part II of Larry Rohter's *Into the Amazon: The Life of Cândido Rondon, Trailblazing Explorer, Scientist, Statesman, and Conservationist* (New York: W. W. Norton, 2023).

5 Cherrie, *Dark Trails*, 249; Todd A. Diacon, *Stringing Together a Nation: Cândido Mariano Da Silva Rondon and the Construction of a Modern Brazil, 1906–1930* (Durham, NC: Duke University Press, 2004), 32–39.

6 Davis, *Released for Publication*, 434.

7 Millard, *River of Doubt*, 106.

8 Theodore Roosevelt, *Through the Brazilian Wilderness* (New York: Charles Scribner's Sons, 1914), 241, 223, xiii. Arsène Lupin, the popular creation of French writer Maurice Leblanc, was a witty and charming gentleman thief. He featured in more than a dozen novels as well as several movies, films, and stage plays; in a 1906 story, he met an aged Sherlock Holmes. Ever popular, the character inspired *Lupin*, which premiered on Netflix in January 2021 for a multiyear run.

9 Ibid., 269–70.

10 Ibid., 291, 298; Cherrie, *Dark Trails*, 264.

11 Roosevelt, *Through the Brazilian Wilderness*, 309; Morris, *Colonel Roosevelt*, 338.

12 Kermit Roosevelt, *The Happy Hunting-Grounds* (London: Hodder & Stoughton, 1920), 47; Cherrie, *Dark Trails*, 250.

13 Roosevelt, *Through the Brazilian Wilderness*, 307.

14 Henry L. Stoddard, *As I Knew Them: Presidents and Politics from Grant to Coolidge* (New York: Harper & Brothers, 1927), 320; Wood, ed., *Roosevelt as We Knew Him*, 394.

58: Wilson's Washington

1 William Appleman Williams, *The Tragedy of American Diplomacy* (New York: W. W. Norton, 1988), 70. On "butchers," see the *New York Times*'s Washington correspondent Charles Willis Thompson's comments to a colleague in May 1913: "While I was in Washington I got the first line I have had on the President's attitude toward the Huerta Government in Mexico. He hasn't given a hint whether he will recognize it or not. But a friend of mine, Jim Doyle, who represents the Huerta folks, went to see the President to urge recognition, and the President replied, 'I will not recognize a government of butchers.'" Arthur S. Link, ed., *The Papers of Woodrow Wilson*, vol. 27 (Princeton, NJ: Princeton University Press, 1978), 465.

2 Herring, *From Colony to Superpower*, 393.

3 *Letters*, 7:763.

4 Ibid., 3:52, 6:1447.
5 Ibid., 8:834, 8:823.
6 Ibid., 7:790, 7:809.
7 *The Outlook* 108 (September–December 1914), 169.
8 *Letters*, 8:903.
9 *Selections from the Correspondence of Theodore Roosevelt and Henry Cabot Lodge*, vol. 2, 449.
10 Theodore Roosevelt, *America and the World War* (New York: Charles Scribner's Sons, 1915), vii, 12, 247, 98, 27, 127, 130. "The Prince of Peace" was the title of Bryan's most popular Chautauqua series lecture—see *New York Times*, September 7, 1913.
11 *Letters*, 8:898–99, 8:879; Jukes Morris, *Edith Kermit Roosevelt*, 407.
12 Roosevelt, *The Naval War of 1812*, 153, 199.

59: Rumors of War

1 *Letters*, 8:922–23.
2 Theodore Roosevelt, *Fear God and Take Your Own Part* (New York: George H. Doran, 1916), 20; *New York Times*, August 26, 1915; Arthur S. Link, ed., *The Papers of Woodrow Wilson*, vol. 34 (Princeton, NJ: Princeton University Press, 1980), 353.
3 "Theodore Roosevelt Says Wilson Is the Worst President Ever," letter written February 4, 1916 [author unknown], Raab Collection, https://www.raabcollection.com/presidential-autographs/roosevelt-wilson-1916.
4 *Letters*, 8:922; *Selections from the Correspondence of Theodore Roosevelt and Henry Cabot Lodge*, vol. 2, 465.
5 *New York Times*, March 10, 1916.
6 *Letters*, 7:568.
7 Ibid., 8:995, 8:1061.
8 Ibid., 8:1118.
9 Arthur S. Link, ed., *The Papers of Woodrow Wilson*, vol. 30 (Princeton, NJ: Princeton University Press, 1979), 29.
10 Ibid., 8:1087.
11 Hermann Hagedorn, ed., *The Works of Theodore Roosevelt*, vol. 20 (New York: Charles Scribner's Sons, 1925), 515, 520, 525–26.
12 Gould, *Edith Kermit Roosevelt*, 127; *Letters*, 8:1139.
13 *Letters*, 8:1163n3; the insult—"most wretched"—appears in a February 4, 1916, letter from Roosevelt to Charles Bull, Superintendent of Yosemite National Park; see https://www.raabcollection.com/presidential-autographs/roosevelt-wilson-1916.

60: Forever Jingo

1 Pringle, *Theodore Roosevelt*, 412; Joseph Bucklin Bishop, *Theodore Roosevelt and His Time*, vol. 2 (New York: Charles Scribner's Sons, 1920), 311; *Letters*, 8:1153.
2 David Ramsay, *Lusitania: Saga and Myth* (New York: W. W. Norton, 2002), 265. This was at least the sixth meeting between Roosevelt and Wilson. They had spoken at a Baltimore rally for municipal reform in 1896; Roosevelt lectured at Princeton

in 1897; Wilson had stayed for two days as an Oyster Bay guest in 1901; the two met again in 1905 at an Army-Navy football game held at Princeton, and again at the White House for an afternoon in May 1914. For chronology, see Arthur S. Link, ed., *The Papers of Woodrow Wilson*, vol. 42 (Princeton, NJ: Princeton University Press, 1983), 32n1.

3 Pringle, *Theodore Roosevelt*, 416; *New York Times*, April 10, 1917.
4 Pringle, *Theodore Roosevelt*, 419.
5 Roosevelt to Dearest Archie, August 23, 1917, Archibald B. Roosevelt Family Papers, MS AM, 1541.10, Theodore Roosevelt Collection, Harvard Library, https://iiif.lib.harvard.edu/manifests/view/drs:20356292$10i.
6 Link, ed., *Papers of Woodrow Wilson*, vol. 42, 56.
7 Ibid., 56–57.
8 *Letters*, 8:1178–82.
9 Ibid., 8:1183–84n3; 8:1187–91.
10 Ibid., 8:1192; Link, ed., *Papers of Woodrow Wilson*, vol. 42, 324, 325, 346.
11 Teague, *Mrs. L*, 110; *Talks with T.R., from the Diaries of John J. Leary, Jr.* (Boston: Houghton Mifflin, 1920), 237; Kermit Roosevelt, ed., *Quentin Roosevelt: Sketch with Letters* (New York: Charles Scribner's Sons, 1921), 233; Dalton, *Theodore Roosevelt*, 478.
12 Link, ed., *Papers of Woodrow Wilson*, vol. 42, 470, 469.
13 *New York Times*, May 28, 1917.
14 *New York Times*, October 12, 1917; Theodore Roosevelt to Dearest Archie, October 14, 1917, Archibald B. Roosevelt Family Papers, MS AM, 1541.5, Theodore Roosevelt Collection, Harvard Library, https://iiif.lib.harvard.edu/manifests/view/drs:20356294$33i.
15 O'Toole, *When Trumpets Call*, 365, 361; *Roosevelt in* The Kansas City Star: *War Time Editorials by Theodore Roosevelt* (Boston: Houghton Mifflin, 1921), 128, 74; Arthur S. Link, ed., *The Papers of Woodrow Wilson*, vol. 45 (Princeton, NJ: Princeton University Press, 1984), 173. In a June 1918 communication to Henry Stimson, Roosevelt touted his recent attack on the German language: "The tide of anti-German feeling is steadily rising, and it was interesting to be cheered to the echo in Milwaukee when I insisted that there should be no language except the English language used in the schools, and that within a reasonable time all papers should be published in English." *Letters*, 8:1338.
16 Link, ed., *Papers of Woodrow Wilson*, vol. 45, 320; Arthur S. Link, ed., *The Papers of Woodrow Wilson*, vol. 46 (Princeton, NJ: Princeton University Press, 1984), 64n2.

61: *Mortal After All*

1 Morris, *Colonel Roosevelt*, 517–18.
2 *Letters*, 8:1286.
3 *The Autobiography of Lincoln Steffens: Complete in One Volume* (New York: Literary Guild, 1931), 503.
4 *Roosevelt in* The Kansas City Star, 121–22.
5 Kermit Roosevelt, ed., *Quentin Roosevelt*, 160; *Letters*, 8:1351.
6 *Washington Evening Star*, July 18, 1918.
7 Kermit Roosevelt, ed., *Quentin Roosevelt*, 170.

8. Edward V. Rickenbacker, *Fighting the Flying Circus* (Philadelphia: J. B. Lippincott, 1919), 193; *Letters*, 8:1353. TR told Colonel Frank McCoy, stationed in France, that "it was very dreadful to have Quentin die. All I can say is that it would have been worse if he had stayed at home." Theodore Roosevelt to Colonel Frank McCoy, September 12, 1918, Archibald B. Roosevelt Family Papers, MS AM, 1541.10, Theodore Roosevelt Collection, Harvard Library, https://iiif.lib.harvard.edu/manifests/view/drs:20356292$6i.
9. Arthur S. Link, ed., *The Papers of Woodrow Wilson*, vol. 49 (Princeton, NJ: Princeton University Press, 1985), 445; *Letters*, 8:1363. Roosevelt considered himself a candidate in 1920, writing to his friend Joseph Bishop, "If the leaders of the party come to me and say that they are convinced that I am the man the people want and the only man who can be elected, and that they are all for me, I don't see how I could refuse to run." Bishop, *Roosevelt and His Time*, vol. 2, 469.
10. *Letters*, 8:1404–5.
11. Ibid., 8:1415.
12. *Roosevelt in* The Kansas City Star, 227, 244.
13. Ibid., 193; *Letters*, 8:1380. Roosevelt's "let us dictate peace" sentiment echoes Prussian prime minister Otto von Bismarck's 1862 quip, "Not by speeches and resolutions of majorities are the great questions of the time decided . . . but by iron and blood." https://germanhistorydocs.ghi-dc.org/sub_document.cfm?document_id=250&language=english.
14. Arthur S. Link, ed., *The Papers of Woodrow Wilson*, vol. 53 (Princeton, NJ: Princeton University Press, 1986), 117.
15. Amos, *Theodore Roosevelt*, 156–57; David H. Wallace, "Historic Furnishings Report: Sagamore Hill," vol. 1 (Harpers Ferry, WV: Harpers Ferry Center, 1989), 31.
16. Miller, *Theodore Roosevelt*, 566.

Coda: Patrimonies

1. *Letters*, 2:804, 3:613. In fact, Ted, weighing less than 130 pounds, was hurt. His football career ended in college when he shattered an ankle on the gridiron.
2. Ibid., 5:42, 5:214, 3:490; Roosevelt, *Day Before Yesterday*, 52.
3. *Letters*, 5:800; 3:490.
4. Stephen Gwynn, ed., *The Letters and Friendships of Sir Cecil Spring Rice*, vol. 2 (Boston: Houghton Mifflin, 1929), 396–97; Edward J. Renehan Jr., *The Lion's Pride: Theodore Roosevelt and His Family in Peace and War* (New York: Oxford University Press, 1998), 133–34; *Talks with T.R., from the Diaries of John J. Leary, Jr.*, 240; Watts, *Rough Rider in the White House*, 247; *Letters*, 8:1403.
5. Nathalia Holt, *The Beast in the Clouds: The Roosevelt Brothers' Deadly Quest to Find the Mythical Giant Panda* (New York: Atria/One Signal, 2025).
6. *Theodore Roosevelt on Race, Riots, Reds, Crime*, compiled by Archibald B. Roosevelt (West Sayville, NY: Probe, 1968), 12.
7. *Letters*, 7:714.
8. Kenneth W. Hechler, *Insurgency: Personalities and Politics of the Taft Era* (New York: Russell and Russell, 1964), 226; Max Freedman, ed., *Roosevelt and Frankfurter: Their Correspondence, 1928–1945* (Boston: Little, Brown, 1967), 218–19.

9 *Letters*, 7:562; https://www.politico.com/blogs/2016-gop-primary-live-updates-and-results/2016/03/donald-trump-independent-bid-220170; https://www.npr.org/2016/03/30/472394248/why-donald-trump-reversed-his-pledge-to-support-the-gop-nominee.
10 Taft to Mrs. Buckner R. Wallingford [Annie Rives Longworth Wallingford], July 17, 1912, Series 8, Reel 513, William Howard Taft Papers; https://www.forbes.com/sites/saradorn/2023/12/10/human-gumball-machine-mitt-romney-blasts-trump-warns-of-2nd-presidency/?sh=456460c86d1b.
11 *Letters*, 2:918.
12 Roosevelt, *The Strenuous Life*, 21.

Index

Page numbers of photographs appear in italics.

Key to abbreviations: FDR = Franklin Delano Roosevelt; GOP = Republican Party; NY = New York; TR = Theodore Roosevelt; WWI = World War I

Abbott, Lyman, 198
Abdul Hamid II, Sultan, 136
Adams, Abigail, 211, 263
Adams, Brooks, 138, 139, 141–43, 340–41
Adams, Evelyn Davis, 139
Adams, Henry, 5, 24, 43–44, 87, 107, 116–17, 176, 240
    comparing TR and Lodge, 87
    opinions of Taft, 306, 131, 181
    "Teddy's luck," 176, 182
    TR and the presidency, 207, 293, 310
    TR and the Spanish-American War, 149
    TR as indestructible, 202
    TR's Bull Moose "cult," 354–55
    TR's political savvy, 164
    TR's vice-presidential bid, 171
    White House renovations, 212
Adams, John, 13, 211, 417n4
Adams, John Quincy, 41
Addams, Jane, 182, 353, 380
African Game Trails (TR), 317, 335
African safari (1906), *299*, 313–18
    funding for trip, 314–15, 316
    Scribner articles, book, 315, 317, 335
    son Kermit as photographer, 315
    specimens for the Smithsonian, 317
Albany, NY, 71–72, 166, 170
Albert, King, 322
Albion's Seed (Fischer), 420n7
Aldrich, Nelson, 255, 256
Alger, Horatio, 180
Alger, Philip, 146
Alger, Russell, 149
Alienist, The (Carr), 125

Allen, Henry, 348
Alsop, Joseph, 415–16n8
Amazon expedition (1913), 367–74, 442n2
    Brazil's interest in, 5, 369–70
    death of Simplicio, 371
    funding for, 368
    Kermit and, 368, 370, 371
    murder and, 372, 373
    Rio da Dúvida and, 369, 371–74
    Rondon and, 368–72
    successes of the journey, 373–74
    TR's companions, 368–69, 442n3
    TR's leg injury and damaged health, 372–73, 374, 378
    TR's publication deals and, 368, 371
    TR's reading materials, 371, 443n8
    TR's speeches and appearances, 368
America and the World War (TR), 379
American Century, 408
American Historical Association (AHA), 110, 421n13
    TR's address "History as Literature," 109–10, 421n13
American Museum of Natural History, 368, 442–43n3
American Political Tradition, The (Hofstadter), 6
American Revolution, 12, 13, 108
American South
    GOP and, 184, 185, 186, 187, 351
    Jim Crow South, 265, 266, 351
    Lost Cause hagiography, 217
    TR's Bull Moose Party challenge to the Democrats (1912), 351–52

449

Amos, James, 401
Andrew, Millard, 363
Angell, James B., 356
Appeal to Reason, The (newspaper), 256
Army and Navy Register, TR's clash with General Miles reported, 197
Arthur, Chester, 50, 85, 86, 185, 235, 440n13
Atlantic Monthly
    "The Negro Problem" (Shaler), 54
    term "Brahmin" and, 192–93
    TR on Byrnes's corruption, 125
    TR reviews *Influence of Sea Power*, 141
    Wilson's "Ideals of America" essay, 358
Audubon, John James, 34–35

Backus, August, 361
Bacon, Robert, 274–75, 291, 315, 383
Baer, George F., 201, 203, 204
Baker, Newton, 385, 388, 390–91
Baker, Ray Stannard, 271, 313–14, 335, 433–34n16
Balfour, Arthur, 400
Ballinger, Richard, 320
Bancroft, George, 109
Bass, Robert, 337
Beaupré, Arthur, 223, 226
Beecher, Henry Ward, 81
Bell, John G., 34–35
Benton, Thomas Hart, 106
Berenson, Bernard, 355
Berger, Victor, 332
Berryman, Clifford, 215
Beveridge, Albert, 257, 353
Bigelow, William Sturgis "Billy Big," 278
Birds of America, The (Audubon), 34
Bishop, Joseph Bucklin, 191
Bismarck, Otto von, 28, 446n13
Black, Frank, 161, 164, 165
Blaine, James G., 85, 88, 89, 93–94, 99, 113, 131, 163, 234, 348
Blocksom, Augustus P., 266, 269
Bonaparte, Charles, 291–92
Borah, William, 347
Boston Herald, on TR's boater cap, 87
Bostonians, The (James), 34
Bourne, Jonathan, Jr., 296
Boutwell, George, 182
Brandeis, Louis, 89
Breckinridge, John, 362
Brisbane, Arthur, 394
Britain
    Bulloch brothers exiled in, 19, 21, 37

Edward VII's funeral, 322–23
    Hay's canal negotiations, 222–23
    Roosevelt family's tour (1869–70), 29–30, 31, 414n4
    Royal Navy's *Dreadnought*, 284
    sea power and, 140
    TR's honorary degree and Romanes Lecture, 323
    TR's London visit (1910), 322–24
Bronson, Theodore, 19
Brown, John, 329
Brownsville case, 265–72, 433n6
    defense by Booker T. Washington, 268
    Nixon's pardon of the men, 271
    TR's actions in, 268, 271
    TR-Foraker dispute over, 268–71
Bryan, William Jennings, 132, 133, 204, 152, 217, 232, 296, 304–5
    pacifism of, 377, 379
    third presidential run and loss, 307
    TR's note to, 311
Bryce, James, 390
Buchanan, James, 41, 379
Buford, Edward, 398
Bulloch, Anna (aunt), 14, 16, 18
Bulloch, Archibald (ancestor), 13, 14
Bulloch, Daniel (uncle), 14
Bulloch, Irvine (uncle), 18–19, 29, 67, 140
Bulloch, James (uncle), 19, 29, 37
Bulloch, James Stephens (grandfather), 13–14, 18
Bulloch, John (ancestor), 13
Bulloch, Martha "Patsy" (grandmother), 13, 17, 18
Bulloch, Mary De Veaux (ancestor), 14
Bunau-Varilla, Philippe, 225–26
Bunyan, John, 181, 426–27n3
Burt, Andrew S., 268
Burton, Theodore, 271
Bush, George H. W., 215
Butler, Nicholas Murray, 356, 435n5
Butt, Archibald "Archie," 1, 344, 358
Buxton, Edward, 313
Byrnes, Thomas, 125–26

Cajazeira, José, 373
Cameron, Elizabeth, 240
Cammidge, Cannon, 100
Cannon, Joe, 294, 302
Carnegie, Andrew, 182, 232, 315, 316
Carnegie Endowment for International Peace, 315
Carow, Charles (father-in-law), 96

Carow, Emily (sister-in-law), 96, 178
Carow, Gertrude (mother-in-law), 96
Carow, Isaac, 96
Carow, John, 117
Carpenter, Edward, 261
Carr, Caleb, 125
Carranza, Venustiano, 384–85
Cassini, Countess Marguerite, 262
Chanler, Elizabeth Astor Winthrop, 164
Chanler, Margaret, 5
Chapman, John Jay, 159, 163, 164
Charles Scribner's Sons
   TR's African safari and, 315, 317
   TR's Amazon expedition and, 368
   TR's books, 156, 315, 317, 335, 379
   TR's income from, 315, 335, 368
Charleston *News and Courier*, criticism of TR's 1907 message to Congress, 296
Cherrie, George, 368, 370, 372–73
Chicago
   Art Institute of Chicago, 87
   Chicago Auditorium, 347, 384
   Chicago Coliseum, 232, 349, 352, 384
   Congress Plaza Hotel, 337, 352
   Democrat National Convention in, 132
   GOP Conventions in, 86–90, 232, 304, 345–49, 383–84
   Grand Pacific Hotel, 88
   Haymarket Riot, 180
   Interstate Exposition Hall, 87, 88
   Leland Hotel, 88
   Orchestra Hall, 349
   Progressive Party Conventions, 351–54, 384
   Roosevelt National Committee formed (1912), 337
   TR greeted by crowds (1912), 347
Chicago Journal, TR campaigning for McKinley, 173
Chicago Morning News, TR's exposure of corruption, 115–16
Chicago Tribune, 333
   on Lincoln's Senate nomination, 11
   on TR's nomination fight (1912), 347
China
   Great White Fleet and, 284–87
   Qing Dynasty, 238
   Sino-Japanese War, 238–39, 244, 246
   trade with the West, 238–39
Choate, Joseph, 134
Cincinnati Enquirer, Hanna opposing TR vice-presidential bid, 172

Civil War, 11
   assault on Fort Sumter, 18
   assault on Port Royal, 140
   Battle of Hampton Roads, 284
   as a brother-against-brother conflict, 11
   Bulloch family and, 18–19, 140
   division in the Roosevelt family, 18–22
   General Wheeler at Chickamauga, 153
   Miles as Medal of Honor recipient, 196
   "a rich man's war but a poor man's fight," 18
   Rockwell in, 35
   Roosevelt brothers and, 18, 19, 412n2
   Southern states secede, 18
   veterans, 220
Clark, Champ, 271
Clark, Edgar E., 204
Clay, Henry, 131
Clemenceau, Georges, 393, 400
Cleveland, Grover, 73, 89, 94, 113, 133, 139, 162, 181, 217
Cleveland *Plain Dealer*, on TR's 1907 message to Congress, 297
Clinton, William J. "Bill," 162
Coffelt, Leslie, 202
Colombia, 3
   breach with the U.S., 227
   discovery of oil in, 228
   Panama Canal and, 221, 223–24, 227
   president Marroquín, 224
   Wilson's apology, 228
Colorado Springs Gazette, on TR's postpresidential popularity, 324–25
Columbia University, 356
   Law School, 62, 64, 74
Conkling, Roscoe, 50
conservation (environmentalism)
   Taft's rollback of, 320–21, 437n3
   TR's creation of national wildlife refuges, parks, and monuments, 320
Coolidge, Calvin, 235, 303, 344
Cortelyou, George, 202, 233–34, 290
Cortland Democrat, on TR and NY's residence requirement, 165
Cowles, Anna Roosevelt "Bamie" (sister), 14, 17, 19, 21
   assumption of family responsibilities, 24–25, 45
   assumption of TR's business affairs, 85
   deaths of her mother and TR's wife Alice, 82, 85

Cowles, Anna Roosevelt "Bamie" (sister), (*cont.*)
   Elliott's alcoholism and, 120, 121, 122
   family's European tour and, 37, 39, 41
   fostering of TR's daughter, Alice, 85, 92, 95, 101
   home in Washington, D.C., 174
   spinal defect or Pott's disease, 24, 35, 37
   surprise marriage and motherhood, 25
   TR at Harvard and, 44
   as TR's confidante, 24, 25
   TR's correspondence with, 44, 47, 61, 88, 92, 98, 113, 121, 122, 124, 126, 127, 131, 152, 337
   TR's engagement to Edie, 98–99
   TR's relationship with, 24, 49, 85, 363
   TR's rising political career and, 86
   TR's wedding to Edie and, 101
Cowles, William Sheffield (brother-in-law), 174, 282
Craig, William, 202
Crane, Winthrop, 202
Crédit Mobilier scandal, 113
Crimmins, John Daniel, 167
Croly, Herbert, 327, 329, 438n3
Cromwell, William, 224
Cuba, 2, 145, 182
   Bay of Pigs invasion, 157
   first president, 274
   honeymoon of Alice Roosevelt Longworth in, 264
   liberation movements in, 145
   Platt Amendment and, 274
   San Juan Heights, 153, 154, 156
   sinking of the USS *Maine*, 146
   Spanish-American War, 152–57
   TR and the Rough Riders, 153–56
   TR's charge up Kettle Hill, 2, 155, 156, 162
   uprising of 1906, 274–76
   U.S. occupation (1906 to 1909), 273–76
   as U.S. protectorate, 170, 189
Cullom, Shelby, 224–25
Cummings, E. E., 60
Current Literature magazine, "The Average American," 179–80
Curtis, George William, 89
Custer, George Armstrong, 77
Cutler, Arthur, 43, 86
Czolgosz, Leon, 176

da Fonseca, Hermes, 368
Dakota Territory (the Badlands), 5
   disappearance of the buffalo, 77–78
   Hunting Trips of a Ranchman (TR), 91, 93, 94
   Little Missouri (Medora), 75, 92, 218
   TR and the vanishing West, 91, 93
   TR hunts (1883, 1884), 75–79, 92–93
   TR on the native peoples of, 77
   TR's emotional response, 76–77, 79, 92
   TR's final visit, 105
   TR's Great Loop Tour (1903) and, 216
   TR's investment in cattle, 92, 95, 105
   TR's ranches, 79, 90–93, 95, 105, 420n11
   TRs trip (1884), 90, 91–93
   TR's trip (1886), 97–98
   The Winning of the West (TR), 107–9
Dana, Fanny Smith, 99
Dana, Paul, 171
Dario, Rubén, "To Roosevelt," 3
Darrow, Clarence, 204
Darwin, Charles, 53
Darwinism, 140. *See also* social Darwinism
Davis, Oscar, 301
Day, James Roscoe, 296
Debs, Eugene, 257, 357, 362, 394
DeCosta Brown, Dr. Charles, 29
De Kay, John Wesley, 375
Delano, Frederic, 253
Democratic Party
   Bryan and, 132, 133, 152, 187, 204, 232, 296, 304–5, 307
   Cleveland's presidential wins, 94, 307
   coalition with the Populists, 131
   criticism of McKinley and, 145
   Dix elected NY governor, 331
   midterm election (1896), 132
   midterm election (1910), 321, 331
   midterm election (1914), 378
   midterm election (1918), 399
   National Convention (1908), 304–5
   National Conventions in Baltimore, 87
   presidential election (1884), 89
   presidential election (1888), 113
   presidential election (1896), 131
   presidential election (1904), 187, 232–34
   presidential election (1908), 307–8
   presidential election and Congressional sweep (1912), 361–62
   presidential election (1916), 386
   Tammany Hall and, 71, 99, 127

INDEX 453

TR's Bull Moose Party challenge to (1912), 351–52
Wilson elected governor, 332, 357
See also Wilson, Woodrow
Dewey, George, 147, 282
Díaz, Porfirio, 375
Dickens, Charles, 234, 315
Dix, John, 331
Dodge, William, Jr., 19–20, 412–13n1
Dolliver, Jonathan, 255
Douglass, Frederick, 186
Doyle, Arthur Conan, 323
Dresden, Germany, 39–41
Du Bois, James, 227
Du Bois, W. E. B., 270
Dubuque Times, on Havana riots, 145
"dude ranch" term, 74
Dunham, George, 302
Dunne, Finley Peter, 157, 173
Durand, Sir Mortimer, 210
Dyott, George Miller, 374

Edison, Thomas, 27
Edmunds, George F., 85, 88
Edwards, Jonathan, 96
Edward VII, King, 202, 264, 388
  TR attends funeral of, 322–23
Egypt
  Alexandria, 37–38
  Roosevelt family tour (1872), 5, 37–39, 313
  TR and party on the Nile (1909), 319
Ehrman, Felix, 226
Eliot, Charles W., 5, 89, 314, 356, 403
Eliot, T. S., 60
Elkins Act, 254, 311
Elliott, Daniel Stuart, 40
Elliott, Lucinda "Lucy," 40
Ellis, G. B., 352
Emerson, Ellen, 39
Emerson, Ralph Waldo, 5, 38–39, 43
Endicott, William, 388
Estrada Palma, Tomás, 274, 275
Europe
  Belle Epoque, 27
  German Empire, 27
  literature, culture, and governance of 1869, 27–28
  Mahan's naval theory and lesson for the U.S., 140–41
  Roosevelt family's grand tours (1869–73), 26, 28–32, 37–42
  Suez Canal and the mechanical age, 28

TR meeting with Continental leaders and royalty (1910), 321–22
TR's honeymoons in, 63–64, 100–101
TR's travel in (1909–10), 319–25
Victorian age, 27–28
Evans, Robley "Fighting Bob," 284, 285

Fairbanks, Charles, 232
Federalist Papers, 12
Ferris, Joe, 78–79
Fillmore, Millard, 235
Fischer, David Hackett, 420n7
Fitzgerald, F. Scott, 12
Following the Conquistadores (Zahm), 368
Foraker, Joseph, 231–32, 268–71, 275, 302
Ford, John, 166
Forrest, Nathan Bedford, 391
France
  naval courtesy call on Russia, 283
  Roosevelt family in (1869–70), 30, 31
  Sino-Japanese War and the Triple Intervention, 238–39, 244
  TR and family visit (1910), 321–22
  See also Jusserand, Jean Jules
Frankfurter, Felix, 406
Franklin, Benjamin, 180
Franz Joseph I., Emperor, 321
Frick, Henry Clay, 2, 233, 291
Fuller, Melville, 236

Gardner, Frederick, 399
Garfield, Harry, 394
Garfield, James, 66, 88, 205, 209, 431n4
Garlington, Ernest A., 267, 268
Garrison, William Lloyd, 163
Gary, Elbert, 291
George, Henry, 59, 99, 100
George V, King, 396, 422n1
Germany
  naval courtesy call on NY, 283
  Sino-Japanese War and the Triple Intervention, 238–39, 244
  TR's visit of 1910, observations of, 322
  See also World War I; World War II
Gilbert, Cass, 308
Glasscock, William, 337
Goldwater, Barry, 232
Gorringe, Henry Honychurch, 75, 76
Gould, Jay, 73
G. P. Putnam's Sons
  publishes TR's books, 69, 94, 107
  TR's investment in, 79
Gracie, James King, 121

Grant, Ulysses S., 65, 196, 212, 234, 314, 440n13
Gray, Horace, 192
Great Gatsby, The (Fitzgerald), 12
Great Loop Tour (1903), 215, 216–21
Great White Fleet, 284–88, 408, 435n8
 return and TR's address, 310
Greeley, Horace, 81
Green-Wood Cemetery, Brooklyn, 28, 82
Grey, Sir Edward, 280
Griscom, Lloyd, 240
Grosscup, Peter, 290
"Growth of Socialism, The" (Debs), 257
Guerrero, Manuel Amador, 227
Guiteau, Stalwart Charles, 66

Haakon VII, King of Norway, 322
Hale, Eugene, 283
Hamilton, Alexander, 12, 255
Hanna, Mark, 132, 172, 173–74, 177, 185, 191, 203, 254, 431n4
 presidential election (1904), 230–32, 347
Harding, Warren G., 235, 303, 332, 344
Harper's, TR's speech at the Naval War College, 136–37
Harper's Weekly, Kemble's bull moose TR caricature, 354
Harriman, E. H., 190, 291
Harris, Joel Chandler, 6, 14, 351
Harris, Julian, 351
Harrison, Benjamin, 113–14, 205, 217, 302, 440n13
 TR in his administration, 114, 115–18
Harrison, William Henry, 230
Hartford Times, criticism of TR's 1907 message to Congress, 296
Harvard Advocate, 60
Harvard Graduates' Magazine, "Theodore Roosevelt's College Rank and Studies" (Ranlett), 54
Harvard Lampoon, 341
Harvard University, 43–48
 Eliot as president, 5, 89, 314, 356, 403
 FDR and, 406
 high-born Bostonians at, 45
 Lodge at, and dissertation by, 86–87
 Longworth at, 261
 notable historians, 109
 notable professors, 43
 notions of "Teutonic" supremacy, 53–54
 number of students, 44
 pedigree of students' families, 44
 Porcellian Club, 52, 60, 142, 163, 261, 404, 415–16n8
 "President's Report for 1876–77," 44
 Shaler's influence on TR, 53–54
 TR and athletics, boxing, 46, 47, 59
 TR attends, 9, 42, 43–49, 51–54, 59, 60
 TR considered for president of, 314
 TR's classmates and friends, 46, 47, 57–58, 64
 TR's clubs and societies, 52, 59, 60
 TR's description of a day at, 45–46
 TR's interactions with women, 58
 TR's sons and, 315, 336, 392, 403–4, 446n1
 TR's wealth and class advantage, 47–48
 tuition and expenses, 44
Hawaii, 132
 Great White Fleet and, 285
 Japanese immigration and, 277, 279
 U.S. acquisition of, 139, 182, 189
 U.S. Navy in Oahu, 144
Hawthorne, Julian, 38, 125
Hay, Clara Stone, 20
Hay, John, 309, 413n5, 431n4
 background, 20, 116
 friendship with Adams, 116, 176, 240
 health decline and death, 240, 431n3
 Lincoln and, 20, 107
 as McKinley's secretary of state, 177
 Open Door policy and, 238, 239
 Panama Canal and, 221, 222, 225, 226
 ring given to TR, 21, 236
 Roosevelt family and, 20–21, 116
 Russo-Japanese War and, 238–40
 Spanish-American War and, 156
 TR backed by, 134
 TR's first secretary of state, 20, 177, 202
 TR's friendship, 116, 117, 131, 181–82
 TR's Great Loop Tour and, 219–21
Hayes, Rutherford B., 49–50, 205, 213, 217, 302, 440n13
Hazel, John, 177
Hearst, William Randolph, 145
Heffelfinger, Pudge, 213
Hendricks, Thomas, 169
Henry, Prince of Prussia, 283
Hepburn, William, 255, 256, 258, 311
Hewitt, Abram, 99
Higginson, Henry Lee, 314
Hill, David B., 127, 134
Hill, James J., 190–94, 212
History of England, The (Macaulay), 67

INDEX

History of the Conquest of Mexico, The (Prescott), 109
History of the Standard Oil Company, The (Tarbell), 181
History of the United States of America, from the Discovery of the American Continent (1854–1878) (Bancroft), 109
HMS *Dreadnought*, 284
Hofstadter, Richard, 6
Holmes, Oliver Wendell, 43, 192–93
Holmes, Oliver Wendell, Jr., 6, 192–93, 310, 324
Hoover, Herbert, 213
Horizon, editorial on Brownsville, 270
Hotel Wentworth, New Castle, Maine, 247
How the Other Half Lives (Riis), 126
Hubbard, John, 226
Huerta, Victoriano, 375–76, 384, 443n1
Hughes, Charles Evans, 74, 302–3, 383–84, 386
Hulbert, Mary Allen, 361
Humboldt, Alexander von, 53
Hunting Trips of a Ranchman (TR), 91, 93, 94, 105

immigration, 73, 107–8, 113, 276–80
  anti-Asian sentiment, 277–80
  Asian Exclusion Act, 280
  Chinese Exclusion Act, 277
  Gentlemen's Agreement, 279, 280, 281
  Irish in NYC, 113
  Japanese, through Hawaii, 277, 279
  TR's policy, 189, 277–80
Indian Wars, 196, 197
Influence of Sea Power upon History, The: 1660–1783 (Mahan), 140, 141
Interstate Commerce Commission (ICC), 112, 253, 255
Italy, 30
  Roosevelt family Christmas in Rome, 31
  Roosevelt family tour (1869–70), 30–31
  TR's encounter with Pius IX, 5, 31

Jackson, Andrew, 3, 69, 112, 189, 216, 217, 234, 255
James, Henry, 34, 212
James, Jesse and Frank, 27
James, William, 44, 314
Japan
  Asian immigration to the U.S., 277–80
  Great White Fleet and, 286
  interest in the Pacific, 144
  Japanese-U.S. relations, 277–82
  Korea and, 245
  navy of, 144
  popularity of Alice Roosevelt, 245
  Prime Minister Katsura Tarō, 245
  pro-war party, 281
  Russo-Japanese War, 239–49, 281
  Satsuma battleship, 281
  Sino-Japanese War, 238–39, 246
  as threat to the Philippines, 280
  TR "goodwill cruise" to, 245
  TR on its international standing, 242–43
  U.S. show of strength and, 282
  U.S. treaty of 1894, 278
Jay, John, 12, 163
Jefferson, Thomas, 1, 2, 41, 69, 75, 145, 210, 414n2, 417n4
  slaves brought to Washington, 185–86
  TR's assessment of, 69, 417n13
jingoism, 139, 145, 223, 273, 388
Johnson, Andrew, 217, 235
Johnson, Hiram, 352, 363, 378
Johnson, Lyndon B., 2, 235
Johnson, Tom, 179
Julien, Honoré, 186
Jungle, The (Sinclair), 256–57
Jungle Book, The (Kipling), 234
Jusserand, Jean Jules, 210, 213, 388, 413n5, 442n8

Kaneko Kentarō, 248, 278
Kansas City Star
  changes in the Republican party, 326
  TR's attacks on Wilson, 394, 397, 400, 401
Katsura Tarō, 245
Kelsey, Clarence, 345–46
Kemble, Edward Windsor, 354
Kennedy, John F., 144, 235
  Resolute desk, 213
  speech, American Society of News Editors, 157
King, Martin Luther, Jr., 270
Kipling, Rudyard, vii, 6, 234, 323, 399, 405
Kissinger, Henry, 144
Knox, Philander, 191, 201, 203, 227, 255, 332
Knudsen, Gunnar, 269
Kohlsaat, H. H., 302
Komura Jutarō, 246, 249
Korea, 245, 246

labor unions and strikes, 180
  Battle of Homestead, 180
  coal strike of 1902, 199, 200–204
  Haymarket Riot, 180
  Pullman railroad strike, 180–81
  TR and government's new status as broker in disputes, 205
  TR's fair treatment of, 203
La Farge, John, 182
La Follette, Robert, 179, 296, 333–34, 337
  disastrous speech of, 338–39
  presidential try (1912), 337, 338–39, 343
  TR and, 334–35
Lambert, Alexander, 404
Landis, Kenesaw Mountain, 290
Landon, Alfred, 362
Lang, Gregor, 76
Lang, Lincoln, 76, 95
Lansing, Robert, 393
Law of Civilization and Decay, The (B. Adams), 141–42
Lawrence, Amos, 62
Lee, Arthur, 332, 442n2
Lee, George Cabot (father-in-law), 58, 89
Lee, Henry, 89
Lee, Rooney, 52
Letters of John Hay and Extracts from Diary, 309
Life of Thomas Hart Benton (TR), 106
Liliʻuokalani, Queen of Hawaii, 139
Lincoln, Abraham, 1, 2, 6, 11, 217, 234, 440n13
  assassination of, 205
  association with "Thee" Roosevelt, 20
  biographers, Hay and Nicolay, 20, 107
  call for volunteer forces, 18
  Cooper Union speech, 385
  election of 1860, 362
  Emancipation Proclamation, 211
  remembered by Frederick Douglass, 186
  as a Republican, 88
  Senate nomination, 11
  TR's hero, 20, 69, 379
  TR witnesses funeral cortège, 5, 29
Lincoln, Mary Todd, 11
Lincoln, Robert, 86
Lindsey, Benjamin, 336
Literary Digest, Northern Securities antitrust case, 192
Littauer, Lucius, 187
Lloyd George, David, 400

Lodge, Anna, 114
Lodge, Henry Cabot, 86
  antipathy for Wilson, 420n8
  backs Holmes for Supreme Court, 192, 193
  Colombia–Panama treaty and, 228
  GOP and, 88–89
  GOP National Convention (1896), 132
  GOP National Convention (1908), 304
  Harrison presidency and, 114
  at Harvard, 86–87
  loss of Congressional campaign, 94
  Panama Canal and, 223
  Philippine home rule and, 198
  Senate investigation of Philippine atrocities, 197–98
  as senator, 178, 228, 255
  on Taft presidency, 317
  TR and, 86–87, 99, 114, 115, 117, 125, 128, 131, 133, 181, 275, 333, 367, 446n13
  TR as assistant navy secretary and, 135
  TR as popular hero and, 156
  TR as president and, 178, 182
  TR as vice president and, 169, 170, 171
  TR on the 1916 elections, 382
  TR's "Charter of Democracy," 339–41
  TR's direct line to Washington and, 152
  TR's governor bid and, 162, 163–64
  TR's "New Nationalism" and, 329–30
  TR's political career pushed by, 133–35
  TR's political future, 125, 170, 326, 383
  TR's postpresidential travel (1909–10) and, 324
  TR's reelection (1904) and, 231
  TR's Rough Riders and, 151, 155–56
  TR's WWI aspirations and, 391
Lodge, Nannie Davis, 139
Loewenthal, Henry, 167
London Morning Post, on TR's diplomacy, 242
Long, John D., 134–35, 136, 144–47
Longfellow, Henry Wadsworth, 43
Longworth, Alice Lee Roosevelt (daughter), 95
  "Alice Blue," 259
  appearance in London (1910), 323
  beaux of, 261
  child, Paulina, 347
  christens the *Meteor*, 283
  courtship and marriage to Nicholas Longworth, 261–63

financial independence, 260
fostered by her aunt Bamie, 85, 92, 95
GOP convention (1908) and, 304
honeymoon in Cuba and Europe, 264
Lee family financial support, 117
life at Sagamore Hill, 260–61
life in the White House, 209, 212, 259, 260–61, 429n3
long life of, 83, 262, 406
lover, William Borah, 347
mother's death and her birth, 83, 406
popularity, 245, 259–60
presidential race of 1912 and damage to her marriage, 348, 362–63
rejection of the Tafts, 310, 311
relationship with her stepmother, 101, 260, 416n1
sense of displacement, 259–60
social life and celebrity, 260, 263
on Taft's personality, 440n15
TR as her father, 83, 92, 95, 97, 221, 237, 259, 260, 363
on TR's "A Charter of Democracy," 340
TR's desire to fight in WWI, 388, 392
TR's goodwill cruise to Japan and, 245
TR wounded by an assassin and, 360
Washington town house, 388
White House wedding, 263–64, 310, 433n10
Longworth, Nicholas, 261, 264, 348, 362–63, 388, 442n15
Louisville Courier-Journal, 197
Lounsbury, Thomas, 384
Low, Seth, 62, 163
Lowell, James Russell, 43
Lupin, Arsène, 371, 443n8
Lyman, Charles, 115

MacArthur, General Arthur, Jr., 195
Macaulay, Thomas Babington, 67, 234
Madden, Euclid, 202
Madero, Francisco, 375
Madison, Dolley, 210–11
Madison, James, 12, 149
Mahan, Alfred Thayer, 138, 139, 140, 282
Malone, Dumas, 69
Manifest Destiny, 106
Mann, Katy, 120
Manney, Henry Newman, 281, 282
Marroquín, José Manuel, 224
Martin, Edward, 341
Martin, Edward Sandford, 47
Martin, Elbert, 359

Marxism, 140
Matterhorn, the Alps, Switzerland, 63–64
Maud, Queen, 322
McCain, Henry P., 385
McCormick, Medill, 333
McKim, Charles, 211, 213
McKim, Mead & White, 211, 308
McKinley, William
  as "advance agent of prosperity," 180
  appearance, 129–30
  appointment seekers, 133–34
  appoints Long as navy secretary, 135
  appoints Root to War Department, 169
  assassination, 175–77, 205
  business-first Republicanism of, 170
  election of 1896, 129, 131, 132, 133
  funeral train, 178
  Philippine-American War and, 195–96
  reelection of 1900, 169, 173–74, 440n13
  TR as assistant navy secretary, 129, 135
  TR as vice president and, 172–74
  TR's Kettle Hill heroics and, 162
  TR's opinion of, 131, 132
  TR's Rough Riders and, 151
  vice president Hobart dies, 169
  warship sent to Cuba, 145
McNamara, Robert, 144
Metropolitan Magazine, 378–79
  TR on the U.S. entering WWI, 380, 381
  TR on WWI restrictions, 394
Mexico, 3
  Battle of Veracruz, 376, 384
  revolution and Pancho Villa, 375, 384–85
  Tampico Affair, 375–76
  TR and Rough Rider revival, 376, 385
  Wilson's foreign policy and, 375–76, 379, 384–85, 443n1
  Wilson's Punitive Expedition, 385
Meyer, George von Lengerke, 241–42, 248
Michtom, Morris, 215
Milburn, John, 177
Miles, Nelson A., 196–97
Minkwitz family of Dresden, 39, 40
Minot, Harry, 53
Mitchell, John, 200–201, 202–3
Monroe, James, 2, 41, 145, 216, 217
Monroe Doctrine, Roosevelt Corollary, 3, 273

Moody, William, 257
Morgan, J. P., 176, 190
   coal strike settlement (1902) and, 204
   "Morganization," 190
   Northern Securities anti-trust case, 192
   Panic of 1907 and, 291
   TR's governor race donation, 191–92
   TR's presidential run (1904), 233, 234
   TR's trustbusting and, 190
   White House meetings with TR (1902, 1907), 191, 289
Morley, John, 235–36
Morse, Samuel, 81
Morton, Levi, 169
Motley, John Lothrop, 109
Mugwumps/Mugwumpery, 89, 108, 234
Muir, John, 216, 220
Murray, Joe, 66–67
"muscular Christianity," 34, 106
Münsterberg, Hugo, 377

Napoleon III, 28, 67
Nast, Thomas, 50
Nation magazine, review of TR's *Life of Thomas Hart Benton*, 106
Native Americans
   encroachment by ranches/railroads, 77
   Indian Wars, 77
   Miles and Wounded Knee massacre, 196
   TR's depiction in *The Winning of the West*, 107
   TR's opinion of, 77
Natus, Frank, 265
Naval War of 1812, The (TR), 6, 66–70, 79, 380, 417n13
"Negro Problem, The" (Shaler), 54
Newberry, Truman Handy, 281
New Nationalism, 327, 329, 354, 357, 361
New York Age (black newspaper), 269
New York City (NYC)
   creation of the NY Public Library, 67
   Irish immigration and, 113
   letter bomb sent to TR, 128
   Little Italy, 125
   Lunatic Asylum, Blackwell's Island, 66
   Tammany Hall and, 72, 113, 127, 128
   TR as police commissioner (1895–97), 124–29, 134, 422n4, 422n6, 422n7
   TR as trustee, NY Infant Asylum and the Orthopedic Dispensary, 62
   TR–Parker enmity, 129, 134
   TR's anti-corruption fights, 115, 125–26, 422n4
   TR's election to State Assembly and, 66
   TR's father's philanthropy in, 26, 50, 62
   TR's GOP meetings, Morton Hall, 64–66, 114
   TR's mayoral campaign (1886), 99–100
   TR's Mulberry Street office, 125
   TR's Sunday saloon shutdown, 126–28, 422n7
   U.S. Customs House, 115
New-York Commercial Advertiser, TR meets with J. P. Morgan, 191
New York Evening Mail, TR encourages the U.S. to enter WWI, 380
New York *Evening Post*
   "Negro Issue a Blunder," 352
   Northern Securities anti-trust case, 192
   on TR–Taft schism, 330–31
New York Evening World, TR's bull moose image, 354
New York Herald
   the Great White Fleet in Japan, 285
   on a "Pacific century," 285
   Panama's independence, 224–25
   Twain on the Philippines, 196
New York Journal
   criticism of TR, 394
   on riots in Havana, 145
   TR–Parker clash covered, 129
New York Mail, on TR's boater cap, 87
New York Press, on TR's Army commission to fight Spain, 150
New York Republican Party (GOP)
   gubernatorial election (1898), 161–65
   gubernatorial election (1910), 331
   Platt–TR clash, 127, 129, 134, 169, 170
   state and city elections (1896), 128
   State Assembly and, 79
   State Convention (1884), 85
   State Convention (1910), 331
   TR attends meetings, Morton Hall, Manhattan's 21st District, 64–66, 114
   TR elected State Assemblyman from the 21st District, 66
   TR's appointment as police commissioner and, 124
   TR's governorship and Platt relationship, 163–64, 166–67
New York state
   Democrat Dix elected governor, 331
   Ford Franchise Tax Bill, 166

governor spot as stepping stone to presidency, 162
TR as governor, *159*, 166–68
TR's progressive reforms, 166–68
New York State Assembly, 73, 79
 TR granduncle James Roosevelt in, 72
 TR resigns, 84, 85
 TR's activism, 72, 74
 TR's appearance, as a "dude," 71, 72, 73
 TR's terms in, *55*, 66, 79–82
New York *Sun*, 331
 comments on TR's vice president chances, 171–72
 criticism of TR's 1907 message to Congress, 296
 report on TR's mayoral chances, 99–100
 TR and 1912 GOP losses, 331
 TR and Sunday saloon closings, 127
 TR puts the navy on war footing, 145
 TR's support from suffragists, 339–40
New York Times
 on the Brownsville case, 268
 calls 1912 Progressive Party convention "a Methodist camp meeting," 352
 criticism of TR's 1907 message to Congress, 296
 Davis as Washington correspondent, 301
 on fining of Standard Oil, 290
 Hunting Trips of a Ranchman review, 94
 managing editor Loewenthal, 167
 obituary of Alice Roosevelt Longworth, 262
 report on General Wheeler, 153–54
 report on TR's "A Charter of Democracy," 340
 on the shooting of McKinley, 176
 site for Russo-Japanese War negotiations, 244
 TR caricatured in, 173
 TR–Parker enmity reported, 129
 TR reported at Jack Cooper's health farm, 389–90
 TR's statement on Wilson, 389
 TR's teeth, 4
 Wilson on WWI volunteer divisions, 389
 on Wilson's progressivism, 357
 on Zimmermann note and Germany, 387

New-York Tribune
 TR's nomination for NY governor, 163
 The Winning of the West review, 109
New York World
 interview with TR (1884), 88
 on the Panama Canal, 224
 quoting J. P. Morgan, 190
 on riots in Havana, 145
 on the Roosevelt Corollary to the Monroe Doctrine, 273
 tags TR "a little tin Czar," 127
 on TR as a demagogue, 192
 TR as police commissioner, 126
Nicholas II, Czar, 241, 242, 246, 248
Nicolay, John, 20, 107
Nixon, Richard, 186
Norris, Frank, 175
North, Newton Dexter, 327
North American Review, criticism of TR, 394
Northern Securities Company, 190, 191, 204, 234
 TR's trustbusting and, 190–94, 289

Octopus, The (Norris), 175
O'Neil, Charles, 146
Open Door policy, 238, 239
Osborn, Chase Salmon, 337–38
Osler, Sir William, 148
Outlook magazine, 327
 office for TR, 327, 335, 337
 TR as contributing editor, 327
 TR's Amazon expedition and, 368
 TR's essays on WWI in, 377–78
Oyster Bay, NY, 35, 62
 Roosevelt estate "Tranquility," 41–42, 62
 See also Sagamore Hill, Oyster Bay, NY

Panama, 3
 constitution and flag created, 225
 first president, 227
 TR and independence of, 225–27
 TR severs from Colombia, 3
Panama Canal, 3, 132, 221, 222–29
 Clayton-Bulwer Treaty of 1850, 222
 Colombia reneges on agreement, 221, 223–24
 difficulties of building, 222
 Hay-Bunau-Varilla Treaty, 227
 Hay-Herran Treaty, 223, 224
 Hay's negotiations, 221, 222, 225
 TR's inspection of, 6
 U.S. purchases French interests, 222

INDEX

Pan-American Exposition, Buffalo, 175
    McKinley shot, 175–76, 177
Parker, Alton B., 172, 232
Parker, Andrew D., 129, 134
Parkman, Francis, 107, 109
Parrington, Vernon, 65
Paterson, John Henry, 313
Pauncefote, Sir Julian, 222, 223
Payne–Aldrich tariff (1909), 321, 324
Pendleton Act (1883), 112
Penrose, Charles, 265, 266
Perkins, George W., 294
Perry, Thomas, 47–48
Pershing, John J., 155, 199, 385, 389
    cable to TR on death of his son, 397–98
Pettigrew, Richard, 195
Philadelphia
    Exposition Auditorium, 173
    GOP National Convention (1900), 171–73
    Hotel Walton, 173
Philadelphia *Evening Bulletin*, on La Follette's speech, 339
Philadelphia Press
    opinion of TR's 1907 message to Congress, 296
    on TR's budding political career, 86
Philippine-American War, 194–99
    Battle of Balangiga, 198
    Battle of Bud Bagsak, 199
    Battle of Manila, 195
    cessation of hostilities, 199
    reports of American misconduct and atrocities, 196, 197–98
    Senate investigation of atrocities, 197–98, 199
    TR challenged by General Miles, 196–97
Philippine Organic Act, 199
Philippines, 170
    Filipino transition to civil rule, 195–96, 198, 199
    Great White Fleet and, 287
    independence and, 195
    Japanese threat to, 280
    Spanish-American War and, 148
    Taft as governor-general, 195–96, 198, 199
    TR on, 407
    U.S. acquisition of, 3, 182, 189, 245, 311
    U.S. military in, 282

Philips, J. Van Ness, 261
Phillips, David Graham, 255–56
Phillips, Wendell, 52
Pierce, Franklin, 145
Pilgrim's Progress, The (Bunyan), 181, 426–27n3
Pinchot, Gifford, 319–21, 336, 437n3
Pingree, Hazen, 179
Pittsburgh Leader, on TR's postpresidential popularity, 324
Pius IX, Pope, 31
Pius X, Pope, 321
Platt, Thomas, 127, 129, 134, 135
    backs TR's governor bid, 163–64
    criticism of Erie Canal expansion, 161
    loathing for TR, 127, 161, 315–16
    NY governor's race (1898), 161–62, 163
    TR's governorship and, 166–71
    TR's progressive reforms and, 254
Polk, James, 145
Pollock, Sir Frederick, 324
Populism and Populist Party, 131, 132, 143, 167, 255, 357, 441n11
    Bryan's 1908 campaign slogan, 307
    crusade against the "money power," 179
    questioning of corporatism, 181
Portsmouth Naval Shipyard, Kittery, Maine, 247
Portsmouth Peace Conference, 247–49
Prescott, William, 109
president, office of, 328
    assassinations, 205
    black leaders at the White House, 186
    children born in the White House, 186
    choices for vice president and, 169
    deaths of vice presidents and, 169–70
    expansion of executive power, 4, 205, 357
    facial hair of presidents, 34
    first "accidental" president to win the office in his own right, 235
    first occupants of the White House, 211
    first secret service agent to die while protecting a president, 202
    last president in the Civil War, 177
    presidential salary, 178
    presidential yacht *Mayflower*, 246, 284
    presidents with sustained contact with Europe prior to taking office, 41

INDEX

Republican presidents seeking reelection, nomination of, 342, 440n13
ritual of pardoning a turkey, 215
shortest presidency, 230
third-party candidates and, 355, 441n11
tradition of presidential tours, 216–17
TR as first sitting president to travel abroad, 6
TR–Booker T. Washington dinner as a first, 186
two term limit and, 235–36
Prime Minister, The (Trollope), 422n4
Princeton University, 356, 357
Princip, Gavrilo, 376
Progress and Poverty (George), 59, 99
Progressive Party, 351–62
   TR and 1916 election, 382–83, 384
   TR campaigning for (1914), 377–78
   TR presidential run (1912), 351–54, 358–62
   TR's running mate Hiram Johnson, 352
   TR's speech "Progressive Cause Greater Than Any Individual," 359
   women's suffrage and, 353, 441n5
progressivism/progressive reforms
   corruption-exposing periodicals, 181
   Croly's influential book and, 327
   exposés on price rigging and, 181
   GOP and, 232, 236–37, 254, 304, 321, 326, 329, 333–34, 349, 382
   growth of, 230, 327
   increasing state centralization and, 327
   La Follette and, 337–39
   midterms of 1910 and, 332
   National Progressive Republican League, 333–34
   New Deal liberalism and, 205
   organized labor and, 200
   reforms of Wall Street and, 295
   rural style of, 338
   Taft's abandonment of, 320, 321
   TR as champion of GOP's, 232, 236–37, 329–36, 439n7
   TR as NY governor and, 166–68
   TR as police commissioner and, 125–29
   TR on Civil Service Commission and, 113, 115–16
   TR opposing rapid industrialization and machine politics, 172
   TR's brand of, 182
   TR's breaks with pacifist Progressives, 380
   TR's "A Charter of Democracy," 339–40
   TR's mixed-minded reaction to corruption exposés, 181
   TR's Osawatomie "New Nationalism" speech, 329
   TR's presidency and, 2, 7, 294–97
   TR's regulatory legislation, 253–58, 295
   TR's Square Deal and, 2, 74, 203, 205, 240, 295
   TR–Taft schism, 326–32
   Wilson and, 332, 333, 351, 357
   See also La Follette, Robert
Promise of American Life, The (Croly), 327, 438n3
Pulitzer, Joseph, 145
Pure Food and Drug Act, 256–58, 311
Putnam, George Haven, 25, 107

Quigg, Lemuel, 124, 161, 163

racial issues, 264
   anti-Asian sentiment, 276, 277–80
   Atlanta race riots, 267, 268
   Brownsville case, 265–72, 433n6
   Jim Crow South, 265, 266, 351
   skin color intolerance in America, 280
   South Carolina Democrat Tillman, defender of lynch law, 255, 266
   TR's dinner with Booker T. Washington and press response, 184–88, 266
   TR's views on black Americans, 266, 268–69
   TR's views on Cubans, 276
   "yellow peril" concerns, 286
railroads
   American economy and, 253
   ICC and rail rates, 255
   monopolistic practices, 253
   Northern Securities trust-busting case, 190–94, 289
   transcontinental lines, 253
   TR's regulatory legislation, 253–54, 289
Ranlett, Frederick, 54
Ransdell, Joseph, 400
Reed, Susan, 132
Reed, Thomas, 114, 131, 132, 134

Reid, Whitelaw, 243, 308
Republican Party (GOP), 73
   attack on cronyism and, 113
   contest between liberals and
      conservatives in, 232
   East Coast financial aristocracy and,
      131–32
   election losses of 1900, 173
   election losses of 1912, 361–62
   Independent Republican faction, 163
   McKinley and, 131, 170
   midterms (1902) 182, 214
   midterms (1910), TR and, 328–32
   National Convention (1896), 132
   National Convention (1900), 171, 172
   National Convention (1904), 232,
      440n13
   National Convention (1908), 304–5
   National Convention (1912), 345–49
   National Progressive Republican
      League, 333–34
   Old Guard wing, 50, 230, 232, 236,
      237, 249, 254, 255, 256, 268, 309,
      320, 321, 329, 333, 334, 344, 347,
      358, 408
   presidential election (1884), TR
      campaigning for Blaine, 93–94,
      131, 234, 348
   presidential election (1888), TR
      campaigning for Harrison, 113–14
   presidential election (1896), TR
      campaigning for McKinley, 132–33
   presidential election (1900), TR
      campaigning for McKinley and
      vice- presidential run, 169–74
   presidential election (1904), TR
      reelected, 185, 187, 196, 229,
      230–37
   presidential election (1908), Taft wins,
      306–8
   presidential election (1912) Taft loses,
      326, 336
   presidential election (1916) Evans
      loses, 382, 385–86
   presidential nomination (1884), 85–90
   presidential nomination fight, TR
      against Taft (1912), 337–49
   presidential nomination (1916), 302
   progressives of, 232, 236–37, 254, 304,
      321, 326, 329, 333–34, 349, 382
   the South and, 184, 185, 186, 187, 217
   Stalwarts/Half-Breeds feud, 66, 73, 232
   Taft as president, 317–18
   Taft handling party patronage, 271
   "Thee" Roosevelt and, 50, 64
   TR–Lodge alliance, 86–87
   TR's commitment to, 113, 376
   TR's endorsement as powerful, 304
   TR's open war with, 348–49, 351–62
   TR's progressivism and, 172, 294–97,
      337–49
   TR's reconciliation with, 384, 385
Reyes, Rafael, 227
Richardson, Henry Hobson, 347
Rickenbacker, Eddie, 398
Riis, Jacob, 126, 422n6
Rise of the Dutch Republic, The (Motley),
   109
Rixey, Marion, 378
RMS *Lusitania*, 381, 382
Robinson, Corinne Roosevelt (sister),
   12–13, 14, 17, 20, 24
   brother Elliott and, 122
   deaths of her mother and TR's wife, 82
   describes her mother, 14–15
   family's second European tour and, 39
   father's death and, 50
   friendship of Edie Carow, 29, 42, 50, 57
   opinion of Elihu Root, 165
   Roosevelt family in Italy (1869), 31
   on TR's childhood ailments, 24, 25
   TR's correspondence with, 45, 59, 61,
      63, 64, 122, 154, 316–17
   TR's masculine resolution and, 36
   TR's 1904 presidential election and,
      235
   TR's relationship with, 49, 363
Robinson, Douglas, 122, 154
Robinson, Edwin Arlington, 182
Rockefeller, John D., 4, 132, 233, 290, 291,
   431n4
Rockefeller, John D., Jr., 255
Rockefeller, Nelson, 232
Rockwell, Dr. Alphonso D., 35
Rondon, Cândido, 368–72
Roosevelt, Alice. *See* Longworth, Alice
   Lee Roosevelt
Roosevelt, Alice Hathaway Lee (wife),
   57–62, 367, 416n1
   absence from TR's memoir, 83
   appearance, 58, 60
   first meets TR at Saltonstall's estate, 59
   honeymoon and TR's scaling the
      Matterhorn, 5, 63–64
   lack of common interests with TR, 59,
      416n5

married life, 74
tragic death of, 81–82, 97
TR's absence during her pregnancy, 76
TR's ardent courtship, 59
TR's correspondence with, 60, 76, 81
as TR's first love, 58, 63
TR's proposals, 59–60
wedding, 61–62, 97
Roosevelt, Anna Rebecca Hall (Eleanor's mother), 119–21, 122
Roosevelt, Archie (son), 117, 335–36, 380, 389, 392, 394, 402, 404, 405, 406
cable to his brothers on TR's death, 401
compiles *Theodore Roosevelt on Race, Riots, Reds, Crime*, 406
war injuries of, 405
Roosevelt, Cornelius Van Schaack "C.V.S." (grandfather), 12, 21, 26, 35, 42
Roosevelt, Edith Kermit Carow "Edie" (wife)
as Alice's stepmother, 101, 260, 416n1
Alice's White House wedding and, 263
attempted assassination of TR and, 360
birth, 96
Carow-Roosevelt family friendship, 29, 42, 50
character and personality, 29
childhood friendship with TR, 29, 42, 57
children of, 117, 118, 148
courtship by TR, secret engagement, wedding, and honeymoon, 96–99, 100–101
family and background, 29, 96
fears for TR's safety as president, 178
finances and handled by, 117, 178, 209
first First Lady to give her successor a White House tour, 310
impact of election loss of 1912, 363
inheritance from an uncle, 117
Kermit's death and, 406
mother and sister in Italy, 96, 97
move to the White House, 178
opinion of Woodrow Wilson, 386
passion for TR, 97
Progressive Party convention of 1912 and, 352
proposal by TR refused, age nineteen, 57, 96, 416n1
serious illness of 1897, 148–49
TR's Amazon expedition and, 368

TR's damaged health and, 393–94
TR's mayoral run squelched by, 124
TR's postpresidential travel and, 319, 323
TR's preferences for her appearance, 118
TR's vice-presidential bid and, 172
TR's western U.S. tour and (1937), 335–36
Washington, D.C., home on Jefferson Place, 116
Washington, D.C., society and, 116
White House entertaining and, 212, 310
Roosevelt, Eleanor (niece), 52, 119
TR and her wedding to FDR, 237
Roosevelt, Eleanor Alexander (daughter-in-law), 324, 336, 404–5
Roosevelt, Elliott (brother), 14, 17, 24, 29, 39, 40, 50, 61, 119–23, 367
affairs and mistresses, 120, 122
despondence of, 82
European stay (1890), 120–21
handsome, charming, popular, 61, 119
health issues, 61, 119
illegitimate son of, 120, 121
marriage to Anna Hall, 119
Midwest trip with TR (1879), 61
personal tragedy, suicide attempt, and fatal seizure (1894), 122
residence "Half Way Nirvana," 120
treatment for alcoholism and opiates, 120, 121, 122
TR's concern about his drinking, 61, 120
TR's criticism of his wife, 120
TR's legal actions against, 121–22
TR's response to his death, 122
yearlong hunting expedition in India, 76
Roosevelt, Ethel (daughter), 117, 212, 218, 260, 319, 397, 404
Roosevelt, Franklin Delano (FDR), 6, 144, 235
Alice's White House wedding and, 263
as assistant navy secretary, 388, 406
New Deal, 2, 406
non-election to the Porcellian Club, 415–16n8
reelection of 1936, 362
relationship to TR, 6, 406
wedding of, 237
White House renovations and, 213

INDEX

Roosevelt, Isaac (ancestor), 12
Roosevelt, James (granduncle), 72
Roosevelt, Jimmy (uncle), 164
Roosevelt, Kermit (son), 117, 182, 363, 396, *402*, 404
    accompanies TR in Europe, 321
    Asian expedition to search for the giant panda, 405
    suicide of, 405–6
    TR's correspondence with, 214, 234, 241, 242, 248, 276, 295, 303, 427n7
    TR's African and Amazon expeditions and, 315, 368, 370, 371, 405
    WWI and, 404
    WWII and, 405
Roosevelt, Martha "Mittie" Bulloch (mother), 13–15, 17
    bequest to TR, 83
    Civil War and family strife, 18–22, 413n7
    death from typhoid fever, 81–82
    family estate in Roswell, Georgia, 14, 15, 18, 21
    family's European tour (1869), 28–29
    family's European tour (1872), 39, 40–41
    health and retreat from active life, 28, 36
    obsessions and compulsive habits, 21
    reunions with her brothers exiled in Liverpool, England, 29, 32, 37
    Thee Roosevelt's courtship and wedding, 14–17
    TR at Harvard and, 45
    TR's childhood illnesses and frailty, 22–25, 30, 40
    TR's correspondence with, 58, 60
    TR sells the family home, 85
    TR's relationship with, 49, 62
Roosevelt, Nicholas (cousin), 2, 347
Roosevelt, Quentin (son), 118, 148, 209, 380, 392, *402*, 403, 404
    death in aerial combat, 397–99, 445n8
Roosevelt, Theodore, Jr. "Ted" (son), 226, 318, 331, 336, 380, 392, *402*, 403–5, 446n1
    Asian expedition in search of the giant panda, 405
    birth, 101
    on Utah Beach, D-Day, 405
Roosevelt, Theodore, Sr. "Thee" (father), 12
    boxing gloves for his sons, 40
    character and personality, 12–13
    Civil War and Lincoln appointment, 18–22, 412n2
    collector of the Port of New York, 50
    commissioner to the Vienna World's Fair, 37, 39
    estate left to his heirs, 51
    family's tours abroad (1869–73), 5, 26, 28–32, 37–42, 414n4
    as a father, 24, 26, 28, 31–32, 49
    health decline and death, 50–51, 367
    Lincoln letters and White House dinner, 20
    Manhattan homes, 17, 23, 35–36, 41
    meets and marries Mittie Bulloch, 14–17
    Oyster Bay summer estate, 41–42
    philanthropic enterprises, 26, 50, 62
    relationship with John Hay, 20
    sickness as a shame, or sin, and, 36
    TR's asthma and edict given to, 35–36
    TR's relationship with, 13, 20, 23–24, 25–26, 49
    wealth of, 26, 41–42
Roosevelt, Theodore (TR)
    appearance and physical characteristics, *iv*, *xiv*, 4, 25, 39, 44, 71, 72, 73, 87, 117, 126, 150, 217, 419n4
    birth, 11, 17
    Butt on TR as a world citizen, 1
    caricatures of, 4, 173, 215, 354
    character, personality, and "dude" persona, 4, 5, 25, 45, 58, 71, 72, 73, 87, 118, 122, 128, 150, 210, 237, 283, 350, 360, 404, 413n5, 419n4, 431n3, 433–34n16
    charisma, 4, 5, 76, 166, 188, 383, 393
    children of, 92, 95, 97, 117, 118, 148, *402*, 403–8, 446n1
    family and background, 5, *9*, 11–17, 31
    fatherhood and, 49, 118, 403–8, 429n3, 446n1
    "first truly national political hero," *xiv*, 1, 2, 407–8
    hunting and hunting trips, 4, 38, 39, 76–79, 84, 92–93, 174, 214, 241, 290, 291, *299*, 313–18, 367–74
    impulsive actions, 62, 74, 79, 91, 92
    income sources and investments, 79, 105–6, 117, 315, 327, 335, 378–79
    lasting popularity, 6
    "the life of strife," 6

INDEX

Lincoln as hero, 20, 21, 379
moral code of, 6, 26, 47, 120, 121, 259, 420n8, 422n1
political moralism of, 89–90
posthumous Medal of Honor, 162
religion and, 31, 46–47, 58
response to tragedy, 83
"strenuous life" ideal, 2, 33, 84, 110, 210, 259, 289, *365*, 379, 395
successors: FDR and Trump, 406–7
temperament, 32, 114
voice of, 4, 71, 126, 217
wealth and privilege, 41–42, 51, 73–74, 83
Roosevelt, Theodore (TR): 1858 to 1881, personal life, *xv*
asthma and illnesses, 23–26, 28–30, 32, 35, 39, 40, 60–61
birth of first son, 101
boxing and, 45, 46, 61
brother Elliott and, 118, 119–23
called "Teedie," 17
childhood companion and wife: Edie Carow, 29, 42, 57, 96–101, 148–49
Civil War's effect on his family, 18–22
Columbia University Law School, 62, 64
contemporary descriptions of, 25
Dakota Badlands and, 5, 55, 70, 74, 75–79, 88, 89, 91–93, 95, 420n11
daughter Alice and, 92, 95, 97
deaths of his mother and first wife, Alice, same day, 81–84, 91–92, 97
in Dresden (1873), 39–41
education and reading choices, 25, 35, 43, 416n12
escape from grief, 83, 90–93, 111 (*see also* Dakota Territory)
European and Asia Minor family tours (1869–73), 5, 26, 28–32, 37–42, 414n4
European honeymoons, first and second, 63–64, 100–101
falling in love: marriage to Alice Lee, 57–62, 74, 97
family's wealth, 41–42
father as hero, 13, 20, 23–24, 46, 49, 83
father's death and, 50–51, 83, 91, 367
father's influence on values, 25–26
father's responsibilities left for, 62
first firearm, 35
at Harvard, *9*, 42, 43–48, 49, 51–54
impact of foreign travel, 41
influence of his parents' personalities, 31–32
inheritances, 51, 83, 92
Lincoln's funeral cortège and, 5, 29
Maine hiking, 61, 92
Manhattan brownstone with Alice, 74, 85
Manhattan family homes and "cursed" house, 23, 35–36, 41, 81, 82, 85
masculine ideal of, 33–36
Midwest trip with Elliott (1879), 61
nature, science, and collecting, 34–35, 40, 43, 45, 52–53
pantheon of greats for, 69
physical regimen, 33, 35–36, 40
Sagamore Hill built, 95 (*see also* Sagamore Hill, Oyster Bay, NY)
scaling the Matterhorn, 5, 63–64, 417n2
self-discovery and, 62
shooting a neighbor's dog, 51
taxidermy and, 34–35, 40, 43, 45, 414n3
Roosevelt, Theodore (TR): 1881 to 1901, rising political career
ability to capture public's attention, 188
advantageous friendships, 116
American expansion and, 106, 139
anti-corruption fights, 115–16, 125–26, 422n4
anti-labor positions, 74
backers for, 134–35
belief in American greatness, 143
big-navy position, 131, 138–39, 142
concern about urban reform and socialism, 181
foreign policy and jingoism, 139
GOP and, 64–66, 85–90, 93–94, 112, 233–34
GOP and clash with Platt machine, 127, 129, 171
GOP National Convention (1884), 85–90
GOP National Convention (1896), 132
GOP National Convention (1900), 171, 172
governorship, *159*, 161–65, 166–68
incorruptible image, 165–66
Lodge's role in his political career, 125, 133–35, 156, 162–64, 169–71
mayoral run, 99–100, 124
newsworthy actions, 115–16

Roosevelt, Theodore (TR): 1881 to 1901, rising political career (*cont.*)
  opinions on government and industry, old and new money, 181–82
  opposition to patronage and spoils politics, 112, 113, 129
  police commissioner appointment, 124–29, 134–35, 422n4, 422n6, 422n7
  political ambition, 64, 65, 99, 101, 123, 169, 171
  political debut, state assemblyman, 55, 66, 71–74, 81–82
  as a political realist, 132
  political savvy of, 156, 167
  presidential election, 1884, campaigning for Blaine, 93–94, 131, 234
  presidential election, 1888, campaigning for Harrison, 113–14
  presidential election, 1896, campaigning for McKinley, 129, 131, 132–33
  presidential election, 1900, campaigning for McKinley and vice-presidential run, 169–74
  progressivism of, 2, 7, 113, 115–16, 125–29, 166–68, 172
  relationship with J. P. Morgan, 191–92
  reputation as law-and-order Republican, 130
  rising political career, 68, 71–74, 84, 85–90, 129–30, 136–37
  route to the White House, 169
  Stoker's prediction of his presidency, 129
  sworn in as vice president, 174
  "Teddy" used by the press, 133
  as a "trustbuster," 189–94, 234
  war hero: Spanish-American War and the Rough Riders, 151–57, 161, 173
  Washington entrée: Civil Service Commission appointment, 111, 112–18
  Washington return: assistant secretary of the U.S. Navy, 129–37
Roosevelt, Theodore (TR): 1901 to 1909, presidency, *207*
  absence of war, 3
  accomplishments and legacy, 311
  annual messages to Congress, 189–90, 254–55, 268–69, 279, 294–97, 303, 309–10
  Asian immigration and, 276, 277–80
  attitude toward the job, 207, 311
  big-stick diplomacy, 3, 287, 292, 311, 367
  Bonaparte as attorney general, 291
  books read for pleasure, 234
  Brownsville case, 265–72, 433n6
  bully pulpit and, 251, *251*, 293, 295, 309–10
  cabinet members, 177, 290, 291, 315
  campaign contributions from Wall Street, 233–34
  coal strike of 1902, 199, 200–204
  concerns about socialism, 257
  conservation and creation of national wildlife refuges, parks, and monuments, 320
  control of corporations and, 201, 289, 292–97, 336
  Cuban occupation and, 273, 275–76
  dinner with Booker T. Washington and press response, 184–88, 266
  election of 1904, 1–2, 185, 187, 196, 229, 230–37, 440n13
  Elkins Act, 254, 290
  executive power and, 4, 205, 357
  Fairbanks as vice president, 232
  family life in the White House, 83, 209–15
  final months in office, 288, 306–12
  first dinner at the White House, 178
  first sitting president to travel abroad, 6
  foreign policy, 2–3, 236, 273, 275–76, 277–82
  Great Loop Tour, 215, 216–21
  Great White Fleet world voyage, 284–88, 310, 408
  Gridiron Dinner speech of 1907, 270–71
  Hay as secretary of state, 20, 177, 202, 309
  Hay's ring and, 21, 236
  Hepburn Bill, 255, 256, 258, 311
  immigration policy, 189, 277–80
  Joint Army and Navy Board, 281, 282
  Knox as attorney general, 191, 201, 227, 255
  leadership limits, 292
  legacy of, 7, 194
  legend of the Teddy Bear, 214–15
  Lincoln Dinner of 1905, 185
  Lodge as confidant, 178, 182, 231, 275
  McKinley's death and swearing in as president (1901), 177

INDEX

modern presidency and, 3–4
Moody as attorney general, 257
naval expansion, 211, 273–74, 280, 284, 408
near-fatal accident, 202, 214
Nobel Peace Prize, 249, 269
Northern Securities case, 190–94, 289
"one man only" theme, 309
Open Door policy, 238, 239, 287
Panama Canal, 3, 221, 222–29
Panama independence and, 225–28, 311
Panic of 1907, 288, 289–93, 435n5
Philippine-American War, 196–99
popularity of, 2, 215, 229, 230, 231
progressive agenda, 2, 7, 253–58, 294–97, 311
Pure Food and Drug Act, 256–58, 311
reactions to ending of, 310
regulatory legislation, 253–58
Roosevelt Corollary to the Monroe Doctrine, 3, 273
Root as possible successor, 301–2, 436n2
Root as secretary of state, 242, 278, 279, 282, 291
Root as secretary of war, 238
ruling in McKinley's shadow, 177–78
Russo-Japanese War, 7, 238–43, 244–49
second inauguration, 236
speech of 1906: "the man with the muck-rake," 181, 426–27n3
Square Deal of, 2, 74, 203, 205, 240, 295
style of leadership and a rising generation, 182–83
Taft as secretary of war, 241, 242
Taft as successor, 301–5
Taft's inauguration and, 311
Tennis Cabinet, 213
third presidential term and, 235–36, 303
trust-busting, 188, 189–94, 233–34, 289
waning power of, 293
White House meetings with J. P. Morgan, 192, 289–90
White House renovations, 211–13, 308
White House wedding of daughter, Alice, 263–64
zenith of his presidency, 249
Roosevelt, Theodore (TR): 1909 to 1919: post-presidency and final years

addressed as "Colonel," 315
African self-imposed exile (1909), 299, 312, 313–18
Amazon expedition (1913), 5, 363, 367–74, 378, 442n2
attempted assassination (1912), 359, 442n8
"bull moose" image, 354
campaigning for Hughes (1916), 385
campaigning for Progressive candidates (1914), 376
Caribbean vacation (1916), 383
death (1919), 401
dissolving his relationship with pacifist Progressives, 380
European travel (1910), 319–25
first grandchild, 336
Fourth Avenue office, 327, 335, 337
GOP and, 320, 329–32, 399
GOP breach, 348–49, 351–62
GOP nomination fight (1912), 337–49, 407
GOP nomination of Hughes (1916) and, 383–84
GOP reconciliation, 384, 385
hat-in-the-ring theme, 341–42
health crisis (1918), 396
health damaged by Amazon expedition, 365, 374, 378, 389, 393–94, 399–400
honorary degree from Cambridge, 323
judiciary criticism, 328–30, 340, 343–44
Kelsey suggests "a new party," 346
last hunting trip, 374
last piece of writing, 401
in London, "special ambassador" at Edward VII's funeral (1910), 322–24
memoir written, 367
military career resurrection sought, 384–85, 387, 388–93
most controversial speech: "A Charter of Democracy," 339–40
New Nationalism and, 329–30, 354, 357, 361
Pinchot and conservation, 320–21
popularity and cheering crowds, 324–25, 328–29, 333, 347
presidential election (1920), 399, 445n9
Progressive Party presidential candidate (1912) and loss, 351–63

Roosevelt, Theodore (TR): 1909 to 1919: post-presidency and final years (*cont.*)
  progressivism and, 328, 329–36, 357, 439n7
  remark on leaving the presidency, iv, 7
  revolver carried by, 359
  Romanes Lecture given at Oxford, 323
  son Quentin's death in aerial combat, 397–99, 445n8
  speaking tour (1910), 328–32, 439n7
  speech: "New Nationalism," 329–31
  speech: "The Soul of the Nation," 385
  Taft's presidency and, 317–18, 324, 325, 326–32, 384
  third term and, 324, 326, 331, 332, 334, 336
  western U.S. tour, 335
  Wilson's presidency and, 6–7, 375–76, 379, 381–87, 389, 394–97, 400, 444n2, 444n13
  women's suffrage and, 441n5
  WWI and, 376–79, 381, 386–94, 445n15, 446n13
Roosevelt, Theodore (TR): writing
  African Game Trails, 317, 335
  America and the World War, 379
  beliefs about inspiration, 109
  compared to other historians, 107
  criticism of Norris's *The Octopus*, 175
  first book completed, 66
  historians as artists, 109–10
  historical imagination of, 106
  "History as Literature" speech, 109–10
  Hunting Trips of a Ranchman, 91, 93, 94, 105
  Kipling friendship, 234, 323, 399, 405
  Life of Thomas Hart Benton, 106
  literary ambitions, 66–67, 101, 106
  Metropolitan Magazine articles, 378–79, 380, 381–82
  The Naval War of 1812, 6, 66–70, 79, 380
  Outlook articles, 327, 377–78
  relationships related to, 6, 181–82, 313
  review of Mahan's *Influence of Sea Power*, 141
  The Rough Riders, 156–67
  The Summer Birds of the Adirondacks in Franklin County, N.Y., 53
  Theodore Roosevelt: An Autobiography, 292, 367
  Through the Brazilian Wilderness, 371
  Wilderness Hunter, 6
  The Winning of the West, 6, 94, 106, 107–11, 420n7, 421n12
  Wister friendship, 175
  See also specific books
Roosevelt, Tweed (great-grandson), 162
Roosevelt, Weir (uncle), 14
Roosevelt Corollary to the Monroe Doctrine, 3
Root, Clara, 242
Root, Elihu, 165, 169, 170, 177, 301, 333
  considered as TR's successor, 301–2, 436n2
  presidential hopes, 383
  Taft presidency and, 308, 317–18
  TR's nomination fight (1912) and, 339, 341, 345, 346, 349
  as TR's secretary of state, 242, 278, 279, 282, 291
  as TR's secretary of war, 192, 196, 197, 198, 204, 239
  as U.S. Senator, 302
Rosen, Roman, 246, 247–48, 249
Rosenvelt, Claes Martenszen and Jannetje Samuels van (ancestors), 12
Rough Riders, 151–57, 216, 324
  Battle of Las Guásimas, 153–54
  casualties, 155
  charge up Kettle Hill, 2, 155, 162
  horse, Little Texas, 152, 155, 425n6
  training in Texas, 151
  TR's African American servant and, 152
  TR's description of, 151–52
  TR's desire for glory, 155–56, 162
  TR's letters from Cuba, 152, 154
  TR's posthumous Medal of Honor, 162
  TR's *The Rough Riders*, 156–67
Russia
  Manchuria and, 238, 239, 249
  railways built, 239
  Sino-Japanese War and the Triple Intervention, 238–39, 244
Russo-Japanese War, 7, 239–49, 277
  Battles of Mukden and the Tsushima Strait, 239, 241, 242, 244
  peace negotiations, 244–49
  settlement meeting aboard the yacht *Mayflower*, 246–47
  site for negotiations, 244, 246, 247
  Treaty of Portsmouth, 249
  TR's Nobel Peace Prize, 249, 269

INDEX

Sagamore Hill, Oyster Bay, NY, 42, 54, 85, 214
    Chapman visit, 164
    cost of construction, 95
    pet cemetery at, 425n6
    taxes and, 164, 165
    telephone and electricity added, 346
    TR plants hedge clippings from Lincoln's Springfield home, 20
    TR's family at, 211
    TR's guests, WWI, 379–80
    TR's plans for, originally "Leeholm," 76
    TR's presidential meetings at, 224, 246, 282
    TR's time spent at, 95, 174, 274, 306, 327, 328, 346, 358, 376, 383
    yearly expense of, 117
Saint-Gaudens, Augustus, 182
Saltonstall, Dick, 57–58
Saltonstall, Rose, 58
Samoan Islands, 106
San Francisco
    anti-Asian sentiment, 277–80
    earthquake of 1906, 277
    school board's decision to segregate Japanese students, 277, 278, 279
San Francisco Chronicle
    on anti-Asian sentiment, 244
    on quotas for Japanese immigration, 280
Sartoris, Nellie Grant, 263
Satterlee, Henry Yates, 263
Saturday Evening Post, profile of Henry Cabot Lodge, 86
Schiff, Jacob, 289
Schmitz, Eugene, 279
Schrank, John, 359–61
Schurz, Carl, 81, 128
Scribner's Monthly, Scudder on Harvard, 45
Scudder, Horace E., 44–45
Seattle, Washington, 220
Seitz, Donald, 339
Selections from the Correspondence of Theodore Roosevelt and Henry Cabot Lodge (1925), 275
Sewall, William, 92
Seymour, Horatio, 162
Shafter, William, 152, 156
Shaler, Nathaniel Southgate, 53–54
Sheard, Titus, 79
Sherman, Florence Bagley, 120
Sherman, William Tecumseh, 21, 171, 217

Sherman Antitrust Act, 189–90, 192, 253–54
"Significance of the Frontier in American History, The" (Turner), 110
Sinclair, Upton, 6, 256–57
Sino-Japanese War, 238–39, 244, 246
slaves/slavery
    Bulloch family as slaveowners, 13, 14, 15
    murder of a slave by Daniel Bulloch, 14
    TR's views on, 185
    Uncle Remus stories and, 14
Smedes, Mississippi, Teddy Bear legend and, 214–15
Smith, Edward North, 393
Smith, Jacob H., 198
Smithsonian Institution
    specimens for TR's safari, 317
    TR's African safari and, 314–15, 316
social Darwinism, 3, 74, 108, 185
Socialist Party, 357–58, 362
Spain
    Havana riots and U.S. warship sent to Cuba, 145
    sinking of the *Maine* and, 146–47, 148
    U.S. demands Cuban withdrawal, 149
Spanish-American War, 2, 144–57, 194
    Admiral Dewey's Asiatic Squadron in Hong Kong, 148
    Admiral Dewey's victory at Manila Bay, 149
    American flotilla to Cuba, 152–53
    assault on Kettle Hill, Cuba, 155, 156
    Battle of Las Guásimas, 153–54
    Byran recruits the Nebraska Guard, 152
    establishes a pattern for U.S. wars of choice, 157, 407
    fruits of, for the U.S., 182
    General Pershing in Cuba, 155
    General Wheeler in Cuba, 153–54
    Miles and Puerto Rico invasion, 196
    peace treaty signed in Paris, 156
    sinking of the USS *Maine*, 146–48
    as a "splendid little war," 157, 173
    TR and the U.S. Navy, 145, 146, 147–48
    TR commissioned as lieutenant colonel, 1st U.S. Volunteer Cavalry, 150
    TR resigns from navy to fight, 149
    TR's officer's uniform, 150
    TR's posthumous Medal of Honor, 162
    TR's Rough Riders and, 151–57
    U.S. as a global power and, 283
    U.S. unpreparedness for, 152

INDEX

Spring Rice, Cecil "Springy," 5, 101, 114, 117, 135, 239, 241, 323, 388
  TR's note on leaving office, 311
SS *Celtic* (White Star steamer), 63
SS *Etruria* (liner), 100
SS *Kaiserin Auguste Victoria* (luxury liner), 324
SS *Russia* (Cunard liner), 37
SS *Scotia* (Cunard steamer), 29
St. Botolph Club, Boston, 86
St. Louis, 132
  GOP National Convention (1896), 132
St. Louis Globe-Democrat, criticism of TR's 1907 message to Congress, 296
St. Paul Pioneer Press, opinion of TR's 1907 message to Congress, 297
Staats-Zeitung (newspaper), accuses TR of snobbery, 128
Standard Oil, 194
  Tarbell's exposé, 181
  TR backed by (1904), 233–34
  violation of the Elkins Act and fine, 290
Stanford, Leland, 27
Steffens, Lincoln, 397
Sternburg, Hermann Speck von, 283
Stevens, Wallace, 60
Stewart, Philip B., 184, 185
Stimson, Henry, 213, 331
Stoddard, Henry, 374
Stoker, Bram, 129
Stone, William, 201, 394, 396
Storer, Bellamy, 134
Storer, Maria, 134
Straus, Oscar, 315
"strenuous life" ideal, 2, 33, 84, 110, 210, 259, 289, *365*, 379, 395
Strew, W. W., 66
Strong, William Lafayette, 124, 129
Stubbs, Walter Roscoe, 337
Sturgis, Russell, 41
Sumner, Charles, 52

Taft, Alphonso, 307
Taft, Charles, 307, 330
Taft, Helen "Nellie" Herron, 302, 303–4, 310, 324, 342, 358
Taft, Horace, 343
Taft, William Howard, 134–35, 228, 292, 245, 301, 306, 307, 416n12
  Adams tags him "a fat mush," 306
  antitrust suits by, 194
  appointments and patronage, 327–38
  calls TR a "honeyfugler," 349
  cooling of relations with TR, 310
  corporate protectionism and, 321
  correspondence with TR on his presidency, 324, 333
  "goodwill cruise" to Japan and, 245
  inauguration of, 311
  midterms of 1910, TR and, 332
  Payne-Aldrich tariff and, 321, 324
  personality, 343, 440n15
  Philippines and, 195–96, 198, 199
  presidency of, 317, 343, 344
  presidential election (1908), 306–8
  presidential race and historic loss (1912), 336, 342–44, 357, 362, 363
  running mate (1912), 356
  sheds progressive agenda, 317–18, 320, 321, 325, 333–34
  as Supreme Court chief justice, 363
  TR challenges for GOP nomination (1912), 337–49, 407
  TR declines White House visit, 325
  TR's chosen successor, 294, 301–5, 326
  TR's dissatisfaction with, 326–32
  TR's meetings with, 328
  TR's offer to fight in Mexico, 388
  TR's reconciliation with, 384
  TR's secretary of war, 241, 242, 269
Takahira Kogorō, 246
Tarbell, Ida, 181
Thayer, William Roscoe, 64
Theodore Roosevelt: An Autobiography (TR), 292, 367
Theodore Roosevelt Dam, 336
Theodore Roosevelt on Race, Riots, Reds, Crime (ed. Kermit Roosevelt), 406
"Theodore Roosevelt's College Rank and Studies" (Ranlett), 54
Thompson, Hugh, 115
Through the Brazilian Wilderness (TR), 371
Tilden, Samuel, 162
Tillman, Benjamin, 255, 256, 266
"To Roosevelt" (Dario), 3
"Treason of the Senate, The" (Phillips), 256
Trevelyan, George Otto, 110, 241, 297
Trimble, William, 66
Trollope, Anthony, 422n4
Truman, Harry, 2, 202, 235
Trump, Donald J., 406–7
Turner, Frederick Jackson, 110–11

INDEX

Twain, Mark, 6, 40, 315, 417n2
   opinion of TR, 427n6
   on the Philippines, 196
   on TR's dinner with Booker T. Washington, 186–87
   TR's opinion of, 187, 427n7
Tweed, William "Boss," 81
Two African Trips with Notes and Suggestions on Big Game Preservation in Africa (Buxton), 313
Tyler, John, 235

United Mine Workers of America (UMWA)
   coal strike of 1902, 200–205
   president John Mitchell, 200–203
United States
   academics who entered politics, 356–57
   American mobility, 180
   anti-imperialism, 182, 195, 196, 199
   assassination of Garfield, 66
   "Average American" (1901), 179–80
   Banana Wars, 3
   Brooklyn Bridge and technology, 28
   clashes between capital and labor, 73
   control of the Samoan Islands and, 106
   corporate monopolization, 1, 74, 179, 189–94, 238, 291, 361
   Crédit Mobilier scandal, 113
   economic growth, 138
   economic inequality, 73, 189–90, 254–55
   employment and industry (1900), 180
   factory labor system and identity, 33–34
   federal employees, 112–13
   foreign policy and jingoism, 139, 145
   Founding generation, elite "natural aristocracy," 65
   Gilded Age, 33–34, 59
   as global power, 283
   gold standard, 132, 143
   "Grantism," 65
   gunboat diplomacy, 228, 273
   Hamiltonians vs. Jeffersonians, 438n3
   immigration, 73, 107–8, 113, 276–80
   increasing urban industrialization, 93
   industrial oligarchy in, 2, 138
   influence of big business, 230
   as "an international police power," 3
   laborer's average salary (1871), 42
   labor unrest and strikes, 180–81
   military capacity increase, 280
   minuteman tradition, 149
   most populous states (1867), 71
   movement toward empire, 138
   national identity, 141, 180
   as a Pacific power, 182, 195, 281–82, 311
   Panic of 1873, 181, 293
   Panic of 1893, 131, 181, 293
   Panic of 1907, 288, 289–93, 435n5
   pattern for wars of choice, 157
   Philippine-American War, 194–99
   political corruption (1870s), 65
   population growth (1900), 214
   population growth (1860 to 1900), 138
   population of major cities (1880 to 1900), 180
   post–Civil War culture and progress, 27
   poverty in (1904), 180
   Progressive Era and regulatory state model, 74, 165
   racial issues, 183, 184–88
   rise of mass democracy, 65
   Spanish-American War, 2, 144–57, 194
   sports and "muscular Christianity," 34, 106
   states entering the Union (1876–90), 106
   territorial expansion, 106, 131, 132, 139, 141, 145, 182, 189
   Transcontinental Railroad, 27
   TR's "distinctly and intensely American stock," 108, 420n7
   TR's Square Deal, 2, 74, 203, 205, 240, 295
   wealthiest families, 73
   Western territories, 75
   Whiskey Ring, 113
   women's suffrage, 179, 353, 357, 441n5
   Woolworth Building, 308
   WWI, 376–77, 386, 399–401, 445n15
   yellow journalism in, 145
   See also Civil War; *specific events and locations*
U.S. Army
   Brownsville case, 265–72, 433n6
   Buffalo Soldiers, 153
   Miles as commanding general, 196
   Rough Riders and the Spanish-American War, 151–57
   size of regular army, 149
   Spanish American War and, 149, 153

U.S. Civil Service Commission, 112, 114–15
   TR appointment, 114–18
U.S. Congress
   Census of 1900 and increase in representatives, 214
   Democrat losses (1918), 399
   Democrat majority (1914), 378
   Democrat sweep (1912), 326
   Elkins Act, 254, 290
   Federal Reserve Act, 293
   first socialist congressman, 332
   funding White House renovation, 211
   Great White Fleet appropriations, 283
   Hepburn Bill, 255–56, 258
   Interstate Commerce Commission created, 253
   national depositories (banks) and, 293
   nation's policymaking and, 205
   Panama Canal and, 223
   Pendleton Act, 112
   Philippine Organic Act, 199
   Platt Amendment, 274
   Progressives in, 378
   Pure Food and Drug Act, 256–58, 311
   ratification of the Hay-Bunau-Varilla Treaty, 229
   Senate Committee on the Philippines, 197
   Senate Foreign Relations Committee, 197
   Senate investigation of the Brownsville case, 269–70, 271
   Sherman Antitrust Act, 253–54
   TR's annual message (1901), 189–90
   TR's annual message (1905), 254–55
   TR's annual message (1906), 268–69, 279
   TR's annual message (1907), 294–97, 303
   TR's progressive agenda and, 295
U.S. Geological Survey, 112
U.S. Marine Corps, 3, 198
U.S. Military Academy, West Point, 69, 416n12
U.S. Navy
   Asiatic Squadron, 146, 147
   balance of Pacific power and, 287
   creation of West Coast bases, 281
   expansion, 135, 273–74, 280, 284, 408
   Great White Fleet, 284–88, 408, 435n8
   Naval War College, 135–36, 140
   Secretary Long as small-navy cautionary, 135, 136
   Spanish American War and, 145–50
   tonnage compared to other nations, 280
   TR as acting secretary, 144–45, 147–48
   TR as assistant secretary, 70, 129, 135–40
   TR's cablegram to Dewey, 147
   TR's speech, Naval War College (1897), 135–36
USS *Connecticut*, 310
USS *Dixie*, 225, 226
USS *Florida*, 376
USS *George Washington*, 400
USS *Illinois*, 283
USS *Maine*, 145, 146, 148
USS *Nashville*, 226
USS *Utah*, 376
USS *Yucatán*, 153
United States Steel, 291, 292, 315
U.S. Supreme Court
   Northern Securities case, 192, 193
   Taft appoints White as chief justice, 343
   Taft as chief justice, 363
   TR appoints Holmes, 6, 192
U.S. Treasury Department, 293
University of California at Berkeley, 219
   campus's Greek Theatre, 228
   TR Charter Day address, 228
Utica Press, Root on his future, 302

Van Alstyne, Egbert, 341–42
Van Buren, Martin, 34
Van Wyck, Augustus, 166
Venezuela, 273
Victor Emmanuel III, King, 321
Victoria, Queen, 27–28, 67, 202, 213, 322
Vienna, Austria
   Roosevelt family in, 39
   Thee Roosevelt appointed commissioner to the Vienna World's Fair, 37
Villa, Francisco "Pancho," 384–85
Virginian, The (Wister), 175

Walcott, Charles, 316
Waller, Littleton, 198
Wallingford, Annie Longworth, 349
Wanamaker, John, 114
War of 1812, 136, 213, 217
Washburn, Charles, 374

Washington, Booker T., 184–88
    Brownsville case and, 268
    rising-people theme and, 185
    TR's Progressive Party run and, 352
    Tuskegee Institute and, 184
    White House dinner with TR, 184, 185–87, 255, 266
Washington, D.C.
    City Hall building, 115
    Lafayette Square, 211
    Metropolitan Club and TR, 144, 146
    New Willard Hotel, 270
    Republican literary-minded group, 131
    Townsend House, 211
    TR and Rock Creek Park, 209–10
    TR arrives (May 1889), 115
    TR declares as legal residence, 164–65
    TR family residence, Jackson Place, 211, 212
    TR residence, Jefferson Place, 116
    TR returns as vice president (1901), 174
    TR's expenses, Commission years, 117
    TR's sister Bamie's home in, 174
    TR's social/political connections in, 116–17, 131, 142–43, 144
    See also White House, 1600 Pennsylvania Avenue
Washington, George, 6, 69, 196, 216–17
Washington Bee, protest poem, 270
Washington Herald, TR's bull moose image and, 354
Washington Post
    legend of the Teddy Bear, 215
    TR and Rock Creek Park, 210
    TR Naval War College speech, 136–37
Washington Star, Morgan–TR meeting (1907) reported, 289
Washington Times, "Man of the Hour" story on Hanna, 230
Watkins, Dora, 82
Watson, James, 203–4
Watterson, Henry, 197
Weber, Max, 4
Weld, Stephen M., 135
Wells, H. G., 4
West, Henry Litchfield, 210
West, Hilborne (uncle), 14
West, Susan Elliott (aunt), 14
Wharton, Edith, 5, 96, 182
Wheeler, "Fighting Joe," 153
Wheeler, William, 169

Whiskey Ring, 113
White, Edward Douglass, 343
White, Henry, 327
White, William Allen, 332, 334, 349, 353
White House, 1600 Pennsylvania Avenue
    African American labor and, 185
    architects for, 211
    Blue Room, 263–64
    British invasion and, 211
    East Room, 263
    FDR's White House renovations, 213
    fire damage under Hoover, 213
    first First Lady to give her successor a tour, 310
    first occupants, 211
    formerly the Executive Mansion, 209
    Garfield's children at, 209
    historical events at, 210–11
    interior decorating for, 212
    Red Room, 212
    Resolute desk, 213
    Taft's additions and Oval Office, 213
    TR's changes (1908), 308
    TR's children and animals at, 83, 209, 310, 429n3
    TR's custom of opening to well-wishers on New Year's Day, 310
    TR's entertaining in, 209
    TR's family moves in, 209
    TR's renovations (1902), 211–13, 308
    wedding of Alice Roosevelt, 263–64, 310, 433n10
    wedding of Nellie Grant, 263
    West Wing, 213
Wilcox, Ansley, 177
Wilderness Hunter (TR), 6
Wilhelm II, Kaiser, 242
Wilhelmina, Queen, 321
Williams, Harry, 341–42
Williams, Marie Selika, 186
Wilson, Edith Galt, 382, 420n8
Wilson, Ellen, 382
Wilson, Woodrow, 6–7, 228, 299, 356–58
    appearance, 357
    background, 356, 357
    elected New Jersey governor, 332, 357
    foreign policy, 379
    Fourteen Points and peace program, 400
    "Ideals of America" essay, 358
    League of Nations and, 228–29
    Mexico and, 375–76, 379, 384–85, 443n1

Wilson, Woodrow (*cont.*)
   as a "New Freedom" reformer, 361, 378
   presidency of, 375–76
   presidential election (1912), 341, 349, 351, 358, 361–62
   as Princeton University president, 356, 357
   progressivism and, 332, 333, 351, 357
   reelection race (1916), 384, 385–86
   Shadow Lawn summer estate, 385–86
   TR calls neutrality policy "diluted-mush policy," 6–7
   Treaty of Versailles, 400–401, 420n8
   TR's desire to fight in WWI, 388–93, 444n2
   TR's disdain for, 385, 387, 420n8, 444n13
   TR's health crisis and, 396–97
   wife's death and remarriage to Edith Galt, 382, 420n8
   women's suffrage and, 357
   WWI and, 6–7, 377, 381, 384
Winning of the West, The (TR), 6, 94, 106, 107–11, 420n7, 421n12
   TR as a frontiersman and, 108–9
Wister, Owen, 6, 175, 185, 257
Witte, Sergei, 246, 247, 248–49
Wood, Leonard, 149–50, 162, 175, 234, 380, 383
World War I (Great War), 381–82
   armistice (Nov. 11, 1918), 399
   casualties, 399
   Germany sinks the *Housatonic*, 386
   Germany sinks the *Lusitania*, 381, 382
   sedition laws and, 394
   TR and, 376–79, 387–93, 394, 445n15
   Treaty of Versailles, 400–401
   TR's relationship with pacifist Progressives and, 380
   TR's sons and, 380, 392–93, 397–99, 401, 404–5
   Wilson and, 6–7, 377, 379, 381
   Wilson's peace program, 400, 446n13
   Zimmermann note, 386–87
World War II, TR's sons and, 405

Yale, 41, 96, 151, 209, 213, 320, 345
   bicentennial celebrations, 186–87
Yellowstone National Park, 216, 218
Yosemite National Park, 216, 220

Zahm, John Augustine, 368, 370, 442n3
Zimmermann, Arthur, 386–87

About the Author

David S. Brown teaches history at Elizabethtown College in Pennsylvania. He is the author of eight books, including *A Hell of a Storm: The Battle for Kansas, the End of Compromise, and the Coming of the Civil War*; *The First Populist: The Defiant Life of Andrew Jackson*; *The Last American Aristocrat: The Brilliant Life and Improbable Education of Henry Adams*; and biographies of F. Scott Fitzgerald and Richard Hofstadter.